Lecture Notes in Artificial Intelligence 10596

Subseries of Lecture Notes in Computer Science

More information about this series at http://www.springer.com/series/1244

Ruslan Mitkov (Ed.)

Computational and Corpus-Based Phraseology

Second International Conference, Europhras 2017 London, UK, November 13–14, 2017 Proceedings

Editor
Ruslan Mitkov
University of Wolverhampton
Wolverhampton
UK

ISSN 0302-9743 ISSN 1611-3349 (electronic)
Lecture Notes in Artificial Intelligence
ISBN 978-3-319-69804-5 ISBN 978-3-319-69805-2 (eBook)
https://doi.org/10.1007/978-3-319-69805-2

Library of Congress Control Number: 2017957565

LNCS Sublibrary: SL7 – Artificial Intelligence

Printed on acid-free paper

This Springer imprint is published by Springer Nature
The registered company is Springer International Publishing AG
The registered company address is: Gewerbestrasse 11, 6330 Cham, Switzerland

Preface

Computational and Corpus-Based Phraseology: Recent Advances and Interdisciplinary Approaches

As the late and inspiring John Sinclair (1991, 2007) observed, knowledge of vocabulary and grammar is not sufficient for someone to express himself/herself idiomatically or naturally in a specific language. One has to have the knowledge and skill to produce effective and naturally phrased utterances, which are often based on phraseological units (the idiom principle). This is in contrast to the traditional assumption or open choice principle that lies at the heart of generative approaches to language. As Pawley and Syder (1983) stated more than three decades ago, the traditional approach cannot account for nativelike selection (idiomaticity) or fluency.

Language is indeed phraseological and phraseology is the discipline that studies phraseological units (PUs) or their related concepts referred to (and regarded largely synonymous) by scholars as multiword units, multiword expressions (MWEs), fixed expressions, set expressions, phraseological units, formulaic language, phrasemes, idiomatic expressions, idioms, collocations, and/or polylexical expressions. PUs or MWEs, are ubiquitous and pervasive in language. They are a fundamental linguistic concept that is central to a wide range of natural language processing and applied linguistics applications, including, but not limited to, phraseology, terminology, translation, language learning, teaching and assessment, and lexicography. Jackendoff (1977) observes that the number of MWEs in a speaker's lexicon is of the same order of magnitude as the number of single words (Jackendoff 1977). Biber et al. (1999) argue that they constitute up to 45% of spoken English and up to 21% of academic prose in English. Sag et al. (2002) state that they are overwhelmingly present in terminology and 41% of the entries in WordNet 1.7 are reported to be MWEs.

PUs do not play a crucial role only in the computational treatment of natural languages. Terms are often MWEs (and not single words), which makes them highly relevant to terminology. Translation and interpreting are two other fields where phraseology plays an important role, as finding correct translation equivalents of PUs is a pivotal step in the translation process. Given their pervasive nature, PUs are absolutely central to the work carried out by lexicographers, who analyse and describe both single words and PUs. Last but not least, PUs are vital not only for language learning, teaching, and assessment, but also for more theoretical linguistic areas such as pragmatics, cognitive linguistics, and construction grammars. All the aforementioned areas are today aided by (and often driven by) corpora, which makes PUs particularly relevant for corpus linguists. Finally, PUs provide an excellent basis for inter- and multidisciplinary studies, fostering fruitful collaborations between researchers across different disciplines, which are, for the time being, unfortunately still largely unexplored.

This volume features a selection of papers written by the invited speakers as well as regular papers presented at the international conference "Computational and Corpus-Based Phraseology: Recent Advances and Interdisciplinary Approaches" (Europhras 2017). The conference, which is organised jointly by the European Association of Phraseology (Europhras) and the Research Institute in Information and Language Processing of the University of Wolverhampton, and sponsored by Europhras, the Sketch Engine, ELRA and the University of Wolverhampton, provides the perfect opportunity for researchers to present their work, fostering interaction and collaboration between scholars working in disciplines as diverse as natural language processing, translation, terminology, lexicography, languages learning, teaching and assessment, and cognitive science, to name only a few. I organised the volume thematically into the following sections, which demonstrate the breath of the topics represented at Europhras 2017: (1) Keynote and Invited Papers, (2) Phraseology in Translation and Contrastive Studies, (3) Lexicography and Terminography, (4) Exploitation of Corpora in Phraseological Studies, (5) Development of Corpora for Phraseological Studies, (6) Phraseology and Language Learning, (7) Cognitive and Cultural Aspects of Phraseology, (8) Theoretical and Descriptive Approaches to phraseology, and (9) Computational Approaches to Phraseology. In fact, the variety of topics at Europhras 2017 is even more remarkable if we take into account other conference presentations that are not included in this volume – in addition to the regular papers, the conference also featured short papers and posters, which are published separately as e-proceedings with ISBN and DOI numbers assigned to every contribution.

Every submission to the conference was evaluated by three reviewers – i.e., members of the Programme Committee consisting of 46 scholars from 23 different countries, or 12 additional reviewers from eight countries, who were recommended by the Programme Committee. The conference contributions were authored by a total of 91 scholars from 24 different countries. These figures attest to the truly international dimension of Europhras 2017.

I would like to thank everyone who made this truly interdisciplinary and international event possible. I would like to start by thanking all colleagues who submitted papers to Europhras 2017 and travelled to London to attend the event. I am grateful to all members of the Programme Committee and the additional reviewers for carefully examining all submissions and providing substantial feedback on all papers, helping the authors of accepted papers to improve and polish the final versions of their papers. A special thanks goes to the invited speakers – both the keynote speakers of the main conference (Ken Church, Gloria Corpas, Dmitrij Dobrovol'skij, Patrick Hanks, Miloš Jakubíček) and the invited speakers of the two accompanying workshops (Carlos Ramish and Jean-Pierre Colson). Words of gratitude go to our sponsors – Europhras, the Sketch Engine, ELRA, and the University of Wolverhampton.

Last but not least, I would like to use this paragraph to acknowledge the members of the Organising Committee, who worked very hard during the last 12 months and whose dedication and efforts made the organisation of this event possible. I would like to mention (in alphabetical order) the following colleagues whom I would like to highlight for competently carrying out numerous organisational tasks and being ready to step in and support the organisation of the conference whenever needed. My big thank you goes out to Amanda Bloore, Martina Cotella, Arianna Fabbri, April Harper, Sara Moze, Nikolai Nikolov, Ivelina Nikolova, Rocío Sánchez González, Andrea Silvestre Baquero, Shiva Taslimipoor, and Victoria Yaneva.

November 2017 Ruslan Mitkov

Organisation

Europhras 2017 was jointly organised by the European Association for Phraseology EUROPHRAS, the University of Wolverhampton (Research Institute of Information and Language Processing), and the Association for Computational Linguistics, Bulgaria.

Programme Committee

Julio Bernal	Caro and Cuervo Institute, Colombia
Douglas Biber	Northern Arizona University, USA
Nicoletta Calzolari	Institute for Computational Linguistics, Italy
María Luisa Carrió-Pastor	Polytechnic University of Valencia, Spain
Sheila Castilho	Dublin City University, Ireland
Kenneth Church	IBM Research, USA
Jean-Pierre Colson	Université catholique de Louvain, Belgium
Gloria Corpas	University of Malaga, Spain
František Čermák	Charles University in Prague, Czech Republic
Anna Čermáková	Charles University, Czech Republic
Dimitrij Dobrovol'skij	Russian Academy of Sciences, Russian Language Institute, Russia
Jesse Egbert	Northern Arizona University, USA
Thierry Fontenelle	Translation Centre for the Bodies of the European Union, Luxembourg
Kleanthes K. Grohmann	University of Cyprus, Cyprus
Patrick Hanks	University of Wolverhampton, UK
Ulrich Heid	University of Hildesheim, Germany
Miloš Jakubíček	Lexical Computing and Masaryk University, Czech Republic
Kyo Kageura	University of Tokyo, Japan
Valia Kordoni	Humboldt University of Berlin, Germany
Simon Krek	University of Ljubljana, Slovenia
Pedro Mogorrón Huerta	University of Alicante, Spain
Johanna Monti	Naples Eastern University, Italy
Sara Moze	University of Wolverhampton, UK
Preslav Nakov	Qatar Computing Research Institute, HBKU, Qatar
Michael Oakes	University of Wolverhampton, UK
Marija Omazić	University of Osijek, Croatia
Petya Osenova	Sofia University, Bulgaria
Magali Paquot	Université catholique de Louvain, Belgium
Giovanni Parodi Sweis	Pontifical Catholic University of Valparaíso, Chile
Alain Polguère	University of Lorraine, France

Carlos Ramisch	Marseille Laboratory of Fundamental Computer Science, France
Ute Römer	Georgia State University, USA
Agata Savary	François Rabelais University, France
Barbara Schlücker	The University of Bonn, Germany
Violeta Seretan	University of Geneva, Switzerland
Kathrin Steyer	Institute of German Language, Germany
Yukio Tono	Tokyo University of Foreign Studies, Japan
Cornelia Tschichold	Swansea University, UK
Benjamin Tsou	City University of Hong Kong, SAR China
Agnès Tutin	University of Grenoble, France
Aline Villavicencio	Federal University of Rio Grande do Sul, Brazil
Eveline Wandl-Vogt	Austrian Academy of Sciences, Austria
Tom Wasow	Stanford University, USA
Eric Wehrli	University of Geneva, Switzerland
Stefanie Wulff	University of Florida, USA
Michael Zock	Marseille Laboratory of Fundamental Computer Science, France

Additional Reviewers

Verginica Barbu Mititelu	Romanian Academy, Research Institute for AI, Romania
Archna Bhatia	Language Technologies Institute, CMU, USA
Ismail El Maarouf	Adarga Limited, Oxford University Press, UK
Voula Giouli	Institute for Language and Speech Processing, Athena RIC, Greece
Václava Kettnerová	Charles University, Czech Republic
Rogelio Nazar	Pontifical Catholic University of Valparaíso, Chile
Irene Renau	Pontifical Catholic University of Valparaíso, Chile
Ioannis Saridakis	University of Athens, Greece
Inguna Skadina	University of Latvia, Latvia
Shiva Taslimipoor	University of Wolverhampton, UK
Veronika Vincze	Hungarian Academy of Sciences, Hungary
Victoria Yaneva	University of Wolverhampton, UK

Keynote Speakers Main Conference

Kenneth Church	Johns Hopkins University, USA
Gloria Corpas	University of Malaga, Spain
Dmitrij Dobrovol'skij	Russian Academy of Sciences, Russian Language Institute, Russia
Patrick Hanks	University of Wolverhampton, UK
Miloš Jakubíček	Lexical Computing and Masaryk University, Czech Republic

Invited Speakers of Europhras 2017 Workshops

Jean-Pierre Colson	Université catholique de Louvain, Belgium
Carlos Ramisch	Marseille Laboratory of Fundamental Computer Science, France

Organising Committee

Amanda Bloore	University of Wolverhampton, UK
Martina Cotella	University of Genoa, Italy
Arianna Fabbri	University of Genoa, Italy
April Harper	University of Wolverhampton, UK
Sara Moze	University of Wolverhampton, UK
Rocío Sánchez González	University of Malaga, Spain
Andrea Silvestre Baquero	Polytechnic University of Valencia, Spain
Shiva Taslimipoor	University of Wolverhampton, UK
Victoria Yaneva	University of Wolverhampton, UK

Conference Chair

Ruslan Mitkov	University of Wolverhampton, UK

Sponsors

EUROPHRAS

EUROPHRAS

EUROPÄISCHE GESELLSCHAFT FÜR PHRASEOLOGIE

Sketch Engine

University of Wolverhampton

ELRA

Contents

Keynote and Invited Talks

Phraseology in Translation and Contrastive Studies

Lexicography and Terminography

Exploitation of Corpora in Phraseological Studies

Development of Corpora for Phraseological Studies

Phraseology and Language Learning

Keynote and Invited Talks

Corpus Methods in a Digitized World

Kenneth Ward Church(✉)

IBM, Yorktown Heights, NY, USA
Kenneth.Ward.Church@gmail.com

Abstract. Data is available like never before. We believed that back in the 1990s, but corpora are even larger today than they were then, and corpora will continue to grow for some time to come. Thus far, corpus sizes have been limited by our ability to collect data, but we are rapidly approaching a fundamental limit on supply of written and spoken language. There are only so many people in the world, and they have only so much time to communicate with one another. It is becoming feasible to digitize a non-trivial fraction of the world's communication. This ability is creating new opportunities for new audiences to join in on the fun. Google Ngrams makes it easy for anyone to apply corpus-based methods to half a trillion words (4% of all books ever printed). The popular press is referring to corpus methods and Google Ngrams as "addictive." Computer Scientists are talking about "digital immortality" (recording much of human communication and storing it forever). Digital immortality may not be a reality just yet, but psychologists are currently recording most of what children say and hear between 2 months and 2 years of age in order to better understand language acquisition. As the world becomes digitized, there will be many applications of corpus-based methods that include lexicography (and so much more).

Keywords: Corpus methods · Digitalized world · Google Ngrams

1 MyLifeBits and Digital Immortality

It is becoming feasible to digitize a non-trivial fraction of the world's communication.

> MyLifeBits is a project to fulfill the Memex vision first posited by Vannevar Bush in 1945. It is a system for storing all of one's digital media, including documents, images, sounds, and videos... Gordon Bell, our apha user, has digitized nearly everything possible from his entire life, and will have eliminated all paper (except those legally required) by the time this paper is published [1].

How much disk space are we talking about? Table 1 is a simplified version of Table 1 from [2]. Disk space used to be expensive; a gigabyte cost $500,000 in 1981, but today, a gigabyte costs just $0.03. It has been suggested that the race to zero

R. Mitkov (Ed.): Europhras 2017, LNAI 10596, pp. 3–15, 2017.
https://doi.org/10.1007/978-3-319-69805-2_1

is over,[1] but even so, the cost of (spinning)[2] disk is no longer an issue for most of us. We could afford the disk space to store a DVD movie of our lifetime (uncut and uncompressed), if we wanted to (which we don't).

Table 1. Bell and Gray's estimates of lifetime storage requirements [2]

Data-types	Lifetime
Text	60–300 GB
Photos	150 GB
Speech	1.2 TB
Music	5.0 TB
DVD video	1 PB

Gray has worked on a number of large data projects including [3] which may have inspired Google Earth[3] and the World-Wide Telescope [4].[4]

2 Spoken Data

Massive amounts of speech are being digitized because of technologies such as Apple Siri, Amazon Alexa, Google Now, etc. Google,[5] Microsoft Bing,[6] IBM Watson[7] and others offer APIs where anyone can upload their speech data and transcribe it. Medical transcription applications are taking off with the need to create electronic medical records under Obamacare.[8] Obviously, much of this data is extremely sensitive and can't be shared widely, but the existence of so much data will create incentives to do many interesting things.

Popup archive[9] has 5.5M minutes (90k hours) of less sensitive audio, largely from public radio stations. That's hundreds of times larger than popular speech corpora such as Fisher [5][10], Switchboard [6][11] and CallHome [7].[12]

---

[1] https://www.backblaze.com/blog/hard-drive-cost-per-gigabyte.

[2] Storage on phones tends to use more expensive solid state disk. Those prices are also falling, though not as rapidly.

[3] https://www.google.com/earth.

[4] http://www.worldwidetelescope.org.

[5] https://www.google.com/intl/en/chrome/demos/speech.html.

[6] https://azure.microsoft.com/en-us/services/cognitive-services/speech/.

[7] https://speech-to-text-demo.mybluemix.net.

[8] Two examples of speech companies in the medical business are: https://www.nuance.com and https://mmodal.com.

[9] https://www.popuparchive.com/.

[10] https://catalog.ldc.upenn.edu/ldc2004t19.

[11] https://catalog.ldc.upenn.edu/ldc97s62.

[12] https://catalog.ldc.upenn.edu/ldc97s42.

Deb Roy popularized the idea of digitizing the first few years of a child's life. His Ted Talk[13] has 2.4M views. When the Human Speechome Project[14] started, it was necessary to install a machine room in Deb Roy's basement. Since then, the technology has made considerable progress. Caitlin Fausey's corpus [8] was collected with a head cam worn by kids 2 months to 2 years. SEEDLingS[15] (Study of Environmental Effects on Developing Linguistic Skills) is recording children between 6 and 18 months, combining well-controlled studies in the lab that assess what words infants know, with in-the-home audio and video recordings of what words infants hear, and what they see when they hear these words.

A community is developing around DARCLE (Daylong Audio Recordings of Children's Linguistic Environments).[16] There is interest in collecting audio of child development across a wide range of diverse languages and social backgrounds. Given the scope of this ambitious project, various consortia are emerging such as HomeBank,[17] which is part of TalkBank,[18] which is part of CLARIN.[19] These consortia are reaching out in all sorts of new directions: video,[20] aphasia,[21] etc.

3 Digital Libraries

Digital libraries have a long history dating back to Vannevar Bush's Memex described in "As we may think" [9].[22] Brewster Kahle is best known for the "Way back machine."[23] Many people have referred to the web as the largest corpus there is, though a crawl of the web is only a few tens of terabytes. Crawls tend to be smaller than query logs. The economics of the web depend on a healthy mixture of readers and writers, with more readers than writers. Thus, logs of what readers are reading tend to be larger than crawls of what authors are writing.

The Wayback Machine, though, is considerably larger than a single web crawl because the Wayback Machine takes snapshots of the web periodically (every few weeks/months) and stores them forever. According to Wikipedia,[24] the Wayback machine grew from 3 petabytes in 2009 to 15 petabytes in 2016, increasing about 100 terabytes per month. Actually, the increase is probably super-linear. Figure 1 fits an exponential to some points from Wikipedia, predicting that the Wayback Machine will soon contain a trillion pages (if it hasn't done so already).

[13] https://www.ted.com/talks/deb_roy_the_birth_of_a_word.
[14] https://www.media.mit.edu/cogmac/projects/hsp.html.
[15] http://bergelsonlab.com.
[16] http://darcle.org.
[17] http://homebank.talkbank.org.
[18] http://talkbank.org/.
[19] https://www.clarin.eu.
[20] https://nyu.databrary.org.
[21] http://aphasia.talkbank.org.
[22] https://en.wikipedia.org/wiki/As_We_May_Think.
[23] https://archive.org/web.
[24] https://en.wikipedia.org/wiki/Wayback_Machine.

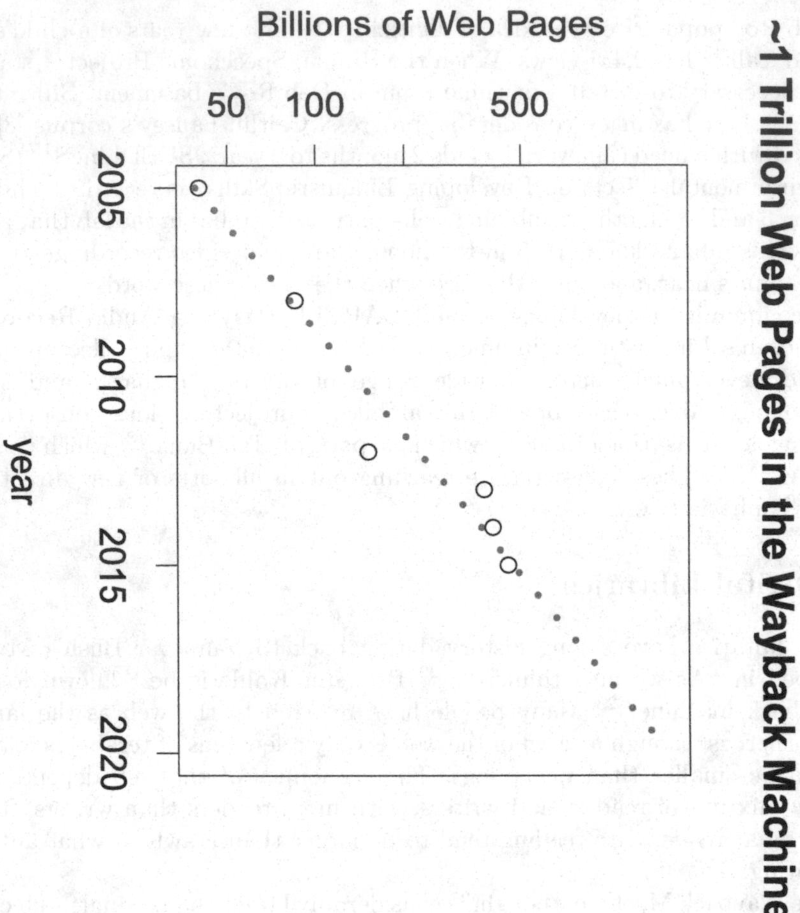

Fig. 1. The Wayback Machine is growing quickly, probably more than linearly. (Note that the y-axis is using a log scale.) The dashed red line is fit to the points (from Wikipedia entry for "Wayback Machine."). Extrapolating the line out to 2020 suggests the Wayback Machine will soon contain a trillion pages. (Color figure online)

In 2007, Brewster Kahle gave a Ted Talk[25] outlining an even more ambitious effort to digitize books, videos, TV and more. That Ted Talk received more than 400k views.

4 Google Books

Google Books and Google Ngrams have upped the ante with an article in Science [10] and a 2011 Ted Talk[26] (with 1.8M views). What makes a word real?

[25] https://www.ted.com/talks/brewster_kahle_builds_a_free_digital_library.
[26] https://www.ted.com/talks/what_we_learned_from_5_million_books.

In another popular Ted Talk[27] (1.6M views), Anne Curzan explains how the American Heritage Dictionary decides such questions. Apparently, they have a usage panel of experts (including people like her) that vote on such decisions. In the Ted Talk, she describes the process she uses to cast her votes (she turns to Google Ngrams).

The Science article makes it clear that it is now possible for anyone to search $\frac{1}{2}$ trillion words (4% of all books ever printed). And the popular press is referring to what we do as "addictive."[28]

Not all of the press is positive. One of the more critical stories starts out nicely before they get to their criticism, which we will return to shortly.[29]

> With Google Ngram, you could easily track the fame of Mickey Mouse versus Marilyn Monroe, the evolution of irregular verbs, censorship in Nazi Germany, and the decline of God. And so, so, so much more. At least, that was the promise from researchers who published a splashy paper in the prestigious journal Science. They even went ahead and gave their new field a name: "culturomics."

Now that Google is making it easier and easier for anyone to do corpus analysis, we will see more and more articles like this summary of the weddings sections of the New York Times.[30] Other articles in the popular press[31] teach the public how to take advantage of features that lexicographers have been using for years such as morphology, parts of speech and wild cards:

> Anyone who has spent time delving into databases knows how much flexibility you can get with wildcards: use an asterisk to stand in for any word, and suddenly your search horizons have expanded. In the new Ngram Viewer, using the asterisk as a wildcard will display the top ten most frequently appearing words that fill the slot over the range of time you have selected. The asterisk can be combined with parts of speech, too, so "*_NOUN" will find only the nouns that could appear in the sequence of words you're searching on.

This article encourages the general public to join in on the fun, and try their hand using corpus-based methods to address classic questions in lexicography. What are frequent objects for "drink" (in English and German)?

> All of this wildcard goodness isn't restricted to the English section of the corpus, either. In English, you can discover that the nouns that most often

---

27 https://www.ted.com/talks/anne_curzan_what_makes_a_word_real.

28 http://www.networkworld.com/article/2197233/applications/google-s-ngram-viewer--clever-and-addictive.html.

29 https://www.wired.com/2015/10/pitfalls-of-studying-language-with-google-ngram.

30 https://genius.com/Atodd-when-harvard-met-sally-n-gram-analysis-of-the-new-york-times-weddings-section-annotated.

31 https://www.theatlantic.com/technology/archive/2013/10/googles-ngram-viewer-goes-wild/280601.

serve as the object of the verb drink include water, wine, coffee, beer, and tea. But you can do the same search on the German verb trinken to find a different ranking of beverages: Kaffee (coffee) and Bier (beer) are on top, followed by Wein (wine), Wasser (water), and Tee (tea).

To encourage readers to try out Google Ngrams, the article contains a number of links that produce output such as Fig. 2. In this case, the query

```
trinken=>*_NOUN
```

was applied to the German corpus.

The article points out that many of these features are available elsewhere [11],[32] but "the peculiar interface can be off-putting to casual users."

Google Ngrams is particularly useful for investigating changes over time. Words enter the language and words leave (and some words take on new meanings). We are all aware of obvious cases. The word, "gay," for example, changed meaning. The word is about as common today as it was 200 years ago, but there a significant dip in the 1950s for obvious reasons. That much is pretty obvious, but I was surprised to see that the word was even less common 300 years ago than it was in the 1950s.

For another example, consider "Prague," "Czechoslovakia" and "Czech Republic." Google Ngrams shows what we would expect. The word "Czechoslovakia" first appeared in the 1920s, and became important during WW II and the Cold War, but became less frequent after the country split into two countries. The rise of the term "Czech Republic" coincides with the decline of "Czechoslovakia." In contrast to "Czechoslovakia" and "Czech Republic," "Prague" has a long history going back hundreds of years. The usage of "Prague" is fairly constant over time, though it also spiked during WW II and the Cold War.

As suggested above, there are many reasons for changes over time. Not only are languages constantly changing, but so are societies. Expletives are more common today than they were in the 1950s, as one would expect. But surprisingly, it appears that many of those 4-letter words were also quite common 300 years ago, though that may be (partially) the result of OCR errors.[33]

The data behind the Google Ngrams interface is available for download.[34] There are links there for ngrams from 1 to 5 words. There is also a link labeled "total counts" that was used to create Figs. 3 and 4.[35]

---

[32] https://corpus.byu.edu.

[33] It is suggested in https://www.wired.com/2015/10/pitfalls-of-studying-language-with-google-ngram/ that the f-word appears to be more common than it is in older books because of a common OCR error involving "f" and "s" discussed in [12]. While that might explain why the f-word appears to be so much more common in the 1700s than the 1800s, it doesn't explain why so many taboo 4-letter words are more common in the 1700s than the 1800s.

[34] http://storage.googleapis.com/books/ngrams/books/datasetsv2.html.

[35] It is reported in [10] that the collection contains over 5 million books and 500 million words, but we find that the collection is about 10% smaller than that.

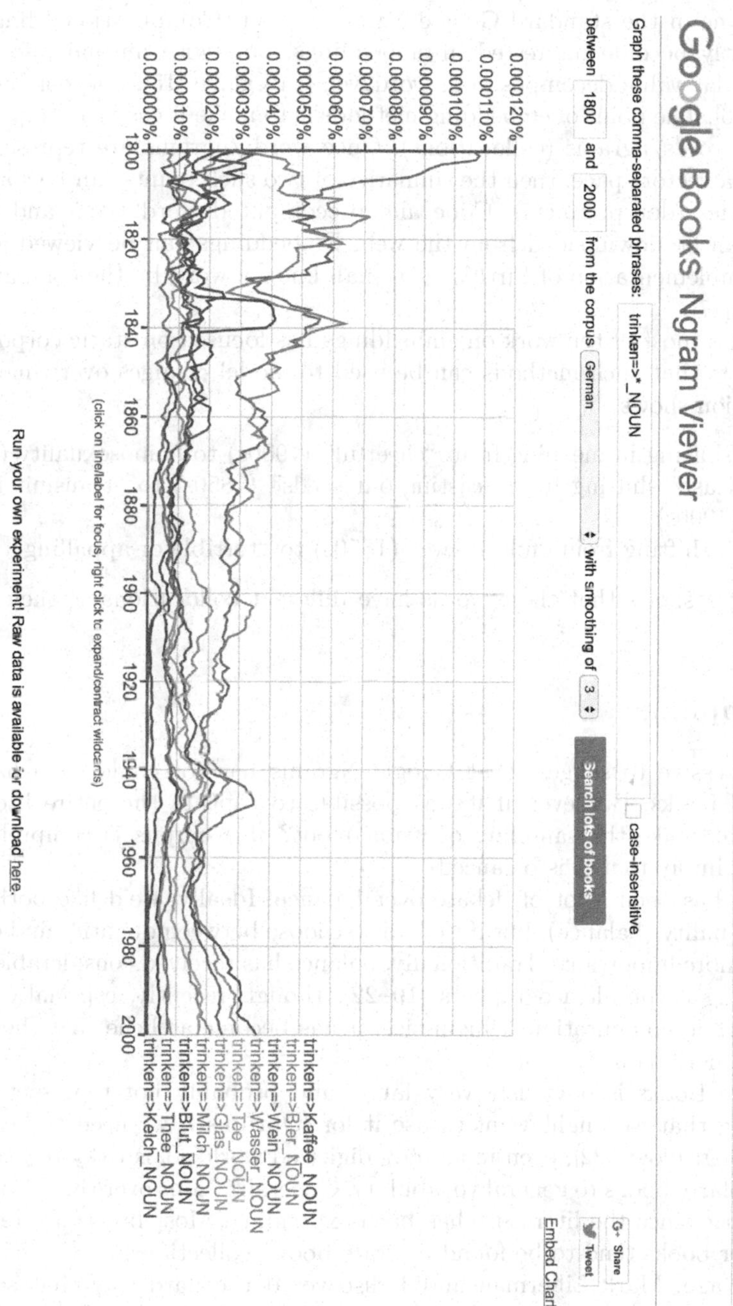

Fig. 2. Example of Google Ngram Viewer to find frequent objects of "trinken" (German for drink). Coffee is increasing in popularity over time; water and wine are declining.

Downloading the data makes it possible to do analyses that go beyond what can be done in the standard Google Ngram Viewer. Computational linguistics has recently become interested in embeddings: pointwise mutual information [13], singular value decomposition, word2vec [14], glove [15], and combinations thereof [16]. The point of embedding methods is to make it easy to compute similarity of words/ngrams (collocations). Once words/ngrams are represented as points in a vector space, then the similarity of two such points can be computed with cosines (dot products). Code and precomputed word2vec[36] and glove[37] vectors can be downloaded from the web. Embeddings can be viewed as engineering implementation of Firth's "you shall know a word by the company that it keeps" [17].

To date, most of the work on embeddings has focused on static corpora, but [18] reports that such methods can be used to model changes over time. Their visualization shows

1. "gay" shifting in meaning from "cheerful" (1900s) to homosexuality (1990s)
2. "broadcast" shifting from "casting out seeds" (1850s) to "transmitting signals" (1900s)
3. "awful" shifting from "full of awe" (1850s) to "terrible or appalling" (1990s)

Their Fig. 1 shows that these words have different collocations as they change meaning.

5 Sampling

It is impressive to suggest that Google Ngrams has (or could soon have) all published books. But even if it was possible to capture the entire literature, would that make the sampling question moot? If a corpus is comprehensive, does that imply that it is balanced?

There has been a lot of debate over balance. Ideally, we'd like both quantity and quality (balance), but if we had to choose between quantity and quality, which is more important? Traditionally, balance has received considerable attention among corpus lexicographers [19–22], though recently, especially among engineers and computational linguistics, it has become a cliche that there is no data like more data.

Google Books is obviously very large, and probably not representative of everything that we might want to use it for. Obviously, we need to be careful about Googleology [22], even in a 100% digitized world. It is risky to generalize from scholarly books to general vocabulary. Generalizations over time can also be problematic since the literature has been expanding. Most books are relatively new; older books tend to be found in "rare book" collections.

Years ago, Mark Liberman and I discovered the hard way that scholarly books aren't very representative of general vocabulary. We agreed to help Chapman when he was updating Roget's from the fourth edition [23] to the fifth

[36] https://code.google.com/archive/p/word2vec.
[37] https://nlp.stanford.edu/projects/glove.

[24]. We thought it would be easy to search recently published books for words that had recently entered the language (between 1977 and 1992). We started with catch-as-catch-can, whatever books the publisher happened to have around. Unfortunately, those books happened to be fairly scholarly, and they were full of words that weren't in the fourth edition, but Chapman didn't want those words. Scholars speak in their own language, with lots and lots of jargon and technical terminology that isn't appropriate for general reference. Chapman made it clear to us that he wasn't going to look at our lists unless 10% of them were good enough to make it into the fifth edition. It quickly became clear that lists based on scholarly books weren't going to make that cut.

After failing miserably with scholarly books, we turned in desperation to news, and discovered, much to our surprise, that the news is much more

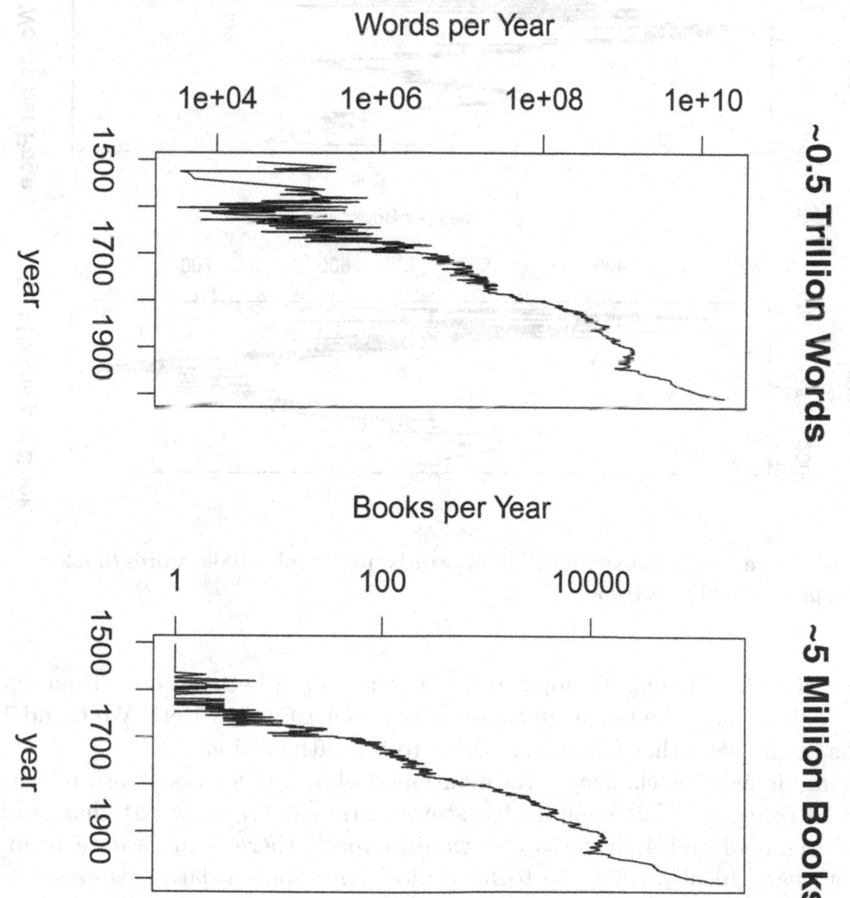

Fig. 3. How big is the Google Ngrams corpus? There are about half a trillion words (in 5 million books), published between 1505 and 2008. The corpus is growing about 3% per year, or 35% per decade.

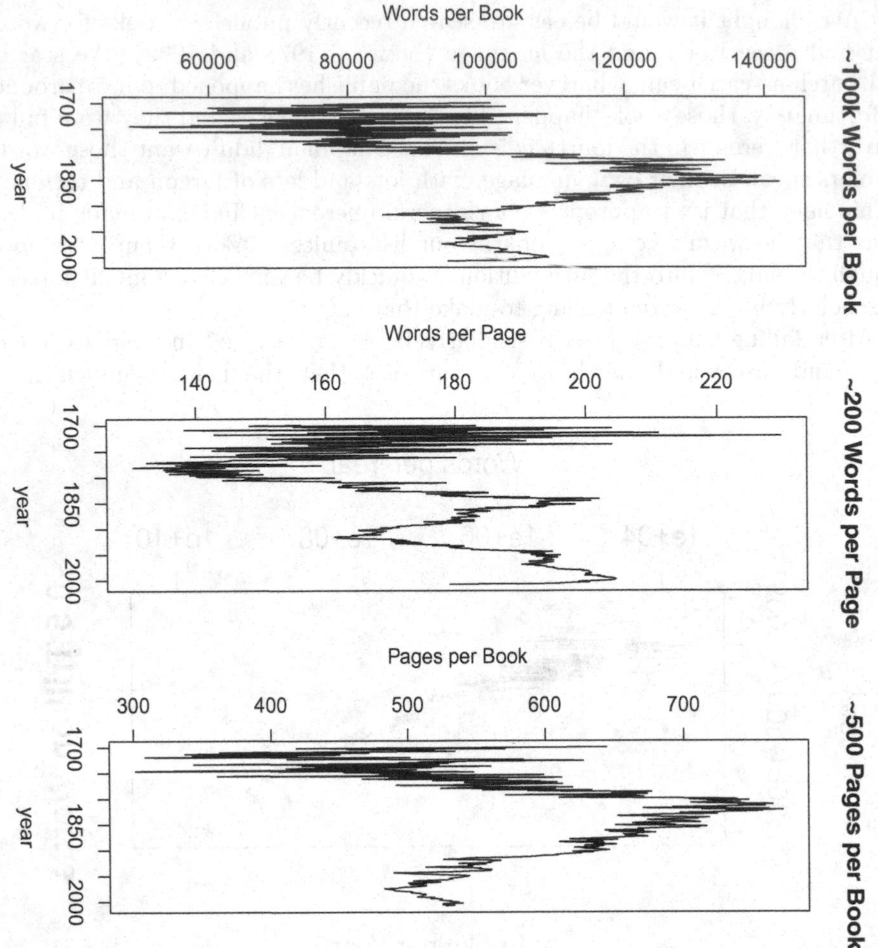

Fig. 4. There are approximately 100k words per book. 100k words/book ≈ 200 words/page × 500 pages/book.

appropriate for Chapman's application. The news is a better sample than scholarly books of how the language changed between 1977 and 1992. We found 10k words in the news that Chapman added to the fifth edition.

Time is another challenge. As mentioned above, older books are relatively hard to come by. That complicates statements about how words change over time. Figures 3 and 4 show, as one would expect, there is more data in more recent years. Ideally, we'd like to have nicely distributed data (regression typically introduces various normality assumptions), but unfortunately, the world isn't always nice.

If we were to estimate error bars on statements about word frequencies, it would quickly become obvious that error bars also depend on time. Estimates based on larger samples (more recent years) are more reliable than estimates based on smaller samples (less recent years). Figures 3 and 4 show more consistency from one year to the next in more recent years. A similar pattern has been observed here,[38] where frequencies of common function words are more consistent from one year to the next in more recent years.

It is actually pretty easy to show that the collection, despite its size, is biased in all sorts of ways. That doesn't mean that we should dismiss it. Data aren't always pretty. We should be thankful for what we have, and make the most of what we have. That said, it should be a relatively straightforward class exercise to download a bunch of ngrams and find words/patterns/collocations that are more salient in one way or another. That is, it should be fairly easy to find significant differences in frequency over time and/or collection.

Here are some fun examples of what one might expect to find from such an exercise. Consider "France" and "America" in two corpora, British English[39] and American English.[40] In the British corpora, "France" has always been more frequent than "America," though the gap has been narrowing in recent years. In contrast, in the American corpora, "France" was on top before 1900, but since then, "America" rules (at least, according to American authors).

There are also differences involving WW I and WW II. In the British corpus, "France" has two peaks (one for each of the two wars), but "America" has a single peak (for WW II, but not WW I). In contrast, in the American corpus, "America" has two peaks peak, but "France" has just one (for WW I). As the cliche goes, we are two nations divided by a common language.

6 How Large Do Corpora Need to Be?

How large do the corpora have to be to learn what? When can we expect to learn frames? In the 1980s, corpora were about 1 million words [19]. That was large enough to make a list of common content words, and to train part of speech taggers. A decade later, we had the 100 million word corpora such as the British National Corpus (BNC).[41] The BNC is large enough to see associations between common predicates and function words such as "save" + "from." Since then, with the web, data has become more and more available (possibly indexed to the price of disks with a growth rate of 100x to 1000x per decade).

If you take the numbers from our papers in the 1990s and look them up in Google today, you'll see that the counts are increasing by 100x to 1000x per decade. The larger counts make it easier to see all sorts of interesting patterns. A rising tide lifts all boats.

---

38 https://digitalsinology.org/when-n-grams-go-bad.

39 https://books.google.com/ngrams/graph?content=France,America&year_start=1800&year_end=2000&corpus=17.

40 https://books.google.com/ngrams/graph?content=France,America&year_start=1800&year_end=2000&corpus=18.

41 http://www.natcorp.ox.ac.uk.

What could we do with a million million words? A million million is a trillion. That should be enough to associations between pairs of content words. We need about 1 million words to see what's going on with a single content word, and a million million to see what's going on with a pair of content words.

Google Ngrams isn't as large as the web, but it is impressive nevertheless. Google Ngrams has half a trillion words (and it is growing quickly, though not nearly as quickly as disk prices are falling).[42] Google Ngrams is probably already large enough to find associations of many pairs of content words (collocations, typical predicate argument relations, Fillmore-style frames). Now that Google Ngrams is available for download, (See footnote 34) machine learning methods should be able to learn many of the patterns that lexicographers have been talking about such as: risk < *valued object* > for < *purpose* > [25].

7 Conclusions

When I was first introduced to corpus linguistics in the late 1980s by Patrick Hanks, I found it exciting, though somewhat out of fashion. As a student at MIT in the 1970s and 1980s, I learned about many things, but empiricism wasn't among those things. Much of that has changed, at least in professional meetings. It is hard to remember that there was a time when it was hard to publish a statistical paper in a computational linguistics venue.

But much more is about to happen as the world becomes digitized. Now that is becoming feasible to digitize a non-trivial fraction of the world's communication (text, speech and video), the mainstream media are becoming interested in what we do. Google Ngrams makes it easy for anyone to apply corpus-based methods to half a trillion words (4% of all books ever printed). Psychologists are studying language acquisition by recording most of what children say and hear for their first few years of life. Corpus-based methods are no longer out of fashion.

References

1. Gemmell, J., Bell, G., Lueder, R., Drucker, S., Wong, C.: MyLifeBits: fulfilling the memex vision. In: Proceedings of the Tenth ACM International Conference on Multimedia, pp. 235–238 (2002)
2. Bell, G., Gray, J.: Digital immortality. CACM **44**(3), 28–31 (2001)
3. Barclay, T., Gray, J., Slutz, D.: Microsoft TerraServer: a spatial data warehouse. ACM SIGMOD Record **29**(2), 307–318 (2000)
4. Szalay, A., Gray, J.: The World-wide Telescope. Science **293**(5537), 2037–2040 (2001)

[42] http://storage.googleapis.com/books/ngrams/books/googlebooks-eng-all-totalcounts-20120701.txt reports the number of words in the corpus by year between 1505 and 2008. Based on those numbers, the corpus is growing about 3% per year, or 35% per decade.

5. Cieri, C., Graff, D., Kimball, O., Miller, D., Walker, K.: Fisher English Training Speech. Linguistic Data Consortium, Philadelphia (2004)
6. Godfrey, J., Holliman, E., McDaniel, J.: SWITCHBOARD: telephone speech corpus for research and development. In: ICASSP, pp. 517–520 (1992)
7. Canavan, A., Graff, D., Zipperlen, G.: Callhome American English Speech. Linguistic Data Consortium, Philadelphia (1997)
8. Fausey, C., Jayaraman, S., Smith, L.: From faces to hands: changing visual input in the first two years. Cognition **152**, 101–107 (2016)
9. Bush, V.: As we may think. Atl. Monthly **176**(1), 101–108 (1945)
10. Michel, J., Shen, Y., et al.: Quantitative analysis of culture using millions of digitized books. Science **331**(6014), 176–182 (2011)
11. Davies, M.: The Corpus of Contemporary American English as the first reliable monitor corpus of English. Lit. Linguist. Comput. **24**(4), 447–464 (2010)
12. Pechenick, E., Danforth, C., Dodds, P.: Characterizing the Google Books corpus: strong limits to inferences of socio-cultural and linguistic evolution. PLoS ONE **10**(10), e0137041 (2015)
13. Church, K., Hanks, P.: Word association norms, mutual information, and lexicography. Comput. Linguist. **16**(1), 22–29 (1990)
14. Mikolov, T., Sutskever, I., Chen, K., Corrado, G., Dean, J.: Distributed representations of words and phrases and their compositionality. In: NIPS, pp. 3111–3119 (2013)
15. Pennington, J., Socher, R., Manning, C.: GloVe: global vectors for word representation. In: EMNLP, pp. 1532–1543 (2014)
16. Levy, O., Goldberg, Y.: Neural word embedding as implicit matrix factorization. In: NIPS, pp. 2177–2185 (2014)
17. Firth, J.: A Synopsis of Linguistic Theory, 1930–1955. Studies in Linguistic Analysis. Basil Blackwell, Oxford (1957)
18. Hamilton, W., Leskovec, J., Jurafsky, D.: Diachronic word embeddings reveal statistical laws of semantic change. In: ACL, pp. 1489–1501 (2016)
19. Francis, N., Kucera, H.: Frequency Analysis of English Usage. Houghton Mifflin Company, Boston (1982)
20. Sinclair, J.: Looking Up: An Account of the COBUILD Project in Lexical Computing and the Development of the Collins COBUILD English Language Dictionary. Collins, London (1987)
21. Aijmer, K., Altenberg, B.: English Corpus Linguistics. Routledge, London (2014)
22. Kilgarriff, A.: Googleology is bad science. Comput. Linguist. **33**(1), 147–151 (2007)
23. Chapman, R.: Roget's International Thesaurus, 4th edn. Harper and Row, New York (1977)
24. Chapman, R.: Roget's International Thesaurus, 5th edn. Harper and Row, New York (1992)
25. Fillmore, C., Atkins, B.: Toward a frame-based lexicon: the semantics of RISK and its neighbors. In: Frames, Fields, and Contrasts: New Essays in Semantic and Lexical Organization, pp. 75–102. Lawrence Erlbaum Associates, Hillsdale (1992)

The *IdiomSearch* Experiment: Extracting Phraseology from a Probabilistic Network of Constructions

Jean-Pierre Colson(✉)

Université catholique de Louvain, 1348 Louvain-la-Neuve, Belgium
jean-pierre.colson@uclouvain.be

Abstract. This paper reports the preliminary results of an experiment carried out on a large scale for the extraction of PUs (phraseological units, also called idioms) from large web corpora in four languages (English, Spanish, French, Chinese). The use of a new algorithm based on metric clustering techniques, of optimized database storage and of interaction with users and researchers by means of a web application, made it possible to reach high precision scores for most common PUs in the four languages, while further experimentation is still necessary for establishing recall levels with long n-grams. In the meantime, the freely accessible web application makes it possible to visualize the high proportion of phraseology in the broad sense (or of formulaic language): about 30 to 60% of the newspaper articles tested in the experiments consisted of PUs. The most surprising results, however, came from Chinese: as the algorithm had to be changed for taking into account the associations between morphemes, the methodology used made it possible to partly confirm, from a statistical point of view, one of the major claims of construction grammar: the existence of a probabilistic network of constructions, from morphemes to idiomatic phrases.

Keywords: Collocation extraction · Construction grammar · Statistical Semantics · Information retrieval · Collostructions

1 Introduction: Theoretical Background

One of the paradoxes of recent research in corpus and computational linguistics is that the theoretical underpinnings are rarely addressed in detail, as if applying algorithms to an object (language) whose very structure is so controversial were a matter of evidence. In such a complex matter as recurrent linguistic sequences, it is besides necessary to have recourse to huge linguistic corpora and to take linguistic diversity into account.

Foreign language learners and translators are often impressed by the overwhelming importance of prefabricated elements and figurative senses in language. For more than 50 years, corpus and computational linguists have therefore been trying to extract those elements automatically from corpora. However, as pointed out by [13], the results of the automatic extraction of *collocations* in the broad sense are still disappointing, and new avenues of research ought to be explored. Indeed, another paradox of the research on automatic extraction of recurrent sequences in language is that *you don't know exactly what you (and the algorithm) should actually extract*.

R. Mitkov (Ed.): Europhras 2017, LNAI 10596, pp. 16–28, 2017.
https://doi.org/10.1007/978-3-319-69805-2_2

Phraseology as defined by [4] encompasses all *phraseological units* or *phraseologisms*, from *collocations* (weakly idiomatic phrases) to proverbs, but *collocation* is widely used in corpus or computational linguistics [13] as a generic term (covering all *phraseological units*). In the same way, *idiom* has sometimes been used for very idiomatic phrases [4] but is also a generic term for all set phrases of a language [17].

Yet another way of describing all language blocks that are accessed as one element of meaning is the notion of *formulaic language* [22]: a *heteromorphic* lexicon makes it possible to store linguistic material of different sizes (morphemes, words, multiword strings); besides, [22] claims that, by default, native speakers will use formulas and will only break down linguistic material into smaller components when they have specific needs (the principle of NOA, Needs Only Analysis). Adults will, on the whole, tend to analyze input and store smaller lexical units. Using formulaic language is considered as a way of promoting the speaker's own interests, because larger and holistic units, with pragmatic and cultural associations, make it possible to exercise a better control over the interpretation of the message by the hearer. In other words, formulaic language is a way of manipulating the hearer. The secondary and somehow artificial character of written language, as opposed to original dialogues, is stressed.

In addition to the great terminological diversity around the notion of phraseology, its extraction raises another thorny issue: where does a phraseological unit (PU) start and where does it end? On the one hand, many PUs are discontinuous (as in *the more you ... the more you* or *X take Y into account*); on the other hand, the exact beginning or the end of the PU are not always straightforward (as in *to VERB (and to VERB) (...) was with N/Pro the work of an instant*).

Finally, developments in cognitive linguistics over the past 30 years and among constructionist approaches in particular [17] have proposed a radical new approach to the study of constructions in general. For construction grammar [10, 12], all *constructions* are Saussurean signs, i.e. conventional and learned pairings of form and function at varying levels of complexity and abstraction. Thus, constructions include partially filled words or morphemes (e.g. *pre*-N or V-*ing*), words, but also idioms in the generic sense of PUs: filled (*spill the beans*), partially filled (*take X for granted*), minimally filled (*the more... the more*), and even abstract constructions such has the Ditransitive Verb Construction (*give X to Y)*, or the Passive Construction.

The constructionist approaches to language have fundamentally changed the vision of PUs, because of the proposed continuum between lexicon and syntax, the *constructicon* [9, 11]: all language sequences are basically of the same type, as they are all *constructions*, ranging from very schematic and abstract constructions such as the passive, to *substantive* or specific constructions (morphemes and words), some of which are complex (idioms, i.e. PUs). According to this approach, PUs are in no fundamental way different from ordinary words of from syntactic constructions; on the opposite, as pointed out by [23], all constructions are in a sense *idioms*. Thus, partially schematic complex constructions (e.g. X SPILL the beans (on/about Y)) are traditionally labelled idioms (or PUs), but this is for [23] simply due to the fact that such constructions make the effects of idiomatic variation very clear, the main point being that they are not fundamentally different from other constructions.

An even more radical view is taken by [7]: all constructions are language-specific, and categories are besides construction-specific. On the basis of a rigorous analysis of various languages of the world, the author comes to the conclusion that there is no such thing as, for instance, a universal passive construction (similarities can only occur between cognate languages) or a universal *verb* category.

Those fascinating and challenging insights were not only gained through introspection and comparison of relevant examples, but also by means of rigorous psycholinguistic experiments, and were besides confirmed by the *collostructional* approach.

This methodology [14, 15, 21], makes it possible to quantify association strength in and between constructions, and is derived from collocational approaches used in corpus linguistics. For instance, [21] shows that there is a statistical association between verbs and Argument Structure constructions and that verbs display very different association strengths within those constructions.

In constructionist approaches, grammar is conceived as a network of constructions, of which the nature is largely probabilistic [8, 21].

These theoretical and practical issues were the starting point of the *IdiomSearch* experiment. In this paper, a summary is given of its methodology, main results, and possible further developments.

2 Methodology

In order to gain fresh insights into both the practical aspects and the theoretical underpinnings of extracting PUs from corpora, we chose to use a *big data* approach. In the first place, it has been demonstrated by several studies such as [5, 19] that large linguistic corpora (of 100 million tokens or more) are necessary in order to be confronted with various examples of the most common PUs. Besides, as pointed out by [13], the dispersion across corpora has not sufficiently been taken into account, and many studies are of a very limited scope, as opposed to the huge number of PUs in a single language.

[13] also lays stress on additional limitations of current methods for extracting PUs from a corpus: most statistical measures are not directional (they consider *that you* and *you that* as the same PU), they are not easy to reconcile with psycholinguistic or cognitive principles, and they are not easily extendable to longer sequences such as trigrams, fourgrams, let alone 6-grams.

Within the framework of the *IdiomSearch* experiment, it was therefore decided to use the *cpr-score (Corpus Proximity Ratio)* described in [6]. This experimental score is non-parametric and directional, as it is derived from information retrieval [1], and more specifically from metric clustering techniques (Fig. 1):

$$\boldsymbol{cpr} = \frac{\boldsymbol{n}\,(\boldsymbol{x_{i_1} x_{i_2} x_{i_3} \ldots x_{i_n}})}{\boldsymbol{n}(\mathbf{max}\,(||\boldsymbol{x_i} - \boldsymbol{x_j}||) \leq \boldsymbol{W} \atop \boldsymbol{x_{i_1}, x_{i_2}, x_{i_3}, \ldots x_{i_n}}}$$

Fig. 1. The *cpr-score*

It basically corresponds to the average distance between the component grams of an n-gram, given a window W, set between 20 and 50 tokens according to the language. In order to compute it, it suffices to keep a trace of all the offsets (positions in the text file) of the n-gram and its component grams in a corpus. For instance, the PU *spill the beans* occurs 14 times on a 200 million token web corpus of English; this exact frequency is then divided by the frequency of *spill the beans* within a window of a maximum of 20 tokens between the grams, which yields 15 occurrences. Dividing 14 by 15 gives a *cpr-score* of 0.93. The significance threshold for PUs has been set experimentally at 0.40, while scores as low as 0.065 still yield partly fixed phrases or elements of phrases, as explained in [6].

Table 1. *cpr-score* for a few English idioms

Idiom	Frequency	*cpr-score*
Add insult to injury	47	0.96
At the drop of a hat	40	1.00
Back to the drawing board	67	0.97
Barking up the wrong tree	7	0.88
Beat about the bush	13	1.00

Bigrams such as *easy rider*, *New York*, *sharp criticism* etc. are easy to explain to informants having to evaluate the results of automatic extraction. Once the level of trigram is reached, and in particular for longer n-grams, making clear to non-linguists what we mean exactly by PUs (or collocations, or formulas and so on) is not an easy matter, especially if the diversity of languages is taken into account.

This is the reason why *recall* was difficult to measure, in the absence of reliable gold standards in several languages, as is the case for most automated tasks in NLP (natural language processing). *Precision* on the basis of native speaker judgment or dictionaries, on the other hand, is very high for very idiomatic phrases (*cpr* > 0.40). The novel feature of *cpr* is that it is very stable, *no matter what the length of the n-gram is* (at least between bigrams and 7-grams). Thus, in Table 1, the very fixed PUs or *idioms* chosen randomly in the dictionary all yielded a very high *cpr-score* on a 200 million token web corpus[1].

At the lower end of the spectrum, however, linguistic structures yielding partly significant association scores (with a *cpr* between 0.065 and 0.40) were problematic. As a rule, separating the wheat from the chaff at the left hand of the phraseological spectrum is nigh on impossible, as already pointed out by [4].

In order to shed new light on the interplay between lexis and grammar, and particularly with respect to phraseology [4], formulaic language [22] and construction grammar [17], the *cpr-score* was computed on large web corpora of 200 million tokens.

[1] The web corpora used in the *IdiomSearch* experiment were assembled using the WebBootCat tool provided by the Sketch Engine (http://sketchengine.co.uk), on the basis of seed words and following the methodology described in [2].

As mentioned in note 1, assembling the corpora happened in an automated way, with a balanced list of seed words. Web corpora of 200 million tokens were created for English, French, Spanish and Chinese[2] (Mandarin, simplified spelling).

For each language, all n-grams ranging from bigrams to 7-grams were extracted from the corpus, with a frequency threshold of 3 occurrences (for 200 million tokens). The *cpr-score* was computed for each selected n-gram. Thanks to an optimization of the database requests by means of a query likelihood model [18], this took no more than one week per language, with an average time for each request of 0.07 second on a Linux machine. Several regex-based algorithms were passed through the results, in order to deal with the problem of phraseological encapsulation: smaller n-grams (bigrams, trigrams) may be included in the results of longer n-grams (e.g. *take the rough* as a partial result for *take the rough with the smooth*); in this case, n-grams included in larger n-grams were discarded, except if their association score was high, which is sometimes the case if competing PUs are at stake (e.g. *take a walk* and *take a walk down memory lane*).

In order to allow easy access to researchers and students, all selected n-grams were put in a database, freely accessible from a web application[3]. The user is presented with results highlighted in colors ranging from pale yellow (partly fixed and frequent) to deep red (very fixed and not frequent). The number of words in the results is also indicated, as well as the number of phrases per word (PW ratio) and the number of phrases in the text (PT ratio). The PT ratio is computed by checking how many words (tokens) of the text are included in PUs. Thus, a PT ratio of 0.45 means that just 55% of the words of the text are not included in phrases.

3 Results and Discussion

3.1 The Proportion of Phraseology in Texts

Before providing an overview of the results produced by the IdiomSearch experiment, it may be useful to start from a small text fragment, in order to show what types of PUs the algorithm is able to extract: a few lines from an opinion piece on Brexit, published in a British newspaper[4].

> *"Don't get me wrong, I – and I'm sure many other Labour voters – consider Brexit to be the biggest act of political self-sabotage in my lifetime, with stark consequences for my generation and those following it. Were it to be miraculously cancelled I would be over the moon. But there's a sense that some would like everything to be about Brexit and only Brexit. When it comes to what people care about in 2017 – and vote on the basis of – that simply is not the case."*

The algorithm used by the IdiomSearch application makes it possible to extract the following PUs on the fly.

---

[2] For Chinese, the corpus does not consist of 200 million Chinese characters (*hans*), but of 200 million Chinese words (as tokens).

[3] IdiomSearch is accessible on the web at: http://idiomsearch.LSTI.ucl.ac.be.

[4] The Guardian, http://www.theguardian.com, 7 August 2017.

Table 2. Examples of extracted PUs

PUs	Frequency	*cpr-score*
Don't get me wrong	124	0.99
Many other	3507	0.55
Be the biggest	179	0.20
In my lifetime	56	0.66
Consequences for	407	0.52
Would be over the moon	3	0.75
Sense that	2365	0.26
Would like	12456	0.80
When it comes to	2026	0.57
Care about	1714	0.46
On the basis of	2752	0.73
Is not the case	449	0.23

As one of the aims of the experiment is to receive feedback from users, and to improve the algorithm and the selection of corpora, no systematic survey of different registers or text types has been carried out so far, but more than 200 newspaper articles have been tested in the different languages, confirming that such a method yields a high percentage of phraseology (as expressed by the PT ratio) in newspaper articles. For opinion pieces published by British or American newspapers, the overall PT ratio, reflecting in other words the total percentage of phraseology that could be extracted by the algorithm, lies between 0.30 and 0.55. For the whole of the example text above (803 tokens), it was precisely 0.50 (i.e. roughly half of the text consisted of PUs). Table 3 presents the results (number of tokens and PT ratio) for 5 newspaper articles (comments on the news).

A comparison was also made with about 200 fragments (of comparable length) from available corpora of spoken English. An example with 5 texts is given in Table 3, comprising 5 randomly selected passages from the *Corpus of Spoken, Professional American-English (Athelstan)*[5].

A word of caution is necessary in the interpretation of these results. It should be stressed again that the extraction of PUs by means of the *cpr-score* crucially depends on the reference corpus used. As mentioned in the preceding section, a balanced English corpus of 200 million tokens was used for the experiment, but there is no guarantee that all phrases from a specific text are also present on the reference corpus; if that is not the case, they can of course not be extracted by the program. The PT ratio is therefore an indication of the minimal percentage of phraseology (in the broad sense).

It may also come as a surprise that fragments from spoken corpora did not show major differences with written corpora as far as the total percentage of phraseology (PT ratio) is concerned. This is partly due to the topics that were discussed during the interviews: the Athelstan fragments (Table 4), for instance, contain interviews about university topics. Many differences appear in the types of PUs used, with many typical

[5] Athelstan Homepage, http://www.athel.com/cspatg.html, last accessed 2017/08/09.

Table 3. *PT ratio* (percentage of phraseology) for 5 newspaper articles in English

	Tokens per text	*PT ratio*
Article one[a]	743	0.41
Article two[b]	789	0.41
Article three[c]	730	0.48
Article four[d]	660	0.56
Article five[e]	769	0.55

[a]The Guardian Homepage, http://www.theguardian.com, 2015/10/05.
[b]The Guardian Homepage, http://www.theguardian.com, 2015/03/31.
[c]The New York Times Homepage, http://www.nytimes.com, 2016/01/13.
[d]The Daily Telegraph Homepage, http://www.telegraph.co.uk, 2015/04/04.
[e]The Daily Telegraph Homepage, http://www.telegraph.co.uk, 2015/05/16.

phrases of spoken English (*Thank you very much, I would strongly suggest, I'm not sure, I wondered if*), but the average percentage is not very different from the results obtained for the written texts.

From a theoretical point of view, these results partly confirm the hypothesis that about 50% of all texts consist of phraseology in the broad sense, the *idiom principle* [20], as the PT ratio (see examples in Tables 3 and 4) reaches figures between 0.35 and 0.60.

Table 4. *PT ratio* (percentage of phraseology) for 5 texts from the *Athelstan* corpus

	Tokens per text	*PT ratio*
Text one	830	0.50
Text two	795	0.56
Text three	793	0.39
Text four	809	0.49
Text five	759	0.48

The examples of extracted PUs, as illustrated in Table 2, also provide convincing evidence for the existence of a network of statistical association between the elements of complex structures such as idioms (*spill the beans*), grammatical collocations (*care about, consequences for*), communicative formulas (*don't get me wrong, when it comes to*), which is compatible with construction grammar [17].

3.2 Experiments with Spanish, French and Chinese

Within the framework of the IdiomSearch experiment, similar tests were conducted for Spanish, French and Chinese (Mandarin, simplified spelling).

For Spanish and French, the results were comparable to those obtained for English, with roughly the same percentages of phraseology in the broad sense. As often in computational linguistics, the main difficulties were technical ones: compiling web corpora by means of the robot required special attention for possible errors of encoding[6]. As Spanish and French are also Indo-European, segmented and inflectional languages, it comes as no surprise that the algorithm was able to work in much the same way as for English. Chinese, on the other hand, represented in many regards a daunting challenge for the IdiomSearch experiment.

Chinese is, in the first place, an *unsegmented* language: there are no blanks between words. Modern Mandarin Chinese remains largely an isolating language (there is a very low morpheme per word ratio, and no inflectional morphology). In classical Chinese, one character (*han*) corresponded to one word, but most words in modern Chinese consist of two characters, and sometimes more. The situation is therefore rather complex, which makes it also particularly interesting for testing linguistic hypotheses.

According to [7], constructions but also categories are language-specific, and Chinese is often cited as an example of a language apparently functioning in a totally different way for grammatical categories such as Noun and Verb. As pointed out by [22], several studies have besides confirmed that Chinese native speakers make different decisions when they have to segment a text into words, and that even the same persons do not always confirm their first choices. Therefore, words –if they exist at all, function in a very different way in Chinese.

For these reasons, it was not an easy matter to adapt the IdiomSearch algorithm to Mandarin Chinese, as the *cpr-score* is based on the average distance between words in a corpus. As a temporary solution, it was decided to consider the distance between Chinese characters, which made it possible to reach very high precision scores on the basis of established Chinese phrases. Table 5 shows the frequency and the *cpr-score* for a few common chengyus, the 4-syllable idioms [16], from which study the examples are borrowed.

The examples of *chengyu* in Table 5 clearly show the achievements of the *cpr-score* for very fixed Chinese phrases: contrary to what might have been expected, the score works particularly well. Being non-inflectional, mostly isolating and having under-gone few influences from other languages, Mandarin Chinese is actually well suited for testing linguistic extraction algorithms, in spite of some technical adaptations.

An important finding of the IdiomSearch experiment, thanks to extensive testing with Chinese, is that statistical association of morphemes/words is partly discontinuous, **even within established phrases**. This contradicts the intuition that adding one element at a time to a n-gram allows to narrow down the probabilities. Not only is frequency of minor importance in the statistical association of words or morphemes,

[6] The computational issue is well known: many web pages contain Unicode errors; the robot assumes that the downloaded web page is in Unicode, but the errors remain and appear in the web corpus.

Table 5. *cpr-score* for a few Chinese *chengyu*

Chengyu	Frequency	*cpr-score*
小心翼翼 *xiǎo-xīn-yì-yì*[a]	1442	1.00
自怨自艾 *zì-yuàn-zì-yì*[b]	100	0.99
趁热打铁 *chèn-rè-dǎ-tiě*[c]	87	1.00
孤掌难鸣 *g -zhǎng-nán-míng*[d]	33	1.00
杯弓蛇影 *bēi-gōng-shé-yǐng*[e]	33	0.97
破釜沉舟 *pò-fǔ-chén-zhōu*[f]	153	0.99

[a]Literally: small-heart-respectful-respectful; meaning: being careful, with respect, taking precautions [16].
[b]Literally: self-hate-self-refrain; meaning: to repent, to be sorry for one's deeds [16].
[c]Literally: profit-heat-beat-iron; meaning: strike while the iron is hot [16].
[d]Literally: solitary-palm-difficult-resonate; meaning: who is without support is doomed to fail [16].
[e]Literally: cup-bow-snake-reflection; meaning: be alarmed for nothing [16].
[f]Literally: break-cauldron-sink-ship; meaning: be decided to win or lose, cross the Rubicon [16].

but there is no strict continuity between the elements. Suppose, for instance, that ABCD is a common PU or *constructional idiom* in English. Thanks to the *cpr*-score, it is possible to measure the statistical association between A + B + C + D. It is also possible to compute the score for A + B + C. Intuitively, one may be tempted to think that A + B + C is incomplete (as D is missing), and that the statistical score for ABC will therefore be lower than for ABCD. This is indeed often the case, but there are many counterexamples showing that the statistical association is much more complex, as internal PUs may interact with the overall score.

Table 6 illustrates this point for the communicative English phrases *long time no see* and *the next thing I knew*, and for the Chinese proverb 书中自有黄金屋[7].

For both English phrases and for the Chinese proverb in Table 6, one can clearly see that adding a gram to the sequence, although it brings the sequence closer to the complete phrase, does not necessarily yields a higher statistical score at each level. These examples also suggest that the best method for extracting longer PUs is not bottom-up but top-down: starting at the level of a gram, adding one gram at a time, and checking the statistical association on the corpus at each level, will not yield good results, because the association is sometimes discontinuous, as between *long time* and *long time no*. On the contrary, the method used in the IdiomSearch experiment was top-down, in the sense that all n-grams (ranging from bigrams to 7-grams) were extracted (with a frequency threshold of 3 occurrences for 200 million tokens); the association was measured for each n-gram at all levels, which made it possible to

---

[7] shū zhōng zì yǒu huángjīn wū, *A book holds a house of gold.*

Table 6. *cpr-score* for successive n-grams within the phrases *long time no see* and *the next thing I knew*

n-gram	Frequency	*cpr-score*
long time	3604	0.68
long time no	15	0.12
long time no see	4	0.80
the next	16344	0.56
the next thing	95	0.20
the next thing I	24	0.20
the next thing I knew	13	0.46
书中	6731	0.47
书中自	57	0.17
书中自有	51	0.66
书中自有黄	28	0.72
书中自有黄金	28	0.72
书中自有黄金屋	28	0.72

extract even idiomatic 7-grams. The difficulty, however, remains for cases such as the Chinese proverb in Table 6, because the maximum frequency and association scores are already reached at the level of the 5-gram, whereas the full proverb is a 7-gram. This is one of the reasons why the algorithm has to be slightly adapted for each language, applying the general principle of the *baboushka* (Russian nesting dolls), or *encapsulation*: for long PUs such as 7-grams, a fine-tuned analysis of the associations between the internal grams is crucial.

3.3 A Probabilistic Network of Constructions

As mentioned in the introduction, constructionist approaches view grammar as a complex network of constructions, and several researchers hold the view that this network is based on probabilistic principles [8, 21].

Thanks to the specific problems posed by the Chinese language (as it is non-inflectional and unsegmented), some additional experiments were carried out within the framework of IdiomSearch.

In the first place, applying the statistical association score to an unsegmented language poses the question of the artificial segmentation in European languages. *Tea cup*, for instance, can be written in one word or two words, *à l'aéroport* is considered as a sequence of 3 words in French but the Spanish equivalent *al aeropuerto* as a two word sequence.

A widely accepted view in construction grammar [3] is precisely that *constructional idioms* exist both at syntactic and morphological level. A constructional idiom is then defined as a syntactic or morphological schema in which at least one position is fixed [3]. This is, for instance, the case in *This is the life*, but also in adjectives such as *un-believable* (in which *-able* cannot be replaced by *-ible* or other suffixes). Constructional morphology views complex words just as complex syntactic constructions.

Table 7. *cpr-score* for the association of morphemes in a few English words

Morphemes	Frequency	*cpr-score*
Accept-able	3855	0.97
Afford-able	2030	0.99
Approach-able	365	0.73
Circum-scrib-ed	107	1.00
Friend-ship	1399	0.97
Ir-respons-ible	505	0.92
System-atic	1893	1.00
Un-intellig-ible	104	0.74
Un-precedent-ed	104	1.00

All constructions are partly fixed, but there is a cline from schematic to substantive constructions.

The specific claims about constructional morphology [3] have been made on the basis of solid examples and of cognitive experimentation, but the question arises of their statistical foundation in corpora. In order to test this hypothesis on a wide scale, it would be necessary to apply morphological segmentation to a whole corpus. In the meantime, preliminary experiments with the *cpr-score* indeed confirm that many words composed of several morphemes display association scores that are quite comparable to those obtained for PUs, especially for fully idiomatic PUs or *idioms*.

In the examples presented under Table 7, a number of English words were treated as separate morphemes, and the *cpr-score* was computed for their association.

As illustrated by the examples from Table 7, there is indeed very little difference between the statistical associations prevailing within idiomatic PUs (Table 1) and within morphological constructs (Table 7).

One may actually go one step further, as [3] does, and consider that constructions such as the English past tense construction *'have + past participle'* are also constructional idioms, in which the auxiliary is fixed and the participle slot schematic. Again, this hypothesis can be supported by the *cpr-score*. We may, for instance compute the score for a given form, say *has*, followed by a maximum of two tokens, followed by the suffix –ed, indicating many regular past participles. If the above mentioned structure is indeed a constructional idiom, we will expect a very significant score (*cpr* > 0.40). This is indeed the case: our 200 million token corpus yields a score of 0.58 for 52350 occurrences. In other words, the *construction itself* can somehow be captured by the *cpr-score*, as it can be extended to 7-grams or even higher.

4 Conclusion

As the extraction of phraseological units/idioms that consist of more than two words is fraught with a wide range of difficulties, both practical and theoretical, the IdiomSearch Experiment sought to determine if a corpus-driven experimental score, the *cpr-score* [6], based on techniques derived from information retrieval, could yield acceptable results for different languages. The experiment was carried out on English, Spanish, French and (Mandarin) Chinese.

The recourse to large web corpora of 200 million tokens each, to optimized data-base storage and to a user-friendly web application has already made it possible so far to receive extensive feedback from students and other researchers, while also shedding fresh light on the theoretical underpinnings of any attempt to derive associative meaning from n-grams.

Although the statistical score can still be improved, as well as the qualitative and quantitative aspects of the web corpora, the preliminary results indicate that most common PUs and even a high number of relatively rare and very fixed PUs can be extracted by the *cpr-score* for European languages such as English, Spanish and French. The fact that the results are at present slightly better for English than for Spanish and French may be due to two main reasons. First, there are many more pages in English on the Web[8], which might explain that robots assembling pages on the basis of seed words in specific combinations yield more representative results for English; the second reason has to do with technical issues around the encoding of special characters in languages other than English.

The results obtained for Chinese are however particularly interesting, because they confirm that we should relativize our Eurocentric vision of language as being assembled from words and syntax. The whole cline of statistical associations, measured by the *cpr-score*, starts at the level of morphemes and ends up in schematic constructions, which is quite compatible with and may even serve as evidence for the claims made by the constructionist approaches to language. Thus, extracting phraseology from corpora looks like an achievable target, but the whole enterprise may only make sense against the backdrop of a probabilistic network of constructions.

References

1. Baeza-Yates, R., Ribeiro-Neto, B.: Modern Information Retrieval. ACM Press/Addison Wesley, New York (1999)
2. Baroni, M., Bernardini, S., Ferraresi, A., Zanchetta, E.: The WaCky wide web: a collection of very large linguistically processed web-crawled corpora. J. Lang. Res. Eval. **43**, 209–226 (2009)
3. Booij, G.: Morphology in construction grammar. In: Hoffmann, T., Trousdale, G. (eds.) The Oxford Handbook of Construction Grammar, pp. 255–273. Oxford University Press, Oxford/New York (2013)
4. Burger, H., Dobrovol'skij, D., Kühn, P., Norrick, N. (eds.): Phraseologie/Phraseology. Ein internationales Handbuch der zeitgenössischen Forschung/An International Hand-book of Contemporary Research. De Gruyter, Berlin/New York (2007)

[8] According to Wikipedia, English is good for 51.6% of all web pages, Spanish for 5.1%, French for 4.1%, and Chinese for 2.0%. Wikipedia homepage, https://en.wikipedia.org/wiki/Languages_used_on_the_Internet, last accessed 2017/08/17.

5. Colson, J-P.: The World Wide Web as a corpus for set phrases. In: Burger, H., Dobro-vol'skij, D., Kühn, P., Norrick, N. (eds.) Phraseologie/Phraseology. Ein internationales Handbuch der zeitgenössischen Forschung/An International Handbook of Contemporary Research, pp. 1071–1077. De Gruyter, Berlin/ New York (2007)
6. Colson, J.-P.: Set phrases around globalization: an experiment in corpus-based computational phraseology. In: Alonso Almeida, F., Ortega Barrera, I., Quintana Toledo, E., Sanchez Cuervo, M.E. (eds.) Input a Word, Analyze the World. Selected Approaches to Corpus Linguistics. Cambridge Scholars Publishing, Newcastle, pp. 141–152 (2016)
7. Croft, W.: Radical Construction Grammar: Syntactic Theory in Typological Perspective. Oxford University Press, Oxford (2001)
8. Croft, W.: Radical construction grammar. In: Hoffmann, T.H., Trousdale, G. (eds.) The Oxford Handbook of Construction Grammar, pp. 211–232. Oxford University Press, Oxford/New York (2013)
9. Fillmore, C.H.: The mechanisms of construction grammar. Berkeley Linguistic Soc. **14**, 35–55 (1988)
10. Goldberg, A.: Constructions: A Construction Grammar Approach to Argument Structure. University of Chicago Press, Chicago (1995)
11. Goldberg, A.: Constructions: a new theoretical approach to language. Trends Cogn. Sci. **7** (5), 219–224 (2003)
12. Goldberg, A.: Constructions at Work: The Nature of Generalization in Language. Oxford University Press, Oxford (2006)
13. Gries, S.: 50-something years of work on collocations. What is or should be next .... Int. J. Corpus Linguist. **18**, 137–165 (2013)
14. Gries, S.: Data in construction grammar. In: Hoffmann, T.H., Trousdale, G. (eds.) The Oxford Handbook of Construction Grammar, pp. 93–108. Oxford University Press, Oxford/New York (2013)
15. Gries, S., Stefanowitsch, A.: Extending collostructional analysis: a corpus-based perspective on 'Alternations'. Int. J. Corpus Linguist. **9**(1), 97–129 (2004)
16. Henry, K.: Les chengyu du chinois: caractérisation de phrasèmes hors norme. Yearb. Phraseology **7**, 99–126 (2016)
17. Hoffmann, T.H., Trousdale, G. (eds.): The Oxford Handbook of Construction Grammar. Oxford University Press, Oxford/New York (2013)
18. Manning, C.H., Raghavan, P., Schütze, H.: An Introduction to Information Retrieval. Cambridge University Press, Cambridge (2009)
19. Moon, R.: Fixed Expressions and Idioms in English. Clarendon Press, Oxford (1998)
20. Sinclair, J.: Corpus, Concordance, Collocation. Oxford University Press, Oxford (1991)
21. Stefanowitsch, A.: Collostructional analysis. In: Hoffmann, T.H., Trousdale, G. (eds.) The Oxford Handbook of Construction Grammar, pp. 290–306. Oxford University Press, Oxford/New York (2013)
22. Wray, A.: Formulaic Language: Pushing the Boundaries. Oxford University Press, Oxford (2008)
23. Wulff, S.: Words and idioms. In: Hoffmann, T.H., Trousdale, G. (eds.) The Oxford Hand-book of Construction Grammar, pp. 274–289. Oxford University Press, Oxford/New York (2013)

Collocational Constructions in Translated Spanish: What Corpora Reveal

Gloria Corpas Pastor[1,2(✉)]

[1] Department of Translation and Interpreting, University of Malaga, Málaga, Spain
gcorpas@uma.es
[2] RIILP, University of Wolverhampton, Wolverhampton, UK

Abstract. In recent years, Construction Grammar has emerged as an enhanced theoretical framework for studies on phraseology in general, and particularly for collocational analysis. This paper aims at contributing to the study of collocational constructions in translated Spanish. To this end, the construction [V PP$_{_de\ miedo}$] is analysed in detail. Our methodology is corpus-based and compares subtitled translations with general Spanish, American Spanish and Peninsular Spanish. The findings suggest that collocational constructions in translated Spanish have a clear preference for the Peninsular standard. They reflect features of translationese, as well as universal traits such as simplification, normalisation, and convergence. Another interesting finding refers to corpus selection, as giga-token corpora appear to provide more fine-grained analysis that conventional, balanced corpora.

Keywords: Collocation · Collocational construction · Translated spanish · Simplification · Normalisation · Subtitled translations · Corpus

1 Introduction

In Phraseology, the term *collocation* refers to a linguistic phenomenon by which words tend to occur together and exhibit idiosyncratic combinatory and semantic properties. The term also covers a type of phraseological unit (*collocation*) and the actual instances (*collocations*). By default, collocations are arbitrary and non-isomorphic, semantically transparent but formally unpredictable. Some examples are *outright insult* (*absolute insult) and *highly intelligent* (*highly unintelligent but *remarkably unintelligent*). Collocation components show a different semantic status: bases are semantically autonomous (*insult, intelligent*), whereas collocates tend to be determined, their actual senses being selected by their bases. Even though collocations undergo some degree of semantic specialisation or grammaticalisation, they differ from other types of phraseological units that exhibit a fixed form and a non-decomposable, unitary meaning. Idioms like *fly off the handle, on cloud nine* or *bite the dust* are semantically opaque and pose both comprehension and production problems.

In computational approaches, the term *collocation* has been used to refer to a distinct type of multiword expression (MWE) that is statistically idiomatic, i.e. a particular combination of words that "occurs with markedly high frequency, relative to the component words or alternative phrasings of the same expression" [1]. For instance, the verbs

R. Mitkov (Ed.): Europhras 2017, LNAI 10596, pp. 29–40, 2017.
https://doi.org/10.1007/978-3-319-69805-2_3

inflict and *impose* are more likely to combine with the noun object *punishment* than *administer*, which in turn is more probable than *prescribe* or *sanction.* Statistical idiomaticity is reminiscent of Halliday's probabilistic definition of collocation [10] and is deeply rooted in the early work on computer-assisted analysis of collocational patterns in large corpora based on frequency [12, 17].

Quantitative methods for the automatic identification and extraction of collocations require large corpora. Corpus-based methods that are based on n-gram frequency can only indentify continuous co-occurrences. This type of collocations have been variously termed *collocational networks*, *lexical bundles*, *clusters*, *recurrent word combinations*, etc. Statistical corpus-based methods use various association measures in order to uncover discontinuous co-occurrences. Hybrid methods rely on linguistic analysis and annotation for refining of results [15]. A more sophisticated version of a hybrid method is *collostructional analysis*, i.e. 'a family of quantitative corpus linguistic methods for studying the relationship between words and the grammatical structures they occur in' [16]. These methods can detect not only discontinuous occurrences of words in various syntactic relationships within a given pattern, but they can also identify words significantly attracted by a particular grammar structure (akin to the notion of colligation) or compare the association strengths of all collocates of two partially synonymous patterns.

Different approaches to collocation agree on co-occurrence and frequency as distinctive features, whether semantically-based, statistically-based or psychologically-based [5]. However, none of those approaches is integrative enough or sufficiently explanatory; nor is there a set of defining features or proper definition of collocation that is generally accepted. In this paper we explore some aspects of the relationship between collocations, idioms, linguistic constructions and grammaticalisation.

The organisation of the paper is as follows. We start with a characterisation of the construal nature of collocations (Sect. 2), with special reference to cross-lingual anisomorphism and potential consequences for translation. Then we provide a case-study in translated Spanish (Sect. 3). Our methodology is corpus-based and compares subtitled translations with general Spanish, American Spanish and Peninsular Spanish. In Sect. 4 we summarise the main findings of the study and some thoughts are presented as how the material discussed might be relevant for further studies on collocational constructions in translated Spanish.

2 Rationale and Background

In recent years, Construction Grammar has emerged as an enhanced theoretical framework for studies on phraseology in general, and particularly for collocational analysis. The constructionist approach views language as an idiomatic continuum of which constructions are the building blocks. Constructions are defined as usage-based pairings of form and (semantic or discourse) function that exhibit different degrees of complexity, schematisation and entrenchment [6, 8]. These symbolic units emerge through repeated experience with actual instances and their generalisations [9]. Frequency plays a key role in the mental representations and storage strength of constructions in the neural network [11].

Collocations possess a distinctive construal nature, as evidenced by their internal lexical restrictions and interpretative accommodation. In this light, collocations can be conceived as partially specified constructions that are semantically predictable. In other words, *collocational constructions* could be described as symbolic units that span various phrasal patterns and contain slots to be filled by a restricted set of lexical items (slot fillers) in a cline of bondness and coercion [3]. The actual instances of collocational constructions would be termed *collocations*. Such a flexible framework fosters a powerful explanatory model of idiomaticity that allows idioms, collocations and other related phenomena to count as constructions in their own right, linked to each other within complex networks.

Collocational peculiarities have serious consequences for cross-language analysis and translation. Monolingual anisomorphism can be observed in (partial) synonyms and lexical sets, as seen in the above examples. It is especially relevant in certain types of semantic processes that are particularly liable to collocational idiosyncrasies, such as intensification. Degree modifiers that refer to a high degree or a high level on a scale are usually lexically restricted to their bases. For instance, adjectives like *huge, tremendous, overwhelming*, *enormous* collocate with *success* ('big success'), but not with *failure*, that usually combines with other intensifiers, such as *complete, utter* and *dismal* in the same sense ('big failure'). Further intervarietal differences arise from discipline-specific collocations and levels of formality: e.g., *give an injection* (general) versus *administer an injection* (medicine), *swear an oath* (formal) versus *take an oath* (neutral), as well as language varieties: e.g., *have a bath, have a rest* (British English) and *take a bath, take a rest* (American English).

To complicate the picture even more, collocational differences are also affected by crosslingual anisomorphism. This phenomenon occurs when the direct translation equivalents of the individual elements of a given collocation in the source language do not constitute collocations in the target language. By way of illustration, consider collocations with *commit*: while *commit a crime/a sin* translate word-for-word in Spanish (*cometer un delito/un pecado*), *commit a mistake* does not translate as **commit a mistake* but as *make a mistake.* As we have previously stated [5], "even completely transparent collocations can pose problems in translation due to the arbitrary, non-isomorfic nature of collocates". This is frequently the case, as collocates are usually polysemous items that depend on their bases for disambiguation and translation (collocation translational equivalents). For instance, the translation into Spanish of collocations with the verb *gain* will depend on its object nouns collocates: ***gain*** *advantage* (***sacar*** *ventaja*), ***gain*** *control* (***hacerse con*** *el control*), ***gain*** *independence* (***conseguir/obtener*** *la independencia*), ***gain*** *port* (***llegar/arrivar*** *a puerto*), ***gain*** *strength* (***cobrar*** *fuerza*), ***gain*** *weight* (***coger*** *peso*), etc. This is the reason why straightforward equivalents (system translation equivalents), such as *gain* ≈ *ganar,* do not hold in translation [5]. In other words, straightforward equivalents when used as individual lexical items may turn into potential false friends as slot fillers of collocational constructions. See, for instance, the large number of bitexts in Linguee where *gain advantage* has been wrongly translated as **ganar ventaja*.

When metaphor is at play, translation choices appear to be even more diverse and complex. For instance, verb-noun collocations with the verbs *kindle* and *spark* are based on the 'lightning/start a fire' metaphor. However, collocations with *kindle* usually have a positive prosody (e.g., *kindle enthusiasm, interest*), whereas the prosody associated with *sparkle* tends to be negative (e.g., *sparkle outrage, controversy*). Neither figurative metaphors nor prosodies are easily conveyed in the target language. For instance, both verb-noun collocations are primarily translated by the same set of prosody neutral and non-figurative collocates: *causar/suscitar/provocar* + *entusiasmo/interés/controversia/indignación*; and secondarily by the collocate verb *despertar* ('wake up, awake'): *despertar entusiasmo/interés/controversia/indignación*. In the second case, the verb *despertar* is prosody-neutral (cf. *despertar* + negative feelings and emotions: *odio/recelos/envidia*) but figurative, although with a different underlying metaphor ('awakening', as opposed to the 'lighting' source metaphor). In addition, other types of differences (diatopic, diastratic, diaphasic) and degree of equivalence may result in cases of infra- or overtranslation. For example, this is the case when collocations pertaining to particular language varieties, levels of formality or specific domains or disciplines are rendered by neutral collocations, and vice versa.

3 Methodology

As a consequence of the translation process, translated texts tend to exhibit characteristic linguistic features, regardless of the source and the target languages. Translations are believed to be simpler, more explicit, closer to the standard prototype and more 'typical' than non-translated texts. These distinctive lexico-grammatical and syntactic characteristics are attributable to widespread translation trends (*universals*) and have been explained by Toury's laws of growing standardisation and interference [20]. The tension between these two laws gives rise to the unique nature of translated language (*translationese*).

This paper contributes to the study of collocational constructions in translated Spanish. To this end, the construction [V $PP_{\_de\ miedo}$] will be analysed in detail. Our starting point will be the lexicographical information provided about this construction by the *Diccionario combinatorio práctico del español contemporáneo* (DCPEC) [2]. This Spanish combinatory dictionary provides a separate entry for the lemma **de miedo**, which is classed as a polysemous idiom with adverbial or adjectival function ("loc. adv./loc. adj."). When combined with verbs *de miedo* has an adverbial function and two main senses: "[de terror]" (lit., 'out of fear') and "[muy bien] (lit., 'very well'). The DCPEC indicates that the first sense is actualised with the verbs *morirse, cagarse, descomponerse*, *encogerse, temblar*; and the second sense, with the verbs *estar*, *pasárse(lo)* and *sentar (a alguien)*.

These two types of disambiguating verbs indicated in DCPEC will constitute the list of verbal slot fillers to be analysed against the various corpora of translated and non-traslated Spanish used in this study (see below).

In a previous study [4], we have reported patterns of simplification and normalisation in translated Spanish as regards idiomaticity and diatopy. A similar corpus-based research protocol will be adopted in this study. For the purpose of this study, non-translated Spanish data will be collated from giga-token Web (sub)corpora and then compared with data stemming from a balanced, conventional reference corpus of Spanish and two subcorpora. Translated Spanish data will be retrieved from a giga-token parallel corpus of fiction subtitles. Slot fillers will be extracted (semi)automatically.

3.1 Corpora

Several (sub)corpora have been selected for the study:

1. ***OpenSubtitles*** – a 8.31 giga-token multilingual parallel corpus that has been downloaded from the *OpenSubtitles.org* repository in 2011 [19]. It comprises 54 languages, but only the bilingual parallel subcorpus has been analysed (50 million aligned sentences of English-Spanish film subtitles). The Spanish component size is over 870 million words.
2. **esTenTen** – a 10.99 giga-token Web corpus of global, standardised Spanish. It was created automatically in 2011 [13]. It comprises the *esEuTenTen* [2011] and the *esAmTenTen* [2011], plus some other documents not classified by their national top level domain (Wikipedia, some Spanish newspapers, etc.).[1]
3. **esEuTenTen** – a 2.3 GT subcorpus of European Spanish (Peninsular variety, 21%).
4. **esAmTenTen** – a 8.6 GT subcorpus of Latin American Spanish (American Variety, 79%). It comprises 18 different varieties that have been identified by their national top-level domains (.ar,.es,.uy,.ve, etc.): Argentina, Bolivia, Chile, Colombia, Costa Rica, Cuba, Dominican Republic, Ecuador, El Salvador, Guatemala, Honduras, Mexico, Nicaragua, Panama, Paraguay, Peru, Uruguay and Venezuela.[2]
5. **CORPES XXI** – a pan-Spanish reference corpus of over 225 million words (1975-2017) [14]. It includes Peninsular and American varieties (*esEuCORPES* and *esAmCORPES*).
6. **esEuCORPES** – a subcorpus of Peninsular Spanish (67 million words).
7. **esAmCORPES** – a subcorpus of Latin American Spanish (168 million words). It comprises the 18 Spanish varieties included in esAmTenTen, plus the varieties spoken/written in Puerto Rico, southern parts of United States, Philipines and Ecuatorial Guinea.

Corpora 1–4 are available through SketchEngine [18], whereas corpora 5–7 can be web-searched through an in-built corpus query system.

Web-crawled (sub)corpora (1–4) and conventional (sub)corpora (5–7) offer advantages and disadvantages. The CORPES XXI corpus and its subcorpora have been carefully designed and compiled in order to be representative of the global, standard language spoken/written across the Spanish-speaking world. However, they present several problems [4]: their size is too small to study low-frequency collocational constructions and phraseological units in general, and not all national varieties are sufficiently covered. In addition, the CORPES in-built corpus system is rather unstable and slow in terms of processing, data downloading is not possible and access to the data is not flexible enough. Another shortcoming is that this corpus is under construction, which could compromise

[1] It has been web-crawled with Spiderling, (pre)processed and tagged with Freeling 4.0.

[2] The Spanish varieties spoken in Puerto Rico or southwestern United States are not covered.

data stability and the results since they may vary significantly according to the access date (it is expected to reach over 500 million words in 2018).

By contrast, Web corpora provide a wealth of information thanks to their giga-token size, the stability of the data, the reproducibility of the research, and the reliability of the results [7]. Major drawbacks of corpora 1-4 are the question of 'representativeness' and 'balance' (document selection) and the number of (pre)processing problems they present.

3.2 Results and Discussion

The selected collocational construction (V PP$_{_de\ miedo}$) has been studied in all corpora. This section will discuss the main findings of the study. In order to establish whether Web crawled (sub)corpora provide reliable data, the slot fillers licensed by this particular construction have been checked against the TenTen corpora and the CORPES XXI.

Tables 1, 2 and 3 illustrate raw and normalised frequencies of selected verbal slots (senses 1 and 2) in the esTenTen corpora, the CORPES XXI (general, American and Peninsular Spanish) and the OpenSubtitles corpus. Verbs have been ordered according to normalised frequencies; raw frequencies have been taken into account only when normalised frequencies coincided.

Table 1. Verbal slot fillers in the TenTen corpora (raw and normalised frequencies).

V PP$_{_DE\ MIEDO}$	esTenTen	esEuTenTen	esAmTenTen
[SENSE 1]			
Morirse	2,564	563	1,994
	0.23	**0.24**	**0.23**
Cagarse	1,072	250	820
	0.10	**0.11**	**0.10**
Descomponerse	4[a]	–	4
	0.00	–	**0.00**
Encogerse	43	6	37
	0.00	**0.0**	**0.00**
Temblar	1,283	245	1,070
	0.12	**0.10**	**0.12**
[SENSE 2]			
Estar	288	59	3
	0.03	**0.03**	**0.00**
Pasar(se)(lo)[b]	140	302	68
	0.01	**0.13**	**0.01**
Sentar [a alg]	371	59	6
	0.03	**0.03**	**0.00**

[a]The four examples in esAmTenTen and esTenTen are even the same ones.

[b]There are also some cases of *pasar(se)(la)*

Table 2. Verbal slot fillers in CORPES XXI (raw and normalised frequencies).

V PP_DE MIEDO	CORPES XXI	esEuCORPES	esAmCORPES
[SENSE 1]			
Morirse	268	34	163
	0.97	**0.13**	**0.65**
Cagarse	93	10	44
	0.33	**0.04**	**0.17**
Descomponerse	–[a]	–	–
	0.00	**–**	**0.00**
Encogerse	2	–	1
	0.00	**0.0**	**0.00**
Temblar	57	13	28
	0.48	**0.05**	**0.11**
[SENSE 2]			
Estar	3	1	3
	0.01	**0.00**	**0.01**
Pasar(se)(lo)[b]	9	4	68
	0.03	**0.01**	**0.27**
Sentar [a alg.]	4	3	6
	0.01	**0.01**	**0.02**

[a]The four examples in esAmTenTen and esTenTen are even the same ones.
[b]There are also some cases of pasar(se) (la).

Table 3. Verbal slot fillers in OpenSubtitles (Raw and normalised frequencies).

V PP_DE MIEDO		OPENSUBTITLES	
[SENSE 1]		[SENSE 2]	
Morirse	207[a]	*Estar*	14
	0.23		**0.01**
Cagarse	134[b]	*Pasar(se)(lo)*	35
	0.14		**0.04**
Descomponerse	–	*Sentar [a alg.]*	–
Encogerse	9		
	0.01		
Temblar	75		
	0.08		

[a]*Morirse de miedo* (207 occurrences); *estar muerto de miedo* (209 occurrences).
[b]*Cagarse de miedo* (134 occurrences); *estar cagado de miedo* (4 occurrences).

The TenTen corpora provide far more occurrences of individual slot fillers than the CORPES. For instance, there are 2,564 cases of *morirse* in the esTenTen corpus as compared to 188 in the CORPES; or 43 of *encogerse* in the esTenTen, and only 2 in the

CORPES XXI. In general, the American variety (esAmTenTen) appears to be closer to general Spanish than the Peninsular variety. In fact, the general and American varieties share the same rankings:

- [SENSE 1]. 1. *morirse*; 2. *temblar*; 3. *cagarse*; 4. *encogerse*; 5. *descomponerse*
- [SENSE 2]: 1. *sentar*; 2. *estar*; 3. *pasar(lo/la)*

In the Peninsular variety (esEuTenTen) this construction licenses only 4 of the verbal slot fillers (*descomponerse* in not found) for sense 1. The ranking is similar to the other two at the top and bottom positions (1. *morirse*; 4. *encogerse*), but changes at the middle positions: 2. *cagarse*; 3. *temblar* (0.02 difference in normalised frequencies). In the esTenTen the ranking appears completely different for sense 2: 1. *pasar(lo/la)*; 2.*sentar*; 3.*estar*.

The similarities between general Spanish and the American variety in the TenTen corpora might be explained by the high proportion of American Spanish documents (seven billion words) in the general corpus, as compared to less than two billion words of Peninsular Spanish.

Not all 5 verbal slot fillers appear to be licensed for this construction in the CORPES family. The CORPES XXI retrieves only 4, ranked as in the esTenTen: 1. *morirse*; 2. *temblar*; 3. *cagarse*; 4. *encogerse* (*descomponerse* is missing). The American variety contains the same 4 verbal slots as general Spanish; it also coincides in the top and bottom positions of the rank (1. *morirse*, 4. *encogerse*), with a slightly difference in the middle positions (2. *cagarse*; 3. *temblar*; 0.15 difference in normalised frequencies). The Peninsular Spanish variety exhibits less lexical richness and different rank of verbal slot fillers, with the only coincidence of *morir* at the top position: 1. *morirse*; 2. *temblar*; 3. *cagarse* (*descomponerse* and *encogerse* are missing).

The ranking of verbal slot fillers for sense 2 is identical for general Spanish and the two varieties analysed: [SENSE 2] 1. *pasar(lo/la)*; 2. *sentar*; 3. *estar*. This rank coincides with the Spanish variety in the TenTen corpus. A possible explanation could be the different composition of the general corpus, as it also includes varieties spoken in Philippines, Ecuatorial Guinea, Puerto Rico and southern parts of United States. Those corpus components might be closer to the European standard. Or else, it could be explained because of a low number of occurrences (and consequently very low normalised frequencies), which might have compromised the results, due to small coverage and lack of representativeness. For this reason, comparative results below will only take into account the data from the TenTen corpora.

The picture depicted by the OpenSubtitles corpus is quite suggestive (see Table 3).

The rank of slot fillers for sense 1 is identical to the euEsTenTen rank: 1. *morirse*; 2. *cagarse*; 3. *temblar*; 4. *encogerse*. This means that Peninsular Spanish would be the variety preferred in subtitled translations. The ranking of verbal slot fillers licensed by the construction for sense 2 points in the same direction. Compare esEuTenTen: 1. *pasar(lo/la)*; 2.*sentar*; 3.*estar* and OpenSubtitles: 1. *pasar(lo)*; 2.*estar*. The main difference is that subtitled translations do not contain the filler *sentar* and only the pronoun *lo* can be found as direct object of *pasar* in the construction under study. This could be also seen as a trait of simplification (lower lexical richness of subtitled translations).

When individual fillers are considered, the data also suggest that translated Spanish tends to gear towards the Peninsular standard, with some exceptions. For instance, the verb *morir* (OpenSubtitles: 0.23) presents a uniform distribution in all three varieties, that is identical to general Spanish and American Spanish (0.23), just 0.01 less than Peninsular Spanish. By contrast, *encogerse* appears slightly higher (+ 0.01) than in all three TenTen corpora. This might be indicating that *morirse de miedo* could be truly considered pan-Spanish, whereas *encogerse* could be suggesting translationese. Normalised frequencies for the rest of fillers in sense 1 are closer to Peninsular Spanish (*cagarse*: 0.14/0.11, + 0.3 difference; *temblar*: 0.08/0.10, −0.02 difference). And *descomponerse* does not occur as filler in both OpenSubtitles and esEuTenTen, possibly because it indexes general and American Spanish.

A similar situation is presented by the fillers for sense 2. Their normalised frequencies are 0.00 in American Spanish, as they seem to be restricted to the Spanish variety (*estar*: 0.03 and *pasárselo*: 0.03), and, therefore, are present with the same values in general Spanish. Their normalised frequencies in the OpenSubtitles corpus simply show minor differences as regards to Peninsular Spanish: *estar* (−0.02) and *pasárselo* (+0.01). The verb *sentar* is not licensed by this construction in the OpenSubtitles corpus, possibly because it is more frequent in the American variety (0.02) than in Peninsular and general Spanish (0.01). It could be the case that its distributional area be covered by *pasárselo* in subtitled translations.

Other examples of normalisation and simplification can be found as regards the lexical richness of the verbal slot fillers licensed by the collocational construction (V $PP_{\_de\ miedo}$). As we have already mentioned, two slot fillers are missing in the Spanish subtitled translations: *descomponerse* (sense 1) and *sentar* (for sense 2). This could be indicative of lower lexical richness in subtitled translations. A comparison between the fillers licensed in translated and not translated Spanish confirms this assumption. The esTenTen corpus registers up to 25 different verbal types (6 happax legomena) for this construction (sense 1); 21 types in American Spanish (10 happax legomena) and 15 types (6 happax legomena) in Peninsular Spanish. Those verbal fillers in non-translated Spanish function as intensifiers that refer to body reactions to fear, such as shivering, sweating, crying, mictioning, etc. (e.g., *tiritar*, *llorar*, *gritar*, *sudar*, *estremecerse*, *mearse* ….) or metaphorical ways of expressing having experienced emotions of intense fear (*paralizarse, desmembrarse, agarrotarse, disolverse, desfallecer*, etc.). In OpenSubtitles there are only 9 fillers (1 happax legomena) which refer to body reactions (*orinarse, sudar, chillar*, etc.), and only one refers to consequences after having experienced extreme fear (*paralizarse*).

As to the number of alternative verbs found for sense 2 of this construction, the situation is as follows. The esTenTen corpus registers 10 (4 happax legomena) for general Spanish, 5 (4 happax legomena) for Peninsular Spanish and 9 (6 happax legomena) for American Spanish. Some verbs exhibit a much stronger bond, as they seem to select secondary, figurative senses in this construction: *ir* and *venir*; *caer,* and *quedar* (synonyms of *sentar* [a alg. *algo de miedo*]; and *dar* (*dársele* a alg. algo *de miedo*). Others appear to be used in their literal senses (*jugar, besar, venderse*, etc.) which are then intensified by the fixed part of the construction. In OpenSubtitles there are 6 more verbal types (5 happax legomena), but the choice of fillers is more restricted: the verb *ir* (*irle* a alg. algo *de miedo*) seems to occupy the area of *sentar*, and together with *pasar* and *estar* are the verbs primarily licensed by this construction in translated Spanish.

The collocational construction [V $PP_{\_de\ miedo}$] shows a process of grammaticalisation by which the PP functions as an adverbial modifier, substitutable by an intensifier adverb or adverbial phrase (e.g., 'very much', 'terribly well'). The PP is perspectivised as in the foreground: an extremely intense emotion which was originally negative but of which only the intensity remains. The degree of lexicalisation of slot fillers is proportional to the degree of grammaticalisation and coerced meanings of this semi-schematic construction.

In this light, *de miedo* is not just an idiom with two different senses, but a semi-schematic collocational construction V PP composed of a variable slot (verb fillers) and a fixed slot (*de miedo*). The choice of verbal slot fillers determines the meaning accommodation of both variable and fixed components. Verbs which denote a physical reaction of weakness or unwellness to the feeling of the emotion trigger a metonymic interpretation of intense fear: e.g., *temblar de miedo* ('tremble with fear') → *tener mucho miedo* ('to be very frightened'). The more intense the fear, the more intense the physical reaction (e.g. *morirse de miedo*, lit. 'die out of fear'). In this case, the interpretation of the verbal filler is coerced by the fixed slot (*morirse* does not literally mean 'die', but be terribly frightened). Bondness and grammaticalisation also affect the interpretation of the fixed slot, which undergoes a process of delexicalisation toward intensification ('in high degree'). Once the fixed slot denotes intensification, it is ready for other verbal slot fillers and further lexicalisations (e.g. *pasarlo de miedo*).

Translated Spanish also reflects this intricate process but in a more restricted way, as regards the lower number slot fillers and the degree of bondness of lexicalised and non-lexicalised verbs (simplification). This grammaticalisation process can be seen in the actual choice of lexical fillers for the construction in Spanish subtitled translations. In this respect, a marked preference for the Peninsular Spanish standard is observed (normalisation).

Simplification seems to be also at work when translation choices and procedures are examined. For instance, we have identified over 50 different ways to express the meaning of 'getting/being terribly frightened' in the English component of OpenSubtitles: e.g., *be shitting, be scared shitless, be scared to death, take a shit, wet one's pants, scare the muggers stiff, shit one's pants, be plain chicken shit, be fucking scared, shit oneself, wait for shit to happen, be fucking scared, pee one's kilt, shit bricks, piss on oneself, be shit-scared, be scared out of one's wits, be piss-scared, crap one's pants, be chicken shit, chicken out, crap in a sock, be really afraid*, etc. The number of examples illustrates the lexical richness of the English subtitles. Many of them also represent creative uses of the language. Interestingly enough, all of them have been translated systematically as *cagarse de miedo*. This makes the Spanish subtitled translations look not only simpler (simplification), but also more homogeneous and closer to the standard (convergence) and more 'typical' or less creative (normalisation).

Finally, this study presents a series of limitations as regards corpora. In addition to the (pre)processing errors of Web-crawled corpora (parsing errors, incomplete deduplication, misrecognition of characters, etc.), *OpenSubtitles* presents problems concerning bitexts (alignment across language pairs only). Another issue is the degree of comparability and/or (a)symmetry between the Spanish corpora, both translated and non-translated. Besides, the technical constrains of subtitling can influence translators' choices. Elements such as the number of lines in a subtitle, the length of subtitles, the structure of line breaks, the number of characters (per second/line) allowed, etc. are an essential facet of subtitled translations that should be regarded as a differential factor.

4 Conclusion

Construction Grammar provides a powerful explanatory model of idiomaticity that caters for different clines of complexity, formal restrictions, semantic coercion and grammaticalisation processes. In this framework, traditional concepts such as collocation, idiom or phraseological unit converge into collocational constructions.

This paper has examined a particular collocational construction in both translated and non-translated corpora. The analysis reveals that [V $PP_{-de\ miedo}$] has undergone a process of grammaticalisation that has affected bondness and meaning accommodation (coercion) of slots (and fillers) in a gradual way. This provides the basis for the creative choice of lexical fillers, bondness and subsequent semantic change. Translated Spanish also reflects this process but in a more restricted way, as the number of lexicalised slot fillers and choice of actual fillers unveil simplification and normalisation traits. Within this process, translated Spanish tends to shows a clear preference for the Peninsular Spanish standard, as well as other features of translationese.

Finally, the corpus-based analysis has revealed that Web-crawled giga-token corpora, like the TenTen family, enable researchers to perform more fine-grained analyses and get more representative results than a balanced, reference corpus like CORPES XXI. The future lies with big data.

Acknowledgements. The research presented in this paper has been partially carried out in the framework of the research projects INTELITERM (FFI2012–38881), TERMITUR (HUM2754) and VIP (FFI2016-75831-P).

References

1. Baldwin, T., Kim, S.N.: Multiword expressions. In: Indurkhya, N., Damerau, F.J. (eds.) Handbook of Natural Language Processing, 2nd edn, pp. 267–292. CRC Press, Boca Raton (2010)
2. Bosque, I. (dir.) Diccionario combinatorio práctico del español contemporáneo: las palabras en su contexto. Madrid, SM (2006)
3. Pastor, G.C.: Register-specific collocational constructions in english and spanish: a usage-based approach. J. Soc. Sci. **11**(3), 139–151 (2015)
4. Pastor, G.C.: Translating English verbal collocations into spanish: on distribution and other relevant differences related to diatopic variation. Lingvisticæ Investigationes **38**(2), 229–262 (2015)

5. Pastor, G.C.: Collocations in e-bilingual dictionaries: from underlying theoretical assumptions to practical lexicography and translation issues. In: Torner, S., Bernal, E. (eds.) Collocations and Other Lexical Combinations in Spanish. Theoretical and Applied Approaches, pp. 139–160. Routledge, London (2017)
6. Croft, W.: Radical Construction Grammar. In: Hoffmann, T., Trousdale, G. (eds.) The Oxford Handbook of Construction Grammar, pp. 211–232. Oxford University Press, Oxford (2013)
7. Gatto, M.: The 'body' and the 'web': The web as corpus ten years on. ICAME J. **35**, 35–58 (2011)
8. Goldberg, A.E.: Constructions: a construction grammar approach to argument structure. University of Chicago Press, Chicago (1995)
9. Goldberg, A.E.: Constructions at Work: The Nature of Generalization in Language. Oxford University Press, New York (2006)
10. Halliday, M.A.K.: Lexis as a linguistic level. In: Bazell, C.E., Catford, J.C., Halliday, M.A.K., Robins, R.H. (eds.) Memory of John Firth, pp. 148–162. Longman, London
11. Hoffmann, T.: Abstract phrasal and clausal constructions. In: Hoffmann, T., Trousdale, G. (eds.) The Oxford Handbook of Construction Grammar, pp. 307–328. Oxford University Press, Oxford (2013)
12. Jones, S., Sinclair, J.: English lexical collocations. A study in computational linguistics. Cahiers de Lexicology **24**, 15–61 (1974)
13. Kilgarriff, A., Renau, I.: esTenTen, a Vast Web Corpus of Peninsular and American Spanish. Procedia Soc. Behav. Sci. **95**, 12–19 (2013)
14. Real Academia Española (n.d.). Banco de datos (CORPES XXI). Corpus del español del siglo XXI. http://www.rae.es. Last accessed 10 Aug 2017
15. Seretan, V.: Syntax-Based Collocation Extraction. Springer, Dordrecht (2011)
16. Stefanowitsch, A.: Collostructional analysis. In: Hoffmann, T., Trousdale, G. (eds.) The Oxford Handbook of Construction Grammar, pp. 290–306. Oxford University Press, Oxford (2013)
17. Stubbs, M.: Two quantitative methods of studying phraseology in English. Int. J. Corpus Linguist. **7**(12), 215–244 (2002)
18. SketchEngine Homepage. https://www.sketchengine.co.uk. Last accessed 16 Aug 2017
19. Tiedemann, J.: News from OPUS - a collection of multilingual parallel corpora with tools and interfaces. In: Nicolov, N., Bontcheva, K., Angelova, G., Mitkov, R. (eds.) Recent Advances in Natural Language Processing V. Selected Papers from RANLP 2007, pp. 237–248. Amsterdam and Philadelphia, John Benjamins (1999)
20. Toury, G.: Descriptive Translation Studies and Beyond. John Benjamins, Ámsterdam (1995)

Constructions in Parallel Corpora: A Quantitative Approach

Dmitrij Dobrovol'skij[1(✉)] and Ludmila Pöppel[2]

[1] Russian Language Institute of the Russian Academy of Sciences, Volkhonka18/2, 119019 Moscow, Russia
dobrovolskij@gmail.com

[2] Department of Slavic and Baltic Studies, Finnish, Dutch and German, Stockholm University, 10691 Stockholm, Sweden
ludmila.poppel@slav.su.se

Abstract. The primary goal of the present study is to find an adequate method for the quantitative analysis of empirical data obtained from parallel corpora. Such a task is particularly important in the case of fixed constructions possessing some degree of idiomaticity and language specificity. Our data consist of the Russian construction *дело в том, что* and its parallels in English, German and Swedish. This construction, which appears to present no difficulty for translation into other languages, is in fact, language-specific when compared with other languages. It displays a large number of different parallels (translation equivalents) in other languages, and possesses a complex semantic structure. The configuration of semantic elements comprising the content plane of this construction is unique. The empirical data have been collected from the corpus query system Sketch Engine, subcorpus OPUS2 Russian, and the Russian National Corpus (RNC). We propose to use the Herfindahl index as a tool for quantitative analysis in order to measure the degree of uniformity in the frequency distribution of the various translations of the construction under investigation. This tool is not universal and does not enable us to answer all the questions that arise in connection with determining the specificity of language units. However, it clearly helps to obtain more objective results and to refine the quantitative analysis of idiomatic constructions on the basis of corpus data.

Keywords: Construction · Contrastive corpus analysis · Parallel corpus · Russian · English · German · Swedish · Language specificity · Quantitative analysis · The Herfindahl Index

---

This paper is based on work supported by the Russian Science Foundation (RSF) under Grant 16-48-03006 "Semantic Analysis of Translated Texts for Comparative Cultural Studies and Cultural Specificity in Language Learning".

R. Mitkov (Ed.): Europhras 2017, LNAI 10596, pp. 41–53, 2017.
https://doi.org/10.1007/978-3-319-69805-2_4

1 Goals, Methods and Data

The present investigation employs quantitative methods with the goal of enhancing the reliability of findings obtained from parallel corpora. As materials for analysis we use the Russian construction *дело в том, что* (*delo v tom, čto*),[1] which has a great many translation equivalents in other languages. This study will examine its parallels in English, German and Swedish.

Empirical data are taken from the parallel corpora of the Sketch Engine search system, the subcorpus of parallel texts OPUS2 Russian (307 709 872 tokens) and the Russian-English, English-Russian, Russian-German and German-Russian corpora of parallel texts in the Russian National Corpus (RNC). The construction *дело в том, что* was searched in Sketch Engine in the pairs of corpora OPUS 2 Russian and OPUS2 English, OPUS2 Russian and OPUS2 German, OPUS2 Russian and OPUS2 Swedish. None of the Sketch Engine OPUS2 subcorpora mark the direction of the translation – the English-Russian and Russian-English parallels, for example, are in the same corpus – so that this distinction is not indicated in the description of the Sketch Engine data. The quantitative data cited in the present study were obtained in July 2016.

The following methods were used:

- a quantitative research method based on an analysis of parallel text corpora;
- a quantitative method using the Herfindahl index as a statistical tool that allows us to identify the degree of uniformity in the frequency distribution of the various translations of the item under investigation.

Thus our work represents a contribution to the development of contrastive corpus studies and methods for the quantitative analysis of corpus data.

2 Previous Research

We have previously examined the construction *дело в том, что* in (Dobrovol'skij and Pöppel 2016a; 2016b). These works did not use any statistical apparatus, i.e. the analysis was qualitative rather than quantitative.

Dobrovol'skij and Pöppel (2016b) tested the following hypothesis:

The Russian expression *дело в том, что* displays a unique configuration of semantic components; that is, it possesses a certain language-specificity. It has a large number of various parallels in other languages, and the choice of each variant depends on specific contextual conditions.

Dobrovol'skij and Pöppel (2016a) tested the hypothesis that discursive constructions based on the same pattern do not have the same linguistic status. *Дело в том, что*, for example, should be regarded as a unit of the lexicon, whereas the constructions *проблема в том, что* and *правда в том, что*[2] are free co-occurrences.

---

[1] Literally: *the thing is that*.

[2] Literally: *the problem is that* and *the truth is that*.

Language-specificity is examined in earlier studies such as Wierzbicka (1992; 1996), Zaliznjak et al. (2005; 2012), Zaliznjak (2015), and Šmelev (2002; 2014; 2015). Šmelev (2015) distinguishes three parameters of the phenomenon.

The first is connected with the number of languages, which lack a unit that at least approximately corresponds to the source expression. The more such languages that can be identified, the greater degree to which the expression can be considered language-specific.

The second parameter consists in the specificity of the content aspect of the expression, including connotations, background components of meaning, etc. (Šmelev 2015), from which it follows that the degree of distinctiveness of the semantic configuration of an expression is directly proportional to its degree of language-specificity.

The third parameter is a corollary of the second: the more distinctive the semantic configuration of a lexical unit, the more difficult it is to find an adequate translation equivalent of this unit in another language.

Šmelev (2015) notes that the object of translation is not individual words but texts, so that the translator can deviate from exact equivalence on the lexical level without regard to the language-specificity of the corresponding units. Nevertheless, it is natural to interpret the presence of a large number of different translation equivalents as indicating the absence of a systematic equivalent. This allows us to measure quantitatively the degree of language-specificity in accordance with this third parameter, which is in fact the focus of the present study.

Previous investigations have also pointed to the need for quantitative analysis to identify the degree of language-specificity. Thus Buntman et al. (2014) note that it is necessary to determine how many translation equivalents exist for potentially language-specific lexical units. It then proposed to evaluate their dispersion, but there is no discussion there of any concrete means for such an evaluation. Sitchinava (2016) does suggest such a tool for quantitatively analyzing the degree of language specificity, namely the Herfindahl index.[3] This method is used in the present study.[4]

3 Qualitative Analysis

Analysis of the corpus data allows us to identify only the degree of variety in the means of translating a given expression into other languages. When one or another expression lacks a generally accepted standard context-independent translation equivalent, we can speak of an absence of systematic equivalents, i.e., a kind of non-equivalence. Whether such non-equivalence is connected with the category of language specificity remains an open question.

Our qualitative analysis uses data obtained in Dobrovol'skij and Pöppel (2016b). The following English correlates were found in Sketch Engine:

---

[3] For more detail see Sitchinava (2016).

[4] The quantitative method for analyzing fixed expressions in monolingual corpora is used in such studies as Zhu and Fellbaum (2015), Steyer (2015).

zero equivalents [154];[5]
the fact is (that) [123];
the thing is (that) [98];
the point is (that) [70];
(it's/this/that is) because/because of [40];
it's just (that)/it's that/just/this is that [27];
in fact [26];
the truth is (that) [26];
however [16];
the fact of the matter is (that) [15];
indeed [13];
the problem is (that) [12];
you see [9];
the reason is (that) [8];
as a matter of fact [5];
for [5];
it's/this is about [5];
it happens that/as it happened/what has happened is/what is happening is [5];
the matter is (that) [5];
but [4];
since [4];
it's a fact that [4];
well [3];
basically [3];
what's true is (that)/it was true (that) [3];
the consequence is (that) [3].

The following parallels occurred twice: *the truth of the matter is (that)*; *the answer is (that)*; *the concern is (that)*; *the crux of the matter is (that)*; *the question is (that)*; *you know*; *look*; *the position is (that)*; *the thing about; in effect.* We also found more than 43 single English correlates: *the situation is; that means that; my story is; the issue is; the reality is; the content is; the explanation is; the fact remained that; the fact that; this is due to; it has everything to do with; what I'm trying to say is that; except that; that is; in reality; actually; in practice; the word is; the plan was; here's the thing; this is the situation; sort of; the point being; the purpose of; it is not that; thus; it should be noted that; in truth; for the reason that; as it was; rather; in that it is; that is; instead; namely; in that connection; in this regard; it is which; to be blunt; here too; it is a matter of; accordingly; the trouble is.* A total of 80 different types of equivalents were found.

The RNC Russian-English parallel corpus contained 26 translation equivalents, among which the zero equivalent was the most frequent:

zero equivalent [27];
the fact is (that) [14];

[5] Figures in brackets indicate total number of hits.

the thing is (that) [14];
the point is (that) [10].
Less common was:
you see [3];
actually [2];
in point of fact [2];
the matter is (that) [2].

18 equivalents occurred only once – *this came about in the following way*; *well*; *for*; *the fact of the matter was that*; *the truth of the matter was that*; *it was exactly that*; *the trouble was that*; *it is that*; *the important point is that*; *the chief thing is that*; *it all lies in the fact that*; *all that matters is that*; *it was true that*; *it was because that*; *the difficulty was that*; *the question is*; *the whole point is*; *the fact remains that.*

These results partly coincide and partly diverge. Four of the most frequent equivalents – zero equivalent, *the fact is (that); the thing is (that) and the point is (that)* – completely coincide, which indicates that the findings are non-random. At the same time, the relatively frequent constructions found in Sketch Engine – *in fact; the truth is (that)* and *however* – do not occur in the RNC, whereas *(it's/this/that is) because/because of; it's just (that)/it's that/just/this is that and the fact of the matter is (that)* – occur only once. These divergences are entirely due to the different sizes of the corpora. Sketch Engine is much larger than the RNC. In addition, the texts in these corpora differ with respect to genre. The RNC contains almost exclusively fictional texts, whereas non-fiction dominates in Sketch Engine.

In Sketch Engine we found 20 German parallels:

zero equivalent [19];
die Sache ist die (dass) [8];
aber [5];
es geht darum, dass [4];
es ist (doch) so, dass [3];
die Wahrheit ist, dass [3];
wissen Sie [2];
nur (dass) [2];
Tatsache ist (nun mal) [2];
es ist nur (dass) [2];
ich meine [2];
der Punkt ist [2];
weil [1];
es ist, was [1];
um die Wahrheit zu sagen [1];
jedoch [1];
das passiert [1];
der Grund dafür ist, dass [1];
das Schlimme ist, dass [1];
wichtig ist nur [1].

The search in the RNC yielded 13 correlates. Some of them coincide with the correlates found in Sketch Engine, some of them not:

die Sache ist die (dass) [18];
zero equivalent [11];
nämlich [9];
es handelt sich darum, dass [3];
die Hauptsache ist, (dass) [3];
doch [2];
der Grund war, (dass) [2];
es kommt (vielmehr/doch nur) darauf an [2];
der Kernpunkt ist vielmehr, dass [1];
die Sache liegt so, dass [1];
es hängt ganz davon ab [1];
es geht darum, dass [1];
weil [1].

Two of the most frequent parallels in Sketch Engine – the zero equivalent and *die Sache ist die (dass)* – coincide with the most frequent ones in the RNC, although in reverse order. The most important difference is the absence of *nämlich* in Sketch Engine, whereas in the RNC it occurs 9 times. This difference is significant because even a superficial analysis of the word *nämlich* shows that its communicative function is very close to that of the Russian construction *дело в том, что*. On the whole, the German parallels display considerable scatter.

The Swedish equivalents are examined only on the basis of the Sketch Engine data, since this is the only text corpus at our disposal. We found 25 Swedish parallels:

zero equivalent [45];
saken är den att [16];
men [8];
problemet är att [7];
faktum är att [4];
det viktiga är (att)/det är viktigt att [4];
det är för att [4];
sanningen är att [3];
grejen är den att [3];
poängen är att [3];
för (att) [3];
det handlar om att [2];
det vad jag vill säga är att [2];
i själva verket [2];
jag/han menar att [2];
det beror på att [1];
det är vad [1];
om [1];
bara [1];
då [1];

faktiskt [1];
det var inte meningen att [1];
oron är att [1];
läget är att [1];
vad jag menar är [1].

The most frequent are the zero equivalent and *saken är den att*. In the intermediate zone (from 10 to 2) there are 13 equivalents, while 10 equivalents are used only once. Here as well we can speak of considerable scatter.

We also consulted the RNC English-Russian and German-Russian parallel corpora, since the objectivity of the findings is increased by testing the hypothesis on materials in which the source texts are not Russian. In the English-Russian corpus we found 54 different English stimuli for the Russian *дело в том, что,* of which 6 equivalents occur more than 10 times each:

zero equivalent [38];
the fact is (that) [36];
for [34];
it's just (that)/it's that/just/this is that [16];
(that is) because [14];
(as) you see [11].

Besides, we found 15 less frequent equivalents, they occur between 10 and 2 times:

well [7];
the thing is (that) [7];
but [5];
it happens (that) [4],
actually [4];
the truth is (that) [4];
the point is (that) [4];
in fact [4];
the reason is (that) [3];
the problem is (that) [3];
I mean [2];
as a matter of fact [2];
I tell you [2];
in truth [2];
to begin with [2].

33 equivalents were found only once: *apparently; it should be understood that; you should understand (that); it appears that; to all appearance; listen; so; I think; it seemed; it depends on; I happen to be; it so happens; it's something in the way; it was the feeling that; the trouble is that; we are asking how; it was due to the fact that; it just amounts to; you know; I may say; it's like this; in the first place; merely; it was a case of; I suppose; that's the proposition; and; you must know; let it suffice to say; now; that's the matter; I believe; nevertheless.*

It is natural to compare these findings with those of the RNC Russian-English parallel corpus, where the corresponding figures are as follows: 3 correlates occur more than 10 times, five range from 10 to 2, and 18 are found only once. Only two equivalents are among the most frequent – the zero equivalent and *the fact is (that)*. This comparison indicates that when translating from Russian to English, translators tend to follow the form of the original, using constructions such as *the fact is (that); the thing is (that)* and *the point is (that)*. Going from English to Russian, however, they are inclined to use the discursive construction *дело в том, что* in places where it is not dictated by form. Thus the most frequent group of English correlates includes lexical units such as *for, just, because, you see*. Actively employed as well are syntactic means such as the cleft. Cf. (1).

(1a) "[…] I'm sorry about this –" My voice was shaking a little, but I couldn't get it under control. "– *it's just that* we can't seem to find Mr. Lagerfeld. [Lauren Weisberger. The Devil Wears Prada]

(1b) […] Я прошу прощения, но… – мой голос слегка дрожал, и я никак не могла унять эту дрожь, – *дело в том, что* мы, кажется, не можем отыскать мистера Лагерфельда.

The following correlates were found in the RNC German-Russian corpus:

nämlich [27];
zero equivalent [11];
die Sache ist die, (dass) [10];
denn [8];
eben [3];
aber [3];
es kommt darauf an [2];
gerade [1];
eigentlich [1];
die Tatsache [1];
doch [1].

A comparison of the RNC German-Russian and Russian-German parallel corpora yields very similar results. The following features stand out. The formal correlate *die Sache ist die, (dass)* dominates in translations from Russian to German, while in the German-Russian corpus the word *nämlich* often correlates with *дело в том, что,* fulfilling the same function even though the two expressions have nothing in common in terms of form. This confirms what was stated earlier. Cf. (2).

(2a) Prinzessin Momo hatte *nämlich* einen Zauberspiegel, der war groß und rund und aus feinstem Silber. (Michael Ende. Momo (1973))

(2b) *Дело в том, что* у принцессы Момо было большое круглое Волшебное Зеркало из чистейшего серебра.

(2c) *You see,* Princess Momo had a magical mirror. It was big and round, and it was made of the finest silver.

Another feature of the German-Russian corpus is that the group of relatively frequent parallels includes the causal conjunction *denn*, which is similar in frequency to the English conjunctions *because* and *for* in the English-Russian corpus.

The empirical data presented in the study indicate the following:

1. The construction *дело в том, что* has many different translation equivalents in English, German and Swedish. Most of these are not mutually synonymous, and choice depends on contextual conditions. This means that *дело в том, что* should be regarded not as a free co-occurrence, but as a unit of the lexicon.
2. The construction *дело в том, что* is characterized by a complex configuration of semantic features. Its semantic structure includes at least the following meanings: substantiation of something stated previously; indication of the reason something has taken place; emphasis on the special significance of the following clause.

Selection of equivalents from the various groups depends on which of these meanings is being highlighted in the utterance. Thus the English equivalent *you see* in the translation of the sentence *Дело в том, что сегодня рождение моей матери – You see, it's my mother's birthday today*; German *nämlich* in *Дело в том, что ночью произошла небольшая катастрофа – In der Nacht nämlich geschah eine kleine Katastrophe* and Swedish *nu är det så* in *Дело в том, принцесса, что у меня есть приказ – Nu är det så, Prinsessan, jag har order* all explain what was stated previously.

In cases where the focus is on the reason or cause, English, German and Swedish translations use causal subordinating conjunctions such as, for example, English *because* in *Ну, дело в том, что у меня есть сюрприз для тебя – Well, because I have a surprise for you*; German *denn* in *Дело в том, что тот, кто заглядывал в, Волшебное Зеркало и видел в нем свое отражение, становился смертным. – Denn wer sein eigenes Spiegelbild darin erblickte, der wurde davon sterblich.* or Swedish *för* in *Дело в том, что если я должен вам, то собрать такую сумму мне будет трудновато. – För att jag är skyldig dig pengar, som jag inte kan få fram.*

When the following clause is emphasized as being especially important, English, German and Swedish employ focusing particles or constructions such as, for example, English *the point is* in *Но дело в том, что я уверен, что это место действительно существует – But the point is, I'm convinced the place definitely exists;* German *der Punkt ist* in *Дело в том, что я влюблен в неё, и это сводит меня с ума – Der Punkt ist, ich bin in sie verliebt und es macht mich wahnsinnig* and Swedish *det viktiga är* in *Но дело в том, что я уверен, что это место действительно существует – Men det viktiga är, jag är övertygad att den platsen verkligen existerar.*

The Russian expression *дело в том, что* simultaneously explains what was said previously, points to the reason something has taken place, and singles out the following statement as especially significant.

4 Quantitative Analysis

The Herfindahl index was used to measure the degree of uniformity in the frequency distribution of the various translations of the construction under investigation. This index is used in economics to indicate the extent of market monopolization. In linguistics its uses include identification of the level of language specificity of various words (Sitchinava 2016). Our study has similar goals. The more uniform the frequency distribution, i.e., the lower the Herfindahl index, the more language-specific the given unit. The higher the Herfindahl index, the lower the degree of language specificity of the expression, since some particular method of translation dominates and is thus standard.

The non-normalized Herfindahl index (H) is calculated using the following formula:

$$H = \sum_{i=1}^{n} f_i^2 \tag{1}$$

where n is the total number of translation equivalents and f_i^2 is the squared relative frequency of an equivalent.

The normalized Herfindahl index (H*) is calculated as:

$$H^* = \frac{H - 1/n}{1 - 1/n} \tag{2}$$

The Herfindahl index ranges from 1/n to 1, the normalized Herfindahl index ranges from 0 to 1.

Our calculations according to the Herfindahl index are presented in Table 1.

Table 1. The Russian construction *дело в том что* in parallel corpora

Subcorpus	H	H*
Sketch Engine Russian-English-Russian	0,1036	0,0922
RNC Russian-English	0,1489	0,1148
Sketch Engine Russian-German-Russian	0,1342	0,0887
RNC Russian-German	0,1855	0,1176
Sketch Engine Russian-Swedish-Russian	0,1798	0,1470
RNC English-Russian	0,0851	0,0678
RNC German-Russian	0,2249	0,1474

All figures are rounded to 4 digits after the comma.

As is evident from Table 1, the non-normalized index (H) and the normalized one (H*) yield different results. Index H depends not only on the degree of uniformity in the frequency distribution, but also on the number of translation equivalents. Index H* allows us to compare the degree of uniformity in the frequency distribution for various language units regardless of the number of different translations of each of them. Thus if it is necessary to compare data obtained from corpora of different sizes, it is preferable to use H*. The H* indices are practically identical, showing that the degree of diversity among translations is the same (rather low in all cases) despite how many different translation approaches are used.

5 Discussion

The data obtained on the degree of translation variety can be meaningfully interpreted only when compared with findings obtained about other language units with the help of similar tools. Sitchinava (2016) uses the Herfindahl index to determine the degree of uniformity in the frequency distribution of translations into English and Ukrainian of words such as *пошлость* [banality/vulgarity], *удаль* [daring/bravado], *тоска* [melancholy/yearning], *пространство* [space], *уют* [coziness/comfort], *страсть* [passion], *простор* [expanse/vastness]. One of the goals of his study was to determine whether this uniformity of frequency distribution corresponds to the degree of language specificity. It was shown that on the whole, such a correspondence exists. A majority of the words analyzed that are traditionally considered to be language-specific display lower H and H* indices than do those which are not regarded as language-specific. This can be demonstrated on the basis of *простор* and *пространство*. *Простор* carries cultural meanings, whereas *пространство* denotes a universal category. Consequently, the Herfindahl index can be expected to be lower for *простор* and higher for *пространство*. Sitchinava's (2016) findings are presented in Tables 2 and 3.

As is evident from the tables, *простор* is language-specific relative to English, but not to Ukrainian, which is due to the proximity of Russian and Ukrainian and shared cultural roots. As for *пространство,* despite the universality of the corresponding concept, the Herfindahl index is lower for the English correspondences than for the Ukrainian ones. From this it can be concluded that even words expressing universal notions possess a certain degree of language specificity when more distant languages are compared. In the present study *дело в том, что* is not compared with equivalents in related languages, which is why Sitchinava's findings based on English materials are of interest to us. The results we have obtained from English, German and Swedish parallel corpora are similar to his findings based on English-Russian and Russian-English parallel corpora. There is reason to assume that *дело в том, что* possesses a high degree of language specificity.

Table 2. The Russian word *простор* in parallel corpora

Subcorpus	H	H*
RNC Russian-English	0,1327	0,0659
RNC English-Russian	0,0718	0,0613
RNC Russian-Ukranian	0,8306	0,8225
RNC Ukranian-Russian	0,7806	0,7795

Table 3. The Russian word *пространство* in parallel corpora

Subcorpus	H	H*
RNC Russian-English	0,3379	0,3217
RNC English-Russian	0,4495	0,4409
RNC Russian-Ukranian	0,6550	0,6494
RNC Ukranian -Russian	0,8611	0,8600

6 Conclusion

We have employed the Herfindahl index as a statistical method of analysis. Our findings show that the normalized Herfindahl index works best for similar linguistic investigations. Comparison with other words demonstrates that the results we obtained tend to resemble earlier findings based on language-specific words. Nevertheless, it cannot be unequivocally asserted that this construction is language-specific, since what the Herfindahl index measures is not the degree of language-specificity, but the degree of uniformity of frequency distribution.

References

Buntman, N.V., Zaliznjak, A.A., Zatsman, I.M., Kruzhkov, M.G., Loshchilova, E.J., Sitchinava, D.V.: Informacionnye texnologii korpusnyx issledovanij: principy postroenija kross-lingvističeskix baz dannyx (Informational technology in corpus-based studies: towards a cross-linguistic database). Inf. Appl. **8**(2), 98–110 (2014)

Dobrovol'skij, D., Pöppel, L.: Diskursivnaja konstrukcija *N в том, что* i ee paralleli v drugix jazykax: kontrastivnoe korpusnoe issledovanie. (The discursive construction *N в том, что* and and its correlates in other languages: A contrastive corpus analysis). Novosibirsk State Pedagogical Univ. Bull. **6**, 164–175 (2016a)

Dobrovol'skij, D.O., Pöppel, L.: The discursive construction *дело в том, что* and its parallels in other languages: A contrastive corpus study. In: Computational Linguistics and Intellectual Technologies: Papers from the Annual International Conference "Dialogue 2016", issue 15 (22), pp. 126–137. RGGU, Moscow (2016b)

Günthner, S.: Die "die Sache/das Ding ist"-Konstruktion im gesprochenen Deutsch – eine interaktionale Perspektive auf Konstruktionen im Gebrauch. In: Stefanowitsch, A., Fischer, K. (eds.), Konstruktionsgrammatik II. Von der Konstruktion zur Grammatik, pp. 157–177. Tübingen, Stauffenburg (2008)

Sitchinava, D.: Parallel corpora as a source of defining language-specific lexical items. In: Margalitadze, T., Meladze, G. (eds.) Proceedings of the XVII EURALEX International Congress: Lexicography and Linguistic Diversity, pp. 394–401. Ivane Javakhishvili Tbilisi University Press, Tbilisi (2016)

Šmelev, A.D.: Russkaja jazykovaja model' mira. Materialy k slovarju. (The Russian language picture of the world). Jazyki slavjanskoj kul'tury, Moscow (2002)

Šmelev, A.D.: Jazyk i kul'tura: est' li točki soprikosnovenija? (Language and culture: do they have points of interaction?). In: Proceedings of the V.V. Vinogradov Institute of Russian Language, issue 1, pp. 36–116. Russian Language Institute, Moscow (2014)

Šmelev, A.D.: Russkie lingvospecifičnye leksičeskie edinicy v parallel'nyx korpusax: vozmožnosti issledovanija i "podvodnye kamni" (Russian language-specific lexical units in parallel corpora: prospects of investigation and "pitfalls"). In: Computational Linguistics and Intellectual Technologies: Papers from the Annual International Conference "Dialogue 2015", issue 14(21), vol. 1, pp. 584–594. RGGU, Moscow (2015)

Steyer, K.: Patterns. Phraseology in a state of flux. Int. J. Lexicogr. **28**(3), 279–298 (2015)

Wierzbicka, A.: Semantics, Culture, and Cognition. Universal Human Concepts in Culture-Specific Configurations. Oxford University Press, Oxford (1992)

Wierzbicka, A.: Semantics: Primes and Universals. Oxford University Press, Oxford (1996)

Zaliznjak, A.A.: Lingvospecifičnye edinicy russkogo jazyka v svete kontrastivnogo korpusnogo analiza (Russian language-specific words as an object of contrastive corpus analysis). In: Computational Linguistics and Intellectual Technologies: Papers from the Annual International Conference "Dialogue 2015", issue 14(21), vol. 1, pp. 683–695. RGGU, Moscow (2015)

Zaliznjak, A.A., Levontina, I.B., Šmelev, A.D.: Ključevye idei russkoj jazykovoij kartiny mira (Key ideas of the Russian language picture of the world). Jazyki slavjanskoj kul'tury, Moscow (2005)

Zaliznjak, A.A., Levontina, I.B., Šmelev, A.D.: Konstanty i peremennye russkoj jazykovoj kartiny mira (Constants and variables of the Russian language picture of the world). Jazyki slavjanskoj kul'tury, Moscow (2012)

Zhu, F., Fellbaum, C.: Quantifying fixedness and compositionality in chinese idioms. Int. J. Lexicogr. **28**(3), 338–350 (2015)

Mechanisms of Meaning

Patrick Hanks(✉)

University of Wolverhampton, Stafford Street, Wolverhampton, WV1 1LY, UK
patrick.w.hanks@gmail.com

Abstract. Word meaning is at best a very vague phenomenon – some lexicographers, including the present writer, have gone so far as to claim that word meanings do not exist. So how is it possible that people can achieve precision in the meaning of their utterances? And how is it possible to use language creatively, to talk about new concepts or to talk about old concepts in new ways? The answer is surprising; it calls into question most previous work in computational linguistics on the so-called 'word sense disambiguation problem', which, I shall argue, is still unresolved because it is based on unsound theoretical assumptions. If word senses do not exist, they surely cannot be disambiguated (or processed in any other way). The hypothesis to be explored in this paper is that meanings are associated with the phraseological patterns associated with each word in normal usage, rather than with words themselves.

Keywords: Lexicography · Corpus linguistics · Semantics · Word sense disambiguation · Phraseology

1 Introduction: The Need for Critical Examination of Received Theories

A guideline for researchers of any subject, whether grand or humble, could be this: "Descartes refused to accept the authority of previous philosophers." – Wikipedia.

In this paper I propose to explore some aspects of the phenomenon that is meaning in language. The hypothesis to be investigated is that meanings reside, not in words alone, but also in the phraseological patterns associated with each word. To put it another way, in natural language different aspects of a word's meaning potential are activated by different collocations. I shall illustrate this concept with corpus-based case studies of the verbs *grin* and *repair*.

Moreover, I shall argue that precision of meaning is achieved, not by a concatenation of words (in ways that have been traditionally envisioned for thousands of years by grammarians and logicians), but rather by a concatenation of phraseological patterns, the meaning of each of which is no more than a set of contrastive probabilities. At first, as pattern elements accumulate around a word in a text, its semantic entropy diminishes. But then, as a text becomes more extensive, entropy become resurgent. Considerable skill is required by writers of scientific and factual reports to keep entropy in perspective. The second law of thermodynamics says that entropy always increases with time. By

R. Mitkov (Ed.): Europhras 2017, LNAI 10596, pp. 54–68, 2017.
https://doi.org/10.1007/978-3-319-69805-2_5

analogy, a law of dynamic semantics might state that semantic entropy always increases with text extent. The immediate environment of each word is critical.

As scientists and critics, it behaves us to be always prepared to re-examine the received theories of the past. This is particularly true of linguistics, for which a new kind of evidence suddenly became available during the last quarter of the 20th century, in the form of electronic corpora—very large collections of text in machine-readable form. This kind of evidence has supplemented and in many ways superseded previous ways of collecting evidence, which were of two kinds: evidence invented by introspection (researchers consulting their intuitions to imagine how they themselves use language) and citations painstakingly collected by hand. It is now clear that both these traditional kinds of evidence tend to introduce bias into the data. This is because both introspection and manual citation collection tend to favour the unusual, while failing to point out regular patterns of lexical co-occurrence.

Corpus evidence is not without dangers and biases of its own, but they are different in kind from the previous shortcomings, The main danger is of falling into the trap of believing that authenticity alone guarantees the existence of a meaningful pattern. It does not. In the words of Firth (1957), "We must separate from the mush of general goings-on those features of repeated events which appear to be part of a patterned process." Corpora enable us to do this.

From the 1980s onwards it became possible, for the first time ever, to use a computer to analyse statistically trends in patterns of usage. Statistical analysis of phraseology, in turn, opens up new possibilities for the analysis of meaning. It might have been the case that the new kind of evidence for phraseological norms would merely confirm received theories. Case studies show that this is not always the case. Occasionally, dictionaries get it wrong. For example, pre-corpus dictionaries typically define the transitive verb ***file*** as "to place (papers, records, etc.) in convenient order for storage or retrieval", while failing to notice the emergent role of this verb in talking about activating a procedure, as in phrases such as 'file a lawsuit', 'file a complaint', and 'file a flight plan'. These are very different meanings from putting papers into a filing cabinet.

Similarly, even the best linguists sometimes get it wrong. For example, Deignan (2005: 121) pointed out that the metaphor theorist Kövesces (1991) cites "Amusement gleamed in his eyes"—an invented example—as a realization of the conceptual metaphor HAPPINESS IS LIGHT. Corpus evidence, from both the Bank of English, which Deignan uses, and the British National Corpus (which I use) shows that Kövesces is right to imply that *eyes* is a normal collocate of *gleam*, but wrong to imply that it is normally associated with happiness. More regular collocates are *crazy, snarling, malicious,* and *mischievous*.

For reasons such as this, I would like to suggest that corpus evidence could and should have a profound effect on theories of meaning. Before going any further, therefore, I will attempt a brief summary of some salient points in the history of theories of meaning in European linguistics. Then we can discuss them.

2 Background: 100 Years of Linguistic Semantics in a Few Short Paragraphs

Throughout the 20th centuries, linguistics in the English-speaking world made steady and occasionally valuable contributions to the understanding of speech sounds (phonetics and phonology) and grammar (syntax and morphology). However, the study of meaning (semantics) was both confused and neglected. A distinction was made between lexical semantics and logical semantics. Lexical semantics was concerned with relationships such as synonymy, antonymy (various kinds of opposites), hyponymy (building hierarchies of semantic types on the basis of introspection) and meronymy (part-whole relations). It was not concerned with analysis of empirical evidence, such as the question of how people use words to make meanings. Logical semantics included topics such as Montague grammar, which I will not attempt to summarize here because, despite some hours of intensive effort since 1981, I do not understand it. Logical semantics also included truth-conditional semantics (very popular in the 1970s), which attempted to equate the meaning of a sentence with its truth conditions. The slogan of the truth-conditionalists was

"Snow is white" is true if and only if snow is white.

This sort of thing is fine as a starting point for any philosophers of language who may be interested in distinguishing true from false statements of fact about the world. It is not useful for the study of language as a phenomenon of social interaction, and the attempt to convert the slogan into a statement about meaning (*"Snow is white" means snow is white,* sometimes unhelpfully extended to translations such as *"Snow is white" means la neige est blanc)* must now be seen for what it is, a resounding and content-free failure.

The European mainstream in linguistics goes back to Roman rhetoricians such as Quintilian (1st century CE) and grammarians such as Priscian (6th century CE). Quintilian was interested in meaning from a practical point of view – essentially, his job as a rhetorician was to teach people how to make effective and persuasive speeches. For this reason, his work is potentially of considerable interest to present-day semanticists and metaphor theorists, though few of them bother to mention him. Priscian, who lived five hundred years later, was the last and best of a long line of Latin grammarians, who saw it as part of their task to impose order on chaos, i.e. to ensure that the Latin usage of writers and public speakers was logical and as well-formed as a Roman sewer. For this reason, surviving Latin prose works, being written according to the rules developed by Priscian and his predecessors, are of great interest for the development of logic and grammar, but of very little interest to modern lexical semanticists. After Priscian, there is an eerie silence for 1200 years. Throughout the Middle Ages and the early years of the Enlightenment, European intellectuals were more concerned with issues in logic and theology than with natural-language semantics. Even grammar was neglected until the 19th century, when a great crowd of scientific philologists, including Wilhelm von Humboldt (1767–1835), Rasmus Rask (1787–1832), and Otto Jespersen (1860–1943), to name but three, burst upon the world, initiating the scientific study of languages and their history.

From the point of view of lexical semantics, the European mainstream runs from Humboldt through Ferdinand de Saussure (1857–1913) and the numerous German semantic field theorists of the 1920s and 30s. Humboldt's main importance lies in his focus on words and meanings and his recognition that all natural languages are rule-governed systems for making meanings—although since his time there have been (and still are, continuing to the present day) many furious disagreements about what sort of rules govern natural language systems. Gradually, it came to be recognized that Latin grammar is not the only kind of grammar that is possible and that other languages have different grammatical structures and even different word classes or components. (This message has still not reached some American and British dictionary publishing houses.) Saussure is widely hailed as the founder of modern scientific linguistics. His four basic dichotomies (langue vs. parole; and synchronic analysis vs. diachronic analysis; linguistic signs vs. what is signified; paradigmatic relations vs. syntagmatic relations) provide an essential foundation on which the analysis of linguistic meaning can be based. The relevance of these dichotomies to lexical analysis is discussed in Chapter 12 of Hanks (2013), which links Saussure's work to that of the semantic field theorists, mostly German, of the 1920s and 30s, and links them in turn to the Sapir-Whorf hypothesis, which argues that "the world is presented [to the individual human being] in a kaleidoscopic flux of impressions which has to be organized by our minds—and this means largely by the linguistic systems in our minds. We cut nature up, organize it into concepts, and ascribe significances as we do, largely because we are parties to an agreement to organize it in this way—an agreement that holds throughout our speech community and is codified in the patterns of our language." (Whorf 1940)

For purposes such as meaning analysis, the Saussurean theory of signs and its successors in various manifestations provided a foundation that needed to be complemented and integrated with a theory of valency. This was provided by the posthumously published work of Lucien Tesnière (1959), which underpins modern dependency grammar. The version of dependency grammar used in current on Corpus Pattern Analysis (CPA) in English is colloquially known as SPOCA (an acronym for *Subject – Predicator – Object – Complement – Adverbial*), of which the best available account is Young (1980). The theoretical foundations of this grammar go back not only to Tesnière but also to Halliday (1961). Halliday's seminal article is the foundation of the systemic-functional tradition in linguistics, to which both CPA and distributional semantics are indebted.

To conclude this lightning survey of lexical semantics, one further name must be singled out, namely that of John Sinclair (1933–2007), a leading exponent, alongside Michael Halliday, of the empirical tradition in the European mainstream, which focuses on meaning as well as structure. Sinclair was the founder and editor-in-chief of the Cobuild series of publications in lexicography and English linguistics, adhering to a remarkably prescient plan that he set out in Sinclair (1966). His relevance to our present theme can best be summarized in the following quotation:

"Many if not most meanings require the presence of more than one word for their normal realization. … Patterns of co-selection among words, which are much stronger than any description has yet allowed for, have a direct connection with meaning." (Sinclair 1998).

Current corpus-driven work in English aims to give an empirically well-founded account of the patterns and to make explicit their connections with meaning. This will require, among other things, discovering reliable links between stereotypical patterns of word use and stereotypical meanings, of the sort described by Putnam (1975), which are very similar to the cognitive prototypes of Rosch (1975). This word (linking meanings to patterns of word use) is in its infancy.

3 The Purpose of Corpus Linguistics

What is the purpose of corpus linguistics? Why should we study and analyse empirical evidence for language use, rather than relying on our intuitions and knowledge of a language to provide examples?

To teach a class of students the difference between the active and passive voice, or singular and plural countable nouns in English, you don't need a corpus. Invented examples will suffice. However, corpus-based exercises can be useful for such activities as teaching the middle voice in ancient Greek - distinguishing the middle from passive. Does *luetai* mean 'he is set free' (passive) or does it mean 'he sets something free for his own benefit' (middle)? A corpus-based exercise could invite student to seek a collocating noun in the accusative case, which would mean that the verb must be in the middle voice. (I wish such an exercise had been available sixty years ago, when I was struggling with A Level Greek).

Corpus exercises may also be helpful for grammatical purposes such as reminding students of the many different ways in which German plural nouns are formed, or the distinction in different languages between countable nouns and mass nouns – for example to remind students that whereas English *money* is a mass noun (e.g. 'How much money have you got?'), Swedish *pengar* is a plural noun ('*Hur mycket pengar har du?*', literally 'How many coins have you got?').

Such pedagogical applications of corpus linguistics are useful enough, but they are trivial compared with 'the elephant in the room', namely the fact that corpus evidence constantly challenges some of our most basic received theories about language and meaning. To engage seriously with this problem, we need to analyse corpus evidence, i.e. the unbiased evidence of patterns of usage. A first step in this direction was the grammar patterns of verbs and nouns by Hunston, Francis, and Manning (1996, 1998).

4 Basic Patterns and Regular Alternations

It is now customary to divide the lexicon into 'function words' (determiners, auxiliary verbs, pronouns, prepositions, and conjunctions: so-called 'closed-class items') and content words (also known as 'open-class items': verbs, nouns, and adjectives). As with all linguistic categorizations, the boundary between these two classes is fuzzy, with some borderline cases. For example, prepositions are closed-class items that share certain properties—especially semantic properties —with open-class items, while the class of so-called 'adverbs' is a ragbag of heterogeneous lexical items, some of which have very little in common. Content words (open-class items) are used to make meanings, while function words are used to show relationships among the content words.

A striking fact about content words (notably nouns and verbs) is that they are used in two quite different ways to make meanings. In the first place, they are used normally and conventionally, in syntactically regular valency structures with semantically regular collocates, whose regularity is immediately apparent in any large concordance to a corpus of ordinary texts. But in the second place, content words are occasionally used in unusual syntactic structures or with unusual, non-recurrent collocations. Such usages exploit the norms. Hanks (2013) demonstrates in some detail that exploitations are also rule-governed, but the rues for exploiting norms are not the rules of grammar. Instead, they are rules governing the creative use of ordinary language.

The remainder of this paper will focus on the corpus analysis of verbs, because the verb is the pivot of the clause. If we can get the phraseological analysis of verbs right, it is reasonable to expect that most of the nouns and noun phrases will fall into place. People interested in the phraseological analysis of nouns using corpus data are invited to consult Hanks (2000, 2004, and 2012), publications all of which have more to say about the corpus analysis of noun patterns.

One of the verbs selected for analysis, summarized in the *Pattern Dictionary of English Verbs* (PDEV), was ***repair*** (**see** Fig. 1). This provides material for our first case study, which will illustrate the relationship between subtly different patterns of normal usage, also the relationship between normal usage and exploitations. As is usual for PDEV entries, a sample of 250 corpus lines was extracted from the British National Corpus (BNC) and each line in the sample was analysed semantically and syntagmatically. The aim of such an analysis is to discover stereotypical patterns of usage and to map them onto stereotypical meanings. These stereotypical meanings take the form of so-called 'implicatures', which include entailments and presuppositions, among other things. A question that this procedure, called Corpus Pattern Analysis (CPA; see Hanks 2004, 2013; Hanks and Pustejovsky 2005) sets out to answer, for each sentence analysed, includes questions such as 'Who did what to whom?' (or, for intransitive verbs, 'What happened?'). A follow-up question, answered by the mapping of patterns onto implicatures, is, "How do we know?".

In the discussion that follows, the terms in double square brackets represent lexical sets that share a semantic type. They are listed in a hierarchical ontology of semantic types, publicly accessible as the CPA Ontology (http://pdev.org.uk/#onto). A lexical set may be vast, as in the case of [[Human]], which designates all the names of all the human beings who have ever lived, all the human beings who ever will live, and all the terms denoting a human being, including their different properties and roles, etc. Lexical sets consisting of only one word (or very few words) also exist; they are typical of idioms. An example of a lexical set of only one word is found in the idiom '[[Human | Institution]] grasp {nettle}'. The verb *grasp* is used in collocation with the noun *nettle* to make the meaning 'deal decisively with a difficult problem'. If someone talks about 'grasping the nettle', it is extremely unlikely (though possible) that they area talking about wild plants that sting passers-by (the usual meaning of the noun *nettle*). It is much more likely that they are using an idiom (which is nothing more than a conventionalized metaphor).

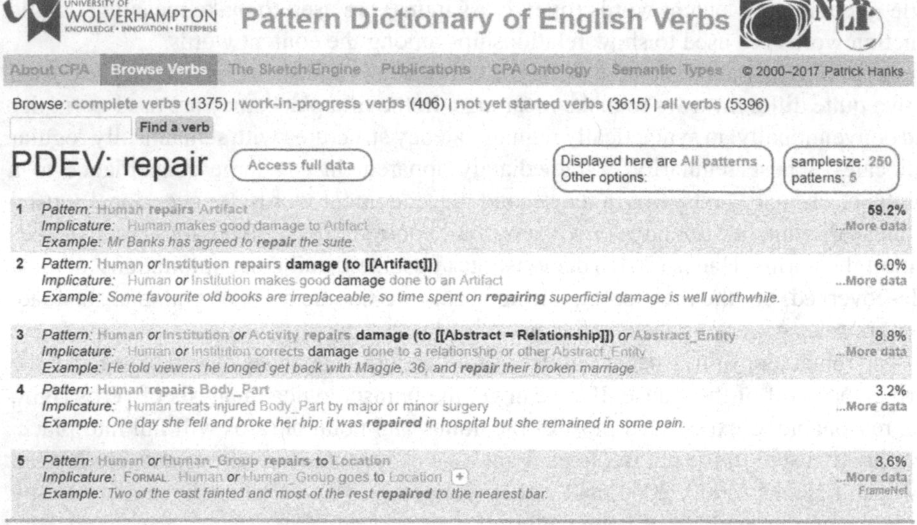

Fig. 1. PDEV entry for 'repair'.

Pattern 1 of *repair* is by far the most frequent, accounting for very nearly 60% of the corpus lines in the sample. Some basic stereotypes are: *repair a computer, an car, a building*. In these examples, the noun that is the direct object denotes a whole artefact, some part or parts of which are broken or damaged. These nouns alternate with others sets of nouns, each of which denotes a part rather that the whole artifact. These alternations include: *repair a keyboard, a wing mirror, a carburettor, the roof, the central heating system, a boiler*. In this set of examples we have the same pattern with the same meaning, but the focus is on the damaged part, not on the artifact as a whole. The implicature records a presupposition (that the [[Artifact]] or, more specifically, a part of it, has been damaged by some event) and an entailment (that the action of repairing puts the [[Artifact]] back into satisfactory working order).

Examples from BNC of terms denoting artifacts in the direct object slot, creating instances of pattern 1 at its most normal are 1, 2, and 3:

(1) the owner's wish to *repair* the aircraft.
(2) it took eight weeks to *repair* a motor vehicle.
(3) a large company, with plenty of in-house techies to *repair* a computer if it goes wrong.

Examples from BNC of part-whole alternations in pattern 1 include:

(4) *Repairing* the damaged cable took workmen about two hours.
(5) Leaky taps are not expensive to *repair*.
(6) Kalchu … began beating down the mud to *repair* the leaking roof.

Cable, taps, and *roof* are nouns that denote parts of a larger entity, rather than the entity itself. However, this difference does not justify making a separate pattern.

Pattern 2 ([[Human]] repair {damage}) is nothing more than a syntagmatic alternation of Pattern 1. That is to say, it has precisely the same meaning as Pattern 1. However, the focus is different, in that this pattern selects the word *damage* as the direct object, Thus, in this pattern, the presupposition has been selected as direct object, rather than the artifact that has been damaged. PDEV regards this admittedly subtle difference as sufficiently different to justify a separate pattern. In this way, the semantic integrity of lexical sets is preserved: despite regular occurrence in the direct object slot, we must recognize that damage is not an artifact; it is something that happens to an artifact. This must therefore be classed as a different pattern from Pattern 1.

Pattern 3 accounts for 8.8% of the 250 lines in our BNC sample. It denotes dealing with damage, not to a physical object, but to an abstract entity, namely a relationship among people or human institutions. This pattern relates to both Pattern 1 and Pattern 2. It could in principle be regarded as an exploitation of the first two patterns, in that a word that normally takes a physical object as its grammatical object is extended to an abstract entity. This sort of alternation (between physical object and abstract entity) is very common in English—and presumably other languages too. Classification into separate patterns is justified on grounds of frequency and regularity.

Pattern 4 (3.2% of the BNC sample) is a conventionalized metaphor. It is normal to talk of *treating* injured body parts, and unusual to talk of *repairing* a body part. By selecting the verb *repair*, the speaker or writer has assigned the human body the status of a machine. But with four or five examples in a 250-sentence sample, the metaphor can be regarded as a pattern (a norm or convention), rather than a creative exploitation.

Associated with pattern 4, we find two examples in the same paragraph of an unusual syntactic exploitation (7).

(7) His consultant was impressed with the speed that the arm was *repairing* in places. Mr Martinson was especially grateful for a modern medical process which may mean that his skin will *repair* without having skin grafts.

This is an intransitive use of what is normally a transitive verb. This may simply be a one-off exploitation. An alternative explanation is that it may be the tip of a domain-specific iceberg. Perhaps it is normal among doctors to talk of limbs and skin repairing, apparently without human intervention. The human body, after all, has a wonderful capacity for self-healing if left to itself in a favourable environment. These are questions that can be answered by assembling additional evidence for the use of this word, both general and domain-specific.

Finally, we come to pattern 5 (3.6% of our BNC sample). This is something completely different. It is a well-evidenced intransitive verb, whereas the preceding four patterns are transitive. And it requires an adverbial of direction governed by the preposition *to*. Pattern 5 is the only representation of the word *repair* in FrameNet (in the Self_motion frame). This means that FrameNet has nothing (yet) to say about 96% of uses of *repair*. This kind of problem is very common in FrameNet, due to its lexicographical methodology: it proceeds frame by frame on a speculative basis, rather than word by word in the light of corpus evidence. FrameNet never asks, "What are the different meanings of this or that word?".

To summarize: for the verb *repair,* PDEV recognizes four very closely related transitive patterns, plus an intransitive one that is very different.

As it happens, pattern 5 is classified by OED as a different word (a homograph), etymologically distinct from the senses of the other four patterns associated with this word. This distinction is made, not on the grounds of the very obvious syntagmatic or semantic differences, but on the basis of an extremely subtle difference in the spelling of the Anglo-Norman French source word(s): *reparer* in the case of the 'restore to good working order' senses, as opposed to *repeirer*, *reparier*, *repairir*, etc., for the verb of motion.

5 Different Kinds of Choice and Contrast

A contrasting verb is *replace.* Nowadays, for example, it is more normal to ***replace** a laptop than to attempt to **repair** it*. A language user makes a choice of the relevant word to express the intended meaning. *Repair* and *replace* denote choices of action the actant within the sentence (typically, the subject of the sentence). Such choices contrast with a different kind of choice, namely one that is made by the speaker or writer, not by a person involved in the event being described.

Repair, *mend, treat*, and *cure* express similar meanings: logically, one might say that the language does not need all of them. The choices are determined by context. Typically, you *repair* an artefact (a manufactured physical object that has a functional purpose), whereas you *treat* a human being or an animal. But *treat* does not imply that the treatment was successful, only that the attempt was made. For successful treatment, we have the verb *cure*. This is just one tiny example of the vast network of contrasts and choices offered by any natural language.

The contrasts just mentioned (*repair, replace, treat, cure*) constitute a paradigmatic set. Other contrasts resolve into meronymic sets, which are syntagmatic. For example, we may ask, what, typically, do you treat? The lexical set of nouns that includes the words *{patient, casualty, man, woman, child, animal}* as direct objects of the verb *treat* also includes words such as *{disease, illness, infection, ulcer, cancer, arthritis, diabetes, malaria}* and a vast number of other terms denoting diseases and ailments, which are meronyms denoting properties of patients receiving or requiring medical treatment. The Sketch Engine (https://www.sketchengine.co.uk/) is a tool that enables the user to instantly identify the statistically salient collocates of any word in almost any natural-language corpus. Associating these statistically salient collocates with particular meanings is a lexicographical task. In the current state of our knowledge, it cannot be automated. Attempts to do so have been premature. However, it is entirely possible that, given a large corpus of pre-tagged training data and advanced machine-learning techniques, automatic sorting of sentences into sense categories will before too long become possible.

6 Using Language Creatively

Creative use of language takes many forms. As far as the identification of patterns is concerned, it may involve unusual syntax, anomalous arguments, or figurative usage (Fig. 2).

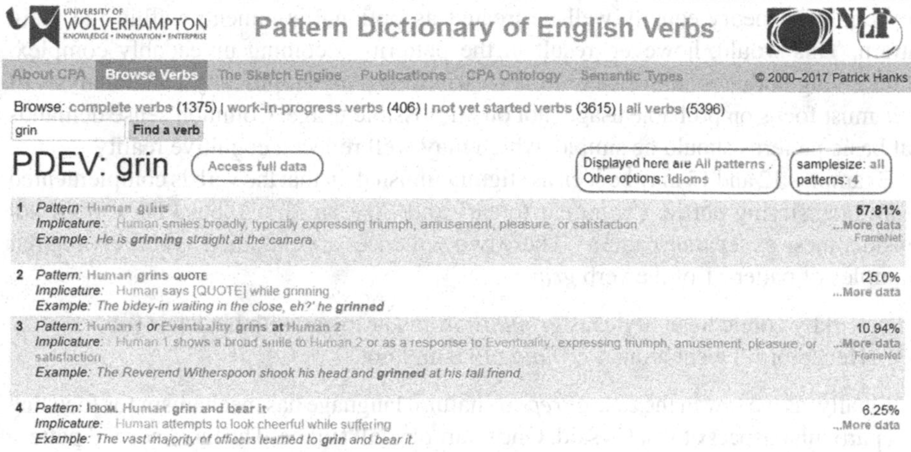

Fig. 2. PDEV entry for 'grin'.

Our second case study illustrates the nature of creative usage. The verb grin is almost always intransitive. Apparently transitive uses, as in examples 8 and 9 (one with a cognate object, the other with a reflexive pronoun), may be regarded as syntactic exploitations of the intransitive norm. Because only one example of each of these syntactic structures was found in our BNC sample, they were easy to classify as exploitations of the norm.

(8) He *grinned* an uncomfortable grin.
(9) Ian McCann *grins* himself to death for a cosy tour round the home of Billy Bragg …

Other cases are more difficult to classify. CPA takes simple statistics seriously, so a group of frequent occurrences of a syntactic structure may be classified as a separate pattern in its own right if it is comparatively frequent, whereas, in the analysis of some other verb, the same grammatical alternation, if rare, may be classified as an exploitation of a norm. PDEV contains two alternations of *grin* as a verb that are separate patterns, plus one ("[[Human]] grin and bear it") that is an idiom with a particular meaning that has little to do with the core sense of *grin*. Thus, although PDEV records four patterns for this verb, there is only one basic literal sense, which is given first. Three of the patterns record subtly different semantics, each of which is associated with a subtly different phraseology.

The first of the regular alternation is the use of *grin* as a verb governing a speech act, as in 10.

(10) ‘No,’ she *grins*, ‘this is far more sophisticated.’

The second regular alternation is the introduction of a second argument governed by the preposition *at*, as in 11:

(11) We all shook hands and *grinned* stupidly *at* one another.

For convenience, PDEV treats both of these alternations as separate patterns, but they could in theory equally well be treated as optional arguments within the main pattern. This would, however, result in the patterns becoming unreadably complex, while giving undue prominence to minor variations. Any empirically valid analysis of lexis must focus on probable usage, not on all possible usage. Common sense demands that basic patterns should be simple, which may well reflect a cognitive reality.

Examples 12 and 13 may be seen as slightly unusual, in that the verb is complemented by an intensifying phrase (‘from ear to ear’ and ‘like an idiot’), but PDEV does not consider these as separate patterns. These two sentences are classified as entirely regular examples of pattern 1 of the verb *grin*.

(12) Kirkby comic Sean Styles is *grinning* from ear to ear with his latest job.
(13) Henceforth I went around *grinning* like an idiot.

Finally, as we saw in the case of *repair*, natural language has mechanism for focusing on a particular aspect of what is said. One example will suffice. The most normal pattern for this verb is that *people grin*. A body part is not a person. However, it is quite unremarkable to select the relevant body part (the face or mouth) and focus on that as the subject of the sentence, as in 14.

(14) The faces *grinning* from the tatty punk regalia looked … depraved and hollow-eyed.

There is a vast literature on metaphor, but the focus on metaphor is misleading in two ways. Firstly, metaphors are not the only kind of figurative language that exist. Chapter 8 of Hanks (2013) identifies several ways in which normal phraseological patterns can be exploited. These include not only metaphors, but also anomalous argument (not all of which are metaphors), similes, exaggeration (hyperbole), understatement (meiosis and litotes), euphemism, sarcasm, irony (saying the opposite of what you mean), and other tropes.

Secondly, as suggested in Bowdle and Gentner (2005), metaphors are of two kinds: conventional and creative. Conventional metaphors are nothing more than secondary conventions. The vast majority of metaphors are conventional, e.g. 15.

(15) the *antibodies* that are the *front-line troops* of the immune system.

When I first read this, it struck me as a fine example of a freshly created metaphor. I was soon disillusioned. A few seconds with Google were enough to show that, in the literature of immunology.

7 Psycholinguistic Implications

Corpus pattern analysis is an exercise in sociolinguistics. The corpus lexicographer compares hundreds of different recorded uses, by many different writers and speakers, of the same word or phrase, and attempts to discern some underlying patterns of linguistic behaviour shared by many members of a speech community. Each of these observed patterns of linguistic behaviour is associated with a particular meaning: more precisely, with a particular set of implicatures, including presuppositions and entailments. On this basis, predictions can be made about what the word or phrase will mean when used in the same or similar contexts by anyone at any time in the future.

The corpus pattern analyst is not interested in trying to predict all possible meanings of a word or phrase; instead, he or she focuses mainly on predicting the *probable* meaning of the word or phrase when it is used in different contexts.

How does this work? According to Hoey's theory of lexical priming (2005), every member of a speech community is primed from the very first moment of exposure to linguistic utterances to recognize patterns of word use and to associate each one with a particular meaning or set of meanings. Moreover, he or she will also learn to make meanings, expressing his or her needs, observations, and questions by uttering different patterns and by ringing the changes on them.

In this way, every member of a speech community has got, stored in his or her brain, a subset of the normal patterns of word use in the language. When a person is listening to or reading a text uttered by someone else, some form of pattern matching is going on inside his or her head—matching the patterns uttered against the set of patterns stored, and seeking the best match. When a match is found, a hearer's meaning is activated. This may be something logical such as an entailment, but it can equally often be an emotion or evocation of an experience.

The patterns are recognized, among listeners and readers, for purposes of understanding at least some of what is said or written. The patterns are also available to the individual in order to express his or her needs, observations, and questions. Some people are very good at pattern recognition; others are better at pattern activation (without necessarily taking much notice what other people way or write). As a result, it is possible —indeed, perfectly normal—for users of the same language, who may never have met each other before, to achieve the mutual satisfaction of believing that they understand each other.

Societies have effective and sometimes brutal ways (including, principally, mockery) of eradicating anomalous uses of phraseological patterns and beliefs about their interpretation. Despite this, language change proceeds inexorably. New patterns and beliefs become established, old ones are driven into literary obsolescence, as each succeeding generation takes over the language for its own purposes and begins to elbow the older generation off the planet. Figurative language is a major component of the process of language change. Most figurative uses die as soon as they are born, but occasionally one will catch on and become established. Thus, today's metaphor may become tomorrow's literal meaning. It is in this way that the word ***dope*** progressed in the twentieth century from denoting a toxic-fume-emitting varnish used to stiffen the canvas fuselages of early aeroplanes (still used, I believe, on model aircraft) to denoting a stupefying drug, and hence a stupid or stupefied person. An unusually rich set of other senses of this word are recorded, including “a thick gooey liquid used as a lubricant for skis and snowshoes or as food”. The entry currently available in OED on-line is a mess, which is not surprising, as it was first published in 1897 and tinkered with, rather unsatisfactorily, in 1989. This was a period during which the word was undergoing sequences of ever more extraordinary, even baffling, meaning changes. It will be interesting to see what the OED lexicographers make of it when they get around to revising it, which cannot be far away.

8 Conclusion

Almost all content words (in all languages) are associated with a variety of different phraseological patterns, which are used by speakers and writers to create meanings. Patterns are established in a language over long periods of time, and (especially in a literary language such as English), they are fairly stable; i.e. a natural language contains a central core of phraseological patterns, which changes only gradually. Most of the phraseology used 200 years ago by writers such as Jane Austen is still in use today. Nevertheless, phraseological patterns do change; the changes are always unpredictable and sometimes sudden. An example that is quietly becoming established right now is the use of the preposition *of* in quantitive questions such as “How big of a bank loan do you need?” which would have been regarded as ungrammatical until the beginning of the present century.

The advent of corpus linguistics in the 1980s has provided us with a vast wealth of possible new ways of studying the extraordinary phenomenon that is natural language. But during the past twenty or thirty years, linguists have been remarkably slow to respond to the challenges. Largely for practical reasons, exacerbated by constraints on research funding, they have confined themselves to developing practical applications – in particular, practical pedagogical applications.

But now, the challenge is to take the opportunity to examine in detail the mechanisms of meaning in natural languages and to test any theoretical conclusions that emerge from such examinations against the evidence of actual usage, which can only be done with the aid of a computer. The theoretical foundations for such examinations were laid (on a necessarily speculative basis) in the second half of the 20th century by philosophers of language such as Wittgenstein and Putnam, literary critics such as I. A. Richards, and anthropologists such as Eleanor Rosch.

The dream of the Semantic Web (Berners-Lee, Hendler et al. 2001) is to “enable computers to manipulate data meaningfully.” Up till the time of writing (September 2017), work on realizing the dream has done little more than construct ontologies and add tags to documents and elements of documents, to structure them and improve their machine-tractability, without engaging fully with their semantic content. As Wilks (2008) put it, the Semantic Web is “the apotheosis of annotation—but what are its semantics?” In the long term, if the dream is to be realized, something very like a pattern dictionary will be needed to explicate the relationship between word use and meaning for every content word in every language in the world. This is not such an impossible dream as it may sound, for much work in distributional semantics, in many languages, is already under way. What is needed is a unifying theory of lexical semantics that will motivate and coordinate these efforts.

One essential future step—perhaps it will not be taken in full earnest until a decade or two from now—will be to examine, in the light of corpus evidence, the theoretical speculations about the nature of language and meaning by the great minds of the past, from Wilkins, Descartes, and Leibniz to Fillmore, Lakoff, and Chomsky. These great thinkers of the past did not have the benefit of corpus evidence or, if they did, they preferred not to use it. Fillmore's use of the corpus was satirized by the late John Sinclair as 'the fish-pond approach" (first dream up a theoretical point by introspection; then go fishing in a corpus for an example that fits the theory; if it does not fit the theory, throw it back and fish out another one).

The generative grammarian Noam Chomsky has been more forthright in his rejection of corpus linguistics, characterizing it as an accumulation of data without theoretical consequences. Chomsky has also said, "The smart way to keep people passive and obedient is to strictly limit the spectrum of acceptable opinion, but allow very lively debate within that spectrum—even encourage the more critical and dissident views. That gives people the sense that there's free thinking going on, while all the time the presuppositions of the system are being reinforced by the limits put on the range of the debate." Nowhere is this more true than of the aggressively constrained field of generative grammar. Chomskyans like to keep university departments of linguistics passive and obedient. The spectrum of acceptable opinion in such departments is limited to speculation about syntax and phonology, based on the evidence of introspection. Chomkyan linguistics, which has so little to say about lexis and meaning, might justly be characterized as "an impoverished and thoroughly inadequate conception of language", which, as it happens, is how Noam himself characterized Saussure's work.

References

Berners-Lee, T., Hendler, J., Lassila, O.: The Semantic Web. Scientific American (2001)

Bowdle, B., Gentner D.: The career of metaphor. Psychol. Rev. **112**(1) (2005)

Deignan, A.: Metaphor and Corpus Linguistics. John Benjamins Publishing, Amsterdam/ Philadelphia (2005)

Firth, J.R.: Personality and language in society. Sociological Review 62. Papers in Linguistics, pp. 1934–1951. Oxford University Press, London (1957)

Halliday, M.: Categories of the theory of grammar. Word **17**(3) (1961)

Hanks, P.: Do word meanings exist? Comput. Humanit. **34**, 205–215 (2000)

Hanks, P.: Corpus pattern analysis. In: Euralex Proceedings, Université de Bretagne-Sud, Lorient, France (2004)

Hanks, P.: How people use words to make meanings: semantic types meet valencies. In: Boulton, A., Thomas, J. (eds.) Input, Process and Product: Developments in Teaching and Language Corpora. Masaryk University Press, Brno, CZ (2012)

Hanks, P.: Lexical Analysis: Norms and Exploitations. MIT Press, Cambridge (2013)

Hanks, P., Pustejovsky, J.: A pattern dictionary for natural language processing. Revue française de linguistique appliquée **10**(2), 335–368 (2005)

Hoey, M.: Lexical Priming. Routledge, Abingdon (2005)

Hunston, S., Francis, G., Manning, E.: Collins Cobuild Grammar Patterns, vol. 1: Verbs; vol. 2: Nouns and adjectives, HarperCollins, London/Glasgow (1996; 1998)
Kilgarriff, A.: I don't believe in word senses. Comput. Humanit. **31**, 91–113 (1997)
Kilgarriff, A., Rychlý, P., Smrž, P., Tugwell, D.: The sketch engine. In: Williams, G., Vessier, S. (eds.) Proceedings of the 11th Euralex International Congress, Université de Bretagne sud, Lorient (2004)
Kövesces, Z.: Happiness: a definitional effort. Metaphor Symbolic Act. **6**(1) (1991)
Putnam, H.: The meaning of meaning and is semantics possible? In: Putnam, H.: Mind, Language, and Reality: Philosophical Papers. Cambridge University Press (1975)
Rosch, E.: Cognitive representations of semantic categories. J. Exp. Psychol. **104**(3) (1975)
Sinclair, J.: Beginning the study of lexis. In: Bazell, C.E., Catford, J.C., Halliday, M.A.K., Robins, R.H. (eds.) In Memory of J.R. Firth, Longman, London (1966)
Sinclair, J.: The lexical item. In: Weigand, E. (ed.) Contrastive Lexical Semantics. John Benjamins, Amsterdam/Philadelphia (1998)
Tesnière, L.: Eléments de Syntaxe Structurale. Klincksieck, Paris (1959)
Whorf, B.L.: Language, Thought, and Reality. MIT Press, Cambridge (1940)
Wilks, Y.: The Semantic Web: The apotheosis of annotation - but what are its semantics? Inst. Electr. Electron. Eng. (2008)
Young, D.J.: The Structure of English Clauses. Routledge, Abingdon (1980)

Putting the Horses Before the Cart: Identifying Multiword Expressions Before Translation

Carlos Ramisch[(✉)]

Aix Marseille Univ, CNRS, LIF, Marseille, France
carlos.ramisch@lif.univ-mrs.fr

Abstract. Translating multiword expressions (MWEs) is notoriously difficult. Part of the challenge stems from the analysis of non-compositional expressions in source texts, preventing literal translation. Therefore, before translating them, it is crucial to locate MWEs in the source text. We would be putting the cart before the horses if we tried to translate MWEs before ensuring that they are correctly identified in the source text. This paper discusses the current state of affairs in automatic MWE identification, covering rule-based methods and sequence taggers. While MWE identification is not a solved problem, significant advances have been made in the recent years. Hence, we can hope that MWE identification can be integrated into MT in the near future, thus avoiding clumsy translations that have often been mocked and used to motivate the urgent need for better MWE processing.

1 Introduction

Translation is probably one of the most complex tasks in language processing, both for humans and computers. One of the reasons why translation is challenging is the arbitrary and non-categorical nature of human languages. In other words, while general grammatical and semantic composition rules are useful abstractions to model languages in computer systems, actual language use is permeated by exceptions that are often at the root of errors in language technology. Multiword expressions (MWEs) represent such exceptions to general language rules when words come together. They can be defined as combinations of at least two lexemes which present some idiosyncrasy, that is, some deviation with respect to usual composition rules at some level of linguistic processing [2]. Therefore, their automatic processing is seen as a challenge for natural language processing (NLP) systems [5,32,35].

I would like to thank the chairs of MUMTTT 2017 for inviting me to the event and for giving me the oportunity to publish this invited contribution. This paper includes materials published in other venues and co-written with: Mathieu Constant, Silvio Cordeiro, Benoit Favre, Marco Idiart, Gülşen Eryiğit, Johanna Monti, Lonneke van der Plas, Michael Rosner, Manon Scholivet, Amalia Todirascu, and Aline Villavicencio. Work reported here has been partly funded by projects PARSEME (Cost Action IC1207), PARSEME-FR (ANR-14-CERA-0001), and AIM-WEST (FAPERGS-INRIA 1706-2551/13-7).

R. Mitkov (Ed.): Europhras 2017, LNAI 10596, pp. 69–84, 2017.
https://doi.org/10.1007/978-3-319-69805-2_6

If MWEs are a pain in the neck for language technology in general [32], this is especially true for machine translation (MT) systems. The automatic translation of MWEs by current MT systems is often used as a compelling argument for the importance of dealing with them in NLP systems [23,26,40]. For example, the two sentences below in English (EN) and in French (FR) contain an equivalent multiword expression which means carrying out a task with precipitation, in the wrong order, by inverting priorities:

- EN: *He puts the cart before the horses.*
- FR: *Il met la charrue avant les bœufs.*

While the FR expression is equivalent in meaning to the EN one, it translates word-for-word into EN as *He puts the plough before the oxen.* As a consequence, even though the automatic translation succeeds in translating the individual words, the translation of the whole expression fails, as we show in the examples below:[1]

- EN$\overset{MT}{\rightarrow}$FR: *Il met le chariot devant les chevaux.*
- FR$\overset{MT}{\rightarrow}$EN: *He puts the cart before the oxen.*

MT can be seen as a process of analysis and generation, that is, a source text is first *analysed* to create an abstract intermediate representation of its meaning, and then a target text is *generated* from this abstract representation so that the meaning of the source text is preserved in the target text [45]. Even though modern MT systems do not always explicitly model translation using Vauquois' triangle, the analysis/generation model is useful to understand the role of MWEs in MT. That is, MWE processing for MT means not only analysing them and getting their meaning correctly, but also generating them in the target text to ensure fluency and naturalness.

We focus only on the first step of translation, that is source text *analysis*, and on the role of MWE identification in the analysis step of MT. While generation is also important to confer naturalness to the output of the system, most research contributions to date in the MWE community have focused on text analysis, and work investigating MWE-aware text generation is quite rare. Therefore, we will explore the landscape of existing monolingual MWE identification methods that could be useful for MT.

This paper gathers methods and experimental results on MWE identification previously published in collaboration with colleagues (see the acknowledgements). Its structure is based on a survey on MWE processing [8], which distinguishes rule-based and statistical tagging methods. First, we briefly list and exemplify resources required and useful for MWE identification (Sect. 2). Then, we summarise previously published models for rule-based MWE identification (Sect. 3) and for sequence-tagging MWE identification (Sect. 4). We conclude by discussing the applicability of these systems as preprocessing steps for MT, and perspectives for future work in the field (Sect. 5).

---

[1] Translations obtained using Google's online translation service (http://translate.google.com) on September 6, 2017.

2 MWE Identification Resources

Automatic MWE identification is a task that consists in finding MWEs in running text, on the level of word occurrences or tokens. Figure 1, taken from [28], shows an example of sentence, with MWEs annotated in bold and additionally containing a category label on the last token. Notice that we use the term *identification* referring to in-context MWE identification, as opposed to MWE *discovery*, where the goal is to extract MWEs from text and include them in lexicons, as explained in [8]. Both tasks are similar, being given as input text where MWEs should be located. However, they differ in their output: while discovery generates MWE lists, identification generates annotations on the input sentences. Often MWE discovery can be considered as a prerequisite for identification, as the latter usually relies on lexicons built with the help of corpus-based MWE discovery.

More$_B$ **often**$_I$ **than**$_I$ **not**$_I$$^{\text{MW-adverbial}}$,$_O$ however$_O$,$_O$ it$_O$ is$_O$ not$_O$ so$_O$ straightforward$_O$ to$_O$ **figure**$_B$ **out**$_I$^{VPC} how$_O$ to$_O$ **make**$_B$ segmentation$_o$ **decisions**$_I$^{LVC} ,$_O$ **in**$_B$ **order**$_I$ **to**$_I$$^{\text{MW-prep}}$ split$_O$ sentences$_O$ into$_O$ **lexical**$_B$ **units**$_I$$^{\text{MW-term}}$ that$_O$ **make**$_B$ **sense**$_I$^{idiom}

Fig. 1. Example of a sentence with MWEs identified (in bold), marked with BIO tags (subscripts) and disambiguated for their categories (superscripts). Source: [28].

Identification methods take text as input and, in order to locate MWEs, also require additional information to guide the process. This additional information is of two types: (a) more or less sophisticated *lexicons* containing MWE entries and sometimes contextual information about their occurrences, and (b) *probabilistic models* learned using machine learning methods applied to corpora where MWEs were manually annotated. In this section we discuss some existing lexicons and annotated corpora for MWE identification.

Lexicons. The simplest configuration of MWE identification requires only a list of entries that are to be treated as single tokens. Many parsers contain such lexicons, especially covering fixed MWEs such as compound conjunctions (e.g. *as well as*, *so that*) and prepositions (e.g. *in spite of*, *up to*). Lists of MWEs with associated information can be found on language catalogues such as LDC and ELRA, but are also freely available, for instance, on the website of the SIGLEX-MWE section.[2] When the target constructions allow some morphological and/or syntactic variation, though, more sophisticated entry representations are required. Among the

[2] http://multiword.sf.net/.

information given in MWE lexicons one usually founds the lemmas of the component words. This allows identifying MWE occurrences in inflected forms, if the text is lemmatised before identification. A complete survey of lexical resources containing MWEs is out of the scope of this work. For further reading on this topic, we recommend the excellent survey by Losnegaard et al. [20].

Annotated corpora. Identification of MWEs in running text can be modelled as a machine learning problem that learns from MWE-annotated corpora and treebanks. Many existing treebanks include some MWE annotations, generally focusing on a limited set of categories, as discussed in the survey by Rosén et al. [31]. However, treebanks are not required for annotating MWEs in context. Minimally, tags can be used to delimit MWE occurrences. Additional tags or features can be used to classify MWE categories, as shown in Fig. 1. Shared tasks often release free corpora for MWE identification. For instance, the SEMEVAL DIMSUM shared task focused on MWE identification in running text, releasing corpora with comprehensive MWE annotation for English [37].[3] The PARSEME shared task on verbal MWE identification released MWE-annotated corpora for 18 languages, focusing on verbal expressions only [34].[4] Other examples of annotated corpora with MWE tags include the English Wiki50 corpus [46], the English STREUSLE corpus [38], and the Italian MWE-anntoated corpus [42]. Some datasets focus on specific MWE categories, such as verb-object pairs [43] and verb-particle constructions [1,44]. More rare but extremely relevant for MWE-aware MT, freely available parallel corpora annotated with MWEs also exist [22,27,47].

3 Rule-Based MWE Identification

In rule-based identification, generally a lexicon is used to indicate which MWEs should be annotated in the text. In the simplest case, the lexicon contains only unambiguous fixed expressions that do not vary in inflection and in word order (e.g. *in fact, more often than not, even though*). In this case, a greedy string search algorithm suffices to match the MWE entries with the sentences. Special care must be taken if the target expressions are ambiguous, such as the fixed adverbial *by the way*, whose words can co-occur by chance as in *I recognise her by the way she walks* [8,24]. Ambiguous fixed expressions, that can have compositional readings and/or accidental co-occurrence, require more sophisticated identification methods (e.g. the one described in Sect. 4).

Among semi-fixed unambiguous expressions that present only morphological inflection, nominal compounds such as *ivory tower* and *red herring* are frequent in many languages. The identification of this type of MWE is possible if the lexicon contains lemmatised entries, and if the text is automatically lemmatised prior to identification [17,26]. Another alternative is to represent morphological

[3] http://dimsum16.github.io.
[4] http://multiword.sf.net/sharedtask2017.

inflection paradigms and restrictions in the lexicon, so that all alternative forms can be searched for when scanning the text [7,33,41].

We have developed and evaluated several strategies for rule-based MWE identification, depending on the language, available resources and MWE categories. The following subsections summarise these methods, whose details can be found in previous publications [12,13].

3.1 Lexicon-Based Matching

In [12], we propose a lexicon-based identification tool, developed as part of the mwetoolkit [26].[5] It was inspired on `jMWE` [15], a Java library that can be used to identify MWEs in running text based on preexisting MWE lists.

Proposed method. The proposed software module allows more flexible matching procedures than `jMWE`, as described below. Moreover, the construction of MWE lists can be greatly simplified by using the MWE extractor integrated in the `mwetoolkit`. For example, given a noun compound pattern such as `Noun Noun`$^{+}$ and a POS-tagged corpus, the extractor lists all occurrences of this expression in a large corpus, which can in turn be (manually or automatically) filtered and passed on to the MWE identification module.

We propose an extension to the `mwetoolkit` which annotates input corpora based on either a list of MWE candidates or a list of patterns. In order to overcome the limitation of `jMWE`, our annotator has additional features described below.

1. **Different gapping possibilities**
   - Contiguous: Matches contiguous sequences of words from a list of MWEs.
   - Gappy: Matches words with up to a limit number of gaps in between.
2. **Different match distances**
   - Shortest: Matches the shortest possible candidate (e.g. for phrasal verbs, we want to find only the closest particle).
   - Longest: Matches the longest possible candidate (e.g. for noun compounds).
   - All: Matches all possible candidates (useful as a fallback when shortest and longest are too strict).
3. **Different match modes**
   - Non-overlapping: Matches at most one MWE per word in the corpus.
   - Overlapping: Allows words to be part of more than one MWE (e.g. to find MWEs inside the gap of another MWE).
4. **Source-based annotation**: MWEs are extracted with detailed source information, which can later be used for quick annotation of the original corpus.

[5] http://mwetoolkit.sf.net/.

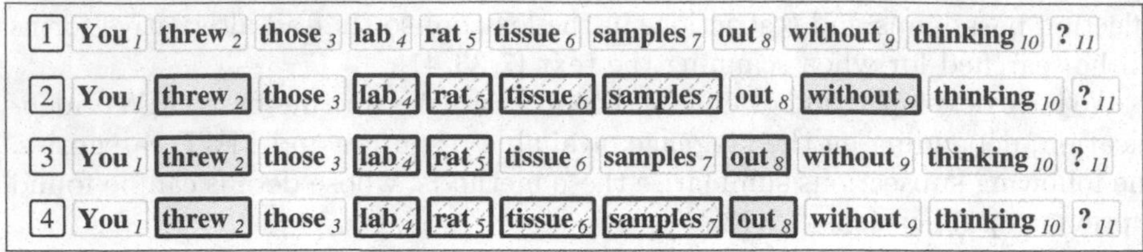

Fig. 2. Lexicon-based MWE identification with the `mwetoolkit` using different match distances. Source: [12].

Examples. Consider two different MWE patterns described by the POS regular expressions below:[6]

- `NounCompound` → `Noun Noun`$^+$
- `PhrasalVerb` → `Verb (Word*) Particle`

Given an input such as Sentence 1 (Fig. 2) the gappy approach with different match distances will detect different types of MWEs. In Sentence 2, we show the result of identification using the *longest* match distance, which although well suited to identify noun compounds, may be too permissive for phrasal verbs combining with the closest particle (*out*). For the latter the *shortest* match distance will yield the correct response, but will be excessively strict when looking for a pattern such as the one for noun compounds, as shown in Sentence 3.

Discussion. The proposed lexicon-based MWE identification module combines powerful generic patterns with a token-based identification algorithm with different matching possibilities. A wise choice of the best match distance is necessary when looking for patterns in corpora, and these new customisation possibilities allow identification under the appropriate conditions, so that one can achieve the result shown in Sentence 4 of Fig. 2. With this module, one can either annotate a corpus based on a preexisting lexicon of MWEs or perform MWE type-based extraction, generate a lexicon and subsequently use it to annotate a corpus. When annotating the same corpus from which MWE types were extracted, source-based annotation can be used for best results.

One limitation of this approach concerns the occurrence of ambiguous expressions. Accidental co-occurrences would require contextual rules that might be tricky to express, and probably a context-dependent module would perform better for this kind of expression [24]. Moreover, since the module does not perform semantic disambiguation, an expression such as *piece of cake* would be annotated as an MWE in both sentences below:

1. *The test was a piece of cake*
2. *I ate a piece of cake at the bakery*

[6] In this toy example, the "lexicon" is formed by abstract POS patterns. In our implementation, lexicons can contain lemmas, surface forms, POS patterns or a mix of all these.

3.2 Corpus-Based Matching

While the proposal above has been tested only using preexisting MWE lexicons, we have subsequently employed it in a system submitted to the DiMSUM shared task and described in [13]. In this shared task, the competing systems were expected to perform both semantic tagging and MWE identification [37]. A training corpus was provided containing annotated MWEs, both continuous and discontinuous (or gappy). The evaluation was performed on a test corpus provided to participants without any MWE annotation.

For MWE identification, we used a task-specific instantiation of the `mwetoolkit`, handling both contiguous and non-contiguous MWEs with some degree of customisation, using the mechanisms described above. However, instead of using preexisting MWE lexicons, our MWE lexicons were automatically extracted from the training corpus, without losing track of their token-level occurrences. Therefore, we could guarantee that all the MWE occurrences learned from the training data were projected onto the test corpus.

Proposed method. Our MWE identification algorithm uses 6 different rule configurations, targeting different MWE categories. While 3 of them are based on lexicons extracted from the training corpus, the other 3 are unsupervised. The parameters of each configuration are optimised on a held-out development set, consisting of $\frac{1}{9}$ of the training corpus. The final system is the union of all configurations.

For the 3 supervised configurations, annotated MWEs are extracted from the training data and then filtered: we only keep combinations that have been annotated often enough in the training corpus. In other words, we keep MWE candidates whose proportion of annotated instances with respect to all occurrences in the training corpus is above a threshold t, discarding the rest. The thresholds were manually chosen based on what seemed to yield better results on the development set. Finally, we project the resulting MWE lexicons on the test data, that is, we segment as MWEs the test-corpus token sequences that are contained in the lexicon extracted from the training data. These configurations are:

- CONTIG: Contiguous MWEs annotated in the training corpus are extracted and filtered with a threshold of $t = 40\%$. That is, we create a lexicon containing all contiguous lemma+POS sequences for which at least 40% of the occurrences in the training corpus were annotated. The resulting lexicon is projected on the test corpus whenever that contiguous sequence of words is seen.
- GAPPY: Non-contiguous MWEs are extracted from the training corpus and filtered with a threshold of $t = 70\%$. The resulting MWEs are projected on the test corpus using the following rule: an MWE is deemed to occur if its component words appear sequentially with at most a total of 3 gap words in between them.
- NOUN^2-KN: We collect all noun-noun sequences in the test corpus that also appear at least once in the training corpus (known compounds), and filter

them with a threshold of $t = 70\%$. The resulting list is projected onto the test corpus.

Additionally, we used 3 configurations based on POS patterns observed only on the test corpus. without looking at the training corpus.

- NOUN^2-UKN: Collect all noun-noun sequences in the test corpus that never appear in the training corpus (unknown compounds), and project all of them back on the test corpus.
- PROPN$^{2..\infty}$: Collect sequences of two or more contiguous words with POS-tag `PROPN` and project all of them back onto the test corpus.
- VP: Collect verb-particle candidates and project them back onto the test corpus. A verb-particle candidate is a pair of words under these constraints: the first word must have POS-tag `VERB` and cannot have lemma *go* or *be*. The two words may be separated by a `N`[7] or `PROPN`. The second word must be in a list of frequent non-literal particles.[8] Finally, the particle must be followed by a word with one of these POS-tags: `ADV`, `ADP`, `PART`, `CONJ`, `PUNCT`. Even though we might miss some cases, this final delimiter avoids capturing regular verb-PP sequences.

Examples. We have analysed some of the annotations made by the system and we show a sample of this analysis below:

- `N_N` Since our system looks for all occurrences of adjacent noun-noun pairs, we obtain a high recall for them. In 19 cases, however, our system has identified two `N`s that are not in the same phrase; e.g. **when I have a problem customer services don't want to know*. In order to realise that these nouns are not related, we would need parsing information. 17 cases have been missed due to only the first two nouns in the MWE being identified; e.g. **Try the memory foam pillows!* – instead of *memory foam pillows*. A similar problem occurred for sequences including adjectives, such as **My sweet pea plants arrived 00th May* – instead of *sweet pea plants*. In 24 cases, our system identified a compositional compound; e.g. **Quality gear* guys, excellent! Semantic features would be required to filter such cases out.
- **`VERB`-particles** Most of the `VERB_ADP` expressions were caught by the VP configuration, but we still had some false negatives. In 7 cases, the underlying particle was not in our list (e.g. *I regret ever going near their store*), while in 9 other cases, the particle was followed by a noun phrase (e.g. *Givin out* Back shots). 5 of the missed MWEs could have been found by accepting the particle to be followed by a `SCONJ`, or to be followed by the end of the line as delimiters. Most of the false positives were due to the verb being followed by an indirect object or prepositional phrase. We believe that disambiguating these cases would require valency information. 4 false positives were CONTIG

[7] In the remainder of the paper, we abbreviate the POS tag `NOUN` as `N`.

[8] The 13 most frequent non-literal particles: *about*, *around*, *away*, *back*, *down*, *in*, *into*, *off*, *on*, *out*, *over*, *through*, *up*.

cases of go to being identified as a MWE (e.g. **In my mother's day, she didn't go to college*). In the training corpus, this MWE had been annotated 57% of the time, but in future constructions (e.g. *Definitely not going to purchase a car from here*). Canonical forms would be easy to model with a specific contextual rule of the form *going to* **verb**.

Discussion. In spite of its simplicity, among the 9 submitted systems, our method was ranked 2nd in the overall results of the shared task. Three systems were ranked first, with two of them being submitted in the open condition (i.e. using external resources such as handcrafted lexicons).

In addition to simplicity, the system is also quite precise. Coverage is limited, though, to MWEs observed in the training corpus. Another limitation is that high-quality lemma and POS annotations are necessary to be able to extract reliable MWE lists from the training corpus and projecting them correctly on the test corpus. The manual tuning of rules and thresholds on a development set is effective, but also corpus-specific. Statistical methods like the ones described in Sect. 4 can be used to bypass this manual tuning step and build more general identification models.

4 Taggers for MWE Identification

A popular alternative, especially for contiguous semi-fixed MWEs, is to use an identification model that replaces the MWE lexicon. This model is usually learned using machine learning from corpora in which the MWEs in the sentences were manually annotated.

Machine learning techniques usually model MWE identification as a tagging problem based on BIO encoding,[9] as shown in Fig. 1. In this case, supervised sequence learning techniques, such as conditional random fields [10] or a structured perceptron algorithm [36], can be used to build a model. It is also possible to combine POS tagging and MWE identification by concatenating MWE BIO and part-of-speech tags, learning a single model for both tasks jointly [11,19].

We have developed and evaluated a statistical tagger for MWE identification based on conditional random fields. The following subsection summarises this method, whose details can be found in a previous publication [39].

4.1 CRF-Based MWE Identification

Linear-chain conditional random fields (CRFs) are an instance of stochastic models that can be used for sequence tagging [18]. Each input sequence T is composed of $t_1 \dots t_n$ tokens considered as an observation. Each observation is tagged with a sequence $Y = y_1 \dots y_n$ of tags corresponding to the values of the hidden states that generated them. CRFs can be seen as a discriminant version of hidden Markov models, since they model the conditional probability $P(Y|T)$. This

[9] B is used for a token that appears at the Beginning of an MWE, I is used for a token Included in the MWE, and O for tokens Outside any MWE.

makes them particularly appealing since it is straightforward to add customised features to the model. In linear-chain CRFs, the probability of a given output tag y_i for an input word t_i depends on the tag of the neighbour token y_{i-1}, and on a rich set of features of the input $\phi(T)$, that can range over any position of the input sequence, including but not limited to the current token t_i. CRF training consists in estimating individual parameters proportional to $p(y_i, y_{i-1}, \phi(T))$.

Proposed model. The identification of continuous MWEs is a segmentation problem. In order to use a tagger to perform this segmentation, we use the well-known Begin-Inside-Outside (BIO) encoding [29]. In a BIO representation, every token t_i in the training corpus is annotated with a corresponding tag y_i with values `B`, `I` or `O`. If the tag is `B`, it means the token is the beginning of an MWE. If it is `I`, this means the token is inside an MWE. `I` tags can only be preceded by another `I` tag or by a `B`. Finally, if the token's tag is `O`, this means the token is outside the expression, and does not belong to any MWE. An example of such encoding for the 2-word expression *de la* (*some*) in French is shown in Fig. 3.

i	-2	-1	0	1	2
w_i	*Il*	*jette*	*de*	*la*	*nourriture*
y_i	O	O	B	I	O
	He	*discards*	*some*		*food*

Fig. 3. Example of BIO tagging of a French sentence containing a *de*+determiner MWE, assuming that the current word (w_0) is *de*. Adapted from [39].

For our experiments, we have trained a CRF tagger using CRFSuite [25].[10] We additionally allow the inclusion of features from external lexicons, such as the valence dictionary DicoValence [14],[11] and an automatically constructed lexicon of nominal MWEs obtained from the frWaC corpus [3] using the mwetoolkit [26]. Our features $\phi(T)$ contains 37 different combinations of values, inspired on those proposed by Constant and Sigogne [10]:

- Single-token features (t_i):[12]
  - w_0 : wordform of the current token.
  - l_0 : lemma of the current token.
  - p_0 : POS tag of the current token.
  - w_i, l_i and p_i: wordform, lemma or POS of previous ($i \in \{-1, -2\}$) or next ($i \in \{+1, +2\}$) tokens.
- N-gram features (bigrams $t_{i-1}t_i$ and trigrams $t_{i-1}t_it_{i+1}$):
  - $w_{i-1}w_i$, $l_{i-1}l_i$, $p_{i-1}p_i$: wordform, lemma and POS bigrams of previous-current ($i = 0$) and current-next ($i = 1$) tokens.

[10] http://www.chokkan.org/software/crfsuite/.

[11] http://bach.arts.kuleuven.be/dicovalence/.

[12] t_i is a shortcut denoting the group of features w_i, l_i and p_i for a token t_i. In other words, each token t_i is a tuple (w_i, l_i, p_i). The same applies to n-grams.

  - $w_{i-1}w_iw_{i+1}$, $l_{i-1}l_il_{i+1}$, $p_{i-1}p_ip_{i+1}$: wordform, lemma and POS trigrams of previous-previous-current ($i = -1$), previous-current-next ($i = 0$) and current-next-next ($i = +1$) tokens.
- Orthographic features (ORTH):
  - hyphen and digits: the current wordform w_i contains a hyphen or digits.
  - f-capital: the first letter of the current wordform w_i is uppercase.
  - a-capital: all letters of the current wordform w_i are uppercase.
  - b-capital: the first letter of the current word w_i is uppercase, and it is at the beginning of a sentence ($i = 0$).
- Lexicon features (LF): These features depend on the provided lexicon and constitute either categorical labels or quantised numerical scores associated to given lemmas or lemma sequences.

Examples. The CRF model described above was tested on French data, based on the French Treebank and on the French PARSEME shared task corpus. Experimental results can be found in [39]. Here, we present some examples of expressions identified and missed by the CRF tagger in the PARSEME shared task corpus.

In our error analysis, we wondered whether the CRF could predict MWEs that were never encountered in the training corpus. In the PARSEME test corpus, for instance, we can find the idiomatic expression *La musique n'adoucit pas toujours les moeurs* (*Music does not always soften the mores*). This expression was never seen in the training corpus and contains discontinuous elements, so the CRF could not identify it at all. Another interesting case is the continuous expression *remettre la main à la pâte* (lit. *to-put-again the hand in the dough*). Even though similar expressions occurred in the training test, such as mettre la dernière main (lit. *to-put the last hand*), this was not sufficient to identify the expression in the test set. In short, the CRF cannot locate expressions that were never seen in the training corpus, except if additional external lexicons are provided (which was not the case in this experiment).

Inversion of elements can also be problematic to identify for the CRF. For example, the sentence *une réflexion* commune est *menée* (lit. *a common reflection is lead*), contains an occurrence of the light-verb construction *mener réflexion* in passive voice. In the training corpus, we only see this expression in the canonical order, in active voice. Therefore, the CRF was not able to identify the expression, even though a variant had been observed in the training corpus.

Discussion. This model can deal with ambiguous constructions more efficiently than rule-based ones, since it stores contextual information in the form of n-gram features. Moreover, there is no need to set thresholds, as these are implicitly modelled in the stochastic model. The discussion above underlines some of the limitations of the model: limited generalisation for constructions that have never been seen, and limited flexibility with respect to word order and discontinuities.

These limitations can be overcome using several techniques. The limited amount of training examples can be compensated with the use of external lexicons [10,30,36]. Discontinuities can be taken into account to some extent using more sophisticated encoding schemes [36], but the use of parsing-based MWE identification methods seems like a more appropriate solution [9]. Finally, better generalisation could be obtained with the use of vector representations for tokens, probably with the help of recurrent neural networks able to identify constructions that are similar to the ones observed in the training data, even though they do not contain the same lexemes.

5 Challenges in MWE Translation

We have presented three examples of systems performing monolingual MWE identification. Significant progress has been made in this field, including the construction and release of dedicated resources in many languages and the organisation of shared tasks. Current MWE identification systems could be used to detect expressions in the source text prior to translation. However, as we have seen in this paper, identification is not a solved problem, so care must be taken not to put the cart before the horses.

As noted by Constant et al. [8], MWE identification and translation share some challenges. First, discontinuities are a problem for both identification and translation. Continuous expressions can be properly dealt with by sequence models, both for identification and translation. However, many categories of expressions are discontinuous (e.g. verbal MWEs, as the ones in the PARSEME shared task corpora). Structural methods based on trees and graphs, both for identification and translation, are promising solutions that require further research.

Additionally, ambiguity is also a problem. For instance, suppose that an MT system learns that the translation of the English complex preposition *up to* into a foreign language is something that roughly corresponds to *until*. Then, the translation of the sentence *she looked it up to avoid confusion* would be incorrect and misleading. Context-aware systems such as the CRF described in Sect. 4 could be used to tag instances of the expression prior to translation. However, current MWE identification strategies for MT seem to be mostly rule-based [4,6,7,27].

Identifying MWEs prior to translation is only part of the problem. Finding an appropriate translation requires access to parallel corpora instances containing the expression, external bilingual MWE lexicons and/or source-language semantic lexicons containing paraphrases and/or synonyms. Therefore, methods to automatically discover such resources could be employed as a promising solution to the MWE translation problem.

A final challenge concerns the evaluation of MWE translation. Many things can go wrong during MT, and MWEs are just one potential source of problems. Therefore, it is important to assess to what extent the MWE in a sentence was correctly translated. Dedicated manual evaluation protocols and detailed error typologies can be used [27], but automatic measures of comparison could also be designed, such as the ones proposed for MWE-aware dependency parsing [8].

References

1. Baldwin, T.: Deep lexical acquisition of verb-particle constructions. Comput. Speech Lang. **19**(4), 398–414 (2005). doi:10.1016/j.csl.2005.02.004
2. Baldwin, T., Kim, S.N.: Multiword expressions. In: Indurkhya, N., Damerau, F.J. (eds.) Handbook of Natural Language Processing, 2nd edn., pp. 267–292. CRC Press, Taylor and Francis Group, Boca Raton (2010)
3. Baroni, M., Bernardini, S. (eds.): Wacky! Working papers on the Web as Corpus. GEDIT, Bologna, 224 p. (2006)
4. Barreiro, A., Monti, J., Batista, F., Orliac, B.: When multiwords go bad in machine translation. In: Mitkov, R., et al. [21], pp. 26–33
5. Calzolari, N., Fillmore, C., Grishman, R., Ide, N., Lenci, A., MacLeod, C., Zampolli, A.: Towards best practice for multiword expressions in computational lexicons. In: Proceedings of the 3rd International Conference on Language Resources and Evaluation (LREC-2002), pp. 1934–1940. Las Palmas (2002)
6. Cap, F., Nirmal, M., Weller, M., im Walde, S.S.: How to account for idiomatic German support verb constructions in statistical machine translation. In: Proceedings of the 11th Workshop on Multiword Expressions (MWE 2015), pp. 19–28. Association for Computational Linguistics, Denver (2015). http://aclweb.org/anthology/W15-0903
7. Carpuat, M., Diab, M.: Task-based evaluation of multiword expressions: a pilot study in statistical machine translation. In: Proceedings of Human Language Technology: The 2010 Annual Conference of the North American Chapter of the Association for Computational Linguistics (NAACL 2003), pp. 242–245. Association for Computational Linguistics, Los Angeles, June 2010. http://www.aclweb.org/anthology/N10-1029
8. Constant, M., Eryiğit, G., Monti, J., van der Plas, L., Ramisch, C., Rosner, M., Todirascu, A.: Multiword expression processing: a survey. Computational Linguistics (2017)
9. Constant, M., Nivre, J.: A transition-based system for joint lexical and syntactic analysis. In: Proceedings of ACL 2016, Berlin, Germany, pp. 161–171 (2016)
10. Constant, M., Sigogne, A.: MWU-aware part-of-speech tagging with a CRF model and lexical resources. In: Proceedings of the ACL 2011 Workshop on MWEs, Portland, OR, USA, pp. 49–56 (2011)
11. Constant, M., Tellier, I.: Evaluating the impact of external lexical resources into a CRF-based multiword segmenter and part-of-speech tagger. In: Proceedings of LREC 2012, Istanbul, Turkey (2012)
12. Cordeiro, S., Ramisch, C., Villavicencio, A.: Token-based mwe identification strategies in the mwetoolkit. In: Proceedings of the 4th PARSEME General Meeting. Valetta, Malta, March 2015. https://typo.uni-konstanz.de/parseme/images/Meeting/2015-03-19-Malta-meeting/WG2-WG3-CORDEIRO-et-al-abstract.pdf
13. Cordeiro, S., Ramisch, C., Villavicencio, A.: UFRGS&LIF at SemEval-2016 task 10: rule-based MWE identification and predominant-supersense tagging. In: Proceedings of the 10th International Workshop on Semantic Evaluation (SemEval-2016), pp. 910–917. Association for Computational Linguistics, San Diego, June 2016. http://www.aclweb.org/anthology/S16-1140
14. van den Eynde, K., Mertens, P.: La valence: l'approche pronominale et son application au lexique verbal. J. Fr. Lang. Stud. **13**, 63–104 (2003)
15. Finlayson, M., Kulkarni, N.: Detecting multi-word expressions improves word sense disambiguation. In: Kordoni, V., et al. [16], pp. 20–24. http://www.aclweb.org/anthology/W/W11/W11-0805

16. Kordoni, V., Ramisch, C., Villavicencio, A. (eds.): Proceedings of the ACL Workshop on Multiword Expressions: from Parsing and Generation to the Real World (MWE 2011). Association for Computational Linguistics, Portland, June 2011. http://www.aclweb.org/anthology/W11-08
17. Kulkarni, N., Finlayson, M.: jMWE: A Java toolkit for detecting multi-word expressions. In: Kordoni, V., et al. [16], pp. 122–124. http://www.aclweb.org/anthology/W/W11/W11-0818
18. Lafferty, J.D., McCallum, A., Pereira, F.C.N.: Conditional random fields: probabilistic models for segmenting and labeling sequence data. In: Proceedings of the Eighteenth International Conference on Machine Learning (ICML 2001), pp. 282–289. Morgan Kaufmann Publishers Inc., San Francisco (2001). http://dl.acm.org/citation.cfm?id=645530.655813
19. Le Roux, J., Rozenknop, A., Constant, M.: Syntactic parsing and compound recognition via dual decomposition: application to French. In: the 25th International Conference on Computational Linguistics: Technical Papers, Proceedings of COLING 2014, pp. 1875–1885. Dublin City University and Association for Computational Linguistics, Dublin, August 2014. http://www.aclweb.org/anthology/C14-1177
20. Losnegaard, G.S., Sangati, F., Escartín, C.P., Savary, A., Bargmann, S., Monti, J.: Parseme survey on MWE resources. In: Proceedings of LREC 2016, Portorož, Slovenia (2016)
21. Mitkov, R., Monti, J., Pastor, G.C., Seretan, V. (eds.): Proceedings of the MT Summit 2013 Workshop on Multi-word Units in Machine Translation and Translation Technology (MUMTTT 2013), Nice, France, September 2013
22. Monti, J., Sangati, F., Arcan, M.: TED-MWE: a bilingual parallel corpus with mwe annotation: Towards a methodology for annotating MWEs in parallel multilingual corpora. In: Proceedings of the Second Italian Conference on Computational Linguistics (CLiC-it 2015). Accademia University Press, Trento, Torino (2015)
23. Monti, J., Seretan, V., Pastor, G.C., Mitkov, R.: Multiword units in machine translation and translation technology. In: Mitkov, R., Monti, J., Pastor, G.C., Seretan, V. (eds.) Multiword Units in Machine Translation and Translation Technology. John Benjamin (2017)
24. Nasr, A., Ramisch, C., Deulofeu, J., Valli, A.: Joint dependency parsing and multiword expression tokenization. In: Proceedings of the 53rd Annual Meeting of the Association for Computational Linguistics and the 7th International Joint Conference on Natural Language Processing (v 1: Long Papers), pp. 1116–1126. Association for Computational Linguistics, Beijing, July 2015. http://aclweb.org/anthology/P15-1108
25. Okazaki, N.: CRFsuite: a fast implementation of conditional random fields (CRFs) (2007). http://www.chokkan.org/software/crfsuite/
26. Ramisch, C.: Multiword Expressions Acquisition: A Generic and Open Framework, Theory and Applications of Natural Language Processing, vol. XIV. Springer, Cham (2015). doi:10.1007/978-3-319-09207-2
27. Ramisch, C., Besacier, L., Kobzar, O.: How hard is it to automatically translate phrasal verbs from English to French? In: Mitkov, R., et al. [21], pp. 53–61
28. Ramisch, C., Villavicencio, A.: Computational treatment of multiword expressions. In: Mitkov, R. (ed.) Oxford Handbook of Computational Linguistics, 2nd edn. Oxford University Press (2016)
29. Ramshaw, L., Marcus, M.: Text chunking using transformation-based learning. In: Third Workshop on Very Large Corpora (1995). http://aclweb.org/anthology/W95-0107

30. Riedl, M., Biemann, C.: Impact of MWE resources on multiword recognition. In: Proceedings of the 12th Workshop on Multiword Expressions (MWE 2016), pp. 107–111. Association for Computational Linguistics, Berlin, Germany (2016). http://anthology.aclweb.org/W16-1816
31. Rosén, V., De Smedt, K., Losnegaard, G.S., Bejcek, E., Savary, A., Osenova, P.: MWEs in treebanks: from survey to guidelines. In: Proceedings of LREC 2016, pp. 2323–2330, Portorož, Slovenia (2016)
32. Sag, I.A., Baldwin, T., Bond, F., Copestake, A., Flickinger, D.: Multiword expressions: a pain in the neck for NLP. In: Gelbukh, A. (ed.) CICLing 2002. LNCS, vol. 2276, pp. 1–15. Springer, Heidelberg (2002). doi:10.1007/3-540-45715-1_1
33. Savary, A.: Multiflex: a multilingual finite-state tool for multi-word units. In: Maneth, S. (ed.) CIAA 2009. LNCS, vol. 5642, pp. 237–240. Springer, Heidelberg (2009). doi:10.1007/978-3-642-02979-0_27
34. Savary, A., Ramisch, C., Cordeiro, S., Sangati, F., Vincze, V., QasemiZadeh, B., Candito, M., Cap, F., Giouli, V., Stoyanova, I., Doucet, A.: The PARSEME shared task on automatic identification of verbal multiword expressions. In: [48], pp. 31–47
35. Savary, A., Sailer, M., Parmentier, Y., Rosner, M., Rosén, V., Przepiórkowski, A., Krstev, C., Vincze, V., Wójtowicz, B., Losnegaard, G.S., Parra Escartín, C., Waszczuk, J., Constant, M., Osenova, P., Sangati, F.: PARSEME - parsing and multiword expressions within a European multilingual network. In: Proceedings of LTC 2015, Poznań (2015)
36. Schneider, N., Danchik, E., Dyer, C., Smith, N.A.: Discriminative lexical semantic segmentation with gaps: running the MWE gamut. In: TACL, vol. 2, pp. 193–206 (2014)
37. Schneider, N., Hovy, D., Johannsen, A., Carpuat, M.: Semeval-2016 task 10: Detecting minimal semantic units and their meanings (diMSUM). In: Proceedings of SemEval 2016, pp. 546–559, San Diego, CA, USA (2016)
38. Schneider, N., Onuffer, S., Kazour, N., Danchik, E., Mordowanec, M.T., Conrad, H., Smith, N.A.: Comprehensive annotation of multiword expressions in a social web corpus. In: Proceedings of LREC 2014, Reykjavik, Iceland, pp. 455–461 (2014)
39. Scholivet, M., Ramisch, C.: Identification of ambiguous multiword expressions using sequence models and lexical resources. In: [48], pp. 167–175. http://aclweb.org/anthology/W17-1723
40. Seretan, V.: On translating syntactically-flexible expressions. In: Mitkov, R., et al. [21], pp. 11–11
41. Silberztein, M.: The lexical analysis of natural languages. In: Finite-State Language Processing, pp. 175–203. MIT Press (1997)
42. Taslimipoor, S., Desantis, A., Cherchi, M., Mitkov, R., Monti, J.: Language resources for italian: towards the development of a corpus of annotated italian multiword expressions. In: Proceedings of Third Italian Conference on Computational Linguistics (CLiC-it 2016) & Fifth Evaluation Campaign of Natural Language Processing and Speech Tools for Italian, Final Workshop (EVALITA 2016), Napoli, Italy, 5–7 December 2016
43. Tu, Y., Roth, D.: Learning English light verb constructions: contextual or statistical. In: Kordoni, V., et al. [16], pp. 31–39. http://www.aclweb.org/anthology/W/W11/W11-0807
44. Tu, Y., Roth, D.: Sorting out the most confusing english phrasal verbs. In: Proceedings of the First Joint Conference on Lexical and Computational Semantics - v 1: Proceedings of the Main Conference and the Shared Task, and v 2: Proceedings of the Sixth International Workshop on Semantic Evaluation, SemEval 2012, pp. 65–69. Association for Computational Linguistics, Stroudsburg (2012)

45. Vauquois, B.: A survey of formal grammars and algorithms for recognition and transformation in mechanical translation. In: IFIP Congress (2), pp. 1114–1122 (1968)
46. Vincze, V., Nagy, I., Berend, G.: Multiword expressions and named entities in the Wiki50 corpus. In: Proceedings of RANLP 2011, pp. 289–295, Hissar, Bulgaria (2011)
47. Vincze, V.: Light verb constructions in the SzegedParalellFX English-Hungarian parallel corpus. In: Proceedings of LREC 2012, pp. 2381–2388, Istanbul, Turkey (2012)
48. Proceedings of the 13th Workshop on Multiword Expressions (MWE 2017). Association for Computational Linguistics, Valencia, Spain (2017). http://aclweb.org/anthology/W17-17

Phraseology in Translation and Contrastive Studies

A Web of Analogies: Depictive and Reaction Object Constructions in Modern English and French Fiction

Susanne Dyka[1(✉)], Iva Novakova[2], and Dirk Siepmann[1]

[1] Universität Osnabrück, University of Osnabrück, Neuer Graben 40, 49069 Osnabrück, Germany
susanne.dyka@uni-osnabrueck.de, dirk.siepmann@uos.de
[2] Université Grenoble Alpes, Université Stendhal Grenoble3, BP25, 38040 Grenoble Cedex 9, France
iva.novakova@univ-grenoble-alpes.fr

Abstract. This paper looks at the cross-linguistic complexity of two fiction-specific English-language constructions involving descriptive key words, viz. (a) depictive constructions and (b) reaction object constructions (ROCs). The English constructions in question were subjected to a detailed, corpus-based analysis in terms of their lexical realizations and complementation patterns. A comparison was then made (a) with French constructional equivalents in literary texts written by French authors and (b) with translations of literary texts from English into French and vice versa. The results show that, compared to English, French literary style has limited options for expressing descriptivity. However, whilst there is an almost total absence of full equivalents of depictives in French novels, the situation is more varied in the case of ROCs, with some types being fairly productive in French (e.g. *hurler*, *murmurer*) but others non-existent.

Keywords: Depictive constructions · Reaction object constructions · Fictional key words · Descriptive verbs

1 Introduction

1.1 Descriptive Fictional Key Words in Contrast

One key feature of modern fiction is the frequent use of descriptive lexis, especially descriptive verbs, i.e. verbs such as *jerk*, *stiffen*, *huddle*, or *gasp* which, besides having a core lexical meaning, contain a complex of semantic features that may "express modality of action (direct descriptivity), (…) characterize one or more of the participants or (…) specify circumstances surrounding the action (indirect descriptivity), or (…) combine all three perspectives" (Snell-Hornby 1983: 43). Although most such words are also found in everyday language, their frequency of occurrence and the patterns in which they occur in fiction are usually specific to that genre.

Previous contrastive research on constructions entered into by literary key words (Siepmann 2016) has shown that a distinction can be made between fully equivalent

R. Mitkov (Ed.): Europhras 2017, LNAI 10596, pp. 87–101, 2017.
https://doi.org/10.1007/978-3-319-69805-2_7

('his thoughts were interrupted as' – 'il en était là de ses réflexions quand') and language-specific constructions. The latter are doubly interesting in that they provide insights into interlingual differences, which in turn reveal something about the intralingual constraints under which literary authors operate. Examples are verbs such as *pour*, *slant* and *break*, which are commonly used to describe the passage of sunlight through a particular medium. The English constructions based around these items can be labelled 'discreetly conventional' because their structural and lexical properties are firmly rooted in the general language. This is far from the case in French, where expressing *exactly* the same content requires far more cognitive processing. In other words, it is the language system itself that motivates particular choices in literary expression, coaxing the literary author into well-trodden semantic paths and often defying even the most inspired translation.

Talmy (2000: 49) has tried to capture such facts in terms of typological differences between languages, claiming that Romance languages conflate motion and path, whereas Germanic languages conflate motion and co-event. The cross-linguistic situation is a little more complex than that, especially in literary text (cf. Siepmann 2016). While Talmy's assumptions would be true of the French equivalents of *trickle* and *slant,* and to a lesser extent of *pour/spill/stream*, they would not apply to the equivalents of *shimmer* and only partly to those of *break*.

This short paper will adduce more such evidence on the cross-linguistic complexity of constructions involving descriptive key words. It looks at two types of constructions, viz. (a) depictive constructions and (b) reaction object constructions (henceforth ROCs). The English constructions in question will be subjected to detailed analysis in terms of their lexical realizations and complementation patterns. Particular attention will be given to metaphorical uses. On the basis of the typical target domains used in metaphorization, a comparison will be made (a) with French constructional equivalents in literary texts written by French authors and (b) with translations of literary texts from English into French and vice versa.

2 Corpora and Methodology

The present study is essentially based on data from two comparable corpora of English-language and French-language novels, comprising crime, science, fantasy, sentimental, historical and general fiction, as well as a parallel corpus containing novels that have been translated from English into French or vice versa; the corpora in question were compiled as part of the PHRASEOROM project (http://turing3.u-grenoble3.fr/phraseorom/index.php/en/author/phraseorom/) and partly analysed using the Sketchengine (www.sketchengine.co.uk). The corpora can be partitioned into a section containing highbrow novels and one containing lowbrow novels. The novels, most of which were published in the late twentieth century or in the early years of the present century, were classified with the aid of publishers' catalogues. The informative section of the British National Corpus (BNC) was used as a reference corpus in investigating English ROCs. Table 1 provides detailed information about the corpora in question.

Table 1. Corpora used in this study.

	Texts	Tokens
English comparable corpus	766	93 Millions
French comparable corpus	1164	110 Millions
Parallel corpus EN-FR	395	19 532 554
Informative section of the BNC	2665	68 419 979

As can be seen, the English and French corpora differ in size. However, since we do not intend to make direct comparisons between absolute frequencies, the fact that one corpus is somewhat larger than the other will not have any significant impact on our findings.

The corpora were automatically parsed to carry out lemmatization and part-of-speech tagging as well as to mark syntactic dependencies between words. Two different tools were used: Connexor (Tapanainen and Järvinen 1997) for the French texts, and XIP (Aït-Mokhtar et al. 2002) for the English texts. Three main procedures were applied:

(a) search for constructions in monolingual corpora
(b) matching of constructions found in monolingual corpora
(c) search for translated constructions in parallel corpora.

3 Depictive Constructions

One typical fiction-specific construction is the use of the descriptive key word *jerk* with a prepositional object designating a change of state, such as *jerk into wakefulness* (cf. Siepmann 2016). On one side, this construction is analogically related to other patterns of the type motion/auditory/visual verb+ADJ (denoting a state); on the other, it is related to a whole class of constructions centred around the lexico-grammatical pattern V+*into*+N (denoting a state: *wakefulness, consciousness, life*), which in turn give rise to variants on the result phrase such as *to life*, *to action*, *into existence*, *to lifelessness*, *out of existence*, etc. It is important to note that the patterns in question are not specific to *jerk*. Underlying them is a complex web of analogical creations (cf. Hanks 2013: 429 on the interplay between logic and analogy in language), all of which take the same or similar patterns and most of which are highly fiction-specific. This web, which is far more complex than any set of synonymic constructions found in speech or newspaper language, is instrumental in creating the illusion of creativity in literary text.

Although there is a vast linguistic literature on constructions of this type (cf. Beaver 2012), there is a lack of consensus on how to classify them. Whereas a prototypical resultative such as (1) indicates a causal link between the two events denoted by the verb and the resultative complement, resultatives with intransitive verbs as in (2) defy a causative reading:

(1) *He hammered the metal flat.*
(2) *The pond froze solid.* (The pond did not solidify by freezing.)

Examples of the type *jerk/snap/bolt/etc. awake* are similar to example (2) in that the motion events involved are concomitant with the state denoted by *awake*. Variants of the *V into life* pattern such as (3) exemplify resultatives where the prototypical order is reversed: the change of state denoted by *into life* causes the auditory impression denoted by the verb:

(3) *The radio crackled into life.*

Such instances, which are commonly found in literary text, contradict Beaver's claim (2012) that "if the sound denoted by the V cannot be caused by motion, a resultative is unacceptable" (such unacceptability is claimed for '*the car honked down the road' vs. 'the truck rumbled into the driveway'). Acknowledging the bewildering variety of resultatives in English, Goldberg and Jackendoff (2004) view them as a family of constructions, each of which encodes a different bi-eventive relationship.

Other authors (Himmelmann and Schulze-Berndt 2005) describe the constructions in question as 'depictive'. In depictive constructions the result complement is participant-oriented, denoting a property of the participant that is true for at least part of the duration of the event denoted by the main predicate, rather than event-orientated, i.e. denoting a property of the event itself by means of (e.g.) a manner adverb (*he shouted at them angrily*).

It is evident that the constructions under discussion, by virtue of being based on complex 'descriptive' verbs, do not need to lexicalize a manner co-event by means of an adverb. We are thus dealing with a kind of double process of composition and densification, with the descriptive verb lexicalizing both action and manner/characterization and the resultative construction combining the verb and the result complement into a single event. On top of this, the depictive constructions coined by novelists are frequently metaphorizations, where target and source domains merge to form a single conceptual entity. A further point to note is that, while descriptive verbs such as *stir* would normally be taken to be atelic, resultatives such as *stir into life* are telic and inchoative. As will be seen, it is difficult to accommodate this diversity of factors in translation.

Table 2 shows the most common variants in abstracted form of the intransitive V *into/to life* construction[1] found in the PHRASEOROM corpora; Table 3 lists the actual verbs that occur at least ten times in one construction in frequency order.

The variability of construct(ion)s would merit further investigation, which is beyond the scope of this paper. The data show quite clearly that some V+result complement constructions admit of a greater variety of subjects and meanings than others; *spring to life*, for example, can be found with people, places, machines, sounds, symbols, but also with flames, faces, topics, blood, etc. It is fair to assume that the construction in question probably originated from the lexicalized expression *come to life* and its causative variant *bring to life*.

A few full-length examples may suffice to illuminate the typical contextual environment in which the construction occurs:

[1] Space in the present article precludes a discussion of the transitive variant (e.g. *unpleasant glimpses jerked him into life*).

Table 2. Intransitive V *into/to life* construction.

	participants		into/to life
non-metaphorical	**[person or other fictitious entity]**	V	
	proper noun/pronoun	*jerks*	*into life*
	the gargoyle	*springs*	*to life*
metaphorical	[**place**: city, jungle, etc.]	motion verb	
	the city	*stirred*	*into life*
	[**device**: radio, machine, heater, etc.]	visual verb, auditory verb, motion verb	
	the radio	*crackled*	*into life*
	a frosted wall panel	*glowed*	*into life*
	the machine	*burst*	*into life*
	[sound or symbol]		
	the voice	*sprang*	*to life*
	the words of the Bible	*sprang*	*to life*
	[person]		
	the servants	*surged*	*into life*
		core meaning: wild movement as caused by the elements	core meaning: start to perform one's habitual function

(4) *Herbie scrambled up to the bow to flash a light ahead of them. As soon as he flicked it on, the grand sweeping semicircle of the beach sprang* ***to life*** *as if they were seeing it on a movie screen* (T.C. Boyle, *San Miguel*)

(5) *Then she picked up Annette's blouse and skirt from the place where they had been carelessly left on the floor and thrust them at her with a gesture of violence. Annette sprang* ***to life****, and in a moment she had slipped them on.* (Iris Murdoch, *The Flight from the Enchanter)*

The abstract forms of the construction listed in Table 2 provided a useful point of embarkation into the search for its natural French equivalents. A trawl was made through the French monolingual corpus to look for the constructions which follow prototypical subjects such as *ville* ('city'), *engin* or *machine* ('engine'), *radio* or *talkie-walkie* and *lumière* (light). Table 4 juxtaposes the results of this search against the correspondences found in the PHRASEOROM parallel corpus of translated texts.

It is evident from the large number of gaps in the second column as well as from the close correspondence between 'natural' equivalents and translation equivalents that French writers are loath to use expressions that would achieve the same degree of

Table 3. Verbs used in intransitive V *into/to life construction* with absolute frequencies.

	+to life	+into life
come (lexicalized)	+(1180)	
spring	+(320)	+(33)
roar	+(129)	+(34)
cling	+(91)	
bring	+(93)	
return	+(78)	
flare	+(56)	+(23)
crackle	+(54)	+(31)
flicker	+(53)	+(42)
hum	+(37)	+(12)
glow	+(34)	+(16)
stir	+(33)	+(14)
rumble	+(29)	+(12)
sentence	+(24)	
blink	+(24)	+(6)
whir	+(22)	+(7)
restore	+(22)	
cough	+(20)	+(9)
leap	+(19)	+(6)
spark	+(17)	+(6)
jangle	+(17)	
blaze	+(17)	+(16)
flash	+(16)	+(20)
sputter	+(15)	+(9)
wink	+(12)	+(9)
purr	+(11)	+(7)
burst		+(22)
explode		+(18)
kick		+(10)

descriptivity as English depictives. Such findings are consistent with Siepmann's (2016) aforementioned results on light effects.

Turning now to a more detailed consideration of the correspondences found in published translations, it is found that English metaphorical depictive constructions are most commonly rendered into French by intransitive verbs whose metaphorical origins are no longer apparent (*s'allumer, se rallumer, s'animer, se ranimer, s'illuminer, s'éveiller, s'embraser, se réactiver*); these verbs tend to express a change of state and are used with telic, punctual and inchoative meanings. If we compare these translation solutions with their commonest natural equivalents found in French novels on the one hand, and with fully equivalent but very infrequent renditions on the other, it becomes clear that, in the majority of cases, translators adopt a target-oriented approach to translating English depictive constructions. Far less frequently do they opt for more

Table 4. Natural French equivalents and translations found.

General pattern	English example	Most common, natural equivalent	Attested fully equivalent item	Correspondence found in translated text
place Vmotion into life	*The city stirred into life*	*la ville s'éveilla (s'éveille)*	*La ville commença à s'animer./La ville commença paresseusement à vivre.* (Simenon, Les dossiers de l'agence)	–
	The chamber sprang to life	*La salle s'anima.*	–	*La salle s'anima subitement.*
object Vvisual/motion into life	*The gargoyle sprang to life*	*La gargouille s'anima.*	–	*La gargouille s'anima.*
	The candle flared to life	*La bougie s'alluma/se rulluma.*	–	*La bougie s'embrasa toute seule.*
device Vauditory/visual into life	*The engine roared into life*	*le moteur rugit*	–	*Le moteur démarra avec un rugissement/dans un vrombissement; le moteur se mit à rugir; s'éveilla/s'anima en rugissant*
	The walkie-talkie crackled into life	*Le talkie-walkie grésilla/se mit à grésiller.*	–	*Son talkie-walkie grésilla.*
	The screen (monitor) glowed to life	*L'écran s'alluma.*	–	*L'écran s'alluma/se mit en marche.*
device Vmotion into life	*The machine burst into life*	*la machine se mit en marche/l'engin s'éveilla/se mit à tourner.*	*Le moteur se mit soudain à tourner à plein régime.* (Stefan Mani, *Noir Karma*, Gallimard)	*La machine s'éveilla alors avec force gargouillis* (Amanda Coe, *translator Sarah Gurcel)*

metaphorical, source-oriented renditions such as *Les murs et les plafonds revinrent soudain à la vie.* The latter equivalent and a number of variants (*revenir à la réalité*, *renaître*, *revivre*) are also found in cases where the subject slot is filled by a noun denoting a person that has previously been alive. Such equivalents are of course ruled out if the subject is an inanimate entity that becomes animate in particular types of fiction. In these cases *s'animer* is the most obvious equivalent:

(6a) *The gargoyle* ***sprang to life*** *and jumped aside.* (J.-K. Rowling, *Harry Potter and the Goblet of Fire, 2000*)

(6b) *La gargouille* ***s'anima*** *soudain et s'écarta en faisant glisser le mur derrière elle. (Translator Jean-François Menard)*

Such fiction-specific constructions, notably common in science or fantasy fiction, are instrumental in creating a fictional universe that presupposes a vocabulary of its own which is "accessible to readers but slightly different from the vocabulary they are accustomed to" (Bozzeto 2007: 60–61; our translation).

A greater variety of equivalents is found in cases where the subject slot is filled by a noun designating a device such as a motor or engine. Here target-oriented translators make ample use of auditory verbs (*rugir, cliqueter, gronder*) without any further support to specify the meaning. An example:

(7a) *The Jeep* ***rumbled to life****, and he spun us around, the tires squealing. (*Stephenie Meyer, *Twilight 0, 2005)*

(7b) *La Jeep* ***gronda*** *et fit demi-tour dans un hurlement de pneus. (Translator Luc Rigoureau)*

By contrast, source-oriented translators opt for deverbal nouns (*vrombissement*, *rugissement du moteur*) or combinations of verbs denoting motion or change of state with gerund constructions functioning as manner adjuncts (Riegel et al. 1993: 339). The following examples illustrate both options:

(8a) *The engines* ***roared to life*** *beneath him, sending a deep shudder through the hull.* (Dan Brown, *Angels and demons,* 2000*)*

(8b) *Le vrombissement des moteurs qui faisait vibrer toute la coque le ramena à la réalité. (Translator Daniel Roche*)

(9a) *I glanced back to find Nathaniel in the Jeep, with Caleb and Gil in the back. The engine* ***roared to life.*** *(*Laurell Kaye Hamilton, *Anita Blake 10 - Narcissus in chains,* 2001*)*

(9b) *Jetant un coup d œ il par-dessus mon épaule, je vis que Nathaniel était monté dans la Jeep, et que Caleb et Gil se faufilaient sur la banquette arrière. Le moteur* ***s'éveilla en rugissant****.* (*Translator Isabelle Troin)*

Source orientation of the kind observed by Siepmann (2016) can be seen in the following example, which provides further evidence suggesting that, in French literary style, the expression of manner may sometimes be effected by a modification of the subject noun (in this case *lueur*) rather than being limited to independent, usually adverbial or gerundial type constituents, as claimed by Talmy (2000: 49).

(10) *Titus' small eyes flared to life.*
(11) ... *une lueur de colère passa dans ses petits yeux.*

4 Reaction Object Constructions

Reaction Object Constructions (henceforth ROCs) bear some resemblance to resultative constructions in that they form a family of different but related constructions (cf. Bouso 2017: 7, Goldberg and Jackendoff 2004) centred around descriptive verbs – usually manner of speaking or gesture verbs (Martínez Vázquez 2014b) – that are transitivized to acquire the meaning "express (a reaction) by V-ing" (Levin 1993: 98), as illustrated in (12) and (13):

(12) *The vicar nodded agreement.* (Julian Barnes, *England, England*, 1998)
(13) *Her jaw ached with smiling her appreciation.* (Beryl Bainbridge, *An awfully big adventure*, 1989)

Examples of manner of speaking verbs used in this construction are *bark*, *groan*, *hum*, *moan*, *murmur*, *snort*, *yowl*, *shout*, *howl*, *cough* and *spit*; gesture verbs include *smile*, *nod*, *blink*, *grin*, *shrug*, *frown*, *clap* (cf. Martínez Vázquez 2014b and Levin 1993: 89). The object can be preceded by a co-referential pronoun (*The woman snorted her contempt.*), the indefinite article (*..., grinning a welcome.*), the zero article (*She was murmuring reassurance...*) or an adjective (*He blinked rueful acknowledgement*) (Bouso 2017: 6). ROCs are closely related to alternative constructions in which the object noun of the corresponding ROC occurs in a prepositional phrase introduced by *in* which functions as an adjunct:

(14) *Sheila nodded in vigorous agreement.* (John McGahern, *Amongst Women*, 1990)

Like the depictive constructions discussed above, ROCs are highly specific to fictional prose. Of the verbs examined here, only *shout* and *nod* were found to occur in the informative section of the BNC; ROCs based on verbs such as *frown, grin, howl, snort, shout,* and *spit* thus appear to be highly fiction-specific.

Table 5 shows the most common object nouns found in ROCs in the PHRASEOROM highbrow and lowbrow corpora. The nouns in question are conventionalized speech acts (*hello*, *thanks*), deverbal speech nouns (*appreciation*, *encouragement*) or emotion nouns (*frustration*, *triumph*) (cf. Martínez Vázquez 2014a: 186–188).

It is evident that there are significant differences between verbs with respect to the range of nouns they accept, with *nod*, *smile* and *murmur* being among the most flexible. Another interesting finding is that, generally speaking, popular fiction exhibits a higher proportion of ROCs than highbrow fiction, with some verbs, such as *shrug* and *blink*, being exclusive to popular fiction.

Although not entirely absent from French, ROCs appear to be less frequent than in English, confirming findings on Spanish (Martínez Vázquez 2014b) and Romance languages generally (Real Puigdollers 2008). A query was made of the PHRASEOROM French literary corpus for potential English equivalents of the English ROC verbs (see Table 5). The findings show that the verbs *hurler, crier, grommeler,*

Table 5. Most common reaction object nouns found in the English literary corpus.

	PHRASEOROM	
	Lowbrow	Highbrow
bark	acknowledgement, approval, encouragement	–
groan	apologies	resignation, delight, relief
hum	approval	–
moan	encouragement, pleasure	–
murmur	apology/apologies, greeting(s), assent (s), delight, good morning, agreement, approval, thanks/thank you, assurance, denial, love, gratitude, reassurance(s), acceptance, welcome, envy, good bye, sympathy, consent, objection, regret, release, excuse	admiration, assent, sympathy, consolation, acknowledgement, concern, regret, disapproval, greeting, excuse, agreement, thanks, good night
snort	contempt, amusement, terror, frustration, impatience, scorn, derision, upset, exasperation, disapproval, sketpicism	derision, contempt, astringency
yowl	protest	–
shout	defiance, contempt, encouragement, abuse, triumph, surprise, rage, confusion, exhilaration, bewilderment, apologies, gratitude, congratulations, agreement, disagreement, frustration, approval, disappointment	abuse, accusations, relief, agreement
howl	glee, distraught, frustration, rage, disapproval, welcome, victory, abuse, displeasure, anger, triumph, defiance	abuse, ignorance, eagerness
spit	disgust, insult, scorn	–
smile	welcome(s), thanks/thank you, gratitude, comprehension, consent, acknowledgement, encouragement, greeting, agreement, apology approval, gratitude, farewell, relief, challenge, amusement, sympathy, pleasure, goodbye(s), congratulations	agreement, goodbye, welcome, thanks, appreciation, reassurance, acknowledgement, greeting, approval, readiness, No
nod	agreement, farewell(s), greeting, thanks, approval, assent, gratitude, affirmation, hello, understanding, acknowledgement, encouragement, satisfaction, consent, acquiescence, permission, goodbye, confirmation, good morning, welcome, respect, comprehension, apology/apologies, appreciation, affirmative, approval,	thanks, satisfaction, acknowledgement, welcome, approval, agreement, assent, greeting, good morning, goodbye, encouragement, understanding, acquiescence, affirmative, gratitude, consent, apology, dismissal, permission

(*continued*)

Table 5. (*continued*)

	PHRASEOROM	
	Lowbrow	Highbrow
	dismissal, appreciation, attention, acceptance, admission, submission	
blink	agreement	–
grin	acknowledgement, defiance, approval, delight, exasperation, thanks	delight, acknowledgement, approval, relief, complicity
shrug	apology, ignorance, indifference, agreement, impotence, approval, bewilderment	–
frown	warning, protest, irritation, disdain, disappointment, impatience, puzzlement, reproach	interest
clap	appreciation, pleasure, approval	–

murmurer, grogner have common transitive uses with speech nouns, such as *murmurer des mots/phrases/paroles/prières; hurler des mots, son nom; grommeler des mots inaudibles, cracher les mots*. Just like their English counterparts, the verbs in question also combine with nouns denoting conventionalized speech acts ('merci'), some of which constitute deverbal nouns (cf. Martínez Vázquez 2014b) such as *hurler des félicitations* ('congratulations'), *grommeler un remerciement* ('thank you'), *grogner une série d'injures* ('insults'). Another commonality is the use of emotion nouns, as in *hurler son angoisse, son indignation, son mécontentement, crier son désespoir, sa colère, sa joie, son amour*.

(15) *Des larmes coulent sur son visage, elle* ***murmure «Merc»***. (Frédérique Deghelt, *Les brumes de l'apparence*, 2014)

(16) *Je* ***grognai ma satisfaction*** (Philippe Djian, *Echine,* 1998).

Just as in English, these ROCs can be described and paraphrased as double predicate constructions: 'dire merci en murmurant', 'remercier en grommelant', 'exprimer sa satisfaction en grognant', 'féliciter en hurlant', 'dire son amour en criant'. Note, however, that such constructions are uncommon in real literary text; there seems to be a preference for using gerund constructions with motion verbs (e.g. 'il se lève/tombe par terre en grognant'), something which awaits further investigation. There are also examples in evidence that denote "the cathartic liberation of a negative emotion" (Martínez Vázquez 2014b: 208):

(17) *Dans le silence je l'ai regardé, le monde, ébranlé, violé, déchiré, tanguant et vacillant et, dans ma tête où les noms propres déferlaient en tourbillon, le monde* ***a crié sa misère***... (Yves Berger, *Les matins du Nouveau Monde,* 1987).

By contrast, gesture verbs such as *sourire* ('smile' or 'grin') or *applaudir* ('applaud' or 'clap') are not used transitively in the French comparable (i.e. monolingual) corpus. English constructions of the type *Richard smiled his encouragement* correspond to V+adjunct (PP or adverb) in French: *sourire tendrement, avec tendresse* rather than **sourire sa tendresse* Given the large number of ROCs involving *smile* found in the English comparable (i.e. monolingual) corpus *(smile satisfaction, pleasure, encouragement, delight, agreement, gratitude, approval* etc.; see Table 5 above), the inference is that in this regard English and French differ considerably (just like English and Spanish; see Martínez Vázquez 2014b: 205).

Another divergence between the two languages concerns the verbs *nod* ('hocher la tête'), *shrug* ('hausser les épaules'), *blink* ('cligner des/les yeux'), *frown* ('froncer les sourcils'). These verbs are invariably transitive in French and take objects denoting body parts *(la tête, les épaules, les yeux, les sourcils*). The object of the English ROC is generally found to correspond to an adjunct in French: *il hocha la tête en signe d'approbation, avec approbation.*

(18) *Il vit clairement les reptiles, autour de lui,* ***hocher la tête avec approbation***. (Romain Gary, *Les racines du ciel*, 1956).

(19) *Capitini* ***cligna les yeux avec étonnement***. (Dominique Fernandez, *Pise 1951*, 2011)

The discussion so far has been limited to potential equivalents of English ROCs, with no consideration given to their frequency of occurrence in French text. It is worth bearing in mind, however, that, even though ROCs can be attested in very large corpora of French fiction, English ROCs are both far more frequent and far more flexible in terms of the range of objects they accept, as illustrated by a comparison of *murmurer* and *murmur* (see Table 6).

Table 6. Occurrences per ten million words of *murmurer/murmur*+reaction objects in French and English corpora (sample).

murmurer		*murmur (lowbrow)*		*murmur (highbrow)*	
merci	1.16	thanks/thank you, agreement	1.17	assent	2.28
amour	0.58	apology/apologies	1.04	greeting	1.14
		greeting(s), assent(s)	0.52		
		assurance(s), good bye, approval	0.39		

The comparative paucity of French ROCs based on verbs such as *murmurer* raises the question of how French fiction writers typically express the same kind of content. If our above discussion was along the right lines, the theoretical possibilities would seem to be limited to four options:

1. a double predicate construction of the type V+*en murmurant*
2. the combination of *murmurer* with an adjunct:
   (a) *murmurer avec*+N/*en signe de*+N
   (b) *murmurer* *ment
3. a class shift which combines the noun *murmure* with an appropriate verb and adjectival or nominal postmodification: *avoir/émettre un murmure de* N/ADJ

4. a class shift which combines the prepositional phrase *dans un murmure* with a verb: V+*dans un murmure*

Oddly enough, none of these constructions occur with any frequency in contexts where they might be viewed as equivalent to English ROCs; only type 3 is found very occasionally:

(20) *Ainsi, il pourrait me faire relire et signer ma déposition avant de partir; j'eus un murmure d'approbation*. (Michel Houellebecq, *Plateforme*, 2001)

If the same situation were found to obtain in the case of other verbs (this would require a more detailed study), this would mean that while writers in both languages may choose to express the same content, French writers do not do so as regularly as English writers. It would be tempting to conclude from such evidence that literary writers use constructions for the sake of constructions; in other words, English writers make ample use of ROCs not because they express significant content, but because they are readily available and almost infinitely malleable.

The results obtained from the parallel corpora provide some confirmation of the tendencies observed in the comparable corpus. Thus, English ROCs involving *murmur* ('murmurer') are usually translated into French as ROCs, confirming the patterns found in the French comparable corpus (see above). This means that, with *murmur*, the translators have adopted a source-oriented strategy.

(21a) *Others* ***murmured their agreement***. (Laurell Kaye Hamilton, *Anita Blake 06, The killing dance*, 1997)

(21b) *Les autres* ***murmurèrent leur approbation***. (Translator Isabelle Troin)

In some cases, however, the ROCs involving murmur are broken down into constructions of the type verb+prepositional phrase built around the deverbal *un murmure*. This translation solution, which may be described as target-oriented, is less frequent, however.

(22a) *Althea* ***murmured an assent****, but said no more.* (Robbin Hobb, *Ship of Destiny*, 2000)

(22b) *Althéa* ***acquiesça dans un murmure****, mais n'ajouta rien.* (Translator Véronique David-Marescot)

Similarly with *howl his pain and rage*: le verbe *howl* has been rendered into French as the deverbal noun *hurlement* followed by a prepositional phrase denoting emotion (*de douleur, de rage*):

(23a) *The guard* ***howled his pain and rage***. (Isaac Asimov, *Foundation 4 - Foundation and Empire*, 1952)

(23b) *Le garde* ***poussa un hurlement de douleur et de rage***. (Translator Jean Rosenthal)

With regard to ROCs centred around gesture verbs such as *shrug, blink, frown, nod* – for which no attested equivalents were found in the comparable corpus (see above) – a search of the parallel corpus reveals a predilection for translation equivalents involving a double predicate structure: *incliner la tête en signe d'approbation ('bend one's head in agreement')/avec satisfaction ('with satisfaction')*:

(24a) *No one, said Harry, and Dumbledore* ***nodded his satisfaction***. (JK Rowling, *HP 07*, 2007)

(24b) *«Personne» indiqua Harry, et Dumbledore* ***inclina la tête avec satisfaction.*** (*Translator Jean-François Ménard*)

Another equivalent of *nod*+reaction object can be seen in the deverbal noun construction *hochement de tête*:

(25a) *She watched her older son, and when* ***he nodded approval***, *she breathed a secret sigh of relief*. (Robin Hobb, *Mad Ship*, 1999).

(25b) *Elle regarda son aîné et, quand* ***il eut approuvé d'un hochement de tête***, *elle poussa un imperceptible soupir de soulagement.* (*Translator Véronique David-Marescot*)

Table 7 provides a summary, and additional examples, of French equivalents of the ROC construction other than ROCs. The gerund construction has been omitted because it rarely constitutes a real textual equivalent of an English ROC.

Table 7. French equivalents of ROC constructions.

	Pattern	Equivalents
murmur +agreement, smile +satisfaction	verb-noun shift, verb +noun collocation; V +(+de+N/+ADJ)	*émettre un murmure d'approbation, arborer un sourire satisfait/avoir un sourire de satisfaction*
He frowned his puzzlement	extraposed ADJ+VP	*Perplexe, il fronça les sourcils.*
The display blinked fresh acknowledgement	V+adjunct (often *en signe de*)	*L'écran clignota derechef en signe d'assentiment., Elle sourit de/avec satisfaction/d'un sourire satisfait.*

5 Conclusion

The picture emerging from this study is one of considerable complexity. It has been shown that, compared to English, French literary style has limited options for expressing descriptivity. However, whilst there is an almost total absence of full equivalents of depictives in French novels, the situation is more varied in the case of ROCs, with some types being fairly productive in French (e.g. *hurler, murmurer*) but others being non-existent. Even potentially productive patterns, such as *murmurer* +reaction object, occur with considerably lower frequencies than their English counterparts. One reason for this may be that in French intransitive verbs lend themselves less readily to transitivization than is the case in English; the same applies to the causative transitivization of inaccusative verbs (Levin and Rappaport Hovav 1995), which is frequent in English but less so in French.

With regard to translation, there is evidence that most translators adopt a target-oriented approach that is in keeping with functionalist theories of translation according to which the target text should read like an original. Only a few translators attempt to recreate the formal or semantic characteristics of English ROCs by opting for a source-oriented approach.

References

Aït-Mokhtar, S., Chanod, J., Roux, C.: Robustness beyond shallowness: incremental deep parsing. J. Nat. Lang. Eng. **8**(2/3), 121–144 (2002)

Beaver, J.: Resultative constructions. In: Binnick, R. (ed.) The Oxford Handbook of Tense and Aspect. Oxford University Press, Oxford (2012)

Bouso, T.: Muttering contempt and smiling appreciation: disentangling the history of the reaction object construction in English. Engl. Stud. **98**(2), 194–215 (2017)

Bozzeto, R.: La Science-fiction. Armand Colin, Paris (2007)

Goldberg, A., Jackendoff, R.: The English resultative as a family of constructions. Language **80** (3), 532–568 (2004). https://ase.tufts.edu/cogstud/jackendoff/papers/EnglishResultative.pdf. Accessed 28 May 2017

Hanks, P.: Lexical Analysis: Norms and Exploiatations. MIT Press, Cambridge (2013)

Himmelmann, N., Schulze-Berndt, E. (eds.): Secondary Predication and Adverbial Modification: The Typology of Depictives. Oxford University Press, Oxford (2005)

Levin, B.: English Verb Classes and Alternations: A Preliminary Investigation. The University of Chicago Press, Chicago, London (1993)

Levin, B., Rappaport Hovav, M.: Unaccusativity: At the Syntax-Lexical Semantics Interface. MIT Press, Cambridge (1995)

Martínez Vázquez, M.: Expressive object constructions in English: a corpus based analysis. Revista Canara De Estudios Ingleses **69**, 175–190 (2014a). https://www.researchgate.net/profile/Montserrat_Martinez_Vazquez/publication/303523978_EXPRESSIVE_OBJECT_CONSTRUCTIONS_IN_ENGLISH_A_CORPUS_BASED_ANALYSIS/links/5746cadd08aea45ee856d00a.pdf. Accessed 28 May 2017

Martínez Vázquez, M.: Reaction object constructions in English and Spanish. E.S. Revista de Filología Inglesa **35**, 193–217 (2014b). https://revistas.uva.es/index.php/esreview/article/view/732/714. Accessed 29 Aug 2017

Real Puigdollers, C.: The nature of cognate objects: a syntactic approach. In: Proceedings ConSOLE XVI, pp. 157–178 (2008). http://media.leidenuniv.nl/legacy/console16-real-puigdollers.pdf. Accessed 28 May 2017

Riegel, M., Pellat, J.-C., Rioul, R.: Grammaire méthodique du français. Presse Universitaires de France, Paris (1993)

Siepmann, D.: Lexicologie et phraséologie du roman contemporain: Quelques pistes pour le français et l'anglais. Cahiers de lexicologie, No. 108 (2016)

Snell-Hornby, M.: Verb-Descriptivity in German and English: A Contrastive Study in Semantic Fields. Carl Winter, Heidelberg (1983)

Talmy, L.: Towards a Cognitive Semantics, vol. 2. MIT Press, Cambridge (2000)

Tapanainen, P., Järvinen, T.: A non-projective dependency parser. In: Proceedings of the Fifth Conference on Applied Natural Language Processing, pp. 64–71. Association for Computational Linguistics, Washington D.C. (1997). http://delivery.acm.org/10.1145/980000/974568/p64-tapanainen.pdf. Accessed 28 May 2017

Brazilian Recipes in Portuguese and English: The Role of Phraseology for Translation

Rozane Rodrigues Rebechi(✉) and Márcia Moura da Silva

Universidade Federal do Rio Grande do Sul, Porto Alegre, RS, Brazil
rozanereb@gmail.com, marciamouras@hotmail.com

Abstract. Although recurrent in TV shows, blogs and magazines, not to mention in a number of cookbooks, culinary texts, including recipes, restaurant reviews and menus, remain academically underexplored. As a matter of fact, according to Capatti and Montanari [4] this textual genre has long been considered inferior to literature and other arts. As a consequence, the area suffers from scarcity of reference materials, especially with regard to the Portuguese-English language pair, which surely has a significant impact on translation. Analyses of translated texts show misleading choices of terms and adaptations that result in de-characterization of cultural references and mistranslations. Moreover, in isolation terms are, in general, insufficient to guarantee fluent texts. Specialized phraseologies are also essential for writing and translating texts. Using corpus linguistics as our methodology, this study aims to identify typical phraseologies used in Brazilian recipes and propose functional equivalents in English. In order to reach our objectives, we built a comparable corpus of Brazilian cuisine cookbooks written originally in Brazilian Portuguese and in North-American English. Results show that appropriate translation goes far beyond prima facie equivalents. We believe that linguistic and cultural differences should be taken into account when creating culinary reference material directed at translators and writers working with this genre.

Keywords: Specialized phraseology · Brazilian cooking · Translation · Corpus linguistics

1 Introduction

Driven by events of international scope hosted in the country[1], as well as worldwide recognition of Brazilian chefs[2] who favor local ingredients in their recipes, Brazilian cooking has attracted growing attention, and as a result a number of cookbooks have been either translated into English or written in this language.[3] Nevertheless, the theme lacks reliable reference material that could help translators and those who write in this

[1] Brazil hosted FIFA World Cup in 2014 and the Olympic Games in 2016.

[2] Alex Atala's D.O.M. has been one of the World's 50 Best Restaurants since 2010, and Helena Rizzo's Maní was included in this list from 2013 to 2015.

[3] A search carried out on May 19th 2017 with the words 'Brazilian' and 'cooking' on Amazon.com resulted in 183 books.

R. Mitkov (Ed.): Europhras 2017, LNAI 10596, pp. 102–114, 2017.
https://doi.org/10.1007/978-3-319-69805-2_8

specialized area. If indeed there are few studies devoted to culinary writing as a whole [2], Brazilian cooking suffers from the same neglect.

Strong cultural aspects such as local ingredients, techniques and utensils of Brazilian cuisine are usually reduced to a small number of entries in general language dictionaries or are restricted to lists of terms aligned to possible equivalents. Not only are these sources insufficient to account for much of the Brazilian cuisine terminology, but they also err in not contextualizing these terms, which can mislead translators and writers on how to use them. Because cooking is often considered as not belonging to a specialized area, and the translation of culinary texts may be delegated to either non-professional translators or automatic tools, the consequences range from lack of standardization of equivalents - especially of cultural references - and naturalness, to plain errors, which obviously hinder reader's understanding [18]. Hardly would a foreigner understand that a dish called 'boyfriend in the oven' refers to a type of roasted fish, or that 'bread with cold' is a cheese and ham sandwich, to number but a few of recurrent translation inadequacies found in bilingual restaurant menus and displays used to identify dishes served at self-service restaurants[4].

However, as previously mentioned, equivalence of terms is far from being the only obstacle to the proper task of translating and writing about food. The way these terms are used in the texts highlights other gender specificities in different cultures. Finding in a list of ingredients expressions such as *cabos de salsão* [sticks of celery] and *cebola cortada em quartos* [onion cut in quarters], instead of the conventionalized *talos de salsão* [celery stalks] and *cebola cortada em quatro* [onion, quartered], respectively, would surely intrigue a reader who has modest knowledge of cooking.

This study aims to identify recurring phraseologics in authentic recipes written in Portuguese and in English in order to propose functional equivalents which could assist translators and those who write about cooking to produce more natural texts. The final product is a Portuguese-English dictionary of Brazilian cooking under construction, which is detailed in [18].

2 Translation, Terminology and Corpus Linguistics

Although autonomous, each with its own specific principles and purposes, specialized translation and terminology converge in many ways. Just as specialists rely on glossaries to ensure accurate communication in their fields, translators use this lexicon to convey specialized knowledge from one language/culture to another. Nevertheless, despite targeting unambiguity and homogeneity, specialized language is far from unequivocal, and equivalence of specialized lexicon is not the only aspect to be considered in translation. Contrary to traditional studies in translation, the specialized text is also subject to the cultural context of production and reception, and these elements should also be observed during the translation process [23].

---

[4] In Brazil, self-service restaurants, known as *restaurantes por quilo*, are food establishments where customers serve themselves the food that they want and proceed to have their plates weighed, as payment is made based on the quantity of food consumed.

When differentiating between 'intention' and 'function' as discussed in translation functionalist approaches, Nord [15] points out that while intention is defined from the sender's point of view - good intentions do not guarantee an adequate translation, though, it is the receiver who uses the text with a certain function "depending on their own expectations, needs, previous knowledge and situational conditions" [p. 28]. Therefore, a recipe, for example, must be seen by its user as such, which means that it needs to have the same characteristics that this genre in this user's cultural setting has. In addition to that, equivalent terms do not guarantee an appropriate translation either, since words tend to appear in groups [8].

Specialized phraseology, or relatively fixed structures, has been receiving special attention in terminological studies (see, for example, [12]), making us aware of the difficulties of delimiting terms and phraseologies of specialized texts in a single language. Adapting them to the target language/culture is even more challenging, and that is why the translation of terms and phraseologies from one language to another needs to be adequate, aiming at conceptual precision through lexical views toward standardization [11], albeit in an idealized way, since there is no way to guarantee it in practice.

Just like any other specialized text, a recipe contains lexical and syntactic specificities [3]; for example, the use of specialized vocabulary such as 'cup', 'spoon', 'add'; and characteristic combinations of words, such as 'finely chopped', 'stirring constantly', 'bring to a boil', are immediately associated with the genre. In addition, the instructions, usually presented by verbs in the imperative such as 'stir', 'let', 'mix', at least in Portuguese and English languages, confirm the operational nature of the recipe [16]. Considering that specialized texts are repositories of terminology, we used the assumptions underlying Corpus Linguistics to assist us in the semiautomatic survey of phraseologies which are characteristic of Brazilian cooking and their respective equivalents in English.

The use of parallel corpora in translation is not a new practice. The comparison of original texts and their translations enables the identification of previously used translation equivalents in a relatively simple way, through the alignment of the sentences of the original text with those of the translated text. However, translated texts do not always reveal terms and phraseologies used conventionally in the target language, since they have been mediated by a translator, who may not be an expert in the area for which s/he translates. Comparable corpora, on the other hand, can reveal terms and phraseologies used naturally in the source language, and also help in the identification of discrepancies between textual types produced in different languages and cultures [17]. As specialized texts, recipes can be used for the extraction of terms and phraseologies, thus contributing to the construction of bi- or multilingual terminology reference material. Next, we describe how the authentic texts served the purpose of this research.

3 Study Corpus: Compilation and Analysis

The criteria underlying the choice of the study corpus should be guided by the objectives to be achieved. Thus, we tried to be very specific in the choice of the texts representing both languages in order to meet our objective of identifying typical phraseologies in Brazilian recipes and their functional equivalents in English. The corpus was compiled with recipes from twenty two Brazilian cookbooks, eleven of which were originally written in Brazilian Portuguese and eleven in North-American English[5]. Table 1 gives a summary of the study corpus:

Table 1. Study corpus

	Number of cookbooks	Number of recipes	Number of words (tokens)
Portuguese subcorpus	11	1,225	234,704
English subcorpus	11	1,449	282,977

There is no consensus regarding the ideal size of a study corpus [22]. Sinclair [20] argues that a corpus should be as extensive as possible; whereas Koester [10] claims that more important than its size is its representativeness. Although not very extensive, specialized corpora, which are commonly used for conducting specific research, may lead to quite significant results, as long as they have been built under strict criteria, always considering the purpose of the investigation.

Koester [10] points out that small corpora have the advantage of allowing a closer relationship between the corpus and the contexts in which their texts were produced. In addition, as in research with small corpora the compiler is usually also the analyst, the degree of familiarity with the context tends to be higher, allowing the quantitative data revealed by the corpus to be complemented by manual analysis. Although it is difficult to guarantee that a particular corpus is ideal for any research (See [13]), and since our study corpus is very specific, we believe that its relatively small size was not an impediment for the analyses carried out.

In this research we are concerned especially with the recurrent phraseological units in Brazilian recipes. So, using WordSmith Tools 6.0 [19] we identified the most significant combinations, i.e. key-clusters, in the study corpus by comparing Brazilian recipes to general recipes, the latter accounting for over 1,000,000 tokens, being used as our reference corpus. The processing of key-clusters is similar to the one of key-words, in such a way that the tool presents us with the most statistically recurrent combinations in the study corpora when compared to the reference corpora. Tables 2 and 3 respectively show the first twenty key-clusters identified in Portuguese and in English in decreasing order of keyness, considering combinations of three to six words which recur at least ten times in the corpora.

It seems important to emphasize that the tool solely shows statistical results based on recurrence. It is the researcher's task to distinguish between combinations of words that do not constitute complete units of meaning, e.g. *de farinha de mandioca* [of manioc flour], *sem pele nem* [peeled and], 'to a boil', 'cook over low', etc., from the ones that form complete units of meaning, be they compound terms, collocations or

[5] The corpus is available for consultation at http://comet.fflch.usp.br/cortec, under the title 'Culinária Brasileira'.

Table 2. First twenty key-clusters in Portuguese.

N	Key word	Freq.
1	de mandioca	411
2	porções tempo de preparo	334
3	porções tempo de	334
4	porções tempo	334
5	farinha de mandioca	318
6	leite de	423
7	de coco	507
8	leite de coco	379
9	xícara de chá de	239
10	xícara de chá	248
11	kg de	602
12	o cheiro-verde	122
13	de cheiro-verde	122
14	camarão seco	91
15	de chá de	393
16	de farinha de mandioca	122
17	de jambu	61
18	de oliveira	59
19	do Thiago	59
20	de chá	413

Table 3. First twenty key-clusters in English.

N	Key word	Freq.
1	add the	3.080
2	in a	4.036
3	salt and	1.942
4	and pepper	1.196
5	salt and pepper	1.128
6	and cook	1.118
7	olive oil	1.110
8	until the	1.100
9	a large	1.108
10	place the	888
11	and add	832
12	in a large	824
13	egg yolks	796
14	teaspoon salt	780
15	or until	734
16	the pan	726
17	remove the	730
18	the mixture	710
19	heat and	638
20	to taste	638

phraseologies such as [*xícara de chá de*] *farinha de mandioca* [cup manioc flour], [*tomate*] *sem pele nem sementes* [tomato, peeled and seeded], etc.

Naturally, had the corpora been POS-tagged, the results could have been optimized, since the processing could start from content words, ignoring grammar words, for instance. Nevertheless, due to the size of the corpora, it was possible to manually analyze the clusters presented by the tool, along with the analysis of those combinations in the context they appear by using the 'concordance' tool, in order to identify phraseological differences in the two languages. This will be explained in the next section.

4 Brazilian Recipes in English and in Portuguese: Phraseological Differences

A recipe is usually "incomplete, inexact and inconsistent" [16, p. 174]. For example, in instructions such as 'stirring constantly' and 'egg whites, beaten', it is assumed that, respectively, a spoon and a mixer, or other similar utensils, will be used so that the tasks are accomplished. Diemer [6] explains that, historically, recipes were shared among cooks and, therefore, dispensed details. Over time, this textual genre expanded its scope to include the layperson and, as a result, the lexical complexity was gradually minimized, and more precise measures and more detailed information were introduced. However, incompleteness still underlies this textual genre, albeit in varying degrees, in different languages/cultures. When comparing recipes in four variants - American and British English, and European and Brazilian Portuguese - Tagnin and Teixeira [21] concluded that Portuguese and British recipes tend to be more precise in terms of measurements, using ounces and pounds, for example, while those from the 'younger' countries - Brazil and the United States – prefer the 'looser' spoon(s) and cup(s). Such differences have an impact on the translation and writing of texts in the area, at least when naturalness and conventionality are sought in the translated text. Next, we will detail differences found in the study corpora and their consequences for translation.

4.1 Inaccuracy

While reporting his insecurities as a casual cook, Barnes [1] complains that cookbooks are not accurate. Referring to a British cookbook, he mentions the problem with onion size, which, in these books appears to have only three - small, medium and large, when in reality it may vary quite substantially. Had this British cook/writer analyzed Brazilian cookbooks written in Portuguese, he would certainly have been even more perplexed by the level of imprecision found in this material.

Among the keywords of the subcorpus in Portuguese, we were struck by the adjective *bom/boa* [good]. We then searched for their contexts, using the *Concordance* tool. Figure 1 shows a sample of this search.

By analyzing the combinations with *bom/boa*, we concluded that, besides referring to quality, this adjective is used to refer to what is ideally expected in terms of size, consistency and quantity in the recipes in Portuguese. For example, Fig. 1 shows occurrences such as *bom espaço* [good space], *bom pedaço* [good piece], *bom molho* [good sauce], and *bom tamanho* [good size]. In the English subcorpus, on the other

Concord

File Edit View Compute Settings Windows Help

N	Concordance
1	afiada o osso da ponta da coxa para dar um bom acabamento. Tempere com sal e
2	: 30 minutos Esta salada é também um bom acompanhamento para carne de porco.
3	, aos poucos, até cozinhar. Deixe formar um bom caldo. Corte a abóbora também em
4	em uma panela grande e alta, deixando um bom espaço em cima, para evitar que
5	numa assadeira untada, deixando um bom espaço entre eles. Leve ao forno e asse
6	o feijão cozinha, prepare em outra panela um bom guisado com a carne de porco e o
7	1 pimenta malagueta esmagada (opcional) 1 bom maço de couve 2 colheres (sopa) de
8	, coloque os ovos por cima. Cubra com um bom molho de tomate e polvilhe com o queijo
9	de peixe e deixe tomar gosto. Faça um bom molho com os tomates, a cebola, o
10	no Pirão mexido (pág 114). Sirva com um bom molho de pimenta. Se preferir, pode
11	Farinha de mandioca, o suficiente Escalde um bom pedaço de charque. Escorra e volte ao
12	manteiga da terra 6 cebolas roxas Escolha um bom pedaço de carne-de-sol, inclusive com
13	> Um bom pedaço de cordeiro Limão Alho socado
14	de cheiro-verde. Em outra panela, faça um bom refogado com a cebola e o tomate
15	no fogo por bastante tempo, até obter um bom refogado. Encha o bucho do animal com
16	> 1 bagre escalado de bom tamanho 200 ml de leite de coco
17	Tire o sumo do coco Escolha um coco de bom tamanho e rale-o. Coloque-o sobre uma
18	de sal Açúcar a gosto Rale um coco de bom tamanho, coloque-o sobre uma peneira
19	de patinhas de caranguejo sem casca e de bom tamanho MODO DE FAZER 1. Retire as
20	a metade do leite de coco em uma panela de bom tamanho e leve ao fogo para cozinhar

Fig. 1. Sample of the concordance lines with the search word *bom* in the Portuguese subcorpus

hand, similar concepts are expressed by adjectives such as 'large' and 'thick', e.g. 'large green bell pepper' and 'make a thick sauce', whereas 'good' is used mostly to indicate high quality as in 'a good substitute' and 'a good chocolate' (see Fig. 2):

4.2 Implicit and Explicit Information

The level of explanation of the instructions to be followed in recipes also differs in recipes written in Portuguese and in English. For example, among the key phraseologies in Portuguese we have *limpe os camarões* [clean shrimp], in which the steps involved in the process remain implicit. In English, a recurring phraseology is 'shell, devein and wash/clean shrimp'.

Another example of explicitness refers to caution in the English subcorpus: 'using a pair of tongs, remove * from the pan'. In the subcorpus in Portuguese, instructions are restricted to the action – *retire * da panela* [remove * from the pan], not mentioning how the action should be carried out. Thus, we can conclude that in addition to the more detailed description of the process, there is more concern with safety in the English texts, as the cook is instructed to use appropriate utensils and to be careful when handling hot ingredients.

Concord

File Edit View Compute Settings Windows Help

N	Concordance
1	. Serve immediately with Brazilian Rice and a good Farofa.
2	or with just a fresh green salad and a good vinaigrette.
3	the strings and serve with the pan gravy. A good accompaniment to this dish is mashed
4	and cayenne pepper. When the oxtails are good and brown, pour off excess drippings,
5	handwriting. I tried the recipe, found it very good, and I am happy to pass it on to you.
6	Risoto de peru Turkey risotto is also very good and very typical too, and a good way to
7	this makes a great snack, it's especially good as a dessert when paired with rhubarb
8	Flour Soup Sopa de Farinha de Arroz 1 quart good beef broth • 2 tablespoons rice flour • 2
9	cooked sweet potatoes • 1 cup milk • 1 quart good beef stock • salt and pepper Melt butter
10	Cevadinha com Maçã 3/4 cup barley • 8 cups good beef stock • 2 bayleaves • 1 sliced
11	Yields approximately 36. The translation is "a good bite of mouthful." anslation is "a good
12	otherwise the shell will break. Working with good brands of chocolate is a mantra, but
13	Most beans will cook in 2 1/2 to 3 hours. The good Brazilian cook removes one bean from
14	cuts. Your best bet for finding these are a good butcher or ethnic markets, including
15	4 tablespoons rice flour • 1 cup milk • 6 cups good chicken or beef stock • seasoning 1 1/2
16	• 1/4 cup milk • 2 egg yolks • salt 1 quart good chicken stock • 1 1/2 cups cooked
17	when bonbons, it is pivotal. That's because a good chocolate will not only have a superb
18	prefer. The Shrimp sauce (see page 83) is a good choice er sauce you prefer. The Shrimp
19	, malagueta, and serrano peppers make good choices. If you ore not used to eating
20	, it can be incorporated into several very good cocktails and punches. In the hope that

Fig. 2. Sample of the concordance lines with the search word 'good' in the English subcorpus

4.3 Technicality

Although recipes can be classified as technical texts, gastronomic material is aimed at different users, such as laypeople, chefs, children, newlyweds, among other enthusiasts; additionally, recipes are also shared in blogs, with their own specificities (See [7]). All these variables certainly interfere in the choice of the terminology used in the texts. In his linguistic analysis of recipes, Cotter [5] concludes that those aimed at laypeople are more explicit and detailed than the ones aimed at professional chefs, for example. But in addition to the aforementioned variables, the degree of technicality in the recipes also varies according to the language/culture in which they are produced.

Having compiled a comparable corpus which is homogeneous in what regards (i) mode – written cookbooks, (ii) authorship – native speakers of the languages involved, (iii) medium – printed, (iv) target audience – laypeople, and (v) amount of texts – eleven cookbooks in each language; we also expected to identify a balance in relation to the degree of technicality used. However, results showed that it was not always the case. For example, significantly recurring in the English subcorpus, the term 'mandoline' is used in phraseologies such as 'cut * (into julienne), using a mandoline' and 'thinly slice * (preferably) using a mandoline'. In the Portuguese subcorpus, the prima facie equivalent – *mandoline(a)* – has no hit. In order to designate a similar concept, the Portuguese subcorpus offers *cortador de legumes* (vegetable cutter), yet with only two occurrences. In general, recipes in Portuguese do not specify the utensil with which the task should be carried out.

Another term present only in the English subcorpus is 'cheesecloth', found in phraseologies such as 'allow to cool in the cheesecloth' and 'place the mixture in cheesecloth and squeeze'. Similar instructions are given in Portuguese by using *pano (bem) fino* [(very) thin cloth] – *ponha * sobre um pano bem fino* [place * on a very thin cloth], *esprema bem em um pano fino* [squeeze well using a thin cloth]. A more technical term – *morim* – was not found in the Portuguese subcorpus.

Another commonly mentioned utensil in the subcorpus in English is cocktail shaker, part of the combinations 'shake well in/transfer to/pour into the cocktail shaker'. Its prima facie equivalent in Portuguese – *coqueteleira* –, on the other hand, is not used at all in the Portuguese subcorpus. We can infer, therefore, that the use of more technical terms in cooking phraseologies in English is considered acceptable by North-American nonprofessional cooks, but not by their Brazilian counterparts, as they may interpret it as excessive use of technicality.

4.4 Semantic Differences

Another feature that differentiates phraseologies used in the recipes in Portuguese and English refers to the semantics underlying the verbs characteristic of this textual genre. In English, verbs used to describe cooking are usually imbued with full meaning, such as 'dice', 'julienne', 'slice', 'half', 'quarter', 'peel', used in phraseologies such as 'tomatoes, peeled and diced'; 'olives, pitted and sliced'; and 'onion, julienned'. Similar instructions in Portuguese are frequently expressed by verb phrases with *cortar* [cut]: *cebola cortada em rodelas* [onion cut in slices]; *batatas cortadas em cubos* [potatoes cut in dices]; *corte os palmitos ao meio* [cut the palm hearts in half]. Even when there is a single verb in Portuguese to express a certain action, in recipes it seems that preference is still given to verb phrases. For example, the Brazilian Portuguese prima facie translation for 'slice' is *fatiar*. In the recipes, however, the verb is used basically as a participial adjective, in sentences such as *bacon fatiado* [sliced bacon] and *maçã fatiada*; the noun *fatia* is also used, as in *fatia de presunto/queijo/pão* [slice of ham/cheese/bread].

5 Different Cultures, Different Amount of Information

Drawing on the anthropologist Edward Hall's concept of 'contexting', Katan [9] claims that "[…] individuals, groups, and cultures (and at different times) have differing priorities with regard to how much information (text) needs to be made explicit for communication to take place." [p. 177]. The researcher designates 'high context cultures' those which rely more on prior knowledge, thus requiring less text to convey information. Low context cultures, on the other hand, assume that common knowledge is insufficient to guarantee communication, demanding more explicitness. Figure 3 summarizes the contexting cline:

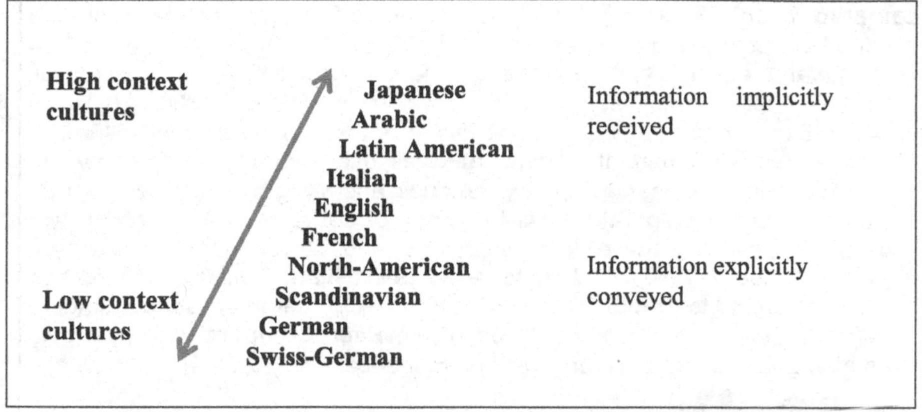

Fig. 3. Context classification of cultures [Adapted from Katan, 1999]

According to the cline, Latin American cultures, including Brazilian culture, are higher than North-American in relation to contexting, requiring fewer words to accomplish successful communication. This helps explain why the instructions found in Brazilian recipes written in English, as shown above, are more detailed than those written in Portuguese, corroborating Navarro's [14] assertions. Using Corpus Linguistics to analyze hotel sites in Brazil and the United States, the researcher concluded that the latter are more detailed. In relation to recipes, not surprisingly, we reached similar results since our English subcorpus is composed of books written by North-Americans. We did not research other English speaking cultures to verify whether they fit into either low or high context cultures because it would escape the scope of this study

Naturally, other factors may influence the amount of information revealed or implied during communication. Recipes aimed at a foreign culture are expected to bring more comments on the local ingredients and preparation, for example. Even the choice of recipes may be different (See [18]). However, since the two subcorpora compiled for this study focus on nonprofessional cooks, we believe that the difference between the amount of information expressed in the phraseologies and the degree of technicality of terms may relate to the different languages/cultures involved.

In order to assist translators and writers in producing recipes that sound natural to English-speaking readers, the phraseological differences herein discussed is taken in account in the creation of a bilingual terminological material in this specialty area. In order to illustrate the proposed translator-targetted dictionary of Brazilian cooking, we present below the entry *camarão* [shrimp]. In addition to the fields dedicated to translation equivalent (TE.), definition (Def.), example (Ex.), and comment (Comment.), we included phraseology (Phrase.), aiming at facilitating the user's choice of a functional equivalent in English (Fig. 4).

camarão *(noun)* TE.: shrimp//**Def.**: Found dried or fresh, this sea shellfish can be fried or cooked and is an essential ingredient in many Afro-Bahian dishes such *vatapá, acarajé, bobó, moqueca, abará* etc.//Ex.: *Shell, devein and clean shrimp and sauté in hot oil with onions, tomato and green pepper. [Brazilian Cooking]*Ex.: *Add the shrimp and cook until pink, stirring continually. [Brazil: a Culinary Journey]*//**Comment**.: Appreciated all over Brazil, especially by the seashore, shrimp is found in many varieties and sizes and is also used as ornament. During preparation, stir-fry, cook or sauté shrimp for about two minutes or until they are pink. Overcooking leads to rubbery and flavorless shrimp.//**Phrase**. *shrimp, shelled* [camarão descascado]; *shrimp, peeled and deveined* [camarão limpo]; *(ground) dried shrimp* [camarão seco (moído)]; *shell, devein and wash shrimp* [limpe o camarão]. **Compare with** pitu, aviú **See also** abará, acarajé, caruru, vatapá, moqueca

Fig. 4. Dictionary entry *camarão*

6 Concluding Remarks

Although interest in cooking has been on the increase all over the world, reliable reference works in the area are still scarce. As far as Brazilian cooking is concerned, reference materials in the Portuguese-English language pair are non-existent. Consequently, texts of this domain written in English or translated into this language show a series of problems, among them multiplicity of translation equivalents, lack of characterization of cultural references and lack of naturalness in the target language.

Due to lexical and syntactic specificities, a recipe is a repository of terminology and phraseology typical of the area and, therefore, constitutes appropriate source for the construction of a bilingual terminological resource for translation purposes. The semiautomatic analysis of the corpus of study, namely Brazilian cookbooks written in Portuguese and in English, revealed, in addition to simple and compound terms, prototypical phraseologies of the recipes produced in both languages. This survey, which combines qualitative and quantitative analyses, evidenced differences that go beyond terminological equivalence.

Although incomplete, since they presuppose prior knowledge on the part of the reader for its correct accomplishment, this incompleteness is unequally revealed in recipes in the two languages/cultures herein analyzed. The processes underlying Brazilian recipes in English indicated a greater tendency for detail and warning than the Portuguese processes, corroborating Katan's [9] conclusion that North-Americans need more text in order to achieve understanding. In contrast, verbs in English used in recipes are more semantically charged than those used in this genre in Portuguese, a language which makes higher use of verbal phrases in recipes, even though it has single verbs that play the same role. In addition, the degree of technicality also varies in this textual genre intended for similar audiences. The aforementioned aspects corroborate Zavaglia et al.'s conclusions [23], according to which the technical text goes far beyond terminological equivalence, since it involves other variables that must be adapted in the target language/culture so that the translation results in a fluent text.

In addition to the compilation of a Portuguese-English dictionary of Brazilian cooking, which we expect to directly assist translators and those who write on gastronomy, our study could also have an impact on the formation of specialized translators. Translation students must be made aware that, when translating a recipe into English, they have to consider that this language requires more detail [as highlighted in Katan's cline], that special attention must be paid to variation in degree of technicality, and that cultural aspects are as important as linguistic ones. By so doing, we believe that they will be able to produce more adequate texts; texts that will be better accepted by target audiences.

References

1. Barnes, J.: The Pedant in the Kitchen. Atlantic Books, London (2003)
2. Brien, D.L.: Writing about food: significance, opportunities and professional identities. In: Proceedings of the 12th Annual Conference of the Australian Association of Writing Programs, pp. 1–15. University of Canberra, Canberra (2007)
3. Bubel, C., Spitz, A.: The way to intercultural learning is through the stomach. In: Gerhardt, C., Frobenius, M., Ley, S. (eds.) Culinary Linguistics: The Chef's Special, pp. 157–187. John Benjamins, Amsterdam, Philadelphia (2013)
4. Capatti, A., Montanari, M.: La Cucina Italiana. Storia di una cultura. Editori Laterza, Roma Bari (1999)
5. Cotter, C.: Claiming a piece of the pie: how the language of recipes defines community. In: Bower, A. (ed.) Recipes for Reading: Community Cookbooks, Stories, Histories. University of Massachusetts Press, Massachusetts (1997)
6. Diemer, S.: Recipes and food discourse in English – a historical menu. In: Gerhardt, C., Frobenius, M., Ley, S. (eds.) Culinary Linguistics: The Chef's Special, pp. 139–155. John Benjamins, Amsterdam, Philadelphia (2013)
7. Diemer, S., Frobenius, M.: When making pie, all ingredients must be chilled. Including you. In: Gerhardt, C., Frobenius, M., Ley, S. (eds.) Culinary Linguistics: The Chef's Special, pp. 53–81. John Benjamins, Amsterdam, Philadelphia (2013)
8. Firth, J.R.: A Synopsis of Linguistic Theory 1930–1955. Studies in Linguistic Analysis, pp. 1–32. Blackwell, Oxford (1957)
9. Katan, D.: Translating Cultures: An Introduction for Translators, Interpreters and Mediators. St. Jerome, Manchester (1999)
10. Koester, A.: Building small specialised corpora. In: O'Keeffe, A., McCarthy, M. (eds.) The Routledge Handbook of Corpus Linguistics, pp. 66–79. Routledge, New York (2010)
11. da Krieger, M.G., Finatto, M.J.B.: Introdução à Terminologia: teoria e prática. Contexto, São Paulo (2004)
12. L'Homme, M.-C., Bertrand, C.: Specialized lexical combinations: should they be described as collocations or in terms of selectional restrictions? In: Proceedings of the 9th EURALEX International Congress, pp. 497–506. EURALEX, Stuttgart (2000)

13. McEnery, T., Hardie, A.: Corpus Linguistics: Method, Theory and Practice. Cambridge University Press, Edinburgh (2012)
14. Navarro, S.L.M.: Glossário bilíngue de colocações de hotelaria: um modelo à luz da Linguística de Corpus. 2011. Dissertation (Master in English Language and Literature)—Faculty of Philosophy, Languages and Literature, and Human Sciences, São Paulo, University of São Paulo (2011)
15. Nord, C.: Translating as a Purposeful Activity: Functionalist Approaches Explained, 2nd edn. St. Jerome, Manchester (2001)
16. Norrick, N.: Recipes as texts: technical language in the kitchen. In: Jongen, R., et al. (eds.) Sprache, Diskurs und Text, pp. 173–182. Niemayer, Tübingen (1983)
17. Philip, G.: Arriving at equivalence: making a case for comparable general reference corpora in translation studies. In: Beeby, A., Inés, P.R., Sánchez-Gijón, P. (eds.) Corpus use and translating, pp. 59–73. John Benjamins, Amsterdam, Philadelphia (2009)
18. Rebechi, R.R.: A Tradução da Culinária Típica Brasileira para o Inglês: um Estudo sob o Enfoque da Linguística de Corpus. 2015. Thesis (PhD in English Language and Literature)—Faculty of Philosophy, Languages and Literature, and Human Sciences, University of São Paulo, São Paulo (2015)
19. Scott, M.: Wordsmith Tools Version 6.0. Oxford University Press, Oxford (2012)
20. Sinclair, J.: Corpus evidence in language description. In: Wichmann, A.S., Fligelstone, S., McEnery, T., Knowles, G. (eds.) Teaching and Language Corpora, pp. 27–39. Longman, London, New York (1997)
21. Tagnin, S.E.O., Teixeira, D.: Linguística de *Corpus* e tradução técnica: relato da montagem de um *corpus* multivarietal de culinária. *TradTerm*, São Paulo, vol. 10. pp. 313–358 (2004)
22. Viana, V.: Linguística de Corpus: conceitos, técnicas e análises. In: Viana, V., Tagnin, S.E. O. (eds.) Corpora no ensino de línguas estrangeiras, pp. 25–95. HUB Editorial, São Paulo (2010)
23. Zavaglia, A., Azenha, J., Reichmann, T.: Cultural markers in LSP translation. In: Baumann, K.-D. (ed.) Fach – Translat – Kultur: Interdisziplinäre Aspekte der vernetzten Vielfalt, vol. 2, pp. 785–808. Frank und Timme, Berlin (2011)

Pragmatic Parameters for Contrastive Analyses of the Equivalence of Eventive Specialized Phraseological Units

Óscar Javier Salamanca Martínez[1(✉)] and Mercedes Suárez de la Torre[2]

[1] Universidad del Rosario, Bogotá, Colombia
[2] Universidad Autónoma de Manizales, Manizales, Colombia

Abstract. This paper discusses the pragmatic aspects that affect the phraseological equivalence in the translation of the Eventive Specialized Phraseological Units (Eventive SPUs). These results were obtained from a descriptive analysis of data in a parallel Spanish > English corpus of semi-specialized texts in the area of renewable energies. The pragmatic parameters to analyze the phraseological equivalence were established to explain the phenomena observed in previous contrastive analyses at the morphosyntactic and semantic levels [13]. It was found that there were complex interrelations between these pragmatic parameters and the parameters set to analyze the phraseological equivalence at the morphosyntactic and semantic levels. It shows how communicative, usage, textual and discourse factors determine the syntactic and conceptual treatment of specialized phrasemes in translation.

Keywords: Phraseological equivalence · Eventive specialized phraseological units · Specialized phrasemes · Translation · Pragmatic analysis · Terminology

1 Introduction

1.1 Eventive Specialized Phraseological Units (Eventive SPUs)

Bevilacqua [2] described the formation rules and structure of the Eventive SPUs in the area of solar energy by using a corpus of semi-specialized texts that were originally written in Spanish.

This author established that Eventive SPUs represent and transmit specialized knowledge in a particular communicative situation [2]. These SPUs are named 'eventive' as they are syntagmatic structures that have an Eventive Nucleus (EN), a unit of relational properties denoting specific processes for a particular field of specialization, and a Terminological Nucleus (TN): a noun unit that has a referential denominative function.

The TN comprises the knowledge nodes that make part of the solar energy conceptual structure (e.g. energía, calor, potencia, electricidad, etc.). According to their location on the conceptual structure of the Renewable energies' field, there are two types of Eventive SPUs: nuclear and peripheral [2].

R. Mitkov (Ed.): Europhras 2017, LNAI 10596, pp. 115–127, 2017.
https://doi.org/10.1007/978-3-319-69805-2_9

This author found that the EN has three derivative underlying structures in Spanish:
(verb structure) [[EN]Verb + [TN]N]: producir energía
(deverbal structure) [[EN]Deverbal Noun] + [TN]Prepositional Syntagma: producción de energía
(participle structure) [[TN]N + [EN]Participle]: energía producida

The semantic properties of the Eventive SPUs are given by (a) the conceptual structure of the TN, (b) the basic meaning of the EN, (c) the domains, (d) their thematic structure and (e) the restriction in the selection of the arguments [2].

In the area of solar energy, the EN denotes processes and actions that are specific for this theme. Nuclear Eventive SPUs in the area of solar energy are categorized into the following stages: initial processes (1.1 capturing, 1.2 accumulation and 1.3 storage), intermediate processes (2.1 creation, 2.2 changes and 2.3 results) and final processes (3.1 supply and 3.2 utilization). Below we can find an example level scheme (Table 1):

Table 1. Creation level scheme of an Eventive SPU and its corresponding domain, ENv and formation rules. (The complete list schemes of these units cf. Bevilacqua [2].).

Level	Domain	EN_{verb}	Rules
2.1 Creation	ACTION	*crear, generar, producir*	**4.** (X1) Force/Engineering/Energy [(ENv) Process 2.1 (X2) Goal/Effected Object/Energy] **Intransitive variant:** [(X1) Goal/Effected Object/Energy (ENv) Process 2.1]

For instance: (turbina convencional para) producir electricidad.
Rule: (X1) Force/Engineering/Energy [(ENv) Process 2.1 (X2) Goal/Effected Object/Energy][1]

In this Eventive SPU, the first argument (X1: turbina convencional) is a device characterized by its thematic structure of 'Engineering'. The EN (producir) shows a process in the second level and first stage of the process of energy creation. The second argument or TN (X2: electricidad) is characterized by its thematic structure of energy and by being 'Goal' and 'Effected Object' at the same time. The TN is an object that did not exist before and was created by the process that the EN denotes [2].

1.2 Background Research on the Translation of the Eventive SPUs

Salamanca [13] accounted for Bevilacqua's work [2] and described the phraseological equivalence in the translation of these units at the morphosyntactic, semantic and pragmatic levels. In this research work, Salamanca [13] analysed data from a parallel corpus Spanish > English in the field of the Renewable Energies in order to set parameters for the contrastive analysis of the Eventive SPUs.

[1] X1 is the first argument of the Eventive SPU; ENv refers to the Eventive Nucleus with a verb structure; X2 is the second argument which is the same TN.

Based on the notion of Functional Phraseological Equivalence (FPE) proposed by Gladrow and Dobrovol'skij [5] and the formation rules of the Eventive SPUs [2], Salamanca [13] established the following contrastive parameters:

(a) Morphosyntactic level: it refers to [M1] transformation of the EN underlying structure (NFPE of Gladrow and Dobrovol'skij in [5]); [M2] changes in the argument structure (argument structure, [2]); and [M3] changes in the surface syntactic realization between the EN and the NT (surface realizations, [2]).
(b) Semantic level: it refers to [S1] changes in the thematic composition of the argument structure (formation rules, [2]); [S2] changes in the lexical composition of the Eventive SPUs (conceptual structure, [2]); [S3] conceptual variation (set from the observations made in [S1] and [S2]); and [S4] changes from the eventive character of the SPUs to a resultative meaning in the translated text (set from the observations made at the morphosyntactic level).
(c) Pragmatic level: it refers to [P1] communicative implications (set to explain the denominative and conceptual variations found at the semantic level); [P2] frequency (suggested by the formation rules of the Eventive SPUs and the NFPE of Gladrow and Dobrovol'skij [5]); and [P3] textual and discursive implications (set to explain different phenomena found at the morphosyntactic and semantic levels). This paper aims at analyzing the pragmatic level since morphosyntactic and semantic levels were previously described in Salamanca and Suárez [14].

Corpus Selection and Methodology

To carry out the work, two corpora (parallel and comparable) with the same level of specialization (semi-specialized texts) were selected. The parallel corpus comprised 12 articles taken from a catalog and 92 news articles from *Renovables Made in Spain* [10], a web site sponsored by the Spanish Ministry of Industry and the Instituto para la Diversificación y Ahorro de la Energía (IDAE). This parallel corpus had a total number of 65,035 words and the texts were originally written in Spanish and had their corresponding translation into English. The comparable corpus was selected in order to analyze the frequency [P2] in the contrastive analysis. This corpus had 32,783 words, and comprised articles found at the Renewable Energy Magazine [11].

Eventive SPUs were extracted by using a semiautomatic methodology. For such purpose, the TNs were identified in the Spanish texts of the parallel corpus by using PhraseFinder [16], which is an automatic term extraction tool based on linguistic patterns. A manual validation was necessary to exclude those candidates that did not have any relation with main conceptual node (the energy). The conceptual map elaborated by Bevilacqua [2] was used for such validation. Only four TNs with a relative high frequency and close relation with the thematic node were identified: TNEnergía, TNPotencia, TNBiomasa and TNElectricidad. The parallel corpus was then aligned and processed by means of WordSmith Tools [15]. An advanced concordance search was run between these four TNs and the stems of the ENs determined by Bevilacqua [2]. Only those collocations with verbal underlying structure were selected to narrow data for subsequent analyses. The TNbiomasa was excluded for not having shown concordances with any EN of verbal underlying structure, and the TNpotencia did not show any concordances with the EN proposed by Bevilacqua [2].

30 concordances between the TNenergía and TNelectricidad and the ENgenerar, ENproducir, ENconsumir, ENalmacenar and ENaumentar were identified. These contexts were manually tagged by using the formation rules (predicate schemes) established by Bevilacqua [2]. This tagging process allowed us to identify 29 contexts (corpus of analysis) as proper Eventive SPUs.

2 Pragmatic Parameters for a Contrastive Analysis of the Eventive SPUs

2.1 Communicative Implications [P1]

To analyze the pragmatic parameters, four communicative criteria were taken from The Principles of the Terminology (Communicative Theory of Terminology, [3]), the Translation Theory (translemic analysis, [9] and, Structure of Sense, [7]):

(a) Theme [3, 7] and the level of specialization of communication: level of specialization of texts [3].
(b) Situationality taken as the register: field, tenor and mode [7, 9].
(c) Sender's intention [7, 9] and text function [3, 7].
(d) Acceptability: recipient and translation purpose [3, 7, 9].

(a) Theme and the Level of Specialization of Communication
Renewable energy is a topic or theme related to pure sciences, technology, engineering and economics. The texts which were part of the parallel corpus in this research focused on the thematic node of 'engineering and fuels', and hence, different content dimensions emerged. For instance, economics, the environment, multidisciplinary engineering, natural resources, operative research and management sciences.

Cabré [3] stated that the terms had a multidimensional and multidisciplinary nature: firstly, they were linguistic, cognitive and communicative units regardless of the perspective they were being addressed; secondly, they were the object of analysis of different disciplines that were explained by them or they explained some of their facets due to the multifaceted nature of terms. Concepts were, thus, polyhedral in nature as they could be part of different disciplines and, within a particular theme, they could be addressed from different perspectives. This could lead to linguistic variations.

This multidisciplinary approach to the theme and terms explains the variations that were found in the morphosyntactic and semantic analyses (e.g. changes in the argument structure [M2], conceptual variation [S3]). These denominative and conceptual variations led to levels of false, partial and null phraseological equivalence in the translation of Eventive SPUs.

There was denominative variation in the TNelectricidad (e,g. 'energía eléctrica', 'la eléctrica') within texts in Spanish, but this denominative variation was also present in translations. For example (Table 2):

This inter-linguistic denominative variation could be explained by the multidisciplinary nature of terms as discussed above. However, the polysemic nature of the TNelectricity' granted its semantic features (e.g. resource, electric charges, flow of

Table 2. Example of a context in which there was an inter-linguistic denominative variation of the TN between the source and the target texts.

ST	TT
(X1) [Ingeniería] **La planta de Lakeview**, de 26,8 MW, se ubicará en un área rural de la zona oriental del Estado de Oregón, y *[(NEV) Proceso intermedio 2.1 (creación) [**generar** ES v]* **generará** *(X2) (NT) [energía]* **energía eléctrica***]* mediante la biomasa forestal que se obtenga de la limpieza y poda de los bosques de las áreas meridional y oriental del mismo Estado	*(X1) [Engineering]* The 26.8-MW **Lakeview plant** will be located in a rural area in the eastern part of Oregon State, and *[(Verbal EN) Intermediate Process 2.1 (creation) [**generate** Verbal Underlying Structure]* **will generate** *(X2) (NT) [Energy]* **electricity***]* from forestry biomass to be obtained from cleaning and pruning operations in the Southern and Eastern Oregon forests

charges) that were different from those of the TNenergía eléctrica: exchanged energy by means of electrical currents [13]. There was also a difference in the level of specialized communication in the use of these TNs. This, therefore, resulted in a partial phraseological equivalence at the sematic level in the translated text.

There was conceptual variation in the TNelectricity due to the polysemic nature of the term. Specialized dictionaries defined electricity as a property of the atomic particles which excluded the other definitions found in less specialized situations. There was also an ‘every day’ definition that stated that ‘electricity’ was the electromagnetic field of energy sent out by batteries and generators, which was equivalent to ‘electrical energy’. It was also found that in these popularized scientific texts on renewable energies, the term ‘electricity’ had meaning attributes of ‘resource’, since it was used with complements such as ‘clean’ (i.e. clean electricity) (Table 3).

Table 3. Example of a context in which conceptual variation of the TN could be observed.

ST	TT
(X1) [Energía] **Las energías limpias** *[(NEV) Proceso intermedio 2.1 (creación) [**generar** ES v]* **generaron** el 36% de la *(X2) (NT) [energía]* **electricidad***]* en España en lo que va de año	*(X1) [Energy]* **Clean energy** *[(Verbal EN) Intermediate Process 2.1 (creation) [**generate** Verbal Underlying Structure]* has **generated** 36% of *(X2) (TN) [Energy]* **electricity***]* in Spain to date this year

In this context, we could trace semantic properties of TNelectricity as a ‘resource’ due to the phraseological relation with the ‘X1energías limpias’ that granted its meaning attributes of an endless natural resource, and at the same time there was a phraseological relation with the EN that gave it the properties of quantity and magnitude of the electric energy. These different facets of the term were given by the multidisciplinary nature of the theme. While the first meaning could be attained from the environmental sciences, the latter came from the management and engineering sciences. The disambiguation of the polysemic nature between ‘electricity’ taken as a ‘resource’ and ‘electricity’ taken as ‘electrical energy’ in these popularized scientific texts depended on the recipient’s content schemata (*e.g.* general reader, technician, business administrator, etc.) Thus, this polysemic nature gave the term cohesive properties that resulted in partial semantic equivalence between the TNelectricidad in the ST and the TNelectricity in the translated text (TT).

Following the classification of the scientific communication set by Rodriguez [12], the texts of our parallel corpus were classified at the level of scientific popularization. Rodriguez [12] stated that this level was characterized by a form of translating the codified language of specialists on a theme into a language that could be understood by a particular receptor. This popularization of science was carried out by following a logic of knowledge appropriation in relation to the culture and the conditions of the receptors.

If we take into account that general readers are among the receptors of these texts, the conceptual negotiations presented at the semantic level (e.g. changes in the thematic composition of the argument structure [S1] and changes in the lexical composition of the Eventive SPUs [S2]) between X1 s and NTs in the translation of Eventive SPUs can be explained. The following example illustrates this (Table 4):

Table 4. Example of a context in which there were changes in the thematic composition of the argument structure of the X1 and the TN.

ST	TT
Según datos de Iberdrola, *(X1) [Energía-producto]* **la potencia** ahora autorizada en Rumanía permitirá *[(NEV) Proceso intermedio 2.1 (creación) [**generar** ES v]* **generar** *(X2) (NT) [energía]* **energía** suficiente*]* "como para suministrar electricidad a cerca de un millón de hogares, evitando además la emisión a la atmósfera de 2,6 millones toneladas anuales de CO2"	According to Iberdrola, *(X1) [Energy-property]* **the capacity** for which approval has been granted in Romania *[(Verbal EN) Intermediate Process 2.1 (creation) [**generate** Verbal Underlying Structure]* **will generate** enough *(X2) (TN) [product of energy]* **power***]* "to supply electricity to about one million households, avoiding the emission into the atmosphere of 2.6 million tonnes of CO2 per annum"

Ciapuscio [4] also stated that, texts that were not highly specialized and had the function of popularizing the science, were prone to focus on the informative conceptual node rather than the terminological/scientific conceptual node. Therefore, conceptual treatment in these types of texts was rather partial.

This conceptual treatment between X1potencia and its translation as X1capacity and between TNenergía and TNpower in the target text caused null phraseological equivalence of this Eventive SPU at the semantic level.

(b) Situationality

The analysis confirmed some facts, which were evident when examining the theme and level of specialization.

When analyzing the theme, it was concluded that the text of the corpus was oriented towards the node of 'engineering and fuels' and, from here, different subdisciplines emerged (e.g. economics, environmental studies, multidisciplinary engineering, natural resources, operative research and management sciences; among others).

The analysis of the tenor revealed that there was not only a sender (IDAE), but also text producers (journalists specialized in the theme of renewable energies). It was confirmed that the receptors were general readers, technicians and, professionals in the area of technology and production of renewable energies. This gave the texts a popularized nature due to the variables of shared knowledge between the sender, the text producers and the wide range of receptors.

(c) Sender's Intention and Text Function
These texts had a popularized purpose to disseminate information regarding the production and technological development of the renewable energies in Spain. This could be confirmed by the high rate of EN in the level of creation found in the detection and extraction process of the Eventive SPUs. Their function was to disseminate this information and were, therefore, addressed from a journalistic perspective. Ciapuscio [4] stated that this type of text had the subfunction of moulding the receptor's beliefs and attitudes, which adopted behavioral modalities according to the text: convince, assess or shape an opinion. These texts tried to form a positive attitude towards science and catch the receptor's attention.

(d) Acceptability
Translated texts not only have to meet the translations requests (function of the target text, content, space, textual style, sentence structure, lexical choice), but they also must adjust to the norm of reception established by the receptor. Thus, lexical and conceptual choices are defined by the receptor. The texts of our parallel corpus were addressed to general and semi-specialized readers. Ciapuscio [4] highlighted that a newspaper article had its own restrictions, not only in format and extension, but also, in the modality and time for reading it. All this explained the lack of accuracy in the conceptual treatment, but only through it could information could be accessible.

2.2 Frequency [P2]

Frequency is taken as a pragmatic parameter to both identify the Eventive SPUs in the corpus and validate preferences of their use.

Bevilacqua [2] explained that frequency was a criterion to identify SPUs as proper units that transmitted specialized knowledge of an area of expertise. Salamanca [13] also used frequency as a criterion to identify the TNs and ENs in the corpus and to narrow data.

On the other hand, in the Notion of Functional Phraseological Equivalence of Gladrow and Dobrovol'skij [5] frequency was related to the familiarity and preference of use, regarding a particular text gender. In the analysis of the phraseological equivalence in parameter [S3], we found semantic content incoherence of Eventive SPUs like 'to produce energy' or 'to generate electricity' if we take into account the law of conservation of energy and the way generators operate. We contrasted the frequency of use of these specialized phrasemes in the comparable corpus and found that the concordance between ENproduce and the TNenergy had a high percentage of use (Table 5):

Table 5. Number of ocurrences between ENproduce + TNenergy in the comparable corpus.

EN + TNenergy	No of ocurrences	Three underlying structures	No verbal EN	% V EN	No deverbal EN	% Dev EN	No Part EN	% Part EN
produce	25	yes	5	20.0	13	52.0	7	28.0

This indirect intertextuality allowed us to observe that the frequency of this concordance that contradicts the law of conservation of energy was accepted in the target culture at similar levels of specialized communication and in equivalent text genres.

We could observe that there was also a higher proportion of nominalization of ENs in the target culture in comparison to the texts analyzed, in the source culture. This was another factor that could determine the phraseological equivalence of the Eventive SPUs at the morphosyntactic and semantic levels. For example, for the following Eventive SPU, there could be two possible translations:

– [(NEV) Proceso final 3.2 (aprovechamiento) [consumir ES v] **consumir** (X2) (NT) [energía] **energía eléctrica**.

A first choice would be to preserve the underlying structure of the EN as a verb:

– [(Verbal EN) Final Process 3.2 (utilization) [consume Verbal US] **consume** (X2) (TN) [Energy] **electrical energy**].

A second choice would be to change the verbal underlying structure to deverbal noun structure, so here we could have two types of constructions in English:

– [(Verbal EN) Final Process 3.2 (utilization) [consume Dev US] **consumption** (prep) **of** (X2) (TN) [Energy] **electrical energy**]:
  NEdev + prep + TN.
– [(X2)(TN) [Energy] **electrical energy** [(Verbal EN) Final Process 3.2 (utilization) [consume Dev US] **consumption**]:
  TN + Dev EN.

Two criteria were established to validate this second choice: (a) the semantic implications when changing the underlying structure of the EN to a deverbal noun structure since this change could lead to the loss of the eventive meaning (parameter [S4]), and (b) the frequency of use regarding the situationality and the text genre.

An advanced concordance search of the two syntagmas ‘consumption of energy’ and ‘energy consumption’ in the comparable corpus showed that the TN + Dev EN form was more frequent. It was observed that it occurred when it came after a verb (e.g. reduce, cut, lower, optimize, etc.) or a possessive form (e.g. its, their, sector’s, etc.). The NEdev + prep + TN was less frequent and it was used when the prepositional syntagma had two complementary nouns (in the consumption of energy and materials) or, there were two noun nuclei (the distribution and consumption of energy).

2.3 Textual and Discourse Implications [P3]

A previous analysis done at the morphosyntactic and semantic level (Salamanca and Suárez, in press) showed that the equivalence in the translation of the Eventive SPUs was affected by textual and discourse implications such as the text genre, cohesion and coherence.

2.3.1 Text Genre

It was found that there were tense changes in the translation of the EN in one context to adjust text conventions, not only in the source text, but also in the target text. In the source text, the Eventive SPU was part of a heading and its EN was in simple past to follow the convention of syntactic economy proper of the culture of origin, although it was followed by a time marker that did not indicate finished time. In the translation, the tense of the EN was changed to agree with the time marker, but not with the textual conventions. This lack of agreement to the textual norms of the target culture created a rather artificial translation that affected the phraseological equivalence.

2.3.2 Cohesion

2.3.2.1 Reference

Baker [1] highlighted there was a different type of reference relation that was not strictly textual (called co-reference), but a matter of real-world knowledge.

In this context, there was a case of repetition of X1Solnova 4 with the superordinate 'plant' in a new sentence. The relation between 'Solnova 4' with the co-referent 'plant' is situational and implied knowledge on what Solnova 4 was. According to Baker [1], there was also lexical cohesion in this context by the selection of vocabulary in organizing relations within a text. Phraseological equivalence was not affected by this co-reference.

Table 6. Example of a context in which there was a case of anaphoric co-reference by the use of a superordinate in X1 in the target text.

ST	TT
(X1) [Ingeniería] **Solnova 4** tiene 50 megavatios de potencia, está compuesta por unos 300.000 m2 metros cuadrados de espejos que ocupan una superficie total de unas 115 hectáreas, *[(NEV) Proceso intermedio 2.1 (creación) [**producir** ES v]* **producirá** la *(X2) (NT) [energía]* **energía** suficiente*]* para abastecer la demanda de 25.700 hogares, y evitará la emisión a la atmósfera de aproximadamente 31.400 toneladas de CO2 anuales	**Solnova 4** has a capacity of 50 MW and comprises approximately 300,000 square metres of mirrors covering a total area of about 115 hectares. *(X1) [Engineering]* **The plant** *[(Verbal EN) Intermediate Process 2.1 (creation) [**generate** Verbal Underlying Structure]* **will generate** enough *(X2) (TN) [Energy]* **energy***]* to meet the electricity needs of 25,700 homes, while eliminating the emission of approximately 31,400 tonnes of carbon dioxide into the atmosphere each year

2.3.2.2. Substitution and Ellipsis

In the source text, the X1 is substituted by a demonstrative and an adjectival proform (estas últimas/this latter). In the translated text, the translator decided to use 'plants' in

X1 to trace reference. In this case phraseological equivalence at the semantic level was affected since the translator failed to identify that the antecede was 'stations' instead of 'plants' (Table 7).

Table 7. Example of a context in which there was a case of substitution of the X1 in the source text.

ST	TT
(X1) [Ingeniería] **Estas últimas** representan una de las grandes ventajas de la hidráulica: su capacidad para *[(NEV) Proceso Inicial 1.3 (almacenamiento) [**almacenar** ES v]* **almacenar** *(X2) (NT) [energía]* **energía***]*	*(X1) [Engineering]* **This latter type of plants** provides one of the great advantages of hydropower: its *[(X2) (NT) [Energy]* **energy** *Initial Process 1.3 (storage) [**store** Deverbal Noun Underlying Structure]* **storage***]* capability

Table 8. Example of a context in which there was a case of partial ellipsis in the X1 in the source text.

ST	TT
Pues bien, el pasado mes de noviembre *(X1) [Energía]* **la eólica** llegó a *[(NEV) Proceso intermedio 2.1 (creación) [**generar** ES v]* **generar** más del 50% de la *(X2) (NT) [energía]* **electricidad***]* durante cinco horas seguidas, con picos del 53% y media mensual del 22,7%	Nevertheless, last November, *(X1) [Energy]* **wind power** was used to *[(ENV) Intermediate Process 2.1 (creation) [**generate** Verbal Underlying Structure]* **generate** more than 50% of the *(X2) (TN) [Energy]* **electricity output***]* over a five-hour period, with peaks of 53% and a monthly average of 22.7%

An example of ellipsis could be observed in the following text (Table 8):

The nucleus of the terminological phrase (X1) was ellipted in the source text. The translator traced back the antecede that was ellipted but failed since it was 'energy'. This conceptual change led to a false phraseological equivalence degree at the semantic level if the conceptual negotiations that occur in semi-specialized communication are considered [13] .

2.3.3 Coherence

Castellà (in [6]) stated that coherence could be analyzed from two different perspectives: as a product and as a process. In the first, the features that could be regulated and classified were observed. In the latter, a dynamic perspective was adopted, in which the actions of both the text producer (construction) and the receptor (interpretation) as individuals were analyzed; the traces of participants (text producer and receptor) were also studied.

Castellà (in [6]) claimed that the rules for analyzing coherence as a product (Charolles, in [6]) were closely related to the rules of cohesion. In Table 6, we discussed the conceptual relations between 'Solnova 4' and the co-referent 'plant'. This co-referent was used to help the target culture receptor to repair the concept of the X1, who might not be familiarized with the type of engineering ‘Solnova 4’ in the source culture. It also presented a coherence relation since it helped the receptor to interpret the concept that underlay for the X1 in the source text due to its explanatory function. This relation corresponded to the rule of repetition of Charolles (in [6]) since a real-world element was stated and, at the same time, it was linked to a concept previously presented in the text.

Van Dijk [17] established four macro-rules that helped us analyze coherence as a process, as they showed the operations the receptor must do to understand the macrostructure. Coherence was approached as a process when analyzing parameter [S3] (conceptual variation). When the complement of a terminological phrase was ellipted the key factor to determine its degree of polysemy within the polysemy/monosemy *continuum* proposed by Cruse (in [8]) was the easiness to identify this ellipted element (Table 9).

Table 9. Example of a context in which there was a case of partial ellipsis of the TN in the source text.

ST	TT
El ITE está analizando el ciclo de vida de *(X1) [Ingeniería]* **cuatro modelos de paneles fotovoltaicos de diferentes tecnologías** (silicio amorfo, monocristalino, policristalino y CIS) para conocer qué cantidad de *[(X2) (NT) [energía]* **energía** *(NEV) Proceso final 3.2 (aprovechamiento) [**consumir** ES v]* **consumen***]* en cada una de las etapas de su vida útil y analizar la posibilidad de reciclar por separado el vidrio, el aluminio y los semiconductores de los que están compuestos	The ITE is analysing the lifecycle of *(X1) [Engineering]* **four models of photovoltaic solar panels of different technologies** (amorphous silicon, monocrystalline, polycrystalline and CIS) to determine the amount of *[(X2) (TN) [Energy]* **energy** *(X1) [Engineering]* **each** *(Verbal EN) Final Process 3.2 (utilization) [**consume** Verbal Underlying Structure]* **consumes***]* during each stage of their useful life and explore the possibility of recycling the glass, aluminium and semiconductors that make them up separately

In the source text of the context above, the identification of the ellipted complement of the noun phrase depended on the receptor’s content schemata to determine that the type of ‘energy’ (TN) affected was the solar energy. It was not possible to trace the antecede ‘solar’ in the surface of the source text and, thus, it was closer to polysemy in the polysemy/monosemy *continuum*. However, in the target text, it could be observed that this antecede was used in the X1.

By following Van Dijk’s macro-rules [17], it was concluded that in the construction of the text, the text producer used the operations of ‘deletion’, ‘selection’ and ‘generalization’ of the specialized knowledge and took what was relevant to the concept. To understand the semantic content of the text, the ‘general reader’ receptor also used particular macro-rules. Due to a less structured content schemata, this general reader preserved the ‘generalization’ of the concept over the other macro-rules. Therefore, from the discourse point of view, it led to a partial semantic equivalence with the target text, which had ‘solar’ in the X1 and made the ellipted complement of the noun phrase easier to be traced by the receptor. The identification of the type of energy of the TN (semantic content) implied 'general reader' receptors to use macro-rules at different levels in both texts.

3 Conclusions

Phraseological equivalence of the Eventive SPUs was presented as a *continuum* between total equivalence and null equivalence. In his research, Salamanca [13] determined that there was not such presumed total equivalence that some authors claim to exist when translating terminological phrasemes [5]. Phraseological equivalence of Eventive SPUs also presented an intricate network of interrelations between the established parameters at the morphosyntactic, semantic and pragmatic levels. This made the translation of Eventive SPUs a complex task if the translator were dealing with different levels of specialization of communication. When analyzing the equivalence of translated texts, there should be a more flexible notion to approach the intricate interrelations at the different levels of the language rather than turning to a restricted notion of degrees of equivalence. It was possible to establish such clear degrees of equivalence at the morphosyntactic level. However, it was a rather difficult task at the semantic level, since what could be considered as a partial degree of equivalence was also possible to be classified as a false degree, or even led to null equivalence due to conceptual changes and negotiations that occurred at this level of semi-specialized communication. It was not possible to establish degrees of equivalence at the pragmatic level due to the intersubjective nature of communication according to the principles of the structure of sense proposed by [7].

Communicative, usage, textual and discourse factors determined the syntactic and conceptual treatment of the Eventive SPUs in their translation. Communicative implications such as the acceptability (receptor, the norm of reception and translation requests) played a crucial role in the intercultural specialized communication as they directly affected the relations of equivalence found across different levels and parameters of analysis. The frequency could be used to validate the translation of the Eventive SPUs against their use in real texts in the target culture (comparable corpus), so that the translation would be in accordance to the norm of reception for that particular text, gender and level of specialization. Textual implications such as text conventions (*e.g.* text genre) could affect the equivalence of these units since their translation must be adapted to what was textually accepted in the target culture. Cohesion also had an important role by determining the equivalence relations at the morphosyntactic level (ellipsis and substitution that resulted in changes in the argumental structure) and at the semantic level (partial ellipsis of the terminological phrase which could result in polysemy). Coherence was at the cognitive level of the receptor and when there was a partial ellipsis of terminological phrase, it could be difficult for the receptor to attain the semantic content of the text and this resulted in false interpretations and textual ambiguity. This also affected the phraseological equivalence when receptors in both cultures had to use different operations to understand the semantic content.

To sum up, translators should take into account how these pragmatic aspects can affect the phraseological equivalence at the morphosyntactic and semantic levels to shape their decisions when translating specialized phraseology.

Acknowledgements. The authors would like to express their sincere gratitude to Thomas Lock, who works at the Translation Center of the Autonoma University of Manizales, for reviewing the final manuscript.

References

1. Baker, M.: In Other Words: A Coursebook on Translation. Routledge, London (1992)
2. Bevilacqua, C.: Unidades frascológicas especializadas eventivas: descripción y reglas de formación en el ámbito de la energía solar. Ph.D. Thesis. Instituto Universitario de Lingüística Aplicada (IULA). Barcelona–Porto Alegre: Universidad Pompeu Fabra (2004)
3. Cabré, T.: Terminología: representación y comunicación. Elementos para una teoría de base comunicativa y otros artículos. Electronic Edition. Barcelona: Universitat Pompeu Fabra, Institut Universitari de Lingüística Aplicada. (1999, rev. 2005)
4. Ciapuscio, G.: Textos especializados y terminología. Universitat Pompeu Fabra, Institut Universitari de Lingüística Aplicada, Barcelona (2003)
5. Corpas, G.: Diez años de investigación en Fraseología: análisis sintáctico-semánticos, contrastivos y traductológicos. Lingüística Iberoamericana, Madrid (2003)
6. Hurtado, A.: Traducción y traductología: Introducción a la traductología. Ediciones Cátedra, Madrid (2001)
7. Lvovskaya, Z.: Problemas actuales de la traducción. Granada Lingvistica, Granada (1997)
8. Martí, M.: Consideraciones sobre la polisemia. In: Martí, M., Fernández, A., Vázquez, G. (eds.) Lexicografía computacional y semántica, pp. 103–161. Edicions Universitat de Barcelona, Barcelona, España (2003)
9. Rabadán, R.: Equivalencia y traducción: problemática de la equivalencia translémica inglés-español. Universidad de León, León (1991)
10. Renovables Made in Spain. Ministerio de Industria, Energía y Turismo a través del Instituto para la Diversificación y Ahorro de la Energía (IDAE). http://www.renovablesmadeinspain.com/index/. Accessed 14 Oct 2013
11. Renewable Energy Magazine. http://www.renewableenergymagazine.com/. Accessed 11 May 2014
12. Rodriguez, E.: Terminología y traducción. Universidad del Valle, Santiago de Cali (2004)
13. Salamanca, O.: La equivalencia en la fraseología especializada: análisis contrastivo de las UFE eventivas en un corpus paralelo en el ámbito de las energías renovables. Magister Thesis. Universidad Autónoma de Manizales, Manizales, Colombia (2014)
14. Salamanca, O., Suárez, M.: The Equivalence of Specialized Phraseology: A Contrastive Analysis of the Translation of Eventive Specialized Phraseological Units. In Phraseology, Diatopic Variation and Translation. IVITRA Research in Linguistics and Literature. John Benjamins Publishing Company (in press)
15. Scott, M.: WordSmith Tools, versión 5. Lexical Analysis Software, Liverpool (2008)
16. SDL International: PhraseFinder, versión 1.1. Terminological Extraction Software, Maidenhead (2005)
17. Van Dijk, T.: Macrostrcutures: An Interdisciplinary Study of Global Structures in Discourse, Interaction, and Cognition. Lawrence Erlbaum Associates, Inc., Hillsdale (1980)

Phraseological Units and Subtitling in Television Series: A Case Study *The Big Bang Theory*

Esther Sedano Ruiz(✉)

University of Malaga, Malaga, Spain
esther.sedano@gmail.com

Abstract. This work is framed into the studies of translation and interpretation and more specifically in the field of Audiovisual Translation (AVT) and Phraseology. In this study we will focus on one of the brands within AVT: Subtitling. Script translation is one of the more special in the range of Audiovisual Translation. Likewise, we find that the complexity that subtitling implies, joined to the appearance of the different phraseological units and the way they are translated into subtitles are totally worth of study. Our main goal is to classify the phraseological units following Corpas Pastor [12] in the American series *The Big Bang Theory* and analyse, according to Martí Ferriol [29], the different techniques that are used in order to translate these phraseological units into the subtitles.

Keywords: Audiovisual translation · Phraseological units · Translation techniques · Subtitling

1 Introduction

This work studies the subtitling proposal of the North American series *The Big Bang Theory*. This series belong to the genre called as situation comedy (sitcom), in it we find humorous elements such us sarcasm, colloquialisms and idioms, which are important to the plot or characterisation of the characters and therefore it is necessary to reflect them properly.

Audiovisual translation has enjoyed an exponential growth in the academic field in recent years; however this particular field has not developed as much as others so far. Likewise, the intrinsic complexity involved in the subtitling of audiovisual material, together with the process of translation and adaptation of phraseological units, have some characteristics worthy of study. For this reason, our motivation is based on the need to analyse the different strategies that appear in order to translate the phraseological units (PU) in the subtitles and see the possible equivalences that may or may not exist into the Spanish language.

On the other hand, we believe that the matter of subtitling is relevant because of the fame that the series in original version and from other countries have experimented in recent years. This way, we encounter the problem that the subtitles must be condensed from an oral to a written context, so the phraseological units may be translated by other

R. Mitkov (Ed.): Europhras 2017, LNAI 10596, pp. 128–142, 2017.
https://doi.org/10.1007/978-3-319-69805-2_10

structures or even not be translated. In this paper we intend to go through all the phases, translation and adaptation stages until the final product. In order to accomplish that, in this work we will follow the classification of Hurtado Albir [24] which includes specifications about strategies and Martí Ferriol [27] who adapts these strategies to this type of subtitling.

In this study, firstly, we will present the status of the issue according, among others, to Lorenzo and Pereira [27] and Díaz Cintas [15], and we will frame subtitling inside Audiovisual Translation (AVT), its characteristics and subtitling phases, as Chaume Varela [9] and Díaz Cintas and Remael [21] state in their works. Next, we will focus on the translation strategies following Hurtado Albir [24] as we have said before and more specifically Martí Ferriol [29], who adapts these strategies to the audiovisual translation. Finally, we will analyse the results obtained from the chosen corpus following the classifications proposed by Corpas Pastor [12] related to the phraseological units and their translation in the subtitles. This classification is divided into four sections that we will see more specifically later on: Collocations, locations or idioms, proverbs and speech act formulae. We will also review technical specifications of the subtitling and adaptation proposal, challenges of the translation, challenges of the script adaptation and technical challenges. The final aim is to present a descriptive analysis of an audiovisual material, and in certain way we expect to clarify the obstacles that may exist in the translation of phraseological units in subtitling and do our part in the struggle for accessibility. We intent to classify the different types of phraseological units (PU) that appear in the subtitles in English-speaking series, taking as corpus the American series *The Big Bang Theory* and analysing the strategies used in the subtitles in Spanish.

2 Theoretical Foundation

2.1 Audiovisual Translation

Audiovisual translation has received special attention in translation studies in latest years since its establishment in the 90's as an academic discipline. The process of subtitling includes different phases that must follow a predetermined order. First of all, the translator produces a text that will pass through numerous and complex operations, at the same time this translation will pass through many hands which will be more or less respectful with the original text and the one produced by the translation. All this process must be connected and respect the author's intention, mainly concerning the reception of the original message.

Audiovisual narration and language are nourished by common rules and codes that have been established along more than a century of existence of the cinema. It has given rise to a worldwide accepted grammar that we could call universal language and that the spectators understand naturally. A language is defined as a set of signs and of rules that enable communication, therefore human language is able to build messages that the interlocutor can decode because of his linguistic competence. In this aspect we can affirm that in the current society and due to technology, signs and symbols are very efficient in order to produce a quick answer thanks to its structural simplicity.

If we focus on subtitling as a modality of audiovisual translation, we have to mention what we mean by subordinated translation. This type of audiovisual translation is submitted to certain restrictions and therefore we can say that subtitling is framed into this kind of AVT. According to Díaz Cintas [15] "all subtitled movies are assembled around three main components: the spoken word, the image and the subtitles" (p. 32).

Following Díaz Cintas [15] and Díaz Cintas and Ramael [21] we can consider subtitling as a type of audiovisual translation that consists on the presentation of a text, normally placed in the lower part of the screen, and that tries to reflect the dialogue of the characters, as well as elements that can appear on the screen such us letters, inserts, inscriptions, etc. or the information contained in the songs. Additionally we can distinguish three essential components in all subtitled programmes: verbal discourse, image and subtitles, moreover it is necessary to synchronise them properly concerning form and content.

Main Characteristics in AVT

When we talk about subtitling and before we analyse it, we must take into account that there exist some characteristics which are distinctive of this field. This way there are some special features within the audiovisual translation. According to the classification of Díaz Cintas [15] about the subtitling discourse we can emphasise the following: reduction, condensation, omission, cohesion and coherence, segmentation of the subtitles and the change from oral to written discourse. This latest feature is the one that seems more interesting to us for this study and for the study of phraseological units in particular, so we will develop it further on next.

As we have pointed out, subtitling presents an added difficulty, the step from the oral to the written discourse. This change implies some restrictions that the translator will have to have in mind, such as linguistic conventions that must be followed in written language, so the subtitles will have a more formal nature, so we find the impossibility of expressing all what it is said in the subtitles due to the limitation of space, paralinguistic elements that appear in the oral discourse or dialectal marks of the characters. All these elements and the strategies that the translator will have to use, will make the subtitles more uniform and homogeneous.

The way of speaking of the characters gives us an idea of their personality and it is very hard to transmit it in another language, since we can observe how the speakers perceive the reality around them paying attention to how the express things, and furthermore every linguistic system is intimately bounded to the society around it. According to Karamitroglou [26], «translation is the forcible replacement of the linguistic and cultural difference of the foreign text with a text that will be intelligible to the target-language reader» (p. 18). In this way, cultural references, slang and vulgarisms are important examples of it, as we can see in our corpus, and the translator will have to pay more attention sometimes to the form than to the content of phraseological units when this situation is presented.

Influence of the Image on Subtitles

Another relevant aspect is the influence that the image applies to the subtitles, therefore to the way the phraseological units are translated and the strategies used in order to accomplish that. According to Díaz Cintas [16],

> the addition of one (image) plus one (word) is not equal to two (image-word), but a wide range of extrafilmic relations and referents that implicit or explicitly are coded in the film through the image, the word or both. (p. 193)

This way, the translator must respect what appears on the screen and cannot contradict it, since what it is said must be supported by the images that are present all the time. The relation between dialogue and the image affect directly to the amount of subtitles and how they are translated. According to this, what appears in the images causes in many cases that less subtitles are needed. We will study if this phenomenon applies when phraseological units are translated and the strategies that are more common.

The image in translation, according to Yuste Frías [33], is considered more as a sign. He states that the western culture has given too much importance to the word, so the image has been placed in a back position, therefore it has not only a secondary place but also it has meant that the image has become an equivalent of a type of sign. The image in translation must be read and interpreted in a symbolic way, since the special dimension of the image invites the translator to go beyond and not only remain superficial.

2.2 Translation Techniques

After laying the foundations referring Audiovisual Translation, we need to define the translation techniques that we will use for our study. As we have stated before, Díaz Cintas [15] presents what he calls "subtitling discourse", from which we understand the importance of reduction as an intrinsic pattern in subtitling. Later on, based on the previous work of Hurtado Albir [24] who has been a reference in Spain, Martí Ferriol [29] presents a classification of translation techniques that are expanded until 20 different techniques. We find this classification appropriate for our study, since Martí Ferriol's classification is adapted to Audiovisual Translation, considering both dubbing and subtitling. According to this, the translation in subtitles will tend to be more literal than communicative and the most frequent techniques will be literal translation and modulation.

The translation techniques presented by Martí Ferriol [29], in which the practical part of this work will be based, are the following:

- **Borrowing**. It happens when we integrate a word or an expression from another language into the target language without modifying it. The change can be pure if there is no change in the word or neutralised if the word is normalised in the target language.
- **Calque.** We find this technique when we translate literally a foreign word or phrase. It can be from the lexical or structurally point of view.
- **Translation word by word**. This is called when the translation maintains the grammar, the order and the meaning of all the words of the original. The words have the same order and number.
- **Translation one by one**. Every word of the of the original text has its corresponding one in the translation, but the original and the translation contains words with different meaning out of context.

- **Literal translation**. The translation represents exactly the original, but the number of words do not coincide and/or the order of the phrase has been modified.
- **Coined equivalent**. We use this technique when we use a recognised term or expression as an equivalent in the target language.
- **Omission.** It is when we delete completely in the target language some element of information present in the source text.
- **Reduction.** We use this technique when we delete in the target text some part of the information present in the source text.
- **Compression.** It occurs when some linguistic elements are synthetised. It is a resource specially used in subtitling.
- **Particularisation**. We find this technique when it is used a more precise and concrete term in the translation.
- **Generalisation.** In this technique occurs the opposite, it is used a more general or neutral term.
- **Transposition.** It is when we change the grammatical category or the tense voice (active o passive) of the verb.
- **Description**. It is found when a term or expression is replaced by the description of its form and/or function.
- **Extension.** In this technique we add linguistic elements that accomplish the phatic function of the language or elements that are not relevant.
- **Amplification**. It occurs when precisions that are not formulated in the source text are introduced, as explicative paraphrases or information added to the text.
- **Modulation**. It is when we change the point of view of the phrase, the focus or category of thinking in relation to the source text, it can be lexical or structural modulation.
- **Variation.** Change of linguistic or paralinguistic elements, intonation, gesture that affect to the linguistic variation: changes in textual tone, style, social dialects, etc.
- **Substitution**. It is the change of linguistic elements for paralinguistic ones or vice versa.
- **Adaptation**. Replace a cultural element by another in the target culture.
- **Discursive creation**. It is to establish a brief equivalence, totally unpredictable out of context.

2.3 Phraseological Units

Due to the prefabricated orality of the discourse, we believe that our corpus is a suitable material to find the different types of phraseological units (PU). In order to accomplish that, we will use the classification by Corpas Pastor [12] since we find it is the most suitable for our study.

According to Corpas Pastor [12], the units are divided into those which are full speech acts and those which are not; this is an element which is combined with the particularities of the PU that are determined by the restriction. Each of the areas is subdivided, in various types of PU according to a series of additional criteria:

grammatical category, syntactic function, nature of textual statement, etc. Following Corpas Pastor [12], a phraseological unit:

- is an expression made of various words
- is institutionalized (institutionalization)
- presents some kind of semantic or syntactic specificity (idiomaticity)
- has different degrees of stability (graduality and stability)
- is possible a certain variation of its components (variation)
- is usually characterized by an high frequency of use

Type I includes *collocations*, speech acts that are in accordance with the rules of the language, but they have a different degree of fixation according to the rules of use; the restriction is lower than in the other two areas. The subtype of collocations is carried out on the basis of the internal structure, according to the grammatical categories. This way we can find 6 different subtypes of collocations: V + N; V + (prep. +) N; Adj./N + N; N + prep. + N; V + Adv; Adj. + Adv.

Type II collects the *locutions (idioms)*, speech acts that were not completed formed by combinations of words whose meaning is not the sum of the components; therefore they have an idiomatic character that we often find closed paradigms. Here Corpas Pastor [12] distinguishes between 6 types of locutions: nominal locution, adjective locution, adverbial locution, verbal locution, conjunctive locution and clausal locution.

In type III we can find the PU's which constitute complete speech acts, *proverbs* and *routine formulae or expressions*. The first can be used to convince, persuade, and instruct the receiver. Concerning the routine formulae, as they are conventionally established to perform certain speech acts, they have social purposes and facilitators of the interaction. Most of them are limited only to be the expression of feelings and attitudes socially appropriate accepted. The degree of fixation is lower than that of the phrases and proverbs.

3 Practical Application

3.1 Methodology

This study is structured in various blocks joined by the main theme, the study and description of the phraseological units. In our work the methodology intents to be eclectic and complete, in order to do so the main aim will be to identify the phraseological units presented in the source language, in this case English. Then we will classify them following Corpas Pastor [12] and finally we will follow Martí Ferriol [29] referring to the techniques used in the translation of the subtitles into Spanish.

The corpus that we have chosen to accomplish this analysis is the American series *The Big Bang Theory*, we have taken the season 5, 6 and 7 since we find that it is a representative corpus for this study. *The Big Bang Theory* is a so-called comedy of situation (sitcom) that was released in 2007 by the American channel CBS. It was created by Chuck Lorre and Bill Prady and produced by Warner Bros and Chuck Lorre.

The series has been gaining followers throughout the years. It has been broadcast in many countries, although North America and Europe are areas where we can find more countries who have acquired copyrights. In terms of the genre, it clearly comes within the framework of comedy, each chapter has a duration of twenty minutes and they are issued weekly.

3.2 Analysis of the Phraseological Units in the Subtitles

I order to carry out our analysis, we have chosen a representative selection of the most frequent techniques. We have visualised the episodes from the three seasons, identifying and selecting the fragments where the phraseological units appeared and later on we transcribed the official subtitles in Spanish from the DVD corresponding with those fragments in the source language in English. The corpus is formed by the different episodes within the seasons, each one has 24 episodes and each episode has around 4500 words. Then we have classified all the fragments that appeared in every episode according to the kind of strategy that has been used in order to translate them into Spanish.

Next we will divide the selection of the most recurrent phraseological units that we have found in our corpus according to the classification of translation techniques of Martí Ferriol [29]. Now we will present the selection of examples extracted from the corpus, divided according to the different techniques used in the translation of the subtitles, for this purpose we will present next the different charts where there will be three different columns: first the source language in English (SL), then the target language in Spanish (TL) of the subtitles, and finally in the last column the type of Phraseological Unit (PU) studied in English.

Translation word by word

SL	TL	PU
Howard: **Zero gravity**	Howard: **Gravedad cero.**	Idiom
Amy: Really? Are you willing to draw a moustache on your finger to **break the ice**? I am.	Amy: ¿De verdad? ¿Estás dispuesto a dibujarte un bigote en el dedo para **romper el hielo**? Yo sí.	Idiom
Mrs Cooper: It is said that **a cat can have kittens in the oven but that don't make 'em biscuits.**	Mrs Cooper: Se dice que **una gata puede tener gatitos en el horno pero eso no los convierte en galletas.**	Proverb

According to the Oxford Dictionary of Idioms published [13], "break the ice" is defined as "do or say something to relieve tension or get conversation started at the start of a party or when people meet for the first time".

Translation one by one

SL	TL	PU
Dr Hofstadter: And we're back to the obvious. Now, **what's up?**	Dr Hofstadter: Vuelves a comentar lo obvio. Bueno, **¿qué pasa?**	Routine expression

Literal translation

SL	TL	PU
Leonard: Let it go, Sheldon Sheldon: **If I could, I would, but I can't, so I shan't**	Leonard: Olvídalo, Sheldon Sheldon: **Si pudiera lo haría, pero no puedo así que no lo haré.**	Routine expression
Raj: Oh. **All right.**	Raj: **Vale.**	Routine expression

Coined equivalent

SL	TL	PU
Sheldon: You're good friends with Penny, right? Amy: Best friends, besties, BFFs, **peas in a pod**, sisters who would share travelling pants. Go on.	Sheldon: Penny y tú sois buenas amigas, ¿verdad? Amy: Superamigas, íntimas, inseparables, **uña y carne**, hermanas que comparten hasta los pantalones. Continúa.	Idiom
Mrs Cooper: Sheldon, your friend is hurtin'. What do we do when someone's hurtin'?	Mrs. Cooper ¿Qué hacemos cuando alguien está sufriendo?	
Sheldon: Offer them a hot beverage. Mrs Cooper: And when they're **drunk as a skunk**, what beverage do we offer? Sheldon: Coffee.	Sheldon: Ofrecerle una bebida caliente. Mrs. Cooper: Y cuando está **borracho como una cuba,** ¿qué ofrecemos? Sheldon: Café.	Collocation
Sheldon: Nice. **Kick a man when he's down**	Sheldon: Genial. **Haz leña del árbol caído.**	Proverb
Penny: Okay, good, because there's this one guy I used to date who's about to be force-fed wine and cheese if he doesn't **get to the point.**	Penny: Vale, bueno, porque hay un tío con el que solía salir que se va a tragar el vino y el queso como no **vaya al grano.**	Collocation
Leonard: Before I come in, you should know, I have gas. (Holds up gas canister) Penny: **For the record**, not your worst opening line	Leonard: Antes de entrar debes saber que tengo gases. Penny **Para que conste,** no es tu peor entrada.	Idiom

In the example we find the PU "for the record", translated in Spanish in the subtitles as "*para que conste*". According to the Oxford Dictionary of idioms [13], it means so that the true facts are recorded or known. In this case we need to highlight the importance of the context and above all of the image, since it is an essential element in order to understand what the characters are saying. Yuste Frías [33] states that the "reading" and the interpretation of the image in translation must always take into account the conditions and effects of its reception in the symbolic structures of the target culture.

Omission

SL	TL	PU
Man: You realise you **just lied your ass off to** your wife and your mother.	Man: Te das cuenta de que acabas de **mentirles** a tu mujer y a tu madre.	Collocation

Reduction

SL	TL	PU
Barry: **What's going on with** Amy?	Barry: **¿qué pasa con** Amy?	Routine expression
Raj: I didn't wanna be a **third wheel**	Raj: No quería **estorbar.**	Idiom

Compression

SL	TL	PU
Leonard: **Let it go**	Leonard: **Olvídalo**	Routine expression
Penny: **I'm done with** this	Penny: **estoy harta** de esto	Idiom

Generalisation

SL	TL	PU
Sheldon: Now, knowing Penny, the obvious answer is, they engaged in coitus. But, since that's what it looked like, we can rule that out. Let's put on our thinking cap, shall we? (Mimes doing so) Raj is from India, a tropical country. Third World hygiene. Parasitic infections are common, such as pinworms. Mm-hmm. The procedure for diagnosing pinworms is to wait until the subject is asleep, and the worms crawl out of the rectum for air. Penny could have been inspecting Raj's anal region for parasites. Oh, boy. That's a **true blue friend.**	Conociendo a Penny, la respuesta obvia es que realizaron el coito, pero dado que eso era lo que parecía, podemos descartarlo. Pongámonos el casco de pensar, ¿quieres? Raj viene de la India, un país tropical de higiene tercermundista invadido por parásitos infecciosos como las lombrices. La clave para diagnosticar lombrices es esperar a que el sujeto esté dormido y que salgan a buscar aire por el recto. Tal vez Penny estuviera inspeccionando la zona anal de Raj buscando parásitos. Vaya, eso **sí que es un amigo.**	Collocation
Mrs Cooper: You're missing out. It's gonna be **wall-to-wall** fun. It's all themed. There's Jonah and the Whale Watching, all-you-can-eat Last Supper Buffet, and my personal favourite, Gunning with God.	Tú te lo pierdes. Será **muy divertido**. Habrá de tofo: avistamiento de Jonás y la Ballena…buffet libre "La última cena". Y mi actividad preferida: "Disparando con Dios".	Idiom

Description

SL	TL	PU
Sheldon: Look at the two of us. Me, a highly regarded physicist. The kind of mind that comes along once, maybe twice in a generation. You, the common man, tired from your labours as a stockbroker, or vacuum cleaner salesman, or bootblack. But deep down inside, apparently we're just **two peas in a pod**. A regular pea, and the kind of pea that comes along once, maybe twice in a generation.	Míranos a los dos. Yo, un físico de prestigio, con un cerebro que sólo surge una vez o quizá dos veces en una generación. Tú, un hombre corriente, cansado de tu trabajo porque eres agente de bolsa o vendedor de aspiradoras o limpiabotas. Pero en el fondo, me temo que **los dos somos exactamente iguales.** Un tipo normal y el tipo de hombre que surge una vez o dos en una generación.	Idiom

Extension

SL	TL	PU
Sheldon: Excuse me. It's Major Sheldon Cooper. With my last breath, I awarded myself a battlefield promotion. It's kind of a **big deal.**	Sheldon: Disculpad, soy el comandante Sheldon Cooper. Con mi último aliento, me he concedido a mí mismo un ascenso militar. **Es algo muy importante.**	Idiom

Modulation

SL	TL	PU
Leonard: **What the hell is wrong with you?**	Leonard: Pero, **¿es que te has vuelto loco?**	Routine expression
Sheldon: Oh, the walls are dripping blood, which looks nothing like a phenolphthalein indicator exposed to a sodium carbonate solution. (*Reading message on wall)* See you in hell Sheldon. The most frightening thing about that is the missing comma. *(A luminous skeleton rushes towards him)* Ah. Okay, all right. That one was clever. Skeleton with phosphorous on a zip line. Come on out, merry pranksters. **Take a bow.**	Sheldon: Ah, ahora sale sangre por las paredes. Aunque solo parece un indicador de fenolftaleína que reacciona antes una solución de carbonato sódico. "Nos veremos en el infierno Sheldon". Lo más aterrador de todo es que falta una coma. Muy bien. Ya vale. Muy astuto. Un esqueleto de fósforo colgado de una tirolina. Salid de ahí bromistas, **que yo os vea**.	Idiom
Howard: Well, too bad, you already did. It's a **done deal**. Oh, well. But I forgive you.	Howard: Bueno, vaya, ya está hecho. **No tiene remedio.** Pero te perdono.	Collocation
Raj: Anyway, I was hoping I could, uh, **pick your brains a little**. I'm supposed to take Lucy out Friday and I need a killer first date.	Raj En fin, quería **pediros algún consejo**. He quedado con Lucy el viernes y quiero una cita increíble.	Idiom

In the example "take a bow", this idiom has been translated as "*que yo os vea*". We can see here that there is not any equivalence in terms of phraseological units, since in the Spanish subtitles the point of view has been changed related to the original.

According to the Oxford Dictionary of Idioms [13], "pick somebody's brain" means question someone who is better informed about a subject than yourself in order to obtain information, in a more informal way. On the contrary, in the subtitles the informal register is lost since "*pedir un consejo*" seems more neutral than the original expression.

Adaptation

SL	TL	PU
Mrs Cooper: Leonard, you're up. Wasserman, you're **on deck.**	Mrs Cooper: Leonard, te toca. Wasserman, **luego tú.**	Idiom

According to the Oxford dictionary of idioms, "on deck" means "ready for action or work". In this particular case the term has to be adapted in Spanish since it is a North American cultural expression and it is almost impossible to find an equivalent in the target language and culture.

Discursive creation

SL	TL	PU
Raj: And, Leonard, you go and propose to this poor girl in the middle of sex? That was some **weak tea,** dude	Raj: Y Leonard, ¿le pides matrimonio a esta pobre chica mientras lo estáis haciendo? Tío, eso es un **golpe bajo.**	Idiom

In the example of "weak tea", translated as "*golpe bajo*" in Spanish does not correspond exactly with the meaning in English. The former means something unpleasant or an unconvincing argument, so only attending to the rest of the conversation we can see that the translation fits, but it would be unsuitable out of context.

4 Conclusion

After this study of the translation techniques of phraseological units in subtitling we can conclude that this combination is worthy of attention, since it connects two main fields inside Translation: Audiovisual Translation, specially subtitling and Phraseology.

As a result of our analysis we can conclude some aspects referring to the translation techniques and the language used to translate the phraseological units in subtitles. Generally, the language used in the translation into Spanish seems more standarised than in English. On the contrary, the register in the original text is more familiar, maybe due to the orality of the studied text. As we know, oral texts have some special features and moreover in this context of sitcoms and comedy, where elements like familiar language, fixed expressions or proverbs are very common, that is why this corpus has been very enlightening in the study of how the phraseological units in oral language are translated into subtitles.

We have also noticed that the phraseological units presented in English are more neutralized in Spanish, that is to say that in a large number of cases we find that the PU's are not translated as an equivalent in the target language, normally we find that the PU has been lost in the subtitles or it has been adapted, so in this special case it seems that in Spanish the phraseological units are not as frequent as in English. However we think that this is caused by the nature of the subtitles themselves, since their main characteristic is reduction. Due to the lack of space, we are not able to add all the examples we have extracted from the corpus, however we can observe the frequency and the percentage of the strategies found in the following table.

Translation word by word	3%
Translation one by one	4%
Literal translation	18%
Coined equivalent	21%
Omission	1%
Reduction	12%
Compression	9%
Generalisation	6%
Description	2%
Extension	1%
Modulation	15%
Adaptation	7%
Discursive creation	1%

As we can see, there are 4 techniques that are more frequent in the examples of our corpus. First of all we find that the "coined equivalent" technique is very recurrent in our corpus as a translation strategy. The next technique we find is "literal translation" and that could be because of the tendency of using this kind of technique when we talk about subtitling since we pass from an oral to a written language. Then we have "modulation" technique, which is used in a large number of cases due to the combinations of languages that we study, the point of view is normally changed in order to cause a more natural language in the translation. Another important technique that we should highlight is "reduction", since as we said before the images affect directly to the amount of subtitles, so this technique is even more used in the field of subtitling.

Finally we should notice that in the Spanish subtitles there are more modulation that in English and furthermore, we find adaptations due to the cultural meaning of the phraseological units that come from another country or a specific region, in this case we find expressions which are typical from North America, so the solution found in the translation is to adapt those terms into the target culture.

References

Primary References

1. Cendrowski, M.: Season 5. [Episodes on DVD]. Warner Bros and Chuck Lorre, USA (2011)
2. Cendrowski, M.: Season 6. [Episodes on DVD]: Warner Bros and Chuck Lorre, USA (2012)
3. Cendrowski, M.: Season 7. [Episodes on DVD]: Warner Bros and Chuck Lorre, USA (2013)

Secondary References

4. Agost Canós, R.: Investigación descriptiva en traducción audiovisual: el estudio de las normas. In: Zabalbeascoa, P., Santamaría, L., y Chaume Varela, F. (eds.) La traducción audiovisual: Investigación, enseñanza y profesión. Comares, Granada (2005)
5. Banos, R; Chaume, F.: Prefabricated Orality: A Challenge in Audiovisual Translation. In: TRAlinea. Special Edition: The Translation of Dialects in Multimedia (2009)
6. Brondel, H.: Teaching subtitling routines. Meta **34**(1), 26–33 (1999)
7. Carroll, M.: Subtitling: changing standards for new media?. In: The LISA Newsletter: Globalization Insider, vol. XIII(3), 5 (2004)
8. Chaume Varela, F.: Cine y Traducción. Cátedra, Madrid (2004)
9. Chaume Varela, F.: Film studies and translation studies two disciplines at stake in audiovisual translation. Meta: Le J. des Traducteurs 49(1), 12–24 (2004)
10. Cómitre, I.: Algunas consideraciones sobre la traducción del texto audiovisual. In: Santamaría, J.M., Pajares, E., Olsen, V., Merino, R., Eguiluz, F. (eds.) Trasvases culturales: literatura, cine y traducción, pp. 89–95. Departamento de Filología inglesa y alemana de la Universidad del País Vasco, País Vasco (1997)
11. Cómitre, I.: Retraducción y traducción audiovisual: estudio descriptivo del doblaje y subtitulado de Peau d'âne de J. Demy. In: Varela Salinas, M.J. (ed.) Panorama actual del estudio y enseñanza de discursos especializados, pp. 165–181. Peter Lang, Bern (2009)
12. Pastor, G.C.: Manual de Fraseología española. Gredos, Madrid (1996)
13. Geall, D.: Oxford Dictionary of English Idioms (3rd edition), Reference Reviews, vol. 25. OUP, Oxford (2001)
14. Díaz Cintas, J.: La traducción audiovisual. el subtitulado. Salamanca: Almar (2001)
15. Díaz Cintas, J.: Teoría y práctica de la subtitulación. Inglés-español. Ariel Cine, Barcelona (2003)
16. Díaz Cintas, J.: Audiovisual translation today: A question of accessibility for all. Translation Today [e-journal] 4, 3–5 (2005)
17. Díaz Cintas, J.: Por una preparación de calidad en accesibilidad audiovisual. Trans, Revista de traductología, 11, 56–59. Available through Roehampton University, London (2007)
18. Díaz Cintas, J.: Traducción audiovisual y accesibilidad. In: Hurtado, C.J. (ed.) Traducción y accesibilidad. Subtitulación para sordos y audiodescripción para ciegos: nuevas modalidades de Traducción Audiovisual, pp. 9–23. Peter Lang, Frankfurt (2007)
19. Díaz Cintas, J.: La accesibilidad en los medios de comunicación audiovisual a través del subtitulado y la audiodescripción. Revista Virtual Cervantes. Roehampton University, Londres (2008)
20. Díaz Cintas, J., Remael, A.: Audiovisual translation: subtitling (Translation Practices Explained Series). St. Jerome Publishing, Manchester (2007)
21. Ellis, N.: Vocabulary acquisition: word structure, collocation, word-class, and meaning. In: Schmitt, N., McCarthy, M. (eds.) Vocabulary: Description, Acquisition and Pedagogy, pp. 122–139. CUP, Cambridge (1997)
22. Flavell, L.R.: Dictionary of idioms and their origins. Kyle Cathie Limited, London (1994)
23. Hurtado Albir, A.: Traducción y Traductología: Introducción a la traductología. Cátedra, Madrid (2001)
24. Siefring, J.: Oxford Dictionary of Idioms. OUP, Oxford (2004)
25. Karamitroglou, F.: Towards a Methodology for the Investigation of Norms in Audiovisual Translation. Rodopi, Amsterdam (2000)
26. Lorenzo García, L., Pereira Rodríguez A.M.: Traducción subordinada (5II) El subtitulado (inglés-español/galego). Universidade de Vigo, Vigo: Servicio de Publicacións (2000)

27. Mansel, M.H.: Dictionary of Proverbs. Facts of File, New York (2007)
28. Martí Ferriol, J.L.: Estudio empírico y descriptivo del método de traducción para doblaje y subtitulación. Publicacions de Universitat Jaume I, Castellón (2006)
29. Martínez Montoro, J.: La fraseología en J. Casares. ELUA. Estudios de Lingüística. N. 16 (2002)
30. Mayoral Asensio, R.: Aspectos epistemológicos de la traducción. Universidad Jaume I, Castellon (2001)
31. Remael, A.: A place for film dialogue analysis in subtitling courses. In: Orero, P. (ed.) Topics in Audiovisual Translation, pp. 103–126. John Benjamins, Amsterdam (2004)
32. Yuste Frías, J.: Leer e interpretar la imagen para traducir. Trabalhos em Lingüística Aplicada, vol. 50(2), pp. 257–280 (2011)
33. Zuluaga, A.: Los "enlaces frecuentes" de María Moliner. Observaciones sobre las llamadas colocaciones. LEA **24**(1), 97–114 (2002)

Lexicography and Terminography

A Semantic Approach to the Inclusion of Complex Nominals in English Terminographic Resources

Melania Cabezas-García([✉]) and Pamela Faber

University of Granada, Granada, Spain
{melaniacabezas,pfaber}@ugr.es

Abstract. Complex nominals (CNs) are characterized by the omission of the semantic relation between their constituents due to noun packing. Despite their frequency in specialized texts written in English [1] their representation and inclusion in knowledge resources has received little research attention. This paper presents a proposal for the inclusion of CNs in an English terminographic resource on renewable energy. For that purpose, we used knowledge patterns and paraphrases to access the meaning of CNs in a wind power corpus. We then filled the definitional templates proposed by Frame-based Terminology [2]. Our main goal was to conceptually organize a term entry to facilitate knowledge of the domain while keeping the entry length to a minimum. Furthermore, this proposal is a valuable starting point toward the development of bilingual and multilingual resources since translation should be based on meaning. Our results also afforded insights into compound term formation in English, as reflected in the addition of specific values to the semantic relations encoded by the hypernym. Term instability and multidimensionality were also prevalent.

Keywords: Complex nominal · Semantics · Terminography

1 Introduction

Renewable energies have led to the creation of new terms that should be included in knowledge resources. Complex nominals (CNs) are of particular importance since these phraseological units are very frequent in scientific texts [1, 3–7]. Noun packing, the omission of constituents, and the non-specification of the semantic relation between the units forming the CN, often result in a lack of compositionality and transparency in these terms [8, 9]. In other words, the meaning of a CN cannot always be predicted from its head and modifiers [10]. The only clear information is that "it denotes something (conveyed by the head) that is somehow related to something else (conveyed by the modifier)" [8: p. 100].

This paper describes how CNs can be included in an English terminographic resource on renewable energies. For that purpose, a corpus of specialized texts on wind power was used to extract paraphrases and knowledge patterns [11, 12] (see Sect. 3), which facilitated access to the semantics of these phraseological units. Furthermore, a specialized corpus on the environment (available in Open Corpora in Sketch Engine)

R. Mitkov (Ed.): Europhras 2017, LNAI 10596, pp. 145–159, 2017.
https://doi.org/10.1007/978-3-319-69805-2_11

provided a larger amount of data. We then filled out the definitional templates proposed by Frame-based Terminology [2], which include the semantic relations encoded by the CNs and permit the clustering of related terms.

Our objectives were to access the semantics of CNs, verify whether their meaning could be understood in terms of similar CNs [10], and conceptually organize the term entry on the basis of this shared meaning. To the best of our knowledge, the semantic organization of specialized CNs, and the inclusion and description of CNs formed by more than two terms have not received sufficient research attention. Moreover, this proposal facilitates knowledge representation of the domain while keeping the entry length to a minimum. It is also a valuable starting point toward the development of bilingual and multilingual resources [3, 13].

2 Complex Nominals in Dictionaries

Complex nominals (CNs), e.g. *power plant*, are very frequent in English specialized texts [1, 3–7]. They are expressions with a head noun preceded by one or more modifiers (i.e. nouns or adjectives) [14]. These multi-word terms are characterized by their syntactic-semantic complexity since two or more concepts are juxtaposed without any explicit indication of the relation between them [10]. This usually entails the formation of long CNs that may be difficult to understand [15], which highlights the need to describe them in specialized resources. CNs can be endocentric (the focus of our study), when one term is the head and the other constituents modify it [1], e.g. *wind power*. Alternatively, they can be exocentric, when the CN is not a hyponym of one of its elements, and thus appears to lack a head [16], e.g. *saber tooth*.

One of the essential characteristics of CNs is the existence of underlying propositions that can be inferred in the term formation processes, as highlighted in Levi [14]: predicate deletion (e.g. *power plant* instead of *a plant produces power*) and predicate nominalization (e.g. *power generation* instead of *power is generated*). Along these lines, Mel'čuk et al. [17] argue that argument structure is fundamental when describing predicates. Given that CNs have concealed or nominalized verbs, the study of micro-contexts (i.e. the relation between a predicate and its argument structure [18]) is crucial in terminographic descriptions.

In the last twenty years, research on CNs has addressed the formation and use of these multi-word units, their semantics, and different methods for interpreting them [14, 19–24]. More recently, CNs have been investigated for translation purposes [5], and special attention has been paid to their formation and interpretation [7, 25], namely by means of paraphrasing verbs and prepositions [1, 26]. However, the focus has been on two-term CNs. Furthermore, CNs have not been systematically treated in dictionaries [27] though most authors agree on their inclusion as sublemmas of a main entry [11, 28] because other locations could prevent readers from finding the right information [11]. Whereas some authors point out that multi-word units should appear under the first content word [29], others defend that CNs should be a sublemma of the head noun [28, 29]. Nonetheless, there is general consensus that the inclusion and treatment of phraseological units depends on user needs [11, 27].

3 Meaning Access in Complex Nominals

The non-specification of the semantic relation between CN constituents often makes it difficult to understand the meaning of these phraseological units. Traditionally, inventories of semantic relations have been the preferred way of accessing this conceptual link ([19, 20, 30, 31] *inter alia*). However, these classifications can pose problems such as the choice of the best set of relations, their abstract nature, and the existence of more than one possible relation in the same CN [1].

For these reasons, Downing [21] argues that current inventories of semantic relations cannot capture the conceptual relation between the constituents of a CN. In this respect, authors such as Nakov and Hearst [32] suggest that the best way of ascertaining the meaning of a CN is by means of multiple verb paraphrases. For instance, *malaria mosquito* can be paraphrased using different verbs such as *carry*, *spread*, *cause* or *transmit*, which specifically convey the action carried out by the mosquito (for more examples, see Hendrickx et al. [4], Butnariu et al. [26], and Nulty and Costello [33] *inter alia*). In our opinion, inventories of semantic relations and paraphrases are complementary approaches since the informativity of conceptual relations can be enhanced by means of fine-grained verb paraphrases [18].

Knowledge patterns (KPs) are also very useful for the extraction of semantic relations [34–36]. They are lexico-syntactic patterns that encode semantic relations in real texts [11, 12]. Table 1 shows some of the most frequent KPs in the environmental domain (as well as in general language) [37: p. 8].

Table 1. Knowledge patterns in León-Araúz and Reimerink [37: p. 8].

Semantic relation	Knowledge pattern
IS_A	such as, rang* from, includ*
PART_OF	includ*, consist* of, formed by/of
MADE_OF	consist* of, built of/from, constructed of, formed by/of/from
LOCATED_AT	form* in/at/on, found in/at/on, tak* place in/at, located in/at
RESULT_OF	caused by, leading to, derived from, formed when/by/from
HAS_FUNCTION	designed for/to, built to/for, purpose is to, used to/for
EFFECTED_BY	carried out with, by using

Another kind of KP are ‘grammatical knowledge patterns’ (e.g. noun + verb), that coincide to a great extent with verb paraphrases and are very useful when identifying functional relations [11].

Nevertheless, KPs also have difficulties such as noise and silence, pattern variation, anaphora, linguistic and domain dependence, etc., which must be taken into account [36]. Section 4 describes the use of paraphrases and KPs in this research.

4 Materials and Methods

For the purpose of the study, a corpus[1] on wind power of approximately 1 million words was manually compiled. It was composed of highly specialized texts, namely scientific articles and PhD dissertations, originally written in English and published in high-impact academic journals. The corpus was uploaded to Sketch Engine (https://www.sketchengine.co.uk/) [38], a corpus analysis tool that can generate concordance lines, word sketches (frequent word combinations), wordlists, etc.

The 'Keywords/Terms' function of Sketch Engine was then used to extract a list of the single-word (keywords) and multi-word lexical units (terms) most typical of the wind power corpus, which was automatically contrasted with a reference corpus. Given the limited scope of this study, the maximum number of keywords and terms was set at 100. We observed that *turbine* was ranked first in the keywords list and *wind turbine* appeared in third position on the terms list. The high prevalence of these terms was confirmed in a term extractor, TermoStat (http://termostat.ling.umontreal.ca/) [39], where *wind turbine* was the second most frequent term of a list of 8,533[2] CNs of the wind power corpus. After consulting specialized resources [40–42], it was found that *wind turbine* was not uniformly treated, and more often than not, its hyponyms were not described, despite the fact that they are recurrent terms in the domain.

As a solution, we analysed the word sketches generated in Sketch Engine. These sketches showed the terms that usually modify *wind turbine* and thus allowed us to select term candidates that were hyponyms of *wind turbine*. We selected those CNs with a higher frequency[3], which did not belong to an extended, irrelevant CN, and whose constituents were linked by semantic relations, with a view to conceptually organizing them and to facilitating knowledge acquisition. CNs formed by general words were rejected (e.g. *prospective wind turbine*, *offshore wind turbine*, *three-bladed wind turbine*) since the *differentiae* with other cohyponyms could be easily inferred. However, other CNs such as *variable speed wind turbine*, apparently easy to understand, convey information that is relevant to their meaning and which cannot be directly elicited from their surface form. They were thus included in our proposal. Our list of term candidates was then composed of 12 CNs, which were hyponyms of *wind turbine*, such as *lift force wind turbine*, *upwind turbine,* and *shroud wind turbine*.

According to Frame-based Terminology [2], each conceptual category has a prototypical template composed of the semantic relations activated by this category. Definitional templates, which were used in Frame-based Terminology since the OncoTerm research project [2], are thus the basis for homogeneous category-specific definitions that make the semantic relations explicit, as well as the logical organization

---

[1] This corpus is planned to be annotated with CNs occurrences and made available in Open Corpora (Sketch Engine).

[2] Even though TermoStat is an excellent term extractor, it often offers some noise due to the inclusion of wrong CNs (e.g. *page u*) or irrelevant parts of longer CNs (e.g. *mw wind*).

[3] Since we focused on CNs that were hyponyms of *wind turbine*, the search was limited to CNs mostly formed by three or more constituents. This explains the relatively low frequency of term candidates (35 occurrences on average). However, since they are key concepts of the domain, they should be described in a resource specialized in wind power.

of the microstructure of a term entry. First, the template of the hypernym *wind turbine* was filled with the information extracted by means of KPs and paraphrases, as detailed below, and later applied to its hyponyms. Property inheritance was evidently present, and subtypes added specific values that distinguished them from their cohyponyms. Table 2 shows the template of *wind turbine*, whose properties are inherited by its hyponyms, which add specific values (Table 3), such as the attributes of the parts (*axis of rotation parallel to the ground*). Although, this has some similarities with traditional ontologies, as previously mentioned, it advances the idea of a category-specific template that acts as a blueprint for the definitions of category members.

Table 2. Definitional template of *wind turbine*.

Wind turbine	
IS_A	Device
HAS_PART	Blade, rotor, shaft, generator, nacelle, gearbox, bearings, yaw control, tower
USES_RESOURCE	Wind
HAS_FUNCTION	Convert wind energy to electrical or mechanical power

Table 3. Definitional template of *horizontal axis wind turbine*.

Horizontal axis wind turbine	
IS_A	Wind turbine
HAS_PART	Axis of rotation parallel to the ground

With a view to accessing the meaning of CNs and filling in these templates, KPs were applied to the wind power corpus in order to ascertain the semantic relations encoded by *wind turbine*. For that purpose, the KP-based grammars developed by León-Araúz et al. [36] were implemented in the wind power corpus. This facilitated the grouping of related terms in word sketches that specify the semantic relation between the terms (e.g. PART_OF, HAS_FUNCTION, LOCATED_AT, etc.). Subsequent CQL queries of the KPs collected in León-Araúz et al. [36] were performed in order to find further knowledge-rich contexts (KRCs), i.e. "a context indicating at least one item of domain knowledge that could be useful for conceptual analysis" [11]. Nevertheless, it was impossible to extract sufficient data because of the reduced size of the corpus (which will be expanded in future work) and the limited number of linguistic forms that a semantic relation can have in specialized texts [35].

Therefore, we decided to use the EcoLexicon English Corpus, a corpus of specialized environmental texts, consisting of more than 23 million words pertaining to different environmental subdomains, which is now available in Open Corpora (Sketch Engine). By using the KP grammars [36] and CQL queries of KPs, the semantic relations activated by *turbine* were ascertained, such as its parts and its function. Even though future work will further refine these grammars and enhance them with more KPs and restrictions, these word sketches permitted us to access the conceptualization of *wind turbine* (essential in the formation of specific hyponymic CNs) and thus elaborate the definitional template of this CN. This template was complemented with and confirmed by the data extracted by means of paraphrases, as subsequently explained, and the information in specialized resources [40–42].

Thus, paraphrases were also used to query the corpus. As argued in Auger and Barrière [35], when elucidating the semantic relation implicit in CNs, KPs must be complemented by an analysis of the syntactic relations that show semantic relations. This can be accomplished by means of paraphrases, which specify the relation between the constituents of the CN [1]. We thus performed CQL queries in Sketch Engine, which allows more sophisticated queries for the optimal extraction of paraphrases with specific lexical or grammatical patterns. Table 4 shows a query to extract words between *turbine* and *lift* and vice versa, in a span of 10 tokens. As can be observed, the paraphrases reveal the semantic content that is concealed in CNs because of noun packing, and they also give access to explanatory segments. Furthermore, they permit the identification of related terms (e.g. *lift force wind turbine* and *drag force wind turbine* are terminological antonyms, as reflected in the use of *instead* and *either*).

Table 4. CQL query of paraphrases of *lift force wind turbine*.

(meet [lemma= "turbine"] [lemma="lift"] −10 10) within <s/>
Modern wind **turbines** are predominantly based on aerodynamic **lift**. Lift force use aerofoils (blades) that interact with the incoming wind
Wind **turbines** using aerodynamic **lift** can be further divided according to the orientation of the spin axis into horizontal-axis and vertical-axis type turbines
Turbines can be divided into **"lift"** machines and "drag" machines according to which force is generated by the wind and exploited as "motive force"
In the **"lift" turbines**, with respect to the "drag" type, the wind flows on both blade surfaces, which have different profiles, thus creating at the upper surface a depression area with respect to the pressure on the lower surface
The design of these modern **turbines** uses **lift** instead of drag to spin the blades
Depending on the design of the **turbine**, either drag or **lift** moves the blades

wind turbine
[HAS_PART (DIRECTION)]
horizontal axis wind turbine; vertical axis wind turbine
[HAS_PART (LOCATION)]
upwind turbine; downwind turbine
[MOTIVE_FORCE]
lift force wind turbine; drag force wind turbine
[HAS_PART]
shroud wind turbine; gearless wind turbine
[HAS_PART (SPEED)]
variable speed wind turbine; fixed speed wind turbine
[HAS_PART (MOVEMENT_CONTROL)]
variable pitch wind turbine; stall-regulated wind turbine

Fig. 1. Organization of hyponyms based on the semantic relations between their constituents.

As previously mentioned, our objective was to verify whether the semantics of specialized CNs could be at least partly derived from the meaning of similar CNs [10, 15, 25, 43]. To this end, hyponyms were organized in different groups based on the semantic relation between their constituents. The groups were alphabetically arranged, whereas the CNs in each group were listed according to their frequency. For example, *horizontal axis wind turbine* had 33 occurrences and thus appeared before *vertical axis wind turbine*, which had 27 occurrences (see Fig. 1, where indentation shows hyponymic relations, semantic relations appear in small caps in square brackets, and attributes are in brackets).

Finally, we performed CQL queries to find KPs that revealed synonyms of the CNs, such as *is a synonym of, also called, referred to as*, etc. (see Fig. 2 below). Other synonyms were found by the identification of synonymic KPs when reading parallel documents (i.e. online texts and websites on wind power) for documentation. For instance, *diffuser augmented wind turbine* was found to be a synonym of *shroud wind*

wind turbine: *turbine* [USES_RESOURCE] *wind.*
Wind-driven device that converts wind energy to electrical or mechanical power (*syn.* wind generator, windmill, aerogenerator). Usage examples.

horizontal axis wind turbine: *wind turbine* [HAS_PART (DIRECTION)] *horizontal axis.*
Wind turbine whose axis of rotation is parallel to the ground (*syn.* HAWT). Usage examples. *Related terms*: vertical axis wind turbine (*syn.* VAWT). Usage examples.

upwind turbine: *horizontal axis wind turbine* [HAS_PART (LOCATION)] *upwind.*
Horizontal axis wind turbine whose rotor faces the wind. Usage examples. *Related terms*: downwind turbine. Usage examples.

lift force wind turbine: *wind turbine* [MOTIVE_FORCE] *lift force.*
Wind turbine that uses lift forces (perpendicular to the direction of the air flow) to spin the blades and turn the rotor. Usage examples. It contrasts with **drag force wind turbine** (*syn.* impulse wind turbine), which uses drag forces (parallel to the direction of the air flow). Usage examples.

shroud wind turbine: *wind turbine* [HAS_PART] *shroud.*
Wind turbine protected by a shroud that accelerates the incoming wind, significantly increasing the mass and power available to the turbine (*syn.* ducted wind turbine, diffuser augmented wind turbine, DAWT). Usage examples. *Related terms*: gearless wind turbine. Usage examples.

variable speed wind turbine: *wind turbine* [HAS_PART (SPEED)] *variable speed.*
Wind turbine in which the rotor speed increases and decreases with changing wind speeds. Usage examples. *Related terms*: fixed speed wind turbine (*syn.* constant speed wind turbine). Usage examples.

variable pitch wind turbine: *variable or fixed speed wind turbine* [HAS_PART (MOVEMENT_CONTROL)] *variable pitch.*
Variable or fixed speed wind turbine that adjusts the angle of the blades out of the wind when experiencing high operational wind speeds in order to control the output power (*syn.* pitch controlled wind turbine). Usage examples. It contrasts with **stall-regulated wind turbine** (*syn.* passive stall-regulated wind turbine, fixed pitch wind turbine), whose blades respond to high wind speeds by stopping turning. Usage examples.

Fig. 2. Term entry proposal for *wind turbine* and its hyponyms.

turbine, as revealed in concordances such as *A shroud wind turbine, often referred to as a diffuser augmented wind turbine* (…).

5 Semantic Organization of a Term Entry

At first glance, a user of a specialized resource might think that all the CNs based on *wind turbine* are subtypes of this concept without any internal differences. However, after an in-depth conceptual analysis of CNs by means of KPs and paraphrases, hyponyms of *wind turbine* were found to belong to different hierarchical levels. In other words, they established different semantic relations, and some of them were found to be hyponyms of other terms. An effective specialized resource should reflect these differences to facilitate understanding and the eventual translation of the terms.

We thus propose the inclusion of CNs as sublemmas of a main entry. Since they are subtypes of a superordinate concept, a logical structure would presumably reflect this conceptual hierarchy. Furthermore, CNs usually designate very specific concepts, which explains the relatively low number of occurrences in the corpus that would validate their inclusion as main entry terms. On the other hand, the head of these CNs is a noun, which is the part of speech most often consulted by users [29], thus avoiding difficulties in finding the CN in question.

Our proposal focuses on the conceptual organization[4] of the microstructure of a term entry. Hyponyms are usually CNs, which, despite their formal similarity, may have quite different meanings, as reflected in the concealed semantic relation between their components. Many authors defend a semantic approach to lexicographic and terminographic resources [2, 17, 44] since this reveals domain structure, facilitates understanding of the concepts, and provides the basis for translation. This is extremely important because English texts are often translated for knowledge dissemination purposes. Furthermore, in our opinion, hyponymic CNs must be defined since they are often formed by more than three constituents with no specification of the relation between them. This evidently makes their comprehension more difficult.

With a view to conceptually organizing a term entry, we studied whether in specialized CNs, similar modifiers complemented the head in the same way [10, 15, 25, 43]. For instance, given the semantic relation CAUSES in *wind erosion*, *water erosion* is expected to establish the same semantic relation [25] since the slots opened by similar heads tend to be filled by similar modifiers [43], and *vice versa*. This would indicate that the semantics of CNs could be partly derived from the meaning of similar CNs [10]. In other words, our assumption was that CNs modified by similar terms (e.g. *variable speed wind turbine* and *fixed speed wind turbine*) establish the same semantic relation between their constituents. Thus, if one of the CNs were defined, it would not be necessary to define the other. Nevertheless, after analysing the meaning of CNs and their implicit semantic relations by means of KPs and paraphrases, it was found that this hypothesis was not satisfactory for all specialized CNs. This occurred because

[4] The overlap in the CNs of this study is not a general rule since many hyponyms do not show the same linguistic form as their hypernyms, e.g. *abrasion* as a hyponym of *erosion*.

many of the specialized CNs were not compositional, i.e. their meaning could not be directly construed from the meaning of their parts [8–10], because there were often concealed constituents that were required for an accurate understanding of the CN. For instance, *stall-regulated wind turbine* is not fully compositional because there is information missing (namely, the high wind speed conditions necessary for the turbine to stall). Without further clarification, the meaning of the CN is opaque since it cannot be understood from the meaning of its parts [10].

Therefore, our assumption was only applied to compositional (i.e. transparent) CNs, where the only difficulty was the specification of the semantic relation between their parts. This was especially true for CNs that are in opposition to each other (e.g. *horizontal axis wind turbine* and *vertical axis wind turbine*). In these cases, it was possible to infer the meaning of one of the related CNs from the definition of other CNs in the same group (i.e. modified by similar terms and linked by the same semantic relation [10, 15, 25, 43]). As for non-compositional CNs (which does not mean that they are idiomatic), both co-hyponyms were defined (e.g. *variable pitch wind turbine* and *stall-regulated wind turbine*). Despite the fact that their constituents belonged to the same family, the meaning of the second CN was not easily construed from the definition of the first because additional information was required. Therefore, we found that the omission of the semantic relation was not the only problem in CNs. More specifically, domain specificity and excessive noun packing (a source of bracketing complexity) do not support the statement that the semantics of CNs can be partly derived from the meaning of similar CNs [10]. However, this hypothesis is of great importance since it considers essential features of CNs, though its application depends on the purposes of the resource.

Figure 2 shows our proposal for the entry of *wind turbine* in a specialized knowledge resource on renewable energies. This model can be applied to any lexicographic or terminographic entry, both in electronic and printed[5] format. Electronic resources are a frequent option in today's world, given the fact that, unlike printed dictionaries, they have no space restrictions and are easily updated. Furthermore, this format offers different access points to the information [45] (e.g. search for phraseological pattern, conceptual category, lemma, conceptual representation, etc.).

As can be observed, the semantic relation between the CN constituents was specified as a first step towards a full understanding of meaning. Related CNs were grouped together when they were modified by similar terms, and the same relation was established between their constituents. In each group, the phraseological unit with the highest frequency in our wind power corpus was defined. As for compositional CNs, the other CNs in the same group were only included as 'related terms'. A definition was not needed since their meaning can be easily inferred from the definition of the first CN. The only difficulty in compositional CNs was the non-specification of the semantic relation. Some examples are *horizontal axis wind turbine* and *vertical axis wind turbine*, *upwind turbine* and *downwind turbine*, *shroud wind turbine* and *gearless wind turbine*, and *variable speed wind turbine* and *fixed speed wind turbine*. Alternatively, in non-compositional CNs, it was not possible to deduce the meaning of the CN from the

[5] Usage examples should be explicitly stated in printed resources.

definition of other related CNs (mostly because of the omission of constituents relevant to their meaning). Thus, the description of the related CN (e.g. *drag force wind turbine* and *stall-regulated wind turbine*) was preceded by the expression *it contrasts with*. The latter CN does not require a full definition, given that the characteristics differentiating it from its cohyponym are sufficient.

Definitions were based on the templates proposed by Frame-based Terminology [2]. These templates reflect the semantic relations activated by a conceptual category and provide consistency to term entries. The definitions in our proposal are composed of a *genus* and *differentiae*. The *genus* indicates the category to which the term belongs. In this case, all the CNs were hyponyms of *wind turbine*, although there were also more specific subtypes, such as *upwind turbine*, a hyponym of *horizontal axis wind turbine*. Thus, property inheritance is evident in the sense that hyponyms acquire the characteristics in the definition of their hypernym. On the other hand, the *differentiae* are the features that distinguish a hyponym from its hypernym and the other units in its lexical domain [2]. The *differentiae* of the hyponyms of *wind turbine* are usually based on attributes of the parts of a turbine.

Although CNs are characterized by a high degree of instability [46], as shall be explained, our proposal only included abbreviations and those synonyms whose linguistic form was significantly different from the CN in question. Synonyms were presented in brackets, introduced by the reduced expression *syn.* and followed by a full stop. In non-compositional CNs, where all related CNs were defined, their synonyms were placed immediately after the name of the CN to avoid possible misunderstandings. Finally, usage examples can be consulted by clicking on the hyperlink (simulated with underlined characters), which shows concordance lines of each CN in the EcoLexicon English Corpus, available in Open Corpora (Sketch Engine).

As previously highlighted, the semantic organization of term entries facilitates translation, because meaning is the starting point when rendering terms into another language. English is the *lingua franca* of specialized communication, but there is a need for translation for purposes of knowledge dissemination. For these reasons, this proposal can be the basis for creating resources in other languages, especially given the proliferation of renewable energy solutions in many different countries. In particular, this model can be used for the implementation of multi-word terms in the phraseological module of EcoLexicon (www.ecolexicon.ugr.es), a terminological knowledge base on environmental science that is conceptually organized.

6 Term Formation

The hyponyms of *wind turbine* were analysed as an example of CN formation in specialized domains. In English, the creation of CNs is the order of the day [5, 7, 46]. CNs are generally created to name more specific concepts, and thus are usually hyponyms of a superordinate term. The hyponyms of *wind turbine* were created by adding specific values to the semantic relations encoded by *wind turbine*, which appear in its definitional template. The CNs studied refer to different parts of a turbine, namely to specific features of these parts, but such components are not explicitly mentioned in the CN. This adds extra syntactic-semantic complexity to these phraseological units.

A distinguishing feature of new CNs is their instability, as reflected in their variants [28, 46]. This instability is clearly evident in the concordance lines of the CNs, where the frequent omission of some of the constituents of the CN is noteworthy. This elision usually occurs as longer CNs with a high frequency in specialized discourse are formed. For instance, in the case of (long) hyponyms of *wind turbine*, the constituent usually omitted is *wind* or the part of the turbine in question since this is the most evident information that can be disregarded. In contrast, the *differentiae* are always present, because these are the distinguishing features of the term.

This instability of complex terms is linked in many cases to multidimensionality, an essential phenomenon in specialized domains. The features of a concept are usually specified from different perspectives and the set of characteristics that define a concept is normally multidimensional [47: p. 120]. Therefore, the hyponyms of *wind turbine* emphasize different features, such as the direction of the axis of rotation, and the location or the speed of the rotor. This conceptual dynamism does not mean that several concepts are involved, but rather that different perspectives are taken in order to highlight one or more characteristics of the same concept. For example, a *horizontal axis wind turbine* can also be regarded as a *variable speed wind turbine* or a *lift force wind turbine*, depending on the information emphasized.

Furthermore, CNs are a special type of term since they have the potential to combine different dimensions in one phraseological unit. The union of these dimensions results in the formation of very long CNs since these dimensions are part of the micro-context of the concealed proposition. In other words, they belong to the argument structure, either as arguments, adjuncts, or attributes of these complements. Different examples of this phenomenon were observed in the wind power corpus. For example, *stall-regulated horizontal axis wind turbine* alludes to the direction of the axis of rotation and the mechanism of movement control in high wind speeds, whereas *horizontal axis offshore wind turbine* refers to the direction of the axis of rotation as well as the location of the turbine. The formation of long CNs adds syntactic-semantic complexity to these units since internal groupings must be identified (i.e. bracketing) in order to ascertain where semantic relations are established.

Because of multidimensionality, the same concept can be involved in different situations, which can affect its relations in the conceptual system, and thus should be considered in knowledge representations [37]. Therefore, the multidimensionality in our CNs underscores the semantic complexity of these phraseological units. It also gives the user a situational picture since it elicits the frame or underlying knowledge structure by making the conceptual dimensions explicit, either by forming long CNs or by highlighting certain dimensions. Frames and multidimensionality thus play a key role in term formation, which is represented in our proposal by means of the conceptual organization of term entries.

Furthermore, micro-contexts are the root of compound term formation since these CNs are the result of concealed propositions. English CNs are characterized by noun packing. However, when translating these phraseological units, this mechanism must be adapted to the term formation rules of the target language. For instance, in Romance languages the underlying semantic relation must be made explicit, namely in long CNs. This usually produces paraphrase structures that make the concealed verb explicit.

The conceptual organization of term entries is thus valuable since translation and idiomatic adaptations must be based on meaning.

7 Conclusions

CNs are very frequent in English specialized texts [1]. These phraseological units are characterized by their syntactic-semantic complexity, which highlights the need to include multi-word terms in linguistic resources. However, up until now CNs have not been systematically treated in dictionaries. This paper presents a proposal for the inclusion of CNs in an English terminographic resource on renewable energies. For that purpose, a wind power corpus was used to extract paraphrases and KPs [11, 12], which allowed access to the semantics of CNs. Also used was an environmental corpus that provided further data. We then filled in the definitional templates proposed in Frame-based Terminology [2], which included the semantic relations activated by the CNs and allowed the clustering of related terms. Our main goal was to conceptually organize a term entry in order to accurately structure knowledge and facilitate the understanding of concepts.

The results of this study showed that the description of CNs in specialized resources is essential, because they play a key role in conceptual systems [5, 7, 47, 48]. As stated by Sager et al. [48], the constituents of a CN are linked by a semantic relation in the conceptual system. Thus, the terminological system is connected to the conceptual system since the semantic relations in CNs (see Fig. 1) allow the reconstruction of the semantic network of a domain [5]. Accordingly, the semantic organization of term entries allows the specification of the different types of hyponym, which are usually CNs. In addition, it favours awareness of the frame or knowledge structure underlying term formation by including related terms, while keeping the entry length to a minimum.

In this research we studied compound term formation based on an analysis of the hyponyms of *wind turbine*. These multi-word terms added specific values to the semantic relations in their hypernyms. A high degree of instability was also observed, since some of the constituents were frequently omitted. Multidimensionality, which is frequent in specialized domains, was found to take part in compound term formation by selecting one dimension in the CN or combining several dimensions, which resulted in long phraseological units.

This proposal for the inclusion of complex terms in specialized resources can be helpful for different users ranging from specialists and semi-experts in the energy domain to language professionals and students. In spite of being a monolingual resource, it provides the basis for the transfer of knowledge to other languages since meaning is the starting point in translation. In particular, when translating CNs into Romance languages, a concept-based approach is particularly useful, because English noun packing is usually rendered in the form of paraphrase structures that make the concealed semantic relation explicit. Accordingly, plans for future research include the analysis of the role of predicates in compound term formation as well as the translation of CNs into Spanish, with a view to implementing these multi-word terms in the phraseological module of EcoLexicon (www.ecolexicon.ugr.es). Although the procedure is mostly done manually, its application to different types of CN will allow the extraction of conceptual information (sets of semantic relations, attributes, conceptual categories) to be implemented in EcoLexicon. This will speed up the inclusion of new CNs in the phraseological module. Moreover, the use of a distributional semantic model [49] will help to identify related terms. Nevertheless, in contrast to phraseological information that is automatically included (without classification or filtering) in other resources such as the word sketches of Sketch Engine, manual work is an added value in EcoLexicon.

Acknowledgements. This research was carried out as part of project FF2014-52740-P, Cognitive and Neurological Bases for Terminology-enhanced Translation (CONTENT), funded by the Spanish Ministry of Economy and Competitiveness. Funding was also provided by an FPU grant given by the Spanish Ministry of Education to the first author. Finally, we would like to thank the anonymous reviewers for their useful comments.

References

1. Nakov, P.: On the interpretation of noun compounds: syntax, semantics, and entailment. Nat. Lang. Eng. **19**(03), 291–330 (2013)
2. Faber, P., López Rodríguez, C.I., Tercedor Sánchez, M.: Utilización de técnicas de corpus en la representación del conocimiento médico. Terminology **7**(2), 167–198 (2001)
3. Daille, B., Dufour-Kowalski, S., Morin, E.: French-English multi-word term alignment based on lexical context analysis. In: Proceedings of the Fourth International Conference on Language Resources and Evaluation (LREC 2004), pp. 919–922 (2004)
4. Hendrickx, I., Kozareva, Z., Nakov, P., Séaghdha, D.Ó., Szpakowicz, S., Veale, T.: SemEval-2013 task 4: free paraphrases of noun compounds. In: Second Joint Conference on Lexical and Computational Semantics (*SEM): Proceedings of the Seventh International Workshop on Semantic Evaluation (SemEval 2013), vol. 2, pp. 138–143 (2013)
5. Sanz Vicente, L.: Análisis contrastivo de la terminología de la teledetección. La traducción de compuestos sintagmáticos nominales del inglés al español. Ph.D. Thesis. University of Salamanca, Salamanca (2011)
6. Fernández-Domínguez, J.: A morphosemantic investigation of term formation processes in English and Spanish. Lang. Contrast **16**(1), 54–83 (2016)
7. Kageura, K.: The Quantitative Analysis of the Dynamics and Structure of Terminologies. John Benjamins, Amsterdam (2012)
8. Grant, L., Bauer, L.: Criteria for re-defining idioms: are we barking up the wrong tree? Appl. Linguist. **25**(1), 38–61 (2004)
9. Smith, V., Barratt, D., Zlatev, J.: Unpacking noun-noun compounds: interpreting novel and conventional food names in isolation and on food labels. Cogn. Linguist. **25**(1), 99–147 (2014)
10. Séaghdha, D.Ó., Copestake, A.: Interpreting compound nouns with kernel methods. Nat. Lang. Eng. **19**, 1–26 (2013)
11. Meyer, I.: Extracting knowledge-rich contexts for terminography: a conceptual and methodological framework. In: Bourigault, D., Jacquemin, C., L'Homme, M.-C. (eds.) Recent Advances in Computational Terminology, pp. 279–302. John Benjamins, Amsterdam (2001)

12. Marshman, E.: Lexical knowledge patterns for semi-automatic extraction of cause-effect and association relations from medical texts: a comparative study of English and French. Ph.D. Thesis. Université de Montréal, Montréal (2006)
13. Morin, E., Daille, B., Prochasson, E.: Bilingual terminology mining from language for special purposes comparable corpora. In: Sharoff, S., Rapp, R., Zweigenbaum, P., Fung, P. (eds.) Building and Using Comparable Corpora, pp. 265–284. Springer, Heidelberg (2013). doi:10.1007/978-3-642-20128-8_14
14. Levi, J.: The Syntax and Semantics of Complex Nominals. Academic Press, New York (1978)
15. Rallapalli, S., Paul, S.: A hybrid approach for the interpretation of nominal compounds using ontology. In: 26th Pacific Asia Conference on Language, Information and Computation, pp. 554–563 (2012)
16. Bauer, L.: Les composés exocentriques de l'anglais. In: Amiot, D. (ed.) La composition dans une perspective typologique, pp. 35–47. Artois Presses Université, Arras (2008)
17. Mel'čuk, I., Clas, A., Polguère, A.: Introduction à la lexicologie explicative et combinatoire. Duculot, Louvain-la-Neuve (1995)
18. Cabezas-García, M., Faber, P.: Exploring the semantics of multi-word terms by means of paraphrases. In: Temas actuales de Terminología y estudios sobre el léxico, pp. 193–217. Comares, Granada (2017)
19. Vanderwende, L.: Algorithm for automatic interpretation of noun sequences. In: Proceedings of the 15th Conference on Computational Linguistics, COLING 1994, vol. 2. pp. 782–788 (1994)
20. Rosario, B., Hearst, M.A., Fillmore, C.: The descent of hierarchy, and selection in relational semantics. In: Proceedings of the 40th Annual Meeting of the Association for Computational Linguistics, ACL 2002, pp. 247–254, July 2002
21. Downing, P.: On the creation and use of English compound nouns. Language **53**, 810–842 (1977)
22. Lauer, M.: Corpus statistics meet the noun compound: some empirical results. In: The Association for Computational Linguistics Conference (ACL), pp. 47–54 (1995)
23. Warren, B.: Semantic Patterns of Noun-Noun Compounds. Acta Universitatis Gothoburgensis, Göteborg (1978)
24. Kageura, K.: The Dynamics of Terminology: A Descriptive Theory of Term Formation and Terminological Growth. John Benjamins, Amsterdam (2002)
25. Kim, S.N., Baldwin, T.: A lexical semantic approach to interpreting and bracketing English noun compounds. Nat. Lang. Eng. **1**(1), 1–23 (2013)
26. Butnariu, C., Kim, S.N., Nakov, P., Séaghdha, D.Ó., Szpakovicz, S., Veale, T.: SemEval-2 task 9: the interpretation of noun compounds using paraphrasing verbs and prepositions. In: Proceedings of the Fifth International Workshop on Semantic Evaluation (SemEval 2010), pp. 39–44 (2010)
27. Parra Escartín, C., Losnegaard, G.S., Samdal, G.I.L., Patiño García, P.: Representing multiword expressions in lexical and terminological resources: an analysis for natural language processing purposes. In: Proceedings of the eLex 2013 Conference, pp. 338–357 (2013)
28. Lew, R.: The role of syntactic class, frequency, and word order in looking up English multi-word expressions. Lexikos **22**, 243–260 (2012)
29. Béjoint, H.: The foreign student's use of monolingual English dictionaries: a study of language needs and reference skills. Appl. Linguist. **2**(3), 207–222 (1981)
30. Nastase, V., Szpakowicz, S.: Exploring noun-modifier semantic relations. In: Fifth International Workshop on Computational Semantics (IWCS-5), pp. 285–301 (2003)

31. Girju, R., Moldovan, D., Tatu, M., Andantohe, D.: On the semantics of noun compounds. J. Comput. Speech Lang. **19**(4), 479–496 (2005)
32. Nakov, P., Hearst, M.: Using verbs to characterize noun-noun relations. In: Euzenat, J., Domingue, J. (eds.) AIMSA 2006. LNCS (LNAI), vol. 4183, pp. 233–244. Springer, Heidelberg (2006). doi:10.1007/11861461_25
33. Nulty, P., Costello, F.J.: General and specific paraphrases of semantic relations between nouns. Nat. Lang. Eng. **19**(3), 357–384 (2013)
34. Condamines, A.: Corpus analysis and conceptual relation patterns. Terminology **8**(1), 141–162 (2002)
35. Auger, A., Barrière, C.: Pattern-based approaches to semantic relation extraction: a state-of-the-art. Terminology **14**(1), 1–19 (2008)
36. León-Araúz, P., San Martín, A., Faber, P.: Pattern-based word sketches for the extraction of semantic relations. In: Proceedings of the 5th International Workshop on Computational Terminology (Computerm2016), pp. 73–82 (2016)
37. León-Araúz, P., Reimerink, R.: Knowledge extraction and multidimensionality in the environmental domain. In: Proceedings of the Terminology and Knowledge Engineering (TKE) Conference 2010. Dublin City University, Dublin (2010)
38. Kilgarriff, A., Baisa, V., Bušta, J., Jakubíček, M., Ková, V., Michelfeit, J., Rychlý, P., Suchomel, V.: The Sketch Engine: ten years on. Lexicography **1**(1), 7–36 (2014)
39. Drouin, P.: Term extraction using non-technical corpora as a point of leverage. Terminology **9**, 99–115 (2003)
40. Park, C., Allaby, M.: Dictionary of Environment & Conservation, 3rd edn. Oxford University Press, Oxford (2013)
41. Jelley, N.: A Dictionary of Energy Science, 1st edn. Oxford University Press, Oxford (2017)
42. Cleveland, C.J., Morris, C.: Dictionary of Energy, 2nd edn. Elsevier, Amsterdam (2015)
43. Maguire, P., Wisniewski, E.J., Storms, G.: A corpus study of semantic patterns in compounding. Corpus Linguist. Linguist. Theory **6**(1), 49–73 (2010)
44. Cohen, B.: Lexique de cooccurrents. Bourse-conjoncture économique. Linguatech, Montreal (1986)
45. Lorente Casafont, M., Martínez Salom, M.A., Santamaría-Pérez, I., Vargas Sierra, C.: Specialized collocations in specialized dictionaries. In: Torner Castells, S., Bernal, E. (eds.) Collocations and Other Lexical Combinations in Spanish: Theoretical, Lexicographical and Applied Perspectives, pp. 200–222. Routledge, Abingdon/New York (2017)
46. Cabezas-García, M., Faber, P.: The role of micro-contexts in noun compound formation. Neologica **11**, 101–118 (2017)
47. Kageura, K.: A preliminary investigation of the nature of frequency distributions of constituent elements of terms in terminology. Terminology **4**(2), 199–223 (1997)
48. Sager, J.C., Dungworth, D., McDonald, P.F.: English Special Languages. Principles and Practice in Science and Technology. Brandstetter Verlag, Wiesbaden (1980)
49. Bernier-Colborne, G., Drouin, P.: Evaluation of distributional semantic models: a holistic approach. In: Proceedings of the 5th International Workshop on Computational Terminology (CompuTerm2016), pp. 52–61 (2016)

Eye of a Needle in a Haystack

Multiword Expressions in Czech: Typology and Lexicon

Milena Hnátková, Tomáš Jelínek, Marie Kopřivová, Vladimír Petkevič, Alexandr Rosen, Hana Skoumalová(✉), and Pavel Vondřička

Faculty of Arts, Charles University, Praha, Czech Republic
hana.skoumalova@ff.cuni.cz

Abstract. We propose a multidimensional taxonomy of multiword expressions (MWEs) as a pattern applicable to entries in a representative lexicon of Czech MWEs. The taxonomy and the lexicon are useful for many reasons concerning lexicography, teaching Czech as a foreign language, and theoretical issues of MWEs as entities standing between lexicon and grammar, as well as for NLP tasks such as tagging and parsing, identification and search of MWEs, or word sense and semantic disambiguation. In addition to the description of various types of idiomaticity, the taxonomy and the lexicon are designed to account for flexibility in morphology and word order, syntactic and lexical variants and even creatively used fragments.

Keywords: Multi-word expressions · Lexicon · Taxonomy · Variabililty

1 Introduction

Multiword expressions (MWEs) are semi-fixed entities, often with a non-compositional meaning, standing astride between lexicon and grammar. They constitute an essential part of language and are relatively frequent. Moreover, they are commonly modified and used in a creative way. Here we propose a typology of Czech MWEs as a basis of a representative lexicon, open to various sorts of users, including NLP tools. The project is motivated by the following factors: (i) Description, typology and classification of MWEs is an essential component of a linguistic model of a language, involving various kinds of MWE idiosyncrasies as opposed to standard grammatical and semantic features and structures. (ii) Explicitly described MWEs can help improve results of tasks such as POS tagging, parsing, word sense disambiguation, or semantic tagging. The improvements may concern not only the analysis of bare MWEs but also of their context within a sentence. (iii) Descriptions of MWEs should allow for the identification and search of MWEs in their standard form, but also of MWE fragments and variants – morphological, syntactic and lexical.

This paper is part of the project *Between Lexicon and Grammar* (2016–2018), supported by the Grant Agency of the Czech Republic, reg. no. 16-07473S.

R. Mitkov (Ed.): Europhras 2017, LNAI 10596, pp. 160–175, 2017.
https://doi.org/10.1007/978-3-319-69805-2_12

Modifications of a MWE occurring in texts as variants of core MWEs can be illustrated by the famous Biblical verse (Matthew 19,24) (1). It is possible to use only the core parts of the quote, as in (2):

(1) Snáze projde velbloud uchem jehly než bohatý do Božího království.
easier goes camel ear.INS needle.GEN than rich into God's kingdom
'... it is easier for a camel to go through the eye of a needle than for a rich man to enter into the kingdom of God.'

(2) velbloud uchem jehly
camel ear.INS needle.GEN

Various other various modifications can be encountered.[1] The variants should be identifiable on the basis of a lexical entry, specifying the core parts, i.e. (*velbloud*) *uchem jehly*:

(3) To by **spíš velbloud vešel do království nebeského**, než abych já navlékl nit **uchem jehly**.
it would rather camel enter into kingdom of heaven, than would I pass thread ear.INS needle.GEN
'A camel would rather enter into a kingdom of heaven than I would thread a needle through its eye.'

(4) Obchvat by se tudy měl protáhnout jak ten **velbloud uchem jehly**.
bypass would REFL this way should thread like that camel ear.INS needle.GEN
'The bypass should be threaded through the area like the camel through the eye of a needle.'

In (3) and (4), *velbloud* 'camel' is preserved, but in (5) it is missing and in (6) it is replaced by *dva slony* 'two elephants':

(5) Je snazší projít **uchem jehly** než získat přístup k unijním fondům.
is easier to go ear.INS needle.GEN than to get access to EU funds
'It is easier to go through the eye of a needle than to get access to EU funds.'

(6) Klaus nutí protáhnout dva slony **uchem jehly**.
Klaus forces to pull two elephants ear.INS needle.GEN
'Klaus forces two elephants to be pulled through the eye of a needle.'

The search for all modifications can be compared to the search for *a needle in a haystack*. However, we want to show that a solid analysis of MWEs and their proper encoding in the lexicon makes it possible to find most variants.

The paper is structured as follows. In Sect. 2, we describe our source data (dictionaries and corpora), criteria, measures and methodology for including candidate MWEs in the lexicon. In Sect. 3, related work is briefly discussed.

[1] Even *velbloud* 'camel' is sometimes missing. Czech is no exception, cf. a similarly creative use in English: *You'd have an easier time getting a camel through the eye of a needle than getting them to agree on the issue* (Farlex Dictionary of Idioms, 2015).

In Sect. 4, principles of the proposed typology are presented, followed by its detailed description in Sects. 5–7. Further, Sect. 8 contains a brief description of a lexicon entry and in Sect. 9 we shortly discuss the use of the lexicon in parsing.

2 Data and Methodology

The lexicon is built to cover the whole range of typologically varied MWEs. The lexical entries are compiled from the following sources:

- A phraseological dictionary of Czech (SČFI) [11].
- *FRANTALEX*, a modified and extended subset of SČFI including 36,000 entries and headword variants, used to support *FRANTA*, a tool for *ph(F)Raseme ANnotation and Text Analysis* [13]. *FRANTA* was used to annotate MWEs in several Czech corpora. A lexical entry in *FRANTALEX* includes information about the lemma and type of the MWE, its variants, lemmas and tags of its components, syntactic and morphological restrictions.
- Several representative CNC corpora of contemporary written Czech.[2] Two measures of MWEs' fixedness are tested for the extraction task: obligatoriness and proximity (cf. [6]), accompanied by other statistical association measures (cf. [12,22]). The candidates for a new entry are then manually screened on the basis of their usage data.
- A valency lexicon of Czech verbs [16], used as a source of default argument structure for lexical components of the MWEs.

The lexicon is compiled as follows:

- Candidates for headwords are selected from the sources above to represent as many diverse MWE types as possible. The MWEs selected from the *FRANTALEX* are converted to the format of the lexicon. Other candidates will be identified primarily on the basis of the obligatoriness and proximity measures (and possibly some other appropriate measures).
- The raw entries are checked and equipped with additional information: coordinates of the MWE within a multidimensional typology including the specification of its syntactic properties, fixedness/flexibility, modifiability, variants, fragments, transformations, morphological restrictions and kinds of idiomaticity – cf. Sects. 4–7.
- Lexical entries specify only nonstandard, idiosyncratic features, i.e. standard/systemic properties are not described.[3]
- The core components of a given MWE are labeled as such to identify variants and fragments.

---

[2] *SYN2010*, *SYN2015* (122 million tokens each), *SYN* release 4 and 5 (4.3 and 4.6 billion tokens, respectively).

[3] Valency is a notable exception from this principle, cf. Sect. 5.4.

The lexicon is due to contain 7000 MWE entries. So far 500 candidate MWEs have been converted from the phraseological dictionary and 300 other candidate MWEs have been identified by obligatoriness and proximity measures in the SYN2015 corpus. Enrichment of these raw entries with detailed classification of their properties is underway.

3 Related Work

MWEs have been studied from many perspectives, often determined by the author's background, research interests or practical goals. Thus results come in very different flavours: theoretical (e.g. [1,10,14,21]), focused on the grammar/lexicon interface (e.g. [24]), or concerned with the building of NLP resources and tools such as lexicons and treebanks (e.g. [3,23]).[4] Our focus is driven by the goal to integrate a MWE lexicon with NLP tools, which includes the need to treat MWEs as units breaking the border between lexicon and grammar. This is also why we are concerned with the variability of MWEs.

However, rather than serving a single purpose, the lexical resource should be open to other viewpoints. Thus our taxonomy is multidimensional, where some categories correlate with those used in the traditional discipline of phraseology. The domain is not without controversy – terminology differs even in the name of the base unit, which varies by language (e.g. German: *Phraseologismus*, English: *idiom*, *collocation*, *set phrase*, Spanish: *unidad fraseológica*, Russian: *фразеологизм*). The term *phraseme* seems to be internationally accepted [5, p. 11]. The situation is further complicated by the concept of collocations in corpus linguistics (e.g., [2,27]).

For the usage type (see Sect. 4.4), we adopt the typology proposed by Moon [20] and Čermák [8]. Moon elaborates a traditional view applied to corpus data. In addition to the traditional categories (*proverbs*, *similes*, *verbal phrases*) she splits up MWEs into *set phrases* (recurrent patterns that have specialized meanings or functions), *idioms* (set phrases which are typically figurative and which have non-compositional meanings), *formulae* (recurrent phrases having specific functions but not necessarily problematic for meaning) and *gambits* (remarks that one makes to someone in order to start a conversation).

Čermák's classification of Czech MWEs, used in SČFI [11], is based primarily on the properties of their components, resulting in the following classes: *propositional* (including proverbs), *similes*, *collocational* (verbal, nominal, grammatical, lexical) and *quasiphrasemes* (verbonominal).

A principled approach to collocations[5] is one of the highlights of the Meaning-Text Theory (MTT) [18]. To model the semantics of collocations, MTT uses more than 60 syntagmatic lexical functions. A function such as *Magn* maps *rain* into *heavy*, with the collocation *heavy rain* as the result. As a promising strategy, lexical functions can be included as a semantic component of our collocation entries. Then we can identify all entries including identical functions such as *Magn* and

[4] For more cf. https://typo.uni-konstanz.de/parseme/index.php/results/papers.

[5] Our taxonomy treats collocations as "statistically idiomatic MWEs" (see Sect. 7.6).

lexical items such as *heavy* or even entries expressing the same concepts across various languages.

The task of extracting collocations undergoing syntactic modifications and transformations is investigated e.g. by Seretan [26].[6] Candidates for collocations are identified in a parse tree built by a symbolic parser and ranked according to syntactic and statistical clues. Instead of using parse trees to extract MWE candidates, we plan to use the MWE lexicon as a lexical resource for a parser to identify MWEs in texts, but using a parser in the extraction task is an interesting and open option.

Most of our taxonomy is based on the taxonomy of MWEs developed in the *PARSEME* project[7] and adapted for Czech, with a stress on the treatment of variants, fragments and the specifics of Czech as a language with rich morphology and relatively free word order.

4 Typology

Multiword expressions can be defined as "lexical items that (a) can be decomposed into multiple lexemes; and (b) display lexical, syntactic, semantic pragmatic and/or statistical idiomaticity" [25]. While the first property is straightforward to identify, at least in a language marking word boundaries, the second property is more complex. In addition to its role in the diagnostics of MWEs, idiomaticity and its types can also be used for their classification. Building upon the proposal of [1], the *PARSEME* project categorizes MWEs according to their (i) syntactic structure, (ii) fixedness/flexibility and (iii) idiomaticity. We adopt and extend this tri-partite taxonomy. Most of the extensions are motivated by the goal to design a lexical template useful to a human user as well as NLP applications, but some extensions are driven by the MWE-relevant properties of Czech as an inflectional and free word order language. The extensions concern the following aspects of MWEs: definition, usage type (MWE type in traditional terms), valency patterns, use of fragments, variants, style/register and a more detailed specification of some types (e.g. morphological idiomaticity).

Some parts of the description assume the standard rules of Czech as default: when describing features of MWEs, it accounts – except for valency – only for deviations and irregularities with respect to Czech grammar. For instance, word order is specified only if it deviates from the standard word order in Czech: e.g. if an attributive adjective follows its head noun or the order of verbal complements cannot be permuted.

According to the multidimensional taxonomy a single MWE is described from all aspects described below. The standard lexical properties (lemma, definition, style/register, usage type) are given first as Sects. 4.1–4.4. Syntactic structure, fixedness/variability and idiomaticity are described in separate Sects. 5–7.

---

[6] Seretan uses the term *collocation* in the linguistic, syntactically motivated sense. For the broader, statistically defined class she adopts the term *co-occurrence*.

[7] Cf. http://typo.uni-konstanz.de/parseme.

4.1 Lemma

A MWE's lemma is a string representing a given MWE in the lexicon and in the annotated/analyzed text, concatenating base forms of inflected components and inflected forms of frozen components in an unmarked order; e.g. *zaklepat bačkorama* 'kick the bucket' (lit. 'shake the slippers').

4.2 Definition

The definition is an explanation of the MWE's meaning; e.g. *na tom nesejde* (lit. 'it does not descend on it') is defined as "it makes no difference"; *vynést někomu spaní* (lit. 'to carry out someone's sleeping') is defined as "a polite saying used as an invitation: *pojď'te dál, ať nám nevynesete spaní* (lit. 'come in, so that you won't carry out our sleeping')"; the verb is always negated.

4.3 Style/Register

Stylistic/register marker characterizing the entire MWE with respect to the register distinguishes between the values below. Note that individual word forms as MWE components are also marked for style/register, but the component values are not necessarily shared by the value for the whole MWE, as in *má to na háku* below, with all forms standard but the whole MWE colloquial.

1. **Standard**, e.g. *člověk člověku vlkem* 'homo homini lupus'
2. **Colloquial**, e.g. [*má*] *to na háku* '[he] couldn't care less'
3. **Expressive** (vulgar), e.g. [*má*] *po prdeli* 'his fun is over/he is off [his] fun' (lit. '[he has] after arse')
4. **Dialect**, e.g. *tož jaká?* 'how are you?' (lit. 'well which?')
5. **Other** – bookish expressions, e.g. *země oplývající mlékem a strdím* 'a land flowing with milk and honey', or translationese, i.e. MWEs appearing originally in translations or transfers of foreign structures

4.4 Usage Type

Usage type characterizes a MWE as being one of the following kinds, out of which (1)–(5) are set phrases [20]:

1. **Proverb** is defined as "a short, generally known sentence of the folk which contains wisdom, truth, morals, and traditional views in a metaphorical, fixed and memorizable form and which is handed down from generation to generation" [19, p. 394], e.g. *komu se nelení tomu se zelení* 'no pains, no gains' (lit. approx. 'who isn't lazy gets green fields').
2. **Weather lore** is an informal folklore saying related to the prediction of the weather; e.g. *studený máj – v stodole ráj*, lit. 'cold May – paradise in the barn'.

3. **Comparison/simile**: A fixed MWE typically constituted by a verbal phrase and usually containing a comparison conjunction, where the subject is a variable: *[Petr] je červený jako rak* '[Peter] is red as a boiled lobster' (lit. 'Peter is red as a crayfish').
4. **Citation** is a part of another text or a saying, typically repeated verbatim. It may be known from the literature or other media, also as the name of a cultural and other entity: *kostky jsou vrženy* 'the die is cast'.
5. **Set phrase**, i.e. "recurrent pattern that has a specialized meaning or function" [20]: e.g. *na tom nesejde* 'it makes no difference'.
6. **Formula**: recurrent phrases with specific functions, not necessarily problematic for meaning [20]; also called grammatical idioms [7,8], i.e. compound function words such as: *v souvislosti s* 'referring to', 'in conjunction with'.
7. **Term** is defined as a "designation of a defined concept in a special language by a linguistic expression" [15] or "a verbal designation of a general concept in a specific subject field" (ISO 1087-1:2000) or "a lexeme used unambiguously for an entity specific to a field of science, discipline, but also to a trade or (hand)craft or a special profession" (translated from [9, p. 132]), e.g. *primitivní funkce* 'primitive function'.

5 Syntactic Structure

5.1 Syntactic Type

Syntactic type concerns a categorization of MWEs according to the syntactic category of the whole unit, usually a constituent. The following kinds of constructions are distinguished, mainly according to the syntactic head:[8]

Noun phrase: *něžné pohlaví* 'weaker sex'; *svatý klid* 'peace and quiet'
Adjectival phrase: *všeho schopný* 'capable of anything'
Verb phrase: *neprodat svou kůži lacino* 'hold one's own', 'sell one's life dearly' (lit. 'not to sell one's skin cheaply')
Light verb construction: *dávat pokyny* 'to give instructions'; *dělat si [z koho] prdel* 'to take the piss [out of sb]'
Adverbial phrase: *volky nevolky* 'willy-nilly'
Prepositional phrase: *pro slepičí kvoč* 'for chicken squat'; *na věky věků[v]* 'for ever and ever'
Conjunctional: *ergo kladívko* 'thus', 'Q.E.D.' (lit. 'ergo gavel') – used before making a conclusion
Interjectional: *ajta krajta!* 'whoops!' (lit. 'aytah python') – (unpleasant) surprise
Clausal: *stokrát nic umořilo osla* 'eight times the donkey squirmed'
Compound and complex sentential: *když ptáčka lapají, pěkně mu zpívají* 'promises, promises!' (lit. 'when they are catching a bird, they are singing to him nicely').

[8] Some of the types below can be binomials, i.e. expressions containing two words that are juxtaposed, or joined by a conjunction (usually *and* or *or*) or preposition: *day and night*, G. *gang und gäbe* 'usual', Cz. *[děvče] krev a mlíko* 'a ruddy, healthy-looking, full-figured [girl]' (lit. '[a girl] blood and milk').

5.2 Basic Pattern

The pattern is derived from the MWE's syntactic tree (a manually checked parse) and represented as a sequence of extended part-of-speech codes, e.g.:

- *s ničím se nemazlit*: (Prep.INSTR PronNeg.INSTR Refl Verb) 'make quick work of something' (lit. 'with nothing to fondle')
- *sedět modelem*: (Verb Noun.INSTR) 'to pose model (for someone)'

5.3 Dependency and Constituency Tree

Each MWE is represented as a dependency and constituency tree annotated with syntactic functions. The tree is built by a parser and then manually checked. For instance, *připravit [někoho] o rozum* (7-a) is represented as (7-b) (dependency tree) and (7-c) (constituency tree), where OBJ, HD, SH and DH denote an object, head, surface head and deep head, respectively.[9] Nodes in the trees may be reference targets of statements in other parts of the lexical entry.

(7) a. *připravit* [někoho] *o rozum*
to rid [someone] of reason
'to irritate someone considerably/to drive someone mad/crazy'
b. (*připravit* (*někoho*.OBJ) (*o*.PREP (*rozum*.OBJ)))
c. [*připravit*.HD *někoho*.OBJ [*o*.SH *rozum*.DH].OBJ]

5.4 Valency

A lexical entry includes information on valency assigned both to the entire MWE and to its component parts, typically verbal and adjectival lexemes. With valency, the principle stating that only idiosyncratic phenomena of MWEs are specified is not observed: valency of MWE components is described even if they take the expected set of arguments or adjuncts with the expected set of morphosyntactic properties. If a verb contained in a MWE is included in the valency lexicon,[10] the corresponding valency frame of the verb is used (a verb can have more valency frames), otherwise – in case the verb or the appropriate valency frame is missing in the valency lexicon – the corresponding valency frame is added. The valency of the entire MWE and of its syntactic head can differ. E.g. a MWE is constituted by a light verb construction (such as *dávat pokyny* 'give instructions' where the verb's Theme (Patient) *pokyny* is part of the MWE and – unlike the MWE's indirect dative object – it is not present in the MWE's

[9] In prepositional phrases (and in some other kinds of phrases), two syntactic heads are distinguished: (i) surface syntactic head and (ii) deep syntactic head constituted by the preposition and the NP's head noun, respectively.

[10] Currently, we use VALLEX [16]. We plan to add entries and/or more information from other electronically available valency lexicons of Czech, such as PDT-VALLEX, and use MWE-related information available in some valency lexicons, cf. [28] and [23].

valency frame). Moreover, a MWE can display idiosyncratic valency behaviour. For instance in *dát na srozuměnou, že* ...'to make clear that ... ' (lit. 'to give on understanding that ... ') – the valency slot for *that*-clause is not specified by any of the component parts. This slot substitutes the original Theme (Patient) slot of the verb *dát* 'to give' while the other slots – Recipient (Addressee) and Agent (Actor) are retained.

6 Fixedness/Flexibility

This section is concerned with the range of options available for a MWE and its parts. Lexical modifications of the headword are the topic of Sects. 6.1 and 6.2. The rest is concerned with restrictions. Any other non-standard but MWE-specific options are presented in Sect. 7. Thus, a MWE acceptable only with a certain colloquial form is a case of morphological restriction (Sect. 6.6, e.g. in *sbaštit to i s chlupama* 'swallow it hook, line and sinker' the colloquial form *chlupama* is used rather than the literary form *chlupy*). On the other hand, a MWE including a form which does not exist outside the MWE is a case of morphological idiomaticity (Sect. 7, e.g. *sloupích* instead of *sloupech*, as in *jména hloupých na všech sloupích*, lit. 'the names of the stupid on all columns').

6.1 Variants

Some elements in MWEs can appear in variants, e.g. in the MWE *hodit/házet/zahodit/zahazovat flintu do žita* 'throw in the towel' (lit. 'throw the gun into a rye field'). The verb *hodit* can appear in its perfective or imperfective form, including prefixed forms. On the other hand, we do not explicitly state the fact that the lexemes can occur in various forms according to the rules of Czech inflectional and derivational morphology.

Variants of a given MWE may share some of its properties. Rather than repeating the shared properties in separate entries, a single entry for multiple variants may provide individual variant-specific properties.

6.2 Fragments

Some MWEs occur in texts as fragments (e.g. *až naprší* instead of the full form *až naprší a uschne* 'never', lit. 'when the rain is over and dries out'). A MWE may also be changed into an expression preserving only very few characteristic words. These core parts of the MWE help to detect the modified MWEs in texts. For example, *pýcha předchází pád* 'pride precedes a fall' has two core words: *pýcha* 'pride', and *pád* 'fall'. A corpus query using these two core words returns, e.g., ... *za pýchou jak stín kluše pád* '... behind pride like a shadow a fall trots'.

Sometimes, MWEs may have two alternative cores. E.g., any variant of *hodit flintu do žita* 'throw in the towel' (see Sect. 6.1 above) must either include *hodit/házet* [*něco*] *do žita*, lit. 'throw [something] into the rye [field]', e.g. *hodit fotoaparát do žita* 'to throw the camera into the rye field', i.e. 'abandon the career of a photographer', or *hodit/házet flintu* [někam], lit. 'throw the gun [somewhere]'.

6.3 Word Order

For Czech as a free word order language we assume that MWEs follow the same general pattern, unless some restrictions specific to a MWE apply.[11] At the same time, word-order restrictions due to the general patterns of Czech apply unless blocked by an explicit statement. The general patterns are often category-specific: verb and its complements can be freely permuted and other constituents may intervene, while prepositions immediately precede their NPs. In line with the division of labour between Sects. 6 and 7, only restrictions on standard word-order patterns are stated. For patterns not occurring outside MWEs, cf. Sect. 7.

6.4 Internal Modifiability

By default, a content word as a MWE element can be modified: *uhodily* [*třeskuté*] *mrazy* 'the [bitter] frost started' (lit. 'struck [bitter] frost'). On the other hand, none of the words in *z cizího krev neteče* 'drive it like a rental' (lit. 'it doesn't bleed from a stranger') can be modified. Such restrictions are stated again in reference to the syntactic structure.

A closed set of words can be used to modify key elements of a MWE (e.g. *příslovečný* 'proverbial'). This option is not explicitly specified in the entries.

6.5 Transformations

Again, only patterns unexpected from the viewpoint of the standard grammar of Czech are specified. The following kinds of transformations are accounted for:

- Passivization/De-passivization:
  - MWE cannot be passivized: *jak si přejete* 'as you wish', although the verb *přát* itself can be passivized.
  - MWE cannot have an active form: *nebylo mu* [*to*] *přáno* 'it was not granted him', although the verb *přát* itself has active forms.
- Nominalization – a verb in the MWE cannot be nominalized:
  - By default, nominalization is possible: *hrát si* [*s někým*] *jako kočka s myší* 'play a cat-and-mouse game [with sb]' (lit. 'play [with someone] like cat with mouse') → *hra*.NOUN *na kočku a myš* 'a cat-and-mouse game' (lit. 'a play at cat and mouse').
  - Nominalization is impossible: in *na tom nesejde* (lit. 'it does not descend on it') 'it makes no difference' – the verb *nesejde* cannot be nominalized.
- Adjectivization – a verb in the MWE cannot be adjectivized:
  - By default, adjectivization is possible: *smrtelně zblednout* lit. 'turn pale mortally' → *smrtelně bledý*.ADJ lit. 'deadly pale'.
  - Adjectivization is impossible: in the proverb *sejde z očí, sejde z mysli* 'out of sight, out of mind' (lit. 'goes from eyes, goes from mind') the verb *sejde* cannot be adjectivized.

[11] Similarly as traditional Czech grammars, we see topicalization as a word-order rather than transformation phenomenon.

6.6 Morphological Restrictions

Morphological restrictions are listed for each component with some morphological constraints such as number or case for nouns, tense and mood for verbs. Some of these restrictions result from the syntactic function of the word (the subject may be only in the nominative case), other morphological restrictions originate in semantics or usage.

E.g., the MWEs *lukulské*.PL *hody*.PL 'Lucullan banquet' is only used in the plural number, *stůj*.IMP *co stůj*.IMP 'at all costs' (lit. 'cost what cost') is used only in the imperative mood. While negation is possible by default, the impossibility of negation/affirmation of a component (verb, adjective, noun or adverb) is stated explicitly, as in ***ber***, *kde* ***ber*** 'take wherever you can' (lit. 'take where take'), or in *v* ***neposlední*** *řadě* 'last but not least' (lit. 'in the non-final row'), where only negated form of the adjective is possible.

Morphological restrictions can apply also to the use of style variants. Some MWEs may contain only colloquial word forms, such as *sbaštit to i s chlup****ama*** 'swallow it hook, line and sinker' (lit. 'to devour it with hair') – the form *chlupama* contains a colloquial morph *-ama* expressing instrumental plural of the lexeme *chlup* 'hair'.

7 Idiomaticity

Idiomaticity describes the degree of MWE's idiosyncrasis/anomaly on the following levels: lexical, morphological, syntactic, semantic, pragmatic and statistical. According to [1, p. 4]:

> "In the context of MWEs, *idiomaticity* refers to markedness or deviation from the basic properties of the component lexemes [...] A given MWE is often idiomatic at multiple levels (e.g. syntactic, semantic and statistical in the case of *by and large*) [...] Closely related to the notion of idiomaticity is *compositionality*, which we consider to be the degree to which the features of the parts of a MWE combine to predict the features of the whole. While compositionality is often construed as applying exclusively to semantic idiomatic [MWEs] (hence by 'non-compositional MWE', researchers tend to mean a semantically-idiomatic MWE), in practice it can apply across all the same levels as idiomaticity."

We adopt this view of idiomaticity and distinguish its types as follows:

7.1 Lexical

Lexical idiomaticity concerns the MWEs including:

- Monocollocable word forms: *křížem krážem* 'crisscross'
- Almost monocollocable word forms (=associated with a very limited set of words): *úhlavní nepřítel* 'arch enemy'

- Negated-only words: *nedílný* ‘integral’ in *nedílná součást* ‘integral part’
- Foreign loans: *mírnyx týrnyx* ‘for no reason’, ‘for/over nothing’ (from German: *mir nichts dir nichts*)
- Macaronic structure: *per hubam* ‘by word of mouth’ (Latin preposition *per* and Czech *huba* ‘mouth’ with the Latin feminine sg. accusative ending *-m*)

Unlike in [1], our lexical idiomaticity does not imply syntactic, semantic, or statistical idiomaticity.

7.2 Morphological

Morphological idiomaticity concerns non-standard morphological forms, e.g.:

- *chca nechca* ‘nolens volens’; this is a variant of the standard form *chtě nechtě*
- *na věky věkův* ‘for ever and ever’ – the form *věkův* ‘ever/time’ is an obsolete genitive plural form of the lexeme’s *věk* ‘time’; this is a variant of the standard contemporary form *na věky věků*

7.3 Syntactic

Syntactic idiomaticity describes syntactic irregularities of the whole MWE:

- Anacoluthon: as in a modified proverb: *kdo po tobě kamenem, ty po něm chlebem* ‘if someone throws stones at you, throw back bread’ (lit. ‘who [throws] a stone at you, you [will throw] bread at him’)
- Attraction: *je širší*.COMP *než delší*.COMP ‘he/she is wider than taller’ – the comparative *delší* ‘taller’ is here only due to the presence of the comparative form *širší* ‘wider’
- Aposiopesis: *já se na to* ... ‘what the f...!’ (lit. ‘I will [shit]... on it’)
- Ellipsis: *nevím, co (dělat) dřív* ‘I do not know what (to do) first’
- Other: *kluk pitomá* ‘stupid chap’, the adjective *pitomá* ‘stupid’ is a non-inflected feminine form, incongruent with the masculine *kluk* ‘chap’
- Word order: e.g. adjective following its head noun – *liška podšitá* ‘crafty devil’ (lit. ‘fox with lining’); preposition following the NP: *všemu navzdory* ‘despite everything’ (lit. ‘everything despite’); PPs where the head noun is premodified by an incongruous attribute: *v pravém slova smyslu* ‘in the strict sense of the word’ (lit. ‘in the strict of word sense’)

7.4 Semantic

MWEs with a non-compositional meaning; the option of literal meaning is also stated:

- **Often**: e.g. *mít holý zadek* ‘be poor’ (lit. ‘to have a naked bottom’), *natáhnout bačkory* ‘to kick the bucket’ (lit. ‘to stretch out/pull on slippers’)
- **Rarely**: e.g. *kočičí hlavy* ‘cobblestones’ (lit. ‘cats’ heads’)

- **Never**: e.g. *nasadit komu psí hlavu* 'heap dirt upon sb' (lit. 'put a dog's head on sb'); [*být*] *zamilovaný/á až po uši* '[to be] head over heels in love with sb' (lit. '[to be] in love up to the ears')

A special type of a semantic idiom is semantic contamination – a combination of two idioms: *mlsný jazýček na vahách* (lit. 'choosy little tongue on the balance') – from [mít] *mlsný jazýček* '[to be] fussy about food' (lit. '[to have] a choosy little tongue') and [být] jazýčkem na vahách 'to hold the balance' (lit. '[to be] a little tongue on the balance'). There is no lexical entry for the contamination, yet the parts are identified in the text and assigned appropriate lemmas.

7.5 Pragmatic

MWEs display pragmatic idiomaticity if they are used in specific situations. E.g. *smím prosit?* 'may I have this dance?' (lit. 'may I [say] please?').

7.6 Statistical

A statistically idiomatic MWE is a fixed but semantically compositional collocation (its components cannot be substituted by synonyms): *silný čaj* 'strong tea' vs. **vydatný čaj* 'substantial tea'; *vydatný oběd* 'substantial lunch' vs. **silná strava* 'strong food'. This group also includes terms, compound prepositions (*vsouvislosti s* 'in connection with') and compound conjunctions (*i když* 'even though'), see compound function words in Sect. 4.4 (6 – Formula).

8 Lexical Entry

The lexical entry[12] of a MWE contains definition of its single slots (representing syntagmatic positions of its components) and their possible fillers (representing possible variable realizations of the components), so that descriptions, features or relations may be assigned separately to the MWE as a whole, or to its single components or their different realizations, as needed. Slots may also be marked as optional or mandatory components of the MWE. Fillers may refer to sequences of other slots, allowing for grouping or construction of tree structures, in order to facilitate assigning descriptions to different partial structures within the MWE.

9 Using the Lexicon of MWEs in Parsing

One example of actual use of the MWE lexicon is dependency parsing of MWEs. We use a stochastic dependency parser (e.g. TurboParser, [17]) to parse any text data. If the parser does not encounter a MWE in its training data, it parses it as a normal text, resulting in a higher percentage of erroneously parsed MWEs. We

[12] The structure of the lexical entry is based on the principles of structured lexical description proposed in [29], though in a substantially simplified way.

solve the problem in two ways, both using the MWE lexicon and the information about the syntactic structures of MWEs it contains. A subset of MWEs, such as compound prepositions (*ve srovnání s*, 'compared to'), that (i) have a fixed word order, (ii) are contiguous, (iii) have a well-defined syntactic structure and (iv) have limited possibilities to be modified by external elements is processed as follows. Before the parsing proper, each MWE of this type is converted into a single token representing the whole MWE. After parsing, the token is reconverted into its constituent parts and assigned a correct syntactic structure specified in the MWE lexicon. In this way, the parser does not need to parse the internal structure of the MWE at all. The other, larger set of MWEs (having free word order, being externally modifiable etc.) is automatically identified in the text already parsed and, if necessary, their syntactic structure is corrected in order to comply with the structure assigned to this MWE in the lexicon.

10 Conclusion

We (1) propose a complex typology of Czech MWEs based on an existing 3D approach classifying MWEs according to their syntactic structure, fixedness/flexibility and idiomaticity, and (2) compile a representative lexicon based on this typology. We have expanded this approach to better suit Czech as an inflectional, free word order language. The lexicon, which is to contain ca. 7000 entries, a part excerpted from a phraseological dictionary, another part extracted automatically from Czech corpora using statistic measures of fixedness, will allow for automatic MWE identification in text including modified MWE forms and fragments. The lexicon can be useful for NLP tools (word-sense disambiguation, lexicography tasks, parsing), and for human users, especially with corpus data linked with the lexicon, which allows for the study of MWEs with their variants in a real context. We plan to refine the typology if new (sub)kinds of MWEs encountered would call for such a refinement, to extend the lexicon and to focus on criteria specifying what are variants of a MWE and what are autonomous MWEs in the lexicon.

The MWE typology with our extensions can be easily adapted to other languages, mainly for those with rich inflection.

References

1. Baldwin, T., Kim, S.N.: Multiword expressions. In: Indurkhya, N., Damerau, F.J. (eds.) Handbook of Natural Language Processing, 2nd edn., pp. 267–292. CRC Press, Boca Raton (2010)
2. Barnbrook, G., Mason, O., Krishnamurthy, R.: Collocation. Applications and Implications. Palgrave Macmillan UK, Basingstoke (2013)
3. Bejček, E., Hajič, J., Straňák, P., Urešová, Z.: Extracting verbal multiword data from rich treebank annotation. In: Proceedings of the 15th International Workshop on Treebanks and Linguistic Theories (TLT 2015), pp. 13–24. Indiana University, Bloomington (2017)

4. Burger, H., Dobrovol'skij, D., Kühn, P., Norrick, N.R. (eds.): Phraseology: An International Handbook of Contemporary Research. Walter de Gruyter, Berlin, New York (2007)
5. Burger, H., Dobrovol'skij, D., Kühn, P., Norrick, N.R.: Phraseology: subject area, terminology and research topic. In: Burger et al. [4], pp. 10–19
6. Cvrček, V.: Kvantitativní analýza kontextu. Nakladatelství Lidové noviny, Prague (2014)
7. Dobrovol'skij, D., Filipenko, T.: Russian phraseology. In: Burger et al. [4], pp. 714–727
8. Čermák, F.: Czech and General Phraseology. Karolinum, Prague (2007)
9. Čermák, F.: Lexikon a sémantika. Nakladatelstí Lidové noviny, Prague (2010)
10. Čermák, F.: Frazeologie a idiomatika: Jejich podstata a proměnlivost názorů na ně. Časopis pro moderní filologii **98**(2), 199–217 (2016)
11. Čermák, F., et al.: Slovník české frazeologie a idiomatiky (SČFI), vol. 1–4. Academia/Leda, Prague (1983–2009)
12. Evert, S.: The statistics of word cooccurrences: word pairs and collocations. Ph.D. thesis, IMS, University of Stuttgart, Stuttgart (2004). http://www.collocations.de
13. Hnátková, M.: Značkování frazémů a idiomů v Českém národním korpusu s pomocí slovníku české frazeologie a idiomatiky. Slovo a slovesnost **63**(2), 117–126 (2002)
14. Klégr, A.: Lexikální kolokace: základní přehled o vývoji pojetí. Časopis pro moderní filologii **98**(1), 95–103 (2016)
15. Lauriston, A.: Criteria for measuring term recognition. In: Proceedings of the Seventh Conference on European Chapter of the Association for Computational Linguistics, EACL 1995, pp. 17–22. Morgan Kaufmann Publishers, San Francisco (1995)
16. Lopatková, M., Kettnerová, V., Bejček, E., Skwarska, K., Žabokrtský, Z.: VALLEX 2.6.3 - Valency Lexicon of Czech Verbs. Institute of Formal and Applied Linguistics, Faculty of Mathematics and Physics, Charles University (2014)
17. Martins, A., Almeida, M., Smith, N.A.: Turning on the turbo: fast third-order non-projective turbo parsers. In: Annual Meeting of the Association for Computational Linguistics - ACL, pp. 617–622 (2013)
18. Mel'čuk, I.: Collocations: définition, rôle et utilité. In: Grossmann, F., Tutin, A. (eds.) Les collocations: analyse et traitement, pp. 23–32. De Werelt, Amsterdam (2003)
19. Mieder, W.: Proverbs Are Never Out of Season: Popular Wisdom in the Modern Age. Peter Lang, New York (2012)
20. Moon, R.: Corpus linguistic approaches with English corpora. In: Burger et al. [4], pp. 1045–1059
21. Nunberg, G., Sag, I.A., Wasow, T.: Idioms. Language **70**(3), 491–538 (1994)
22. Pecina, P.: Lexical association measures and collocation extraction. Lang. Resour. Eval. **44**(1–2), 137–158 (2010)
23. Przepiórkowski, A., Hajič, J., Hajnicz, E., Urešová, Z.: Phraseology in two Slavic valency dictionaries: limitations and perspectives. Int. J. Lexicogr. **30**(1), 1–38 (2017)
24. Richter, F., Sailer, M.: Idiome mit phraseologisierten Teilsätzen: Eine Fallstudie zur Formalisierung von Konstruktionen im Rahmen der HPSG. In: Lasch, A., Ziem, A. (eds.) Grammatik als Netzwerk von Konstruktionen, pp. 291–312. de Gruyter, Berlin (2014)
25. Sag, I.A., Baldwin, T., Bond, F., Copestake, A., Flickinger, D.: Multiword expressions: a pain in the neck for NLP. In: Gelbukh, A. (ed.) CICLing 2002. LNCS, vol. 2276, pp. 1–15. Springer, Heidelberg (2002). doi:10.1007/3-540-45715-1_1

26. Seretan, V.: Syntax-Based Collocation Extraction. Text, Speech and Language Technology, vol. 44. Springer, Dordrecht (2011). doi:10.1007/978-94-007-0134-2
27. Sinclair, J.M.: Corpus, Concordance, Collocation. Oxford University Press, Oxford (1991)
28. Urešová, Z.: Building the PDT-VALLEX valency lexicon. In: On-line Proceedings of the Fifth Corpus Linguistics Conference. University of Liverpool (2009)
29. Vondřička, P.: Formalized contrastive lexical description: a framework for bilingual dictionaries. LINCOM GmbH, München (2014)

Predicate-Argument Analysis to Build a Phraseology Module and to Increase Conceptual Relation Expressiveness

Arianne Reimerink(✉) and Pilar León-Araúz

Department of Translation and Interpreting, University of Granada, Granada, Spain
{arianne,pleon}@ugr.es

Abstract. EcoLexicon, a multilingual and multimodal terminological knowledge base (TKB) on the environment, needs improvements: more expressive non-hierarchical relations and a phraseology module consistent with knowledge representation in the other modules of the TKB. Both issues must be addressed by analyzing predicate-argument structure in text. In this paper, we explain our methodology for predicate-argument analysis with the case study on the conceptual relation *affects*. We take a semi-automatic approach to extract term-verb-term collocates with Sketch Engine [1]. Then the verbs are classified according to the lexical domains proposed by Faber & Mairal [2] and the arguments in conceptual categories based on the knowledge contained in EcoLexicon. To validate the lexical domains and conceptual categories, an automatic clustering method based on word2vec [3] is applied. The analysis of verbs and arguments contributes to the refinement of our semantic relations and categories as well as to the population of the phraseological module.

Keywords: Predicate-argument analysis · Phraseology · Conceptual relation expressiveness

1 Introduction

EcoLexicon[1] is a multilingual and multimodal terminological knowledge base (TKB) on the environment. In the construction of the TKB, two different but related problems have arisen. On the one hand, we are working on the design of a phraseology module that is consistent with the knowledge extraction and representation methodology based on triplets, or conceptual propositions, in EcoLexicon [4]. On the other hand, the semantic expressivity of some of the conceptual relations in the TKB's semantic networks should be improved. For instance, conceptual propositions such as EROSION *affects* LANDFORM would be more meaningful if the relation was *reduces* instead of *affects*. However, the phraseological module of the TKB should also contain other verbs lexicalizing and specifying the nuclear meaning of reduction (e.g. *carve*, *degrade*, *erode*, etc.) as well as other terms that can also fill the

[1] ecolexicon.ugr.es.

R. Mitkov (Ed.): Europhras 2017, LNAI 10596, pp. 176–190, 2017.
https://doi.org/10.1007/978-3-319-69805-2_13

slots of these arguments (e.g. *weathering*, *cliff*, etc.). To solve these problems, the first step is to analyze predicate-argument structure in real text.

We understand phraseology from a broad perspective as all word combinations with certain stability [5, 6]. According to Rundell [7] (vii), collocations are as important as grammar since they make speakers/writers sound fluent. In specialized domains, they are perceived by language users to contribute to the domain-specific flavor of special languages [8]. In this line, recent studies have highlighted the importance of verbs, their collocations and argument structure in specialized terminology [9, 10], but there are currently few terminographic resources that incorporate them (exceptions are DiCoInfo and DiCoEnviro [11] and DicSci [12], for example). If terminological knowledge bases (TKBs) want to be truly helpful for specialized writing, phraseological information should be added in a consistent and user-friendly way.

In an attempt to connect the description of predicative units to the knowledge structure [11: 89] of EcoLexicon and make the phraseological module consistent with the conceptual module, it should be based on the same principles. Therefore, we propose a design based on the categorization of term-verb-term collocates reflecting the different lexicalizations of conceptual propositions. In this way, semantic relations can be further specified according to specialized predicates. In turn, phraseological templates can be generalized based on the semantic types related in conceptual networks. However, these semantic types still need to be extracted in a consistent way. In this paper, we explain our methodology for predicate-argument analysis with the case study on the conceptual relation *affects*. The analysis of verbs and arguments will contribute to the refinement of our conceptual relations and categories as well as to the population of the phraseology module.

In Sect. 2, the EcoLexicon TKB is described in more detail. In Sect. 3, the methodology for predicate-argument analysis is explained. Section 4 describes how the results of predicate-argument analysis affect the representation of conceptual networks and phraseology module design in EcoLexicon. In Sect. 5, word2vec clustering is used to validate the conceptual categories and lexical domains defined in Sect. 3 and to extract new seed terms for further analysis. Conclusions are drawn and future work is proposed in Sect. 6.

2 EcoLexicon

EcoLexicon is a multilingual and multimodal terminological knowledge base (TKB) on the Environment. It currently contains 3,601 concepts and 20,211 terms in English, Spanish, French, German, Russian and Modern Greek. It is the practical application of Frame-based Terminology (FBT), a cognitively-oriented theory of specialized knowledge representation that applies certain features of Frame Semantics [13] to structure specialized domains and create non-language-specific representations. FBT focuses on: (i) conceptual organization; (ii) the multidimensional nature of specialized knowledge units; and (iii) the extraction of semantic and syntactic information through the use of multilingual corpora. FBT operates on the premise that specialized knowledge units activate domain-specific semantic frames that are in consonance with users' background knowledge [14].

EcoLexicon is an internally coherent information system, which is organized according to conceptual and linguistic premises at the macro- as well as the micro-structural level. It targets users such as translators, technical writers, and environmental experts who need to understand specialized environmental concepts with a view to writing and/or translating domain specific texts. Users interact with EcoLexicon through a visual interface (see Fig. 1). The top horizontal bar gives users access to the term/concept search engine. The vertical bar on the left of the screen provides information regarding the search concept, namely its definition, term designations, associated resources, general conceptual role, and phraseology. The center area has tabs that access the following: (i) the history of concepts/terms visited; (ii) the results of the most recent query; (iii) all the terms alphabetically arranged; (iv) the shortest path between two concepts; and (v) concordances for a term. On the center of the screen, the conceptual map is shown as well as the icons that allow users to configure and personalize it for their needs. The standard representation mode shows a multi-level semantic network whose concepts are all linked in some way to the search concept, which is at its center [15].

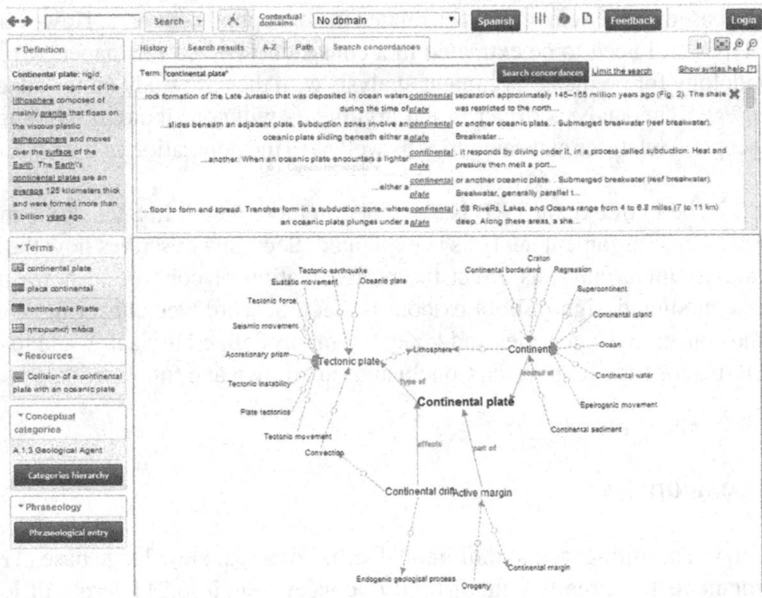

Fig. 1. EcoLexicon user interface.

2.1 Conceptual Relations

Conceptual description in EcoLexicon is based on concept types and their relational behavior. We use a fixed set of conceptual relations (see Table 1) that have been defined according to coherent and systematic criteria in order to make EcoLexicon a consistent resource at its different representational levels.

Table 1. EcoLexicon inventory of conceptual relations.

Relation category	Relation	Example
Generic-specific	Type_of	GROYNE *type_of* COASTAL DEFENSE STRUCTURE
Part-whole	Part_of	SPILLWAY *part_of* DAM
	Made_of	GROYNE *made_of* WOOD
	Delimited_by	STRATOSPHERE *delimited_by* STRATOPAUSE
	Located_at	GROYNE *located_at* COAST
	Takes_place_in	LITTORAL DRIFT *takes_place_in* SEA
	Phase_of	PUMPING *phase_of* DREDGING
Non-hierarchical	Affects	GROYNE *affects* LITTORAL DRIFT
	Causes	WATER *causes* EROSION
	Result_of	ACCRETION *result_of* SEDIMENTATION
	Has_function	AQUIFER *has_function* WATER SUPPLY
	Studies	POTAMOLOGY *studies* SURFACE CURRENT
	Measures	PLUVIOMETER *measures* PRECIPITATION
	Effected_by	DREDGING *effected_by* DREDGER

For instance, meronymy has been split up into six different relations, since not all parts interact in the same way with their wholes. In the same way the expressiveness of meronymy has been increased by splitting it up into six different relations, some non-hierarchical relations need more specification as well. This is the case of *affects*. This conceptual relation has become a catch-all relation in EcoLexicon, where for example ABLATION *affects* GLACIER and WATER DENSITY *affects* WATER. In the first case, the relation expressed would be that GLACIER is a *patient* of ABLATION, whereas in the second WATER DENSITY is an *attribute* of WATER. An example of a predicate-based relation where more expressiveness would be needed is BREAKWATER *affects* BEACH. In this case, it would be interesting to know how one affects the other, as the consequences of having a break-water may be positive for a beach (e.g. *protect*) in some cases and negative in others (e.g. *erode*). One case where the relation is not only inexpressive but also confusing is where EcoLexicon tells its users that ULTRAVIOLET RADIATION *affects* OZONE and OZONE *affects* ULTRAVIOLET RADIATION. We will discuss the latter in detail in Sect. 3. Refining the *affects* relation would greatly improve knowledge acquisition by non-expert end users.

2.2 Phraseology Module

The phraseology module of EcoLexicon is currently under construction. Until recently, phraseological information was stored at the term level, where verbs were related to arguments contained in EcoLexicon as shown in Fig. 2. The verbs that collocate with the term were classified according to the lexical domain and subdomain based on Faber & Mairal [2] (see Sect. 3). The partial phraseology entry for hurricane shown in Fig. 2 includes the lexical domains Action and Change. Within Action, the subdomain "to come against something with sudden force" includes the definition of the phraseological pattern and the verbs *hit*, *batter*, *strike*, and *blast*. By clicking on *hit*, the user accesses four usage examples as well as a note section with information about meaning restrictions. In this case, the note states, among other things, that the natural force is usually an atmospheric agent, water agent, natural disaster or atmospheric condition [10].

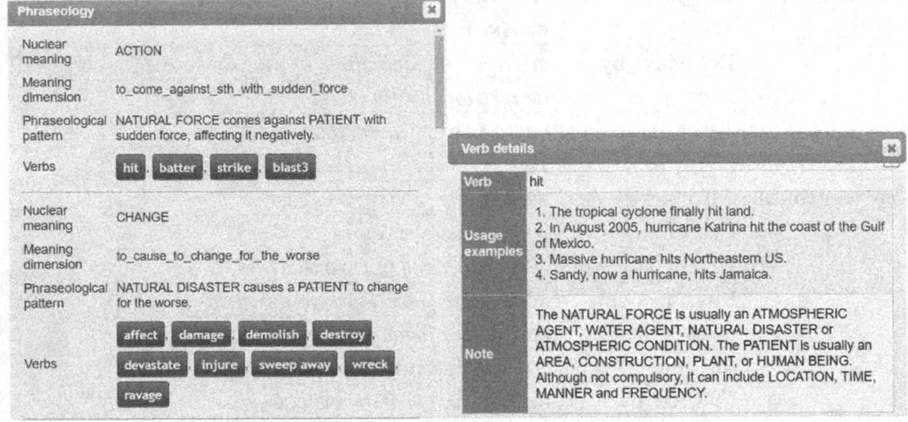

Fig. 2. Current phraseology entry for *hurricane*.

We intend to improve the phraseology module of EcoLexicon by creating phraseological templates that represent a generalization of predicate-argument structure, where lexical domains of verbs are related to the conceptual categories of their arguments.

3 Case Study: *Affects*

The case study on *affects* was carried out along several phases. Firstly, term-verb-term combinations that represent *affects* were analyzed in a 67-million-word specialized corpus on the environment. This was done by selecting all conceptual propositions linked through the *affects* relation in EcoLexicon in need of a predicate-based refinement, which means that patient and attribute-based propositions were ruled out for this study. Then, the verbs lexicalizing the extracted triplets in the corpus were classified into lexical domains. Thirdly, to increase the expressiveness of the relation *affects*, a verb was chosen within the higher level hierarchy of the lexical domain in order to relabel the relation. The rest of the verbs were collected to be stored in the phraseological module. The terms in the argument slots of the verbs were classified in conceptual categories and, finally, the predicate-argument structure of the verbs and their arguments was described for the phraseology module.

3.1 Corpus Analysis

We started out with the terms *ozone* and *ultraviolet radiation* to clarify the confusing example described in Sect. 2.1 where one affects the other and vice versa. We used

Sketch Engine [1] to analyze the corpus, more specifically wordsketch and the simple query with context restrictions (see Fig. 3).

was *observed* between solar *radiation* and	ozone	annual cycles; the latter peaked in springtime
1997]), so as expected, the annual cycle of	ozone	and *radiation are* not in phase (Rowland
absorption of *ultraviolet* radiation by the	ozone	layer , which *restricts* turbulence and
such as temperature, pressure, humidity,	ozone	or *ionising radiation* . The sensor pack
damage by *ultraviolet* radiation. As the	ozone	shield *is* weakened, receipt of ultraviolet
. Additionally, in the stratosphere, the	ozone	*absorbs* the *ultraviolet* rays that would
destroyed ozone. The high, thin layer of	ozone	*blocks* the Sun's *ultraviolet* rays, so removing
(global warming and *increased UV* due to	ozone	depletion). Antarctic fish have been and
maximises near the stratopause (50 km), where	ozone	*absorbs* the Sun's *ultraviolet* radiation
about 10 to 20 miles up in the sky. This	ozone	layer *absorbed* the intense *ultraviolet*
Ozone is found in the stratosphere. Because	ozone	*absorbs* high-energy *UV* rays from the Sun
were sufficient to *create* a substantial	ozone	layer that absorbed dangerous *ultraviolet*
This warming *is* due to concentrations of	ozone	gas that absorb *ultraviolet* radiation from
solar *radiation* UV radiation *absorbed* by	ozone	layer radiation reflected by atmosphere
December Incoming *radiation is* absorbed by the	ozone	layer. Incoming radiation is reflected
law). The major source of OH radicals *is*	ozone	photolysis with short wavelength *UV* radiation
only vibrational mode *is* symmetrical). Thus	ozone	absorbs *UV* radiation without being consumed
main techniques used for the produ ction of	ozone	*are* corona discharge, *UV* irradiation, and
most common way of *producing* commercial	ozone	. B. *UV* irradiation. Ozone produced by the
producing commercial ozone. B. *UV* irradiation.	Ozone	*produced* by the UV-irradiation of air has

Fig. 3. Sample concordances of *ozone* + verb + *UV*, *ultraviolet*, *radiation*, *rays*.

In the concordances, combinations of *ozone* and *ultraviolet radiation* or *UV* or *rays* were found with verbs such as *absorb*, *filter out*, *block*, and *shield*. In this context, ozone was found as part of multiword terms such as *ozone layer*, *stratospheric ozone*, and *ozone shield*. For how *ultraviolet radiation* affects *ozone*, we found instances of ultraviolet radiation interacting with, *creating* or *destroying* ozone. Ultraviolet radiation can create as well as destroy ozone, because ozone is a very instable molecule.

Then we broadened our search to find combinations of *ozone* with different verbs with the basic underlying conceptual meaning of affect and the arguments that go with them. Ozone combines with verbs such as *shield* and *protect*, but also with *damage* and *irritate*. From the concordances with these verbs, it became clear that stratospheric zone (the ozone in the ozone layer) *shields* and, therefore, *protects*, whereas tropospheric (or ground-level) ozone *damages* and *irritates* (see Fig. 4). The second argument for both cases can be *Earth*, the *Earth's surface*, *wildlife*, *us*, *environment*. However, only in the case of ground-level ozone damages or irritates, the second argument refers to human health (*health*, *respiratory system*, *eyes*, *nose*, etc.).

To identify conceptual categories for the arguments and define lexical domains, the corpus queries were further broadened. For example, the verb *absorb* was queried in combination with *radiation*, *energy*, *rays*, *sunlight*, etc. The arguments found were all atmospheric components (*ozone*, *water vapor*, *carbon dioxide* and *greenhouse gases*; see Fig. 5). In another query, we combined synonyms of affect (*influence*, *damage*, *change*, *affect*) with second arguments such as *Earth*, *climate*, *environment* and *health*. In this case, we found greenhouse gases (*ozone*, *carbon dioxide*, *methane*, *nitrous oxide*, etc.) as a more specific semantic category.

warming, sea-level rise, and *reductions* in the stratospheric ozone protection *shields* . It was now imperative
key gases. 4.6 *Stratospheric* Chemistry. Stratospheric ozone *protects* life on the surface of the Earth
not as dramatically as in the *Antarctic* . Stratospheric ozone *protects* life on the surface of the Earth
molecular oxygen and atomic *oxygen* . There, stratospheric ozone provides a protective *shield* against the
appear to be involved with *ozone* depletion. Stratospheric ozone *shields* the earth from solar ultraviolet
health *problems* and *damage* forests and crops. Ground-level ozone affects the respiratory system, aggravating
chief *contributors* to ozone production. Ground-level ozone adversely affects health and *damages* the
They form photochemical *oxidants* (including ground-level ozone) that affect health, *damage* materials,
harmful ultraviolet (*UV*) radiation. However, ground-level ozone can *irritate* the eyes, noses, throats,
environment. Toxic *air* pollutants, rain and ground-level ozone can *damage* trees, crops, wildlife, lakes

Fig. 4. Stratospheric ozone protects and shields, ground-level ozone damages and irritates.

greenhouse gases. Atmospheric gases that absorb and reflect long-wave *radiation* , causing
circulation of *air* . latent heat. *Energy* being absorbed from the air during changes from water
and through photochemical *reactions* , that absorbs ultraviolet *radiation* from the sun, an
greenhouse gases. Atmospheric gases that absorb and reflect long-wave *radiation* , causing
circulation of *air* . latent heat. *Energy* being absorbed from the air during changes from water
and through photochemical *reactions* , that absorbs ultraviolet *radiation* from the sun, an
but most *reaches* the earth, where it is absorbed and re-emitted as long-wave *energy* , also
of our *atmosphere* , the ozone layer, that absorbs the dangerous part of the sun's *radiation*
that takes *place* as the sun's *energy* is absorbed varies greatly. The reason for this comes
infrared *radiation* rising from the surface is absorbed by CO2 in the middle levels of the atmosphere
world, and the *data* he used for how gases absorbed *radiation* were far from reliable. Nevertheless
quantity of *gas* . The reason was that CO2 absorbs *radiation* only in specific bands of the
difference . Moreover, water vapor already absorbed infrared *radiation* in the same region of
took to studying how CO2 in the *atmosphere* absorbed infrared *radiation* , as an adjunct to his

Fig. 5. Sample concordances of *absorb* with *radiation*, *energy*, *rays*, *sunlight*, etc.

3.2 Verb Classification

To classify the verbs found during corpus analysis in broader semantic categories, we applied the lexical domains and subdomains defined by Faber & Mairal [2]. These authors propose a model for lexical classification based on the distinction between syntagmatic and paradigmatic relations, where the most prototypical verbs are those that have the largest combinatory potential from a semantic point of view. They applied the model to over 10,000 verbs of the English language and the lexical domains they propose are: Existence, Movement, Position, Contact, Change, Perception, Cognition, Possession, Action, Feeling, Speech, Sound, and Light. Below, part of the Possession lexical domain hierarchy is reproduced with some example verbs in square brackets [2: 291].

We classified the verbs *absorb* (as in ozone absorbs ultraviolet radiation), *filter out*, and *block* within the lexical domain Possession and its subdomain "to come to have something". We considered *shield* and *protect* meronymic extensions of *block*. The verb *create* (as in ultraviolet radiation creates ozone) was classified in Existence in the subdomain "to cause something to exist". *Destroy* was included in Existence as well of course, but in the subdomain "to cause something to stop existing". *Damage*, *irritate*, and *harm* were classified in Change under "to cause something to change making it worse".

12 Possession
- 12.1 To have something [*possess, own, hold*]
  - 12.1.1 To come to have something [*get, obtain*]
    - 12.1.1.1 To get something as a result of force/skill [*take, capture*]
    - 12.1.1.2 To get something through effort/as a reward [*gain, earn*]
    - 12.1.1.3 To get something after it has been given/sent to you [*receive*]
    - 12.1.1.4 To get a large number of things over a period of time [*collect, accumulate*]
    - 12.1.1.5 To get something back after it has been lost/stolen [*recover*]
  - 12.1.2 To continue to have something [*keep, save*]
    - 12.1.2.1 To have something within as a part [*contain, include*]
    - 12.1.2.2 To cause something to have something as a part [*include, incorporate*]
      - 12.1.2.2.1 To not include [*omit, exclude*]
  - 12.1.3 To stop having [*lose*]

…

To increase the expressiveness of the conceptual relation *affects*, we then chose a verb from the same lexical subdomain that we felt expressed the relation more specifically but would still be applicable in other cases. For Possession ("to come to have something"), we chose *obtain*, for Existence ("to cause something to exist"), *create*, for Existence ("to cause something to stop existing"), *destroy*, and for Change ("to cause something to change making it worse"), *damage*. Further research will show if these choices are the most adequate for the environmental field.

3.3 Argument Classification

From the corpus analysis, several conceptual categories were deducted for the arguments in the predicate-argument structures found. For example, for the lexical domain Possession ("to come to have something"), the Agent was an atmospheric component with members such as *nitrogen*, *oxygen*, *argon* and the so-called trace gases (*stratospheric ozone*, *carbon dioxide*, *methane*, and *nitrous oxide*). The Patient in combination with this same lexical domain was some type of energy: *ultraviolet radiation*, *sunlight*, *sunrays*, *photons*, etc. For Existence and Change, we found the same Agents and Patients. The Agents were ozone-depleting substances, such as greenhouse gases (*water vapor*, *carbon dioxide*, *methane*, *nitrous oxide*, *chlorofluorocarbons*) and the Patients were stratospheric ozone, with its term variants *ozone layer*, *ozone*, *ozone shield*, etc., and the environment, including *Earth*, *climate* and *living beings*. The results are summarized in Table 2.

Table 2. Summary of argument and verb classification.

Argument 1 [Agent]	**Verb**	**Argument 2 [Patient]**
Conceptual category	Lexical domain	Conceptual category
Atmospheric component nitrogen oxygen argon trace gas: stratospheric ozone carbon dioxide methane nitrous oxide	Possession obtain retain absorb filter out block	Energy ultraviolet radiation sunlight sunrays photons
Ozone-depleting substance greenhouse gas: water vapor carbon dioxide methane nitrous oxide chlorofluorocarbons	Existence[a] destroy Change deplete degrade damage	Atmospheric component stratospheric ozone Environment Earth climate living beings humans health animals plants
Energy ultraviolet radiation sunlight sunrays photons	Existence[a] destroy Existence[b] Create	Atmospheric component stratospheric ozone
	Existence[a]	Ozone depleting substance greenhouse gas water vapor carbon dioxide methane nitrous oxide chlorofluorocarbons

[a]Subdomain "to cause something to stop existing"
[b]Subdomain "to cause something to exist"

4 Applying Results

4.1 Conceptual Network Modification

The increased expressiveness of the conceptual relation *affects* will be applied to the conceptual networks of EcoLexicon. Currently, the network of ultraviolet radiation, for instance, shows ULTRAVIOLET RADIATION *affects* OZONE-DEPLETING SUBSTANCE and ULTRAVIOLET RADIATION *affects* STRATOSPHERIC OZONE (see Fig. 6). These relations will be more expressive when changing them to the verbs chosen in Sect. 3.2 (see Fig. 7).

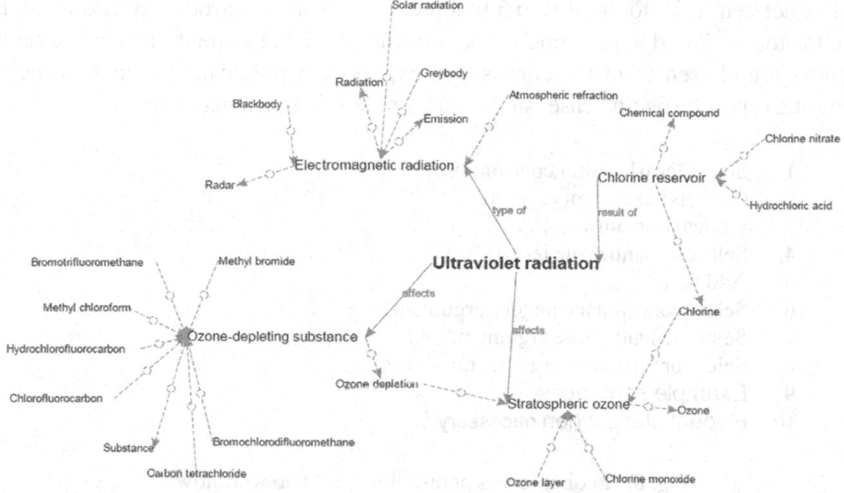

Fig. 6. ULTRAVIOLET RADIATION with inexpressive *affects* relation.

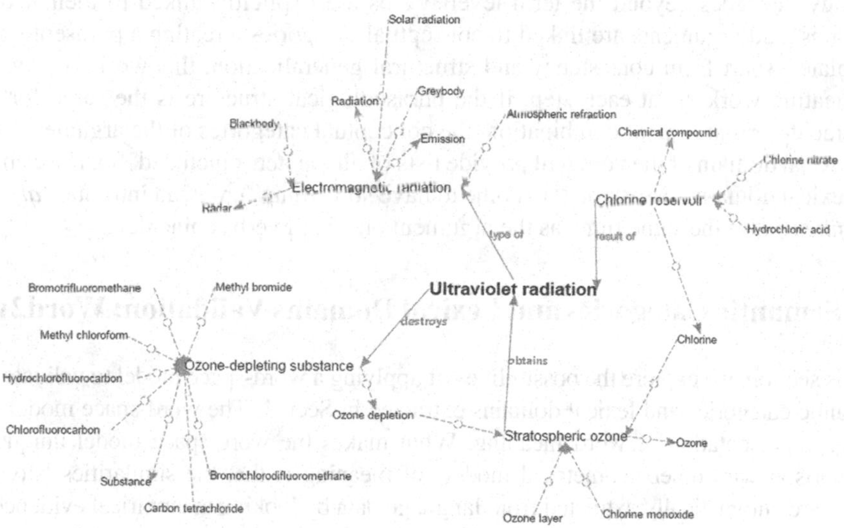

Fig. 7. ULTRAVIOLET RADIATION with increased expressiveness: *destroys* and *obtains*.

4.2 Phraseology Module Workflow

For detailed predicate-argument description in EcoLexicon's future phraseology module, the following workflow has been developed (see Fig. 8). First a term is selected within a concept entry, for example *tropospheric ozone* in the concept entry TROPOSPHERIC OZONE. Then a conceptual category is chosen for that concept (Step 2 in Fig. 8). After that, the lexical domain of the verb is selected (for example Possession) and its subdomain ("to come to have something"). In step 4, the role of the argument of the term in step 1 is defined. It is not until step 5 that the actual verb is introduced (*absorb* in this case). In steps 6, 7 and 8, the same is done for the second argument. In step 9, example sentences are chosen from the corpus that express the predicate-argument structure. Depending on each specific case, steps can be repeated when necessary.

1. Select term1 within concept: tropospheric ozone
2. Conceptual category: greenhouse gas → gas → chemical → substance
3. Lexical domain verb: Possession (to come to have something)
4. Select semantic role term1: Agent
5. Add verb: absorb
6. Select conceptual category argument2: radiation → energy
7. Select semantic role argument2: Patient
8. Select or introduce argument2: ultraviolet radiation
9. Example sentences
10. Repeat steps when necessary

Fig. 8. EcoLexicon's phraseology module workflow.

In this way, the workflow forces consistency as well as a perspective towards phraseology that goes beyond the term level. Verbs are explicitly linked to their lexical domains, and arguments are linked to conceptual categories, creating a phraseological template. Apart from consistency and structural generalization, this workflow avoids duplicating work, as at each step, if the phraseological structure is the same for the argument-verb-argument combination, the conceptual categories of the arguments and the lexical domain of the verb will provide lists of all the items included. So, if we chose the lexical domain Possession ("to come to have something"), we can introduce *absorb* and *filter out* at the same time, as the arguments for both verbs coincide.

5 Semantic Categories and Lexical Domains Validation: Word2vec

In this section, we explore the possibilities of applying a word-space model to validate the semantic categories and lexical domains extracted in Sect. 3. The word-space model is a spatial representation of word meaning. What makes the word-space model unique in comparison with other geometrical models of meaning is that the similarities between words are automatically extracted from language data by looking at empirical evidence of real language use. Words with similar distributional properties are put in similar regions of the word space, so that proximity reflects distributional similarity [16: 21]. The idea behind this is the so-called distributional hypothesis: words with similar distributional properties have similar meanings [idem]. We used the word-space model word2vec [3] provided by Python's open source vector space topic modeling toolkit Gensim[2]. We chose the continuous bag-of-words (CBOW) hierarchy and applied it to our 67-million-word specialized corpus on the environment. Preprocessing included underscoring multiword terms contained in EcoLexicon present in the corpus and tokenizing with NLTK Toolkit[3].

[2] https://radimrehurek.com/gensim/models/word2vec.html.
[3] http://www.nltk.org/.

We created the model and then used the most similar method to obtain clusters of those vectors that are most similar to the search term with varying numbers of 20 or 40 (topn = 20 or topn = 40) different most similar vectors. The results are shown in Table 3. Searches were based, on the one hand, on the arguments *ozone* and *ultraviolet radiation* as well as those that were found accompanying any of the latter with similar predicates. In this way, the phraseological template of each of these terms could be rapidly enriched by adding new arguments belonging to the same conceptual category (note that most terms shown in the clusters are synonyms, hyponyms or cohyponyms of the search term). On the other hand, searchers were also based on the predicates found between ozone and ultraviolet radiation in order to enrich the lexical domains.

Search 1 and 2 provide clusters that coincide quite well with the items we included in the conceptual categories in Sect. 3.3. Search 1, for example, obtains all term variants for *ozone*, the term *greenhouse gases* as well as all of its hyponyms, and other atmospheric components. However, from the cluster only, it would be difficult to deduce the difference in meaning and behavior of stratospheric and tropospheric ozone. Search 3 provides a cluster with names of other planets and astronomical bodies, very different from the category of entities damaged by greenhouse gases we found in Sect. 3. Earth, climate and environment do not seem to be in the same category according the cluster. When looking for other entities damaged by greenhouse gases, *plant* (search 4) and *animal* (search 5), *tree* and *animal* are present in the former and *adult* and *human* in the latter, but the cluster still does not seem to fit our purposes. However, when using *human* as search word (search 6), the cluster includes tokens such as humankind, climate change, health, and global warming, which does give an accurate idea of how these can be included in the same category of the environment.

For the validation of the lexical domains of the verbs, the results of clustering seem to partially coincide with the results of Sect. 3.2, but the clusters would need refining to clearly show certain conceptual differences. For example in search 6 (*absorb*), *penetrate*, *enter*, *retain*, *consume*, *sequester* and *trap* all express the meaning of the lexical subdomain "to come to have something". According to the word2vec results, the opposite meaning is part of the same cluster as well, with verbs such as *emit*, *lose*, *dissipate*, and *radiate*, which are still part of the lexical domain Possession, but not of the same subdomain. Other verbs in the cluster are more closely related to the lexical domain Change, for example *attenuate* and *deplete*. Similar conclusions can be drawn from the other clusters. Further research will be necessary to refine the clustering technique, or to compare word2vec to other clustering algorithms such as Brown clustering [17] or Hierarchical Dirichlet Processing [18].

Apart from coinciding results that provide an approximate validation of the lexical domains and conceptual categories, clustering with word2vec also provides new members for each class, which can be added to the lexical domain or conceptual category in question and therefore enrich the module in a coherent and structured way. For example, *trap* and *sequester* can be added to the lexical domain Possession ("to come to have something"). These new members can then be used as seed words for further research. Thus, combining automatic procedures with manual queries to the corpus facilitates the population of the phraseological module and at the same time ensures coherence during the parallel development of the conceptual module.

Table 3. Clusters for search words in EcoLexicon corpus.

Search	Search word	Cluster
1	Ozone (topn = 20)	O3, stratospheric ozone, tropospheric ozone, CO2, atmospheric, aerosol, CH4, stratospheric, SO2, NO2, N2O, NOx, greenhouse gases, sulphur dioxide, carbon dioxide, ground-level ozone, water vapor, carbon monoxide, GHGs, nitrogen oxide
2	Ultraviolet radiation (topn = 20)	UV radiation, ultraviolet, UVR, UV, radiation, thermal radiation, UV-B, solar radiation, sunlight, irradiances, radiations, UVB, EUV, sunburn, PAR, radiant energy, photochemical reactions, photons, infrared, re-emits
3	Earth (topn = 40)	earth, planet, Earth's, Earthâ\x80\x99 s, surface_of_the_Earth, Moon, earth's, Earth's_surface, earth\x92 s, Earth\\, Sun, sun, Venus, Mars, planet's, earthâ\x80\x99 s, moon, Saturn, magnetosphere, Jupiter, surface, atmosphere, planetâ\x80\x99 s, globe, Uranus, planets, ground, orbit, crust, ocean_floor, sphere, Pluto, above, objects, object, photosphere, Earth's, body, icy, earth\\
4	Plant (topn = 40)	plants, animal, bacterial, tissue, host, microorganism, microbial, microorganisms, crop, biomass, woody, fungus, legume, seed, tissues, fish, weeds, fruit, aquatic, organism, caterpillar, fungal, seeds, parasite, tree, fungi, microbes, bacteria, forest, food_chain, organisms, rice, insect, plant's, microalgae, pathogen, micro-organisms, weed, photosynthetic, yeast
5	Animal (topn = 40)	organism, fish, animals, plant, insect, aquatic, shellfish, excreta, bird, food, faeces, wild, adult, host, edible, living, dung, feces, human, insects, wildlife, carcasses, pets, humans, seaweed, meat, larva, intestines, Elodea, sedentary, mammal, exotic, fishes, herbivores, chicken, eating, reptile, livestock, microorganism, decomposers
6	Human (topn = 40)	humans, humankind, health, natural, environmental, humanity, social, economic, mankind, biological, society, natural_processes, welfare, animal, cultural, Human, climate_change, man, ecological, our, anthropogenic, their, fetus, wildlife, global_warming, life, grave, detrimental, fear, living, technological, well-being, respiratory, peopleâ \x80\x99 s, distress, person's, agricultural, adverse, natural_resources, lifestyle
7	Absorb (topn = 20)	emit, penetrate, photosynthesize, lose, dissipate, evaporate, consume, attenuate, dissolve, redistribute, retain, radiate, absorbs, adsorb, vaporize, enter, disperse, deplete, sequester, trap
8	Create (topn = 20)	produce, generate, develop, make, deliver, provide, induce, impart, give, acquire, accommodate, add, lead, bring, incorporate, drive, offer, handle, render, allow
9	Destroy (topn = 20)	kill, disrupt, impair, disturb, degrade, suppress, threaten, overwhelm, deplete, eliminate, stimulate, infect, displace, regenerate, undermine, pollute, invade, render, resist, eradicate

6 Conclusions and Future Work

In this paper, we have presented a methodology for predicate-argument analysis with two objectives: improving conceptual relation expressiveness and designing a phraseology module. We have shown that semi-automatic and automatic approaches can be combined and reinforce one another. Results have only been provided for a small case study. In the near future, we will apply a combined top-down and bottom-up methodology to establish all basic semantic categories in the environmental domain. The top-down method will consist of a manual classification based on the definitions, conceptual networks, and other information contained in EcoLexicon. This will result in a domain-specific ontology similar to that of CPA semantic types, which is used in the Pattern Dictionary of English Verbs (PDEV) [19] for general language. We will again apply automatic clustering techniques to validate this manual categorization. The bottom-up method will consists of extracting all the verbs from the EcoLexicon corpus with TermoStat[4] (Drouin 2003) and then classifying them into different paradigms based on the concepts they relate and the basic conceptual relations they express, along the lines of the methodology described in this paper, to extract all the necessary information to populate our phraseology module.

Acknowledgments. This research was carried out as part of project FF2014-52740-P, Cognitive and Neurological Bases for Terminology-enhanced Translation (CONTENT), funded by the Spanish Ministry of Economy and Competitiveness.

References

1. Kilgarriff, A., Rychly, P., Smrz, P., Tugwell, D.: The sketch engine. In: Proceedings of the 11th EURALEX International Congress, pp. 105–116. EURALEX, Lorient (2004)
2. Faber, P., Mairal, R.: Constructing a Lexicon of English Verbs. Mouton de Gruyter, Berlin/New York (1999)
3. Mikolov, T., Chen, K., Corrado, G., Dean, J.: Efficient estimation of word representations in vector space. In: ICLR Workshop (2013)
4. Faber, P., León-Araúz, P., Reimerink, A.: Representing environmental knowledge in EcoLexicon. In: Bárcena, E., Read, T., Arús, J. (eds.) Languages for Specific Purposes in the Digital Era. EL, vol. 19, pp. 267–301. Springer, Cham (2014). doi: 10.1007/978-3-319-02222-2_13
5. Hausmann, F.J.: Le dictionnaire de collocations. In: Hausmann, F.J., Reichmann, O., Wiegandand, H.E., Zgusta, L. (eds.) Wörterbücher/Dictionaries/Dictionnaires — Ein internationals Handbuch zur Lexikographie/An International Enyclopedia of Lexicography/Enyclopédieinternationale de lexicographie, pp. 1010–1019. Walter de Gruyter, Berlin/New York (1989)
6. Gläser, R.: Relations between Phraseology and terminology with special reference to English. ALFA **7**(8), 41–60 (1994/1995)
7. Rundell, M.: Defining elegance. In: de Schryver, G.-M. (ed.) A Way with Words: A Festschrift for Patrick Hanks, pp. 349–375. Menha Publishers, Kampala (2010)

[4] http://termostat.ling.umontreal.ca/.

8. Bartsch, S.: Structural and Functional Properties of Collocations in English: A Corpus Study of Lexical and Pragmatic Constraints on Lexical Co-occurrence. Gunter Narr Verlag, Tübingen (2004)
9. Buendía Castro, M.: Verb dynamics. Terminology **18**(2), 149–166 (2012)
10. Buendía-Castro, M., Montero-Martínez, S., Faber, P.: Verb collocations and phraseology in ecolexicon. In: Kuiper, K. (ed.) Yearbook of Phraseology, pp. 57–94. De Gruyter Mouton, Berlin (2014)
11. L'Homme, M.C.: Predicative lexical units in terminogy. In: Gala, N., Rapp, R., Bel-Enguix, G. (eds.) Language Production, Cognition, and the Lexicon, pp. 75–93. Springer, Heidelberg (2015). doi:10.1007/978-3-319-08043-7_6
12. Alonso, A., Millon, C., Williams, G.: Collocational networks and their application to an E-Advanced Learner's Dictionary of Verbs in Science. In: Proceedings of eLex 2011, pp. 12–22 (2011)
13. Fillmore, C.J.: Frames and the semantics of understanding. Quad. di Semant. **6**, 222–254 (1985)
14. Faber, P.: Frames as a framework for terminology. In: Kockaert, H.J., Steurs, F. (eds.) Handbook of Terminology, vol. 1, pp. 14–33. John Benjamins Publishing Company, Amsterdam (2015)
15. Faber, P., León-Araúz, P., Reimerink, A.: EcoLexicon: new features and challenges. In: Kernerman, I., Kosem Trojina, I., Krek, S., Trap-Jensen, L. (eds.) GLOBALEX 2016: Lexicographic Resources for Human Language Technology in conjunction with the 10th edition of the Language Resources and Evaluation Conference, pp. 73–80. Portorož (2016)
16. Sahlgren, M.: The word-space model: Using distributional analysis to represent syntagmatic and paradigmatic relations between words in high-dimensional vector spaces. Dissertation. Stockholm University (2006)
17. Brown, P.F., De Souza, P.V., Mercer, R.L., Della Pietra, V.J., Lai, J.C.: Class-based n-gram models of natural language. Comput. Linguist. **18**(4), 467–479 (1992)
18. Teh, Y.W., Jordan, M.I., Beal, M.J., Blei, D.M.: Hierarchical dirichlet processes. J. Am. Stat. Assoc. **101**, 1566–1581 (2006)
19. Hanks, P.: Mapping meaning onto use: a pattern dictionary of english verbs. In: AACL 2008, Utah (2008)

Exploitation of Corpora in Phraseological Studies

Phrasal Settings in Which the Definite and Indefinite Articles Appear to Be Interchangeable in English: An Exploratory Study

Stephen James Coffey(✉)

University of Pisa, Pisa, Italy
stephen.james.coffey@unipi.it

Abstract. This paper investigates the fact that some English phrases may be used with either the definite or the indefinite article, without any obvious change in meaning or effect. Whereas many types of phrasal variation have been documented in the literature, there is little description of this particular phenomenon. Examples are given of a number of phrasal types, ranging from opaque idiomatic expressions to fairly transparent word strings. Contextualized examples are provided, mainly from the British National Corpus but also from corpus-based reference works.

Keywords: Definite article · Indefinite article · Esphoric NPs · Corpora · Phraseology

1 Introduction

The words *the* and *a* (or prevocalic *an*) are usually mutually exclusive in English text; this is only natural since they have different uses, for the most part; indeed, their functions are often in direct contrast to one another. One area in which they do, partially, overlap, is that of 'generic reference', and here the two words are sometimes interchangeable. Consider, for example, the following extract, from which an article has been deliberately removed and where I would judge both articles to be possible at that point in the text:

> A buzzard's feathers have almost a glossy look to them, and they're more than one shade of brown. If you observe the bird from the front, you'll see that it ranges in hue from the creamy white of the breast and stomach to quite a dark brown with even darker flecks on the neck. When ___ buzzard is in flight, cream is the main colour you see, and if you have good eyesight and know what you are looking for, it's quite distinctive, even from a distance.

[This extract was retrieved from the British National Corpus, where the reader may also check which article was used in the original text.]

The two possibilities in this text correspond to two of five patterns for 'generic reference' listed in Berry [1]; these are, quite simply, 'the indefinite article + singular count noun' and 'the definite article + singular count noun' (p. 35). The example sentences provided are, respectively, 'A dog likes to eat far more than a human being' and 'The gorilla is a shy retiring creature.' Berry, however, warns against assuming that the various patterns for generic reference are always interchangeable.

R. Mitkov (Ed.): Europhras 2017, LNAI 10596, pp. 193–204, 2017.
https://doi.org/10.1007/978-3-319-69805-2_14

As well as being occasional alternatives before single-word units (as with *buzzard* in the above extract), *the* and *a/an* can also be found as alternatives within phrasal units of one sort or another, and it is this aspect of their usage which is the focus of the present paper. In Sect. 2, I exemplify and discuss *specific* phrases in which either article may be found, while in Sect. 3, examples are given of relevant phrases belonging to the lexico-grammatical frame '*a/the* N_1 *of* N_2'. The emphasis in the study is more on British English than other geographical varieties, since the corpus used to investigate phraseology was the British National Corpus; also, the dictionaries consulted, even though including data from the US and other countries, were published by UK-based publishers.

2 Specific Phrases

As is well known, many fixed phrases are only *relatively* fixed. One of the main variation types is that of alternative component words, as in *a piece of the action/a slice of the action*, usually described as two versions of what is essentially the same phraseological item. Many examples of such variation are given in the literature, and in relation to different word types. The following phrasal pairs, for example, include alternative particles and conjunctions: *a bolt from the blue/a bolt out of the blue*; *hit and miss/hit or miss*; these examples are taken from [2] (p. 129). Article variation, by contrast, has received little attention; an example from my own data is *do SB a world of good/do SB the world of good.*

In order to help presentation, and also to reflect the methodology of the study, examples of article variation are divided into two broad groups. Firstly, I discuss phrases which are to some degree semantically opaque when considered from the perspective of their component words, and secondly I give examples of phrases which are reasonably transparent from this point of view. In both cases the article within a phrase is being considered as an integral part of that phrase. To give a clear example of what I mean by this (though not involving article variation), the word *a* is a necessary component of the verbal phrase *come to a head*, and the word *the* is always found in the phrase which has as its lexical nucleus the words *the naked eye* – the presence of the articles in these two particular phrases is commented on by John Sinclair in, respectively, [3] (p. 161) and [4] (pp. 83–89).

2.1 Semantically Opaque, or Partially Opaque, Phrases

One of the sources of phrases in this study was corpus-based dictionaries of idioms. This was considered to be a useful starting point since lexical variation is well attested in the types of phrase typically included in such dictionaries. To this end, searches were carried out in two dictionaries: the *Collins COBUILD Dictionary of Idioms* [5], hereafter CCDI, and the *Cambridge International Dictionary of Idioms* [6], CIDI. According to descriptive information in the dictionaries themselves, the Cobuild dictionary includes 'approximately 4400 current British and American idioms', while CIDI includes 'around 7,000 idioms' covering 'current British, American and Australian idioms'. Both dictionaries were compiled mainly for learners and teachers of English as a foreign language.

Dictionary consultation involved looking at not only the citation forms of phrases, but also examples of usage. This was because sometimes variation was found only in examples, or through a combination of citation form and examples; in the case of the Cobuild dictionary the definitions were also of relevance. Examples of usage come from, or were based on, the corpora used to help compile the dictionaries, respectively, the Bank of English and the Cambridge International Corpus.

The phrases found in either or both of these dictionaries form a heterogenous set from the point of their semantic composition. They include, among others, phrases with more literal counterparts (e.g. *come to a boil*), similes (*as dead as a dodo*), phrases in which one or more words are being used in their usual sense (e.g. *not a ghost of a chance*), and phrases in which a specific sense of a word is associated with a specific structure (e.g. *a model of [politeness, etc.]*).

Not too many relevant examples of article variation were found in the two idioms dictionaries. This may simply reflect the fact that there is not very much variation of this sort in the English language. Another consideration, however, is the fact that in some phrases one of the two alternative forms may be found much more frequently than the other, and for this reason the less frequent form may not have been included in the dictionary, both for reasons of space and so as to keep presentation relatively simple for the dictionary reader. A further factor is the relatively low corpus frequency of many phrases of this sort, and consequent lack of available data (see [7], pp. 311–316, [8], pp. 82–90).

In addition to relevant data found in the two dictionaries, a list was also made of phrases which were judged to be possible candidates for variation of the sort being investigated. These were then looked for in the British National Corpus (BNC), as well as in general corpus-based dictionaries. The BNC was consulted using the University of Lancaster's BNC*web* interface (http://bncweb.lancs.ac.uk/).

Before giving examples of the phrases found, it should be pointed out that in all cases, the articles are being considered as genuine alternatives and the choice of one article or the other is not related to the precise nature of the cotext. This is very different from cases in which the usual form of a phrase has been adjusted in some way so as to fit into a specific context. Noun modification is quite common in this respect. Here is an example, involving the phrase *the thin end of the wedge*, followed by a non-modified example of the same phrase:

> 'I understand the intention – of wanting to try to make a conciliatory gesture – but this could be the thin end of a very dangerous wedge.' [BNC]

> 'Opponents say legalisation would be the thin end of the wedge.' [BNC]

A further example of modification, though slightly different in nature, is the following: 'But I don't speak French or Arabic so I'm going to stick out like the proverbial sore thumb.' [BNC]. Here, the phrase *stick out like a sore thumb* has been adapted so that the expression is not only being used, but is also being referred to metalinguistically through the words 'the proverbial'. One could, perhaps, also have found '... like *a* proverbial sore thumb', but, on the basis of evidence in the BNC, reference to idioms and sayings through use of the word *proverbial* almost always involves the word *the* rather than *a*. The same findings are reported in [2] (pp. 306–7) relating to other corpora.

Some examples of 'genuine' article variation which were found in one or both idiom dictionaries are: *as dead as a/the dodo*, *come/bring to a/the boil*, *jump in a/the lake*, *to play a/the waiting game*, *given half a/the chance*, *not a/the ghost of a chance*, and *a/the model of*. I now discuss each of these pairs in turn.

The first expression has as its citation form in CCDI the form *dead as a dodo*. The definition, however, is more precise regarding form: 'If you say that something is as **dead as a dodo** or as **dead as the dodo**, you mean that it is no longer active or popular'; at the same entry there is also an example of usage for each of the two forms:

'The foreign exchange market was as dead as a dodo.'

'This lugubrious Mozart style is as dead as the dodo everywhere in the world except Vienna and Salzburg.'

The next phrasal pair has the following explanation in CCDI: 'If a situation or feeling **comes to the boil** or **comes to a boil**, it reaches a climax or becomes very active and intense'; 'Someone or something can also **bring** a situation or feeling **to the boil** or **bring it to a boil**' (pp. 39–40). The two examples given are with the verb *come*, and a different article is used in each case:

'Their anger with France came to the boil last week when they officially protested at what they saw as a French media campaign against them.'

'The issue has come to a boil in Newark, where federal prosecutors have warned lawyers that if the chairman is indicted, the government may move to seize the money that he is using to pay legal fees.'

The next two phrases, *Go jump in a/the lake* and *to play a/the waiting game*, are presented with article variation in CIDI, though there is only one example of usage in each case. Two examples of the second phrase, taken from the BNC and with different articles, are the following:

'There is no doubt about Mary of Guise's political ability. She had played a waiting game with great skill in the 1540s ….'

'Think before saying yes — or no. Consider the value of a family contract. Prepare to play the waiting game.'

By contrast, in the following example the presence of a prenominal modifier appears to exclude the possibility of *the*, or at least to make it sound more awkward:

'PETER Coyne is 80 min away from a Sydney Grand Final appearance — leaving Castleford to play a frustrating waiting game.'

The phrase *given half a/the chance* is presented in CIDI in precisely that form, that is with either article, and the same is true for some learner's dictionaries. In the BNC, *given half* ***a*** *chance* is by far the more frequent form. Examples with the two respective articles are:

'It's the trees they go for, given half a chance.'

'I am always happy to work myself up into a great cultural stew, given half the chance.'

Actually, phraseological description is more complex than this, especially since the slightly shorter phrase *half a/the chance* is also found in *if*-clauses, notably with the verbs *give* or *get*:

'Not in an evil way at all, but if you gave him half a chance he'd hammer you into the ground and stamp on you.'

'All women take advantage of the men in their lives if they get half a chance.'

The only example found in the BNC of 'half *the* chance' in an *if* clause is with the verb *have*: 'I never want nothing on the side' – 'You could if you have half the chance' (transcription of a conversation).

A second phrase with the word *chance* is *NOT a ghost of a chance*, where *NOT* indicates any negative word. The citation form in CIDI is with *a* (and not *the*), though the only example given is with initial *the*: 'Against competition like that, they didn't have the ghost of a chance of winning'. There were no examples with *the* found in the BNC, but there again, there were only five tokens with *a*; an example is: 'You would have thought *The Woman In Black* wouldn't have stood a ghost of a chance of survival with just two actors, a simple set and some offstage sound effects going for it.'

The next phrase exemplified is *a/the model of*. It is presented with both articles in CIDI, though there is just one example, with the word *the*: 'Claudia, always the model of good taste, looked elegant in a black silk gown'. Judging from dictionary presentation generally, as well as evidence in the BNC, the phrase appears to be used above all with the word *a*. Examples of both forms from the BNC are:

'Apart from one or two lapses, you've been a model of fidelity.'

'Rangers remain the model of consistency, aiming tonight for their 38th successive match without defeat.'

Generally, this phrase implies approval on the part of the writer or speaker, though not always: 'The Whitehall switchboard was a model of inefficiency, as usual'.

I turn now to phrases which were not found with alternative forms in either dictionary but which were among those found in the BNC. Examples are the following, and in most cases one of the articles (in brackets) was found to be much less frequent than the other: *put a (the) damper/dampener on STH*, *give SB the (a) cold shoulder*, *talk the (a) hind leg(s) off a donkey*, *the (a) lion's share*, *at the (a) drop of a hat*, *a/the ghost of a smile*, *do SB a/the world of good*, and *a (the) means to an end*. The 'hind leg' idiom is interesting, compositionally, in that the only logical possibilities should be *talk the hind legs off a donkey* and *talk a hind leg off a donkey*; however, the form *talk the hind leg off a donkey* is also found (and, indeed, is the citation form in [9]), despite the fact that this wording suggests that donkeys only have one hind leg. The following are short contextualizations for some of the relative corpus examples:

'… it might put a damper on things if you remained tight-lipped and poker-faced.'

'So that put the damper on gigs for a bit.'

'Both Price Waterhouse and now Touche Ross have dallied with the Deloitte domestic partnership and been given the cold shoulder.'

'Where Italy is being given a cold shoulder today, could other deficit countries with particular political problems [….] be jilted tomorrow?'

'Someone who'll argue the hind leg off a donkey just for the sake of it.'

'Aye, and such a one' – she was shaking her head – 'who'd talk a hind leg off a donkey …'

'They fear that having separated post and telecommunications, France Telecom will receive the lion's share of the budget and may ultimately be privatised altogether.'

'Rupert Murdoch's TV Guide could be in the strongest position, to scoop a lion's share of the market, since it is already established.'

'He'll give hundreds away at the drop of a hat.'

'Mr Rodger Bell QC, for Mr Bewick, suggested that his client had a "bee in his bonnet" about surgeons being able to work anywhere at a drop of a hat.'

The phrase *a/the ghost of a smile* was not included in either idioms dictionary, and was investigated because of its similarity to *a/the ghost of a chance* (though without the negative patterning of the latter). It was found with both articles in the BNC, five tokens with *a* and seven with *the* (ignoring one with a prenominal modifier). Examples are:

'He bowed his head a fraction, a ghost of a smile on his mouth.'

'The ghost of a smile glimmered in his eyes.'

The next phrase, *do SB a/the world of good*, is presented in a number of dictionaries in just this way (i.e. with either article), and evidence from the BNC suggests that both forms are used indifferently. There are 31 tokens in all in the BNC, 14 with *a* and 17 with *the*. Examples with each article are:

'… this type of exercise will do you the world of good.'

'A good run in pastures new would do you a world of good.'

The last of the phrases listed above is *a/the means to an end*. In this case the preferred form, both in dictionaries and in the corpus consulted, is clearly the version with *a*. In the BNC there are 65 examples of *a means to an end* and six of *the means to an end*. Examples of the two forms are:

'All this could not have been achieved without Macintosh computers, but again, they were only the means to an end.'

'There is considerable debate about the value of education for its own sake, rather than as a means to an end.'

Lastly in this section I will mention two pairs of related phrases. The first, included in CIDI, is *one way or the other/one way or another*, and the second is *one after another/one after the other*. Of course, these phrases do not contain the word *an*, at least not as a separately written word, so strictly speaking they should not form part of this study. However, it should not be forgotten that there is no a priori reason why the phrase *an other* should not have become the norm in modern English; compare Sinclair's comments regarding the compound nature of the 'phrase' *of course* and the 'words' *maybe*, *anyway* and *another* ([10], p. 321).

The expression with the word *way* is accompanied by one example sentence in CIDI: 'One way or the other, I'm going to finish this job next week.' An example with *another* from the BNC is: 'One way or another, I'll get into the garden. So it doesn't matter what happens!'. It should be noted, however, that the two phrases can be used in different ways, and are not always interchangeable. For example, in the following extract it would not have been possible to use the form with *another*. 'Claims that it shortened the war by several years cannot be proved one way or the other'. For more discussion of the phraseological nature of the word *way*, see [3].

The other pair of phrases involving 'other' are both used quite frequently in English, and appear to be interchangeable in most circumstances. Examples are:

'The usual pattern is that you take several fish one after the other, and then nothing for perhaps an hour…'

'It is depressing to see the predicted problems materialising one after another…'

However, if we allow for an intervening word after the word *one*, which usually means a noun, the comparison between the phrases alters somewhat. The BNC frequency figures for the basic phrases are: *one after the other* 111, and *one after another* 70; however, with one intervening word the figures change considerably, to: *one ___ after the other* 15; *one ___ after another*: 112. Relative examples from the corpus are:

'He had smoked one cigarette after the other, holding them cupped in his palm…'

'… by which time she had calmed down a little, but was smoking one cigarette after another.'

Not all phrases looked for in the BNC were found in alternative forms. Examples of hypothesized alternatives which were *not* found, are: *to talk (etc.) nineteen to **a** dozen*, *in **a** blink of an eye*, *to get **a** hang of sth*, and *to take **the** back seat*. Of course, absence from the BNC does not mean that a hypothetical alternative version is never used in the language or could not be found in another corpus.

2.2 Semantically Transparent Phrases

The specific phrases discussed in this section are examples of items noted by the author over a period of time, and representing different phraseological types. They are: the collocational verb phrase *put sth to a/the vote*, scalar phrases such as *to an/the inch* and *to a/the mile*, the numerical frame *in a/the ratio of [3:5]*, and the phrase *as a/the result of*.

With regard to the first of these phrases, the total number of corpus tokens (with either *a* or *the*) is 72, and *the* is considerably more frequent than *a* (57:15). These overall figures, however, hide an even greater difference, which relates to the spoken texts in the BNC. Actually, 'spoken' here means just certain types of language, since all tokens were found in the transcripts of meetings and discussions of various kinds. Here, the ratio of *the* to *a* increases to 36:2. In quite a number of instances the phrase is introducing an actual vote, which is about to take place or is being suggested (e.g. 'Can I put that to the vote?'). It would seem, then, that *put to the vote* is very much the preferred form in these situations, though the figures may be inflated by repeated use of the phrase by individual chairpersons and similar. It should also be pointed out that the two tokens with *a* are also used to refer to an actual vote: 'So I think we should put that to a vote'; I'll put this to a vote then'.

In the written BNC texts, the ratio of *the* to *a* is 21:13. In the majority of cases, the two forms appear to be interchangeable, as in the following extracts:

'… when a final version of the draft platform, retaining intact the proposals outlined by Gorbachev, was put to a vote by a show of hands on Feb. 7 it was adopted with only one vote against and one abstention.'

'When the issue was put to the vote in the House of Commons we had a majority of 127 and the campaign against us was left in ruins.'

Occasionally there is modification of one sort or another, and *put to a vote* appears to be the only possibility (e.g. 'to put the work of the government to a vote of no confidence', 'Otherwise, the issue will be put to a vote which also includes 20 smaller nations who lack Test status.').

I turn now to the phrases *to an/the inch* and *to a/the mile*, which are mainly used in connection with the scale of maps. Examples of the former are:

'With a scale of twenty-two miles to an inch, the escarpment should be massive…'

'Western Europe is scaled at a useful 12 miles to the inch.'

Examples of the second phrase are:

'Though I had some small scale maps at three inches to a mile for some areas…'

'It is on what was for the period the large scale of almost one inch to the mile.'

The phrases *to an/the inch* were also found in a slightly different use, as in the following examples:

'With synthetic thread, polyester for example, and rather long stitches at 4 to the inch or 6 mm each…'

'… and that usually the eight points, which was meant to say there were eight threads to an inch.'

The next phrase is *in a/the ratio of*. Often, either article may be used, as in the following comparable contexts from the BNC:

'Zero dividend preference shares are also being issued in a ratio of 37 for every 63 ordinary shares.'

'… applicants for the Institute of Advanced Motorists test are in the ratio of one woman to four men.'

Where the word *ratio* is preceded by a classifying premodifier, *a* seems to be the only possibility, as in the following example: 'The labelled Watson and unlabelled complementary strand were mixed in a concentration ratio of 1:2 respectively.' In the case of other premodifiers, *the* is still an option, as in: 'This difference is in the approximate ratio of 2:1.'

Lastly, it is to be noted with regard to *in a/the ratio of*, that the continuation of the phrase (or rather its completion) must be a numerical relationship; it cannot just include the names of the entities being compared, as in the following example, where only the word *the* is possible: '… there is a remarkable constancy in the ratio of one element to the other'.

Turning now to the phrases *as a result of* and *as the result of*, these sometimes appear to be completely interchangeable, as can be seen by comparing the two extracts below.

'If a radiator starts to leak (usually as the result of internal corrosion), try adding a radiator sealant at the feed-and-expansion tank.'

'Where problems associated with water penetration have occurred on mastic asphalt roofs, it is usually as a result of failure from one or more of the following:…'

By far the more usual form of the phrase is *as a result of*, with 5149 tokens in the BNC as opposed to 338 for *as the result of*. These are raw frequency figures for the word strings, and about 20% of tokens of 'as the result of' represent other phenomena, especially the collocation *the result of* preceded by *as*, itself dependent on a previous verb (e.g. 'There are many baffling viral diseases that cannot be readily explained as the result of an acute infection…'). By contrast, in a 10% sample of tokens of 'as a result of' just two items were irrelevant to the phrase *as a result of*.

3 The Frame *a(N)/the* N_1 *of* n_2

The lexico-grammatical frames *a(n)* N_1 *of* n_2 and *the* N_1 *of* n_2 sometimes overlap; that is, they can include the same N_1 without a change in the resulting phrasal meaning or function. One such noun is the word *chance*, as is used in the following corpus extracts:

'I think the best I've qualified has been 12th and I have never finished a race, so I am due something. I believe we have a chance of a good points finish, but of course it all depends on how we qualify on Saturday.'

'But, if all goes according to plan, we have the chance of a title unification fight with even more appeal.'

The following pair of examples, again with the word *chance*, are even closer in their meaning and phraseology:

'… has had the first tablets which may give her a chance of a normal life.'

'He admitted that Estella was his housekeeper's daughter, adopted by Miss Havisham to give her the chance of a better life.'

The word *chance* has a number of slightly different meanings, and in the above examples the sense is, quoting from [9], 'a possibility of something happening, especially something that you want'. If we wish to rationalize the presence of either article in such phrases, the most obvious explanation is the fact that in the versions with *a chance of*, the word *a* is present because new information is being introduced, while in the versions with *the chance of*, the word *the* is being used cataphorically (though on a phrasal level, not textually). This phrasal phoric relationship is discussed by Willemse in some detail in [11], and I will now outline some of the points in this article that are of relevance to the present discussion. (For the use of the term 'esphoric' in Willemse's article, see [12].)

Willemse's study revolves around one specific frame, which can be referred to as *the* N_1 *of a/an* N_2 (e.g. 'the lights of a car'). The focus of the article is 'NPs involving a forward phoric relation', in which there are 'two discourse referents rather than only one'. Of specific relevance to the present paper, is the fact that in all 200 examples analyzed (from the Bank of English),

> '... neither referent had been mentioned at an earlier point in the discourse before the esphoric NP_1, i.e. neither NP_1 nor NP_2 maintained any anaphoric relations with the preceding discourse context. This is of course not unexpected for NP_2, since it is an indefinite NP. However, it is remarkable for the definite NP_1...' (p. 329).

The relevance of this to the current study is the fact that it draws attention to the non-anaphoric nature of phrase-initial *the*. In phrases where this occurs, it would be reasonable to expect that the (often non-anaphoric) word *a* might also sometimes be found instead of *the*, thus allowing for both *the chance of a* and *a chance of a*.

This is not to say, of course, that the two versions will always be used indifferently in the language. As has been seen above in the case of fairly fixed phrases, there will often be restrictions and preferences for one or the other form. In the case of the word *chance*, and with reference just to phrases in which the second noun is preceded by *a/an* (as in Willemse's study), we find that in the BNC there are 27 tokens of *a chance of a* and 123 of *the chance of a*. Very often they appear to be interchangeable, though not always. For example, 'a chance of a' sometimes forms part of the longer phrase *in with a chance (of a...),* while there is no evidence in the corpus of a parallel phrase 'in with the chance (of a...)'.

A number of first nouns can be found with either article in this frame; for the purposes of this paper I will refer to a few of the nouns mentioned by Willemse. In his paper he describes the various 'conceptual relations' which motivate forward bridging in his database. These are divided between the general categories of 'possessive relations' and 'contiguity relations'. One sub-category of the former is 'kinship relations', and a specific contextualized example is, 'A small urchin, pushing a bicycle, was with him. It was Wali Jan, from a mile down the valley; *the son of a smallholder*.' (Willemse's italics). Looking for the phrases *the son of a* and *a son of a* in the BNC, we find, not unexpectedly, that the former is by far the more frequent form. However, the important thing to note is that there are at least a few examples of *a son of a*. Examples of each phrase are:

> 'Mr Morton was born in South Africa, the son of a Scottish oil executive who had married into a local Afrikaner family.'
>
> 'Francis Bacon, well known for his capacity to drink nearly everyone under the table, left his friend John Edward, a son of a publican, £10 million in his will, which was published last month.'

With regard to 'contiguity relations', Willemse tells us that the most frequent type in his database is that of 'causal relations' (p. 348). One of the contextualized examples is, 'He was a tall, gaunt Scott in his mid-fifties with thinning hair and a pronounced limp on his left leg, *the result of an injury sustained during the Korean war*.' (Willemse's italics). In this particular example, 'a result' sounds less probable, and a search in the BNC suggests that the reason is its position in the sentence, grammatically speaking. The frequency figures for the word strings *the result of a* and *a result of a* are, respectively

473 and 350. However, if we make the same searches but with a preceding comma, as in the Willemse example, then we find that there are 28 tokens of '…, the result of a', but none at all for '…, a result of a'.

In contrast to this, there are other situations in which the two phrases do seem to operate in parallel. The following are examples:

'The occupation of the West Bank was a result of a war launched by third parties.'

'Mrs Thatcher's unwilling departure was the result of a combination of factors.'

Lastly in this section, I will give examples of two other words involving causal relations, *consequence* and *product*. Both are found in the BNC with each of the articles, and the following are examples:

'The shortages were primarily a consequence of a blockade by Azerbaijan…'

'This has been shown by lower prevalence of antibodies to toxoplasma in immigrants to Paris than in women of French origin, a factor suggested to be the consequence of a cultural preference for poorly cooked meat.'

'As a gourmet you certainly think of yourself as a product of high civilization…'

'Above all, worker radicalism was not the product of furious démarches by Bolshevik leaders against trade unionism…'

4 Concluding Remarks

The words *a/an* and *the* are usually thought of as being opposites, and their traditional labels, the indefinite and definite article, help to underline their very different functions. However, perceiving them in this way, and as part of a restricted grammatical paradigm, is to ignore their diverse functional and phraseological roles. Sinclair affirms that *the* and *a* each have 'a word class all to itself' ([3] p. 165), and I would fully endorse this opinion. In the same publication he writes that:

'The very frequent words of English form a large proportion of any text, and yet their particular qualities are not fully recognized. They are not given adequate provision in theories of language, and their role is not very clearly described in either grammars or dictionaries, both of which take a somewhat partial view of their behaviour'. (p. 157)

It is in the context of this general research need that I am examining the phraseological overlap between *a* and *the*, which is one more piece in the puzzle of understanding the usage of the two words.

Exemplification of the phenomenon has been varied in this paper, but at the same time it has been limited. A few of the many phrases which have not been mentioned are *to the/a layman*, *(see) a/the need for* STH, and *(have) a/the right to* (DO) STH, and only a few examples have been given of the nouns which make up the combined frame discussed in Sect. 3. Many phrases, and many contexts, would need to be examined in order to have a clear picture of the extent of the phenomenon, and also to understand why alternative articles are possible in some cases but not others.

Methodology-wise, it is to be noted that using corpus evidence to study very specific patterning of the words *a/an* and *the* is by no means straightforward. On the one hand, there is sometimes insufficient data, as is the case with some idioms; on the other hand, where there is an abundance of material, it may be necessary to study many contextual environments, one by one, to discover whether uses with *a/an* and *the* are genuinely comparable. Asking computer software to recognize relatively simple patterns is by no means enough; for example, word strings such as ‘a model of’ and ‘the model of’ have a number of meanings. A further point is that analysis of corpus data involves a degree of personal judgement, since sometimes one has to assess whether a specific example would have been possible, with the same communicative effect, if the other article had been used; there is nothing unusual about this, however, since all corpus-based lexicology involves a degree of human intervention.

Finally, I would point out that it is relatively unusual in corpus-aided research to focus on what specific words have *in common*; we usually use the corpus to tease out the differences between words, phrases and structures, rather than the opposite. At the same time, however, focussing on the similarity between words, in this case the articles, can also show up differences in the phraseology of the words they combine with.

References

1. Berry, R.: Collins Cobuild English Guides: 3 Articles. HarperCollins Publishers, London (1993)
2. Moon, R.: Fixed Expressions and Idioms in English: A Corpus-Based Approach. Clarendon Press, Oxford (1998)
3. Sinclair, J.: A Way with Common Words. In: Hasselgård, H., Oksefjell, S. (eds.) Out of Corpora: Studies in Honour of Stig Johansson, pp. 157–179. Rodopi, Amsterdam (1999)
4. Sinclair, J.: The Search for Units of Meaning. Textus Eng. Stud. Italy **IX**, 75–100 (1996)
5. Collins COBUILD Dictionary of Idioms. HarperCollins Publishers, London (1995)
6. Cambridge International Dictionary of Idioms. Cambridge University Press, Cambridge (1998)
7. Hanks, P.: Dictionaries of Idioms and Phraseology in English. In: Corpas Pastor, G. (ed.) Las Lenguas de Europa: Estudios de fraseología, fraseografía y traducción, pp. 303–320. Granada, Editorial Comares (2000)
8. Moon, R.: Frequencies and Forms of Phrasal Lexemes in English. In: Cowie, A.P. (ed.) Phraseology: Theory, Analysis, and Applications, pp. 79–100. Clarendon Press, Oxford (1998)
9. Oxford Advanced Learner’s Dictionary. 9th edn. Oxford University Press, Oxford (2015)
10. Sinclair, J.: Collocation: A Progress Report. In: Steele, R., Threadgold, T. (eds.) Language Topics: Essays in honour of Michael Halliday, vol. II, pp. 319–331. John Benjamins, Amsterdam (1987)
11. Willemse, P.: Esphoric *the N of a(n) N*-nominals: Forward bridging to an indefinite reference point. Folia Linguistica **40**(3–4), 319–364 (2006)
12. Martin, J.R.: English text: System and structure. John Benjamins, Amsterdam (1992)

Deverbal Nouns in Czech Light Verb Constructions

Václava Kettnerová(✉), Veronika Kolářová, and Anna Vernerová

Faculty of Mathematics and Physics, Institute of Formal and Applied Linguistics, Charles University, Malostranské nám. 25, 118 00 Prague 1, Czech Republic
{kettnerova,kolarova,vernerova}@ufal.mff.cuni.cz

Abstract. In this paper, we provide a well-founded description of Czech deverbal nouns in both nominal and verbal structures (light verb constructions), based on a complex interaction between the lexicon and the grammar. We show that light verb constructions result from a regular syntactic operation. We introduce two interlinked valency lexicons, *NomVallex* and *VALLEX*, demonstrating how to minimize the size of lexicon entries while allowing for the generation of well-formed nominal and verbal structures of deverbal nouns.

Keywords: Deverbal nouns · Valency · Light verb constructions · Valency lexicon

1 Introduction

One of the long-standing interests of phraseology lies in the study of compositionality, i.e., to what extent the syntactic and semantic properties of multiword units can be deduced from the properties of their respective parts. Indeed, compositionality or the lack thereof has a wide range of consequences both in theoretical linguistics and in NLP applications (e.g., information retrieval and machine translation). In this paper, we focus on the syntactic formation of nominal structures of Czech deverbal nouns and verbal structures in which they take part, on light verb constructions representing multi-word units. We show that the deep and surface syntactic structures of light verb constructions can be treated as compositional, being composed by applying simple syntactic rules to the structure of deverbal nouns and the light verbs. Although we only investigate examples in Czech (taken mostly from the Prague Dependency Treebank), we believe the same mechanisms operate in other languages as well.

Czech deverbal nouns, being derived from verbs either by productive suffixes *-ní/tí*, e.g., *podporování* 'supporting', or by non-productive suffixes or the zero suffix, e.g., *podpora* 'support', can denote processes (in a broad sense, covering actions and states) as their base verbs (1), or abstract (2) or concrete (3) results of the processes denoted by their base verbs.

(1) *podporování/podpora pacienta lékařem*
'support(ing) of the patient by the doctor'

R. Mitkov (Ed.): Europhras 2017, LNAI 10596, pp. 205–219, 2017.
https://doi.org/10.1007/978-3-319-69805-2_15

(2) *lékařova podpora pacientovi*
'doctor's support to the patient'

(3) *podpora v nezaměstnanosti*
'unemployment benefits'

Deverbal nouns are typically characterized by valency, i.e., by the ability to open a certain number of valency positions for other dependent units, representing their valency complementations. The description of valency structure of deverbal nouns is of great importance as deverbal nouns referring to processes (1) and to abstract results of processes denoted by their base verbs (2) – along with deadjectival nouns (e.g., *trpělivost* 'patience') or some primary nouns (e.g., *láska* 'love') – form not only nominal structures but verbal structures as well, the latter as parts of light verb constructions. In contrast to constructions with full verbs, the syntactic structure of light verb constructions is not determined solely by the verb but also by the deverbal noun with which the verb combines. Although the participation of light verbs and deverbal nouns in the syntactic structure formation of light verb constructions has attracted much attention of theoretical linguistics, see esp. [1,3,4,13], many aspects of this process still remain unclear.

In this paper, we demonstrate a close interplay between valency structures of light verbs and deverbal nouns in the syntactic formation of Czech light verb constructions. Czech, an inflectional language encoding syntactic relations via morphological forms, provides an excellent basis for studying this mechanism because the forms clearly indicate whether a complementation is syntactically structured as a complementation of the light verb, or as a complementation of the deverbal noun. Our theoretical findings are applied in an extensive annotation of light verbs and deverbal nouns in the valency lexicons *VALLEX* and *NomVallex*, respectively. We show that the information provided by these lexicons is sufficient for generating well-formed light verb constructions.

The paper is structured as follows. First, we lay out the main tenets of the description of the valency structure of deverbal nouns (Sect. 2), with an emphasis on differences between the expression of valency complementations of deverbal nouns in nominal structures (Sect. 3) and in verbal structures (Sect. 4). Second, a lexicographic representation of light verbs and deverbal nouns is proposed (Sect. 5), which, supplemented with grammatical rules, allows for generation of well-formed light verb constructions.

2 Valency of Deverbal Nouns in FGD

In the description of the valency structure of deverbal nouns, we make use of the valency theory formulated within the Functional Generative Description (FGD), a dependency oriented framework which takes a stratificational approach to language description, see esp. [14]. In FGD, valency belongs to the tectogrammatical layer, i.e., a layer of linguistically structured meaning corresponding to the deep syntactic layer, see esp. [10]. The valency theory has been first elaborated for the description of verbs. Corresponding to the argument-adjunct distinction in other linguistic theories, two kinds of valency complementations of verbs are distinguished in FGD – inner participants (actants) and free modifications (adjuncts) [12]. As actants, the valency complementations corresponding to the subject and the direct and indirect object are classified; their morphemic form is typically determined by the verb. Actants occur with a verb only once regardless of coordination and apposition (e.g., *(Jan a Marie)*$_{\mathsf{ACT}}$ *šli do kina.* '(John and Mary)$_{\mathsf{ACT}}$ went to the cinema.' provides only a single occurrence of the relevant complementation). Both obligatory[1] and optional actants characterize a verb in a unique way and in this sense, they have to be listed in its valency frame, see below. Five types of actants are distinguished mostly on syntactic criteria: 'Actor' (ACT), 'Patient' (PAT), 'Addressee' (ADDR), 'Effect' (EFF), and 'Origin' (ORIG) (e.g., *Vláda*$_{\mathsf{ACT}}$ *omezila těžbu*$_{\mathsf{PAT}}$ *uranu ze současných 950 tun*$_{\mathsf{ORIG}}$ *na 500 tun*$_{\mathsf{EFF}}$ *ročně.* 'The government$_{\mathsf{ACT}}$ restricted uranium mining$_{\mathsf{PAT}}$ from the current 950 tonnes$_{\mathsf{ORIG}}$ to 500 tonnes$_{\mathsf{EFF}}$ per year'). Among free modifications fall the valency complementations corresponding to adverbials; in contrast to actants, their morphemic form is not determined by the verb. Free modifications can typically occur more than once with a verb (e.g., *Až v neděli*$_{\mathsf{TWHEN}}$ *dopoledne*$_{\mathsf{TWHEN}}$ *3. září*$_{\mathsf{TWHEN}}$ *v 11 hodin*$_{\mathsf{TWHEN}}$ *oznámila britská vláda světu,...* 'Not before the morning$_{\mathsf{TWHEN}}$ on Sunday$_{\mathsf{TWHEN}}$ September$_{\mathsf{TWHEN}}$ the 3rd at 11 o'clock$_{\mathsf{TWHEN}}$ did the British government announce...'). Just as actants, free modifications are either obligatory, or optional. However, unlike actants, only obligatory free modifications characterize a verb in a unique way (e.g., *Petr přijel domů*$_{\mathsf{DIR3}}$. 'Peter arrived home$_{\mathsf{DIR3}}$.' and *Děti se dobře*$_{\mathsf{MANN}}$ *chovaly.* 'Children behaved well$_{\mathsf{MANN}}$.') and thus they have to be listed in the valency frame.

The same inventory of valency complementations is applied in the description of valency characteristics of deverbal nouns denoting processes and those that refer to abstract results of the processes. The inventory of valency complementations of deverbal nouns referring to concrete entities, especially to concrete results of processes, is broader, comprising other specific complementations such as the actant MATerial (e.g., *jedno balení másla*$_{\mathsf{MAT}}$ 'one package of butter$_{\mathsf{MAT}}$') and the free modifications APPurtenance (e.g., *oddělení odbytu*$_{\mathsf{APP}}$ 'sales department$_{\mathsf{APP}}$') and AUTHor (e.g., *výzdoba od Michelangela*$_{\mathsf{AUTH}}$ 'decoration by Michelangelo$_{\mathsf{AUTH}}$'), see [11].

The valency characteristics of both verbs and deverbal nouns are described in the form of valency frames. A valency frame is modeled as a sequence of valency slots. Each slot stands for one valency complementation and it comprises a functor (labeling the syntactic-semantic relation of the given complementation to its governing word) and the information on its obligatoriness; this information is supplemented with a list of possible morphemic forms which determine the expression of the complementation in the surface syntactic structure.

[1] We refer here to the obligatoriness on the tectogrammatical layer, i.e., on the deep syntactic layer; while being subject to different types of ellipsis on the surface layer, obligatory complementations are still present on the tectogrammatical layer.

3 Nominal Structures

Czech deverbal nouns express the meaning ranging from a process via an abstract result of the process to its concrete result. Those deverbal nouns that are derived from verbs by productive suffixes *-ní/-tí* typically preserve the meaning of the verbs from which they are derived; as a result, they mostly express processes as their base verbs (i). For example, the deverbal noun *plánování* expresses the process of planning just as its base verb *plánovat* 'to plan'. The deverbal nouns derived by non-productive suffixes or the zero suffix express processes only rarely. Typically, they either denote an abstract result of the process expressed by their base verbs (ii), or they refer to a concrete result of the process (iii). For example, the deverbal noun *plán* 'plan' derived by the zero suffix expresses both the abstract result of the planning process (e.g., *Janův plán studovat* 'John's plan to study') and its concrete result (e.g., *plán zahrady* 'a plan of the garden').

(i) The deverbal nouns referring to *processes* typically inherit the valency structure from their base verbs, i.e., the number and type of valency complementations and their obligatoriness remain the same. Only morphemic forms of those valency complementations that are expressed as the nominative subject and the accusative direct object of the base verb undergo systemic changes:

verb	→ deverbal noun
nominative	→ genitive, instrumental, possessive adjective or pronoun
accusative	→ genitive, possessive adjective or pronoun

These changes are regular enough to be described in terms of rules [11]. For example, the valency frame of the deverbal noun *plánování* 'planning' denoting the process of planning, see (5), is identical with the valency frame of its base verb *plánovat* 'to plan', see (4), except for the morphemic forms of individual valency complementations. These morphemic forms exhibit systemic shifts; the form of the ACT is changed from nominative to one of the following forms: genitive, instrumental and a possessive adjective or pronoun, and the form of the PAT changes from accusative to genitive or a possessive adjective or pronoun while other forms remain unchanged.[2]

(4) *plánovat* 'to plan': ACT^{obl}_{nom} $\mathsf{PAT}^{obl}_{acc,inf,dcc}$
Firma$_{\mathsf{ACT}:nom}$ *plánuje výstavbu*$_{\mathsf{PAT}:acc}$ *elektrárny.*
'The firm$_{\mathsf{ACT}}$ is planning the construction$_{\mathsf{PAT}}$ of a power plant.'

(5) *plánování* 'planning': $\mathsf{ACT}^{obl}_{gen,instr,poss}$ $\mathsf{PAT}^{obl}_{gen,poss,inf,dcc}$
plánování výstavby$_{\mathsf{PAT}:gen}$ *elektrárny firmou*$_{\mathsf{ACT}:instr}$
'the firm's$_{\mathsf{ACT}}$ planning of a power plant construction$_{\mathsf{PAT}}$'

(ii) The deverbal nouns denoting *abstract results* of the processes expressed by their base verbs behave similarly to the deverbal nouns expressing processes in

[2] In the labels for morphemic forms, *nom, gen, dat, acc, loc* and *instr* stand for the cases, *inf* stands for an infinitive, *poss* stands for possessive adjectives and possessive noun forms, and *dcc* indicates the dependent content clause.

that they typically exhibit the same valency structure as their base verbs in terms of the number and type of valency complementations (i.e., the functors and obligatoriness of the complementations). However, the morphemic forms of valency complementations of these deverbal nouns are – in addition to systemic shifts – often subject to non-systemic shifts as well [7]. For example, as in case of the deverbal noun *plánování* 'planning', the valency frame of the deverbal noun *plán* 'plan', see (6), referring to the abstract result of the process of planning, consists of the same number of valency complementations as the valency frame of its base verb *plánovat* 'to plan', see above (4). Further, their functors and their obligatoriness are preserved as well. However, in contrast to the deverbal noun *plánování* 'planning', the morphemic forms of the valency complementations of this deverbal noun undergo non-systemic shifts besides systemic ones, see the prepositional groups expressing the PAT *na*+accusative, *o*+locative and *pro*+accusative.

(6) *plán* 'plan': $\mathsf{ACT}^{obl}_{gen,poss}$ $\mathsf{PAT}^{obl}_{gen,poss,na+acc,o+loc,pro+acc,inf,dcc}$
plán firmy$_{\mathsf{ACT}:gen}$ *na výstavbu*$_{\mathsf{PAT}:na+acc}$ *elektrárny*
'plan of the firm$_{\mathsf{ACT}}$ for the construction$_{\mathsf{PAT}}$ of a power plant'

(iii) Valency frames of the deverbal nouns that refer to the *concrete results* of the processes denoted by their base verbs can substantially differ from the valency frames of the verbs. The changes in their valency frames can concern the number of valency complementations, their type with respect to both functors and obligatoriness, as well as possible morphemic forms. For example, the valency frame of the deverbal noun *plán* 'plan' with the concrete meaning (7) comprises an optional free modification AUTH (marked as typ) and an obligatory PAT.

(7) *plán* 'map': $\mathsf{AUTH}^{typ}_{gen,od+gen,poss}$ $\mathsf{PAT}^{obl}_{gen,poss}$
plán města$_{\mathsf{PAT}:gen}$
'map/plan of the city$_{\mathsf{PAT}}$'

4 Verbal Structures

In addition to nominal structures, the deverbal nouns denoting processes (type (i) in Sect. 3) and the deverbal nouns referring to abstract results of processes (type (ii) in Sect. 3) can be employed in verbal structures as well. In this case, the deverbal noun selects a particular light (semantically impoverished) verb to form a complex predicate. This complex predicate exhibits a discrepancy between semantic and syntactic behavior. It is the deverbal noun that represents the semantic core of the given predicate, contributing most if not all of the predicate's semantic participants. However, it is the light verb that syntactically governs the deverbal noun. In Czech, complex predicates of the given type form (idiomatic) light verb constructions.

Complex predicates in which the deverbal noun is expressed as the direct object of the light verb (i.e., by the prepositionless accusative) represent the central type of Czech complex predicates, e.g., *mít plán* 'to have a plan'. Rarely, the deverbal noun can be expressed as the indirect object by a prepositionless case other than accusative, e.g., *dojít újmy*$_{gen}$ 'to come to harm', *podrobit zkoumání*$_{dat}$ 'to put under scrutiny', *zahrnout výčitkami*$_{instr}$ 'to shower with reproaches', see esp. [9]. These predicates form light verb constructions (LVCs); the syntactic structure formation of LVCs is regular to a great extent (Sects. 4.1 and 4.2).

Less frequently, complex predicates in which the deverbal noun is expressed as an adverbial of the light verb occur in Czech, e.g., *mít v plánu* 'to intend, lit. to have in plan'. These predicates form the so-called idiomatic light verb constructions representing the borderline between LVCs and idioms due to a greater degree of irregularities in their syntactic formation (Sect. 4.4), see [2].

4.1 The Deep Syntactic Structure

The deep structure of LVCs is formed by both valency complementations of the light verb and complementations of the deverbal noun within the complex predicate. For example, the deep structure of LVCs with the complex predicate *mít plán* 'have a plan' consists of both valency complementations of the deverbal noun *plán* 'plan', see the valency frame in (6) in Sect. 3, and complementations of the light verb *mít* 'have', see the frame in (9).

The valency frame of the deverbal noun corresponds to the usage of the noun in nominal structures (Sect. 3). Individual valency complementations of deverbal nouns are semantically saturated by semantic participants. For example, the ACT and PAT of the noun *plán* 'plan' are mapped onto 'Agent' and 'Goal', respectively.

The valency frame of the light verb is typically identical with the frame of its full verb counterpart, see the frame of the full verb *mít* 'have' in (8) and the frame of the light verb *mít* 'have' in (9) and examples (10) and (11), respectively. They only differ in that the valency position reserved for the deverbal noun, representing the nominal component of the complex predicate with the light verb, is marked by the functor CPHR.

(8) *mít*$_{Full}$ 'have': ACT^{obl}_{nom} PAT^{obl}_{acc}

(9) *mít*$_{Light}$ 'have': ACT^{obl}_{nom} $\mathsf{CPHR}^{obl}_{acc}$

(10) *Petr* $_{\mathsf{ACT}:nom}$ *má pěkný dům* $_{\mathsf{PAT}:acc}$.
'Peter $_{\mathsf{ACT}}$ has a beautiful house $_{\mathsf{PAT}}$.'

(11) *Petr* $_{\mathsf{ACT}:nom}$ *má plán* $_{\mathsf{CPHR}:acc}$ *přestavět dům.*
'Peter $_{\mathsf{ACT}}$ has a plan $_{\mathsf{CPHR}}$ to rebuild the house.'

While valency complementations of full verbs are mapped onto semantic participants, complementations of light verbs do not correspond to any participants; the only exception is represented by light verbs with causative meaning that provide the semantic participant 'Causator', see below. For example, the ACT and PAT of the full verb *mít* 'have' are mapped onto 'Possessor' and 'Possession', respectively. In contrast, the ACT of the light verb *mít* 'have' (the only valency

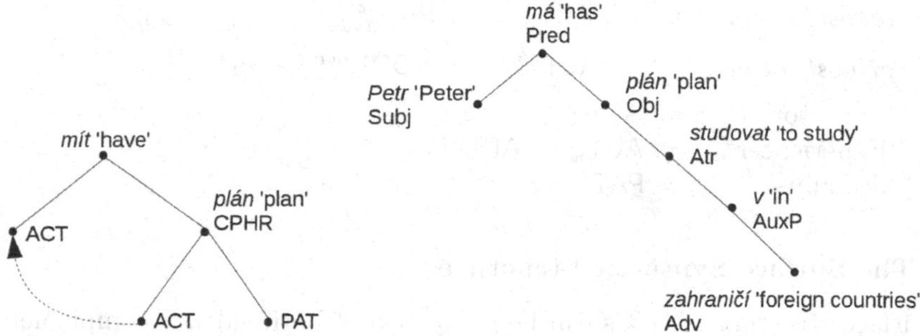

Fig. 1. The deep and surface syntactic structure of the complex predicate *mít plán* 'to have a plan'.

complementation in its valency frame except for CPHR) is not semantically saturated by any participant of the verb.

Although valency complementations of the light verb are not semantically specified by any semantic participants of the verb, they do not remain semantically unsaturated. To acquire semantic capacity, valency complementations of the light verb enter in coreference with complementations of the deverbal noun. For example, the ACT of the light verb *mít* 'have' within the complex predicate *mít plán* 'to have a plan' corefers with the ACT of the noun *plán* 'plan'; both these ACTors thus refer to the 'Agent', see the scheme of the mapping of the semantic participants onto valency complementations in the complex predicate *mít plán* 'to have a plan' provided in (12) ($\Rightarrow$ indicates the mapping of participants, $\rightarrow$ shows coreference). Figure 1 displays the deep syntactic structure of the complex predicate *mít plán* 'have a plan'.

(12) 'Agent'$_n \Rightarrow$ ACT$_n \rightarrow$ ACT$_v$
'Goal'$_n$ $\Rightarrow$ PAT$_n$

In case of *causative light verbs*, the semantic participant 'Causator' is provided by the light verb, being mapped onto one of its valency complementations. For example, within the complex predicate *přinést radost* 'to bring joy' two semantic participants – 'Experiencer' and 'Stimulus' – are provided by the noun *radost* 'happiness, joy'. These participants correspond to the ACT and PAT of the noun, respectively, see the frame of the noun *radost* 'happiness, joy' in (13). In addition, the causative light verb *přinést* 'to bring' contributes the 'Causator', mapped onto its ACT, to the complex predicate *přinést radost* 'to bring joy', see the frame in (14). The ADDR of the light verb – the only remaining semantically unsaturated valency complementation in its valency frame – does not correspond to any participant. To be semantically saturated, the ADDR enters in coreference with the ACT of the deverbal noun *radost* 'happiness, joy', see the scheme of the mapping of the semantic participants within the complex predicate *přinést radost* 'to bring joy' in (15).

(13) *radost* 'happiness, joy': $\mathsf{ACT}^{obl}_{gen,poss}$ $\mathsf{PAT}^{obl}_{nad+instr,z+gen,inf,dcc}$

(14) *přinést* 'bring': ACT^{obl}_{nom} $\mathsf{ADDR}^{obl}_{dat}$ $\mathsf{CPHR}^{obl}_{acc}$

(15) 'Causator'$_v$ $\Rightarrow \mathsf{ACT}_v$
'Experiencer'$_n$ $\Rightarrow \mathsf{ACT}_n \rightarrow \mathsf{ADDR}_v$
'Stimulus'$_n$ $\Rightarrow \mathsf{PAT}_n$

4.2 The Surface Syntactic Structure

The surface structure of LVCs can be composed of both valency complementations of the light verb and complementations of the deverbal noun. Each semantic participant is typically expressed in the surface structure only once. Despite being primarily contributed to LVCs by deverbal nouns, semantic participants tend to be expressed on the surface as valency complementations of light verbs. As corpus evidence shows, the surface structure formation of Czech LVCs is governed by the following principles [5]:

- From the *valency frame of the light verb*, all valency complementations are expressed, namely:
  - the valency complementation with the functor CPHR, indicating the deverbal noun,
  - the valency complementation corresponding to the 'Causator' (if present),
  - all valency complementations which corefer with complementations of the deverbal noun.
- From the *valency frame of the deverbal noun*, those valency complementations are expressed on the surface that are not in coreference with any complementation of the light verb.

For example, from the valency frame of the light verb *mít* 'to have', besides the CPHR reserved for the predicative noun, the ACT coreferring with the ACT of the deverbal noun *plán* 'plan' is expressed in the surface structure of the LVC with the complex predicate *mít plán* 'to have a plan'. From the valency frame of the noun *plán* 'plan', only the PAT, not coreferring with any complementation of the verb, is expressed on the surface; see the valency frames (6) and (9) and the scheme (12). Example (16) illustrates the LVC with the complex predicate *mít plán* 'to have a plan'; see also its surface syntactic structure in Fig. 1.

(16) *Petr*$_{v\mathsf{ACT}:nom}$ *má plán*$_{v\mathsf{CPHR}:acc}$ *studovat*$_{n\mathsf{PAT}:inf}$ *v zahraničí.*
'Peter$_{v\mathsf{ACT}}$ has a plan$_{v\mathsf{CPHR}}$ to study$_{n\mathsf{PAT}}$ abroad.'

The surface structure of the LVC with the complex predicate *přinést radost* 'to bring joy' with the causative light verb *přinést* 'to bring' consists of all valency complementations of the light verb *přinést* 'to bring': the ACT corresponding to the 'Causator', the ADDR coreferring with the ACT of the deverbal noun *radost* 'happiness' (thus expressing the 'Experiencer') and the CPHR standing for the deverbal noun. From the valency frame of the deverbal noun, only the PAT that does not corefer with any complementation of the verb is expressed on the surface, see the valency frames (13) and (14), scheme (15) and example (17).

(17) *Dětem*$_{v\mathsf{ADDR}:dat}$ *akce*$_{v\mathsf{ACT}:nom}$ *přinesla radost*$_{v\mathsf{CPHR}:acc}$ *z pěkných dárků*$_{n\mathsf{PAT}:z+gen}$.
'The event$_{v\mathsf{ACT}}$ brought children$_{v\mathsf{ADDR}}$ joy$_{v\mathsf{CPHR}}$ from beautiful gifts$_{n\mathsf{PAT}}$.'

4.3 A Quantitative Comparison of Nominal and Verbal Structures in Corpus Data

Prague Dependency Treebank (PDT),[3] containing Czech texts with complex and interlinked morphological, surface syntactic and deep syntactic annotation, provides an excellent basis for the study of syntactic behavior of deverbal nouns in nominal and verbal structures. We have divided the instances of nouns in PDT into two groups: the occurrences in which the noun has the CPHR functor,[4] representing verbal structures, and all other occurrences of nouns, representing their nominal structures. We have limited our investigation to the nominal lemmas that appear at least once in a verbal structure; Table 1 gives basic statistics of investigated lemmas and instances.

The graph in Fig. 2 summarizes the frequency of different types of valency complementations of deverbal nouns expressed on the surface relative to all their occurrences; the remaining space to 100% is filled by the occurrences of that functor that are not expressed on the surface.

The figure shows that nominal ACT and ADDR are expressed much more rarely in verbal structures (where they typically corefer with verbal complementations) than in nominal structures. On the other hand, the PAT of productively derived nouns is expressed more often in verbal structures; a preliminary investigation of a sample of the *VALLEX* lexicon (Sect. 5.2) shows that a nominal PAT enters a coreference relation with a complementation of the light verb about three times less than a nominal ACT.

Table 1. Investigated PDT data

	Lemmas	Instances	
		Nominal	Verbal
Productively derived (*-ní/tí*)	57	2265	159
Non-productively derived	265	22028	1950
Total	322	24293	2109

4.4 Remarks on Idiomatic Light Verb Constructions

By idiomatic light verb constructions (ILVCs) we understand the LVCs that are formed by the complex predicates within which the deverbal noun is expressed

[3] http://ufal.mff.cuni.cz/pdt3.0.

[4] The instances of deverbal nouns governed by the verb *být* 'to be', representing a copula verb, were left aside.

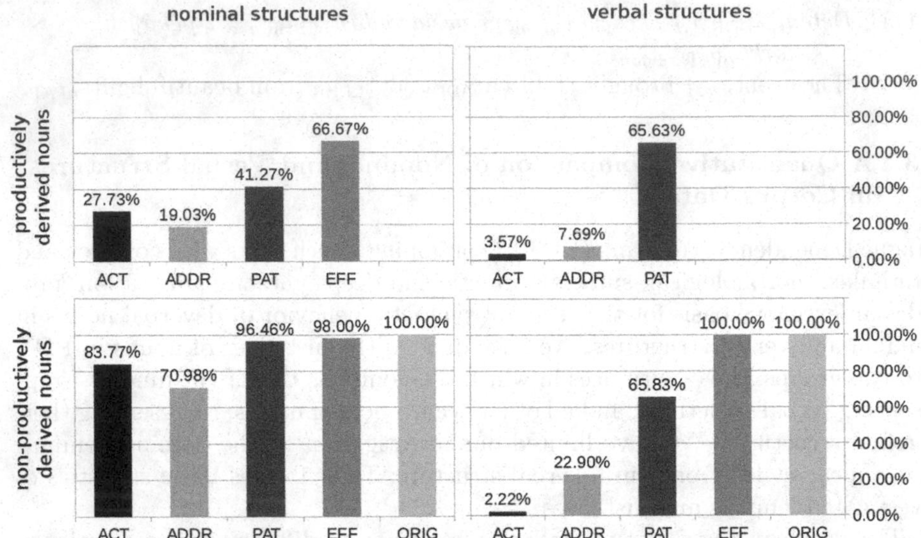

Fig. 2. For each functor, the percentage of its occurrences in which it is expressed in the surface structure of the sentence is given. The missing columns correspond to actants that did not appear with any noun instance in the investigated sample.

as an adverbial of the light verb (i.e., by various prepositional groups, e.g., *dát do pořádku* 'to put in order', *mít pod kontrolou* 'to have under control', *mít na starosti* 'to be responsible, lit. to have on care', *mít v úmyslu* 'to intend, lit. to have in intention').

In ILVCs, semantic participants are primarily provided – as in LVCs – by deverbal nouns that represent their semantic core. The only exception is represented by the complex predicates within which light verbs fulfill the causative function (e.g., *dostat pod kontrolu* 'to get under control', *uvést do chodu* 'to give a start, lit. lead into operation', *dát do ochrany* 'to give under protection, lit. to give in protection'), which contribute the participant 'Causator' initiating the event expressed by the deverbal noun.

The syntactic structure formation of ILVCs is governed by the same principles as that of LVCs:

- the *deep syntactic structure of ILVCs* results from an interplay between the valency frame of the deverbal noun and the frame of the light verb (Sect. 4.1) and it is characterized by coreference between valency complementations of the deverbal noun and complementations of the light verb;
- the *surface syntactic structure of ILVCs* is guided by the same principles as that of LVCs (Sect. 4.2).

For example, the deep structure of the ILVC formed by the complex predicate *mít v plánu* 'to intend, lit. to have in plan' is underlain by the valency frame of the light verb *mít* 'to have' (18) and the frame of the deverbal noun *plán* 'plan' (6) repeated here in (19). This predicate exhibits coreference between the nominal ACT and the verbal ACT and at the same time between the nominal PAT and the verbal PAT, expressing the 'Agent' and 'Goal' provided by the noun, respectively, see scheme (20) and the deep structure of this ILVC in Fig. 3.

(18) *mít* 'to have': ACT^{obl}_{nom} PAT^{obl}_{acc} $\mathsf{CPHR}^{obl}_{v+loc}$

(19) *plán* 'plan': $\mathsf{ACT}^{obl}_{gen,poss}$ $\mathsf{PAT}^{obl}_{gen,na+acc,o+loc,pro+acc,inf,dcc}$

(20) 'Agent'$_n$ ⇒ $\mathsf{ACT}_n \rightarrow \mathsf{ACT}_v$
'Goal'$_n$ ⇒ $\mathsf{PAT}_n \rightarrow \mathsf{PAT}_v$

In the surface structure of the ILVC with the complex predicate *mít v plánu* 'to intend, lit. to have in plan', all valency complementations from the valency frame of the light verb (18) are expressed, namely ACT and PAT coreferring with the nominal ACT and PAT, and the CPHR occupied by the deverbal noun. No valency complementations from the valency frame of the deverbal noun, namely neither the ACT nor the PAT, are expressed on the surface as they corefer with the verbal complementations, see the principles of the surface structure formation in Sect. 4.2 and example (22). The surface structure of the ILVC is displayed in Fig. 3.

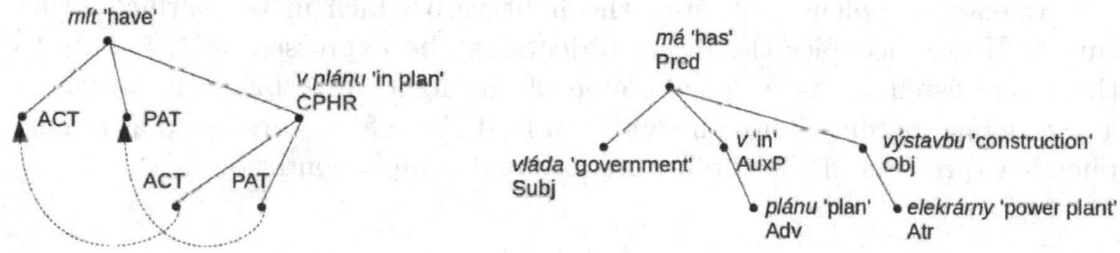

Fig. 3. The deep and surface syntactic structure of the complex predicate *mít v plánu* 'to have a plan, lit. to have in plan'.

However, ILVCs exhibit a lesser degree of regularity in morphemic expressions of valency complementations than LVCs. The irregularities concern morphemic forms of those valency complementations that semantically correspond to participants of propositional character. Corpus evidence shows that information on their morphemic forms cannot be easily inferred from the valency frame of the light verb containing the valency complementation referring to the given participant.

For example, the semantic participant 'Goal' characterizing the complex predicates *mít plán* 'to have a plan' and *mít v plánu* 'to intend, lit. to have in plan' represents a proposition. In LVCs formed by the complex predicate *mít plán* 'to have a plan', the 'Goal' is realized on the surface as an attribute of the deverbal noun *plán* 'plan', i.e., as its PAT (see principles in Sect. 4.2 and Fig. 1). The PAT can be expressed in LVCs by any of the morphemic forms prescribed in the valency frame of this noun, see the valency frame (19) and example (21).

In contrast, in ILVCs formed by the complex predicate *mít v plánu* 'to intend, lit. to have in plan', the Goal is expressed on the surface as the direct object of the light verb *mít* 'to have', i.e., as its PAT. In the valency frame of the light verb *mít* 'to have' (18) – underlying also this verb in the complex predicates without any propositional participant, e.g., *mít v užívání* 'to make use, lit. to have in use', *mít v oblibě* 'to have a liking, lit. to have in liking', only the form of a prepositionless accusative is prescribed for the given PAT. However, the PAT corresponding to the propositional participant 'Goal' in ILVCs with the complex predicate *mít v plánu* 'to intend, lit. to have in plan' can have the form of the infinitive and the dependent content clause as well, see (22).

(21) *Vláda*$_{v\mathsf{ACT}}$ *má plán*$_{v\mathsf{CPHR}}$ *výstavby*$_{n\mathsf{PAT}:gen}$/*na výstavbu*$_{n\mathsf{PAT}:na+acc}$/*o výstavbě*$_{n\mathsf{PAT}:o+loc}$/*pro výstavbu elektrárny*$_{n\mathsf{PAT}:pro+acc}$/*vystavět*$_{n\mathsf{PAT}:inf}$/*že vystaví*$_{n\mathsf{PAT}:dcc}$ *elektrárnu.*

(22) *Vláda*$_{v\mathsf{ACT}}$ *má v plánu*$_{v\mathsf{CPHR}}$ *výstavbu*$_{v\mathsf{PAT}:acc}$/*vystavět*$_{v\mathsf{PAT}:inf}$/*že vystaví*$_{v\mathsf{PAT}:dcc}$ *elektrárnu.*
'The government$_{v\mathsf{ACT}}$ has intention$_{v\mathsf{CPHR}}$ to construct$_{v\mathsf{PAT}}$ a power plant.'

To capture irregularities in the expression of propositional participants in ILVCs, we establish the following principle:

- The valency complementation of the light verb which in the surface structure of ILVCs occupies the direct object may be expressed, additionally to the forms listed in the valency frame of the light verb, by an infinitive or a dependent content clause on condition that these forms are listed as a morphemic expression of the coreferring nominal complementation.

5 Lexicographic Representation of Deverbal Nouns

In this section, we introduce *NomVallex* and *VALLEX*, valency lexicons which provide information on the basis of which nominal (Sect. 5.1) and verbal structures containing deverbal nouns (Sect. 5.2) can be generated.

5.1 Nominal Structures in a Lexicon

The valency lexicon *NomVallex* provides all the information necessary for producing nominal structures governed by Czech deverbal nouns, together with additional syntactic information [6]. This lexicon has adopted the design of the valency lexicon of Czech verbs, *VALLEX*, see Sect. 5.2.

In *NomVallex*, each deverbal noun is described by a lexeme, an abstract twofold unit associating all lexical forms of the noun with lexical units (individual senses of the noun). Each nominal lexeme is represented by a set of lemma(s); it is formed by a set of lexical unit(s) corresponding to the individual senses. The lexical units are specified with respect to their types, i.e., whether they denote processes, abstract results or concrete results of processes.

Key information on the valency structure of each lexical unit is provided by the valency frame, see Sect. 2. Besides the valency frame, each lexical unit is accompanied with a gloss describing the given meaning and an example providing its corpus evidence. Further, each lexical unit can be assigned additional syntactic and semantic information, e.g., on reciprocity, control, and semantic class membership.

Each deverbal noun forming complex predicates with light verbs has the attribute `lvc` providing references to individual valency frames of light verbs with which the noun combines; the particular light verbs are stored in the *VALLEX* lexicon, see Sect. 5.2. On the basis of these references, individual complex predicates can be obtained. See Fig. 4 displaying a simplified entry of the deverbal noun *plán* 'plan'.

*** PLÁN**

: id: blu-n-plán-1 plán
+ $\mathsf{ACT}^{obl}_{gen,poss}$ $\mathsf{PAT}^{obl}_{gen,na+acc,o+loc,pro+acc,inf,aby,že,dcc}$
 -derived: blu-v-plánovat-1
 -gloss: *záměr, úmysl* 'intention, aim'
 -example: *plány vystavět*$_{\mathsf{PAT}}$ *podnik* 'plans to construct a processing plant'
 -lvc: blu-l-mít-2, ...
 -control: ACT, ex
 -class: mental action
 -type: abstract result

: id: blu-n-plán-2 plán
+ $\mathsf{AUTH}^{typ}_{gen,poss}$ $\mathsf{PAT}^{obl}_{gen,poss}$
 -derived: blu-v-plánovat-1
 -gloss: *mapa, nákres* 'map, layout'
 -example: *plán města*$_{\mathsf{PAT}}$ 'city plan'
 -class: mental action
 -type: concrete

Fig. 4. Simplified entry of the noun *plán* 'plan'.

5.2 Verbal Structures in a Lexicon

The derivation of verbal structures with deverbal nouns (LVCs and ILVCs, see Sect. 4) requires a close cooperation between the lexicographic representation of deverbal nouns (see Sect. 5.1) and light verbs on the one hand, and grammatical rules, on the other (see Sect. 4). The representation of LVCs is proposed here for the valency lexicon of Czech verbs *VALLEX*, see [8]. The structure of this lexicon is the same as that of *NomVallex* (Sect. 5.1).

Light verbs in *VALLEX* are treated as specific senses of verbs. Each light verb is assigned its respective valency frame. The valency position reserved in the valency frame for deverbal nouns is labeled by the CPHR functor. Each valency frame of the light verb is assigned three special attributes: `lvc`, `instig`, and map. The attribute map provides a list of pairs of valency complementations of the deverbal noun and the light verb that are in coreference. The attribute lvc provides references to relevant deverbal nouns. If relevant, the attribute instig introduces that valency complementation of the light verb onto which the semantic participant 'Causator' is mapped. See Fig. 5 displaying the simplified entry of the verb *mít* 'to have'.

The lexicon thus economically captures recurring patterns of complex predicates with the given light verb, and the grammatical rules enable users to generate well-formed LVCs and ILVCs.

*** MÍT**

: id: blu-v-mít-1 **impf:** mít **iter:** mívat
+ ACT^{obl}_{nom} PAT^{obl}_{acc} LOC^{typ}
  -gloss: vlastnit 'to possess'
  -example: *Petr má dům v Karpatech.* 'Peter has a house in Carpathians.'

: id: blu-l-mít-2 **impf:** mít **iter:** mívat
+ ACT^{obl}_{nom} $\mathsf{CPHR}^{obl}_{acc}$
  -lvc: blu-n-plán-1, ...
  -map: ACT_v–ACT_n
  -example: *Petr má plán studovat v zahraničí.* 'Peter has a plan to study abroad.'

: id: blu-l-mít-3 **impf:** mít **iter:** mívat
+ ACT^{obl}_{nom} PAT^{obl}_{acc} $\mathsf{CPHR}^{obl}_{v+loc}$
  -lvc: blu-n-plán-1, ...
  -map: ACT_v–ACT_n, PAT_v–PAT_n
  -example: *Petr má v plánu studovat v zahraničí.* 'Peter has a plan to study abroad.'

Fig. 5. Simplified entry of the verb *mít* 'to have', showing the valency frames for the core meaning of the full verb and its corresponding light verbs.

6 Conclusion

In this paper, we have proposed a lexicographic representation of nominal and verbal structures of Czech deverbal nouns, focusing primarily on the verbal ones, i.e., light verb constructions and idiomatic light verb constructions. We have demonstrated that their well-formed syntactic structure can be derived by a complex process requiring a close interplay of information provided by lexicons and grammatical rules, making it possible to better understand the syntactic compositionality of these types of multi-word units.

Acknowledgements. The research reported in the paper was supported by the Czech Science Foundation under the projects GA15-09979S and GA16-02196S and partially by the LINDAT/CLARIN project of the Ministry of Education, Youth and Sports of the Czech Republic (project LM2015071).

This work has been using language resources developed, stored and distributed by the LINDAT/CLARIN project of the Ministry of Education, Youth and Sports of the Czech Republic (project LM2015071).

References

1. Alsina, A., Bresnan, J., Sells, P. (eds.): Complex Predicates. CSLI Publications, Stanford (1997)
2. Baldwin, T., Kim, S.N.: Multiword expressions. In: Indurkhya, N., Damerau, F.J. (eds.) Handbook of Natural Language Processing, pp. 267–292. CRC Press, Boca Raton (2010)
3. Grimshaw, J., Mester, A.: Light verbs and θ-marking. Linguist. Inq. **19**(2), 205–232 (1988)
4. Hinrichs, E., Kathol, A., Nakazawa, T.: Complex Predicates in Nonderivational Syntax. Academic Press, San Diego (1998)
5. Kettnerová, V., Lopatková, M.: At the lexicon-grammar interface: The case of complex predicates in the Functional Generative Description. In: Hajičová, E., Nivre, J. (eds.) Proceedings of Depling 2015, pp. 191–200. Uppsala University (2015)
6. Klímová, J., Kolářová, V., Vernerová, A.: Towards a corpus-based valency lexicon of Czech nouns. In: GLOBALEX 2016: Lexicographic Resources for Human Language Technology, pp. 1–7 (2016)
7. Kolářová, V.: Special valency behavior of Czech deverbal nouns. In: Spevak, O. (ed.) Noun Valency, vol. 2, pp. 19–60. John Benjamins, Amsterdam (2014)
8. Lopatková, M., Kettnerová, V., Bejček, E., Vernerová, A., Žabokrtský, Z.: VALLEX 3.0 - Valenční slovník českých sloves. Karolinum, Praha (2016). http://ufal.mff.cuni.cz/vallex/3.0/
9. Macháčková, E.: Constructions with verbs and abstract nouns in Czech (analytical predicates). In: Čmejrková, S., Štícha, F. (eds.) The Syntax of Sentence and Text, pp. 365–374. John Benjamins, Amsterdam (1994)
10. Panevová, J.: Valency frames and the meaning of the sentence. In: Luelsdorff, P.A. (ed.) The Prague School of Structural and Functional Linguistics, pp. 223–243. John Benjamins, Amsterdam (1994)
11. Panevová, J.: K valenci substantiv (s ohledem na jejich derivaci). In: Zbornik Matice srpske za slavistiku, pp. 29–36 (2002)
12. Panevová, J.: In favour of the argument-adjunct distinction (from the perspective of FGD). Prague Bull. Math. Linguist. **106**, 21–30 (2016)
13. Ramos, M.A.: Towards the synthesis of support verb constructions: distribution of syntactic actants between the verb and the noun. In: Wanner, L., Mel'cuk, I.A. (eds.) Selected Lexical and Grammatical Issues in the Meaning-Text Theory, pp. 97–137. John Benjamins, Amsterdam (2007)
14. Sgall, P., Hajičová, E., Panevová, J.: The Meaning of the Sentence in its Semantic and Pragmatic Aspects. D. Reidel Publishing Company, Dordrecht (1986)

Contribution Towards a Corpus-Based Phraseology Minimum

Marie Kopřivová(✉)

Charles University, Prague, Czech Republic
Marie.Koprivova@ff.cuni.cz

Abstract. This paper represents an attempt to put together a list of the most commonly used (most typical) Czech idioms using corpus data with annotated collocations. Collocations are annotated in corpora of contemporary written Czech as well as in a corpus of spoken Czech containing transcripts of intimate conversations. Idioms are selected based on their frequency in different text types (newspapers and magazines, non-fiction, fiction, spoken language) and the resulting list is compiled based on a criterion of occurrence of the given idiom in at least two different text types. A short characteristic of the individual text types is given in terms of which types of idioms are typical for them (according to formal criteria). This study confirms a substantial divide between idiom use in written and spoken language. A smaller difference can be observed between fiction on the one hand and non-fiction and newspapers on the other. The main reason for this is the interactive nature of fiction texts, which leads to them containing idioms with verbal components. These are employed in a fashion similar to spoken languages, in interactions among the individual characters. By contrast, non-fiction and journalistic language tends to be more descriptive, with more nominal idioms.

Keywords: Idiom · Corpus · Czech idioms · Phraseology minimum

1 Introduction

While the notion of a paremiological minimum[1] is well established and for many languages, there are paremiological minima verified from different sources (for example [2, 16]), it is more difficult to compile a set of the most widely used idioms for a particular language, which we call a phraseological minimum in this paper. This is a wider set of units of various kinds, which cannot be compiled using the tried and tested procedures employed when creating paremiological minima. One of these methods, for

This study was written within the project Between Lexicon and Grammar (2016–2018), supported by the Grant Agency of the Czech Republic, reg. no. 16-07473S.

[1] "A paremiological minimum hinges on the concept of a set of proverbs that all members of society know, or an average adult is expected to know." [6]. The first creator of the paremiological minimum on a demographic basis was Permjakov [15]. Another method of determining paremiological minima is based on large corpora [3].

R. Mitkov (Ed.): Europhras 2017, LNAI 10596, pp. 220–231, 2017.
https://doi.org/10.1007/978-3-319-69805-2_16

example, verifies the participants' knowledge of the proverbial form by omitting part of it and making them complete it. This is not possible with shorter idioms, because if some of their parts are omitted, it will not be clear what idiom it is, or indeed whether it is an idiom at all. Moreover, knowing the proverbial form doesn't necessarily imply being able to use it right, and that the participant uses it actively. Yet frequency of use is very important for the phraseological minimum.

In spite of these difficulties, such a set would be very useful for language teaching and lexicographical purposes, among other things. In this paper, we will try to show how corpora of Czech could serve to this end. Corpora reveal the actual usage of specific idioms in written and spoken language. Use in written language can be considered more representative of passive knowledge, but still, it does affect individual production. Spoken corpora, on the other hand, provide a fairly large number of speakers; they can be thought of as representing active knowledge with some restrictions, because the use of idioms may vary. The question remains, of course, how reliably and exhaustively the idioms can be identified in large corpus data [12]. A few corpora of Czech are among the first to have such annotations, so we used them for our experiment.

2 The Data

As a source of phrasemes for the written language, the SYN2015 100 M-word representative corpus of written Czech [13] will be used. It has the same proportion of newspapers and magazines, non-fiction and fiction [14]. For the spoken corpora, we will employ the ORAL-F 2M-word corpus [8], which was created by merging the ORAL2006 [11] and ORAL2008 corpora [17]. These contain transcriptions of recordings of spontaneous conversations between speakers who know each other well, recorded from 2002 to 2007. ORAL-F contains annotations of idioms and collocations carried out using the FRANTA tool [7, 10]) This tool, based on the *Dictionary of Czech Phraseology and Idioms* (SČFI, [3]), identifies phrasemes in the text of the corpus; it is even able to identify phrasemes with word order permutations, variants and some creatively modified uses. The initial list extracted from the dictionary was extended with some newer phrases and other types of collocations (e.g. multi-word prepositions).

The distribution of phrasemes varies with each type of register,[2] so frequency should not be the sole criterion when establishing the set of most commonly used idioms. Moreover, we will never have a comparatively large subcorpus for the spoken data, yet idioms used in ordinary conversation are an important component of the knowledge of phraseology. Thus, we divided the written corpus into three subcorpora: fiction, journalism and professional literature, all of which are represented by the same amount of words (33M) in the SYN2015 corpus. The fourth part is a 2M corpus of spontaneous conversations among people who know each other well, i.e. very informal spoken language.

[2] For example, in newspapers, a lot of space is dedicated to sports news, which has a specific phraseology. This can then reduce the prominence of other commonly used idioms.

3 Methodology

In all four parts of the corpus, which represent specific registers (journalism, nonfiction, fiction, spoken language), the most common annotated collocations were identified and the list was then narrowed down to contain only idioms: set phrases which are typically figurative and which have non-compositional meanings [1, 10][3]. Therefore, grammatical idioms, verbo-nominal combinations and multi-word prepositions were not included in the selection. Also excluded were cases that may have both literal and figurative meaning in the text (such as *lose one's marbles* in English) that cannot be easily distinguished, which could distort the frequency figures. This applies in particular to somatic idioms, which often serve to report direct speech (*mávnout rukou/ wave one's hand*). On the other hand, those containing words with a restricted collocational profile (so-called monocollocates) have been left in, as even native speakers find it difficult to determine their meaning based on synchronic language use.

In each group, a list of the 100 most common idioms was selected (this number was arbitrarily determined) and these lists were compared to each other. The resulting list, which should contain the most used phrasemes in written and spoken communication in contemporary Czech, included such phrasemes that occurred in at least two genres. This set is far from exhaustive, probably not sufficient in terms of scope or theoretical definition. Still, this corpus-based study gives us interesting insights into the use of phrasemes in different types of text.

4 Characteristics of Idioms by Type of Text (Register)

The following table lists the number of phrasemes and collocations in each part of the corpus. What all types of texts have in common is that the most frequent collocations are relatively short idioms, most of which consist of two components, some of 3 or 4. As can be expected, there are no proverbs between the most frequent idioms; proverbs are usually much longer. Idioms with a verbal component are predominant. The largest proportion of identified collocations is in fiction, the smallest one being in non-fiction (Table 1).[4]

Table 1. Numbers of collocations in the subcorpora.

Subcorpus	Number of coll's (i.p.m)	Number of coll's	Number of types of coll's
Newspapers	11,216	445,782	18,514
Non-fiction	9,871	338,758	17,702
Fiction	16,213	674,796	23,526
Spoken	12,418	–	–

[3] This restriction results in the elimination of some types of very common multi-word expressions, especially in non-fiction (for example, multi-word prepositions). This allows us to focus on the core of phraseology, as represented by idioms.

[4] Specialized multi-word terms are not identified by the automatic extraction procedure.

The following sections give brief characteristics of the individual text types from the point of view of the most common idioms.

4.1 Newspapers and Magazines

In journalistic texts, terms can often be found among the frequent idioms, often created on a metaphorical basis (e.g. *cestovní ruch /tourism*, lit. *travel bustle*, *žlutá karta/yellow card*, *noční můra/nightmare*, *pitný režim /hydration schedule*, lit. *drinking schedule*, *sametová revoluce/Velvet Revolution*, *studená válka/Cold War*). The most commonly used nominal collocations thematically correspond to those areas which appear regularly in journalism, such as politics (*široká veřejnost/the general public*, *vysoce postavený/high-ranking*); sports news (*dostat se do vedení/get in the lead*, *podat výkon/perform (well, bad)*, lit. *give a performance*, *malé vápno/goal area*, lit. *small lime*). Among verbal idioms, verbo-nominal combinations dominate (e.g. *dostat se do vedení/get in the lead*, *spatřit světlo světa/see the light of day*, lit. *see the light of the world*). The frequency of the most common idioms selected ranges from 1565 to 102 occurrences. But more foolish idioms appear in the journalism. Idioms are often creatively repurposed, which shifts them away from their usual use cases. For instance, *říci poslední slovo/to have the last word* is usually associated only with the context of a verbal argument, can be repurposed to fit the context of a sporting event:

... v polovině duelu i vyrovnali, jenže poslední slovo patřilo zkušenému obránci
... they managed to even the score in the middle of the duel, but the last word belonged to an experienced defender.

Likewise, the idiom *spatřit světlo světa /to see the light of day* was originally associated with birth but later came to refer to a moment of appearance in general:

První Mini spatřilo světlo světa v roce 1959.
The first Mini saw the light of day in 1959.

Newspapers often shift the limits of the usage of idioms and have an impact on their employment, or on the introduction of new idioms. Recently, these are mostly coming in as borrowings from English.

4.2 Non-fiction

This subcorpus includes academic, professional and popular science texts. This register is where the smallest amount of set phrases was found. Even more than in the journalistic subcorpus, idioms in this group tend to be also terms (*velký třesk/big bang*, *černá díra/black hole*, *světelný rok/light year*, *krásná literature/fiction*, lit. *beautiful literature*, *skleníkový efekt/greenhouse effect*, *císařský řez/caesarean section*). Many of these are originally calques, mainly from English, and some of them are shifting from terminological use to wider phraseological use. For instance, the astronomical term *black hole* borrowed from English is beginning to be used beyond its terminological meaning and describes any entity that absorbs other entities, especially money, initially appearing as part of a simile, later on its own as a metaphor:

Mnoho projektů se ukázalo jako černá díra na evropské peníze.
Many projects have turned out to be a black hole for European money.
Taková černá díra, se kterou se člověk musí vypořádat.
A sort of black hole which one has to deal with.

The 100 most common idioms are found in the frequency range 1814–74 occurrences. Collocational idioms combining adjective + noun predominate.

4.3 Fiction

Collocations in fiction are the most variegated, which is reflected both in the highest number of identified collocations and the highest number of identified *types* of collocations. The 100 most frequent idioms are found in the frequency range between 884 and 175 occurrences. Few terms are to be found among them, combinations involving verbs are more prominent (*číst myšlenky/to read one's mind*, lit. *read thoughts*, *dát pokoj/to leave alone*, lit. *give peace*, *zlomit srdce/to break one's heart*, *mít sto chutí/to feel like doing sth*, lit. *have one-hundred desires/inclinations*) and even binomials occur occasionally (*ruku v ruce/hand in hand*, *den co den /day by day*). The individual phraseme components tend to be more common words. Some idioms can even play a role in structuring dialogue:

"Proč jsi nic neřekla?" ***skočil jí do řeči*** *Jirka.*
"Why didn't you say anything?" Jirka ***cut in*** (lit. ***jumped into her speech***).

In general, the idioms employed tend to be more figurative or metaphorical, for instance:

Nechtěl bych, aby mé sestře ***zlomil srdce*** *nějaký ničema.*
I wouldn't want my sister to have ***her heart broken*** *by some scoundrel.*

4.4 Spoken Language

The spoken corpus data are much smaller than in the case of the previous three groups, which means we reach fairly low absolute frequencies in our top 100 most common idioms: from 524 to 21 occurrences. Here as elsewhere, short idioms tend to dominate, and a distinctive feature is the conspicuous presence of profanities (*vysrat se na něco/fuck it*, lit. *take-a-shit oneself on sth*, *jít do prdele/fuck off*, lit. *go to ass*). Idiom usage is mostly governed by their pragmatic function, the following being the most typical: surprise (*ty bláho/wow*), advice (*vykašli se na to/let it be*, lit. *cough on it*) and admonitions (*dej si pozor/be careful*, lit. *have yourself attention*) or warnings (*dej pokoj/leave me alone*, lit. *give peace*). The idioms tend to be more often evaluative and intensifying, which is reflected in an increased rate of occurrence of expressive components. Another type of idioms which frequently occur in spoken language is idioms which contain only function words and whose identification also depends on intonation [4]. For both these reasons, these idioms are hard to distinguish from cases where the same sequence of words occurs just by chance within spoken discourse (e.g. as fillers, turn-initiators etc.), so these problematic instances were removed (e.g. *no tak*, which can be both an idiom with a pragmatic function of admonishment/warning and a simple turn-initiator). Another typical component of spoken language idioms is verbs in the imperative mood, for instance:

Bohouši, vykašli se na to.
Let it be, Bohouš.

5 Mutual Comparison of Text Types

5.1 Similarities in Idiom Use

If we compare the individual text types based on the most frequent phrasemes, we find that newspapers and non-fiction are most similar to each other, followed by fiction and non-fiction. The use of similar idioms in newspapers, fiction and non-fiction can at least partially be explained by the fact that non-fiction also includes lifestyle and other magazines, which can include similar topics and treatments, and on the other hand, newspapers may include short prose close to fiction.

Table 2 also shows that written language in general is fairly compact (the individual text types are close to each other) and spoken language is a different beast altogether, with a much smaller overlap in the most frequent idioms. However, from other perspectives (see below), fiction, which often represents or portrays spoken language, is relatively close to the spoken data. It should be stressed at this point that the spoken data employed are highly specific, they include a high number of substandard word forms and regional variants. In all likelihood, more formal spoken language would exhibit a higher similarity to written language.

All four categories share a single idiom, a binomial: *čas od času/from time to time*.

Table 2. Identical idioms in different text types.

Text types	Number of identical idioms
Newspapers × non-fiction	27
Fiction × non-fiction	18
Newspapers × fiction	13
Spoken × fiction	8
Spoken × newspapers	4
Spoken × non-fiction	4

5.2 Cranberry Idioms

The so-called cranberry idioms are idioms containing monocollocates (words with a restricted collocational profile). They generally have a low frequency in language [5]. However, it appears, somewhat surprisingly, that some of these feature among the most common idioms. Therefore, it would be appropriate to incorporate them in the education system.

In our sample, we met them most often in newspapers and fiction, they were almost non-present in spoken language (Fig. 1).

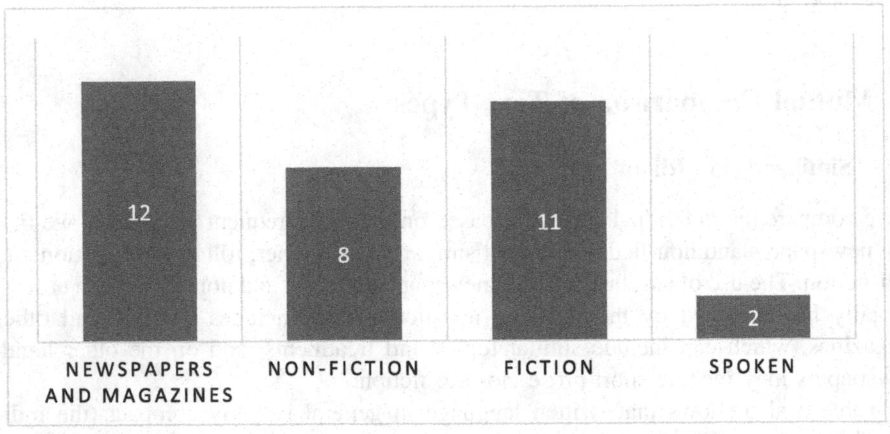

Fig. 1. Number of cranberry idioms by text type.

In Table 4, the monocollocates (components of cranberry idioms) are shown in bold. Here is an example of cranberry idiom usage:

Téměř všechno bylo k mání včetně druhých největších zásob plynu v Latinské Americe.
Almost everything was up for grabs including Latin America 's second-biggest gas reserves.

5.3 Idioms by Number of Components

The following bar chart compares the most common idioms in the individual text types according to the number of their constituent components. In the domain of newspapers and non-fiction, two-component idioms are the most common, which corresponds to the fact that they are mostly terminological appellations consisting of an adjective and noun. In fiction, the amount of two- and three-component idioms is comparable, whereas in spoken language, there is a clear preference for three-component ones (they are mostly very short words, one of them often being a preposition, e.g. *čas od času / from time to time*). Only fiction and spoken language yielded frequent idioms with four components, and only spoken language went as far as five components (three idioms) and one with six – it is a saying attributed to Lenin which people often like to quote in jest (Fig. 2):

jak říkal Lenin učit se, učit se, učit se.
as Lenin said, study, study, study

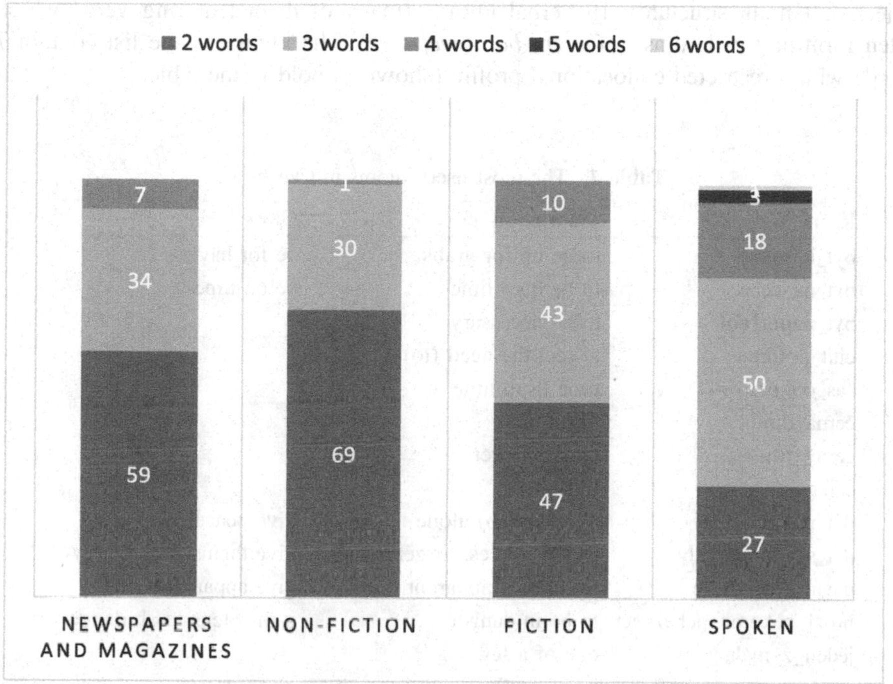

Fig. 2. Proportions of idioms consisting of different numbers of components by text type.

5.4 Idioms by Type of Components

Different types of texts also differ in the dominant type of components in the idioms; nouns dominate in newspapers and non-fiction, while fiction and spoken language contain predominantly idioms with a verbal component, as shown in Table 3. This corresponds to the interactional nature of these two groups.

Table 3. The number of verbal idioms in the text type.

Text type	Number of verbal idioms
Newspapers	36
Non-fiction	33
Fiction	73
Spoken	70

6 The Resulting List

The resulting list is based on the criterion that the phraseme has occurred among the 100 most common idioms in at least two text types. It contains 47 idioms (see Table 3), of which 28 are nominal and 19 are verbal. This list is nicely representative of the usual idiom structures in Czech. It contains 4 binomials,[5] 16 nominal idioms (with a typical adjective + noun structure), 19 verbal idioms (many of them featuring verbs which often form part of idioms in Czech: *be, have, give*). The idioms in the list contain 7 words with a restricted collocational profile (shown in bold in the table).

Table 4. The most used idioms in Czech.

Idiom	Translation	Gloss
být_k_**mání**	to be up for grabs	be for having
být_na_čase	to be high time	be on time
být_**zapotřebí**	to be necessary	
cítit_potřebu	to feel the need (to)	
čas_od_času	time from time	
černá_díra	black hole	
černý_trh	black market	
čerstvý_vzduch	fresh air	
dát_pokoj	to leave (sb) alone	give peace
dát_se_dohromady	to join forces, to get together	give themselves jointly
dávat_najevo,_že	to make it apparent that	give apparently that
hrozí_někomu_nebezpečí	to be in danger	it-threatens to-sb danger
jeden_z_mála	one of a few	
jít_do_toho	to be up for it	go in it
lámat_si_hlavu	to try to figure out	break to-oneself head
lézt_na_nervy	to irritate	climb/crawl on nerves
mít_na_**vybranou**	to have a choice	have on choosing
mít_plné_zuby	to be fed up (with)	have full teeth
mít_to_za_sebou	to be done with it	have it behind oneself
mít_**tušení**	to have a hunch	
na_první_pohled	at first sight	
nemít_**ponětí**	to have no clue	not-have idea
noční_můra	nightmare	night moth
od_rána_do_večera	from dawn to dusk	
onen_svět	the other side	that-other world

(*continued*)

[5] According to [2], similar combinations of two slightly different but conceptually similar word forms can also be described as binomials, e.g. a co-occurring pair of adverbs like *tu a tam/here and there*.

Table 4. (*continued*)

Idiom	Translation	Gloss
otázka_času	a matter of time	question of-time
pod_širým_nebem	outdoors	under wide sky
poslední_slovo	the last word	
přijít_na_svět	to be born	come on world
ruku_v_ruce	hand in hand	
sametová_revoluce	the Velvet Revolution	
silná_stránka	strong suit	strong page/side
spatřit_světlo_světa	to see the light of day	see light of-world
stát_v_cestě	to stand in the way	
studená_válka	the Cold War	
široká_veřejnost	general public	broad public
štědrý_den	Christmas Eve	generous day
tu_a_tam	here and there	
tvrdá_práce	hard work	
velké_peníze	big money	
vysoce_postavený	high-ranking	highly placed
zbrusu_nový	brand new	from-grindstone new
zdravý_rozum	common sense	healthy reason
zorné_pole	field of view	
železná_opona	the Iron Curtain	
živý_plot	hedge	live fence

7 Conclusion

Using the automatic identification of phrasemes and collocations in corpora of Czech, we attempted to identify the most commonly used idioms in Czech. For the time being, this is just a pilot study on a small sample of the most frequent idioms in four different text types. The resulting list contains fairly short idioms, consisting mostly of two or three components. In the future, an expanded overview of idioms of this type would constitute a welcome resource for both lexicographical and teaching purposes.

Based on our study, we can confirm that idiom use differs significantly in spoken and written language. This is probably indicative of a difference between passive knowledge and active use of idioms. The resulting list contains 47 idioms; the criterion for inclusion was that the given idiom had to occur in at least two registers. It also contains eight words with restricted collocational profiles (*být k* ***mání****, být* ***zapotřebí****, dát* ***najevo****, mít na* ***vybranou****, nemít* ***ponětí****, mít* ***tušení****,* ***zbrusu*** *nový,* ***zorné*** *pole*). Synchronically, these occur almost exclusively as components of the phrasemes listed. Since they are used fairly often, they should be part of the passive vocabulary of students of Czech as a foreign language.

Based on the usage of verbal idioms in the individual text types, we can categorize them into interactional registers, where verbal idioms predominate, such as fiction and spoken language, and descriptive registers (newspapers and non-fiction). It turns out that idioms which are simultaneously terms and reflect important geopolitical events in the longer time frame, like *železná opona/the Iron Curtain*, *studená válka/the Cold War*, *sametová revoluce/the Velvet Revolution*, can make it to the top of the frequency list.

Searching for idioms in corpora is complicated by their variability and use in different kinds of text. For example, in actual usage, longer idioms may be reduced to just some of their constituent parts, which are distinctive enough to hint at the intended meaning (represented by the entire idiom).The identification of verbal idioms is complicated by the fact that in Czech, the individual parts of the idiom can be found at different places in the sentence. Some types of idioms have slots which can be filled by one of a series of homonymous verbs. The chosen verb can then express different pragmatic functions or affinity with a particular register. A new database of multi-word units in Czech is intended to capture these features [9].

An important requirement for future work is to lay better theoretical foundations, use more reliable and even better annotated data, and consider various options in verifying speakers' knowledge of idioms.

References

1. Burger, H., Dobrovolskij, D., Kühn, P., Norrick, N.: Phraseology: Subject area, terminology and research topic. In: Burger, H., Dobrovolskij, D., Kühn, P. Norrick, N. (eds.) Phraseology: An International Handbook of Contemporary Research. Walter de Gruyter, Berlin, New York (2007)
2. Čermák, F.: Czech and General Phraseology. Karolinum, Praha (2007)
3. Čermák, F.: a kol.: Slovník české frazeologie a idiomatiky. 1– 4. LEDA, Praha (2009)
4. Čermák, F., Kopřivová, M.: Idioms in Spoken Corpus: A Sample of Czech Data. Computerised and Corpus-based Aproches to Phraseology: Monolingual and Miltilingual Perspectives, Editions Tradulex, Geneva, pp. 194–205 (2016)
5. Čermák, F., Čermák, J., Obstová, Z., Vachková, M.: Language Periphery: Monocollocable Words in English, Italian, German and Czech. John Benjamins Publishing Company, New York, Philadelphia (2016)
6. Ďurčo, P.: Empirical research and paremiological minimum. In: Hrisztova-Gotthardt, H., Varga, A. (eds.) Introduction to Peremiology: A Comprehensive Guide to Proverb Studies (2015)
7. Hnátková, M.: Značkování frazémů a idiomů v Českém národním korpusu s pomocí Slovníku české frazeologie a idiomatiky. SaS 63/2 (2002)
8. Hnátková, M., Kopřivová, M.: Identification of idioms in spoken corpora. In: Gajdošová, K., Žáková, A. (eds.) Natural Language Processing and Corpus Linguistics and E-learning, pp. 92–99. SAV JÚLŠ, Bratislava (2013)
9. Hnátková, M., Jelínek, T., Kopřivová, M., Petkevič, V., Rosen, A., Skoumalova, H.: Eye of a needle in a haystack. (in this book)
10. Kopřivová, M., Hnátková, M.: From dictionary to corpus. In: Jesenšek, V., Grzybek, P. (eds.) Phraseology in Dictionaries and Corpora, pp. 155–168. Filozofska fakulteta Maribor, Maribor (2014)
11. Kopřivová, M., Waclawičová, M.: ORAL2006: korpus neformální mluvené češtiny. Ústav Českého národního korpusu FF UK, Praha (2006). http://www.korpus.cz

12. Moon, R.: Corpus linguistic approaches with English corpora. In: Burger, H., Dobrovolskij, D., Kühn, P., Norrick, N. (eds.): Phraseology, pp. 1045–1059. HSK. Walter de Gruyter, Berlin, New York (2007)
13. Křen, M., Cvrček, V., Čapka, T., Čermáková, A., Hnátková, M., Chlumská, L., Jelínek, T., Kovářiková, D., Petkevič, V., Procházka, P., Skoumalová, H., Škrabal, M., Truneček, P., Vondřička, P., Zasina, A.: SYN2015: reprezentativní korpus psané češtiny. Ústav Českého národního korpusu FF UK, Praha (2015). http://www.korpus.cz
14. Křen, M., Cvrček, V., Čapka, T., Čermáková, A., Hnátková, M., Chlumská, L., Jelínek, T., Kovářiková, D., Petkevič, V., Procházka, P., Skoumalová, H., Škrabal, M., Truneček, P., Vondřička, P., Zasina, A.: SYN2015: representative corpus of contemporary written Czech. In: Proceedings of the Tenth International Conference on Language Resources and Evaluation (LREC 2016), pp. 2522–2528. ELRA, Portorož (2016). ISBN 978-2-9517408-9-1. http://www.lrec-conf.org/proceedings/lrec2016/pdf/186_Paper.pdf
15. Permjakov, G.L.: On the paremiological level and paremiological minimum of language. Proverbium 22, pp. 862–863 (1973)
16. Schindler, F.: Das Sprichwort im heutigen Tschechischen: empirische Untersuchung und semantische Beschreibung. Sagner, München (1993)
17. Waclawičová, M., Kopřivová, M., Křen, M., Válková, L.: ORAL2008: sociolingvisticky vyvážený korpus neformální mluvené češtiny. Ústav Českého národního korpusu FF UK, Praha (2008). http://www.korpus.cz

Estimating Lexical Availability of European Portuguese Proverbs

Sónia Reis[1(✉)] and Jorge Baptista[1,2]

[1] University of Algarve, Campus de Gambelas, 8005-139 Faro, Portugal
reis.soniamm@gmail.com, jbaptis@ualg.pt
[2] L2F/INESC-ID, Lisbon, Portugal

Abstract. This paper relates data on lexical availability with data on textual frequency of proverbs in European Portuguese. Each data source should provide different perspectives on the use of proverbs in the language. This should allow an empirically well-motivated selection of proverbs aiming at the development of NLP resources, specifically for applications for learning Portuguese as a Foreign Language and for the diagnosis/therapy of speech impairments/disabilities. A large database (over 114,000 proverbs and their variants) was independently classified by two annotators, according to intuitively estimated lexical availability. Next, a random, stratified sample was selected and lexical availability was then confirmed with an online survey. Frequency data was gathered from two web browsers and a large-sized, publicly available, *corpus* of journalistic texts. Results from the survey, the web and the *corpus* by and large confirm the initial intuitive classification and a core of commonly used proverbs was defined.

Keywords: European portuguese proverbs · Frequency in *corpus* · Lexical availability

1 Introduction: Using Proverbs

Proverbs are used frequently and in many communicative contexts [1]. In spite of their colloquial/popular status and (mostly) oral transmission process [2], they are found not only in oral communication but also, though perhaps less frequently, in written discourses, and in different text types and genres [3], serving several types of rhetorical functions within discourse [4]. Because of their rich cultural and linguistic content [5], proverbs have been used in many applications, namely, as linguistic material for language learning [6] and language impairment diagnosis or speech therapy [7].

For language learning, proverbs provide a wide spectrum of expressive effects and a cross-cultural perspective on the language community and their symbolic heritage [2]. Furthermore, they are concise, often highly figurative, linguistic structures, naturally yielding to syntactic as well as culturally-oriented exploration in pedagogic context [8, 9].

As linguistic material for diagnosis/therapy of language impairment, particularly in the case of pathologies resulting from trauma, proverbs are deemed as effective tools, since they can be used as stimuli or prompts to exercise different cognitive structures, particularly long-term memory, even when the ability to speak is impaired [10–14].

R. Mitkov (Ed.): Europhras 2017, LNAI 10596, pp. 232–244, 2017.
https://doi.org/10.1007/978-3-319-69805-2_17

Therefore, proverbs have been used in speech therapy, for example in tasks requiring the patient to complete a proverb, to explain its meaning, or the conditions in which it would be adequate to use it.

In spite of the crucial role that the adequate use of proverbs plays in the development of such exercises or tasks, little is said about their selection. Particularly in the case of didactic games involving proverbs, many available exercises could perfectly have used other linguistic material and no proper justification of the selected proverbs is provided [15].

Concerning proverbs, the selection of adequate material by specialist from these two areas faces several difficulties [16]. Selected proverbs should be commonly known, in order to reflect in a representative way, the culture of the language community using them. On the other hand, vocabulary involved in those expressions cannot be too rare or unknown. Furthermore, the choice of phraseological material should provide relevant items for the pedagogic goals of the exercises/activities [15].

As stimuli for speech therapy or language impairment diagnosis, selection of adequate examples is crucial. It is not easy to determine whether the fact of the patient not recognising the proverb, or the failure in producing an adequate answer to a fill-in-the-blank task, is due to a pathologic condition (e.g. dementia), or it is just due to the fact that he/she does not recognise/know the proverb.

Concerning Portuguese, and more specifically European Portuguese, [17] report several on-line resources, already available for learning Portuguese as a Foreign Language (PFL). The *Ciberescola da Língua Portuguesa*[1] and the *Centro Virtual Camões*[2] make available a set of didactic games, some of them involving proverbs. These games consist, basically, in completing a proverb or explaining its meaning.

For speech therapy/diagnosis, on the other hand, there are very few, publicly available, virtual therapists. One of them is the VITHEA system (Virtual Therapist for Aphasia Treatment) [18], which aims at the treatment of aphasia, featuring different types of visual and auditory stimuli, especially for eliciting vocabulary. To date, only a small number of exercises with proverbs have been produced.

Lexical availability is the key concept concerning these selection requirements. Besides other issues that may be task- or domain-specific (that should be used either in language learning or in speech therapy), a lexically available set of proverbs, consists of expressions:

(a) that are easily recognised as such by the linguistic community as whole;
(b) whose meaning and pragmatic conditions of use are widely known by native speakers;
(c) that occur in a broad set of communicative situations.

Linguistic items presenting such requirements are considered to be lexically available, in the sense that they are part of the shared knowledge of the linguistic community, in as much the same way as the meaning and syntax of a commonly used verb is known, with high likelihood, by any native speaker of that given language. Lexically available

[1] http://www.ciberescola.com/, last accessed 2017/05/13.
[2] http://cvc.institutocamoes.pt/, last accessed 2017/05/13.

items are also deemed to show a significant frequency on the language daily use, so that frequency can be viewed as an indirect signal of that availability.

The problem at hand is, thus, a question of devising the appropriate method for selecting a representative sample from the *corpus* of proverbs available for a given language. This problem is somewhat similar to the definition of a common vocabulary from the large lexicon of a language [19]. However, because of their primary oral mode of transmission and their colloquial nature, finding evidence of proverbs' use in written *corpora* is not a trivial task: in several languages, such as Portuguese, many large-sized available *corpora* are built from journalistic texts, and writing and style conventions strongly advise against using such colloquial expressions [20][3]. Besides, proverbs often present lexical and syntactical *variation* [21], which renders the task of finding them in texts much more complex than just looking for simple lexical items (words or phrases).

In view of the above, this paper aims at establishing, on solid empirical grounds, a core set of very commonly used proverbs, widely recognised (and adequately interpreted) by the majority of the (European) Portuguese, native speaking community. This selection could then be used in different scenarios, such as in language teaching and speech therapy, among other practical applications.

The remainder of the paper is structured as follows: Sect. 2 presents the method for manually selecting an initial set of proverbial expressions; then, using a stratified sample, classified according to their estimated lexical availability, that selection was validated using a survey. Next, in Sect. 3 the frequency of that sample is obtained from two popular web browsers, in order to further validate the initial selection. Finally, in Sect. 4 those same proverbs were queried in a large-sized, publicly available, European Portuguese *corpus*. Frequency data from the two types of sources (web and *corpus*) are compared against the estimated lexical availability, in order to produce an empirically well-motivated selection of commonly used proverbs that may be reliably used for different applications. The paper concludes (Sect. 5) by presenting the main findings and suggestions for future work.

2 Lexical Availability and Proverb Selection

In order to tackle the selection of an initial set of proverbs, candidate to the status of lexically available items, a large data base with 114,413 proverbs and their variants was used [22]. These were collected from four dictionaries of European Portuguese, which were digitised and then manually corrected. Each proverb was given a unique identifier (ID), indicating its source. After removing the stop words, each proverb was associated to a set of keywords: full verbs, nouns and adjectives, for the most part.

Two annotators both native speakers of European Portuguese and extensive knowledge of the proverbial stock of the language independently marked the proverbs they recognised and deemed as usual. Annotator 1 marked 739 proverbs, while Annotator 2 marked 379 proverbs. This produced a tiered list of proverbs, ranked by levels (0 to 2).

[3] http://static.publico.pt/nos/livro_estilo/13-rigor-e.html, last accessed 2017/05/13.

In total, 276 expressions were considered usual by both annotators (level 2), 566 proverbs were considered usual by only one of the annotators (level 1), and the remainder forms (113,571) have not been marked by either (level 0).

The initial assumption is that level 2 proverbs are lexically highly available expressions, level 1 are less so (only moderately available), and level 0 items, constituting the bulk of the database, though they are part of the *corpus* of proverbs of the language, are not sufficiently usual (seldom available) to be included in a selection aiming at the applications envisaged in this paper (language learning and speech therapy, for example).

Since only two annotators were involved, it was then deemed necessary to further confirm their selection. Furthermore, since a significant mismatch was found between the two annotations, it should be ascertained which proverbs from level 1 (where the two annotators did not agree) should be integrated in level 2, or left as only moderately available (level 1), or even removed from the selection altogether (and integrated in level 0).

A survey was thus built to confirm this initial selection. However, because the total set of proverbs (and variants) from levels 1 and 2 is too large to be presented in a survey to a wide audience, for it would require a long time to be answered by each participant; a random, stratified sample of the list of proverbs was produced, namely 50 items from levels 1 and 2 (25 from each), and 50 items from level 0. Because of the random selection, the items were manually revised in order to avoid repetition of proverbs from two different sources or using two variants of the same proverb.

Google Forms was used to build the survey and collect the answers. Some personal data was collected to characterise the sample: gender (M/F/undisclosed), age (less than 18, 18 30, 31-50, over 50), school level (basic, secondary, university level, other), nationality (short answer) county of residence (Portugal's 22 counties, including the autonomous regions of Madeira and Azores), area of residence (urban/rural). The detailed analysis of this data is presented elsewhere [16]. The selected proverbs were presented in random order, but always in the same order to every participant. For each proverb, the participant was asked to indicate whether he/she did not know proverb, or knew it but did not use it, or knew it and used it. These answers correspond to the 0 to 2 levels of the tiered selection of the random sample.

The survey was divulged among the authors' list of contacts, both individuals and groups, potentially reaching over 3,600 people. The survey was open for 7 days, and 735 answers were gathered before closing the survey (answer rate: 20,4%).

Figure 1 shows the results from the survey. It can be seen that most answers for the level 2 proverbs (ID-001 to ID-025) were recognised and marked by the subjects, either as in the same level 2 (known and used) or in level 1 (known but not used). A small number of cases do not follow this pattern: In the case of proverb:

ID-002 *Não se apanham trutas a bragas enxutas*
'Trouts cannot be cached/fished with dry trousers'

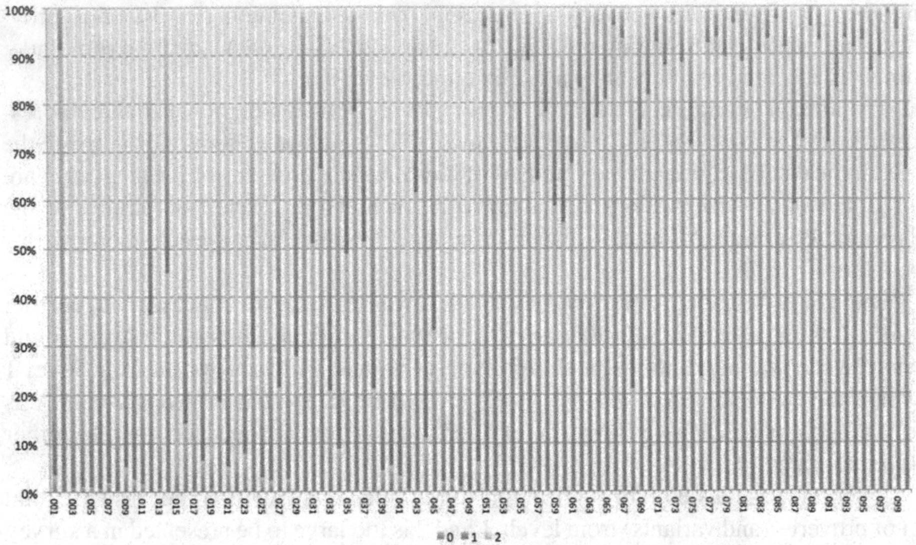

Fig. 1. Assigning lexical availability to proverbs. Horizontal axis: the sample of 100 proverbs, identified by their ID code; from ID-001 to ID-025: reference level 2 (highly available); from ID-026 to ID-050: reference level 1 (moderately available); from ID- 051 to ID-100: reference level 0 (seldom available). Vertical axis: Percentage of answers from the survey (N = 735) as they map onto the reference values: 2: I know and use this proverb; 1: I know but I do not use this proverb; 0: I do not know this proverb.

most participants did not know the proverb and only 8% knew it but did not use it. This proverb includes the archaic word *bragas* 'trousers', which may be one of the reasons for it not being recognized. In fact, common variants of the proverb replace this disused noun either for the modern equivalent *calças* 'trousers' or by a phonetically similar noun *barbas* 'beards', which does not change the overall figurative meaning of the expression. For another four cases, the sum of answers indicating levels 1 and 2 is above 50%:

ID-012 *São mais as vozes que as nozes*
'There are more voices then nuts',

ID-014 *A preguiça morreu de sede à beira da água*
'The sloth died of thirst (sitting) by/next to the water',

ID-020 *A morte não escolhe idades*
'Death chooses no ages', and

ID-024 *Hoje por mim, amanhã por ti*
'Today for me, tomorrow for you'.

In some cases, this can also be a result of the random selection of these proverbs/variants. In the case of proverb ID-020, a much more common variant exists with the noun *amor* 'love', which was confirmed by the queries on the web: the frequency ratio *morte/amor* 'death/love' in Google is 40/70 (0.57), and in Bing 40/237 (0.17).

On the other hand, among the many variants of proverb ID-024, there is one where 1st- and 2nd-person pronouns switch places:

Hoje por ti, amanhã por mim
'Today for you, tomorrow for me'.

This variant (an instance of the so-called 'golden rule') is also almost as frequent as the one shown in the survey. As the survey's variant constitutes an 'inversion' of the golden rule, this may be the cause for the lower availability level assigned by the survey. To sum up, selecting the most lexically available variants of a proverb proves to be almost as much important as choosing the proverbs themselves, in view of defining their lexically availability.

The situation is somewhat fuzzier in the case of level-1 proverbs (ID-026 to ID-050). Notice that this group of proverbs corresponds to a disagreement between the two annotators, as only one selected them as lexically available. Again, the (random) choice of a variant can be the cause for the proverb not being recognised. In the case of proverb:

ID-043 *Morra o gato, morra far*to
'May the cat die, may it die fully satisfied'

the variant

Morra Marta, morra farta,

with the proper noun *Marta* 'Martha', is much more frequent. Queries on the web yielded a *gato*/*Marta* ratio of 3/38 (0.08) in Google and 2/59 (0.03) in Bing. The remaining cases caution for a careful review of the full list of level-1 proverbs (and their variants), using frequency data (from the web and eventually other sources) to support this classification.

Finally, all level-0 proverbs (ID-051 to ID-100) were also assigned the same lexical availability level by the subjects, except for two proverbs (ID-068 and ID-076), since a level 1 was assigned instead.

This data seems to confirm in general the manual assignment of 0- and 2-level of lexical availability to the sample of proverbs. The cases from level 1 must be considered with care, as results do not show a clear-cut distinction between this level and the other two.

3 Proverbs in the Web

The frequency of the same sample of proverbs was obtained from querying two web browsers, Google and Bing. The query was restricted to the exact matches, within the Portugal top domain (.pt), and selecting only pages written in European Portuguese. The matches were manually perused for false positives. Figure 2 shows these results. It is clear that the two web sources produced very similar results (Pearson correlation coefficient: 0.96), although the correlation is much higher for level-2 (0.94) and level-1 (0.91) proverbs, than for level-0 (only 0.86).

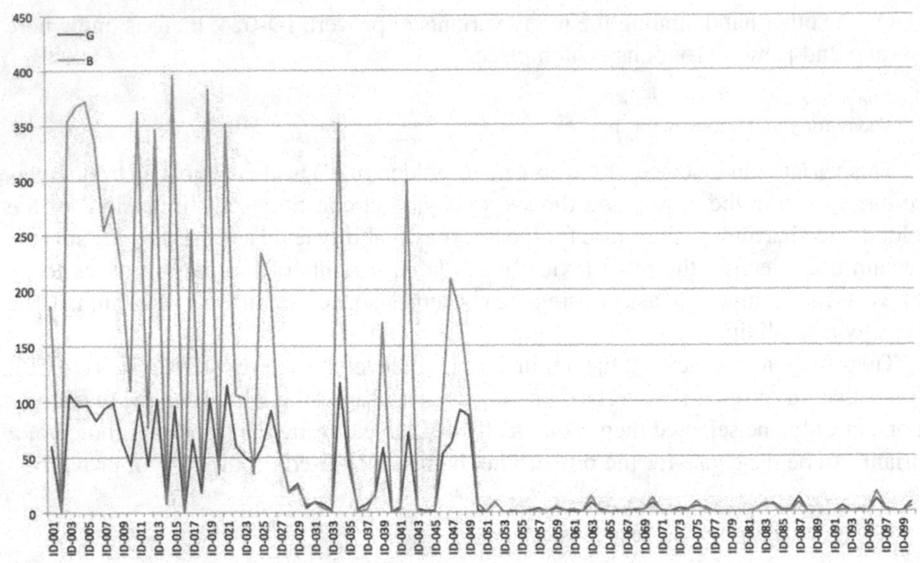

Fig. 2. Proverbs Frequency in two web browsers. Horizontal axis: the sample of 100 proverbs, identified by their ID code; from ID-001 to ID-025: reference level 2 (highly available); from ID-026 to ID-050: reference level 1 (moderately available); from ID- 051 to ID-100: reference level 0 (seldom available). Vertical axis: hit counts, exact match, top domain Portugal (.pt), language: Portuguese (Portugal); values: Google (G, retrieved on 2017/05/03) and Bing (B, retrieved on 2017/05/13).

Table 1 shows the total and the average frequency of proverbs matched by the browsers, and the breakdown by reference level of lexical availability. It is noteworthy that Bing produced 2.7 times more matches than Google. When compared against the reference, the frequency values were slightly higher for the results from Google (Pearson: 0.73) than for those from Bing (0.69), while the sum of the frequency values from both browsers yield an intermediate value (0.70). This corresponds to a relatively high correlation.

Table 1. Total and average frequency of proverbs matched by the web browsers Google and Bing, and their sum (G + B), considering the entire sample (100 proverbs; 'All'), and by reference level ('L-2' to 'L-0').

	Total			Average		
Level	Google	Bing	G + B	Google	Bing	G+B
All	2,594	7,143	9,143	26	71	97
L-2	1,650	5,196	6,846	66	208	274
L-1	833	1,834	2,667	33	73	107
L-0	111	113	224	2	2	4

4 Proverbs in *Corpus*

Finally, the same proverbs were searched in the Cetem*Público corpus* [23][4]. This is a large-sized, publicly available *corpus* of journalistic text, collected from the online edition of the European Portuguese newspaper *Público*, and containing about 9,6 million words.

To process and query the *corpus*, the UNITEX linguistic development platform [24][5] was used. The *corpus* was processed using the European Portuguese language resources distributed with the system. The queries were carried out using finite-state transducers (FST) that are built using this platform formalism. These FST define a linguistic pattern to be matched and output the ID of the proverb corresponding to the matched string. Figures 3 and 4 show the FST used for querying the proverb *Santos de casa não fazem milagres* 'Home saints don't make miracles'.

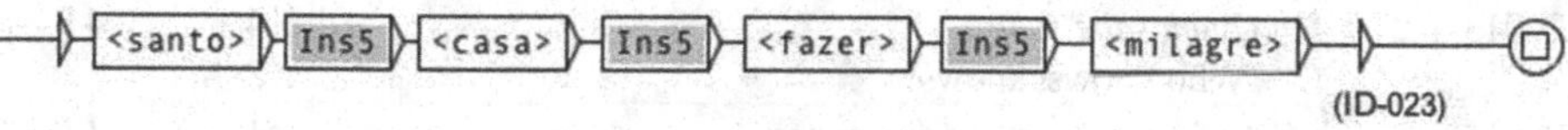

Fig. 3. FST built for querying the proverb *Santos de casa não fazem milagres* 'Home saints don't make miracles' in *corpora*: sequences of keywords. Words inside chevrons represent lemmas. Grey boxes *Ins5* are subgraphs for insertions of 0 up to 5 words.

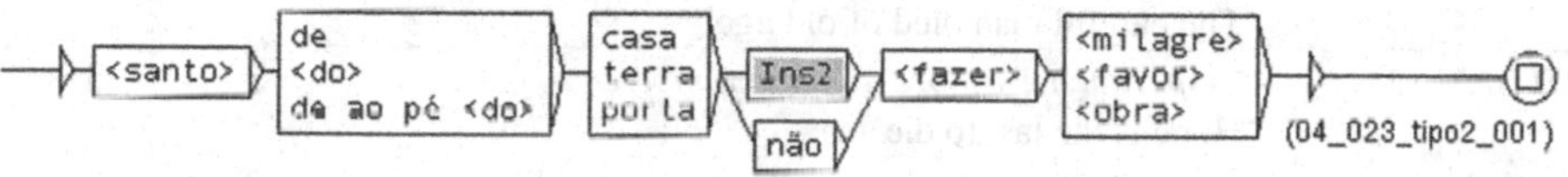

Fig. 4. FST built for querying the proverb *Santos de casa não fazem milagres* 'Home saints don't make miracles' in *corpora*: graph describing lexical variants. Words inside chevrons represent lemmas. Grey box *Ins2* is a subgraph for insertions of 0 up to 2 words.

Two methods of querying were used:

(a) a set of FST describing the sequence of keywords (mainly nouns, verbs and adjectives) that characterise the proverb, allowing for a window of 0 to 5 words between them, and a small set of punctuation marks[6]: <;, ([)] /and. .. >. This type of FST was automatically built from the database. Keywords are represented by their lemmas.

(b) another set of FST, manually built to describe all the variants of a given proverb found in the database, or deemed as reasonably probable to occur, according to the vocabulary involved and the syntactic structure of the proverb. These FST are only available for the 50 proverbs from levels 2 and 1, since level 0 expressions were not considered sufficiently relevant to be represented in this way.

---

4 www.linguateca.pt/cetempublico.

5 http://unitexgramlab.org/.

6 These insertions are reported in the sub-graphs - the grey boxes in Figs. 3 and 4.

Table 2 shows the results from applying the two sets of graphs to the Cetem*Público* *corpus*. As expected, only some few instances (34) of the sampled proverbs were found in the *corpus*, corresponding to 13 different proverbs, from which 30 proverbs (instances) were matched by both methods. The keywords' graphs matched 40 instances (hence 10 false-positives), while the variants' graphs are very precise (no false-positive matches).

Table 2. Sampled proverbs matched in the Cetem*Público corpus*. Column 'Var indicates the number of matches using the proverbs' variants FST, while column 'Key' corresponds to FST with the keywords. An approximate translation of the proverbs (or an equivalent expression) is provided.

ID	Level	Proverb 'equivalent/Translation'	Var	Key
ID-003	2	*Depois da tempestade vem a bonança* 'After the storm comes the calm'	2	2
ID-013	2	*Quem sabe sabe* 'Who knows, knows'	4	4
ID-015	2	*Mais vale tarde do que nunca* 'Better late than never'	1	1
ID-019	2	*O tempo voa* 'Time flies'	1	1
ID-021	2	*O seguro morreu de velho* 'The careful man died of old age'	5	5
ID-022	2	*A esperança é sempre a última a morrer* 'Hope is the last to die'	3	3
ID-023	2	*Santos de casa não fazem milagres* 'Home saints don't make miracles'	7	7
ID-026	2	*O sol quando nasce é para todos* 'The sun when it is born is for everyone'	2	0
ID-034	1	*Nem só de pão vive o homem* 'Man does not live by bread alone'	2	2
ID-038	1	*Um crime não justifica outro* 'One crime does not justify another'	1	0
ID-042	1	*Quem avisa, amigo é* 'He who warns is a friend'	1	1
ID-049	1	*O tempo é dinheiro* 'Time is money'	4	4
ID-050	1	*Não degenera quem sai aos seus* 'He who resembles his own [people] does not degenerate'	1	0
		Total	**34**	**30**

The (small) difference between the results from the variants' graphs and from the keywords' graphs (proverbs ID-026, ID-038 and ID-050) is due to the fact that the variants' graphs include lexical variants of the keywords, while the keywords' graphs only consider one of those lexical variants.

For example, for proverb:

ID-026 *O sol quando nasce é para todos*
'The sun when it is born is for everyone'

the keywords' graph only considers the keywords *sol-nascer-ser-todos* 'sun-rise- be-everyone', but the corresponding variants' graph allows *brilhar* 'shine' instead of *ser* 'be'.

For proverb:

ID-038 *Um crime não justifica outro*
'One crime does not justify another'

the lexical variant *erro* 'mistake' is allowed but it was not a keyword.

Finally, for proverb:

ID-050 *Não degenera quem sai aos seus*
'He who resembles his own people does not degenerate'

the lexical variant *puxar* 'pull/take' was represented in the variants' graph, but not in the keywords.

Only level-2 and level-1 proverbs were matched, 8 and 5, respectively. Though the number of instances is low, the most frequently occurring, level-1 proverbs, namely,

ID-049 *Tempo é dinheiro* (4 matches)
'Time is money'

and (the fragment of) the biblical quote

ID-034 *Nem só de pão vive o homem* (2 matches)
'Man does not live by bread alone' (Mt 4:4)

may lead us to reclassify them as level-2.

Notice that the FST account for morphosyntactic variation of the proverbs' keywords. For example, the gender-number variation of *santo* 'saint', or number variation on *milagre* 'miracle', as well as subject-verb agreement, are all handled by the graphs, using the lexical resources available with the system:

… *Portanto, para a Qualidade Total*, **santo de casa é quem faz milagres**…
'Thus, for the Overall Quality, home saint (masc.-sg.) is the one that does miracles (pl.)'

… *E* **santa de casa não faz milagre**…
'Home saint (fem.-sg.) doesn't do miracle'

… *contrariando a tese de que* **santo de casa não faz milagre**…
'against the thesis that home saint (masc.-sg.) doesn't do miracle (sg.)'

The proverb:

ID-050 *Não degenera quem sai aos seus*
'He who resembles his own people does not degenerate'

is more often used with the subject in the canonic word order, v.g.

Quem sai aos seus não degenera.

This variant had been used in the survey because of the random selection method used for the sampling. The more common variant, showing the basic word order was also checked. However – and quite surprisingly, no match was found in the *corpus*.

Contrasting with the low frequencies observed in this *corpus*, all these proverbs are quite frequent in the web (see Sect. 3). In average, these proverbs occurred 78 times in (Google) and 233 times (in Bing) – standard deviation, approximately 37 and 146, respectively; and totalling 1,017 and 3,034 respectively.

In spite of the low frequency observed in the *corpus*, it seems possible to conclude that:

(a) most probably due to the journalist nature of the *corpus*, the occurrence of proverbs is this type of text is scarce, as expected;
(b) even so, the lexical availability level, manually assigned to the proverbs' sample, has been confirmed, since no level-0 expressions were found, and there are more instances of level-2 than of level-1 proverbs.

5 Conclusion and Future Work

This paper set out to establish the lexical availability of a large-sized database of with over 114,000 proverbs. A preliminary estimation, carried out by two annotators, was confirmed by and large using data obtained through a survey (735 participants) and through queries on two popular web browsers (Google and Bing). Results from queries over a large-sized *corpus* of journalistic text also confirmed the initial expectations that the use of this type of linguistic expressions is often limited by style conventions to oral/colloquial communicative contexts.

In view of the results, it is reasonable to extend the lexically available status to all the level-2 manually selected proverbs. These will constitute the main core of a lexicon of commonly used proverbs. Level-1 proverbs, in general, and certain difficult or interesting cases, both from level-2 and level-0, will have to be studied further. In some cases, only some variants of a given proverb should be assigned level-2 status, while the remainder variants may be attributed to level-1 (moderately available) or even level-0 (seldom available). In other (rarer) cases, level-0 proverbs (or variants) may have to be raised to level-1, too.

The 50 finite-state transducers already built will now be extended to the remainder of level-2 proverbs and, time allowing, to level-1, after careful revision of this list. Eventually, surveying the lexically availability of the remaining entries from level-1 will be useful.

Previous experiments using a Brazilian Portuguese database of approximately 3,500 proverbs (614 types or paremiological units) over a relatively large *corpus* of this language variety [25] showed that the approach of using just the proverb's keywords (surface forms) is a reasonably effective strategy for detecting proverbs in texts.

In this paper, however, the keywords in the FST were (for the most part) lemmatized, which broadened the search area of the queries in the *corpus*.

A similar experiment has already been carried out on a *corpus* of Portuguese textbooks [15], but due to technical shortcomings of the linguistic platform used, it was not possible to build FST with lemmatized keywords for the entire database. As a consequence, only the keywords' surface forms were used, narrowing the queries' search space. Having narrowed down in this paper the set of lexically available (or, at least, moderately available) proverbs of European Portuguese, it should now be possible to produce a new, richer resource, equivalent to that of [25], improving the accuracy and recall of proverb identification in texts.

More importantly, with this paper, an empirically motivated list of lexically available proverb (and variants) has now been produced[7], which can be used in a reliable way to develop many types of applications, for example, for diagnosis/therapy of some speech disorders or for didactic games for language learning.

Acknowledgements. This work was partially supported by national funds through Fundação para a Ciência e Tecnologia (FCT) with reference UID/CEC/50021/2013.

References

1. Charteris-Black, J.: Proverbs in communication. J. Multiling. Multicult. Dev. **16**(4), 259–268 (1995)
2. Mieder, W.: Proverbs – A Handbook. Greenwood Press, London (2004)
3. Rezaei, A.: Rhetorical function of proverbs based on literary genre. Procedia Soc. Behav. Sci. **47**, 1103–1108 (2012). Elsevier Ltd.
4. Meira, A.: Casa de ferreiro, espeto de pau: uma análise das relações retóricas a partir do uso dos provérbios como estratégia argumentativa em textos da internet. (Ph.D. thesis), Faculdade de Letras da UFMG, Belo Horizonte (2015)
5. Hrisztova-Gotthardt, H., Varga, M. (eds.): Introduction to Paremiology: A Comprehensive Guide to Proverb Studies. DeGryuter, Berlin (2015)
6. Council of Europe: Common European Framework of Reference for Languages: Learning, Teaching. Council of Europe (2001)
7. Chaika, E.: Linguistics, Pragmatics and Psychotherapy – A Guide for Therapists. Whurr Publishers, London and Philadelphia (2000)
8. Arif, M., Abdullah, I.: The impact of output communication on EFL learners' metaphor second language acquisition. Soc. Sci. (Pakistan) **11**(9), 1940–1947 (2016)
9. Salbego, N., Osborne, D.: Schema activation through pre-reading activities: teaching proverbs in L2. BELT Braz. Engl. Lang. Teach. J. **7**(2), 175–188 (2016)
10. Gorham, D.: A proverb test for clinical and experimental use. Psychol. Rep. **1**, 1–12 (1956)
11. Benton, A.: Differential behavioral effects in frontal lobe disease. Neuropsychologia **6**(1), 53–60 (1968)
12. Gibbs, R., Beitel, D.: What proverb understanding reveals about how people think. Psychol. Bull. **118**(1), 133–154 (1995)
13. Siqueira, M., Marques, D., Gibbs Jr., R.: Metaphor-related figurative language comprehension in clinical populations: a critical review. Scripta **20**(40), 36–60 (2016)

[7] This list is available to the scientific community at: https://www.researchgate.net/publication/319465467_List_of_100_proverbs_annotated_with_lexical_availability (DOI: 10.13140/RG.2.2.30110.64326).

14. Vas, A., Spence, J., Eschler, B., Chapman, S.: Sensitivity and specificity of abstraction using gist reasoning measure in adults with traumatic brain injury. J. Appl. Biobehav. Res. **21**(4), 216–224 (2016)
15. Reis, S., Baptista, J.: O uso de provérbios no ensino do Português (The use of proverbs in the teaching of Portuguese). In: Proceedings of the 10th Interdisciplinary Colloquium on Proverbs, Tavira, Portugal, November 6–13, 2016 (in print)
16. Reis, S., Baptista, J.: O provérbio como estímulo num terapeuta virtual (Proverbs as a stymulus of a virtual therapist). In: 6th Simpósio Mundial de Estudos sobre o Português (SIMELP), Simpósio 77, A Importância da Aprendizagem Lexical, Santarém, Escola Superior de Educação, Instituto Politécnico de Santarém (2017, accepted for publication)
17. Reis, S., Baptista, J.: Let's Play with Proverbs? – NLP tools and resources for iCALL applications around proverbs for PFL. In: Proceedings of the International Congress on Interdisciplinarity in Social and Human Sciences, 5th-6th May, University of Algarve, Faro, Portugal, 427–446 (2016b)
18. Abad, A., Pompili, A., Costa, A., Trancoso, I., Fonseca, J., Leal, G., Farrajota, L., Martins, I.: Automatic word naming recognition for an on-line aphasia treatment system. Comput. Speech Lang. Elsevier **27**(6), 1235–1248 (2013)
19. Coxhead, A., Nation, P., Sim, D.: Measuring the vocabulary size of native speakers of English in New Zealand Secondary schools. N. Z. J. Educ. Stud. **50**, 121–135 (2015)
20. Martins, E.: Manual de redação e estilo, 3rd edn. O Estado de S. Paulo, São Paulo (1997)
21. Chacoto, L.: Estudo e Formalização das Propriedades Léxico-Sintácticas das Expressões Fixas Proverbiais, (Master thesis), Faculdade de Letras da Universidade de Lisboa, Lisboa (1994)
22. Reis, S., Baptista, J.: Portuguese proverbs: types and variants. In: Corpas Pastor, G. (ed.) Computerised and Corpus-based Approaches to Phraseology: Monolingual and Multilingual Perspectives, 208–217. Editions Tradulex, Geneva (2016)
23. Santos, D., Rocha, P.: Evaluating CETEMPúblico, a free resource for Portuguese. In Proceedings of the 39th Annual Meeting of the Association for Computational Linguistics (Toulouse, 9–11 de julho de 2001), pp. 442–449 (2001)
24. Paumier, S.: Unitex 3.1 User Manual. Université de Paris-Est/Marne-la-Vallée – Institut Gaspard Monge, Noisy-Champs (2016)
25. Rassi, A., Baptista, J., Vale, O.: Automatic Detection of Proverbs and their Variants. In: Pereira, M., Leal, J., Simões, A. (eds.) Proceedings of the Symposium on Languages, Applications and Technologies (SLATE 2014), pp. 235–249. Schloss Dagstuhl - Leibniz-Zentrum fur Informatik, Dagstuhl Publishing, Leibniz (2014)

Development of Corpora for Phraseological Studies

Verbal Multiword Expressions in Slovene

Polona Gantar[1], Simon Krek[2(✉)], and Taja Kuzman[3]

[1] Faculty of Arts, University of Ljubljana, Ljubljana, Slovenia
apolonija.gantar@ff-uni.lj.si

[2] Jožef Stefan Institute, Ljubljana, Slovenia
simon.krek@ijs.si

[3] Ljubljana, Slovenia
kuzman.taja@gmail.com

Abstract. This paper discusses the building of a manually annotated training corpus of Slovene verbal multiword expressions, which was a part of PARSEME shared task that covered eighteen languages from various language families. In the course of the project, annotation guidelines were compiled, describing the notation scope in detail and proposing a multilingual system for verbal MWE categorisation. In this paper, we present the methods of identification, annotation scope and linguistic tests that determine structural, syntactic and lexical characteristics of the verbal MWE candidate lexical units. Furthermore, we highlight examples that specifically apply to the Slovene language. Tools and previously available data that were used in the project are also presented: an annotation tool and syntactically and morphosyntactically annotated training corpus for Slovene.

Keywords: PARSEME shared task · Verbal multiword expressions · Categorisation · Training corpus · Slovene

1 Introduction

As multiword expressions (MWEs) constitute a large part of a speaker's mental lexicon, they are an important topic in linguistic studies, and they are interesting for the development of machine-readable language resources which represent a basis for building NLP-oriented lexicons of multiword expression and tools for their processing.

Many definitions of multiword expressions exist, which vary according to the focus of research. Linguistic, or more narrowly, lexicographic definition, emphasises semantic features of MWEs and defines them as "all the different types of phrases that have some degree of idiomatic meaning or behaviour" (Atkins and Rundell 2008). On the other hand, a definition of MWEs put forward for the purposes of natural language processing stresses their compositionality: "Multiword expressions (MWEs) are lexical items that: (a) can be decomposed into multiple lexemes; and (b) display lexical, syntactic, semantic, pragmatic and/or statistical idiomaticity" (Baldwin and Kim 2010). Although a generally accepted definition does not exist, linguists and NLP experts agree that the most basic characteristic that distinguishes MWEs from free combinations is a special relation between the elements of multiword expressions. This relation is usually defined

R. Mitkov (Ed.): Europhras 2017, LNAI 10596, pp. 247–259, 2017.
https://doi.org/10.1007/978-3-319-69805-2_18

through concepts like collocability (statistical idiomaticity or institutionalization), (semantic) idiomaticity or semantic (non-)compositionality and syntactic flexibility, which includes the problems of internal modification (discontinuity and long-distance dependency issues), and lexical variability. In addition to that, fixedness, figuration and dependence on pragmatic circumstances are considered. Due to all these factors, MWEs pose problems not only for linguistic analyses, but also for natural language processing and automatic identification in text.

One approach to improve processing of MWEs in natural language processing tasks is to develop methods and standards for identification of different types of MWEs in running text. For Slovene, a machine-readable resource which would help in these tasks has not been developed yet, therefore participation in the shared task conducted within the PARSEME European COST action was considered as a welcome opportunity.

The aim of the PARSEME shared task[1] is automatic identification of verbal MWEs (hereinafter VMWEs) in running text, which includes the compilation of universal guidelines[2] providing examples for all included languages, and building a multilingual manually VMWE-annotated corpus released under various Creative Commons licenses.[3] Originally, the task focused on verbal multiword expressions, whereas in the future, the project plans to include other MWEs and to expand the number of languages.

As was mentioned, before this project neither machine-readable resources manually annotated with MWEs were available for the Slovene language, nor a lexicon and adequate classification that would formalize specific features of MWEs in a suitable machine-readable format. The only two resources with lexicographic description of Slovene MWEs are Dictionary of Literary Slovene (DLS) and in the Dictionary of Slovene Phrasemes (Keber 2011), but as they both follow lexicographic concepts from the 1960s, they are not compatible with modern lexicographic methods and they do not reflect modern usage of MWEs that can be found in existing Slovene reference corpora (cf. Gigafida, Kres, Gos).[4] Both resources are not machine-readable and thus cannot be used for the purposes of language technology. Hence, one the main purposes of Slovene involvement in the PARSEME project was also to build a manually annotated training corpus, which is compatible with international (interlingual) standards and takes into account also Slovene specifics, and to create a lexicon of Slovene multiword expressions designed for linguistic description in lexicographic works (dictionaries, grammars), which would be also machine-readable and available for NLP tasks.

2 PARSEME Shared Task Universal Guidelines

The main purpose of annotation guidelines (version 1.6b)[5] is to define the scope of annotation and to propose a classification of VMWEs, based on linguistic tests for

[1] https://typo.uni-konstanz.de/parseme/index.php/results/shared task.

[2] http://parsemefr.lif.univ-mrs.fr/guidelines-hypertext/.

[3] The final corpus, consisting of 5.5 million tokens and 60,000 VMWE annotations in eighteen languages, is available on: https://gitlab.com/parseme/sharedtask-data/tree/master.

[4] http://www.slovenscina.eu/korpusi.

[5] http://parsemefr.lif.univ-mrs.fr/guidelines-hypertext/?page=home.

various languages from different language families. The guidelines define criteria for the identification of VMWEs based on predictable syntactic variants, lexicalized elements and open slots. The annotation includes all lexicalized elements of VMWEs – in both continuous and discontinuous sequences – that can function as individual lexical items, as well as VMWEs embedded in other VMWEs. Categories are divided into universal categories, applicable to all languages participating in the task, quasi-universal categories, applicable only to some of the languages, and language-specific categories, defined for a particular language.

For purposes of identification and categorisation of VMWEs, a decision tree method was devised, as well as generic and language-specific tests.

Decision tree includes three steps. In step one we identify a VMWE candidate, i.e. a combination of a verb with at least one other word, which is a potential verbal multiword expression. In step two we determine which elements of the expression are lexicalized, i.e. without which elements the candidate does not occur. In step three we place the VMWE in one of the categories, using general and language-specific tests. Generic tests consider general criteria that are valid for all languages, while language-specific tests consider structural, lexical, morphologic and syntactic features that are specific for different languages.

In the following sections, we first present general criteria, elaborated in the course of the PARSEME shared task, and then focus on examples that present Slovene particularities.

3 Verbal Multiword Expressions – Slovenian Case

3.1 Scope and Definition of VMWE

As is shown in Fig. 1, generally accepted Slovene classification of MWEs (multiword expressions that differ from free combinations, formed accordingly to general grammatical rules) divides MWEs into (a) phraseological units (PUs), determined by the presence of at least one component with a meaning that differs from one of its denotative "dictionary" senses, and their expressiveness, also described as figuration; and (b) all other multiword expressions (i.e. fixed expressions)[6] that are characterized by a certain degree of fixedness, but with a meaning that can be predicted (relatively well) from the meaning of their elements. Further division of PUs is based on syntax, with clausal or phrasal type, the first including also proverbs and the second all non-verbal PUs.

[6] Fixed expressions differ from collocations, which are usually not independent lexical units. This term mostly includes semi-terminological word combinations, such as *stara mama* 'grandmother', *dnevna soba* 'living room' etc. Collocations, being semantically transparent units, are not included in the categorisation of VMWEs.

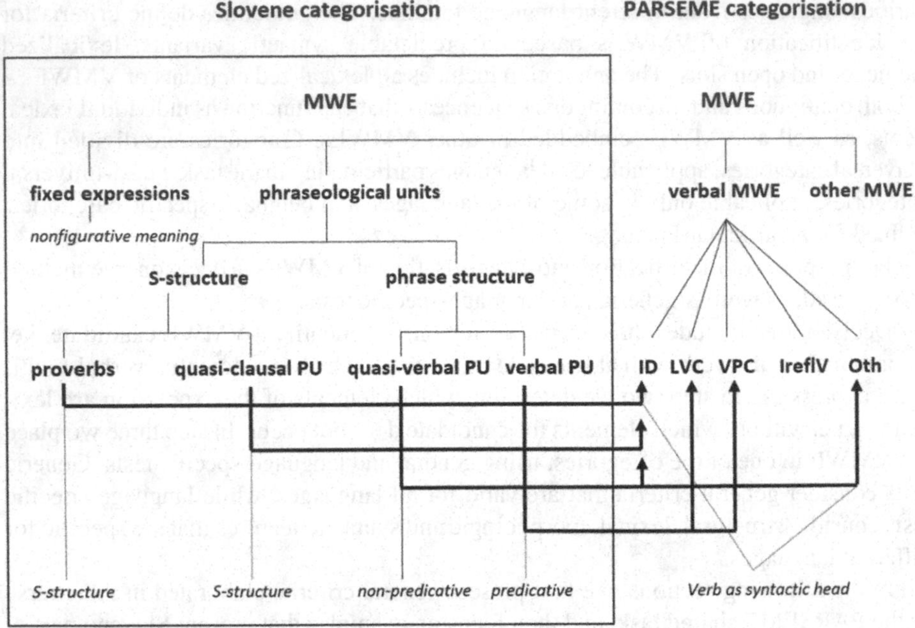

Fig. 1. Comparison of Slovene and PARSEME categorisation of VMWEs.

Furthermore, in Slovene linguistic theory verbal MWEs are determined by morphological features (Toporišič 1973/1974; Kržišnik 1994), meaning that a MWE is classified as a VMWE if (1) its meaning is not the sum of the meanings of its parts, (2) it has metaphorical nature, and (3) it functions as a predicate. However, it remains unclear how to classify MWEs where the verbal MWE does not function as a predicate, e.g. VMWE *voditi za nos* (lit. to lead by the nose 'to deceive') in the sentence: *ne spodobi se takole voditi za nos ubogega otroka* ('it is not nice to deceive (=to lead by the nose) the poor child in this manner') with the MWE part of the sentence (=*voditi za nos*) functioning as the clausal subject in Slovene.

The problem of categorizing MWEs according to their morphological structure and syntactic function was resolved in PARSEME shared task through the definition that the main criterion for VMWEs is that their syntactic head in the prototypical form is a verb, regardless of the fact if it can or cannot fulfil other syntactic roles, as is shown in the example in the previous paragraph. In addition to that, VMWEs should have the following characteristics: (a) they express some degree of orthographic, morphological, syntactic or semantic idiosyncrasy with respect to general grammar rules of a language; (b) their component words include a verbal head word and at least one other syntactically related word; (c) at least two components of the expression are lexicalized.

3.2 Types of Verbal MWEs

MWE types that are identified as verbal MWEs, according to the PARSEME annotation guidelines, are divided into two categories: universal categories, valid for most languages, and quasi-universal categories, valid only for particular language families or individual languages. Universal categories include light verb constructions (LVC) and idioms (ID), whereas quasi-universal categories comprise inherently reflexive verbs (IReflV), verb-particle combinations (VPC) and other verbal MWEs (OTH).

All of the categories above are valid for the Slovene language, but some of them show distinctive features either due to Slovene syntactic or morphological characteristics, or the description of some Slovene grammatical categories partially differs from that of other languages. For example, in the Slovene language, gerunds are categorized as a subcategory of nouns and (adjectival) participles as a subcategory of adjectives, which influences morphosyntactic annotation in our corpus. We will highlight specific Slovene characteristics for each VMWE category.

Idioms (ID). An idiom has at least two lexicalized components: a head verb and at least one of its arguments which can have different functions and can be of different types of speech.

Some examples for Slovene:

subject + head verb (predicate): *srce mu je padlo v hlače* (lit. His heart fell into his pants, meaning 'he has lost courage').[7]
verb + direct object, e.g. *streljati kozle* (shot the goats, meaning 'to say or to do something stupid');
verb + adjunct, e.g. *spati kot ubit* (lit. to sleep like dead, meaning 'to sleep soundly');
verb + complex noun phrase: *biti trn v peti komu* (lit. to be a thorn in somebody's heel meaning 'to be a big problem, obstacle');

In the PARSEME shared task, structures such as "verb + adjectival phrase" are categorized as idioms, e.g. *to come clean, to stand firm*. Similar to other languages, also in Slovene the verb is typically limited to the auxiliary 'to be', as in case of *biti zlata vreden* (to be worth its weight in gold, meaning 'extremely valuable, useful' or *biti zelen od zavisti* 'to be green with envy') but can also occur in a complex noun phrase as a modifier: *zlata vredna zmaga* ('victory, worth its weight in gold'),[8] which is an adjectival MWE. According to the general annotation guidelines, constructions with a copula are

[7] In Slovene categorisation, this VMWE type has been problematised since its syntactic structure consists of a basic relationship between subject and predicate, and such examples are formally categorized "PUs with S-structure" (Toporišič 1973/1974). However, as they function similarly to "verbal PUs", an independent subcategory, "false verbal PUs", vas suggested (Kržišnik 1994, pp. 63, 66) which forms a part of "phrase structure PUs" top category, separating them from "S-structure PUs" such as: *Obleka naredi človeka* 'Clothes make the man' or *Čas je denar* 'Time is money'.

[8] The rule also applies to noun phrases that function as subject complements, e.g. *(biti) mož beseda* '(to be) a man of his word', *(biti) alfa in omega* '(to be) alpha and omega' (meaning '(to be) the basis of something').

considered as VMWEs only if the complement does not retain the idiomatic meaning when appearing without the verb. In our case, additional analysis showed that there are no cases where the modifying role of adjectival phrases would be exclusive, in spite of the perceivable tendency that some of them appear more typically in this role than others. Therefore, such constructions are not considered as verbal MWEs.

The following VMWEs are also considered as idioms:

verb + subordinate clause, e.g. *vedeti, koliko je ura* (lit. to know what time it is, meaning 'to realize the truth'), which are classified as quasi-verbal PUs according to their prevalent non-predicative syntactic function (see Fig. 1) and

verb + non-reflexive personal pronoun, such as *ucvreti jo* (lit. to flee her, meaning 'to run away'). Similar constructions are recorded in the guidelines for other languages, e.g. for German *es gibt* (lit. it gives 'there is'), for English: *to make it*, for Italian: *prender le* (lit. to take it 'to be beaten'). In Slovene, such structures are defined as "minimal verbal phraseme", which are – like verb-particle combinations (VPC) – only conditionally classified as MWEs (cf. Kržišnik 1994).

Furthermore, the idioms category includes all other MWEs with more than one lexicalized argument, for example *beseda mi je ostala v grlu* (lit. a word got stuck in my throat, meaning 'I'm speechless'), including embedded VMWEs, not necessarily of the same category, such as *delati se norca iz koga* (lit. to make (+reflexive clitic) a fool of someone, meaning 'to mock someone'), annotated as ID, which contains an inherently reflexive verb (IReflV) *delati se* (lit. to make + reflexive clitic), which, when standing alone, means 'to pretend'.

Light verb constructions (LVC). In Slovene categorisation, light verb constructions are not regarded as a separate subcategory of verbal PUs, neither does the theory address the issue of their semantic non-compositionality, which is also one of the biggest challenges in their identification. Light verbs, or "verbs with weakened meaning", are discussed primarily in lexicography and as part of lexicological research (Vidovič Muha 2000). Lexicography is concerned mostly with light verbs functioning as auxiliary verbs and with main verbs that function as auxiliaries in certain contexts (Kozlevčar Černelič 1975). Instances of the later are verbs of motion, such as *priti do prodaje/razhajanja/zamenjave* (lit. to come to sale/divergence/substitution, meaning 'sale/divergence/substitution took place') that have a different meaning than in *priti do vrha* ('reach the peak'), where *priti* means 'to reach a destination (by moving)'. According to the PARSEME annotation guidelines, such cases are classified as verb-particle combination (VPC).

LVCs typically consist of a **verb** and a **noun** or **prepositional phrase**. The verb has a purely syntactic operator function (performing an activity or being in a state), whereas the noun expresses the activity or state. In *biti v dvomih* 'to be in doubt' the noun refers to a state and in *dati napoved* 'to give a forecast' it refers to an event. Since the semantics of a light verb can be more or less "light", there are many borderline cases in which the verb partially retains its regular semantics – for instance, in case of *storiti kaznivo dejanje [samomor, prekršek, zločin …]* 'to commit a crime, suicide, minor offence, felony' the verb *storiti* 'to commit' forms LVCs with a relatively extensive range of nouns, but limited to those expressing negatively perceived actions. Universal annotation guidelines provide some guidance to facilitate categorisation of borderline cases and to ensure interlingual comparability. Some examples for Slovene, which comply with the compulsory or sufficient tests:

- *imeti vlogo* 'to have a role', *imeti učinek* 'to have an effect': noun is used in its literal sense, *imeti* 'to have' adds no meaning besides that of having a property; it's a LVC (sufficient test).
- *sprejeti odločitev* 'to make a decision': the denotative meaning of the verb *sprejeti* is 'to receive', but here it is not used in this sense nor does it add any semantics to the event;[9] it's a LVC (sufficient test).
- When the doer of the action, which is expressed by the noun, cannot be realized as the subject and as a modifier of the noun, VMWE is categorized as a LVC, for example *Učiteljica je sprejela odločitev* ('The teacher made a decision') and *dijakova odločitev* ('pupil's decision') cannot appear in the same sentence: **učiteljica je sprejela dijakovo odločitev* '*The teacher made a pupil's decision'; it's a LVC (compulsory test).
- When the noun is not used in its denotative meaning, VMWE is classified as ID, for instance *imeti krompir* (lit. to have a potato, meaning 'to be lucky').

As identification of LVCs is interesting for NLP tasks, they have been included in the annotation. It is important to stress that – although LVCs need to fulfil the compulsory tests described above – they do allow some syntactic and morphologic transformations, e.g. *Direktor mora sprejeti odločitev* 'Director has to make a decision' can be transformed to *odločitev, ki jo direktor mora sprejeti* 'a decision that the director has to make'. This makes them similar to free word combinations with no idiosyncratic semantics, which makes their automatic identification in corpus more difficult (Baldwin and Kim 2016, Sag et al. 2002).

Inherently reflexive verbs (IReflV). Inherently reflexive verbs are a language (family)-specific category of verbal multiword expressions in the annotation guidelines of the PARSEME shared task. They are typical for Germanic languages (except for English), Romance and Slavic languages, whereas no examples of inherently reflexive verbs were found in multilingual PARSEME corpus for Lithuanian, Farsi, Greek, Hebrew, Hungarian and Maltese.

In Slovene, reflexive verbs (REFLV), paired with reflexive clitic *se* (RCLI), play several semantic roles, depending on the context, and the clitic does not always have a reflexive meaning, as is demonstrated below. According to the annotation guidelines, reflexive verbs are annotated as VMWEs, or more precisely, as inherently reflexive verbs (IReflV) only if (a) they never occur without the clitic, or (b) the verb has a different meaning or subcategorisation frame when occurring with the clitic than when appearing without it. Therefore, two criteria for categorisation of IReflV are:

---

[9] Within the shared task, the decision was taken that cases in which the verb has light semantics per se, e.g. *commit a crime* in English or *izkazati interes* ('to show interest') or *vzeti v službo* (lit. to take into the job 'to employ') in Slovene are treated as LVCs, given the different understanding of the notion of »light verbs«, and the possibility to distinguish between support verbs and light verbs, or light verbs and vague action verbs.

- the verb without the RCLI does not exist, as is the case with *sramovati se* 'to be ashamed' and *bati se* 'to be afraid';
- the verb without the RCLI does exist, but has a very different meaning, for instance *pomeriti se* 'to compete' has a completely different sense than *pomeriti* 'to measure'.

In all other instances, where a reflexive clitic defines some kind of syntactic relation between the subject and the object, the combination of a clitic and a verb is not considered as IReflV. Such relations include passivisation or reciprocity, expressing a general doer of the action etc. The following combinations of verbs + reflexive clitics are therefore excluded from the IReflV category:

- **reciprocal:** the clitic has a sense of mutually, it can be translated with 'each other', e.g. *poljubljati se* 'to kiss each other', *srečati se* 'to meet each other';
- **reflexive:** the clitic *se* means 'oneself', e.g. *umivati se* 'to wash oneself', *praskati se* 'to scratch oneself';
- **possessive reflexive** (body part): the clitic functions as the indirect object (in the dative case) and in the role of the direct object is a body part or an inalienable part of the subject, e.g. *zlomiti si roko* (lit. break RCLI (dative) arm, meaning 'break one's arm');
- **synthetic passive:** the clitic expresses the passive voice. The direct object of an active sentence becomes the subject in the *se*-passive and thus the verb agrees with the subject (who is not the doer of the action), e.g. *hiše se dobro prodajajo* (lit. the houses RCLI sell well, meaning 'the houses sell well'). In some languages, alternation with preverbal subject sounds unnatural, hence, alternation with postverbal subject is preferred. Since Slovene has a relatively free word order[10] (as is also the case of Polish, Japanese etc.), a postverbal subject is a regular alternation: *nove hiše se gradijo/gradijo se nove hiše* (lit. new houses RCLI are being built/are being built RCLI new houses for 'new houses are being built');
- **impersonal:** the clitic marks an impersonal verb alternation of either transitive or intransitive verbs (which is not applicable to all languages participating in the shared task). There is no noun phrase before the verb (empty subject slot), the presence of the RCLI indicates a verb interpreted with a generic and underspecified subject and the verb is in the third person singular, even when the object is plural: *govori/govorijo se neumnosti* (lit. says/say (third person singular/plural) RCLI silly things, meaning 'people are saying silly things');
- **inchoative:** the direct object of the transitive version appears as the subject of the REFLV. This type differs from synthetic passives by the fact that the subject is not only absent, but it is also semantically unclear or non-existent. e.g. *vrata se odpirajo* 'the doors open'.

These types of REFLVs are not annotated as VMWEs in the multilingual PARSEME corpus, because in these cases RCLI is not an obligatory (semantic) component of the

[10] Free word order is a feature of a language that has either enough grammatical markers to eliminate any ambiguity in meaning, either easily identifiable verbs and a word order in which the subject always comes first, so it cannot be confused with the object.

verb phrase, it does not directly influence the meaning of the verb, it only relativises the subject in the sentence.

IReflVs that are embedded in idioms are also annotated, e.g. *režati se kot pečen maček* (lit. to laugh RCLI like a baked tomcat, meaning 'to roar with laughter').

As was mentioned under idioms, a separate type of VMWEs are combinations of verbs and non-reflexive clitics similar to *es gibt* (lit. it gives, meaning 'there is') structure in German. In Slovene, such structures are verbs + personal pronouns in non-nominative cases, e.g. *ucvreti jo* (lit. to flee her, meaning 'to flee'), *pihniti ga* (lit. to puff him, meaning 'to be funny'). These types of VMWEs are annotated as IDs, according to the annotation guidelines.

In this category we can highlight a specific combination of a verb-particle construction (VPC) and reflexive clitics (VPC + IReflV) functioning as a lexical unit, for instance *obrniti se na (koga)* (lit. to turn RCLI on (sb.), meaning 'to appeal to (sb.)'), *nanašati se na (koga/kaj)* (lit. to spread RCLI on (sb./sth.), meaning 'to refer to (sb./sth.)'), which have not yet been studied as a separate category in Slovene. In the shared task, these combinations were annotated as VPCs and not as a language-specific category – although this type of VMWEs was considered as a specific construction only in the Slovene corpus.

Verb-particle constructions (VPCs). Unlike other Slavic languages[11] included in the shared task, some combinations of a verb and a "preposition" as in *gre za* (lit. it goes for 'it is about') or a verb and an adverb, as in *pasti dol* (lit. to fall down, meaning 'to faint') and *pasti noter* (lit. to fall in, meaning 'to become absorbed, engrossed') were categorised as VPCs in the Slovene training corpus. This represents a deviation from the shared task guidelines and requires short explanation of differences between English and Slovene. One of the basic rules in relation to VPC identification is "to properly distinguish the particle from a possibly homographic preposition". However, the particle category is defined and understood quite differently in both languages. In Slovene, particles ("členek") are words that modify whole sentences, which is a rough equivalent of English sentence adverbs. The equivalent of English particles in VPCs are called "free verbal morphemes" in Slovene. To make the situation more complex, free verbal morphemes are also homographic with both prepositions and adverbs (in different syntactic roles). Therefore, as we understood the Slovene combinations of a verb and a free verbal morpheme as essentially the same as the English verb + particle constructions, we used the VPC category in annotation of Slovene. In Slovene linguistic theories, these combinations have been problematised in relation to two points. The first one is their general categorisation as MWEs, which has been only conditional, based on their minimal two-word structure; and the second is the degree of their semantic transparency, as there are many borderline cases where a verb frequently appears with a certain preposition and the semantic interpretation of the combination is ambiguous. In Slovene grammars, verb-particle constructions are divided into two main groups, according to their semantic transparency: "phrasal verbs" only show structural fixedness (the

[11] It is interesting that this type of VMWEs was not considered in the PARSEME shared task in other Slavic languages, such as Polish, Czech, Croatian and Bulgarian. VPCs are typical mostly for English and other "Germanic languages.

preposition is a part of a prepositional phrase and not verbal phrase, e.g. *skočiti + čez* 'to jump + over'), but do not form a lexical unit; and "phraseological verbs" ("frazemski glagoli"), such as *priti do* (lit. to came to, meaning 'it occurred or happened') where the combination of a verb and a "preposition" (so-called "free verbal morpheme") has idiomatic meaning. Also other possible morphosyntactic transformations with a "holistic semantic value" (cf. Kržišnik 1994) speak in favour of the categorisation of "phraseological verbs" as verbal multiword expressions. They can be embedded in complex VMWEs, having a different meaning as a construction, e.g. *biti ob* (lit. to be at, meaning 'to lose' = VPC), in *biti ob glavo* (lit. to be at head, meaning 'to die' = ID); or they can show polysemy as a combination: in addition to their literal meaning[12] they have more idiomatic meanings. For instance, *priti do* 'come to' has two different idiomatic meanings: (1) *prišlo je do nesreče* (lit. (it) came (third person singular) to an accident, meaning 'an accident occurred') with no subject (obligatory empty subject slot), and (2) *priti do stanovanja* (lit. to come to an apartment, meaning 'to (manage to) acquire an apartment'), where the subject is obligatory and always animate.

The shared task annotation guidelines categorize all VMWEs with the following general characteristics as VPCs:

- They consist of a lexicalized head verb and a lexicalized particle dependent on verb.
- The meaning of the VPC is non-compositional. Notably, the change in the meaning of the verb goes significantly beyond adding the meaning of particle, as in *gre za* (lit. goes for, meaning 'it is about') and *biti ob* (lit. to be at, meaning 'to lose').

As already mentioned, potential VPC candidates can be identified by differentiating between a particle and a homographic preposition, e.g. *biti za njeno idejo* (lit. to be behind her idea, meaning 'to agree with her idea') in comparison with *biti za zaveso* ('to be behind the curtain').

4 Corpus and Annotation Platform

The aim of the PARSEME shared task was to build a corpus of at least 3,500 annotated VMWEs per language. Since the density of VMWEs is highly dependent on the language, as well as text genre, no reliable estimation of the corpus size in terms of the number of tokens was predefined. It was recommended that the corpus includes newspaper texts, Wikipedia pages and similar texts, dedicated to no specific technical domain and free from copyright issues, in order to be compatible with an open license. The corpus should be lemmatized and – if possible – morphosyntactically tagged.

SSJ500 k training corpus[13] (Krek et al. 2015), which contains 500,000 words from sampled paragraphs originating from the FidaPLUS corpus (Arhar Holdt and Gorjanc 2007) was used for the Slovene MWE-annotated training corpus. All annotation layers in SSJ500 k are manually checked: tokenization, sentence segmentation, lemmatization,

---

[12] E.g. *gre za vodičem* 'he follows the guide' in comparison to *gre za naše temeljno načelo* 'it is about our fundamental principle'.

[13] Accessible on Clarin.si repository: https://www.clarin.si/repository/xmlui/handle/11356/1052.

morphosyntactic tagging, named entities and syntactic dependencies. Furthermore, a segment of this corpus is currently being annotated on the semantic level with semantic roles (Gantar et al. 2016).

In the PARSEME shared task, 8,881 sentences have been annotated by two annotators for Slovene. At the end of the annotation, inter-annotation agreement was measured and the annotators agreed on final decisions in order to achieve maximal consistency of VMWE categorisation. Detailed results are presented on the PARSEME official website.[14]

A web-based annotation platform FLAT (FoLiA Linguistic Annotation Tool)[15] was used for the purposes of the automatic annotation in the shared task. It was adapted for this task and tested on thirteen languages included in the task,[16] whereas other participating languages, including Slovene, were annotated outside FLAT.

For Slovene, a SentenceMarkup tool was used, which had been originally created for syntactic annotation of the Slovene language (Dobrovoljc et al. 2012). The tool was adjusted for the purposes of MWE annotation: another level of annotation was added that can be used in combination with other levels, as Fig. 2 demonstrates.

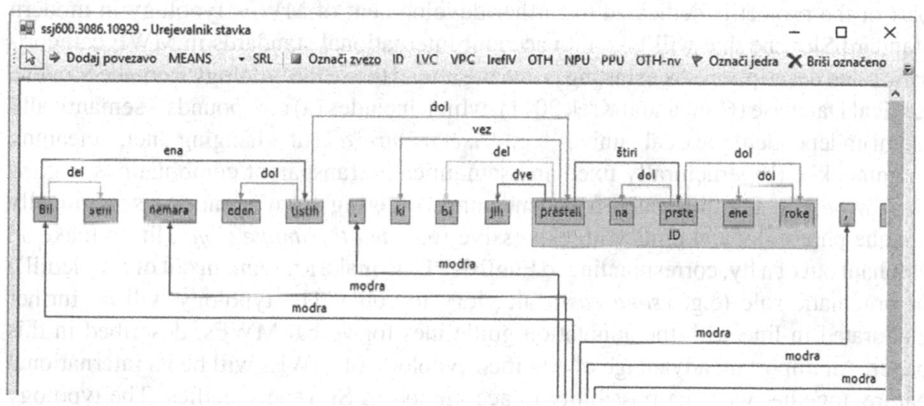

Fig. 2. SentenceMarkup system for MWE annotation in Slovene training corpus

Dependency annotations are marked with green, yellow and red arrows above the words in squares with blue background. Blue arrows link punctuation, syntactically less predictable structures, parentheses etc. to the root. Lexicalised parts of verbal MWEs are tagged with the corresponding category, which can be selected from the menu bar at the top of the annotation window, and is shown in a gray square indicating the VMWE. In the example in Fig. 2, the VMWE *prešteti na prste ene roke* (lit. to count on the fingers of one hand, meaning 'not many') is tagged as ID. In discontinuous MWEs each

14 https://typo.uni-konstanz.de/parseme/index.php/2-general/142-parseme-shared-task-on-automatic-detection-of-verbal-mwes.

15 http://proycon.github.io/folia/.

16 Current state of the annotation in FLAT can be observed at: http://mwe.phil.hhu.de/bot/mwe_count_perlang_html.

lexicalized part is tagged with the same category and recognized by the system as one unit.

The tool provides autonomy in changing the tag set on multiple levels, a possibility of individual as well as combined search in relation to all types of annotations and exports annotations and search results in the tabular and in XML format.

5 Conclusion and Further Work

The fact that the presence of multiword expressions in machine-readable resources is significantly smaller than their frequency in real texts has impact on the development of many areas in human language technology. In this respect, MWEs remain the weak spot in machine translation, semantic role labelling, named entity recognition, automatic generation of text, and also on the lower processing levels such as syntactic parsing, tagging and lemmatisation.

We intend to improve this situation with a new project which aims to develop resources and methods for producing a new grammar of modern standard Slovene. A part of the project is dedicated to further development of MWEs typology in modern standard Slovene that will take into account international standards in MWE categorisation and description. As a starting point, we intend to use the typology from the Slovene Lexical Database (Gantar and Krek 2011), which includes (a) compounds – semantically (semi)independent lexical units, e.g. *viseča mreža* (lit. hanging net, meaning 'hammock'), (b) structurally fixed and semantically transparent combinations, e.g. *za razliko od* (lit. for difference from, meaning 'differing from'), and (c) semantically opaque phraseological units with expressive (e.g. *delati iz muhe slona*, lit. to make an elephant out of a fly, corresponding to English PU 'to make a mountain out of a molehill') or pragmatic role (e.g. *vsaka čast*, 'all glory to you'). The typology will be further elaborated in line with the annotation guidelines for verbal MWEs, described in this paper. An important advantage of a unified typology of MWEs will be its international nature, together with the possibility to accommodate Slovene specifics. The typology will serve as a basis for a formal (grammatical) description of MWEs, and will help determine the methods for the automatic identification of MWEs in text.

A manually annotated training corpus with different types of MWEs will also be synchronized with syntactic dependency annotations. This will result in a machine-readable collection of Slovene MWEs with formal descriptions of their syntactic characteristics as found in real language use. These descriptions will record the syntactic function of the MWE as a whole, variability of MWE components (on lexical and morphological levels), the possibility of incorporating non-lexicalized (lexically independent) elements in MWE structures, flexibility of word order, the limitations of syntactic transformations (e.g. the possibility of forming passive constructions, relative clauses, negation or interrogative structures), as well as the description of its textual (e.g. conjunctional or connective) or discourse roles.

References

Arhar Holdt, Š., Gorjanc, V.: Korpus FidaPLUS: nova generacija slovenskega referenčnega korpusa. Jezik in slovstvo **52**(2), 95–110 (2007)

Atkins, B.T.S., Rundell, M.: The Oxford Guide to Practical Lexicography. Oxford University Press, New York (2008)

Baldwin, T., Kim, S.N.: Multiword expressions. In: Indurkhya, N., Damerau, F.J. (eds.) Handbook of Natural Language Processing, 2nd edn, pp. 267–292. CRC Press, Boca Raton (2010)

Dobrovoljc, K., Krek, S., Rupnik, J.: Skladenjski razčlenjevalnik za slovenščino. In: Erjavec, T., Žganec Gros, J. (eds.) Zbornik Osme konference Jezikovne tehnologije, pp. 42–47. Institut Jožef Stefan, Ljubljana (2012)

Gantar, P., Kosem, I., Krek, S.: Discovering automated lexicography: the case of Slovene lexical database. Int. J. Lexicogr. **29**(2), 220–225 (2016)

Gantar, P., Krek, S.: Slovene lexical database. In: Majchraková, D., Garabík, R. (eds.) Natural Language Processing, Multilinguality: Sixth International Conference, pp. 72–80. Slovenská akadémia vied, Jazikovedný ústav Ľudovíta Štúra, Modra (2011)

Keber, J.: Slovar slovenskih frazemov. Založba ZRC. Inštitut za slovenski jezik Frana Ramovša, Ljubljana (2011)

Kozlevčar Černelič, I.: O funkciji glagolov z oslabljenim pomenom tipa biti. Jezik in slovstvo **21**(3), 76–81 (1975)

Krek, S., Dobrovoljc, K., Erjavec, T.: Training corpus ssj500k 1.4. Slovenian language resource repository CLARIN.SI (2015). http://hdl.handle.net/11356/1052. Accessed 15 June 2017

Kržišnik, E.: Slovenski glagolski frazemi (ob primeru glagolov govorjenja). Univerza v Ljubljani, Doktorska disertacija. Filozofska fakulteta (1994)

Sag, Ivan A., Baldwin, T., Bond, F., Copestake, A., Flickinger, D.: Multiword expressions: a pain in the neck for NLP. In: Gelbukh, A. (ed.) CICLing 2002. LNCS, vol. 2276, pp. 1–15. Springer, Heidelberg (2002). doi:10.1007/3-540-45715-1_1

Toporišič J.: K izrazju in tipologiji slovenske frazeologije. Jezik in slovstvo (8), 273–279 (1973/1974)

Vidovič Muha, A.: Slovensko leksikalno pomenoslovje – Govorica slovarja. Znanstveni inštitut Filozofske fakultete, Ljubljana (2000)

Using Parallel Corpora to Study the Translation of Legal System-Bound Terms: The Case of Names of English and Spanish Courts

Francisco J. Vigier[1](✉) and María del Mar Sánchez[2](✉)

[1] Universidad Pablo de Olavide, Ctra. de Utrera km. 1, 41013 Seville, Spain
fvigier@upo.es

[2] University of Alcalá, Plaza de San Diego, s/n, 28801 Alcalá de Henares, Madrid, Spain
mar.sanchezr@uah.es

Abstract. Corpus-based Translation Studies has opened new avenues to research since Mona Baker published her seminal study back in the 1990s. In comparison to other domains within Translation Studies, in legal translation corpus-based research has not been so widely used despite its incontestable potential and usefulness. In this field, parallel corpora are chiefly used to study the translation process and to identify translation options for problematic terminological and phraseological units. Hence, parallel corpora allow researchers to systematically and objectively study the solutions given to pre-identified translation problems, like legal system-bound terms, which are the quintessential feature of legal translation as clear exponents of legal asymmetry and conceptual-terminological incongruity.

In this contribution, we describe the design, compilation and alignment of a specialised bilingual parallel corpus (English-Spanish) comprising judgments delivered by the European Union Court of Justice. With the main aim of studying the options found for the translation of court names, one corpus is made up of 127 aligned judgments in English and Spanish that refer to English courts, whereas the other corpus consists of 145 aligned files that refer to Spanish courts. The corpus was aligned at sentence level, accounting for 16,012 aligned sentence pairs for the English corpus, and 13,971 for the Spanish corpus. In the following we present the most relevant outcomes of this study (both from a qualitative and quantitative perspective), describe technical aspects related to the compilation process and point to further uses of these corpora, specifically for training purposes.

Keywords: Parallel corpora · Legal system-bound terms · Translation options

1 Introduction: The Use of Corpora to Study Legal Translation-Related Phenomena

Corpus-based approaches have revolutionized Translation Studies (TS) research and practice in the last decades, since corpora enable "the empirical study of the product and process of translation, the elaboration of theoretical constructs, and the training of

R. Mitkov (Ed.): Europhras 2017, LNAI 10596, pp. 260–273, 2017.
https://doi.org/10.1007/978-3-319-69805-2_19

translators" [1]. Despite their widespread use in other fields within TS, where corpora just seem to be *the* methodology, their development has been rather slower in the field of Legal Translation (LT), most probably because of the confidential and private nature of many legal documents (and their translations). However, as pointed out by Soriano [2], some legal texts can be accessed more easily than others: whereas legal scholarly and legislative texts are available for the general public – and hence accessible for LT researchers –, court documentation (except for some judgments) and private documents (for instance, wills, contracts and deeds) belong to the private sphere of individuals and are much more difficult to retrieve for research purposes. It is no wonder, then, that most corpus-based studies on LT-related phenomena undertaken so far have dealt with legislative documents or judgments.

Nevertheless, it is undeniable that corpus-based methodologies "benefit from methodological triangulation and the combination of quantitative and qualitative methods" [3]. Subsequently, corpora have been steadily gaining ground in legal translation research, training and practice, so as to become a fundamental tool for LT researchers – for the study of elements as varied as textual fit of translated EU law [4], legal phraseology [5] or the use of binomials in legal discourse [6], to name but a few recent instances –, LT trainers [7–10] and also LT practitioners [11, 12]. Among the different types of corpora, a parallel corpus, as further explained below, contains documents in a given language (source texts) aligned with their relevant translations into (at least) another language, which allows for the study of translation phenomena. In LT, "parallel corpora offer new vistas to bilingual lexicography and terminography" [13]. Since they reflect translation practice helping identify relevant LT units as well as their *equivalents*, they are used to "complement and validate existing dictionaries" [13].

LT is dominated by the system-specificity of law and, accordingly, legal terminology and legal discourse, which results in the ever-present legal asymmetry and conceptual-terminological incongruity as far as inter-systemic legal translation is concerned. Although "differences in conceptual content pervade legal translation" [14], they are particularly conspicuous in relation to the so-called (legal) system-bound terms, which markedly "refer to concepts, institutions and personnel which are specific to the SL [source language] culture" [15]. As with all other types of culture-bound units, legal system-bound terms from one language can only be rendered in another language by applying one translation technique or procedure taking account of the communicative situation and the purpose (or *skopos)* of the intended target text and on the basis of an exercise of comparative law. Thus, the notion of equivalence in LT is dynamic and context-dependent, and not static and monolithic, like most bilingual legal dictionaries seem to present their translation options, devoid of "any further information on the legal context" [16] or on the type of equivalence and the justification for the relevant translation option [17].

Therefore, with the aim of studying the translation of legal system-bound terms (Spanish <-> English) objectively, systematically and on the light of authentic data, as offered by corpus-based studies [13]), and due to the scarcity of legal parallel corpora and the unavailability of the few ones that have been built in this language pair, as described below in detail, we have compiled an *ad hoc,* parallel corpus with the English and Spanish versions of judgments issued by the European Union Court of Justice

(ECJ)[1]. To be more precise, our corpus comprises judgments on proceedings referred from a national Member State's court in relation to the interpretation or validity of European Union law, but where issues of national law are also raised [18], both in their English and Spanish versions. These documents ensured us that the generated bitexts would be reliable and there would be a translation in the other language of, at least, the referring court.

As noted above, court names are an archetypal example of legal system-bound terms and, therefore, we decided to use our corpus to study the translation of these problematic units. Due to time and resource limitations, we decided to focus our study on the names of civil and criminal courts, as these courts hear the largest number of cases settled in the justice system. In this article, however, we only present our results in relation to the translation of criminal court names, namely, Magistrates' Court, Crown Court, High Court (of Justice), Court of Appeal and Supreme Court – for England and Wales[2] – and Juzgado de Paz, Juzgado de (Primera Instancia e) Instrucción, Juzgado de lo Penal, Audiencia Provincial, Tribunal Superior de Justicia, Audiencia Nacional and Tribunal Supremo – for Spain[3].

The following sections of this article contain a full detailed description of the painstaking compilation and alignment process as well as the analysis of the results obtained, combining quantitative and qualitative approaches and considering the translation techniques used to convey the source legal system-bound court name into the target language. Finally, conclusions are drawn and further uses of the corpus for research and training purposes are highlighted.

2 Design of a Bilingual Parallel Corpus

The use of bilingual and multilingual parallel corpora has been extensively investigated in TS [19–24], since corpora are an excellent means for studying translation phenomena. Specialised research into translation phenomena requires a corpus that can shed light on specific translation issues. Due to the scarcity of legal, bilingual corpora (and the inaccessibility of the few ones that have been built), such specialized *ad-hoc* corpora have to be compiled, and this task is generally arduous and tedious. Designing a corpus requires a procedure or compilation protocol that will guide the research and obtain the desired results. The different phases that we followed in building our corpus were as follows: (1) documentation, in order to establish design criteria and search for original texts; (2) compilation, involving the downloading, logging and naming of original texts, their organization in folders, the conversion of formats and alignment to create bitext files; and (3) corpus analysis. The following subsections describe how we designed an

[1] For a detailed account of translation and multilingualism at the ECJ see [18] and [25] respectively.

[2] For more on the English court system see https://www.judiciary.gov.uk/wp-content/uploads/2012/08/courts-structure-0715.pdf (last accessed: 22 May 2017).

[3] For more on the Spanish court system see http://www.mjusticia.gob.es/cs/Satellite/Portal/es/administracion-justicia/organizacion-justicia/organizacion-juzgados/juzgados-tribunales (last accessed: 22 May 2017).

English-Spanish parallel corpus of ECJ case law in different phases and the current state of the corpus.

2.1 Documentation

The texts that make up a corpus cannot be selected randomly; rather, according to [26], specific criteria need to be pre-determined according to needs and objectives. We followed the set of criteria proposed by these authors, namely, reason for compilation, size, medium, topic, text type, authorship, date of publication and, finally, language. Such criteria optimally delimit how texts are selected for inclusion in a corpus.

We applied the above criteria as follows. The reason underlying the creation of our corpus was to investigate the translation of legal system-bound terms (both from English into Spanish and conversely) in judgments issued by the ECJ. As for size – a subject that has generated a great deal of debate –, a huge corpus is not required in our case. Besides this, as discussed by several authors [11–13], legal discourse and genres are so conservative that a large corpus is not required to determine frequencies and tendencies. The medium in our case is written texts; the topic and text type are delimited to the genre reflected by the ECJ judgments, which also indicates their authorship; the publication date refers to sentences issued between 1990 and 2014; and finally, the languages are English and Spanish. Once the corpus was delimited by these specific criteria, we searched for ECJ judgments referred from English and Spanish national courts along with their translations. The source for these judgments was the repository at http://curia.europa.eu/jcms/. As these were public instruments, we had no problems of copyright or permissions, an issue that hinders the compilation of many corpora in the legal domain [27].

2.2 Compilation

All suitable texts located in the repository were downloaded. The source texts were mostly available as .html and .pdf files. The downloaded texts were organized into two main diatopically delimited sub-corpora, coinciding with the languages of our study (English and Spanish). Each sub-corpus was organized in folders reflecting the institution (court) to which the files belonged, and each of these folders was sub-divided, in turn, into two sub-folders: one for files in English and another for equivalents in Spanish.

The next step was to transparently name and log the texts to enable proper management and analysis. Thus, as texts were saved, they were assigned specific names and were also logged in an Excel spreadsheet with summary data on the parallel corpus. The texts were named as follows: Source_TerritorialJurisdictionOfCourtReferredTo_ReferenceNo_Language. For this particular project, all the texts were coded "ECJ" to reflect their source. In terms of territorial jurisdiction, the England-Wales sub-corpus texts were coded "EW", while the Spain sub-corpus texts were coded "SP". Each text was then assigned a reference number consisting of four digits (starting with 0001), followed by a code for the language of the text: "EN" for texts in English and "ES" for texts in Spanish. Thus, for example, text 0001 in English from the Spain sub-corpus was assigned the name ECJ_SP_0001_EN, while its equivalent in Spanish was named ECJ_SP_0001_ES.

Before alignment, texts were converted to an editable format that could be recognized by corpus management programs, usually plain text (.txt). Since the original texts were obtained as .html and .pdf files, conversion — which can sometimes be onerous and time-consuming — was relatively easy. For conversion we used the programs HtmlAsText — which allows batch conversions — for .html files and Pdf2text for .pdf files. It has to be highlighted that the conversion stage did not find any mayor problems. Main.pdf files were the result of the conversion from word processors. In other cases, when the .pdf files are based upon an image of a document, they must be converted into an editable format by means of Optical Character Recognition (OCR) systems and be manually corrected. Finally, to streamline the alignment process, it was important to ensure that the source and target texts were virtually identical in layout. Therefore all original and translated texts were checked manually to resolve minor layout issues and conversion errors.

English Courts parallel sub-corpus
This sub-corpus is composed of 7 folders containing 127 texts in each language, distributed as described in Table 1. Each folder contains two sub-folders called EN and ES to keep texts in English separate from the corresponding texts in Spanish.

Table 1. English Courts parallel sub-corpus

	Files	Tokens	Types
EN	127	844898	13121
ES	127	938276	20262

Spanish Courts parallel sub-corpus
This sub-corpus is composed of 9 folders containing 145 texts in each language, distributed as described in Table 2. Each folder contains two sub-folders that keep texts in the two languages separate.

Table 2. Spanish case law parallel sub-corpus

	Files	Tokens	Types
EN	145	767661	12259
ES	145	832945	18108

The final corpus building stage was to align the texts for subsequent exploitation and contrastive linguistic analysis. Alignment is defined by [28] as "a process of making symmetric correspondences explicit in order to enable further processing of parallel resources." Originals and their translations are aligned to produce a set of two texts called a bitext. Alignment functions on the basis of identifying segmentation levels, whether paragraph, sentence or word. Segmentation at the sentence level — the typical practice — was applied to our texts.

Original texts and their translations can be aligned using any one of several tools. We tested several to decide which one was the most appropriate, using a test translation memory and the following alignment programs: Intertext, WinAlign, AntPConc, Bitext2tmx, SketchEngine and Bifid. This test translation memory revealed the advantages and disadvantages of each alignment program. We finally chose Intertext for the alignment phase, as it was the program that produced the fewest alignment errors.

Intertext, a free open-source program with a simple interface (available for Windows, MacOS and Linux), was developed by [29] for the InterCorp project. Fast and simple to download and install, it accepts bilingual files in .xml and .txt and offers a choice between two alignment methods: Hunalign or Plain 1:1 aligner. We chose to use Hunalign for this project, as it allows alignment of fragments of a complete text if necessary. The fact that texts are aligned vertically means that looking for a particular alignment is faster. And, as mentioned, the level of error is lower than for the other tested programs. However, before alignment, certain data have to be entered. This stage requires knowing the codes used to indicate specific information for the alignment process (source language, target language, etc.). It should be possible to search for a term in the segments of one of the two aligned texts or in both at the same time. However, Intertext only locates the segments where a term appears and does not indicate the translation. Note that if the translation memory in which the search is to be carried out is not open (that is, not in .tmx format and therefore exchangeable between applications), it cannot be opened from Intertext. Even if it can be opened from Intertext, it has to be located in the repository of the program, but if the number of translation memories is large, then selecting and opening one is a very slow process. For this reason, other programs are better for term searches. Finally, aligned texts can be exported as a single bilingual file with the .tmx extension.

In the alignment process using Intertext, parallel texts in the English Courts parallel sub-corpus were aligned setting English as the source language and Spanish as the target language, while those of the Spanish Courts parallel sub-corpus were aligned setting Spanish as the source language and English as the target language. The source language for each sub-corpus was chosen according to the official language of the territorial jurisdiction represented in the sub-corpus, because, even if the EJC publishes its decisions in all its official languages, only the judgment in the language of the proceedings, which is determined by the language used by the referring Member State's court, is the authentic one [25].

Once the alignment project has been created, Intertext offers a choice between two methods of alignment (Hunalign or Plain 1:1 aligner) and also between aligning the two full parallel documents or a number of consecutive parallel segments of the documents (Fig. 1).

There were few errors in the resulting alignments, which were manually corrected. Other than alignment problems with two pairs of parallel texts, most of the errors found were due to different line breaks and to different segmentation of paragraphs in parallel texts. In most cases it was possible to use Intertext editing options to move segments that were not well aligned up or down and in some cases combine them to ensure that the segments in both texts coincided. As for the two problematic text pairs, the reason

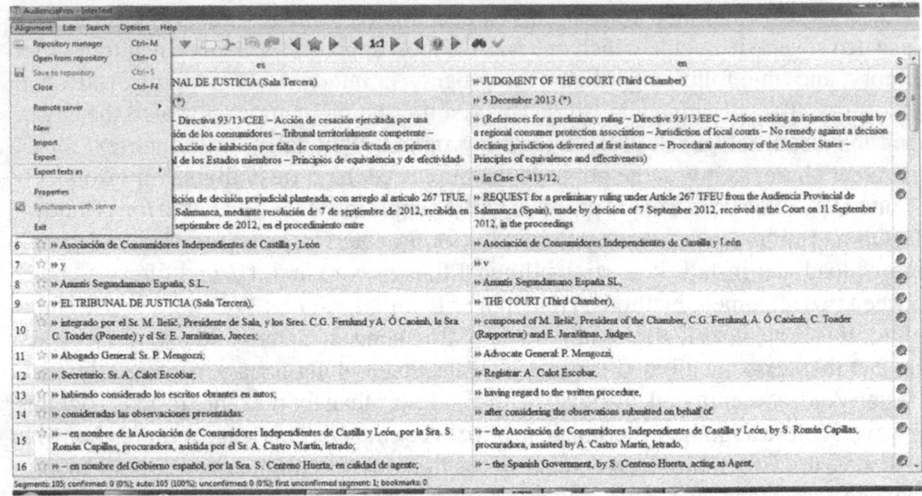

Fig. 1. Alignment process with Intertext

was the type of coding used in them. We solved this problem by converting the texts to UTF-8.

Finally, the aligned texts were stored in the Intertext repository. In order to be able to later use these alignments with other programs, they were exported as translation memories with the extension .tmx, for which it was necessary to specify the name of the translation memory, as well as the source and target languages using the corresponding ISO 639-1 codes (Fig. 2).


```
ECJ_EW_0027_EN_ES.ECJ_EW_0027_EN.ECJ_EW_0027_ES.tmx
<tmx version="1.4b">
    <header creationtool="InterText" creationtoolversion="1.0" datatype="PlainText" segtype="block" adminlang="en-us" srclang="en" o-tmf="XML aligned text"
    ></header>
<body>
<tu><prop type="x-sentbreak">|#|</prop>
    <tuv xml:lang="en"><seg>Avis juridique important </seg></tuv>
    <tuv xml:lang="es"><seg>Avis juridique important </seg></tuv>
</tu>
<tu><prop type="x-sentbreak">|#|</prop>
    <tuv xml:lang="en"><seg>|</seg></tuv>
    <tuv xml:lang="es"><seg>|</seg></tuv>
</tu>
<tu><prop type="x-sentbreak">|#|</prop>
    <tuv xml:lang="en"><seg>61990J0038</seg></tuv>
    <tuv xml:lang="es"><seg>61990J0038</seg></tuv>
</tu>
<tu><prop type="x-sentbreak">|#|</prop>
    <tuv xml:lang="en"><seg>Judgment of the Court (Sixth Chamber) of 10 March 1992. - Criminal proceedings against Thomas Edward Lomas and others. -
    References for a preliminary ruling: Crown Court Maidstone and Crown Court Leeds - United Kingdom. - Common organization of the market in sheepmeat and
    goat meat - Clawback - Method of calculation - Validity. - Joined cases C-38/90 and C-151/90. </seg></tuv>
    <tuv xml:lang="es"><seg>SENTENCIA DEL TRIBUNAL DE JUSTICIA (SALA SEXTA) DE 10 DE MARZO DE 1992. - PROCESOS PENALES CONTRA THOMAS EDWARD LOMAS Y OTROS. -
    PETICIONES DE DECISION PREJUDICIAL: CROWN COURT MAIDSTONE Y CROWN COURT LEEDS - REINO UNIDO. - ORGANIZACION COMUN DEL MERCADO DE LAS CARNES DE OVINO Y
    CAPRINO - CLAWBACK - METODO DE CALCULO - VALIDEZ. - ASUNTOS ACUMULADOS C-38/90 Y C-151/90. </seg></tuv>
</tu>
<tu><prop type="x-sentbreak">|#|</prop>
    <tuv xml:lang="en"><seg>European Court reports 1992 Page I-01781</seg></tuv>
    <tuv xml:lang="es"><seg>Recopilación de Jurisprudencia 1992 página I-01781</seg></tuv>
</tu>
<tu><prop type="x-sentbreak">|#|</prop>
    <tuv xml:lang="en"><seg>Summary</seg></tuv>
    <tuv xml:lang="es"><seg>Índice</seg></tuv>
```


Fig. 2. TMX sample

2.3 Analysis

Intertext was not the best option for opening a translation memory because the memory has to be created by Intertext to be included in the program repository. Additionally, when this repository is full, opening and navigation is a slow process. Thus, although Intertext was the best option for aligning parallel documents and creating the corresponding translation memories, it was not the best option for searching for terms. WinAlign, an alignment program integrated in SDL Trados Studio, is a better option as it is fast and is capable of locating both a term and its equivalent. The translation memories with the .tmx extension created with Intertext were therefore imported into SDL Trados Studio to be able to search for terms using WinAlign.

3 Results Obtained from Our Corpus

Once we had all our translation memories, we searched for our terms to study how they were translated into the other language. As discussed above, legal system-bound terms can only be rendered into the other language after an exercise of comparative law between the source and the target systems and an analysis of the communicative situation of the translation (including the purpose and recipients of the intended translated text) unravel degrees of equivalence, on the one hand, and degrees of adequacy, on the other [17], thus enabling the translator to apply the most appropriate translation technique for the rendition of that given unit under those specific circumstances.

There are different classifications of translation techniques used in LT [15, 30–32] which "range from foreignising (SL-equivalents) to domesticating (TL [target language]-oriented equivalents)" [13, p. 24]. According to [33], who studied the translation of court names from English into Polish, "whatever technique is used, the translator must always bear in mind two translation commandments of a general nature: firstly, the translation must have informative value (the higher the better) and secondly, it cannot be misleading or inaccurate". Keeping this in mind, in order to describe the techniques used in the translation of English and Spanish court names in the texts that make up our corpus, we have limited the procedures to the following: borrowing (i.e., reproducing the SL term in the target text), literal translation (word-for-word rendition), description (using a general term or a paraphrase), amplification (adding new elements in the target text to convey information implicit in the source text) and adaptation (using a TL term to translate the SL term due to their conceptual and functional similarities).

In the following, we present our results from both a qualitative perspective (describing the techniques used to translate the relevant court name) and a quantitative perspective (which technique has been most or least frequently used). In order to illustrate the scope of our study, but due to obvious space restrictions, we present the results regarding two English court names (*Magistrates' Court* and *Crown Court)* and two Spanish court names (*Audiencia Provincial* and *Audiencia Nacional)*, as much clearer exponents of legal asymmetry and conceptual incongruity between the English and Spanish court systems than others (for instance, *Supreme Court* vs *Tribunal Supremo)*.

3.1 Magistrates' Court

This subsubcorpus consists of 8 ECJ judgments (in both English and Spanish) on questions referred from a magistrates' court in England and Wales. All in all, the English corpus has 34 occurrences of this term. Surprisingly, in its Spanish counterpart, it is the borrowing that has been used to convey the term into Spanish on 33 occasions, thus using the SL term in the translated text, and only once was the term translated by *"órgano jurisdiccional nacional"* [national court], thus using a description (Table 3).

Table 3. Translation of "Magistrates' Court" into Spanish

EN	ES [Translation Technique]	Occurrences
Magistrates' Court	Magistrates' Court [borrowing]	33
	órgano jurisdiccional nacional [description]	1

Considering other grammatical, syntactical and orthographic elements in the Spanish translations, the borrowed term was preceded by the article *la* (femenine, singular). This is striking, too, since, in this context, *court* can translate into Spanish as *juzgado* or *tribunal* (both masculine nouns) and, therefore, the article *el* would be expected to be used and not the article *la* – probably influenced by the false friend *corte* (which, in today's European Spanish, makes reference to the place of residence or retinue of a sovereign), but in Latin American Spanish still referring to the place where justice is administered. It is also noteworthy that, in the Spanish translations, the name of the place where the court is located precedes the court name (e.g., *"la Nottingham Magistrates' Court"*), even if it is a plural name (*"la Reading and Sonning Magistrates' Court"*), which makes it really ambiguous for a Spanish reader. Additionally, on 4 occurrences in the same text, the apostrophe was not used in the borrowed term (*"la Richmond Magistrates Court"*), even if the first time the term appeared in the text was correctly spelled.

3.2 Crown Court

This subsubcorpus consists of 9 ECJ judgments (in both English and Spanish) on questions referred from the Crown Court of England and Wales. As can be seen in Table 4, there are 41 occurrences of this term in our corpus of judgments in English and, again, the English term was preserved in the translation into Spanish (borrowing) in those 41 cases, followed by an amplification (namely, *Reino Unido* [United Kingdom]) in 8 cases in 4 different texts (like in *"la Chelmsford Crown Court del Reino Unido"* and *"la Manchester Crown Court (Reino Unido)"*), thus providing information implicit in the source text. Surprisingly, though, this technique was not used to convey more information regarding the court or consistently either in the translation itself or throughout the corpus: in one text (ECJ_EW_0031_ES), amplification was not used the first time the term appeared in the translated text – as otherwise expected and recommended –, but the second; in another text (ECJ_EW_0032), the amplification was used on all the occurrences of the term.

Table 4. Translation of "Crown Court" into Spanish

EN	ES [Translation Technique]	Occurrences
Crown Court	Crown Court [borrowing]	41
	Crown Court (Reino Unido) [borrowing + amplification]	8

From a syntactic and stylistic point of view, again, the feminine article *la* and its plural form *las* antecede the term on 28 and 5 occurrences respectively. As to the name of the places where the Crown Court sits and are referred to in the corpus, it is remarkable that there is no uniformity in how they are treated in the translations into Spanish, probably because there is no uniformity either in how they appear in the source texts (see *"the Crown Court at Maidstone"*, *"Chelmsford Crown Court"* and *"Crown Court Leeds"*). Accordingly, on 13 occurrences in 3 different texts, the term is preceded by the name place (for instance, *"la Rochdale Magistrates' Court"* and *"la Manchester Crown Court"*); on 6 occurrences in 3 different texts, the place name comes right after the court name (for example, *"Crown Court Leeds"*); on 17 occurrences in 5 different texts, the place name comes after the court name preceded by the preposition *de* (e.g., *"la Crown Court de Maidstone"* and *"la Crown Court de Chelmsford"*); and, finally, on 5 occurrences of the same text, the place name comes after the court name with a comma separating both units (*"la Crown Court, Bolton"*).

3.3 Audiencia Provincial

This subsubcorpus consists of 22 ECJ judgments (in both Spanish and English) on questions referred from an Audiencia Provincial in Spain. There are 100 occurrences of this term. As shown in Table 5, borrowing, once again, was the translation technique most frequently used to convey the name of the Spanish court into English, therefore the Spanish term was kept (borrowing) in 92 cases, 21 times followed by a (geographical) amplification (e.g., *"the Audiencia Provincial de Málaga (Spain)"*), and 21 times followed by a description – of the court: such description being *"Provincial Court"* – literal translation – 19 times (like in *"the Audiencia Provincial de Sevilla (Seville Provincial Court)"*, *"Regional High Court*[4]*"* once (in *"the Audiencia Provincial de Salamanca (Salamanca Regional High Court))"* and *"Provincial High Court"* once (in *"the Audiencia Provincial de Barcelona (Provincial High Court, Barcelona)*)". Description was the technique used to translate the term in 7 cases (5 of them in the same text), with translation options including *"national court"*, *"court"*, *"the appellant"* and a very simple *"it"*), whilst only once was literal translation (*"Provincial Court"*) used to convey the term into English.

[4] *Regional High Court* may be especially risky, as, if back-translated into Spanish, could lead to *Tribunal Superior de Justicia* [High Court of Justice], which is a region-level court and not a province-level court like *Audiencia Provincial.*

Table 5. Translation of "Audiencia Provincial" into English

ES	EN [Translation Technique]	Occurrences
Audiencia Provincial	Audiencia Provincial [borrowing]	92
	Audiencia Provincial (Spain) [borrowing + amplification]	21
	Audiencia Provincial (Provincial Court) [borrowing + description]	21
	national court [description]	7
	Provincial Court [literal translation]	1

From a syntactic and stylistic viewpoint, it seems that the name of the place of the court was treated as part of the proper noun, and thus the entire syntagm in Spanish [term + preposition *de* + place name] was subsequently maintained in the translation into English (for instance, *"the Audiencia Provincial de Castellón"*). This was the procedure followed in 78 cases and the only one used when reference to the place name was made in English (otherwise, some of the techniques noted above applied, like description).

3.4 Audiencia Nacional

This subsubcorpus consists of 15 ECJ judgments (in both Spanish and English) on questions referred from Spain's Audiencia Nacional. All in all, there are 68 occurrences to this court in our corpus. As displayed in Table 6, once again, borrowing was overwhelmingly used in the translations into English (67 times) and only on 1 occasion was description used (namely, *"the national court"*). Out of these 67 times the Spanish term was kept, only 20 times was it accompanied, too, by amplification procedures: 11 times followed by *"National High Court"* and 9 times followed by a reference to *"Spain"*, one of them actually by a combination of both.

Table 6. Translation of "Audiencia Nacional" into English

ES	EN [Translation Technique]	Occurrences
Audiencia Nacional	Audiencia Nacional [borrowing]	67
	Audiencia Nacional (Spain) [borrowing + amplification]	20
	national court [description]	1

4 Conclusion and Future Research

In this article, we have described the building and application process of a parallel corpus for the purpose of researching the translation of legal system-bound terms (more specifically, court names). From a technical point of view, we have described the process of designing a parallel bilingual (English-Spanish) corpus of ECJ case law via a protocol with three phases: documentation, compilation and analysis. As part of this protocol, the alignment process is one of the most important steps in successfully creating a parallel corpus. Intertext was chosen as the simplest program that met our research needs. Following a cleanup and a manual check of the files, a bilingual parallel corpus was created, consisting of a sub-corpus each with judgments on cases brought by the said English and Spanish courts.

Content-wise, despite the arduous task of retrieving, compiling and aligning texts in their build-up process, *ad-hoc* parallel corpora prove to be an interesting tool for the study of legal system-bound terms as they allow LT researchers to objectively and systematically assess how a given term has been conveyed in another language, both from a quantitative and qualitative perspective. This methodology has been especially interesting for our specific study, which intended to assess the translation techniques used in the translation of court names in the judgments of the ECJ, thanks to the output offered by our parallel corpus.

After our analysis, we can conclude that there seems to be a preference for borrowings (that is, preserving the source system-bound term in the target language as it is) over other translation procedures, thus keeping a distinctively foreignizing approach. In fact, of the 243 occurrences of the court names in the four subcorpora detailed above, on 233 occasions the term was kept in the target language as it is in the source language, which accounts for over 95% of the cases. Taking into account the binding nature of the decisions taken by the ECJ for all EU member states, this is a surprising result given that borrowings, if not accompanied by an adequate gloss or amplification, make it difficult for the reader to recognize and understand the term [15, p. 5], and this strategy, carried to the extreme, has the danger of "making the translation into a collection of foreign-language words glued together by prepositions, adverbs and verbs from another language" [16]. As we have also demonstrated, there does not seem to be much consistency or clarity in the use of the amplifications of such *borrowed* terms or in their syntactic and stylistic treatment, therefore contravening, as noted above, the recommendations regarding the translation of court names put forward by [33].

As indicated above, we have only presented the results regarding four court names, but our parallel corpus has many more utilities that can be exploited in further studies. From a technical perspective, it may be interesting to grammatically and lexically tag the texts using a program like TreeTagger and to include metadata (tagged in .xml) to provide information about the corpus (court, judgment year of issue, judgment language, etc.) Incontestably, our parallel corpus may be of extreme usefulness in the pursuit of other research aims (to name but a few, a study on the use of phraseology in ECJ judgments Spanish-English or a diachronic study on Spanish and/or English legal *translationese* or a follow-up study on the translation of legal system-bound terms, with a greater number of language combinations), but also for training purposes, in line with our previous contributions regarding monolingual corpora [9].

References

1. Laviosa, S.: Corpora and translation studies. In: Granger, S., Lerot, J., Petch-Tyson (eds.) Corpus-Based Approaches to Contrastive Linguistics and Translation Studies, pp. 45–54. Rodopi, Amsterdam, New York (2003)
2. Soriano Barabino, G.: La creación de corpus de documentos reales por parte del traductor jurídico, del investigador y del docente de traducción jurídica: aspectos jurídicos y prácticos de las dificultades de recopilación. In: II AIETI. Actas del II Congreso Internacional de la Asociación Ibérica de Estudios de Traducción e Interpretación, pp. 196–206. AIETI, Madrid (2005)
3. Biel, L., Engberg, J.: Research models and methods in legal translation. Linguist. Antverp. **12**, 1–11 (2013)
4. Biel, Ł.: The textual fit of translated EU law: a corpus-based study of deontic modality. Transl. **20**(3), 332–355 (2014)
5. Pontrandolfo, G.: Investigating judicial phraseology with COSPE. A contrastive corpus-based study. In: Fantinuoli, C., Zanettin, F. (eds.) New Directions in Corpus-Based Translation Studies, pp. 137–160. Language Science Press, Berlin (2015)
6. Andrades Moreno, A.: Propuesta de equivalencias de binomios en la traducción jurídica inglés-español. Estudios de Traducción **6**, 129–145 (2016)
7. Monzó Nebot, E.: Corpus-based activities in legal translator training. Interpret. Transl. Train. **2**(2), 221–252 (2008)
8. Laursen, A., Arinas Pellón, I.: Text corpora in translator training. A case study of the use of comparable corpora in classroom teaching. Interpret. Transl. Train. **6**(1), 45–70 (2012)
9. Sánchez Ramos, M., Vigier Moreno, F.: Using monolingual virtual corpora in public service legal translation. In: Martín-Monge, E., Elorza, I., García-Riaza, B. (eds.) Technology-Enhanced Language Learning for Specialized Domains, pp. 228–239. Routledge, London, New York (2016)
10. Vigier Moreno, F.: Teaching the use of ad hoc corpora in the translation of legal texts into the second language. Lang. Law/Linguagem e Direito **3**(1), 100–119 (2016)
11. Scott, J.: Can genre-specific DIY corpora, compiled by legal translators themselves assist them in 'Learning the Lingo' of legal subgenres? Comp. Legilinguistics **12**, 87–100 (2012)
12. Scott, J.: Towards professional uptake of DIY electronic corpora in legal genres. In: Salford Working Papers in Translation and Interpreting, pp. 1–22 (2012)
13. Biel, Ł.: Corpus-based studies of legal language for translation purposes: methodological and practical potential. In: Heine, C., Engberg, J. (eds.) Reconceptualizing LSP. Online Proceedings of the XVII European LSP Symposium 2009, Aarhus, pp. 1–19 (2010)
14. Way, C.: The challenges and opportunities of legal translation and translator training in the 21st century. Int. J. Commun. **10**, 1009–1020 (2016)
15. Harvey, M.A.: Beginner's course in legal translation: the case of culture-bound terms. In: ASTTI/ETI, pp. 357–369 (2000)
16. De Groot, R., Van Laer, C.: The dubious quality of legal dictionaries. Int. J. Leg. Inf. **34**(1), 65–86 (2006)
17. Prieto Ramos, F., Orozco Jutorán, M.: De la ficha terminológica a la ficha traductológica: hacia una lexicografía al servicio de la traducción jurídica. Babel **61**(1), 110–130 (2015)
18. Künnecke, M.: Translation in the EU: language and law in the EU's Judicial Labyrinth. Maastricht J. Eur. Comp. Law **20**(2), 243–260 (2013)
19. Baker, M.: Corpora in translation studies: an overview and some suggestions for future research. Target **7**(2), 223–243 (1995)

20. Blum-Kulka, S.: Shifts of cohesion and coherence in translation. In: Venuti, L. (ed.) The Translation Studies Reader, pp. 209–313. Routledge, New York (2004)
21. Calzada Pérez, M.: Five turns of the screw: a CAD analysis of the European parliament. J. Lang. Polit. **16**(3), 412–433 (2017)
22. Kenny, D.: Lexis and Creativity in Translation. Manchester, St. Jerome (2001)
23. Mauranen, A., Kujamäki, P.: Translation Universals. Do they exist? John Benjamins, Amsterdam (2004)
24. Seghiri, M.: Metodología de elaboración de un glosario bilingüe y bidireccional (inglés-español/español-inglés) basado en corpus para la traducción de manuales de instrucciones de televisores. Babel **63**(1), 43–64 (2017)
25. Łachacz, O., Mańko, R.: Multilingualism at the court of justice of the European union: theoretical and practical aspects. Stud. Log. Gramm. Rhetor. **34**(47), 75–92 (2013)
26. Bowker, L., Pearson, J.: Working with Specialized Language. Routledge, London, New York (2002)
27. Koehn, P.: Europarl: a parallel corpus for statistical machine translation. In: Conference Proceedings: The Tenth Machine Translation Summit, Phuket, Thailand, pp. 79–86 (2005). http://homepages.inf.ed.ac.uk/pkoehn/publications/europarl-mtsummit05.pdf. Accessed 05 Oct 2017
28. Tiedemann, K.: Bitext Alignment. Morgan & Claypool, Toronto (2011)
29. Vondřička, P.: Aligning parallel texts with Intertext. In: Calzolari, N. et al. (eds.) Proceedings of the Ninth International Conference on Language Resources and Evaluation, LREC 2014, pp. 1875–1879. European Language Resources Association (ELRA) (2014)
30. Šarcevic, S.: New Approach to Legal Translation. Kluwer Law International, The Hague (2007)
31. Holl, I.: Técnicas para la Traducción Jurídica: Revisión de diferentes propuestas, últimas tendencias. Hermeneus: Revista de Traducción e Interpretación **14**, 1–17 (2012)
32. Orozco Jutorán, M.: Propuesta de un catálogo de técnicas de traducción: la toma de decisiones informada ante la elección de equivalentes. Hermeneus: Revista de Traducción e Interpretación **16**, 233–264 (2014)
33. Goscinski, M.: The names of English judicial offices, courts and tribunals and their translation into Polish. Comp. Legilinguistics **28**, 43–62 (2016)

Phraseology and Language Learning

Towards Better Representation of Phraseological Meaning in Dictionaries for Learners

Elena Berthemet(✉)

Centre de Linguistique en Sorbonne, Paris, France
elenaberthemet@gmail.com

Abstract. The main research question we would like to discuss in this paper is the following: What is the best manner to represent the meaning of idioms in a phraseological dictionary for learners? In order to illustrate our discussion, this paper describes a part of a project whose long-term goal is to supply learners with explicit practical information about idioms, and to give unambiguous examples from which they can build their own competence. The analysis is based on the French idiom *mouton noir* 'black sheep'. Although our focus is on French as a foreign language, it seems that the same method is applicable to the description of any language in the project (Chinese, English, French, German, Italian, Japanese, and Russian).

The paper is divided into five sections. Section 1 provides an overview of the project, defines its tasks and presents its main objective. Following this brief introduction, Sect. 2 explores the theoretical and methodological sources that are useful for the aims of our study. Section 3 shows what the microstructure looks like. Starting from a semasiological perspective, Sect. 4 investigates definition(s) and examples and considers how combining corpus methods, introspection and input from international students can render definitions more precise. Taking the onomasiological perspective, Sect. 5 describes the central organizing principle, based on *notions*. We will conclude with some final remarks and a presentation of issues that are worth exploring in the future.

Keywords: Computational linguistics · Corpora · Language learning and teaching · Lexical semantics · Lexicography · Semantics

1 Main Objective and Summary of the Project

Before we move on to the main research question, it is important to give the reader sufficient information about the main objective of the project. The thoughts described in this paper were inspired by my own frustrations as a student of English, German, and French. Idioms confront the learner with numerous difficulties. My starting point is the observation that the information about idioms available in most dictionaries is fragmented and insufficient.

The primary goal of the project is to develop a multilingual system for describing idioms, and to help non-native speakers in acquiring phraseological proficiency in an L2. *Idioms* are lexical signs which have an opaque meaning in the sense that it cannot

R. Mitkov (Ed.): Europhras 2017, LNAI 10596, pp. 277–289, 2017.
https://doi.org/10.1007/978-3-319-69805-2_20

be deduced from the meaning of individual components. For example, it is not sufficient to know what *poule* 'chicken' and *mouillée* 'wet' mean to understand the French idiom *poule mouillée* 'wet chicken' meaning 'a person who is afraid of everything'. Therefore, idioms are problematic both from the decoding and encoding perspectives. The present research addresses only the problems that idioms pose from the reception.

The idea is to transform tacit native-speaker knowledge into an explicit, well-organized resource by providing a model for a parsimonious and accurate description of idioms. The software is a privately funded online project. The current version is based on Java using Eclipse. The server runs on Windows with MS SQL Server, but it can be run on any operating system with any database. Currently the application supports Chinese, English, French, German, Italian, Japanese and Russian and enables multi-directional searches of phraseological equivalents in any of these languages. Other languages can be added. The microstructure is fixed and symmetrical, i.e., the presentation and content do not differ between languages. A uniform detailed description of idioms helps readability and improved searches in a particular field. All versions are saved, and it is possible to compare and to reverse them. The user is provided with a classic word search or with queries via the notions.

However, the tool is unfinished: it contains about one hundred entries at different levels of development and still needs improvements such as modifications to make it more user-friendly. Work continues on defining its optimal content and structure, and a number of practical and theoretical issues are involved in its production. For this paper, we focused on understanding.

2 Theoretical Framework

The problem is that idioms present a challenge not only to natural language applications, but also to linguistic theory. There is a wealth of excellent literature on phraseology [2–6, 9–11, 14, 16, 20] that we will use to provide a strong theoretical framework. In what follows, we will not attempt to give a full overview of our theoretical background: only the main aspects will be taken into consideration.

This project derives its theoretical and methodological sources from the Moscow Semantic School and Baranov's and Dobrovol'skij's [2, 3] research. Its theoretical starting points are the following:

- Understanding is not universal.
- Idioms have a complicated semantic structure, since understanding them involves many interacting lexical, syntactical, and pragmatic phenomena, as well as the background knowledge of the listener.
- Idioms have a complicated conceptual structure (i.e., it is not limited to any one concrete language); they are motivated and based on principles of human cognition.
- Idioms should be integrally described; that is, they should have parsimonious and accurate explanations.
- Idioms have no perfect equivalents.

The representation of phraseological meaning rests on three pillars of the cognitive linguistic conception of language: "a belief in the contextual, pragmatic flexibility of meaning, the conviction that meaning is a cognitive phenomenon that exceeds the boundaries of the word, and the principle that meaning involves perspectivization" [7].

Scholars who have done similar research are Baranov, Dobrovol'skij [1] and Lubensky [13]. Despite the undoubted quality of these two dictionaries, they are subject to constraints imposed by linear presentation, and do not treat more than two languages.

Although idioms have received a fair amount of attention in the literature, in practice the linguistic information given in dictionaries about idioms often is (tends to be) quite confusing and fragmented. The most substantial criticisms are the following: (a) differences between L1 and L2 equivalents are not explained; (b) idioms are presented out of context; (c) pragmatics is of little consideration, and no consideration is given to the situation, which is not purely linguistic; (d) because learner's dictionaries focus more on reception than on production, it is not clear how to use idioms. With these shortcomings in mind and with the aid of corpus technology, our aim is to explain meaning and usage clearly.

Our phraseological dictionary is intended to be systemic, multilingual, complete, and user-friendly. By *systemic* we mean that the user will be provided with information about an idiom's relationships and links to other units in the dictionary, in particular those with similar and opposite meanings. Since the dictionary is *multilingual* and practically oriented, it will allow a multi-directional search starting from Chinese, English, French, German, Italian, Japanese or Russian. That means that both the input and the output information will be in any of these languages. It will be *complete* because it takes into account all the relevant information on understanding as well as on production. The program will be *user-friendly*, and will help the user to make an informed choice of the best match for the idiom s/he wishes to translate.

3 Microstructure

One of the practical problems concerns the structure of entries. The microstructure is built on two essential requirements: coherence and completeness. In order to understand how idioms are presented in the project, let us enumerate the essentials of this microstructure: (a) headword; (b) variants; (c) definition(s); (d) examples; (e) notions; (f) commentary (lexical, grammatical, temporal, territorial, stylistic and discursive constraints); (g) links (synonyms, antonyms, conversives); (h) etymology (scientific etymological origin, diachronic perspective); (i) popular etymology (naïve native users' interpretation, contemporary perspective). The example below (Table 1) represents the idiom *avoir un chat dans la gorge* 'to have a cat in (one's) throat'.

As can be seen, aside from notions, the article is in the language of the idiom. The main goal of the notions, which are given in English, is to enable the compilation of lists of units possessing a common semantic feature. English helps to establish the coherence of the database and to make automatic the link between idioms.

Table 1. A case study of the French idiom *avoir un chat dans la gorge* ‘to have a cat in (one’s) throat’.

Entry : [French] avoir un chat dans la gorge

Notions : voice, irritation, hoarseness, pain, thickness, throat, health

Polarization : Neutral

Links :

- Equivalent
  - [English] to have a frog in (one’s) throat
  - [German] einen Frosch im Hals haben

Definition : avoir la gorge irritée, la voix cassée

Etymology : L’origine de l’expression est à chercher dans un calembour, comme le suppose Pierre Guiraud, cité dans (Rey A., Chantreau S. (1993) Expressions et locutions, Paris : Dictionnaires Le Robert). Selon ces auteurs, « ‘chat’, ‘marron’, et ‘maton’ désignent toutes sortes de grumeaux et coagulations qui se forment dans diverses substances. Il doit y avoir à l’origine un jeu de mots sur ‘maton’ (chat) et ‘maton’ (lait caillé, grumeau) ; ‘le chat dans la gorge’ est sans doute une sécrétion catarrheuse qui obstrue le gosier ».

Popular Etymology : L’image d’un chat dans la gorge est inhabituelle, elle est renforcée par les griffes de cet animal.

Examples :

1. J’ai du mal à parler, j’ai un chat dans la gorge.

Regrettably, the scope of this paper does not allow for a thorough presentation of the microstructure. Three of the underlined points that constitute the heart of the matter will be considered more elaborately: definition(s), examples, and notions. In fact, because they seem to us particularly interesting from the viewpoint of understanding, we regard them as the most significant aspects. For the sake of organization, the discussion is broken down into two sections: definition(s) and examples are discussed in greater detail in Sect. 4, whereas Sect. 5 is devoted to notions.

As can be seen below (Table 2), the entry *mouton noir* ‘black sheep’ (with simplifications) takes the following form:

We will use this table as a background during the following discussion.

Table 2. The simplified entry *mouton noir* 'black sheep'.

(1) **Headword:** *mouton noir*

(2) **Definition(s):** personne rejetée par les autres membres du collectif car ne correspondant pas aux normes du groupe. La raison de ce rejet n'est pas objective et peut être de caractère temporaire.

(3) **Examples:**

a. Ouais, chaque famille a son *mouton noir*. Souvent, c'est quelqu'un de différent : pas assez intelligent, pas assez beau, pas d'accord avec les autres.

b. Après tout, c'est moi le *mouton noir*, celle qui fait tout de travers et attire les critiques de tout le monde.

c. Lui, il était l'enfant préféré et moi le *mouton noir*. Le rêve pour une mère, il faisait tout comme il fallait, il était sportif et ambitieux. Moi, j'ai toujours été la honte de la famille.

d. Elle n'appelle jamais Patrick par son prénom, mais par Mouton Noir. Elle ne l'aime pas parce qu'il n'a jamais voulu lui obéir, n'était jamais d'accord avec elle et n'avait pas peur de le dire.

Notions: anomaly, community, conflict, difference, disagreement, disapproval, discord, disdain, exception, exclusion, non-agreement, non-conformism, opposition, particularity, protest, refusal, reject, separation, singularity, society, unconformity

4 Definition(s)

4.1 Research Question

As stated above, the main question we address in this section concerns the representation of meaning. We believe that there is no single method for describing and formalizing phraseological meaning. The sole objective of the approach we propose throughout this section is to describe such meaning as accurately as possible.

The principal focus is on the methodology itself: although some discussion of corpus methods, introspection and linguistic experiments are provided, what concerns out here is to point out the importance of the integrated use of these three methods in clarifying the semantics of idioms. We think that corpus methods are best deployed in combination with other approaches.

How do we identify and capture the salient components of meaning? Beyond the strictly semantic factors (Subsect. 4.2), the section examines pragmatic elements (Subsect. 4.3), emotional and evaluative aspects (Subsect. 4.4), as well as motivation (Subsect. 4.5).

4.2 Semantic Description

To illustrate our methodology, let us take the French idiom *mouton noir* 'black sheep'. We first have a look at how it is described in one French dictionary and go on to consider the role of authentic and pedagogical examples and the intercultural viewpoint of students in defining idioms. We then suggest that semantic description needs to be supplemented with other elements of meaning (pragmatic, emotional, evaluative, and motivational aspects).

The above-mentioned idiom is explained in [13] as follows (Table 3): 'black sheep - scabby ewe. Translation from English black sheep'.

This explanation seems interesting as a starting point because it invites a number of

Table 3. *Mouton noir* 'black sheep' in [12].

(Fr.) *mouton noir – 'brebis galeuse. Traduction de l'anglais the black sheep'*

remarks. First, instead of defining the original idiom, the dictionary refers students to another idiom: *brebis galeuse* 'scabby ewe'. Do foreign learners know this synonym? Do these two idioms have the same meaning? Are these two idioms used in the same way? Second, this approach leaves the impression that the French idiom was borrowed from English, while this is not necessarily so. We believe, therefore, that this way of explaining idioms to foreign students is not appropriate.

4.2.1 The Role of Authentic Examples

It seems that both authentic and pedagogical examples are useful in idiom acquisition. For our project, corpus examples have a double value: definitions are derived from corpus examples; pedagogical examples complement definitions and help to refine definitions. In this way, definitions and examples are interrelated.

We believe that to describe idioms, a solid empirical basis is needed. Following Rosamund Moon, we "take it as axiomatic that effective and robust descriptions of any kind of lexical item must be based on evidence, not intuition, and that corpora provide evidence of a suitable type and quality" [14]. That is why we analyze actual usage by conducting a corpus-based study (corpora available at https://the.sketchengine.co.uk). For our project, corpora are a useful tool for idiom analysis in two ways: first, contexts provided by monolingual corpora give semantic and pragmatic contexts, show syntactic patterns and compare the frequencies; and second, parallel corpora refine the description of the meaning by shedding light on nuances. However, we consider corpus-based methods to be just a tool, since the introspection of a lexicographer is needed to provide a detailed description.

4.2.2 The Role of Pedagogical Examples

Examples can be considered to be a missing link between understanding (knowing what) and production (knowing how), because it is not only the meaning of idioms that is learned, but also their behaviour. However, it is worth adding that the problem with examples taken from corpora is that besides their length, they tend to contain unknown words and can confuse the learner even more.

Let us consider some authentic examples of *mouton noir* 'black sheep'. Table 4 gives a selected concordance of this idiom from the OPUS2 French (https://the.sketchengine.co.uk/):

Table 4. A selection of authentic examples of *mouton noir*.

Left context	Node	Right context
1 Mais non, beaucoup de familles ont un	Mouton noir	C'est moi, ton mari, pas lui. Tu sais quoi? Tu es toujours la plus belle
2 William me rappelle quelqu'un. Sûrement un	Mouton noir	dans la famille. Non, un jeune garçon à qui je n'avais même jamais parlé
3 C'est le plus beau jour de ma vie. Qui aurait cru que tu étais le	Mouton noir	de la famille? - On peut parler? - Bien sûr
4 Bienvenue aux Caraïbes, chérie. On est des démons, des	Moutons noirs	de mauvais bougres! Cul sec, les gars! La flibuste, ça me va!
5 Le défi à relever est dès lors plus ambitieux, bien plus ambitieux que la recherche d'un compromis de pouvoir avec deux	Moutons noirs	du Conseil européen. Il est d'oser dépasser les non-dits, les propos lénifiants, la langue de bois communautaire et oser appeler un chat un chat et une crise une crise
6 Deux sauts périlleux, une pyramide.	Moutons noirs	Trois cents nanas à croquer. – Et le camp de foot? – Je m'en tape
7 Ouais, chaque famille a son	Mouton noir	La plupart ont un attardé, ou un mec qui aime porter des robes. Nous, on a un sculpteur
8 Après tout, c'est moi le	Mouton noir	Celle qui fait tout de travers
9 Mais il était l'enfant chéri et moi le	Mouton noir	Il faisait tout comme il fallait, le rêve pour une mère. Travailler dur, sportif, ambitieux
10 Et tu devrais savoir qu'elle n'appelle Patrick que par le	«Mouton Noir»	Mim n'aime pas mon frère parce qu'il a rejeté ses règles et ses valeurs et a le culot de s'en sortir très bien comme ça

Contexts in concordance lines (1–6) are of little use to foreign students in a task as complex as the acquisition of idioms. In fact, they are quite problematic in at least one of the following ways: (1) it is not easy to deduce the meaning of this idiom from their extralinguistic contexts (lines 1–3); (2) they contain vocabulary which is likely to add unnecessary difficulty: (a) words like *flibuste* 'buccaneering' and *lénifiant* 'soothing' are not frequent and belong to a specific lexical area, and (b) idioms such as *mauvais bougre* ‘bad man’, *cul sec* ‘a shot’, *langue de bois* ‘political cant’, *appeler un chat un chat* ‘call a spade a spade’, and *s’en taper de* ‘not to care’ do not further understanding (lines 4–6).

Thus lines (1–6) do not satisfy the extremely important requirement of offering learners enlightening contexts. Examples (7–10), however, seem to be straightforward, because they provide prototypical situations where the idiom is used. How can we be sure that contexts are enlightening? In order to demonstrate how this question was answered for our project, let us take a look at an experiment.

4.2.3 The Role of the Intercultural View of Students in Defining Idioms

This experiment was conducted with a group of fourteen international students (three Spanish, three Brazilian, two Portuguese, one Indonesian, one Vietnamese, one Thai, one Greek, one Polish, and one Romanian). Coming from different cultural backgrounds, they were all learning French as a foreign language at Télécom Bretagne (graduate engineering school and international research centre) in France. Their level of French was intermediate B1+. This multilingual group was asked to write a definition of *mouton noir* ‘black sheep’ for other foreign students based on prototypical examples.

It is not easy to determine a prototypical situation for an idiom. Learners were provided with four examples of the idiom *mouton noir* ‘black sheep’ presented in a surrounding context and modified for pedagogical purposes (Table 5). What is quite important to note is that authentic examples were extended with additional, more explicit words; that is, they were paraphrased by clarifying and strengthening their meaning. Let us take a look at the first authentic example: *Mais il était l’enfant chéri et moi le mouton noir. Il faisait tout comme il fallait, le rêve pour une mère. Travailler dur, sportif, ambitieux.* ‘But he was the darling child and me, the black sheep. He was doing everything right, a mother’s dream. Working hard, sporty, ambitious.’ To highlight the difference between the two children, the personal pronouns *lui* and *moi*

Table 5. Pedagogical examples for *mouton noir*.

Authentic example	Pedagogical example
Mais il était l’enfant chéri et moi le *mouton noir*. Il faisait tout comme il fallait, le rêve pour une mère. Travailler dur, sportif, ambitieux	Lui, il était l’enfant préféré et moi le *mouton noir*. Le rêve pour une mère, il faisait tout comme il fallait, il était sportif et ambitieux. Moi, j’ai toujours été la honte de la famille
Ouais, chaque famille a son *mouton noir*. La plupart ont un attardé, ou un mec qui aime porter des robes. Nous, on a un sculpteur	Ouais, chaque famille a son *mouton noir*. Souvent, c’est quelqu’un de différent: pas assez intelligent, pas assez beau, pas d’accord avec les autres
Après tout, c’est moi le *mouton noir*, celle qui fait tout de travers	Après tout, c’est moi le *mouton noir*, celle qui fait tout de travers et attire les critiques de tout le monde
Et tu devrais savoir qu’elle n’appelle Patrick que par le « *Mouton Noir* » . Mim n’aime pas mon frère parce qu’il a rejeté ses règles et ses valeurs et a le culot de s’en sortir très bien comme ça	Elle n’appelle jamais Patrick par son prénom, mais par Mouton Noir. Elle ne l’aime pas parce qu’il n’a jamais voulu lui obéir, n’était jamais d’accord avec elle et n’avait pas peur de le dire

were included, and additional, more explicit information about the black sheep was added: *j'ai toujours été la honte de la famille* 'I have always been the shame of the family.'

Let us return to our experiment. There was no fixed time limit for the task, and the students were encouraged to work in pairs. The learners first had to understand what *mouton noir* means and then to propose a definition. The students developed the following five definitions in succession:

(1) *être différent* 'to be not like the others';
(2) *être une personne différente* 'to be a person not like the others';
(3) *être une personne différente et séparée des autres* 'to be a person not like the others, separated from others';
(4) *être une personne différente, rejetée par les autres* 'to be a person not like the others, rejected by others';
(5) *être une personne rejetée par les autres membres du collectif car ne correspondant pas aux normes du groupe. La raison de ce rejet n'est pas objective et peut être de caractère temporaire.* 'to be a person rejected by other members of the community because this person is different from what is considered normal. The reason for this rejection is prejudice, and it may be temporary'.

All these definitions were written in simple, easy-to-understand and unambiguous language. The students progressively refined the first definition, which was too vague. The word *de* 'from' in the third version was replaced by the word *par* 'by' to underline the deliberate nature of exclusion by the community. The final definition explains rather successfully the meaning of this French idiom: the word *séparée* 'separated' was replaced with the word *rejetée* 'rejected', which shows who initiated the rejection. Also, the questions asked by curious students allowed them to define more precisely the reason for the rejection and to introduce the factor of subjectivity and temporality. The final definition showed that four pedagogical examples were sufficient to ensure understanding of the idiom's meaning.

We think that foreign students, especially those studying in multinational and multilingual groups, have an outsider's perspective on idioms that is different from that of native speakers of the language. This perspective makes it possible to identify the features that are meaningful to all students regardless of their origin and native language. Thus explanations based on such a view become more precise and the risk of producing definitions reflecting only the monocultural background of the lexicographer is avoided.

It has been shown that to determine the meaning of an idiom we use corpora, introspection and an intercultural point of view. Otherwise, it is very important to emphasise that learners who have found the meaning of the idiom may still need other types of information. For our project, in addition to the informational semantic constituents, we register three other elements of meaning. These three items – pragmatic aspects, an emotional or evaluative part, and a motivational element – will be investigated in greater detail in the next section below. All of them are implicit and must be made explicit. We believe that because understanding these three elements can be of great value in providing insights into the interrelationship of language and culture, it can contribute to learning and memorizing idioms.

4.3 Pragmatic Description

Because idioms are used with a purpose and are conditioned by the pragmatic aspects of communication, they should be regarded as communicative units. In fact, since the situation in which idioms are used is not completely linguistic, their pragmatic properties should also be taken into consideration. This is especially true of formulae, which have a cohesive role in direct speech. Idioms are found in informal dialogic (interactive) speech more often than in monologic speech. The pragmatic part of meaning is conventionalized, i.e., shared by all members of a speech community, who use them as signals. Because foreign language students are unable to recognize these signals, they face an additional difficulty in deducing the message being conveyed and what is expected from them. For instance, knowing the meaning of the French expression *Mon œil* 'My eye', which is 'I do not trust what you are saying, usually said in jest' is not sufficient to know that the person who utters it may expect her interlocutor to admit his lie and may also pull down the lower eyelid with her index finger. If the learner is unable to recognize the signals, communication difficulties are likely to arise, which is why we plan to describe the prototypical dialogic situation where the idiom is used.

4.4 Emotions and Evaluation

The second point that deserves to be described in the definition concerns emotions and evaluations. In fact, speakers choose in many cases to use idioms not only to communicate descriptive information, but also to convey emotions. Another purpose closely related to the evaluative function is to express the speaker's evaluations or attitudes.

Following Sinclair, we retain the term *semantic prosody* to talk about this phenomenon: "Often the use of a word in a particular cotext carries extra meaning of an emotive or attitudinal nature […] This kind of meaning is sometimes called "connotation" […] We will call it *semantic prosody*" [17]. However, we would like to stress that in the case of idioms, emotions and evaluations are an integral, important part of meaning rather than an 'extra meaning', and we therefore intend to explain these aspects in our project. This is an area for further research.

4.5 Motivation

The final question to be treated in this section concerns motivation, a detailed exploration of which, unfortunately, exceeds the scope of this short article. Briefly, motivation is the image structure underlying the semantics of idioms. We would like to underscore that idioms are motivated by conceptual metaphors [6, 15]. In fact, because some idioms are relatively transparent and analysable in metaphorical terms, foreign learners could profit from explanations of metaphors. Information about the motivation of the phraseological unit *copains comme cochons* 'friends like pigs', for instance, would be especially useful to Muslim L2 learners.

In the light of the above discussion, we think that definitions need to be given at various levels: the semantic level should be complemented by pragmatic aspects, emotions and evaluations, as well as motivation. All of these levels are closely interconnected and influence each other. In the following section, we will briefly discuss the third and the last point: notions.

5 Semantic Annotation

In this section we will focus on the final issue that needs to be addressed here, namely the central organizing principle based on *notions*. It involves assigning a number of semantic labels to each idiom, thereby enabling users to find idioms without knowing any of their lexical constituents; in other words, it provides onomasiological access. Notions are comparable to descriptors in the following two dictionaries: Baranov, Dobrovol'kij [1] and Urdang, Hunsinger, LaRoche [18].

How does it work? Let us consider three idioms: *chaud lapin* 'hot rabbit', *vieux cochon* 'old pig' and *coureur de jupons* 'skirt chaser' (Table 6):

Table 6. Definition and notions of *chaud lapin* 'hot rabbit', *vieux cochon* 'old pig' and *coureur de jupons* 'skirt chaser'.

Chaud lapin
Definition: homme connu pour ses brèves relations sexuelles avec de nombreuses femmes, n'ayant pas des sentiments sérieux
Notions: Casanova, coition, copulation, Don Juan, fornication, fuck, lubricity, pleasure, relation, screwing, sex, zeal

Vieux cochon
Definition: vieil homme souhaitant avoir des rapports sexuels et/ou faisant des allusions sexuelles
Notions: allusion, coition, copulation, fantasy, fornication, fuck, imagination, insinuation, invention, lubricity, pleasure, screwing, sex, zeal, unreality, wish

Coureur de jupons
Definition: homme qui aime flirter et séduire les femmes, ne s'engageant pas dans des relations sérieuses
Notions: Casanova, coition, copulation, Don Juan, flirt, fornication, fuck, playboy, pleasure, relation, seduction, sex, zeal

Let us first compare *chaud lapin* and *vieux cochon*. *Chaud lapin* 'hot rabbit' is used to speak about 'a man generally well known as having frequent brief sexual relations with several women, without any serious sentimental relationship', whereas *vieux cochon* 'old pig' means 'an old man who wishes to have sex and/or tells sexual stories'. These two idioms have some semantic constituents in common. However, a computer is not able to automatically find the link between them. That is why every idiom, being anthropocentric, is associated with several *notions* belonging to the domain of human behaviour: *chaud lapin* 'hot rabbit' with *Casanova, coition, copulation, Don Juan, fornication, fuck, lubricity, pleasure, relation, screwing, sex, zeal*; *vieux cochon* 'old pig' with *allusion, coition, copulation, fantasy, fornication, fuck, imagination, insinuation, invention, lubricity, pleasure, screwing, sex, zeal, unreality, wish*. The following common notions - *coition*, *copulation*, *fornication*, *fuck*, *lubricity*, *pleasure*, *screwing*, *sex*, and *zeal* - connect the two idioms, and to a certain degree show semantic relations between idioms.

If we then compare *chaud lapin* 'hot rabbit' with *coureur de jupons* 'skirt chaser', meaning 'a man who loves flirting and seducing women without entering into any serious relationship', we see that these two idioms are semantically closer than the two previous ones. In fact, they can be considered quasi-synonyms: their notions and their definitions are close.

How to assign notions to idioms? Our notions are not pre-established units, but derive from the meaning of each idiom and are attributed intuitively and inductively. The problem is that it is extremely difficult to work out foolproof notions that can be applied by all users. In fact, notions are attributed inconsistently not only by different individuals, but also by the same individual. The difficulty is complicated by the fact that languages share very few universal human concepts [8, 19].

Although notions may be accused of being subjective and arbitrary, they seem to be a helpful complement to definitions, since: (1) they make cross-linguistic comparisons possible; (2) they create links from one idiom to other annotated idioms; (3) they allow the compilation of lists of idioms possessing a common semantic component. Notions can be viewed as labels that enable the primary selection, whereas definitions refine the primary selection and permit us to compare idioms in order to find similarities and to work out differences.

6 Conclusion

What can be concluded from this brief overview? Our primary concern is to create a system that retains the meaning and reflects the real use of idioms, and to organize the information in a pedagogically applicable manner. The above-mentioned program is designed with the foreign language learner in mind. A paper of this sort is inevitably incomplete, and the ideas presented here are preliminary and tentative. It is hoped that they will attract scholarly criticism and advice that will contribute to the development of the dictionary.

It has been shown that multiple problems need to be sorted out in order to make our representation of phraseological meaning adequate and complete: not only is the semantic meaning of idioms ambiguous, but their pragmatic, emotional, evaluative, and motivational aspects also have to be taken into consideration. That is why we incorporate all of these aspects into the definition. Together with examples and notions, definitions allow for semantic description. An idiom can be accessed not only through its lexical constituents, i.e., by means of a traditional semasiological search that is useful for understanding idioms, but also through notions - an onomasiological search, in other words, that is suitable for encoding tasks. Finally, we hope we have shown that the above-mentioned project not only provides a rich resource for phraseological meaning that allows learners to gain information about pragmatics, emotions, evaluations and motivation, but also shows idioms in context.

We hope that the project will be of value to both theoretical and applied linguistics. From the theoretical point of view, it can serve the objectives of linguistic theory: as an instrument for linguistic analysis, it contributes to describing phraseological systems in different languages and to clarifying the theoretical status of idioms. From the applied point of view, its broad goal is to describe and explain idioms in a manner that encompasses all of their particularities and provides the basis for a full understanding and production.

The proposed method seems to solve the problems encountered during our study. It would be interesting to see how it might work if applied to a wide range of idioms in languages belonging to different language families.

References

1. Baranov, A., Dobrovol'skij, D. (eds.): Slovar'-tezaurus sovremennoj russkoj idiomatiki. Mir entsiklopedij Avanta+, Moskva (2007)
2. Baranov, A., Dobrovol'skij, D.: Aspekty teorii frazeologii. Znak, Moskva (2008)
3. Baranov, A., Dobrovol'skij, D.: Osnovy frazeologii. Flinta Nauka, Moskva (2013)
4. Burger, H., Dobrovol'skij, D., Kühn, P., Norrick, N.R.: Phraseology. In: An International Handbook of Contemporary Research. Walter de Gruyter, Berlin, New York (2007)
5. Cowie, A.P. (ed.): Phraseology. Theory, Analysis, and Applications. Clarendon Press, Oxford (1998)
6. Dobrovol'skij, D., Piirainen, E.: Figurative language. In: Cross-Cultural and Cross-Linguistic Perspectives. Elseveir, Amsterdam (2005)
7. Geeraerts, D.: Theories of Lexical Semantics, p. 182. Oxford University Press, Oxford (2010)
8. Goddard, C. (ed.): Cross-Linguistic Semantics. John Benjamins, Amsterdam, Philadelphia (2008)
9. Gonzalez-Rey, I.: La Phraséologie du Français. Presses Universitaires du Mirail, Toulouse (2002)
10. Granger, S., Meunier, F.: Phraseology. An Interdisciplinary Perspective. John Benjamins Publishing Company, Amsterdam, Philadelphia (2008)
11. Grossmann, F., Tutin, A. (eds.): Les Collocations: Analyse et Traitement. Travaux et Recherches en Linguistique Appliquée. De Werelt, Amsterdam (2003)
12. Lafleur, B.: Dictionnaire des Locutions Idiomatiques Françaises. Duculot, Paris (1991)
13. Lubensky, S.: Random House Russian-English Dictionary of Idioms. Random House, New York (1995)
14. Moon, R.: Fixed Expressions and Idioms in English, p. 44. Clarendon press, Oxford (1998)
15. Bertrán, A.P.: Semantic explanations and entry structure in idiom dictionaries. In: Dobrovol'skij, D., Lubensky, S. (eds.) Contents, Contexts, Comments. Round Table Discussion. Oxford University Press, Oxford (2015). International Journal of Lexicography. Special issue: Phraseology and Dictionaries, volume 28, number 3, pp. 351–456
16. Sinclair, J.: Corpus, Concordance, and Collocation. Oxford University Press, Oxford (1991)
17. Sinclair, J.: Reading Concordances: An Introduction, p. 117. Longman, London (2003)
18. Urdang, L., Hunsinger, W., LaRoche, N.: Picturesque Expression. A Thematic Dictionary. Verbatim Books, London (1998)
19. Wierzbicka, A.: Semantics. Primes and Universals. Oxford University Press, Oxford (1996)
20. Wray, A.: Formulaic Language: Pushing the Boundaries. Oxford University Press, Oxford (2008)

Designing a Learner's Dictionary with Phraseological Disambiguators

P.V. DiMuccio-Failla[1,2] and Laura Giacomini[1,2(✉)]

[1] University of Heidelberg, Heidelberg, Germany
laura.giacomini@iued.uni-heidelberg.de
[2] University of Hildesheim, Hildesheim, Germany

Abstract. In this paper, we propose a strategy for sense disambiguation through phraseology in the modelling of a learner's dictionary. The theoretical basis is that, as corpus evidence shows, clusters of similar senses of a verb can be identified by their common collocates.

This paper is part of a study for the design of an Italian advanced learner's dictionary. The present goal is to portray the meaning profile of verbs by explicitly marking the conceptual and phraseological differences between their senses through a multilevel structure of meaning disambiguators that logically guide the user towards the needed data. The top level is constituted by ontological disambiguators, the middle level by common collocates, and the bottom level by normal patterns of usage.

We are currently investigating the feasibility and usefulness of implementing John Sinclair's vision of 'the ultimate dictionary', based on his conception of lexical units. The lexicographic project is in its design stage and is intended as a platform for cooperation between the Zanichelli publishing house and a network of international universities and research institutes.

Keywords: Learner's dictionaries · Phraseological disambiguators · Sinclair's hypothesis · Sinclair patterns

1 Introduction

This paper is part of a project, initiated by Paola Tiberii, author at the Zanichelli publishing house and Laura Giacomini of Heidelberg University, for the design of an Italian advanced learner's dictionary. We are currently investigating the feasibility and usefulness of implementing John Sinclair's vision of 'the ultimate dictionary' (see Sinclair et al. 2004, p. xxv), based on his conception of lexical units. Let us proceed to quickly review the origination of his ideas (a more detailed exposition can be found in DiMuccio-Failla and Giacomini 2017).

1.1 Sinclair's Hypothesis About Lexical Units

At the beginning of the 1980s, advances in computer technology made huge quantities of machine-readable text available to lexicographers and linguists in general.

R. Mitkov (Ed.): Europhras 2017, LNAI 10596, pp. 290–305, 2017.
https://doi.org/10.1007/978-3-319-69805-2_21

John Sinclair, a then leading scholar at the University of Birmingham, started a project[1] to build a large and representative electronic corpus of contemporary English and to produce innovative language reference works (Sinclair 1987, p. 1; Sinclair 1991, p. 2). The wealth of new information extracted from this multi-million-word corpus called into question several long-accepted conventions in lexicography like the idea that a polysemous word could inherently, by itself, have several distinct meanings (Sinclair 1998), and that any occurrence of such a word could signal any of those meanings (Sinclair 1986, p. 60). In fact, evidence gradually accumulated for the alternative hypothesis of a general correspondence between the distinct senses of a word (not considering trivial extensions - cf. for example Sinclair 1991, pp. 55–56) and its observable patterns of usage, every pattern having only one meaning. More specifically, Sinclair came to the following conclusion (see, e.g., Sinclair 1996, 1998, 2004c), which we will refer to as 'Sinclair's hypothesis':

In general, each (major) sense of a word can be associated with a distinctive pattern of normal usage determined by its

(1) collocation, i.e. its tendency to co-occur with other particular words;
(2) colligation, i.e. its tendency to occur in particular grammatical structures;
(3) semantic preference, i.e. its tendency to co-occur with words having particular semantic features;
(4) semantic prosody[2], i.e. its tendency to appear in a co-text implying a particular connotation of the described state of affairs or attitude of the writer/speaker.

Take, for instance, the word *put*. It can be part of a phrasal verb, in which case its meanings are co-determined by other parts of speech, or it can be a non-phrasal verb, in which case its senses mostly correspond to the (choices of the) semantic types of the referents associated with its arguments (i.e. its selectional preferences). As an illustration of this correspondence, we look at the first three senses of *put* in the corresponding entry of the COBUILD (2014) dictionary (see also Moon 1987, p. 91):

1. "When you put something in a particular place or position, you move it into that place or position".
2. "If you put someone… [in a particular place or position], you cause them to go there and to stay there for a period of time".
3. "To put someone or something in a particular state or situation means to cause them to be in that state or situation".

Sinclair's analysis even allows the finding of hidden senses of words. Consider, for example, the word *feeling*. No corpus examination is needed to know that it frequently co-occurs with the adjective *true* in the phrase *true feelings*. Such a collocation would not be considered idiomatic and hardly be given any special treatment in a traditional dictionary (Sinclair 1996, p. 89). An accurate pattern analysis (cf. Sinclair 1996;

---

[1] The Collins Birmingham University Language Database, in short COBUILD.

[2] The notion of semantic prosody was implicitly introduced by Sinclair (1987, p. 155, 1991, p. 75) and first defined by Louw (1993). It is actually rather controversial (see Whitsitt 2005; Stewart 2010) and hard to work with.

Sinclair 2003, 145 ff.) will in fact show statistical restrictions on the choice of its co-text. *True feelings* is usually preceded by a possessive adjective, which is in turn preceded by a verb synonymous with *express*, *show*, or *hide*. This constitutes a syntactic tendency, a colligation, but also a semantic preference for verbs of expression. In the case of semantically 'positive' expressions, there is usually an even broader context, i.e. a semantic prosody, hinting at a reluctance or difficulty in expressing those true feelings. Hence the actual lexical unit here can be presented by

> "to hide one's true feelings or show them with/after some reluctance/difficulty".

Thus, Sinclair arrived at the conclusion that the true units of meaning of a language are largely phrasal and that, as a consequence, phraseology is due to become central in the description of language (cf. Sinclair 2004a). Sinclair used the term '(extended) canonical form' to refer to the most explicit presentation of a lexical unit (Sinclair 2004c, p. 298), like the one we just proposed for *true feelings*. The shortest unambiguous presentation of the lexical unit (in our case, simply *true feelings*) he called 'short canonical form' (Sinclair et al. 2004, p. xxv; see also Sinclair 2004b). In the final years of his career, he was convinced that a new kind of dictionary based on the canonical forms of lexical units "would be the ultimate dictionary", allowing students to truly master a language (Sinclair et al. 2004, p. xxv).

1.2 Our Current Investigation

As explained in DiMuccio-Failla and Giacomini (2017), we believe that Sinclair's concept of lexical units is substantially the right one. We know this is still a controversial issue: many linguists do not even agree on the existence of objective criteria for correctly lumping/splitting the senses of polysemous words (see, for instance, Kilgarriff 1997, p. 100). However, by comparing the results of our present research with ItalWordNet, the Italian wordnet (see Roventini et al. 2003) created in the framework of the EuroWordNet project (see Vossen 2002), we found a remarkable correspondence between Sinclair's lexical units and the single senses of words implicit in the synsets of ItalWordNet. Such senses result from a completely different approach and it is hard to see how this could be a coincidence. We will explain our findings in detail for the Italian verb *seguire* in the following subsection.

We also share Sinclair's opinion that a dictionary extensively describing the canonical forms of each lexical unit would be 'the ultimate dictionary', because it would potentially contain all semantic information about word usage. This is why we started investigating the practicability of Sinclair's vision. The two main problems we encountered are the following:

(1) Extracting lexical units from a corpus and accurately studying their canonical forms can be difficult and time consuming.
(2) It is not easy to present the extended canonical form of a lexical unit without overloading its entry with information of various degrees of importance.

In DiMuccio-Failla and Giacomini (2017), we made some proposals on how to cope with the first problem and then applied our strategies to systematically distinguish all senses of the Italian verb *seguire* (see next subsection). In this paper we will concentrate on the second problem, presenting a strategy to portray the meaning profile of words by explicitly marking the conceptual and phraseological differences between their senses through a multilevel structure of meaning disambiguators.

1.3 The Patterns of Usage of the Italian Verb *Seguire*

As detailed in DiMuccio-Failla and Giacomini (2017), applying Hanks's Corpus Pattern Analysis (see Hanks 2004 and Hanks and Pustejovsky 2005) to the Italian Web itTenTen corpus (2010) on the Sketch Engine (see Kilgarriff et al. 2004), we found (with some minor modifications) the following normal patterns of usage ('Sinclair patterns') for the Italian verb *seguire* (in both the transitive and intransitive variants):

T1. Seguire qu. che sta andando da qualche parte ("to follow sb. who is going some-where")
T2a. Seguire un certo tragitto ("to follow a particular route")
T2b. Seguire una certa descrizione di un tragitto ("to follow a particular description of a route")
T3. Seguire qu. che ha appena fatto qc. ("to follow sb. who has just done sth.")
T4a. Seguire una certa linea di condotta ("to follow a particular course of action")
T4b. Seguire una certa descrizione di una linea di condotta ("to follow a particular description of a course of action")
T5. Seguire con lo sguardo qu. che si sta spostando ("to follow with your eyes sb. who is moving")
T6a. Seguire qu. che sta svolgendo un'attività percepita ("to follow sb. who is performing a perceived activity").
T6b. Seguire una certa attività percepita in corso ("to follow a particular perceived activity in progress").
T7a. Seguire qu. che sta svolgendo un'attività riportata in corso ("to follow sb. who is performing a reported activity in progress")
T7b. Seguire una certa attività riportata in corso ("to follow a particular reported activity in progress")
T8. Seguire qu. che sta narrando, spiegando o argomentando ("to follow sb. who is telling a story, explaining, or making an argument")
T9. Seguire una certa narrazione, spiegazione o argomentazione ("to follow a particular story, explanation, or argument")
I1. A un primo periodo/situazione/evento SEGUE un secondo periodo/situazione/evento ("a second period/situation/event follows a first period/situation/event")
I2. A una prima persona/oggetto SEGUE una seconda persona/oggetto ("a second person/object follows a first person/object")
I3. Una situazione/evento SEGUE DA un'altra situazione/evento ("a situation/event follows from another situation/event"). With this meaning, *seguire* is synonymous with *conseguire*.
I4. Un'affermazione SEGUE DA un'altra affermazione ("a statement follows from another statement"). With this meaning, *seguire* is synonymous with *conseguire*.
I5. Un testo SEGUE IN una parte di supporto testuale diversa dalla presente ("a text continues in a different part of a textual carrier"). With this meaning, *seguire* is synonymous with *proseguire*.

We compared our results with those of existing resources, like traditional Italian dictionaries and ItalWordNet. What follows are the senses of *seguire* found on ItalWordNet, listed in exactly the same order but labelled according to our convention:

T1. Synset: (seguire^1). Gloss: andare dietro a qlcu.
I1. Synset: (seguire^2, succedere^3). Gloss: accadere successivamente…
I3. Synset: (seguire^3, avere origine^2, conseguire^3, derivare^2, nascere^9, procedere^5, provenire^2, resultare^1, risultare^1, sorgere^6, uscire^{11}).

T2a. Synset: (seguire[4], tenere[7]). Gloss: andare per un certo percorso.
T5. Synset: (seguire[5], accompagnare). Gloss: seguire con lo sguardo…
T4b. Synset: (seguire[6], conformarsi[1]). Gloss: accettare un'idea, una dottrina…
I4. Synset: (seguire[7], conseguire[2], susseguire[2]). Gloss: derivare come conseguenza…

As already mentioned, the correspondence is remarkable. The only notable difference is that here senses T3, T6, T7, T8, T9, I2, and I5 are missing. We think that this confirms the validity of our methodology.

As to the traditional dictionaries, all problems lamented by John Sinclair (see, e.g., Sinclair 1991, pp. 37–38) about pre-corpus lexicography can be attested, e.g. the presence of long lost meanings (like sense C3 in ZINGARELLI 2017: "accadere, avvenire: sono cose che seguono!"), abnormal examples, illogical splitting of meanings (like, in DE MAURO 2017, senses 4a vs. 5a: "mettere rigorosamente in pratica una regola, una norma, una convenzione" vs. "stare dietro all'evolversi di una tendenza uniformandosi ai suoi dettami"), and illogical lumping.

2 Extending Sinclair's Hypothesis to Sense Clusters

2.1 The Cognitive Network of the Senses of *Seguire*

Clearly, pattern T1 corresponds to the fundamental meaning of *seguire*. Furthermore, it is easy to discern that the first four transitive senses are linked together by abstraction, metonymy and metaphor relations, as displayed in Fig. 1.

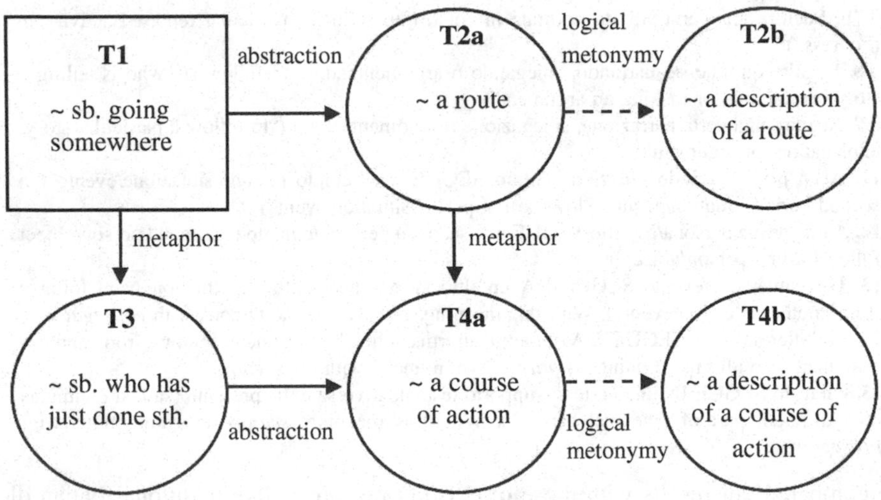

Fig. 1. Senses T1–T4 of *seguire*

Notice in particular that between sense T1 and T2a, and also between T3 and T4a, there is a relation of abstraction, which can be considered a type of logical metonymy (see Pustejovsky 1995). Notice also that between sense T2a and T2b, and between T4a and T4b, there is a logical metonymy in which the verb *seguire* can be thought to coerce (see Pustejovsky 1995) the meaning of the word *description* into assuming the semantic type expected for its argument: "If I tell you to follow my directions, what I really *mean* is that you follow the route I am describing". Whatever the linguistic elucidation, the culminating action denoted by the verb *seguire* does not change. We will consider this kind of polysemy immaterial for learner's lexicography, hence merging, from now on, pattern T2a with T2b and pattern T4a with T4b, since a definition like

T2. To follow a route or a description of a route: to move along a route.

is, for humans, more economical than

T2a. To follow a route: to move along a route.
T2b. To follow a set of directions: to move along the route described by a set of directions.

Let us now move on to the last five senses of *seguire* as a transitive verb. The corresponding logical relations are shown in Fig. 2.

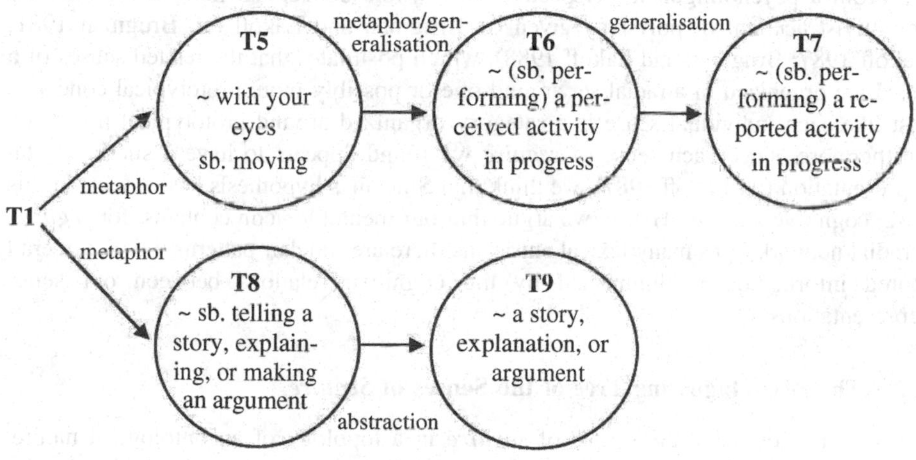

Fig. 2. Senses T5–T9 of *seguire*

Notice that senses T6a and T6b, and also T7a and T7b, have been conflated together since, in this case, when we refer to someone's activity, we are not referring to the proper abstraction of what she/he is doing. To understand why, notice for instance that one cannot play the same game of football more than once. By contrast, sense T9 is a true abstraction of sense T8, since, e.g., the action of explaining something can be distinguished from the resulting explanation, which can be instantiated multiple times and by different people. However, this is an ontological differentiation which has no place in a learner's dictionary. Thus, patterns T8 and T9 will also be merged into one.

All senses of *seguire* hitherto considered have been activities, and this is reflected by their transitivity. Senses I1–I5, displayed in Fig. 3, are static relations, which is signalled by their intransitivity (notice the contrast with English).

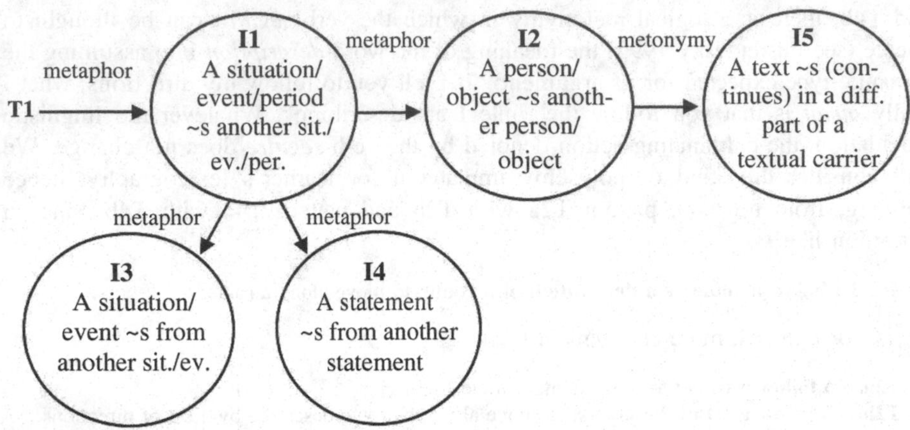

Fig. 3. Senses I1–I5 of *seguire*

From a psycholinguistic perspective, this whole conceptual network verifies the cognitivist account of polysemy given by Brugman and Lakoff (cf. Brugman 1981; Lakoff 1987; Brugman and Lakoff 1988), which postulates that the related senses of a word are organized in a radial set around one or possibly more prototypical concepts, just like each individual sense is a category organized around prototypical members. Furthermore, since each sense of *seguire* we found appears to have a single mental representation (cf. Lakoff 1987), we think that Sinclair's hypothesis has, at least in this case, cognitive validity. Hence, we argue that our mental lexicon contains, for *seguire*, a radial network of as many lexical entries as there are Sinclair patterns, but the overall stored information is diminished by the cognitive relations between our sense representations.

2.2 The Disambiguating Tree of the Senses of *Seguire*

We can also organize the senses of *seguire* in a topology of an ontological nature, grouping them together into sense clusters according to their semantic similarities, by means of what we may call a 'disambiguating tree', as shown in Fig. 4.

By turning back to the Sketch Engine and analysing a wider phraseological context than Sinclair patterns for *seguire*, we found out that such sense clusters are empirically attested by the collocations they have in common. For instance, all senses in the cluster *seguire nelle azioni* ("to follow in one's actions") can be modified by the following adverbial adjuncts: *scrupolosamente, esattamente*, *ciecamente*, *fedelmente*, *pedissequamente*. By contrast, all senses in the cluster *seguire con l'attenzione* ("to follow with one's attention") can be modified by the following adverbials: *attentamente*, *con interesse*, *con trepidazione*, *con preoccupazione*, *con apprensione*, *con entusiasmo*.

This points to the fact that, in general, semantically closer senses share a greater number of collocates and that we can tentatively extend Sinclair's hypothesis by stating that sense clusters, just like individual senses (the true lexical units of language), are identifiable by phraseology.

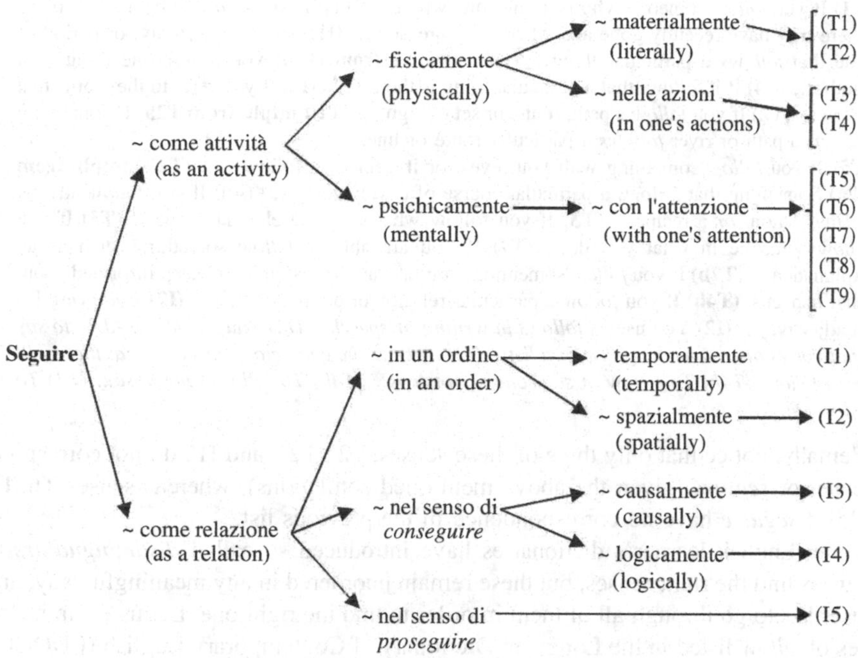

Fig. 4. The disambiguating tree of the senses of *seguire*

Our analysis of corpus evidence also showed that when, in a given discourse, a particular Sinclair pattern is not complete and therefore cannot disambiguate the meaning of a word (as in the sentence "Seguimi!"), such an adverbial is often used as an actual disambiguator ("Seguimi attentamente!").

3 Designing a Sense Disambiguating Dictionary

3.1 The Shortcomings of Sense Enumeration

The shortcomings of the traditional enumerative approach to the representation of word senses are well known (see, e.g., Brugman and Lakoff 1988; Norvig 1989; Pustejovsky 1995). The most common criticism is that enumerations do not make reference to the relations between the senses (Norvig 1989, p. 2; Pustejovsky 1995, p. 48), and do not adequately describe the kind of knowledge at play in the disambiguation process (cf. Pustejovsky 1995, p. 28). Notice that the COBUILD dictionary is no exception in this regard: senses are disambiguated by Sinclair patterns (used as *definienda*), but finding the right one and grasping its relation to other meanings in order to get full knowledge of a word (cf. Miller 1999) is not an easy task, as is confirmed, for example, by the *definienda* of the verb *follow* (COBUILD 2014), here labelled in such a way as to highlight the similarities with the senses we found for *seguire*:

(T1) If you *follow* someone who is going somewhere… (T1) If you *follow* someone to a place where they have recently gone and where they are now… **(I1)** An event, activity, or period of time that *follows* a particular thing… **(I1′: ergative from I1)** If you *follow* one thing *with* another… **(I4)** If it *follows* that a particular thing is the case… **(I2)** If you refer to the words that *follow*… **(T2)** If you *follow* a path, route, or set of signs… **(T2′: mtph. from T2a)** If something such as a path or river *follows* a particular route or line…
(T5) If you *follow* something with your eyes, or if your eyes follow it… **(T2″: mtph. from T2a)** Something that *follows* a particular course of development… (T4b) If you *follow* advice, *an* instruction, *or* a recipe… **(T3)** If you follow what someone else has done… **(T3)** If you *follow* someone in what you do… **(T9)** If you are able to *follow* something such as an explanation… **(T7b)** If you *follow* something, you take an interest in it and keep informed about what happens. **(T4b)** If you *follow* a particular religion or political belief… **(I2)** *Following* [as an adjective]… **(I2)** You use *as follows in writing or speech... **(I2)** You use followed by to say what comes after something else in a list... **(I2)** After... one course of a meal... what there will be to follow. (T4b) To follow in someone's footsteps... **(T4b)** To follow your nose... **(T3)** To follow suit...*

Incidentally, notice that only three of these senses, T2′, T2″, and I1′, do not correspond to senses of *seguire* (given the above mentioned conflations), whereas senses T6, I3, and I5 of *seguire* have no correspondence in the previous list.

Other English learner's dictionaries have introduced so called *disambiguators* to help users find the right senses, but these remain unordered in any meaningful way, and the user has to go through all of them in order to find the right one. Let us examine the senses of *follow* listed in the Longman Dictionary of Contemporary English (LDOCE):

(T1) GO AFTER to go, walk, drive etc. behind or after someone else. **(I1)** HAPPEN AFTER to happen or do something after something else... **(I2)** COME AFTER to come directly after something else in a series, list, or order. **(I2) as follows… (T4b)** DO WHAT SB. SAYS to do something in the way... **(T2b) follow the signs/sb.'s directions… (T3)** DO THE SAME THING... **(T4b)** BELIEVE IN STH. to believe in and obey a particular set of religious or political ideas. **(T2a)** GO IN PARTIC. DIRECTION to continue along a particular road... **(T2′: mtph. from T2a)** ... to go parallel to sth. else. **(T9)** UNDERSTAND to understand something such as an explanation or story... **(I4)** BE A RESULT to be true as a result of something else that is true... **(T7b)** BE INTERESTED to be interested in something and in the way it develops... **(T2″: mtph. from T2a) follow a pattern/course/trend etc… (T3) follow suit… (T4b) follow in sb.'s footsteps… (T6′: mtph. from T6b)** BE ABOUT to show or describe someone's life or a series of events, for example in a film or book. **(T3) be a hard act to follow… (T6)** WATCH CAREFULLY to carefully watch someone do something... **(T9)** THINK ABOUT/STUDY to study or think about a particular idea or subject... **(T4b) follow your instincts/feelings/gut reaction etc… (T3) follow the herd/crowd… (T4b) follow your nose… (T4a) follow a profession/trade/way of life etc…**

Such disambiguators, referred to as 'signposts' by the LDOCE (2009), actually serve the same purpose as the Sinclair patterns in the COBUILD dictionary: to find the right sense. The result is not as precise, but the process is faster, since Sinclair-style definitions tend to be long-winded and repetitious (cf. Heuberger 2015; Herbst 1990, p. 1382).

Again incidentally, notice that, in the previous list, three senses appear which were not found for *seguire*: T2′, T2″, and T6′. In the opposite direction, we see that senses T5, I3, and I5 are absent here. Note also that the COBUILD dictionary lacks sense T6′ of the LDOCE, which lacks sense I1′ of the COBUILD.

Both entries show a high degree of meaning fragmentation. Cognitive links such as those between the prototypical senses of a word and its metonymical and metaphorical extensions are difficult to reconstruct. This is likely to cause some problems for language learners, who naturally rely on cognitive relations in their mental lexicon to comprehend, store and actively access words.

The main reason for such fragmentation is that the COBUILD dictionary, relying for the first time on objective data about the frequency of word usage, started the tradition, later embraced by other learner's dictionaries (Lew 2013, p. 7) like the LDOCE (Wilks and Stevenson 1996), of enumerating senses in order of decreasing frequency. This is thought to give users the best chance of finding the right sense in the shortest time possible. We find this argument unconvincing. As remarked by Lew (Lew 2013, p. 7), it is quite unlikely that an advanced learner will be looking for the most frequent senses of a polysemous word. Furthermore, this approach can lead to unnatural and confusing results, such as the notorious definition of *summit* found in the COBUILD dictionary:

1. A **summit** is a meeting at which the leaders of two or more countries discuss…
2. The **summit** of a mountain is the top of it.

3.2 From Sense Enumeration to Sense Disambiguation

A more traditional approach to sense ordering is to try to group similar senses in a nested structure and then list them starting with the prototypical meanings. A well-known example of such an approach is the (New) Oxford Dictionary of English (ODE), in which a systematic attempt was made to logically group senses sharing a 'core meaning' (cf. the preface to the ODE 1998). Let us look at the entry of *follow* in the ODE online (ODE 2017):

(T1-T2) Go or come after (a person or thing proceeding ahead); move or travel behind. T1. Go after (someone) in order to observe or monitor them. T2a. Go along (a route or path). T2′. (of a route or path) Go in the same direction as or parallel to (another). T5. Trace the movement or direction of.
(I1-I4) Come after in time or order. I3. Happen after (something else) as a consequence. I4. (no object) Be a logical consequence of something. I1′ (with object and adverbial) (of a person) Do something after (sth. else). I1′ Have (a dish or course) after another or others during a meal.
(T3-T4) Act according to (an instruction or precept). T4. Conform to. T4b. Act according to the lead or example of (someone). T3. Treat as a teacher or guide.
(T5-T9) Pay close attention to. T7. Take an active interest in or be a supporter of. T6'. (of a book, film, programme, etc.) Be concerned with or trace the development of. T7a. Track (a person, group, or organization) by subscribing to their account on a social media website or application. T8-T9. Understand the meaning or tendency of (a speaker or argument).
(T4) Practise (a trade or profession). T4a. Undertake or carry out (a course of action or study).
Phrases: (T4b) follow in sb.'s footsteps; (T4b) follow one's nose; (T3) follow suit.

As expected, sense I5 of *seguire* is not present, while among the senses found in the COBUILD dictionary and in the LDOCE, T2″ and T6 are missing.

In our opinion, it is unfortunate that no present English advanced learner's dictionary uses the previous kind of structure because it would allow learners to gain a much better feeling for the meaning profile of complex words. On the other hand, the Oxford Dictionary of English is not based on Sinclair's units of meaning, which, as mentioned, better capture both actual usage and mental representation of words. This is why we propose the following lexicographic structure for an entry of the verb *seguire* in an Italian learner's dictionary:

---

seguìre[attività] **v.trans.**

S. qu. che sta andando da qualche parte [1] Andare dietro a qu., mantenersi dietro qu. ES.: *Abbiamo seguito la guida turistica fino al castello.* COLLOC. s. *da vicino,* s. *a distanza. Segua quella macchina!* **S. qu. in un luogo [est.]** Andare in un luogo dietro o poco dopo qu. (di solito per raggiungerlo lì). ES.: *I tifosi seguirono la squadra dentro gli spogliatoi.* **S. qu. a ruota [sport./fig.]** Seguire... **S. qu. come un'ombra [fig.]** Seguire... ◆ SINONIMI: inseguire; accompagnare; pedinare.

S. (le indicazioni di) un tragitto [2] Andare lungo un tragitto. ES.: *Abbiamo seguito il sentiero e siamo arrivati alla grande quercia.* COLLOC.: s. *una strada/sentiero,* s. *una rotta,* s. *un tracciato,* s. *delle tracce/orme.* **S. una direzione [est.]** Andare in una direzione.

NELLE AZIONI, AD ES. S. *FEDELMENTE/CIECAMENTE/ESATTAMENTE/SCRUPOLOSAMENTE*

S. qu. che ha appena fatto qc. [3] Fare quello che qu. ha appena fatto. ... **S. la corrente [fig.]** Fare quello che... COLLOC.: *Chi mi ama mi segua!* ◆ SINONIMI: imitare; prendere a modello, emulare.

S. (la descrizione/indicazione di) un certo modo di agire [4] Agire in un certo modo. ... COLLOC.: s. *la moda,* s. *la tradizione,* s. *un metodo/strategia;* s. *una dieta,* s. *un consiglio/regola,* s. *l'esempio/modello di qu.* **S. le orme/passi di qu. [fig.]** ... **S. (la spinta di) qu./qc. [fig.]** ... COLLOC.: s. il proprio *cuore/inclinazioni,* s. *l'istinto.* ◆ SINONIMI: conformarsi, uniformarsi.

CON L'ATTENZIONE, AD ES. *S. ATTENTAMEMTE, CON INTERESSE/PREOCCUPAZIONE/APPRENSIONE*

S. con lo sguardo qu. che si sta spostando [5] Mantenere lo sguardo su qu. COLLOC.: *Seguire qu. con la coda dell'occhio.* ◆ SINONIMI: guardare, osservare.

S. (qu. in) un'attività in corso [6] Fare attenzione e avere coscienza del progredire di un'attività di qu. COLLOC.: s. *una trasmissione, un programma, una partita.* **[est.]** Fare attenzione al progredire di qu. (in un'attività) per... ◆ SINONIMI: guardare, ascoltare, osservare; assistere†.

S. (qu. in) un'attività riportata in corso [7] Tenersi aggiornati sul progredire di un'attività di qu. COLLOC.: s. *uno sport, ad* es. *il calcio;* s. *i movimenti/spostamenti di* qu. **Seguire qu. su un social network [idiom.]** ... ◆ SINONIMI: tenersi al corrente, tenersi informati.

S. (qu. in) una narrazione/spiegazione/argomentazione [8] Fare attenzione e capire lo sviluppo di una narrazione/spiegazione/argomentazione di qu. ... COLLOC.: s. *la lezione. Mi segui? Segui quello che dico?* **S. un corso di lezioni [est.]** Frequentare... ◆ SINONIMI: capire, comprendere.

seguìre[relazione: 'venire dopo'] v.intrans. (+ a *ogg. indir.*)

IN ORDINE DI TEMPO **A un primo periodo/evento SEGUE un secondo periodo/evento [1]** Un secondo periodo/evento viene dopo un primo periodo/evento... COLLOC.: *il giorno/anno seguente.* ◆ CONTRARI: precedere.

IN UN CERTO ORDINE SPAZIALE O ASTRATTO **A una prima persona/cosa SEGUE una seconda persona/cosa [2]** Una seconda persona/cosa viene dopo una prima persona/cosa. ... COLLOC.: s. *in ordine alfabetico,* s. *in classifica* **Quanto segue [idiom.]** ... **A seguire [idiom.]** ... ◆ CONTRARI: precedere.

seguìre[relazione: 'conseguire'] v.intrans. (+ *origine*)

CAUSALMENTE **Un evento SEGUE da un altro evento [1]** Un evento è effetto di un altro evento. ... ◆ SINONIMI: conseguire, derivare.

LOGICAMENTE **Un'affermazione SEGUE da un'altra affermazione [2]** Un'affermazione è vera se è vera un'altra affermazione. ... ◆ SINONIMI: conseguire, derivare.

seguìre[relazione: 'proseguire'] v.intrans. (+ *luogo*)

IN ALTRO LUOGO **Un testo SEGUE in un'altra parte di supporto testuale** Un testo...

Our grey signposts are phraseological disambiguators at a more general contextual level than Sinclair patterns and may or may not correspond to sense clusters. They can be used not only to find the desired sense, but also to learn the Sinclairian extended canonical forms of lexical units. At the highest level of generality are the semantic disambiguators in square brackets, which correspond to different morphosyntactic variants of *seguire*, exploiting the relatively tight correspondence, in Italian, between semantic and syntactic categories, as can be verified studying the different argument structures in the entry.

Our version of Sinclair patterns is more compact than the one in the COBUILD, in order to speed up the process of disambiguation. Their identification numbers appear after them, so that the most impatient and unsystematic readers can quickly skim through all definitions. Note also that we introduced *subsenses*, such as trivial domain- or situation-specific generalizations and specializations. We have listed idioms under the subsenses to make them more easily accessible and comprehensible.

As to the claim made by Pustejovsky (1995, p. 48) that lexica should always express the logical relations between the senses of a polysemous word, we do not think that this applies to learner's dictionaries (notice that the ODE does not do this), since most of the time logical metonymies and crystallized metaphors are only subconsciously perceived by native speakers: consciously noticing them can indeed be confusing at first.

It is very important to distinguish the different senses logically, since logical distinctions lead to usage distinctions. It is also important to group meanings according to their relatedness, but explicitly marking the distinctions between all possible types of semantic links could make things more confusing for the learner, instead of clearer.

We think that, most of the time, we activate the right sense of a word for the present situation by phraseological disambiguation, not by a brute force search on a cognitive lexical network. As Sinclair realized 35 years ago, phraseology is the true key to solving the polysemy paradox (cf. Taylor 2003). This is why we are convinced that representing the disambiguating tree of a word is the most appropriate way of presenting the set of its senses.

Our method also works with substantives. In the Italian Web itTenTen corpus (2010) we found the following lexical units containing the Italian word *braccio* ("arm"), here given in extended canonical form: *braccio di un essere umano*; *braccio di sostegno/supporto di uno strumento*; *braccio meccanico o di una macchina*; *braccio di una croce*; *braccio di un'ancora*; *braccio di terra*; *braccio d'acqua*; *braccio di mare*; *braccio di una distesa/corso d'acqua*; *braccio di un carcere*; *braccio di ferro* (see also DiMuccio-Failla and Giacomini 2017).

The major problem here is the extreme lexical fragmentation. For example, *braccio* has the same sense in three fixed phrases, i.e. *braccio di terra*, *braccio d'acqua*, and *braccio di mare*, and also in three phrase templates with an argument referring to any see, river, channel, lake, etc. (as in "Questo è un braccio del Mar Rosso"). Also in this case, our phraseological disambiguators prove to be extremely useful not only at disambiguating, but also at describing the extended canonical form of the lexical units:

il bràccio[parte del corpo] s.num. ⟨plurale: *le bràccia*⟩

Braccio di un essere umano [1] Parte allungata del corpo di un essere umano tra la spalla e la mano... COLLOC.: *braccio teso/alzato; sollevare/* alzare*/allungare/stendere/tendere/agitare un braccio (/le braccia); incrociare/allargare; stare/tenere in braccio; tenere tra le braccia...* **Braccia [fig.]** Lavoratori... *Questo lavoro richiede molte braccia.* **Braccio destro di qu. [fig.] ... A braccia conserte [idiom.] ... Accogliere a braccia aperte [fig.] ... A qu. cascano le...**

il bràccio[cosa materiale] s.num. ⟨plurale: *i bràcci*⟩

B. DI SOSTEGNO/SUPPORTO **Braccio di uno strumento [1]** Parte sporgente e allungata di uno strumento a sostegno di qualcosa. COLLOC.: b. *mobile/ flessibile/snodabile/rotante/estensibile; b. di una bilancia/leva/lampada/ candelabro/lampadario. Candelabro a sei bracci.*

B. MECCANICO **Braccio di una macchina [2]** Parte allungata, articolata† e semovente† di una macchina la cui estremità serve a svolgere una qualche operazione.

Braccio di una croce/ancora [3]...

B. D'ACQUA **Braccio di una distesa/corso d'acqua [4a]** Parte allungata di una distesa/corso d'acqua. COLLOC.: *braccio di mare* (= stretto†).

B. DI TERRA ***Braccio di terra*** **[4b]** Parte allungata di terraferma†, istmo†.

Braccio di un carcere [5] Reparto di un carcere. ... **Braccio della morte [idiom.]** Reparto di un carcere in cui si trovano i condannati a morte, specialmente negli USA.

il bràccio[unità di misura] s.num. (plurale: *le bràccia*)

...

il bràccio di ferro s. solo sing.

...

References

Brugman, C.: Story of over. Master thesis. University of California, Berkeley (1981)

Brugman, C., Lakoff, G.: Cognitive topology and lexical networks. In: Small, S., Cottrell, G., Tanenhaus, M. (eds.) Lexical Ambiguity Resolution, pp. 477–507 (1988)

COBUILD 2014: Collins COBUILD Advanced Learner's Dictionary. Harper Collins, Glasgow (2014)

DE MAURO 2017: Il Nuovo De Mauro (2017). https://dizionario.internazionale.it. Accessed 22 May 2017

DiMuccio-Failla, P.V., Giacomini, L.: Designing an Italian learner's dictionary based on Sinclair's lexical units and Hanks's corpus pattern analysis. In: Proceedings of the Fifth eLex Conference Electronic Lexicography in the 21st Century (2017, forthcoming)

Hanks, P.: Corpus pattern analysis. In: Proceedings of the EURALEX International Congress, pp. 87–98. (2004)

Hanks, P., Pustejovsky, J.: A pattern dictionary for natural language processing. Revue Française de linguistique appliquée **10**(2), 63–82 (2005)

Herbst, T.: Dictionaries for foreign language teaching: English. In: Wiegand, H.E., et al. (eds.) Dictionaries. An International Encyclopaedia of Lexicography, vol. 2, pp. 1379–1385 (1990)

Heuberger, R.: Learners' dictionaries. In: Durkin, P. (ed.) The Oxford Handbook of Lexi-cography (2015)

ItalWordNet. http://www.ilc.cnr.it/iwndb_php. Accessed 22 Oct 2017

Kilgarriff, A.: I don't believe in word senses. Comput. Humanit. **31**, 91–113 (1997)

Kilgarriff, A., Rychly, P., Smrz, P., Tugwell, D.: The sketch engine. Inf. Technol. **105**, 116 (2004)

Lakoff, G.: Women, Fire, and Dangerous Things. University of Chicago Press, Chicago (1987)

LDOCE 2009: Longman Dictionary of Contemporary English for Advanced Learners (2009)

Lew, R.: Identifying, ordering and defining senses. In: Jackson, H. (ed.) The Bloomsbury Companion to Lexicography, pp. 284–302 (2013)

Louw, B.: Irony in the text or insincerity in the writer? The diagnostic potential of semantic prosodies. In: Baker, M., Francis, G., Tognini-Bonelli, E. (eds.) Text and Technology: In Honour of John Sinclair, pp. 157–176. John Benjamins Publishing (1993)

Miller, G.A.: On knowing a word. Annu. Rev. Psychol. **50**(1), 1–19 (1999)

Moon, R.: The analysis of meaning. In: Looking Up: An Account of the COBUILD Project in Lexical Computing and the Development of the Collins COBUILD English Language Dictionary, pp. 86–103 (1987)

Norvig, P.: Building a large lexicon with lexical network theory. In: Proceedings of the IJCAI Workshop on Lexical Acquisition (1989)

ODE 2017: Oxford Dictionary of English. https://en.oxforddictionaries.com. Accessed 15 June 2017

Hanks, P., Pearsall, J. (eds.): New Oxford Dictionary of English, 1st edn. Oxford University Press, Oxford (1998)

Pustejovsky, J.: The Generative Lexicon. MIT Press, Cambridge (1995)

Roventini, A., et al.: ItalWordNet: building a large semantic database for the automatic treatment of Italian. Computational Linguistics in Pisa, Special Issue XVIII–XIX Pisa-Roma IEPI. Tomo II, 745–791 (2003)

Sinclair, J.M.: Trust the Text: Language, Corpus and Discourse. Routledge, London (2004a)

Sinclair, J.M.: In praise of the dictionary. In: Proceedings of the XI EURALEX International Congress, pp. 1–12 (2004b)

Sinclair, J.M.: New evidence, new priorities, new attitudes. In: Sinclair, J.M. (ed.), How to Use Corpora in Language Teaching, pp. 271–299. John Benjamins Publishing (2004c)

Sinclair, J.M.: Reading Concordances: An Introduction. Pearson Longman, London (2003)

Sinclair, J.M.: The lexical item. In: Weigand, E. (ed.) Contrastive Lexical Semantics (Current Issues in Linguistics Theory 171), pp. 1–24. John Benjamins Publishing (1998)

Sinclair, J.M.: The search for units of meaning. Textus: English Studies in Italy **9**(1), 75–106 (1996)

Sinclair, J.M.: Corpus, Concordance, Collocation. Oxford University Press, Oxford (1991)

Sinclair, J.M.: Grammar in the dictionary. In: Sinclair, J.M. (ed.), Looking Up: An Account of the COBUILD Project in Lexical Computing and the Development of the Collins COBUILD English Language Dictionary, Collins COBUILD, pp. 104–115 (1987)

Sinclair, J.M.: First throw away your evidence. In: Leitner, G. (ed.) The English Reference Grammar, pp. 56–65. Max Niemeyer Verlag (1986)

Sinclair, J.M., Jones, S., Daley, R.: English Collocation Studies: The OSTI Report. Continuum, pp. xvii–xxix (2004)
Sketch Engine. https://www.sketchengine.co.uk. Accessed 15 June 2017
Stewart, D.: Semantic Prosody: A Critical Evaluation. Routledge, London (2010)
Taylor, J.R.: Polysemy's paradoxes. Lang. Sci. **25**(6), 637–655 (2003)
Vossen, P. (ed.): EuroWordnet. General Document, Version 3 (2002). http://dare.ubvu.vu.nl. Accessed 22 May 2017
Whitsitt, S.: A critique of the concept of semantic prosody. Int. J. Corpus Linguist. **10**(3), 283–305 (2005)
Wilks, Y., Stevenson, M.: The grammar of sense: is word-sense tagging much more than part-of-speech tagging? Nat. Lang. Eng. **4**(2), 135–143 (1996)
ZINGARELLI 2017: lo Zingarelli. http://dizionari.zanichelli.it. Accessed 22 May 2017

Individual Differences in L2 Processing of Multi-word Phrases: Effects of Working Memory and Personality

Elma Kerz[1(✉)] and Daniel Wiechmann[2(✉)]

[1] RWTH Aachen University, Aachen, Germany
elma.kerz@ifaar.rwth-aachen.de
[2] University of Amsterdam, Amsterdam, The Netherlands
d.wiechmann@uva.nl

Abstract. There is an accumulating body of evidence that knowledge of the statistics of multiword phrases (MWP) facilitates native language learning and processing both in children and adults. However, less is known about whether adult second language (L2) learners are able to develop native-like sensitivity to the statistics of MWP, and more importantly up until now no attempt has been made to determine to what extent variation in this ability is related to individual differences (IDs) in cognitive and affective factors. Using a within-subject design embedded in an individual-differences framework, the aim of the present study was twofold: (1) to replicate the MWP frequency effect reported in Hernandez et al. [1] with another sample of L2 learners, and (2) to determine to what extent variation in online L2 processing of MWP can be accounted for by two IDs measures, working memory (WM) and personality. We could replicate the frequency effect for MWP from the high frequency band but not for MWP from the low frequency band. Our findings revealed that while there was no main effect of WM, the Openness personality trait had a statistically significant impact on online L2 processing of MWP. However, subsequent analyses yielded three significant two-way interactions indicating that the relationship between WM, personality and online L2 processing of MWP is a complex one. Taken together our findings underscore the importance of further investigation of L2 learners' ability to keep track of and build up knowledge of the statistics of MWPs as well as the interrelationships between the cognitive and affective IDs that impact the development of such ability.

1 Introduction

1.1 The Role of Multiword Phrases in Language Acquisition and Processing from a Usage Based Perspective

Usage-based (UB) approaches to both first language (L1) and second language (L2) processing and acquisition have recently gained much attention among language researchers and cognitive scientists. UB is an umbrella term encompassing a broad class of approaches including dynamic system theory, usage-based

R. Mitkov (Ed.): Europhras 2017, LNAI 10596, pp. 306–321, 2017.
https://doi.org/10.1007/978-3-319-69805-2_22

construction grammar, constraint-based accounts, connectionist models of learning and processing and exemplar-models of linguistics knowledge that share the same core assumptions models [2–4]. UB approaches seek to account for language processing and learning in terms of general cognitive mechanisms rather than internalized linguistic constraints. One such mechanism is statistical learning, succinctly defined as the ability to detect and keep track of statistical and distributional regularities in the language input. An accumulating body of evidence has demonstrated that statistical learning mechanisms underlie the acquisition of knowledge at all levels of linguistic organization both in children and adults, and are at work continuously over the lifespan [5]. This implies that language learning does not lead to the establishment of a static knowledge system, but rather that as long as there is exposure to linguistic input an individual's knowledge of a language is in constant flux. These approaches put the emphasis on experience with language input and assume a direct and immediate relationship between processing and learning, conceiving of them as inseparable, rather than governed by different mechanisms. Consistent with a large body of work showing the ubiquity of frequency effects (e.g., [6,7]), UB approaches see input frequency as a key determinant of L1 and L2 processing and acquisition.

Moving away from the traditional words-and-rules approach [8], UB approaches have developed an increasing interest in the role of multi-word phrases (MWP), often defined as variably-sized continuous or discontinuous frequently recurring strings of words [9][1]. This interest stems from an extensive body of evidence demonstrating that children and adults are sensitive to the statistics of MWP and rely on knowledge of such statistics to facilitate their language processing and boost their acquisition (see, e.g., [9–11]). Analyses of corpora of spontaneous adult-child interactions made available through the CHILDES database [12] have shown that child-directed speech is characterized by the frequent use of MWP and that childrens' early productions heavily rely on the use of such MWP [13,14]. This pattern is also observed in recent computational simulations based on the input-output modeling approach [15,16]. Frequency estimates obtained from corpora are shown to be robust predictors of childrens' language behavior in experiments: For example, young children were faster and more accurate at repeating higher frequency MWP (e.g., *sit in your chair*) than lower frequency MWP that differed only in their final word (e.g., *sit in your truck*) ([17] see also [18] for a follow-up study looking at the effects of predictability, semantic density and entropy on childrens' performance in the repetition task). The first study to investigate the role of MWP in adult language processing - particularly relevant for the purposes of the present study - was conducted by Arnon and Snider [19]. Building upon [17], the goal of that study was to provide experimental evidence for frequency effects in the processing of MWP and to compare a threshold approach - where phrasal frequency is defined based on certain frequency threshold - to an approach where phrasal frequency is regarded as a continuum. The stimulus set consisted of matched

[1] MWP have been investigated under various cover terms including multi-word phrases/sequences/chunks or formulaic sequences [9].

pairs of four-word phrases from three different frequency bands (high, medium and low) derived from a 20-million-word corpus of spontaneous speech from telephone conversations. A phrasal decision task was used in which participants had to decide whether a phrase was possible in English or not. Sensitivity to MWP frequency was assessed by comparing reaction times between higher and lower frequency variants. The study demonstrated a direct relation between frequency of occurrence and processing latencies: More frequent MWP (*Don't have to worry*) were processed faster than less frequent MWP (*Don't have to wait*) that were matched for the frequency of the substrings. The frequency effect of MWP was found to be not limited to high frequency band but occurred across the frequency continuum. The finding that adult native speakers are sensitive to the statistics of MWP was corroborated by a number of subsequent studies across a wide variety of paradigms, including self-paced reading and recall studies [20] as well as eye tracking studies [21]. While there has been an increased interest in the role of MWPs in L2 processing, most of the available research has focused on either non-compositional phrases, i.e. idioms (e.g. *kick the bucket*) or shorter compositional MWP including binomials (e.g. *bride and groom*) or collocations, i.e. frequently recurring two-word sequences (e.g. *perfectly natural*) (see, [22] for a review). However, much less is known whether and to what extent adult L2 learners can develop sensitivities to the frequency of larger compositional, i.e. syntactically regular and semantically transparent, MWP. To our knowledge, the only study to address this question is Hernandez et al. [1]. As pointed out by [1], previous L2 studies that have been conducted with non-compositional MWP cannot contribute to the investigation of the role of phrasal frequency during online processing of MWP, simply due to the low frequency of occurrence of such idiomatic expressions. Prior studies on L2 processing of two-word phrases leave open the questions of whether adult L2 learners are able to develop sensitivity to the statistics of larger MWP and whether MWP frequency effect occurs only in high-frequency phrases or across the frequency continuum. Using the same experimental design as in [19] (Experiment 1), [1] set out to investigate whether intermediate-advanced late L2 learners of English (L1 Spanish) were able to learn distributional properties of compositional four-word phrases as efficiently as L1 speakers and whether the sensitivity to MWP frequency is contingent upon the type of language exposure (immersion vs. classroom). Their findings replicated the MWP frequency effect for both L2 learner groups across the entire frequency range. However, these findings are inconsistent with the results reported in a number of studies indicating that L1 and L2 speakers differ in their degree of such sensitivity (see, e.g., [23–25], see also [9] for a recent discussion).

1.2 Individual Differences in Second Language Acquisition

It is common knowledge in L2 acquisition[2] research that there is considerable variability outcomes among adult learners (for overview, see, e.g., [27,28]). This variability persists even when L2 learners share commonalities such as native language, educational level, and experience with the L2. A number of learner-internal psychological factors have been proposed to account for such variability including cognitive-related factors (e.g. working memory (WM)), affective factors (e.g. motivation) and personality. To determine whether and to what extent individual differences (IDs) explain this variability is key for a theoretical understanding of L2 acquisition. Two IDs variables that have recently been the focus of considerable research are WM capacity and personality traits.

WM is commonly conceived of as a multicomponent cognitive system responsible for temporary storage, manipulation, and maintenance of task-relevant information during online cognitive operations such as language comprehension, arithmetic calculation, reasoning and problem solving ([29–31]). The WM system includes two key components, (1) short-term memory responsible for the temporary storage of information, and (2) central executive [32](see also executive attention [33]) concerned with the control of that information. Cognitive science researchers have drawn attention to a close link between putative storage and executive control aspects of WM capacity and language learning and processing (e.g. [34,35]). IDs in WM capacity and language processing have been shown to be systematically related at multiple linguistic levels (cf., e.g., [30,36,37]). Building upon previous work demonstrating the close link between WM capacity and L1 learning and processing, WM is gaining more prominence as an important ID measure in L2 acquisition research (see, [38–40]). Some L2 researchers have proposed WM to be treated as a key component of L2 aptitude or even to equate WM capacity to an L2 aptitude [41,42]. A few studies that have investigated the role of WM on L2 acquisition of MWP have focused on the phonological short-term memory (PSTM) tapping into the short-term storage component of WM [43,44]. These studies have found a positive association between PSTM capacity and L2 acquisition of MWP. To our knowledge no study has been undertaken to examine the role of complex span measures, such as reading span tasks (see, [45] for a seminal methodological paper on WM span tasks). A recent comprehensive meta-analysis [46] indicated that the executive control component of WM measured with complex span tasks is more strongly related to L2 outcomes than is the storage component. The reading span task (RSPAN) is the first span task that was designed to jointly tap into the storage and processing functions of WM capacity by drawing a word or digit span task coupled with an additional sentence processing task. The RSPAN task was originally developed by [30]. In

[2] An important point to make here in connection with Krashen's acquisition/learning hypothesis concerns the alleged distinction between second and foreign languages. There is now general consensus that the latter should be subsumed under the former term, since "underlying learning processes are essentially the same for more local and for more remote target languages, despite differing learning purposes and circumstances" ([26]: 1).

a classical RSPAN task, participants are required to read sentences and verify their logical accuracy. Simultaneously, they store a to-be-remembered item (e.g. the last word of the sentence, a non-word, or a digit) while moving on to further sentences. At the end of a sentence set participants are instructed to recall these to-be-remembered items. A participant's reading span is quantified as the size of the largest set at which the participant can accurately recall all of the sentence-final words.

Personality can be defined as "the dynamic organization within the individual of those psychophysical systems that determine his characteristic behavior and thought" ([47], p. 28). Recent years have witnessed a growing interest in the interrelation of personality and L2 acquisition (cf. [48] for an overview). As personality has been addressed from various points of view, including philosophical, sociological, biological, cognitive, learning theoretical or humanistic one, multiple theoretical perspectives and numerous levels of abstraction have been proposed to study this phenomenon. This has led to the development of a large number of personality concepts and questionnaire scales designed to measure them (cf. [49]). The Five Factor Model – also known as the Big Five – has emerged as the dominant contemporary model of personality and is recognized as the major taxonomy for classifying IDs in personality [50]. The five dimensions are Extraversion vs. Introversion, Neuroticism vs. Emotional Stability, Conscientiousness vs. Lack of Direction, Openness to new Experience vs. Closedness, and Agreeableness vs. Antagonism. These personality dimensions have been assessed with a range of instruments (cf. [50] for an overview). Several studies have looked at the relationship between personality and L2 acquisition (e.g., [51–53]). While it has not yet been conclusively determined which personality traits (or combination of such traits) create a potential for L2 success, there is a trend towards a positive relationship between Openness-to-Experience as well as Extraversion and the acquisition of L2 knowledge at multiple levels of linguistic organization.

1.3 The Present Study

As reviewed above, a large body of evidence has demonstrated that children and adult native speakers are sensitive to the statistics of larger (i.e. four-word) compositional MWP. However, less is known about whether adult L2 speakers are able to develop native-like sensitivity to such statistics. More importantly, no attempt has been made to account for individual variation in online L2 processing of larger MWP. Using a within-subject design embedded in an individual-differences framework, the present study attempts to fill this gap by addressing the following two research questions: (1) Can the MWP frequency effect reported in [1] be replicated with another sample of L2 speakers? (2) Can variation in online L2 processing of MWP be accounted for by IDs in WM capacity and personality traits?

2 Method

2.1 Participants

63 German advanced L2 learners of English participated in this study (43 female and 20 male, M = 25.08 years, SD = 3.00). All participants were college students recruited from the RWTH Aachen University. The participants were classified as having a Common European Framework (CEF) English proficiency level of at least B2 (upper intermediate) or C1 (lower advanced) based on their institutional status, as they all graduated with the German Abitur (higher education entrance qualification). We also estimated our participants' L2 proficiency level through the LexTALE test [54], a useful instrument designed for medium to advanced L2 learners to assess their receptive vocabulary knowledge in English. Participants also filled out the LEAP-Q [55], a questionnaire used to obtain general demographic information and more specific information on self-rated proficiency for three language areas (reading, understanding and speaking) and self-rated current knowledge of L2 English and exposure to the L2. The data gathered from the LEAP-Q instrument and the LexTALE test are reported in Table 1, showing means, standard deviations and ranges of our L2 group. Overall the L2 learners investigated in the present study exhibited comparable levels of L2 acquisition, exposure and proficiency as the classroom exposure group tested in [1]. The proficiency level of our group as estimated by LexTALE scores was slightly above that of the corresponding group in [1] but the difference was not statistically significant ($t(86) = 0.483$, $SE = 0.041$, $p = 0.63$).[3] However, there were statistically significant differences between the two groups with regard to the self-reported amount of current exposure to English: Our group had spent significantly more time in an English-speaking country ($t(86) = 2.47$, $SE = 0.97$, $p = 0.02$) and had higher current L2 experience through interaction with family members ($t(86) = 2.53$, $SE = 0.61$, $p = 0.01$). On the other hand the L2 exposure group in [1] significantly of current L2 exposure resulting from self instruction ($t(86) = 2.35$, $SE = 0.75$, $p = 0.02$).

2.2 Materials

L2 Processing of MWP: L2 learners' sensitivity to the frequencies of MWP was assessed using the same phrasal decision task (PDT) and the same material as those in [1] taken from the original study from [19]: Experiment 1. The material was taken from a 20-million-word corpus constructed from two corpora of authentic Americans' phone conversations, the Switchboard corpus [57] and the Fisher corpus [58]. These corpora were chosen to ensure that the experimental set of MWP was typically used in spontaneous speech. The stimulus material consisted of 26 pairs of MWP. MWP in each pair differed only in the final word

[3] We used Average % correct as the scoring measure for LexTALE performance, as this had the highest correlation with the criterion measure in [54]. [1] report LexTALE performance on the basis of I_{sdt} scores ([56]) The mean LexTALE score of our group of 75.35% correct corresponds to an I_{sdt} score of 0.54.

Table 1. Information on English acquisition, exposure, and proficiency of the L2 group.

	Mean	SD	Range
English acquisition (years)			
Age start acquisition	10.14	1.26	6–13
Age became fluent	16.1	2.43	12–23
Months in an English-speaking country	4.83	4.63	0–18
Current exposure to English			
Family (0–10)	1.9	3	0–10
Friends (0–10)	5.1	2.89	0–10
Reading (0–10)	7.52	2.2	0–10
Self inst. (0–10)	2.57	3.25	0–10
Watching TV (0–10)	7.75	2.49	0–10
Radio/music (0–10)	4.35	3.53	0–10
Self-rated English proficiency			
Speaking	75.10%	15.3	40–100
Reading	81.90%	13.8	30–100
Listening	82.90%	13.8	30–100
LexTALE % correct average	75.35	13.69	47.5–100

and in phrase frequency high vs. low (e.g. *Dont have to worry* vs. *Dont have to wait*). In the original study [19], the 26 phrases were divided into two frequency bands (High and Low) that differed in their cut-off: In the high frequency band, the more frequent variant had a mean frequency of 19.48 per million words and the less frequent variant had a mean frequency of 3.61 per million words. In the low band, the more frequent variant had a mean frequency of 3.5 per million words and the less frequent variant had a mean frequency of 0.2 per million variant. The material also included 12 grammatically correct and 68 grammatically incorrect four-word fillers. The PDT with a total 136 four-word phrases was implemented in OpenSesame, an open-spource program created for generating experiments for psychology and neuroscience [59]. Participants were instructed to decide as quickly as possible whether a visually presented MWP was a possible word sequence in English or not. Response time and accuracy were recorded.

Working Memory: WM capacity was assessed using a modified version of the Waters and Caplan's (1996) [60] RSPAN task described in [61] and implemented in TATOOL, an open source, Java-based framework [62]. The sentence material consisted of 63 simple and easily comprehensible sentences that varied from four to eight words each (M = 5.8 words per sentence). 32 of the sentences were meaningful or correct/right and the other 31 were non-sense or wrong. Participants were instructed to read the sentence and rate whether it made sense or was non-sense as fast as possible by pressing the arrow-keys on the keyboard. They were instructed to press the 'left' key if the sentence made sense and the 'left' key if the sentence was non-sense. Participants were additionally informed about the equal importance of sentence-decision and digit recalling accuracies to prevent them from only focusing on remembering the digits. After the participants had decided whether the sentence was sensible or non-sense, the next screen appeared and showed another digit, again followed automatically by a new sentence to-be-processed. The digits and sentences were presented in ascending order in groups of two, three, four, five and six. After the end of each trial, the participants were instructed to recall the presented digits and enter them successively in order of their appearance. The participants were exposed to a total of 15 trials, three of each consisting of either two, three, four, five or six sentences. Performance in the RSPAN test was assessed using a 'composite score' computed by summing the standardized scores for the speed, (semantic judgment) accuracy, and digit recall components of the task.

Personality: For personality, a paper-and-pencil version of the Big Five Inventory (BFI) questionnaire constructed by [50] was used. The BFI is an efficient and frequently used instrument to assess the five personality traits (Extraversion, Neuroticism, Conscientiousness, Openness to Experience, and Agreeableness). The BFI consists of 44 self-rating statements, such as *I see myself as someone who generates a lot of enthusiasm* or *I see myself as someone who remains calm in tense situations*. Participants were asked to rate each statement on a 5-point Likert-scale ranging from 1 (disagree strongly) to 5 (strongly agree). Participants' scale scores for each of the five dimensions were expressed as person-centered z-scores that were adjusted for differences in acquiescent response styles ('yea-saying' vs. 'nay-saying').

3 Results

An overview of the means, standard deviations and observed ranges of all ID measures investigated in this study is presented in Table 2.

In the PDT, we excluded responses under 200ms or more than two standard deviations from the mean of each condition. This resulted in the loss of 5% of the data. Accuracy for target items was at ceiling for both high (mean 99%) and low (mean 99%) frequency items. Mean accuracy for filler items was 94.6%. To determine the presence of a phrase frequency effect, we analyzed the reaction time data using mixed-effect linear regression models. We fitted three models to the data that corresponded to the models reported in replicated study [1] (Model 1) and the original study [19] (Models 2 & 3). Following [1], Model 1 was fitted to the entire data set (i.e. including both high and low frequency band) and included the phrase frequency predictor as a continuous variable. Following [19], additional models were fitted separately for the high band (Model 2) and the low band (Model 3). In these models, phrase frequency was entered as a binary variable (high vs. low). All models were run with phrase frequency as a fixed effect and random

Table 2. Means, standard deviations and observed ranged of ID measures.

Task	Dependent measure	Mean	SD	Range
Phrasal decision	RT (high)	1220.79	201.77	1390–3892
	RT (low)	275.5	202.81	1449–3982
Reading span	Composite score	−0.06	1.83	−9.53
BFI questionnaire	Agreeableness score	0.47	0.49	−2.12
	Conscientiousness score	0.26	0.61	−4.1
	Neuroticism score	−0.13	0.59	−2.77
	Openness score	0.35	0.36	−1.95
	Extraversion score	0.69	0.44	−2.07

effects for subjects and items. The relevant substring frequency measures, i.e. the log frequency of the final word, final bigram and final trigram, were added as controls. The models had the maximal random-effects structure justified by the data [63]. For each of the three models, we used likelihood ratio tests to determine whether the inclusion of phrase frequency led to a significant improvement in model fit. Collinearity in all reported models was small, i.e. all variance inflation factors were under 2. We found phrase frequency to be a significant predictor only when it was expressed as a binary variable and only in the high frequency bin ($\chi^2(1) = 4.95$, $p = 0.02$). In the high frequency bin, participants responded faster to higher frequency variants (M = 1180ms SD = 188) than to lower frequency ones (M = 1261ms, SD = 210), leading to a phrase frequency effect of 81 ms ($\beta = 0.12$, SE = 0.06, t = 2.09, p = 0.05). None of the control variables was statistically significant. The results of Model 2 are summarized in Table 3.

Table 3. Regression coefficients and test statistics from linear mixed effects model fitted to the reaction time data of PDT.

	β	SE	t	$Pr(>\|t\|)$	
(Intercept)	6.97	0.44	16.01	0	***
Phrase-frequency	0.12	0.06	2.09	0.05	*
Control variables					
Number of characters	0.01	0.02	0.55	0.59	
log(Freq final unigram)	−0.01	0.03	−0.43	0.67	
log(Freq final bigram)	−0.05	0.03	−1.75	0.09	.
log(Freq final trigram)	0.05	0.03	1.73	0.1	.

indicate statistical significance (, P < 0.05; **, P < 0.01; ***, P < 0.001)

To determine whether and to what extent the variability in online L2 processing of MWP can be accounted for by individual differences in WM capacity and personality, we used multiple linear regression. L2 learners' performance in the PDT was assessed by calculating the difference in their mean reaction time to high and low frequency items (ΔRT scores). Before the regression models were run, correlations between the predictor variables were calculated to see if they were moderately-to-strongly correlated ($0.5-1.0$), which could cause collinearity effects in the regression models described below. Correlation coefficients between the ID variables ranged from -0.28 and 0.34. As a first step, we fitted a full model with all variables included. In this model, the ΔRT scores were regressed on vWM and the five personality variables while controlling for participants' overall speed of responding (average RT) and LexTALE scores. The full model was significant ($F(8, 41) = 2.685, p = 0.018$) and accounted for 34% of the variance. The only variable that made a significant contribution to predicting ΔRT scores was Openness ($\beta = 75.37, SE = 30.99, p = 0.02$). No main effect was found for WM ($\beta = -0.39, SE = 5.74, p\, 0.94$). As a second step, the minimal adequate model was identified by stepwise (bi-directional) selection of variables based on Akaike's Information Criterion. The resulting model contained three of the five personality dimensions (Extraversion, Neuroticism and Openness) as well as LexTALE and Average RT. The only variable that remained significant in this model was Openness ($\beta = 73.4, SE = 28.79, p = 0.014$). The model accounted for 34% of the variance in ΔRT scores ($F(5, 44) = 4.567, p = 0.002, multipleR^2 = 0.341, adjustedR^2 = 0.267$). To understand the proportion of the variance in ΔRT scores explained by the personality traits, partial r^2 statistics were computed. The results of the model are summarized in Table 4.

Table 4. Regression coefficients and partial r2 values from the multiple regression model fitted to the ΔRT scores.

	β	SE	t	$Pr(>\|t\|)$	Partial r^2
(Intercept)	154.32	102.37	1.5	0.14	
Personality					
Extraversion	−45.17	27.76	−1.62	0.11	0.057
Neuroticism	−33.91	17.55	−1.93	0.06	0.078
Openness	73.4	28.79	2.55	0.014*	0.257
Control variables					
LexTALE	−1.74	0.96	−1.82	0.08	0.07
Average RT (all items)	0.05	0.03	1.79	0.09	0.068

indicate statistical significance (, P < 0.05; **, P < 0.01; ***, P < 0.001)

To further explore the role of vWM on the L2 processing of MWUs, we fitted additional models that included all two-way interactions between the WM and personality variables. We report the results of the minimal adequate model. This model accounted for 54% of the variance. There were three significant interactions: (1) WM × Extraversion ($\beta = 40.51, SE = 13.9, p < 0.006$), (2) WM ×

Agreeableness ($\beta = -30.49, SE = 11.27, p = 0.01$) and (3) WM × Neuroticism ($\beta = 37.24, SE = 14.41, p = 0.01$). For participants scoring low on the Extraversion, there was a negative relation between WM and L2 processing ability, i.e. ΔRT scores decreased with increasing RSPAN scores. With higher Extraversion scores, the relation between WM and L2 processing became increasingly more positive. The same pattern was observed for Neuroticism: Participants scoring higher on Neuroticism benefitted from higher WM capacity. In the case of Agreeableness, the pattern was reversed: For participants with lower scores on the Agreeableness scale, we observed a positive relationship between WM and L2 processing ability. With higher Agreeableness scores, the relation between WM and L2 processing became increasingly more negative. Figure 1 presents graphical illustrations of the interaction effects. There were no main effects of the two IDs measures.

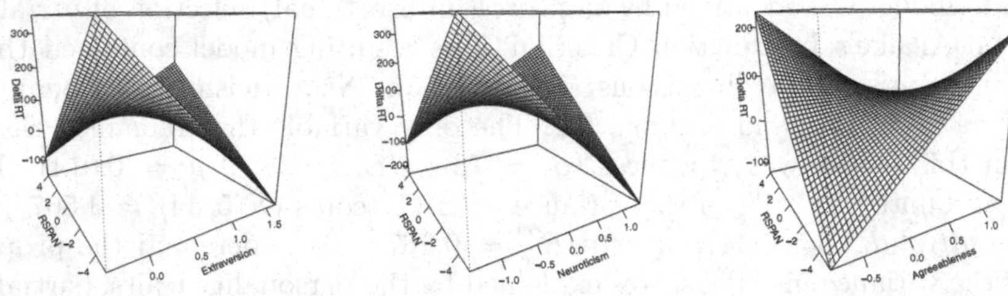

Fig. 1. Effect of WM on RT Deltas depending on personality (left: Extraversion middle: Neuroticism right: Agreeableness).

4 Discussion and Conclusion

The aim of the present study was twofold: (1) to replicate the MWP frequency effect reported in [1] with another sample of L2 learners of English, and (2) to examine whether and to what extent variation in online L2 processing of MWP can be accounted for by two IDs measures, i.e. WM and personality. To accomplish the first aim, we constructed three models using the model specifications from the original L1 study [19](:Experiment 1) and its recent replication [1]. The models differed with respect to (a) the operationalization of the phrase frequency predictor (continuous vs. binary) and (b) the data to which the model was fitted (the entire data set vs. separately to the high- and low-band data). Mixed-effects modeling revealed that our group of L2 advanced learners developed sensitivity to the frequencies of MWP only for the high frequency band with phrase frequency expressed as a binary variable. Thus we could replicate the MWP frequency effect for higher frequency items but not across the entire frequency spectrum. Our failure to replicate the MWP frequency effect across the frequency continuum in another sample of L2 learners can neither be attributed to differences in L2 proficiency level between our participants and those tested in [1] nor a lack of statistical power, as the sample size used in the present study

(N = 63) was more than twice as large as that of the classroom group (N = 25) in [1]. The finding that our L2 learners showed only sensitivities to the frequencies of MWP in the high frequency band is consistent with the results reported in previous L2 studies (see e.g. [23, 64]). These studies have demonstrated that L2 learners tend to rely more on simple overall frequency of MWP, rather than on the statistical association between the component words as is characteristic of L1 speakers. Further support for our findings comes from two more recent studies: [16] provide a direct evidence from large-scale, corpus-based computational modeling that adult L2 learners rely on MWP to a lesser extent than both children and native adult speakers. More indirect evidence comes from an experiment reported in [25] showing age-of-acquisition effects of MWP. In this study, adult native speakers of English responded faster to early-acquired MWP compared to later-acquired ones in phrasal decision task. Given these findings, one would expect difference in the magnitude of MWP frequency effects between L1 speakers and late L2 learners. More generally, our findings are consistent with the predictions of UB accounts of language and acquisition that statistical learning mechanisms underly both both L1 and L2 learning and processing and that input frequency is a key determinant of language outcomes. While our L2 learners did show sensitivity to the statistics of MWP, they were able to develop such sensitivity across the entire frequency spectrum, which is likely to reflect differences in the amount of exposure to spontaneous telephone conversational speech. This calls for further studies investigating L1 and L2 speakers' sensitivity to register-specific frequencies of MWP (e.g. fiction, academic writing) that more closely mirror the statistics of their language experience at different points across their lifespan.

Regarding our second aim, we found a positive significant relationship between the Openness personality trait and online processing of MWP, whereas no such relationship was found for WM. The positive effect of Openness has been observed in several prior studies (e.g.,[52, 53, 65]). In contrast to previous studies that have shown a positive association between phonological short-term memory capacity and L2 acquisition of MWP (see, e.g., [43, 44]), we found no main effect of WM capacity as gauged by a RSPAN task on online L2 processing of MWP. However, in light of previous research showing that complex span measures are stronger predictors of L2 outcomes [46], we fitted additional models that included interactions between WM and personality variables. As evidenced by three significant two-way interactions, the relationship between WM, personality and online L2 processing of MWP appears to be more complex (see Fig. 1): The effects of WM on L2 processing were in opposite directions for introverts and extraverts with the latter benefiting from higher WM capacity. A similar pattern was observed for Neuroticism, whereas a reversed pattern was found for Agreeableness. These findings suggest that the relationship between WM capacity and L2 processing is mediated by personality and underscore the importance of further investigation of the interrelation between the cognitive and the affective IDs that impact L2 acquisition and processing (see, e.g. [66, 67] for research linking personality traits to IDs in WM task-performance and to the macro-configurations of the WM neural circuitry).

In sum, the present study is a first step towards understanding individual differences in L2 processing of MWP and calls for a comprehensive account of L2 processing of MWP based on large-scale investigations of interactions among experiential, cognitive, and affective factors at different points across an individual's lifespan.

References

1. Hernández, M., Costa, A., Arnon, I.: More than words: multiword frequency effects in non-native speakers. Lang. Cogn. Neurosci. **31**(6), 785–800 (2016)
2. Beckner, C., Blythe, R., Bybee, J., Christiansen, M.H., Croft, W., Ellis, N.C., Holland, J., Ke, J., Larsen-Freeman, D., Schoenemann, T.: Language is a complex adaptive system: position paper. Lang. Learn. **59**(s1), 1–26 (2009)
3. McClelland, J.L., Botvinick, M.M., Noelle, D.C., Plaut, D.C., Rogers, T.T., Seidenberg, M.S., Smith, L.B.: Letting structure emerge: connectionist and dynamical systems approaches to cognition. Trends Cogn. Sci. **14**(8), 348–356 (2010)
4. Christiansen, M.H., Chater, N., Culicover, P.W.: Creating Language: Integrating Evolution, Acquisition, and Processing. MIT Press, Cambridge (2016)
5. Armstrong, B.C., Frost, R., Christiansen, M.H.: The long road of statistical learning research: past, present and future. Philos. Trans. R. Soc. B Biol. Sci. **372**(1711) (2017)
6. Diessel, H.: Frequency effects in language acquisition, language use, and diachronic change. New Ideas Psychol. **25**(2), 108–127 (2007)
7. Ambridge, B., Kidd, E., Rowland, C.F., Theakston, A.L.: The ubiquity of frequency effects in first language acquisition. J. Child Lang. **42**(02), 239–273 (2015)
8. Pinker, S., Poeppel, D.: Words and rules: the ingredients of language. Nature **403**(6768), 361 (2000)
9. Christiansen, M.H., Arnon, I.: More than words: the role of multiword sequences in language learning and use. Top. Cogn. Sci. **9**, 542–551 (2017)
10. Bannard, C., Lieven, E.: Formulaic language in L1 acquisition. Annu. Rev. Appl. Linguist. **32**, 3–16 (2012)
11. Conklin, K., Schmitt, N.: The processing of formulaic language. Annu. Rev. Appl. Linguist. **32**, 45–61 (2012)
12. MacWhinney, B.: The CHILDES system. Am. J. Speech Lang. Pathol. **5**(1), 5–14 (1996)
13. Cameron-Faulkner, T., Lieven, E., Tomasello, M.: A construction based analysis of child directed speech. Cogn. Sci. **27**(6), 843–873 (2003)
14. Lieven, E., Salomo, D., Tomasello, M.: Two-year-old children's production of multiword utterances: a usage-based analysis. Cogn. Linguist. **20**(3), 481–507 (2009)
15. Kol, S., Nir, B., Wintner, S.: Computational evaluation of the traceback method. J. Child Lang. **41**(01), 176–199 (2014)
16. McCauley, S.M., Christiansen, M.H.: Computational investigations of multiword chunks in language learning (2015)
17. Bannard, C., Matthews, D.: Stored word sequences in language learning: the effect of familiarity on children's repetition of four-word combinations. Psychol. Sci. **19**(3), 241–248 (2008)

18. Matthews, D., Bannard, C.: Childrens production of unfamiliar word sequences is predicted by positional variability and latent classes in a large sample of child-directed speech. Cogn. Sci. **34**(3), 465–488 (2010)
19. Arnon, I., Snider, N.: More than words: frequency effects for multi-word phrases. J. Mem. Lang. **62**(1), 67–82 (2010)
20. Tremblay, A., Derwing, B., Libben, G., Westbury, C.: Processing advantages of lexical bundles: evidence from self-paced reading and sentence recall tasks. Lang. Learn. **61**(2), 569–613 (2011)
21. Siyanova-Chanturia, A., Conklin, K., Schmitt, N.: Adding more fuel to the fire: An eye-tracking study of idiom processing by native and non-native speakers. Second Lang. Res. **27**(2), 251–272 (2011)
22. Conklin, K., Schmitt, N.: Formulaic sequences: are they processed more quickly than nonformulaic language by native and nonnative speakers? Appl. Linguist. **29**(1), 72–89 (2008)
23. Ellis, N.C., Simpson-vlach, R., Maynard, C.: Formulaic language in native and second language speakers: psycholinguistics, corpus linguistics, and tesol. Tesol Q. **42**(3), 375–396 (2008)
24. Durrant, P., Doherty, A.: Are high-frequency collocations psychologically real? Investigating the thesis of collocational priming. Corpus Linguist. Linguist. Theory **6**(2), 125–155 (2010)
25. Arnon, I., McCauley, S.M., Christiansen, M.H.: Digging up the building blocks of language: age-of-acquisition effects for multiword phrases. J. Mem. Lang. **92**, 265–280 (2017)
26. Mitchell, R., Myles, F., Marsden, E.: Second Language Learning Theories. Routledge, Abingdon (2013)
27. Dörnyei, Z., Skehan, P.: Individual differences in second language learning. In: Doughty, C.J., Long, M.H. (eds.) The Handbook of Second Language Acquisition, pp. 589–630. Blackwell, Oxford (2003)
28. Dewaele, J.-M.: Individual differences in second language acquisition. In: The New Handbook of Second Language Acquisition, vol. 2, pp. 623–646 (2009)
29. Baddeley, A.D., Hitch, G.: Working memory. Psychol. Learn. Motiv. **8**, 47–89 (1974)
30. Daneman, M., Carpenter, P.A.: Individual differences in working memory and reading. J. Verbal Learn. Verbal Behav. **19**(4), 450–466 (1980)
31. Miyake, A., Shah, P.: MoDels of Working Memory: Mechanisms of Active Maintenance and Executive Control. Cambridge University Press, Cambridge (1999)
32. Baddeley, A.: Working Memory, Thought, and Action, vol. 45. OUP, Oxford (2007)
33. Kane, M.J., Conway, A.R., Hambrick, D.Z., Engle, R.W.: Variation in working memory capacity as variation in executive attention and control. In: Variation in Working Memory, vol. 1, pp. 21–48 (2007)
34. Baddeley, A.: Working memory: looking back and looking forward. Nat. Rev. Neurosci. **4**(10), 829–839 (2003)
35. Cowan, N.: Working Memory Capacity. Psychology Press, Hove (2012)
36. Carpenter, P.A., Just, M.A.: The role of working memory in language comprehension. In: Klahr, D., Kotovsky, K. (eds.) Complex Information Processing: The Impact of Herbert A. Simon, pp. 31–68. Erlbaum, Hillsdale (1989)
37. Miyake, A., Just, M.A., Carpenter, P.A.: Working memory constraints on the resolution of lexical ambiguity: maintaining multiple interpretations in neutral contexts. J. Mem. Lang. **33**(2), 175 (1994)
38. Juffs, A., Harrington, M.: Aspects of working memory in L2 learning. Lang. Teach. **44**(02), 137–166 (2011)

39. Williams, J.N.: Working memory and SLA. In: Gass, S., Mackey, A. (eds.) The Routledge Handbook of Second Language Acquisition, pp. 427–441. Routledge, London (2012)
40. Wen, Z., Mota, M.B., McNeill, A.: Working Memory in Second Language Acquisition and Processing, vol. 87. Multilingual Matters, Bristol (2015)
41. Robinson, P.: Effects of individual differences in intelligence, aptitude and working memory on adult incidental SLA. In: Robinson, P. (ed.) Individual Differences and Instructed Language Learning, pp. 211–266. John Benjamins, Amsterdam (2002)
42. Skehan, P.: Theorising and updating aptitude. Individ. Differ. Instruct. Lang. Learn. **2**, 69–94 (2002)
43. Bolibaugh, C., Foster, P.: Memory-based aptitude for nativelike selection: the role of phonological short-term memory. In: Granena, G., Long, M. (eds.) Sensitive Periods, Language Aptitude, and Ultimate L2 Attainment, vol. 35, p. 205. John Benjamins Publishing Company, Amsterdam (2013)
44. Foster, P., Bolibaugh, C., Kotula, A.: Knowledge of nativelike selections in a L2. Stud. Second Lang. Acquis. **36**(01), 101–132 (2014)
45. Conway, A.R., Kane, M.J., Bunting, M.F., Hambrick, D.Z., Wilhelm, O., Engle, R.W.: Working memory span tasks: a methodological review and users guide. Psychon. Bull. Rev. **12**(5), 769–786 (2005)
46. Linck, J.A., Osthus, P., Koeth, J.T., Bunting, M.F.: Working memory and second language comprehension and production: a meta-analysis. Psychon. Bull. Rev. **21**(4), 861–883 (2014)
47. Allport, G.W.: Pattern and Growth in Personality. Holt, Rinehart & Winston, New York (1961)
48. Dewaele, J.-M.: Personality in second language acquisition. In: Chapelle, C.A. (ed.) The Encyclopedia of Applied Linguistics. Wiley-Blackwell, Oxford (2013)
49. Cervone, D., Pervin, L.A.: Personality Psychology. Wiley, Hoboken (2010)
50. John, O.P., Naumann, L.P., Soto, C.J.: Paradigm shift to the integrative big five trait taxonomy. In: John, O.P., Robins, R.W., Pervin, L.A. (eds.) Handbook of Personality: Theory and Research, vol. 3, pp. 114–158. Guilford Press, New York (2008)
51. Ehrman, M.E., Oxford, R.L.: Cognition plus: correlates of language learning success. Mod. Lang. J. **79**(1), 67–89 (1995)
52. Verhoeven, L., Vermeer, A.: Communicative competence and personality dimensions in first and second language learners. Appl. Psycholinguist. **23**(03), 361–374 (2002)
53. Kaufman, S.B., DeYoung, C.G., Gray, J.R., Jiménez, L., Brown, J., Mackintosh, N.: Implicit learning as an ability. Cognition **116**(3), 321–340 (2010)
54. Lemhöfer, K., Broersma, M.: Introducing lextale: a quick and valid lexical test for advanced learners of English. Behav. Res. Methods **44**(2), 325–343 (2012)
55. Marian, V., Blumenfeld, H.K., Kaushanskaya, M.: The language experience and proficiency questionnaire (LEAP-Q): assessing language profiles in bilinguals and multilinguals. J. Speech Lang. Hear. Res. **50**(4), 940–967 (2007)
56. Huibregtse, I., Admiraal, W., Meara, P.: Scores on a yes-no vocabulary test: correction for guessing and response style. Lang. Test. **19**(3), 227–245 (2002)
57. Godfrey, J.J., Holliman, E.C., McDaniel, J.: Switchboard: telephone speech corpus for research and development. In: 1992 IEEE International Conference on Acoustics, Speech, and Signal Processing, ICASSP-92, vol. 1, pp. 517–520. IEEE (1992)
58. Cieri, C., Miller, D., Walker, K.: The fisher corpus: a resource for the next generations of speech-to-text. LREC **4**, 69–71 (2004)

59. Mathôt, S., Schreij, D., Theeuwes, J.: Opensesame: an open-source, graphical experiment builder for the social sciences. Behav. Res. Methods **44**(2), 314–324 (2012)
60. Waters, G.S., Caplan, D.: Processing resource capacity and the comprehension of garden path sentences. Mem. Cogn. **24**(3), 342–355 (1996)
61. Stone, J., Towse, J.: A working memory test battery: java-based collection of seven working memory tasks. J. Open Res. Softw. **3**(1), e5 (2015)
62. von Bastian, C.C., Locher, A., Ruflin, M.: Tatool: a java-based open-source programming framework for psychological studies. Behav. Res. Methods **45**(1), 108–115 (2013)
63. Barr, D.J., Levy, R., Scheepers, C., Tily, H.J.: Random effects structure for confirmatory hypothesis testing: keep it maximal. J. Mem. Lang. **68**(3), 255–278 (2013)
64. Durrant, P., Schmitt, N.: To what extent do native and non-native writers make use of collocations? IRAL Int. Rev. Appl. Linguist. Lang. Teach. **47**(2), 157–177 (2009)
65. Ehrman, M.: Personality and Good Language Learners, p. 6172. Cambridge Language Teaching Library. Cambridge University Press, Cambridge (2008)
66. Gray, J.R., Braver, T.S.: Personality predicts working-memory related activation in the caudal anterior cingulate cortex. Cogn. Affect. Behav. Neurosci. **2**(1), 64–75 (2002)
67. Dima, D., Friston, K.J., Stephan, K.E., Frangou, S.: Neuroticism and conscientiousness respectively constrain and facilitate short-term plasticity within the working memory neural network. Hum. Brain Mapp. **36**(10), 4158–4163 (2015)

Cognitive and Cultural Aspects of Phraseology

Verbal Phraseology: An Analysis of Cognitive Verbs in Linguistics, Engineering and Medicine Academic Papers

María Luisa Carrió-Pastor(✉)

Universidad Politécnica de Valencia, Valencia, Spain
lcarrio@upv.es

Abstract. The main aim of this paper is to study if the phraseology of cognitive verbs used in academic English reveals different discourse patterns in the specific fields of Linguistics, Engineering and Medicine. The objectives of this study are first the identification of cognitive verb patterns in academic English, second the contrastive analysis of the cognitive verbs patterns used in Linguistics, Engineering and Medicine and finally, the study of the patterns used in the different disciplines of academic English. In this analysis, the taxonomy proposed by Marín-Arrese (2015) to identify evidential expressions, i.e. verbs of mental state or cognitive attitude, is used to identify the cognitive verbs in the corpus. The verbs identified in this category were searched with WordSmith Tools 5.0 and the phraseological units including cognitive verbs were compiled and studied. The frequencies of the verbs with the concordances of the cognitive verbs were analysed and examples discussed. The results extracted from the three different specific fields of knowledge were discussed and the conclusions were drawn.

Keywords: Academic English · Cognitive verbs · Phraseology

1 Introduction

The way researchers present their findings and express attitude is important for academic communication. I consider a key issue in language studies the identification of specific patterns and phraseological units used in specific settings, as language variation is important to identify language patterns. In this sense, this paper deals with the analysis of verbal phraseology. Specifically, I focus my study on the phraseology used to express epistemic stance with verbs of cognitive attitude. This study covers academic English papers published in scientific journals in the specific fields of Linguistics, Engineering and Medicine. The different fields of study have been selected as they may represent the use of cognitive verbs phraseology in hard sciences (Engineering), soft sciences (Linguistics) and in a discipline that uses a mixture of both (Medicine).

This paper shows some of the results of the research project FFI2016-77941-P (Ministerio de Economía y Competitividad, Spain).

R. Mitkov (Ed.): Europhras 2017, LNAI 10596, pp. 325–336, 2017.
https://doi.org/10.1007/978-3-319-69805-2_23

Thus, the main aim of this paper is to study if the phraseology of the cognitive verbs used in academic English reveals different discourse patterns in the specific fields of Linguistics, Engineering and Medicine. My hypothesis is that academic writers use different cognitive verbs and phraseological units when showing cognitive attitude to readers. The objectives of this study are, first the identification of cognitive verb patterns in academic English, second the contrastive analysis of the cognitive verbs patterns used in Linguistics, Engineering and Medicine and, finally the study of the patterns used in the different disciplines of academic English. The research questions to be answered after the analysis of the results are the following ones:

(a) Which are the most commonly used cognitive verbs in Linguistics, Engineering and Medicine?
(b) What are the preferred cognitive verb patterns in academic papers? Are they different depending on the discipline?
(c) Do cognitive verb patterns change depending on the specific field of knowledge in academic papers? What are the possible causes?

This paper is organised as follows. First, in the Introduction, a general overview and the objectives of this paper have been set. Second, the section 'Phraseology and epistemic stance' discusses the different concepts and classifications of epistemic modality and phraseology. Third, the section 'Corpus and method' describes the different academic papers compiled and the procedure of the study. Fourth, the quantitative results are shown and some examples from the corpus discussed in the section 'Results and discussion', and finally the conclusions are drawn in the last section.

2 Phraseology and Epistemic Stance

Phraseology is an area of research that has been of interest for several researchers in the last thirty years. Some researchers have focused on phraseology for language teaching and second language learning (Granger and Paquot 2008; Charles 2011a), but most of them have used phraseology to study academic discourse and suggest patterns, as stated by the studies of Howarth (1996), Baranov and Dobrovol'skij (1996), Cowie (1998), Hunston (2002), Geasuato (2008), Charles (2011b), Vincent (2013), Brett and Pinna (2015), Le and Harrington (2015), John et al. (2017) and Fiedler (2017).

In this analysis, I follow the distributional or corpus-driven approach, which has been used by researchers such as Hunston and Francis (2000), Biber et al. (2004), Scott and Tribble (2006), Saber (2012) and Cortes (2013) to study pattern grammar. Corpus studies have proven that certain keywords are typically used in some genres and this fact may be helpful to determine the patterns followed by language users. As Charles (2011b: 48) explains, there are two volumes that should be mentioned as being representative of corpus studies on academic writing, the first by Biber et al. (2004) and the second by Charles et al. (2009). But one of the problems of using corpus techniques and retrieving individual items is that language patterns may not be identified, resulting in a fragmented analysis of discourse (Charles 2011a). This is the reason why I consider a phraseological analysis of units should also be performed to have a wider view of discourse patterns and identify differences in the use of certain structures. Therefore, this paper takes an integrative corpus and discourse approach, showing how cognitive verbs can combine in different specific fields to signal academic discourse patterns. As Vincent (2013: 44) explains, "Findings have consistently shown that phraseology is register specific", but in this study my interest lays on demonstrating that phraseology is also specific in different fields of knowledge.

The second key issue of this paper is the nature of cognitive verbs in academic papers. In fact, this study focuses on the epistemic devices (i.e., the elements of discourse which allows writers to convey their knowledge claims) that act as persuasion strategies (Carrió Pastor, 2014; Alonso-Almeida 2015a, b; Alonso Almeida and Carrió-Pastor 2015) and the phraseological units associated to epistemic-cognitive verbs. I analyse the use of epistemic modality showing Halliday's textual metafunction, which "can be regarded as an enabling or facilitating function, since the others – construing experience and enacting interpersonal relations– depend on being able to build up sequences of discourse, organising the discursive flow, and creating cohesion and continuity as it moves" (Halliday and Matthiessen 2001: 30–31).

As Marín-Arrese (2015: 1) states: "the use of epistemic stance expressions reflects the stance or positioning of the speaker with respect to their assertions and their commitment to the validity of the proposition". In this sense, this article explores the use of epistemic stance through cognitive verbs in academic papers, using a corpus which includes texts from three specific fields of knowledge.

This topic has been studied by Marin-Arrese (2015), this author proposes the taxonomy of epistemic stance strategies that can be observed in Table 1:

Marín-Arrese (2015) includes the categories of epistemic modality (or modals) and cognitive evidentials (or verbs of mental state or cognitive attitude) proposed in 2009

Table 1. Categories of epistemic stance strategies (Marín-Arrese 2015: 2–3)

Categories of epistemic stance	Definition	Expressions
1. Indirect inferential evidence	"It involves personal, indirect justification, based on either perceptual-based or conceptual-based inferences and an additional subcategory of inferential meaning based on information acquired through reports"	*seem, appear, look, clearly, obviously, evidently, apparently*
2. Indirect reportative evidence	"It involves non-personal, indirect access to information, originating in some external source, and where no internal mental processing or inference on the part of the speaker is involved"	*accordingly to x, said, told, seem, appear, apparently, allegedly, reportedly, supposedly*
3. Epistemic modals	"and epistemic sentence adverbs and verbs, involving the expression of degrees of epistemic support for a proposition"	*must, may, might, could, certainly, surely, probably, possibly, perhaps, maybe*
4. Verbs of mental state or cognitive attitude	"They convey the explicit expression of speakers' reflective beliefs and knowledge regarding representations"	*I/we know, I/we think, I/we believe, I/we suppose, it seems to me/us, I would say*

and 2011, but adds two categories. The first category proposed is "Indirect inferential evidence" and the second is "Indirect reportative evidence". Here I focus on the use of phraseological verbs that show cognitive attitude to readers, conveying the explicit expression of beliefs and knowledge. As Marín-Arrese (2015: 10) explains "verbs of mental state or cognitive attitude indicate speakers' reflective attitudes or beliefs regarding representations". Capelli (2007: 123–124) describes these verbs as "the evaluator is certain that a representation of some sort holds, the output is a piece of knowledge, otherwise when the degree is still positive but below the level of certainty, the output is a belief".

In this paper, my intention is to identify the variation in the patterns of verbs that express cognitive attitude and to study the evidential strategies used to convince readers in academic English. In this sense, the most frequent phrases of cognitive verbs may show that there are in fact different patterns in the different specific fields of knowledge of a genre.

3 Corpus and Method

In this study, the corpus was composed of 120 research papers. Forty research papers belong to the specific field of Linguistics, forty were compiled from journals that publish engineering research and forty were published by medicine research journals.

All the research papers meet the following criteria:

- They belong to either Linguistics, Medicine or Engineering.
- They are authored by at least one English native speaker, preferably as the first author.
- They were published in 2016.
- They are listed in the Journal Citation Reports® database (JCR, Thompson and Reuters). This indicates that the journal's quality has been externally evaluated in terms of citation impact.

In this paper, a quantitative analysis of the cognitive verbs was first carried out and then the phraseological units were identified and examples given and discussed. The procedure I followed was the following one. After collecting the research papers, I removed all lists of references, tables and figures. In the corpus of Linguistics journals, the examples that included cognitive verbs were also removed. Then, the corpus was processed with the tool *WordSmith 5.0* (Scott 2010). First, the total occurrences of words were calculated and the cognitive verbs were searched actively, identified and later the results were checked manually. Secondly, the concordances of the cognitive verbs were extracted and those that were identified as phraseological units that contained cognitive verbs were counted and annotated. The results were normalized to a frequency in a ratio per 10,000 words as the total number of tokens of the sub-corpora was different. Then, the concordances of the cognitive verbs were listed and analysed.

The different verbs analysed in this paper, taking into account Marín-Arrese (2015) taxonomy were: *know, think, believe/d, suppose/d, (it) seems/ed (to me/us), would say, means, understand/understood*. After generating concordances for all the detected cognitive verbs, I counted their occurrences and analysed them. In the following sections, I shall present the results of the study, highlighting some of the most interesting and relevant examples found in the corpus. I shall also provide a contrastive analysis of the examples extracted from the three specialized sub-corpora with the aim of identifying potential domain-specific patterns associated with cognitive verbs, and present the final findings in the Conclusion.

4 Results and Discussion

The results of the statistical analysis of the corpus are shown in Table 2:

Table 2. Statistical data from the corpus

Sub-corpora	File size	Running words	Distinct words	Sentences no.
Engineering	3,790,652	277,369	14,778	12,587
Medicine	1,473,300	141,457	9,922	6,147
Linguistics	3,952,950	350,654	16,178	13,195
Total	9,216,902	769,480	40,878	31,929

The corpus included 120 research papers. As can be seen in Table 2, the running words of the three sub-corpora were dissimilar due to the different nature of the specific fields. The Medicine sub-corpus included shorter papers and consequently had a lower frequency in the file size, running words, distinct words and number of sentences, meanwhile the sub-corpus of Linguistics was composed of longer research papers. On the other hand, the academic papers from the Linguistics sub-corpus were longer than the ones in the sub-corpora of Engineering and Medicine. This may be due to the descriptive nature of academic papers that study Linguistics.

After the analysis of the texts, the cognitive verbs were identified and compiled. The raw occurrences of cognitive verbs extracted from the analysis can be seen in Fig. 1:

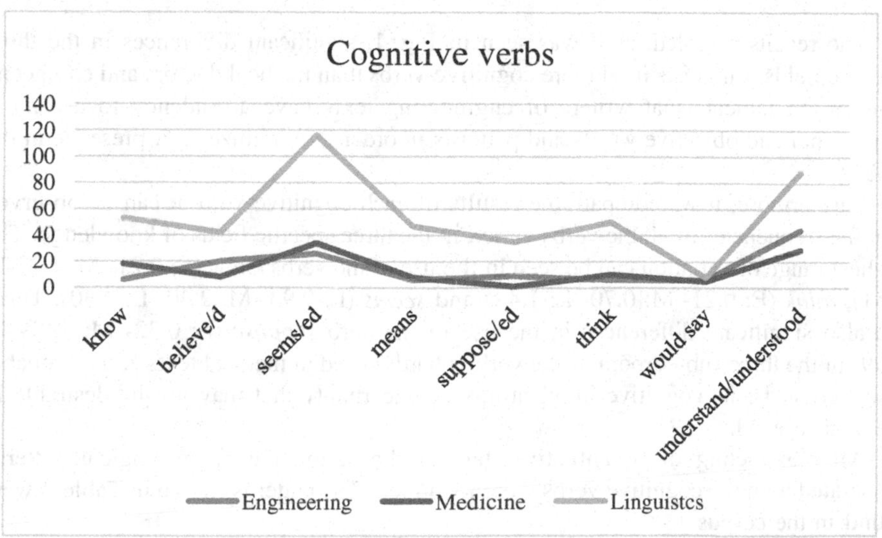

Fig. 1. Comparison of raw occurrences of cognitive verbs in Engineering, Medicine and Linguistics

It can clearly be observed in Fig. 1 that linguists preferred the use of cognitive verbs to make explicit their beliefs. On the contrary, engineers and medical doctors seldom used these verbs to convey the explicit expression of the writers' knowledge. In this sense, it may be proved after these results that there are differences in the use of cognitive verbs among specific fields of knowledge. As stated above, the texts differed in their length (see Table 2), so the raw occurrences were normalized in a ratio per 10,000 words. This step was important to be sure there were differences in the use of cognitive verbs in specific settings of academic English. Table 3 shows the data of each specific field after processing and normalising the results of the corpus:

Table 3. Raw and normalised occurrences of cognitive verbs in the sub-corpora of Engineering, Medicine and Linguistics

Cognitive verbs	Raw occurrences engineering (normalised per 10,000)	Raw occurrences medicine (normalised per 10,000)	Raw occurrences linguistics (normalised per 10,000)
Know	6 (0.21)	18 (1.27)	53 (1.51)
Believe/-d	20 (0.72)	8 (0.56)	42 (1.19)
Seems/-ed	26 (0.93)	34 (2.40)	116 (3.30)
Means	6 (0.21)	8 (0.56)	47 (1.34)
Suppose/-s/-ed	9 (0.32)	1 (0.07)	35 (0.99)
Think	6 (0.21)	10 (0.70)	50 (1.42)
Would say	6 (0.21)	5 (0.35)	8 (0.22)
Understand/-tood	44 (1.58)	29 (2.05)	88 (2.50)
Total	123 (4.43)	113 (7.98)	439 (12.51)

The results revealed, as it was seen in Fig. 1, significant differences in the three specific fields. Linguists used more cognitive verbs than medical doctors and engineers. This might indicate that writers of engineering texts have a tendency to use more impersonal and objective words and patterns in order to minimize their presence in the text.

Furthermore, if we compare the results of each cognitive verb, it can be observed that the frequencies of all the verbs varied in the three specific fields of knowledge. The highest range of variation can be seen in the use of the verbs *know* (E: 0.21- M: 1.27-L: 1.51), *think* (E: 0.21- M: 0.70- L: 1.42) and *seems* (E: 0.93- M: 2.40- L: 3.30). There are also significant differences in the use of the verb *suppose* (E: 0.32- M: 0.07- L: 0.99) in the three sub-corpora as the verb is hardly used in medical texts and a probable cause could be its cognitive implications of uncertainty that may not be desirable in medical research.

After extracting the quantitative data of the study, the phraseological patterns associated with the cognitive verbs were identified. The patterns shown in Table 4 were found in the corpus:

Table 4. Phraseological units of cognitive verbs

Phraseological units of cognitive verbs		
Engineering	Medicine	Linguistics
Impersonal + know + noun Impersonal + know + if Impersonal + know + where	We know + that clause We know + of We know + what We know + how We know + noun I know + as We know + whether	I/we know + noun I/we know + what I/we know + that clause I/we know + about I/we know + whether I/we know + if I/we know + why
I/we believe + that clause I/we believe + verb-ing	I/we believe + pronoun I/we believe + that clause I/we believe + noun	I/we believe + to be I/we believe + sentence I/we believe + that clause I/we believe + what I/we believe + noun To what I/we believe + to be
Impersonal + seems + to infinitive Impersonal + seems + adjective Impersonal + seems + that clause Impersonal + seems + noun	Impersonal + seems + to me/us + noun Impersonal + seems + to infinitive Impersonal + seems + adjective	Impersonal + seems + to me/us + adjective/that clause Impersonal + seems + to infinitive Impersonal + seems + adjective Impersonal + seems + likely
Impersonal + means + that clause	Impersonal + means + that clause	Noun + means + that clause Noun + means + noun Noun + means + verb + ing
I/we think + about I/we think + of I/we think + in I/we think + noun	I/we think + that clause I/we think + of I think + noun	I/we think + about I/we (modal verb) think + of I/we think + noun I/we think + that clause
I/we suppose + that clause	I/we suppose + that clause	I/we suppose + that clause Let +us + suppose + that clause
I/we would say + if I/we would say + that clause	I/we would say + on I/we would say + that clause I/we would say + what	I/we would say + that clause
I/we understand + noun I/we understand + that clause I/we understand + which clause I/we understand + how I/we understand + why I/we understand + whether	I/we understand + noun I/we understand + how Third person + understand + noun	I/we understand + noun I/we understand + how Third person + understand + noun I/we understand + why I/we understand + whether

The patterns identified in the three sub-corpora varied, as can be seen in Table 4. I identified more phraseological units of cognitive verbs in the specific field of Linguistics, these findings being expected, given that linguists used more cognitive verbs. The researchers use first person pronouns to express their attitude through cognitive verbs, by contrast the verbs *mean*, *seem* and *know* are used with the pronoun *it* by academic researchers rather than with first person pronouns. Engineers preferred the use of impersonal patterns to describe their experiments, meanwhile, linguists used more personal forms to mark explicitly the presence of the researchers.

Some examples of each cognitive verb are shown above to illustrate the results of Table 4:

KNOW

Engineering example [1]: "While this modelling might explicitly take co-variates into account, thus possibly benefitting from a large variety of statistical models, it may be difficult to actually formulate the important co-variates and *one might not know their specific values*" (ENG04).

Medicine example [1]: "The need for treatment of fractures of the condylar head remains controversial, *and we know of no* high quality, randomised controlled trials that have examined outcomes" (MED34).

Linguistics example [1]: "such a specific agent and neither does it conform to what *we know about these* experiences which tend to be idiosyncratic in their sensory qualities" (LING34).

BELIEVE

Engineering example [2]: "*We believe that this* is a topic that requires further attention, it links to many system dependability concepts including inedibility and resilience" (ENG02).

Medicine example [2]: "and the temporal pole may also be an indicator of resilience to clinical depression in the future, *we believe this is certainly* worth investigating further" (MED38).

Linguistics example [2]: "Such an opposition *is, I believe, legible* in the terms in which Nolan (2013) and Pearsall (2001) frame their revisionist arguments" (LING17).

"We return to some further important principles from the wider field of historical linguistics research, but ordered according to *what I believe are* priorities for ALH" (LING10).

SEEMS

Engineering example [3]: "From the grouping of cultivars per decades of their release, *it seems that the greatest* change through breeding from the 1919 through 1970-time frame" (ENG05).

Medicine example [3]: "using apps to support their education and clinical practice, *this seems to be where* future means of communication may be heading" (MED17).

Linguistics example [3]: "*It seems to me that this* scalar approach offers more scope to explore the subtle, sustained conceptual effects of extended metaphor alluded to by Werth" (LING06)

MEANS

Engineering example [4]: "This *means that the* operational indices after the priori and posteriori RL update do improve the production rate of concentrate ore in practice" (ENG11).

Medicine example [4]: "*This means that* a staff member began using the keyboard before the cleaning" (MED32).

Linguistics example [4]: "The very fact that sentence metaphor contains only source-frame *language means that attention* to the source-world is, in his words, 'mandatory'" (LING14

THINK

Engineering example [5]: "moved up in levels until *they did not think the project* team could meet anything higher" (ENG21).

Medicine example [5]: "ORIF of fractures of the condylar head, *we think that it* is important to discuss the indications" (MED28).

Linguistics example [5]: "While *we think that typicality* is an important component of many implicatures and thus should ultimately be derived from a complete pragmatic" (LING38). "We *might think of inferential* as something that can be very low-level" (LING28).

SUPPOSE

Engineering example [6]: "First, *suppose that one can* assign a precise probability for the event that the next task is of type r," (ENG25).

Medicine example [6]: "*We suppose the objectives* of the College that demand it be and remain an outward looking" (MED30).

Linguistics example [6]: "*let us suppose that the overall* syntactic behavior of the subject is decisive in determining case assignment, rather than the behavior of either individual coordinate" (LING40).

WOULD SAY

Engineering example [7]: "From our data, *we would not say if the original* fill soil added was much lower in C" (ENG28).

Medicine example [7]: "It would be interesting to see what *we would say on this*" (MED01)

Linguistics example [7]: "rather than on general capacities of social cognition, *we would say that social isolation* leads to a bias in the cognitive system toward detecting agents" (LING27).

UNDERSTAND

Engineering example [8]: "The main reason for this occurrence is unknown, but one *should understand that there are* a number of limitations that can influence the outcome of the results" (ENG30).

Medicine example [8]: "It is the physician's obligation to ensure that *patients understand the purposes,* procedures, alternatives, benefits" (MED02)

Linguistics example [8]: "*we understand the input to the simulation*, which of course is what matters for understanding the results of that simulation (LING30).

The examples clearly show the different uses of the cognitive verbs and the different patterns chosen by linguists, medical doctors and engineers. The data confirm that there are differences in the use of phraseological units not only in different genres but also in specific fields of knowledge. Traditionally, verb phrases are treated as following a general pattern, but in this study, variation in verb patterns can clearly be identified in different specific fields of the same genre. In this vein, Marín-Arrese (2015) identified variation in different languages, but this analysis focuses on the variation of verb phrases in academic English. The novelty of this study is to show that verb pattern identification is not as straightforward as it could seem. Differences in the use of cognitive verb patterns were identified in this study, so the findings may be considered a preliminary action that may help linguists to map verb phrases in different genres and domains.

5 Conclusions

This article has explored the presence and distribution of cognitive verbs in three domain-specific academic English, i.e. Engineering, Medicine and Linguistics. After the analysis of the data and concordances, it was proven that there are differences in specific fields of knowledge in the genre of academic papers. Linguists used cognitive verbs and different patterns to express their reflective attitudes or beliefs more frequently. This may be caused by the nature of the research related to Linguistics, as researchers show their attitude through personal forms of the pronouns, with the use of *I* and *we* and the use of cognitive verbs.

This study has shed light on the variation of verbal patterns in three different domains. This aspect is not taken into account when teaching academic English. I believe non-native researchers should be conscious of the different patterns that could be used when writing a research paper.

The first research question focused on the most frequently used cognitive verbs in Linguistics, Engineering and Medicine. Table 3 shows that *seem* was the most frequently used verb in Linguistics and Medicine. This verb expresses the attitude and beliefs of the researchers, in this case, functioning with an indirect-inferential meaning, as Marín-Arrese (2015) also noticed in her study. On the other hand, engineers prefer the use of *understand* to express their knowledge, as the verb expresses certainty about a fact.

The second research question asked about the preferred cognitive verb patterns in academic papers and if they are different depending on the discipline. As the most commonly used verb in Linguistics and Medicine was *seem*, the phraseological units of this verb are the most frequent. The patterns are: *impersonal form + seems + to me/us + adjective/that clause*; *impersonal + seems + to infinitive*; *impersonal + seems + adjective* and *impersonal + seems + likely*. Examples can be seen in [3] that show that researchers present their ideas epistemically, justifying their claims with the use of the impersonal form *it + seems*. In Engineering, the most common patterns are those connected with understand: *I/we understand + noun; I/we understand + that clause; I/we understand + which clause; I/we understand + how; I/we understand + why* and *I/we understand + whether.*

The last research question enquired if cognitive verb patterns change depending on the specific field of knowledge in academic papers and the possible causes. It was seen in Table 3 that the frequencies of cognitive verbs changed depending on the specific field of academic English. This shows that researchers have different ways of describing their findings and position themselves dissimilarly. This, in turn, shows that a particular field of study has its distinctive use of phraseological units, thus highlighting the importance of corpus analysis.

This study focused on one specific aspect of epistemic stance, i.e. cognitive verbs. The findings benefit the fields of academic writing, academic language teaching and academic English. Future research may examine phraseology in other epistemic stance acts to show how language patterns are constrained by specific discourse.

References

Alonso-Almeida, F.: Introduction to stance language. Res. Corpus Linguist. **2**, 1–5 (2015a)

Alonso-Almeida, F.: Sentential epistemic and evidential devices in Spanish and English texts on computing. In: Zamorano-Mansilla, J.R., Maíz, C., Domínguez, E., Martín de la Rosa, M.V. (eds.) Thinking Modally, pp. 383–408. Cambridge Scholars, Cambridge (2015b)

Alonso-Almeida, F., Carrió-Pastor, M.L.: Sobre la categorización de seem en inglés y su traducción en español: Análisis de un corpus paralelo. Rev. Signos **48**, 154–173 (2015)

Baranov, A., Dobrovol'skij, D.: Cognitive modeling of actual meaning in the field of phraseology. J. Pragmat. **25**, 409–429 (1996)

Biber, D., Conrad, S., Cortes, V.: If you look at: lexical bundles in university teaching and textbooks. Appl. Linguist. **25**(3), 371–405 (2004)

Brett, D., Pinna, A.: Patterns, fixedness and variability: using PoS-grams to find phraseologies in the language of travel journalism. Procedia Soc. Behav. Sci. **198**, 52–57 (2015)

Capelli, G.: I Reckon I Know How Leonardo da Vinci Must Have Felt: Epistemicity, Evidentiality and English Verbs of Cognitive Attitude. Pari Publishing, Pari, Pari (2007)

Carrió Pastor, M.L.: Cross-cultural variation in the use of modal verbs in academic English. Sky J. Linguist. **27**, 153–166 (2014)

Cortes, V.: The purpose of this study is to: connecting lexical bundles and moves in research article introductions. Engl. Acad. Purp. **12**(1), 33–43 (2013)

Cowie, A. (ed.): Phraseology: Theory, Analysis and Applications. Clarendon Press, Oxford (1998)

Charles, M., Pecorari, D., Hunston, S. (eds.): Academic Writing: At the Interface of Corpus and Discourse. Continuum, London (2009)

Charles, M.: Corpus evidence for teaching adverbial connectors of contrast: however, yet, rather, instead and in contrast. In: Kubler, N. (ed.) Corpora, Language, Teaching, and Resources: From Theory to Practice. Peter Lang, Bern (2011a)

Charles, M.: Adverbials of result: phraseology and functions in the problem-solution pattern. J. Engl. Acad. Purp. **10**, 47–60 (2011b)

Fiedler, S.: Phraseological borrowing from English into German: cultural and pragmatic implications. J. Pragmat. **113**, 89–102 (2017)

Gesuato, S.: Acknowledgements: Structure and Phraseology of Gratitude in Ph.D. Dissertations. Unipress, Padova (2008)

Granger, S., Paquot, M.: Disentangling the phraseological web. In: Granger, S., Meunier, F. (eds.) Phraseology: An Interdisciplinary Perspective, pp. 27–49. John Benjamins, Amsterdam (2008)

Halliday, M.A.K., Matthiessen, C.: An Introduction to Functional Grammar. Arnold, London (2001)

Howarth, P.A.: Phraseology in English Academic Writing: Some Implications for Language Learning and Dictionary Making. De Gruyter, Berlin (1996)

Hunston, S.: Corpora in Applied Linguistics. Cambridge University Press, Cambridge (2002)

Hunston, S., Francis, G.: Pattern Grammar: A Corpus-driven Approach to the Lexical Grammar of English, vol. 4. John Benjamins, Amsterdam (2000)

John, P., Brooks, B., Schriever, U.: Profiling maritime communication by non-native speakers: a quantitative comparison between the baseline and standard marine communication phraseology. Engl. Specif. Purp. **47**, 1–14 (2017)

Le, T.N.P., Harrington, M.: Phraseology used to comment on results in the discussion section of applied linguistics quantitative research articles. Engl. Specif. Purp. **39**, 45–61 (2015)

Marín Arrese, J.I.: Effective vs. epistemic stance, and subjectivity/ intersubjectivity in political discourse: a case study. In: Tsangalidis, A., Facchinetti, R. (eds.) Studies on English Modality. In Honour of Frank R. Palmer, pp. 23–52. Peter Lang, Bern (2009)

Marín Arrese, J.I.: Epistemic legitimizing strategies, commitment and accountability in discourse. Discourse Stud. **13**(6), 789–797 (2011)

Marín Arrese, J.I.: Epistemic stance: a cross-linguistic study of epistemic stance strategies in journalistic discourse in English and Spanish. Discourse Stud. **17**(2), 210–225 (2015)

Saber, A.: Phraseological patterns in a large corpus of biomedical articles. In: Boulton, A., Carter-Thomas, S., Rowley-Jolivet, E. (eds.) Corpus-informed Research and Learning in ESP: Issues and Applications, pp. 45–81. John Benjamins, Amsterdam (2012)

Scott, M., Tribble, C.: Textual Patterns: Key Words and Corpus Analysis in Language Education, vol. 22. John Benjamins, Amsterdam (2006)

Scott, M.: WordSmith tools (Version 5.0.) [Computer Software]. Lexical Analysis Software, Liverpool (2010)

Vincent, B.: Investigating academic phraseology through combinations of very frequent words: a methodological exploration. J. Engl. Acad. Purp. **12**, 44–56 (2013)

Cultural Models and Motivation of Idioms with the Component 'Heart' in Croatian

Zvonimir Novoselec(✉)

University of Zagreb, Ivana Lučića 3, 10 000 Zagreb, Croatia
znovosel@ffzg.hr

Abstract. Idioms as lexical constructions are from cognitive linguistic view motivated by conceptual metaphors, metonymies and cultural models [1]. I have chosen to look closely at the motivation of idioms in Croatian that contain the lexeme *srce* (eng. *heart*). The aim of this study is to show that all the 'heart idioms' are systematically motivated by the above mentioned cognitive mechanisms, primarily by cultural models which are a direct result of symbolic meaning of the heart in western civilization. My results show that all idioms are motivated by three cultural models: (1) heart as a site for emotion (2) physical model of the heart and (3) intellectual model of the heart. I will argue that the three cultural models overlap, that is, that they have fuzzy borders and that they are elaborated by conceptual metaphors. On the other hand, most conceptual metaphors are based on conceptual metonymies. I will also raise the point that cultural models, when it comes to emotions, are not completely cognitively independent.

Keywords: Cultural models · Idioms · Motivation

1 Introduction

Cultural models have been recognized as one of the cognitive mechanism, together with conceptual metaphor and conceptual metonymy, that motivate meaning of idioms [1]. The aim of this study is to show whether idioms with the component 'heart' in Croatian are motivated and by which cognitive mechanisms. We shall argue that all idioms with the component heart in Croatian are systematically motivated by a relative small number of cultural models which are, in return, elaborated by different conceptual metaphors and based on conceptual metonymies. Furthermore, borders between the cultural models are fuzzy. We shall look at some of the examples that are excerpted from the real language use of the idioms, e.g. from the Croatian national corpus.

2 Idioms and Cognitive Linguistics

Cognitive linguistics shed a new light on exploring idioms and language in general. The term conceptualization became the most important notion including the formation of meaning, so called construal. It explains how the meaning is formed in the mind of the speakers. Language capability is one of the many other human cognitive capabilities and

R. Mitkov (Ed.): Europhras 2017, LNAI 10596, pp. 337–347, 2017.
https://doi.org/10.1007/978-3-319-69805-2_24

the meaning is formed through a dynamic interaction between people, their mind and the interaction with the world. According to cognitive linguistics language units on different levels are motivated. That applies to all the constructions, including idioms. Idioms are defined as a multiple word combination which meaning as a whole is not a sum of the meaning of separate lexical items forming the combination. However, the meaning is not unmotivated. There are three main cognitive mechanisms that account for the motivation of idioms: conceptual metaphor, conceptual metonymy and cultural models.

2.1 Conceptual Metaphor

Conceptual metaphor is defined by Lakoff and Johnson [2] as one of the mechanisms that help us understand abstract meanings by making them closer to our concrete meanings through the process which they called mapping. Clearly, they are not just a part of poetic texts, but a part of our cognitive systems. Two domains are included in the mapping: source domain and target domain. Target domain is usually an abstract concept that we understand by mapping the source domain, more concrete concept, onto it. For example, in the conceptual metaphor LOVE IS A JOURNEY the concept of journey is mapped onto the concept of love thus making it easier to understand. For example, metaphoric expression *we've gone a long way* can be explained by the above mentioned metaphor. When it comes to idioms, conceptual metaphors are one of the cognitive mechanisms that motivate them. The idiom *spill the beans* is motivated by the conceptual metaphors MIND IS A CONTAINER and IDEAS ARE ENTITIES [4].

2.2 Conceptual Metonymy

Metonymies were recognized already by Aristoteles who defied them as figures of speech in which one thing stands for an another. That is called referential meaning and it took a long time to recognize that metonymies may have cognitive potential in conceptualization and were as such first recognized by Lakoff and Johnson [2]. The mapping involves just one conceptual domain. Radden and Kövecses [4] gave metonymies more conceptual meaning, not only referential. Let us look at the example in which conceptual metonymy motivates an idiomatic expression. For example, the idiom *to lose one's head* is motivated by the conceptual metonymy HEAD STANDS FOR CONTROL. If we lose our head, we are no more in control.

2.3 Cultural Models

Knowledge of the world that is shared by a community was usually referred to as folk-models. The term cultural model comes from the research done by Quin and Holland [5] in which they analyzed cultural models of marriage inherent to the speakers of American English. According to them, cultural models are highly organized knowledge of the world and they define them as '(…) presupposed, taken-for-granted models of the world that are widely shared (although not necessarily, to the exclusion of other, alternative models) by the members of a society and that play an enormous role in their understanding of the world and their behavior in it' [5]. Cultural models are also one of the mechanisms that motivate meanings of idioms. The motivation can be synchronic - for example, the knowledge of the world in which pigs don't fly helps us to understand the idiom *when pigs fly*, meaning 'never', or diachronic - the knowledge is lost nowadays but existed in the past. The idiom *to pull sb's leg* is motivated by the knowledge that in the past relatives to the people who were about to be hanged, pulled their leg from the chair they were standing on in order to end their sufferings sooner.

The question that have been raised is whether the cultural models are cognitively independent, that is, whether they exist on its own, without metaphorical and metonymical mappings. Quinn and Holland [5] and Quinn [6] argue that cultural models are cognitively independent because they consist of our knowledge which is not metaphorical.

Lakoff and Kövecses [7], on the other hand, think that that is not the case. They did a research in a cognitive model of conceptualization of anger that proved that the model is not cognitively independent – it's highly metaphorical in nature.

Kövecses [8] did a research in the concept of anger in different languages and cultures and came to the conclusion that in all of them anger is conceptualized as a pressurized container. Since that cannot be a coincidence, Kövecses [8] explains it through embodiment. He argues that in the case of cultural models for emotions, the physiological factor is the basis of motivation and therefore they cannot be completely cognitively independent, but on the other hand they share common knowledge of the anger that is elaborated by metaphors. It's his approach that we will use as our standpoint in this research.

3 Heart as a Symbol

Heart is the central organ in the body that pumps the blood and as such is one of the vital organs. We are not interested in the organic function of the heart, but its cultural-anthropological perception. Such understanding is necessarily non-scientific and is a part of the so-called naive picture of the world. For example, the shape of the heart that we find at the first drawings in the caves do not correspond to its real form. However, we will see that this is a part of deeply rooted cultural knowledge that surpasses scientific explanations, and even today the hearts as a symbol of love is shown in a non-scientific form (e.g., a heart that is bleeding or pierced by an arrow). In today's Western cultures the dualism of the heart and the mind is often emphasized. The heart is considered to be the seat of emotions and the mind of reason. The beginnings of dualism between the mind and the heart occurs in ancient Greece, but not in such a prominent dualistic relationship as today. Greek philosophers have dealt with the question which part of the body is the center of the soul - the heart or the brain. It is interesting that those who thought that the heart was the center of the soul, put in the heart both emotions and reason [9]. The symbol of the heart as a spiritual-emotional center and the symbol of divine love for God in Europe began with the influence of the Bible [10]. The dualism between the heart as a site for emotions and the mind as a site for reason began in the 17th century with Descartes and rationalism. Interesting enough, the shift could be seen linguistically. For example, the middle Dutch idiom *bi der herten leren* (eng. learn sth by heart) in the meaning of 'learn sth by heart' was replaced by *uit het hoofd leren* (eng. learn sth by head). On the other hand, the English idiom *learn* sth *by heart* is used even today [9]. The dualism of the heart as a site for emotion and a site for reason give rise to two cultural models that are consciously or unconsciously present in our mind today.

4 Methodology and Corpus

For the purpose of this research 110 idioms have been excerpted from the two Croatian phraseological dictionaries: *Frazeološki rječnik hrvatskog ili srpskog jezika*[1] and *Hrvatski frazeološki rječnik*[2]. Since the aim of this research is corpus-driven, we looked at the examples of real usage of the excerpted idioms in the Croatan National Corpus[3] and got 888 examples. The Corpus consist of 1,3 million tokens and is compiled mostly from Croatian daily and weekly newspapers and magazines and from the national literature. All the idioms and the usage examples from the corpus are also translated into English. Due to the lack of space, only most interested examples from the cognitive perspective have been chosen.

5 Cultural Model of Feelings

The cultural model of feelings consists of our knowledge of how we show feelings or how we can notice them. Some feelings are visible on the face, on the posture or in the gestures: EMOTION IS A PHYSICAL SENSATION [11], while some are not: EMOTION IS AN INTERNAL SENSATION [11] As we have already shown most of the human feelings lies in the heart. It is a part of prescientific conceptualization of the world that is extremely productive as one of the cognitive mechanisms that motivates meanings of the idioms.

5.1 Heart is a Container

The heart can be conceptualized as a container. The container schema is one of the fundamental metaphorized conceptual schemas that motivate metaphorical mappings based on direct bodily experience. People can also be conceptualized as a container that are by their skin separated from the outer world. Since the feelings are in ourselves, not outside the body, they can be conceptualized as the contents of the container: EMOTION IS A SUBSTANCE IN A CONTAINER [11].

The basis of conceptualization is a conceptual metaphor HEART IS A CONTAINER FOR FEELINGS [12], that is an elaboration of the conceptual metaphor HEART IS A CONTAINER. In these conceptualizations, we observe other cognitive mechanisms, such as conceptual metaphor, HEART IS A CONTAINER FOR

[1] Matešić, J. Frazeološki rječnik hrvatskoga ili srpskog jezika. Školska knjiga, Zagreb (1982).

[2] Menac, A., Fink-Arskovski, Ž., Venturin, R. Hrvatski frazeološki rječnik. Naklada Ljevak, Zagreb (2003).

[3] www.hnk.ffzg.hr, search engine at http://filip.ffzg.hr/cgi-bin/run.cgi/first_form, both last accessed 2016/8/6.

FEELINGS [11], and all metaphorical conceptualizations are based on the conceptual metonymy of HEART STANDS FOR PERSON [13].

nositi *koga, što* u srcu (to carry *sth, sb* in the heart)

No, mi u srcu nosimo medalju s ovoga prvenstva.

But in our hearts we carry a medal from this championship.

Za slobodu smo se digli, i svaki je nosi u srcu, u ruci.

We rose up for freedom, and each one of us bear it in the heart, in the hand.

If we have or bear something or somebody in our hearts, we love and cherish it, and at the same time we feel an inextricable attachment. In the examples it is a homeland, championship and freedom that we have/bear in our hearts. Of all the examples in the corpus, most of them refer to localities, feelings and persons in the heart. This is a very metaphorical conceptualization motivated by the metaphor HEART IS A CONTAINER FOR FEELINGS [12] and EMOTIONS ARE A SUBSTANCE IN A CONTAINER [11]. The conceptual metaphors are based on metonymies: HEART STANDS FOR PERSON [13] and HEART STANDS FOR FEELINGS [12].

ubosti *koga* u srce (to stab *sb* in the heart)

Doživljavam svaki neuspjeh svoje momčad kao

da me netko ubode nožem u srce.

I experience every failure of my team as if someone

was stabbing me with a knife in the heart.

The emotional pain as heart-stabbing in the container is conceptualized by physical pain as an emotional by metaphorical mapping EMOTIONAL HARM IS PHYSICAL INJURY [14]. The conceptual basis for such metaphorical mapping is the metonymy HEART STANDS FOR PERSON [13] and EMOTIONAL PAIN IS PHYSICAL PAIN [15].

However, examples from the corpus show that we don't deal with emotional pain that would be a result of love or affection because the agent is not a person nor his or hers actions, but of a dynamic movement of an instrument (a knife) that provokes a sense of emotional pain.

otvoriti *komu* svoje srce (to open *one's* heart to *sb*)

Sto puta bila se Dragutinu pružila prilika da joj posve otvori svoje srce, da joj kaže koliko je ljubi i obožava.

For hundred times Dragutin was given an opportunity to open his heart to her completely, to tell her how much he loves and adores her.

If we open our heart, we show our deepest feelings in it. The corpus shows that the heart can be opened to other people or something specific, such as letters or messages, although the largest number of examples in the corpus show that we open our heart to another person. The heart is conceptualized as a prototypical container that can be opened and we can have a look into it, that is, into its content: EMOTIONS ARE A SUBSTANCE IN A CONTAINER [11].

5.2 Heart is a Site for Emotions

There are numerous idioms in which the heart symbolizes a site for emotion in the broadest sense, but it is not conceptualized as a prototypical container. This means that nothing is in the heart nor goes into the heart or comes out of it. In these idioms the metonymic relationship to the conceptual metonymy HEART STANDS FOR PERSON [13] is stronger than in that of the container examples.

nemati srca (not have a heart)

Taj čovjek nema srca ni za koga i zato je jako opasan.

That man doesn't have a heart for anybody and therefore is very dangerous.

If we don't have heart, we are completely emotionally cold as is seen from the example above. The heart is conceptualized as a site for emotions in its broadest sense without specific metaphorical elaborations.

Conceptualization of intensity

nasmijati se od srca (to laugh from the heart)

Antičević-Marinović preuzela ministarsku dužnost. Na pitanje trebamo li joj čestitati, ili joj uputiti riječi utjehe, ministrica se nasmijala od srca.

Antičević-Marinović took over the minister duty. Being asked whether to congratulate her or express words of compassion, the minister laughed from the heart.

The conceptualization of intensity profiles the wholeness of the heart in the way that we take actions with the deepest emotional engagement. The idiom *from the heart* can be found in Croatian phraseological dictionaries only within one collocation – the verb phrase 'to laugh from the heart'. The conceptualization in elaborated with the metaphor INTENSITY IS QUANTITY [8].

Conceptualization of pressure

svaliti se komu na srce (*sth* tumbles down on *sb's* heart)

Ljubomor, težak kao gora, svalio mu se na srce.

Jealousy, heavy as a mountain, tumbled down on his heart.

If something tumbles down on our heart, we suffer terrible emotional discomfort and pain. The heart is conceptualized metaphorically as a site for feelings on which all emotional burden has been loaded off. Burden is a source domain in the conceptual metaphor DIFFICULTIES ARE BURDENS [11], that is in its elaboration EMOTIONAL DIFFICULTIES ARE BURDENS [11].

Conceptualization of hardness

biti kamena srca (to be stone-hearted)

(...) istaknuo prijetvornost vlasti i Crkve, pogotovo nadbiskupa Bozanića, kojeg je nazvao 'čovjekom kamena srca' (...)

(...) pointed out the dissembling of the government and the church, especially of the archbishop Bozanić whom he called 'a stone-hearted man' (...)

In the conceptualization of the heart as a stone we profile its hardness and coldness. The stone itself is though not necessarily cold. However, we would say that this is a prototype characteristic of stones, because we can find it in other phraseological constructions, such as *cold as a stone*. Based on the linguistic data, we argue that the perceived coldness of a stone functions in return as a source domain of the conceptual metaphor EMOTION IS COLDNESS [11] which motivates the idiom together with the conceptual metonymy HEART STANDS FOR FEELINGS [12].

Conceptualization of size

imati veliko srce (to have a big heart)

Još ne znamo koliko smo novca uspjele sakupiti, ali se nadamo iznosu od 400 tisuća kuna. U svakom slučaju Zagrepčani su ponovno pokazali da imaju veliko srce.

We still don't know how much many we managed to raise, but we hope about 400 thousand kuna. In any case, the people of Zagreb has once again shown that they have a big heart.

To have a big heart means to be extremely generous. Conceptual metaphors that underlie the idioms is GENEROSITY IS CHANGE IN SIZE together with the conceptual metonymy HEART STANDS FOR PERSON [13].

Conceptualization of pureness

biti čista srca (to be of a pure heart)

Za osudu su svi oni koji gaze dostojanstvo svih nas što smo čista srca stali braniti domovinu.

For condemnation are all those who trample on the dignity of all of us who with a pure heart began to defend our homeland.

People with pure hart are uncorrupted and honest. The concept of pureness is profiled and becomes a conceptual domain in the conceptual metaphor HEART IS PURENESS. Pureness is symbolically often referred to innocence. The idiom and the underlying metaphor are in the above example used as a counterpart to war. The basis for the metaphorical mapping is the conceptual metonymy HEART STANDS FOR FEELINGS [12].

5.3 Heart is an Object

slomiti komu srce (to break sb's heart)

Ne mogu reći da mi nitko nije uspio slomiti srce, ali posao mi je uvijek bio najvažniji.

I cannot say that nobody has broken my heart, but my job has always been most important to me.

Kelly je priznao da je on bio izvor jedne sporne BBC-jeve vijesti o Iraku, 'slomio mu je srce', rekla je njegova udovica.

Kelly admitted that he was the source of one controversial BBC news on Iraq. 'he broke his heart', said his widow.

The heart is conceptualized as a fragile object [12] - it is possible to manipulate it, and the heart as a seat of the human affective world is extremely sensitive to every form of manipulation resulting in emotional pain. Thus, the cognitive mechanisms in these examples are the conceptual metaphors HEART IS A FRAGILE OBJECT [12] which is the elaboration of conceptual metaphors HEART IS AN OBJECT [12], and the conceptual metonymies HEART STANDS FOR FEELINGS [12] and EMOTIONAL PAIN IS PHYSICAL PAIN that is an elaboration of the conceptual metaphor EMOTIONAL DAMAGE IS PHYSICAL DAMAGE [11].

pokloniti komu svoje srce (to give one's heart away to sb)

Ja ti velim, i sto puta velim, da je Sofija samo jednome poklonila srce, a taj je profesor Vinko.

I tell you, tell you for hundred times, that Sofia gave her heart away only to one man, and he is professor Vinko.

We conceptualize the heart as a valuable object that we can give to those who have deserved our love or special affection. By giving away our heart, we give away part of ourselves.

Cognitive mechanisms that underlie this idiom are the conceptual metaphor HEART IS AN VALUABLE OBJECT [12] that is an elaboration of the metaphor HEART IS AN OBJECT [12], and conceptual metonymies HEART STANDS FOR FEELINGS [12], HEART STANDS FOR PERSON [13] and PART FOR WHOLE [4].

6 Physical Model of the Heart

Pre-scientific view of the world about the function of the heart and its position in the body is the conceptual basis of motivation. It is the knowledge that the heart is mostly metaphorically conceptualized as a living organism [12]. It should be said that some of the above mentioned knowledge is scientifically based, but this kind of knowledge need not scientific confirmation because they are even visible to the eye (for example, the heart really beats, bleeds if it is cut, we know where the chest is located).

kuca komu srce za kim, za čim

Vi, domine admodum reverende, ljubite brata, ljubite njegovu djecu, za njih kuca vam srce živo.

You, domine admodum reverende, love your brother, love his children, for them your hearts beat lively.

If our heart beats for somebody we feel undoubtedly strong affection for that person. The conceptualization of the heart is based on the metonymy A HEARTBEAT STANDS FOR EMOTION which is in direct correlation with the physiological function of the heart. However, the conceptualization is highly metaphorical because the heart is conceptualized as a site for emotions [12].

skoči komu srce (sb's heart leaps)

Skoči mu srce od nade, zapovjedi svojoj četi da se poreda i bude spremna svaki čas na njegovu zapovijed.

His heart leaps of hope and he commands his troop to line up and be ready every moment for his command.

The heart cannot leap so this is a personification in which hearts is seen as a living being. As such, the conceptualization is extremely metonymical – HEART STANDS FOR PERSON [13]. Personifications are the most metonymical conceptualization in all cultural models. The heart leaps in the direction above its usual placement in the body which gives rise to the conceptual metaphor MORE IS UPP [2] and thus its elaboration HAPPY IS UPP [2].

7 Intellectual Model of the Heart

In the intellectual model of the heart we have placed those 'heart idioms' that have to do with the mentioned dichotomy between the heart and the mind, or better to say, those in which heart can be seen as a remnant of the site for reason. We'll represent two of them.

usjeći se *komu* u srce (to become carved in *sb's* heart)

Pojedini prizori iz Svetog pisma usjekli su mi se srce i to sam htjela.

Some scenes from the Bible became carved in my heart, and that's what I wanted.

We don't want to forget something that is carved in our heart. It is obvious then that the heart is conceptualized as a site for memory, but not for 'pure' memory, more for something what we would call emotional memory.

The same mechanism is also seen in the following idiom:

primati *koga* srcu (to take *sb* to heart)

To je nama pouka iz Strasbourga koju valja pomno proučiti i uzeti k srcu.

This is a lesson to us from Strasbourg which should be carefully studied and taken to heart.

We take something to heart we don't want to forget. It is again a clear case of emotional memory. The idiom is then, in return, motivated by the conceptual metaphor HEART FOR EMOTIONAL MEMORY that we regard as an elaboration of the conceptual metaphor HEART STANDS FOR MEMORY [16]. The conceptualization of the heart is also in both idioms motivated by conceptual metonymies HEART STANDS FOR FEELINGS [12] and HEART STANDS FOR PERSON [13].

8 Conclusion

The conceptual analysis of idioms with the component 'heart' in Croatian showed that there are three cultural models that motivate their meaning: cultural model of feelings, physical model of the heart and intellectual model of the heart. Each model is based on conventional knowledge about the heart, the knowledge which the speakers may or may not be consciously aware. Each model is elaborated by numerous metaphorical elaborations.

The cultural model of feelings symbolizes a person's emotional world and conceptualizes feelings like generosity, love, affection, pain, pleasure etc. The most examples from the corpus belong to this model.

In the physical model of the heart, heart's physiological features are metaphorically profiled in conceptualizations, in the mental imagery or in personification. In this model the metonymical basis for metaphorical conceptualizations is most obvious.

The intellectual model of the heart emphasizes the conceptualization of the heart from the past when the heart was seen as a site for memory. In Croatian there are no so direct conceptualization as in English *learn* sth *by heart*, but nonetheless we put in our hearts something we are emotionally attached to and something we don't want to forget. We defined it as emotional memory.

However, borders between the models are fuzzy – each model deals with emotions and conceptualizations depends on what the speaker wants to profile.

We have shown that the cultural models are highly dependent on conventional, folk knowledge. and in this respect they are not cognitively independent. They are furthermore elaborated by numerous metaphors who are very often metonymically based. Taking all we have said into account, the Kövecses [8] definition of cultural models, when it comes to emotions, stand.

References

1. Kövecses, Z.: Metaphor: A Practical Introduction. Oxford University Press, Oxford (2002)
2. Lakoff, G., Johnson, M.: Metaphors We Live By. The University of Chicago Press, Chicago-London (1987)
3. Gibbs, R.W.: The Poetics of Mind: Figurative Thought, Language, and Understanding. Cambridge University Press, Cambridge (1994)

4. Radden, G., Kövecses, Z.: Towards a theory of metonymy. In: Panther, K.U., Radden, G. (eds.) Metonymy in Language and Thought, pp. 17–59. John Benjamins Publishing Co., Amsterdam, Philadelphia (1999)
5. Quinn, N., Holland, D.: Cultural Models in Language and Thought. Cambridge University Press, Cambridge (1987)
6. Quinn, N.: The cultural basis of metaphor. In: Fernandez, J. (ed.) Beyond Metaphor: The Theory of Tropes in Anthropology, pp. 56–93. Stanford University Press, Stanford (1991)
7. Lakoff, G., Kövceses, Z.: The cognitive model of anger inherent in American english. In: Quinn, N., Holland, D. (eds.) Cultural Models in Language and Thought, pp. 195–221. Cambridge University Press, Cambridge (1987)
8. Kövecses, Z.: Metaphor and the folk understanding of anger. In: Russell, J.A. (ed.) Everyday Conceptions of Emotion, pp. 49–71. Kluwer, Dordrecht (1995)
9. Foolen, A.: The heart as a source of semiosis: The case of Dutch. In: Sharifan, F., Dirven, R., You, N. (eds.) Culture, Body and Language, pp. 373–395. Mouton de Gruyter, Berlin, New York (2008)
10. Chevalier, J., Gheerbrant, A.: Rječnik simbola. Naklada Jesenski i Turk, Zagreb (2007)
11. Kövecses, Z.: Metaphor and Emotion: Language, Culture, and Body: Human Feeling. Cambridge University Press, Cambridge, New York (2003)
12. Niemeier, S.: Straight from the heart – metonymic and metaphorical explorations. In: Barcelona, A. (ed.) Metaphor and Metonymy at the Crossroads: A Cognitive Perspective, pp. 195–213. Mouton de Gruyter, Berlin, New York (2003)
13. Yu, N.: The Chinese Heart in a Cognitive Perspective: Culture, Body and Language. Mouton de Gruyter, Berlin (2009)
14. Lakoff, G., Espenson, J., Schwartz, A.: Master metaphor list. Second draft copy. Cognitive Linguistics Group, University of California Berkeley (1991)
15. Kövecses, Z.: Metaphors of Anger, Pride and Love: A Lexical Approach to the Structure of Concepts. John Benjamins, Philadelphia/Amsterdam (1986)
16. Takács, I. C.: Idioms of body parts in English. Doctoral thesis. 'Babes-Bolyai' University, Cluj-Napoca (2014)

Variation of Adjectival Slots in *kao* ('as') Similes in Croatian: A Cognitive Linguistic Account

Jelena Parizoska[1(✉)] and Ivana Filipović Petrović[2]

[1] Faculty of Teacher Education, University of Zagreb, Zagreb, Croatia
jelena.parizoska@ufzg.hr

[2] Croatian Academy of Sciences, Zagreb, Croatia
ifilipovic@hazu.hr

Abstract. This paper deals with variation of Croatian similes which follow the pattern adjective + *kao* ('as') + noun (e.g. *crven kao rak* lit. red as a crab 'having red skin or cheeks'). Previous studies have mostly focused on noun variations and their semantic relations with adjectives (e.g. *crven kao rak/paprika* lit. red as a crab/pepper), while variation in the adjective slot has not been explored. Corpus data suggest that adjectival slots also vary and that variant realizations are not restricted solely to adjectives. The aim of this paper is to show that variations of adjectival slots reflect different construals of the conceptual content of similes and to give a cognitive linguistic account of the mechanisms underlying this process. We performed a study of 98 adjectival similes in the Croatian web corpus hrWaC. The results show that adjectival slots can be filled by adjectives, adverbs and verbs (e.g. *pocrvenjeti kao rak* lit. turn red as a crab 'be sunburnt or embarrassed'). Furthermore, adjectival slots may not be filled altogether or their lexical components vary widely, both of which suggest that similes undergo subjectification (in the Langackerian sense). This indicates that variation is dependent on the interplay of semantic and grammatical factors.

Keywords: Similes · Variation · Adjectival slots · Corpus · Croatian

1 Introduction

Similes are conventionalized expressions which assert a similarity relation between two entities – traditionally labelled the topic and the vehicle [1–5] – and the comparison is signaled by a preposition, e.g. *as* or *like* in English, *wie* in German, *comme* in French, *как* in Russian, etc. The typical pattern is adjective + preposition + noun, for example *(as) clear as crystal* in English, in which the noun identifies the vehicle whose salient property is attributed to the topic, and the adjective expresses the property – the tertium comparationis or the tertium for short – that provides the basis for comparison.[1]

In Croatian similes are signaled by the preposition *kao* ('as') which is commonly shortened to *ko* in informal and spoken language. The typical structure is adjective + *kao* + noun, e.g. *tvrd kao kamen* (lit. hard as stone 'very hard'), *lukav kao lisica*

[1] We will adopt Norrick's [1] labels the vehicle and the tertium for convenience.

R. Mitkov (Ed.): Europhras 2017, LNAI 10596, pp. 348–362, 2017.
https://doi.org/10.1007/978-3-319-69805-2_25

(lit. cunning as a fox 'very cunning'). The other common structure is verb + *kao* + noun, e.g. *spavati kao beba* (lit. sleep like a baby 'sleep very well'), *raditi kao konj* (lit. work like a horse 'work very hard'). Less common patterns are nominal groups, e.g. *vrućina kao u paklu* (lit. heat like in hell 'scorching heat') and constructions in which the tertium is not expressed explicitly, e.g. *biti kao grom* (lit. be like thunder 'terrific') as in *auto je ko grom* ('the car is terrific').

Studies of similes in different languages have shown that they have relatively stable lexical components and syntactic structure [6–8]. Even so, they do exhibit variation to a certain degree. For instance, in adjectival similes variation is common in the noun slot, e.g. *white as a sheet/ghost* ('very pale') in English; *ljut kao ris/pas* (lit. angry as a lynx/dog 'very angry') in Croatian; *голодный как волк/собака* (lit. hungry as a wolf/dog 'very hungry') in Russian. Previous studies and corpus data show that adjectival slots also vary, e.g. *thin/skinny as a rake* ('very thin'); *crn/taman kao noć* (lit. black/dark as night 'very dark'); *чистый/прозрачный как кристалл* (lit. clean/clear as crystal 'completely transparent').

In Croatian there is also evidence of adjectival similes in which the tertium may not be expressed. For instance, *gol kao od majke rođen* (lit. naked as if s/he has just been born by mother 'stark naked') commonly occurs without the adjective *gol* ('naked') as in *slikala se kao od majke rođena* ('she posed naked for a photo shoot'). Even though vehicles in similes are conventionally associated with specific features and therefore form stable collocations with adjectives and verbs, some *kao* + noun structures occur with a wide range of items that do not belong to a specific lexical set. For example, *kao pas* (lit. like a dog) is used to make a number of adjectival and verbal similes, some of which include *gladan kao pas* (lit. hungry as a dog 'very hungry'), *lagati kao pas* (lit. lie like a dog 'lie boldly'), *ljubomoran kao pas* (lit. jealous as a dog 'extremely jealous') and *umoran kao pas* (lit. tired as a dog 'very tired').

Although there are a number of studies of conventionalized similes in Croatian and other languages, variability of adjectival slots has not been explored. The results of previous studies and corpus data suggest that adjectival slots are neither fixed nor restricted solely to adjectives, and that the tertium may not be expressed explicitly. In addition, in some similes lexical components in the adjective slot vary widely and do not belong to a specific set. This raises the following questions:

1. What types of lexical items occur in the adjective slot?
2. What is the nature of the semantic relation between the vehicle and the types of variant realizations of the adjective slot?
3. What mechanisms are involved in the variation of the adjective slot?

The aim of this paper is to show that variant realizations of the adjective slot reflect different construals of the conceptual content of similes and to give a cognitive linguistic account of the mechanisms involved in this process. More specifically, using data from the Croatian web corpus hrWaC, we will show that conceptual content may be construed as a nonprocessual relation or as an event, which is expressed by lexical units belonging to different word classes. We will also show that similes in which the tertium is not expressed as well as those in which the realizations of the adjective slot vary widely both occur as a result of subjectification (in the Langackerian sense). This indicates that variation of adjectival slots in similes is dependent on the interplay of semantic and structural factors.

The paper is organized as follows. Section 2 deals with the theoretical points concerning the structural and semantic properties of adjectival similes and their variability. Sections 3 and 4 present the methods and results of the corpus study. Section 5 is a general discussion of the results. The final section is the conclusion, which also outlines avenues for further research.

2 Theoretical Background

Conventionalized similes relate a topic and a vehicle, the latter of which is typically expressed by a noun. It has been shown that nouns which are commonly used to form similes belong to a relatively small semantic set – typically animals, plants and artefacts [7, 9] – which indicates that they are strongly associated with particular salient properties of the entities they designate. In Croatian and a number of other languages, the salient property of the vehicle which is applied to the topic is most commonly expressed by an adjective.

The meanings of adjectival similes correspond to the meanings of their component adjectives. In some cases the adjective retains its literal meaning and refers to a property which is directly experienced, e.g. snow being white in *bijel kao snijeg* (lit. white as snow 'very white') or to a property that is conventionally associated with the vehicle, e.g. bulls being strong in *jak kao bik* (lit. strong as a bull 'very strong') and mules being opinionated in *tvrdoglav kao mazga* (lit. stubborn as a mule 'very stubborn'). In some similes the adjective meaning is metaphorical, e.g. *čist kao suza* (lit. clean as a teardrop 'completely honest or legal') and *jasno kao dan* (lit. clear as day 'obvious').

Even though conventionalized similes have stable forms, they are nevertheless prone to variation. Corpus-based studies of English similes have shown that items which follow the pattern (*as*) + adjective + *as* + noun tend to be relatively fixed and contain lexical items that belong to a restricted set, while patterns with *like* (e.g. (verb) + *like* + noun) are lexically more flexible [10, 11]. Computational studies of English similes show that they are often creatively exploited in discourse, especially to achieve an ironic tone [12, 13].

In adjectival similes noun variation is the commonest type: the same adjective may occur with alternating nouns and variant realizations have identical or similar meanings. The Croatian web corpus hrWaC provides the following examples of similes referring to speed of movement which contain the adjective *brz* ('fast') and varying nouns: *brz kao munja* (lit. fast as lightning), *brz kao metak* (lit. fast as a bullet), *brz kao zec* (lit. fast as a rabbit), *brz kao strijela* (lit. fast as an arrow) and *brz kao vjetar* (lit. fast as the wind). There is also evidence of adjective variation (e.g. *black/dark as night* in English), which seems to be less common. In some languages there is widespread occurrence of noun-adjective compounds in which the tertium and the vehicle are inverted [7, 14, 15]. A case in point are English compounds such as *crystal-clear* and *rock-solid* which occur alongside the cognate similes *clear as crystal* and *solid as a rock*. Minor types of variation include the use of comparative adjectives (*colder than ice*), insertion of lexical items (*honest as the day/honest as the day is long*), forms with optional items (*točan kao (švicarski) sat* lit. punctual as a (Swiss) watch 'very punctual') and parallel forms without the adjective (*quick like lightning/like lightning*).

As regards variation of adjectival similes in Croatian, previous studies have mainly focused on realizations of the noun slot and their semantic relations with adjectives [6, 16]. For example, the variant forms *crven kao krv/paprika/rak* (lit. red as blood/a pepper/a crab) all designate color, but relate to different entities. The expression *crven kao krv* (lit. red as blood) designates the color of an object (e.g. a red rose, red lips), whereas *crven kao paprika* (lit. red as a pepper) and *crven kao rak* (lit. red as a crab) are used of humans and designate redness in the face and/or body caused by physiological processes or embarrassment. Variability of adjectival slots has not been explored and isolated examples are provided merely to illustrate a motivating link between the noun and varying adjectives, e.g. *blijed/bijel kao kreda* (lit. pale/white as chalk 'extremely pale'). Omazić [6] lists pairs of cognate verbal and adjectival similes that share a common vehicle and labels them synonymous expressions rather than variant forms of an individual item. Examples include *crven kao rak* (lit. red as a crab 'very red in the face') and *pocrvenjeti kao rak* (lit. go red as a crab 'go red in the face'); *problijedjeti kao krpa* (lit. go white as a rag 'go white in the face') and *bijel kao krpa* (lit. white as a rag 'extremely pale'). This also raises the issue of whether such items are individual expressions or variations of a single item.[2] We take the view that pairs or groups of items which have the same conceptual content and share a common vehicle are variant realizations of a single simile.

Other than listing the possibilities for variation, previous studies of similes in Croatian have not investigated the semantic relation between the vehicle and the lexical items which occur in the adjective slot. Furthermore, most studies are based on relatively small, manually collected samples. We will therefore conduct a corpus study of similes to explore the variation of adjectival slots and give a cognitive linguistic account of the mechanisms involved in this process. Given cognitive grammar's central claim that grammar and lexicon form a continuum, structural changes reflect differences in meaning. More specifically, the conceptual structure of word classes will vary from completely thing-like (nouns) to completely relational (verbs). Relational expressions – adjectives, adverbs, verbs and prepositions – may have a different number of focal participants: the primary focal participant is referred to as the trajector, and the second participant is referred to as the landmark [17], which roughly correspond to arguments in the traditional sense. Finally, elements may undergo different degrees of subjectification [18, 19], which means that their conceptual content is attenuated, whereby what was once part of the objective content of an item now needs to be reconstructed by the conceptualizer.

3 Methods

We performed a study of adjectival similes in the hrWaC corpus using the Sketch Engine. The corpus consists of 1.2 billion words and contains texts crawled from the .hr domain [20]. The texts comprise newspapers, magazines, fiction, online

---

[2] For a discussion on different approaches to variation see [7, 10].

forums, blogs and comments sections on news media websites. This corpus was chosen for the study because journalistic texts and online communication forms are an ample source of idiom variation. Furthermore, forums and comments sections are probably the closest to spoken language and provide evidence of creative use of figurative expressions.

The study was performed in three steps. First, we searched for nouns which occur with the preposition *kao* ('as') and its shortened form *ko* within the span of 3 words. We looked at the first 100 most frequent as well as the first 100 most characteristic noun collocates of *kao/ko* using logDice scores [21]. This combined approach was used since high frequency of occurrence does not equal high likelihood of occurrence. Non-metaphorical word combinations were manually removed and *kao/ko* + noun combinations which occur solely in verbal constructions were excluded from the study (e.g. *živjeti kao car* (lit. live like an emperor) 'enjoy a lavish style of living'). In this way we obtained 59 *kao/ko* + noun structures.

Next, we looked at adjectives co-occurring with *kao/ko* + noun structures to find conventionalized adjectival similes. The significance threshold was set at 5 in line with Evert [22], as word combinations which occur in a corpus five or more times are not random occurrences. In this way we obtained 98 conventionalized adjectival similes, some of which contain the same nouns (e.g. *crn kao noć* lit. black as night 'very dark'; *glup kao noć* lit. stupid as night 'very stupid'; *ružan kao noć* lit. ugly as night 'very ugly'). Finally, in order to find variant realizations of adjectival slots, for each of the 98 conventionalized adjectival similes we looked at the types of lexical items co-occurring with *kao/ko* + noun within the span of 5 words.

4 Results

Three types of results were obtained. Firstly, of the 98 similes, 57 (58%) have variant realizations of their adjectival slots and the adjective alternates with one or more lexical items. Secondly, adjectival slots can be filled by items which belong to the same word class (adjectives) or different word classes (verbs and/or adverbs). Finally, some similes have variant forms without the tertium (i.e. they occur as *kao/ko* + noun) and some *kao/ko* + noun structures occur with a range of adjectives and verbs which are not restricted to a specific lexical set. Both are indicative of similes undergoing subjectification (in the Langackerian sense). We will look at each group of results in turn.

4.1 Variability of Adjectival Slots

Of the 98 similes, 41 (42%) occur in a single form. Some examples include *sam kao duh* (lit. alone as a ghost 'without anyone around'), *ćorav kao kokoš* (lit. blind as a hen 'unable to see well'), *lud kao kupus* (lit. crazy as cabbage 'totally crazy'), *slobodan kao ptica (na grani)* (lit. free as a bird (on a branch) 'completely free').

57 similes (58%) have one or more variant realizations of the adjective slot. Each type of variant form has been counted separately. There are 113 types of variant forms altogether. This is shown in Table 1.

Table 1. Variant realizations of the adjective slot.

Types of variant forms	Number of examples	%
adjective + *kao* + noun	58	51.3%
verb + *kao* + noun	41	36.3%
adverb + *kao* + noun	7	6.2%
noun + *kao* + noun	7	6.2%
Total	113	100%

Table 1 shows that conventionalized adjectival similes occur in several different types of variant forms. Of the 98 similes, 16 have one variation type and occur as constructions with alternating adjectives, e.g. *nervozan/živčan kao pas* (lit. nervous/highly-strung as a dog 'very nervous'), *ružan/gadan kao lopov* (lit. ugly/hideous as a thief 'very ugly'), *crn/taman/mračan kao noć* (lit. black/dark as night 'very dark'). One simile, *čist kao suza* (lit. clean as a teardrop), exhibits fixedness or variation of the adjective slot depending on the adjective meaning. If the meaning is literal, *čist* ('clean') alternates with *bistar* ('transparent') and the simile refers to substances (e.g. water). If the adjective meaning is metaphorical ('legal' or 'straightforward') the simile occurs in a single form and is used with abstract nouns such as *pobjeda* ('victory') and *situacija* ('situation').

31 similes occur in two types of structures. Of these, 30 have adjectival and verbal forms. Examples include *pijan kao svinja* (lit. drunk as a pig 'very drunk') and *napiti se kao svinja* (lit. get drunk like a pig 'get very drunk'); *zaljubljen kao tele* (lit. in love as a calf 'madly in love') and *zaljubiti se kao tele* (lit. fall in love like a calf 'fall madly in love'); *mokar kao miš* (lit. wet as a mouse 'soaking wet') and *pokisnuti kao miš* (lit. become soaked like a mouse 'get soaking wet'). In one instance component adjectives alternate with adverbs: *tvrdoglav/uporan kao magarac* (lit. stubborn/persistent as a donkey 'very stubborn') also occurs with the adverbs *tvrdoglavo* ('stubbornly) and *uporno* ('persistently').

9 similes have three types of variant forms. For instance, *kao puž* (lit. like a snail), which designates slow movement, occurs with adjectives, adverbs and verbs. The adjectival form *spor kao puž* (lit. slow as a snail) specifies the extent to which a person or a motor vehicle exhibits slowness. The adverb phrase *sporo kao puž* (lit. slowly like a snail) describes manner of motion (e.g. *ići sporo kao puž* lit. go slowly like a snail 'move very slowly'). Verbal forms designate events, e.g. *vući se kao puž* (lit. drag like a snail 'move very slowly') and *voziti kao puž* (lit. drive like a snail 'drive very slowly').

A minor type of variation are nominal groups. 7 similes occur as constructions which follow the pattern noun + *kao* + noun in which the first noun (i.e. the topic) varies, e.g. *glava/dupe kao trokrilni ormar* (lit. head/bum like a three door wardrobe 'huge'). One construction in this group has a fixed form and occurs with a single noun: *obraz kao opanak* (lit. a cheek like a peasant shoe) is used to describe people who are completely shameless.

In this section we have shown that the majority of similes have one or more realizations of their adjectival slots. The component adjective alternates with other adjectives, adverbs and verbs, and a small number of similes also occur as nominal groups. The specific types of items which occur in adjectival slots and their semantic relations with nouns are dealt with in the following section.

4.2 Types of Lexical Items in the Adjective Slot

Corpus data show that the adjective slot can be filled by items which belong to three word classes: adjectives, adverbs and verbs. In the first type of variation, alternating adjectives are broadly synonymous and the variant realizations have similar meanings:

(1) *snažan/jak kao lav* (lit. strong/powerful as a lion) 'very strong'
(2) *ljut/bijesan kao ris* (lit. angry/furious as a lynx) 'very angry'
(3) *tvrdoglav/uporan kao mazga* (lit. stubborn/persistent as a mule) 'very stubborn'
(4) *hladan/miran kao špricer* (lit. cool/calm as a spritzer) 'very calm and relaxed'
(5) *glup/tup/blesav kao noć* (lit. stupid/thick/silly as night) 'very stupid'

A minor type of variation is where the adjective slot is filled by antonymous adjectives and such expressions can be classified as ironic similes. For example, *dosadan kao proljev* (lit. annoying as diarrhea 'very annoying') also occurs as *zanimljiv kao proljev* (lit. interesting as diarrhea) and *zabavan kao proljev* (fun as diarrhea). All three variant forms are used to refer to annoying or boring people.

In the second type of variation, the component adjective alternates with a cognate adverb. Like their adjectival counterparts, adverbs profile nonprocessual relations. However, in contrast with adjectives, focal prominence is placed on the activity rather than the entity [17, pp. 112–117]. Consider the following examples:

(6) *Vjerujem da bih odreagirala* ***hladno kao led*** *i mirno ga zamolila da se iseli iz stana.*
'I'm sure I would react coldly (lit. coldly like ice) and calmly ask him to move out of the flat.'
(7) *Za vrijeme vožnje* ***mirno ko bubica*** *leži na stražnjem sjedalu.*
'When we're driving, she lies quietly (lit. quietly like a bug) in the back seat.'
(8) ***Uporno ko mazga*** *uvijek dokazujem da mogu sve sama.*
'I always stubbornly try to prove (lit. prove persistently like a mule) that I can do everything on my own.'

The adverb phrases in (6)–(8) assess the rate of the execution of a particular activity. Thus, *hladno kao led* (lit. coldly as ice) in (6) refers to one person acting towards another in an unfriendly fashion, *mirno kao bubica* (lit. quietly like a bug) in (7) refers to a dog lying quietly in the car, and *uporno ko mazga* (lit. persistently like a mule) in (8) designates the manner in which a person is proving a point.

In the third type of variation the component adjective alternates with one or more verbs. The adjectival form specifies a property, whereas the verbal form designates a process or a state. There are three principal subtypes of verb variations. In the first, the adjective alternates with a cognate verb:

(9) *miran kao bubica* (lit. quiet as a bug) 'very quiet'
mirovati kao bubica (lit. be quiet as a bug) 'be very quiet'
(10) *napuhan kao balon* (lit. inflated as a balloon) 'bloated' or 'conceited'
napuhati se kao balon (lit. get inflated like a balloon) 'become bloated'
(11) *crven kao rak* (lit. red as a crab) 'having red skin or cheeks'
crvenjeti se/zacrvenjeti se/pocrvenjeti kao rak (lit. turn red as a crab) 'turn red in the face' or 'one's body turns red'

The similes in (9) refer to a person who is quiet and does not make any noise. In (10) both the adjectival and the verbal form refer to a person that feels swollen (e.g. during pregnancy or after eating too much), while the adjectival form also designates an arrogant person. In (11) the adjective *crven* ('red') and the construction with the verb *pocrvenjeti* ('become red') can both refer to a person's skin which is sunburnt or to their red cheeks because they feel embarrassed. By contrast, the variant forms with the verbs *crvenjeti se* ('blush') and *zacrvenjeti se* ('turn red') are only used to designate a person whose cheeks are red because they feel embarrassed or ashamed. These examples provide evidence of how different grammatical forms reflect differences in meaning.

In the second subtype, the adjective alternates with verbs which are similar in meaning or semantically related:

(12) *brz kao metak* (lit. fast as a bullet) 'very fast'
juriti/izletjeti kao metak (lit. speed/fly out like a bullet) 'move very quickly'
(13) *sretan kao dijete* (lit. happy as a child) 'very happy'
radovati se kao dijete (lit. rejoice like a child) 'rejoice'

The variant realizations in (12) are used of an entity that is moving extremely fast and are expressed by the adjective *brz* ('fast') and motion verbs designating fast movement, respectively. In (13) the adjective *sretan* ('happy') and the verb *radovati se* ('rejoice') both refer to happiness.

In the third subtype, the component adjective alternates with semantically unrelated verbs, but there is a clear association between the verb and the feature associated with the entity denoted by the vehicle. Consider the following examples:

(14) *hrabar kao lav* (lit. brave as a lion) 'very brave'
boriti se kao lav (lit. fight like a lion) 'fight bravely'
(15) *blijed kao duh* (lit. pale as a ghost) 'extremely pale'
izgledati kao duh (lit. look like a ghost) 'look pale'

Examples (14) and (15) show that the alternating verb designates a process or a state in relation to the property assigned by the adjective – courage and pale skin, respectively. Furthermore, the examples show that the adjective slot can be filled not only by verbs which have specific meanings (*boriti se* 'fight' in 14), but also by verbs that have more schematic meanings (*izgledati* 'look' in 15). This is due to the fact that the meaning of a simile is tied to a particular feature associated with the vehicle. The corpus provides evidence of similes designating outward appearance which contain the verb *izgledati* 'look' (as in 15) and occur as parallel adjectival structures in which the adjective explicitly expresses the property that is conventionally associated with the vehicle. Examples include *širok/izgledati kao trokrilni ormar* (lit. wide/to look like a three door wardrobe) and *debeo/izgledati kao svinja* (lit. fat/to look like a pig) which are both used of people who are overweight; *sladak/izgledati kao bombon* (lit. sweet/to look like candy), used of people, objects and places that are attractive; *crven/izgledati kao rak* (lit. red/to look like a crab), used to describe people whose skin is red due to excessive sun exposure. Similarly, adjectival similes which designate motion have variant realizations with the schematic verb *ići* ('go'). For example, *spor kao puž* (lit. slow as a snail) and *brz kao metak* (lit. fast as a bullet) occur in the corpus as *ići kao puž* (lit. go like a snail 'move very slowly') and *ići kao metak* (lit. go like a bullet 'move very fast') respectively. In both cases the manner of motion is specified by the particular type of movement of the entity denoted by the vehicle.

In this section we have shown that the component adjective can be replaced by other adjectives, as well as by items belonging to different word classes, namely adverbs and/ or verbs. This reflects whether the conceptual content of a simile is construed as a nonprocessual relation or an event. The variant realizations with verbs are the most various and include cognate verbs, verbs that are similar in meaning and semantically unrelated verbs. In addition, alternating verbs may have specific or more schematic meanings, but even in the latter case their selection is dependent on the particular feature conventionally associated with the vehicle.

Let us now turn to cases in which adjectival slots are not filled altogether and those in which the items in adjectival slots vary widely and do not belong to any particular lexical set. Both could be attributed to similes undergoing subjectification. This is dealt with in the following section.

4.3 Subjectification of Similes

The corpus provides examples of similes which have variant realizations without the tertium. They commonly occur as the copulative construction with the verb *biti* ('be') in which the structure *kao* + noun functions as the complement. Consider the following examples:

(16) (…) *izuzmemo li zadnje dane uoči porođaja kada sam* ***bila kao balon***.
'(…) except for the last few days before I had my baby when I was really bloated (lit. when I was like a balloon)'

(17) *Hobotnica ispod peke im* ***je ko putar***, *topi se u ustima*.
'Their baked octopus is very soft (lit. is like butter), it melts in your mouth'

(18) *Sa susjedima treba samo lijepo. S njima* ***sam kao med***.
'You should always be nice to your neighbours. I'm super friendly to them (lit. I am with them like honey)'

Sentences (16)–(18) show that a specific property of the vehicle is selected to be the ground for similarity and the subject of the copulative construction is assigned that property. Thus, to be like a balloon is to be bloated (16), to be like butter is to be very soft (17) and to be like honey to people is to be very kind to them (18). The fact that similes occur in structures without the tertium with the highly schematic verb *biti* ('be') suggests that they have undergone subjectification, so the property of the entity denoted by the vehicle is implicitly encoded [19]. This is confirmed by the fact that the similes in (16)–(18) occur in the corpus as parallel adjectival structures in which the tertium is explicitly expressed: *napuhan kao balon* (lit. inflated like a balloon), *mekan kao putar* (lit. soft like butter) and *sladak kao med* (lit. sweet as honey), respectively. The corpus provides other examples of similes which occur as adjectival and copulative constructions with *biti* ('be'). In the latter case, the property assigned by the adjective is subjectively construed and figures only implicitly in a simile's meaning. Some examples are *točan kao sat* (lit. punctual as a clock) and *biti kao sat* (lit. be like a clock) meaning 'arriving at the expected time'; *siromašan kao crkveni miš* (lit. poor as a church mouse) and *biti kao crkveni miš* (lit. be like a church mouse) meaning 'very poor'; *dobar kao kruh* (lit. good as bread) and *biti kao kruh* (lit. be like bread) 'very kind'.

Some similes which have variant forms without the tertium occur in constructions that follow the pattern noun + *kao* + vehicle:

(19) *Kad sam mislio da je to kraj, digli smo se u zadnjim minutama i osvojili* ***bod ko kuća***.
'Just when I thought it was all over, we picked ourselves up in the last few minutes of the game and won a solid one point (lit. a point like a house)'

(20) *Mnogi to uočavaju, ali kada netko ima* ***obraz ko opanak***, *tu nema pomoći.*
'Many people have noticed this, but when a person is completely shameless (lit. when a person has a cheek like a peasant shoe), there's nothing you can do'

Sentences (19) and (20) illustrate variant forms in which the feature denoted by the vehicle is subjectified. Thus, in (19) the property implicitly specified by *ko kuća* (lit. like a house) is large size (here used in the metaphorical sense), hence winning one out of three points in a football championship is considered to be a major achievement. In (20) the structure *ko opanak* implicitly specifies the hardness of the peasant shoe, and thus *obraz ko opanak* is used metaphorically to refer to a person who is not ashamed of their bad behavior. It is worth noting that the items in (19) and (20) occur in the corpus as structures in which the property associated with the vehicle is explicitly expressed by an adjective: *velik kao kuća* (lit. big as a house) and *tvrd kao opanak* (lit. hard as a peasant shoe), respectively. However, the two items exhibit different degrees of subjectification. The expression *velik kao kuća* is used with concrete nouns to designate physical size (e.g. *kofer* 'suitcase') and with abstract nouns to designate intensity or importance (e.g. *bod* 'point', *srce* 'heart', *problem* 'problem', *ego* 'ego'). The simile *tvrd kao opanak* is used of hard objects (e.g. *meso* 'meat') and people who are stern and unyielding. The meaning of *obraz kao opanak* (lit. a cheek like a peasant shoe) has been extended to refer to a person who has no sense of shame. In comparison with *ko kuća*, which can be used with a range of nouns (e.g. *bod* 'point', *srce* 'heart', *penal* 'penalty'), the word combination *obraz ko opanak* has been constructionalized, so that *ko opanak* functions as a postmodifier in a noun phrase.

Corpus data also shows that some *kao* + noun structures occur with a range of adjectives and verbs which may not be related to any specific property conventionally associated with the entity denoted by the vehicle. This is evident in the fact that the varying constituents are not restricted to a specific lexical set. For example, *kao pas* (lit. like a dog) occurs in the following conventionalized forms (the varying items are listed by frequency of occurrence in the corpus): *umoran* ('tired'), *lagati* ('tell lies'), *ljut* ('angry'), *gladan* ('hungry'), *ljubomoran* ('jealous'), *raditi* ('work'), *živčan* ('nervous'), *bijesan* ('furious'), *ružan* ('ugly'), *nervozan* ('nervous'), *živjeti* ('live'), *vjeran* ('loyal'), *bolestan* ('ill'), *žedan* ('thirsty'), *lijen* ('lazy'), *tužan* ('sad'), *zločest* ('naughty'). These constructions show that the lexical components vary widely, which is also the result of subjectification. However, in contrast with examples (16)–(18), where a specific quality conventionally associated with the vehicle is implicitly encoded (i.e. a balloon being inflated, butter being soft and honey being sweet), in the construction *kao pas* there seems to be no particular feature that pertains to dogs exclusively other than perhaps *vjeran* ('loyal'). This could be a result of semantic bleaching [19, p. 21], so the meaning of *kao pas* has become similar to that of intensifying adverbs. For example, *umoran kao pas* (lit. tired like a dog) can be interpreted as 'very tired' and *raditi kao pas* (lit. work like a dog) as 'work a lot'.

Another example of a structure whose function is similar to that of an intensifying adverb is *kao vrag* (lit. like the devil). It occurs with a wide range of semantically unrelated items: *boljeti* ('hurt'), *skup* ('expensive'), *smrdjeti* ('stink'), *peći* ('sting'), *ružan* ('ugly'), *težak* ('heavy' and 'difficult'), *opasan* ('dangerous'). The meaning of *kao vrag* can be interpreted as 'very' (with adjectives) or 'very much/badly' (with verbs). For instance, *skup kao vrag* (lit. expensive like the devil) means 'tremendously expensive' and *boli kao vrag* (lit. it hurts like the devil) means 'it hurts really badly'. This suggests that the structure *kao vrag* (lit. like the devil) has been semantically bleached and largely lost its lexical meaning.

5 Discussion

The results of this study show that the majority of conventionalized similes which follow the pattern adjective + *kao* ('as') + noun have one or more variant realizations of their adjectival slots. The component adjective alternates with other (typically synonymous) adjectives as well as with adverbs and verbs. This shows that the conceptual content of a simile can be construed as a nonprocessual relation – expressed by adjectives and adverbs – or as a process, which is expressed by verbs. All three types of lexical items are relational expressions, but they differ in the number and nature of their focal participants [17, pp. 123-128]: adjectives and adverbs have only one participant (the trajector), while verbs profile a relation between a trajector and a landmark. Thus, a simile which occurs as an adjective phrase indicates the degree to which the trajector exhibits a particular property (e.g. *brz kao metak* lit. fast as a bullet), while a simile which has the form of an adverb phrase assesses the rate of execution of the activity the participant engages in (e.g. *doći brzo kao metak* lit. come fast as a bullet), giving trajector status to the activity itself. On the other hand, verbal forms accord focal prominence to two participants, the trajector and the landmark. For instance, *juriti kao metak* (lit. speed like a bullet) profiles an event in which the trajector moves along a path toward a goal, which is the landmark.

The results also show that alternative construals expressed by verbs are the most variable. Alternating items include cognate verbs and verbs that are similar in meaning to the component adjective. Both types of items profile events in relation to the specific property assigned by the adjective (e.g. *miran kao bubica* lit. quiet as a bug vs. *mirovati kao bubica* lit. be quiet like a bug and *šutjeti kao bubica* lit. be silent like a bug). This shows that there is a recurrent association between the vehicle and the property. Further evidence are variant realizations with schematic verbs such as *izgledati* ('look') as in *izgledati kao rak* (lit. look like a crab) and those that contain semantically unrelated verbs, e.g. *boriti se kao lav* (lit. fight like a lion) which is a variant form of *hrabar kao lav* (lit. brave as a lion). The occurrence of a particular verb relies on the strong association between the vehicle and the property expressed by the component adjective (e.g. crabs being red and lions being brave).

The findings also show that some similes have variant realizations without the tertium. We argue that this is a result of their subjectification: the property that the simile expresses is implicitly encoded and can be "recovered" from the vehicle. For instance, the property that figures implicitly in the meanings of *biti kao bombon* (lit. be like candy) and noun + *kao bombon* (as in *curetak kao bombon* lit. a young girl like candy) is sweetness, which has been extended to designate visual appeal. Further evidence in support of this argument is that similes which have variant realizations without the tertium occur in the corpus as parallel adjectival structures where the property is marked overtly, e.g. *sladak kao bombon* (lit. sweet as candy). Some subjectified similes have been constructionalized so that *kao* + noun functions as a postmodifier in a noun phrase. A case in point is the expression *obraz kao opanak* (lit. a cheek like a peasant shoe). The original meaning 'hard' (as in *tvrd kao opanak* lit. hard as a peasant shoe) has been extended to 'completely shameless'. This is in line with the results of previous studies showing that there are similes which occur solely as *kao* + noun structures, e.g. *kao grom* (lit. like thunder) 'terrific', *kao zmaj* (lit. like a dragon) 'excellent' [16]. This indicates not only that the properties they invoke are subjectively construed, but also that the motivation for their meanings has been lost.

The results also show that lexical components in adjectival slots may vary without any apparent limits and they are not restricted to a particular lexical set. A case in point are structures such as *kao pas* (lit. like a dog) and *kao vrag* (lit. like the devil), which occur with a wide range of semantically unrelated adjectives and verbs. We argue that this is also a result of subjectification. However, in comparison with similes which occur without the tertium, in the latter case the subjective construal seems to be carried one step further: subjectification has led to a loss of the semantic association between the entity denoted by the vehicle and the feature it is conventionally associated with. As a result, structures such as *kao pas* and *kao vrag* have become similar in meaning to intensifying adverbs. Furthermore, corpus evidence suggests that semantic bleaching is an ongoing process and it seems to be affecting a number of conventionalized similes which occur with a wider or different range of lexical items in their adjectival slots. For instance, *kao konj* (lit. like a horse) occurs with adjectives such as *jak* ('strong'), *glup* ('stupid'), *umoran* ('tired'), *uporan* ('persistent') and verbs such as *raditi* ('work'), *učiti* ('study'), *kašljati* ('cough') and *znojiti se* ('sweat'). Consequently, the meanings of such similes shift from lexical to more grammatical ones. Importantly, similes exhibit this change to different degrees, so some expressions are conventionalized structures, while others may yet become institutionalized. Since conventionality is a matter of degree, such expressions are evidence of language change.

6 Conclusion

This paper explored the variation of adjectival slots in Croatian similes which follow the pattern adjective + *kao* ('as') + noun. The aim was to show that variant realizations reflect different construals of the conceptual content of similes and to give a cognitive linguistic account of the mechanisms involved in this process. We performed a study of 98 similes in the hrWaC corpus. The results show that adjectival slots may be filled by lexical items which belong to three types of word classes, namely adjectives, adverbs and verbs. Furthermore, adjectival slots may not be filled altogether or they are filled by a number of semantically unrelated items. We have argued that the occurrence of those two types of constructions is a result of a more subjective construal of the relation between the vehicle and the property it is conventionally associated with. Furthermore, some *kao* + noun structures which occur with a wide range of lexical items seem to have lost their categorial properties as a result of semantic bleaching and have become similar in meaning to intensifying adverbs.

On a more general level, this study has shown that lexical variation of similes in systematic and structural changes to adjectival slots reflect differences in meaning. This indicates that the variation of similes in particular, and idiom variation in general, is dependent on the interplay of semantic and grammatical factors.

A possible avenue for further research is to investigate variation of adjectival slots using corpus data in a cross-linguistic perspective to determine the types of mechanisms underlying this process in different languages. This could show which mechanisms are universal and whether there are any that are specific to a particular group of languages. Expressing similarity through similes is a universal human ability, which raises the following question: what can structural differences in various languages tell us about the nature of this ability? For example, English conventionalized similes are signaled by two prepositions – *as* and *like* – and similes containing *like* are less fixed and restricted than those with *as* [10, pp. 149-151]. In fact, *as*-similes seem to be constructionalized. By contrast, in a number of languages (Croatian being among them) comparison is signaled by one preposition, which appears to affect the variability of similes. Furthermore, structural differences between languages (e.g. Slavic and non-Slavic) could also play a role in the occurrence of different types of variant forms. For instance, in Slavic languages the tertium is omitted altogether in a number of adjectival similes (e.g. *kao na iglama* (lit. like on needles) 'anxious' in Croatian; *как рыба в воде* (lit. like a fish in water) 'be in your element' in Russian). Subjectification of similes could also be explored cross-linguistically to establish in what ways it affects their structure and meaning. For instance, it has been shown that as a result of semantic bleaching, similes in various languages lose their lexical meaning and become similar to intensifiers, e.g. *kao pas* (lit. like a dog) in Croatian; *как чёрт* (lit. like the devil) in Russian [23]; *stone-cold* in *stone-cold sober* ('completely sober') and *stone-cold certain* ('absolutely certain') in English [24]. This could provide valuable insight into the universal mechanisms underlying idiom variation.

References

1. Norrick, N.R.: Stock similes. J. Literary Semant. **15**(1), 39–52 (1986)
2. Ortony, A.: The role of similarity in similes and metaphors. In: Ortony, A. (ed.) Metaphor and Thought, 2nd edn, pp. 342–356. Cambridge University Press, Cambridge (1993)
3. Glucksberg, S.: Understanding Figurative Language: From Metaphors to Idioms. Oxford University Press, Oxford (2001)

4. Chiappe, D., Kennedy, J.M.: Literal bases for metaphor and simile. Metaphor Symb. **16**(3–4), 249–276 (2001)
5. Chiappe, D., Kennedy, J.M., Smykowski, T.: Reversibility, aptness, and the conventionality of metaphors and similes. Metaphor Symb. **18**(2), 85–105 (2003)
6. Omazić, M.: O poredbenom frazemu u engleskom i hrvatskom jeziku. Jezikoslovlje **3**(1–2), 99–129 (2002)
7. Moon, R.: Conventionalized as-similes in English: A problem case. Int. J. Corpus Linguist. **13**(1), 3–37 (2008)
8. Mokienko, V.M. (ed.): Ustojchivye sravnenija v sisteme frazeologii [Fixed similes in the phraseological system]. LEMA, Saint Petersburg/Greifswald (2016)
9. Hanks, P.: Similes and sets: The English preposition *like*. In: Blatná, R., Petkevič, V. (eds.) Jazyky a jazykověda: Sborník k 65. narozeninám prof. Františka Čermáka. Faculty of Philosophy, Charles University, Prague (2005)
10. Moon, R.: Fixed Expressions and Idioms in English: A Corpus-Based Approach. Clarendon Press, Oxford (1998)
11. Wikberg, K.: Phrasal similes in the BNC. In: Granger, S., Meunier, F. (eds.) Phraseology: An Interdisciplinary Perspective, pp. 127–142. John Benjamins, Amsterdam/Philadelphia (2008)
12. Hao, Y., Veale, T.: An ironic fist in a velvet glove: Creative mis-representation in the construction of ironic similes. Mind. Mach. **20**, 635–650 (2010)
13. Veale, T.: A computational exploration of creative similes. In: MacArthur, F., Oncins-Martínez, J.F., Sánchez-García, M., Piquer-Píriz, A.M. (eds.) Metaphor in Use: Context, Culture, and Communication, pp. 329–344. John Benjamins, Amsterdam/Philadelphia (2012)
14. Norrick, N.R.: Semantic aspects of comparative noun-adjective compounds. In: Asbach-Schnitker, B., Roggenhofer, J. (eds.) Neuere Forschungen zur Wortbildung und Historiographie der Linguistik, pp. 145–154. Gunther Narr Verlag, Tübingen (1987)
15. Novoselec, Z., Parizoska, J.: A corpus-based study of similes and cognate adjectival forms in English, Swedish and Croatian. In: Pamies, A., Pazos Bretaña, J.M., Luque Nadal, L. (eds.) Phraseology and Discourse: Cross Linguistics and Corpus-based Approaches, pp. 101–110. Schneider Verlag, Baltmannsweiler (2012)
16. Fink-Arsovski, Ž.: Poredbena frazeologija: pogled izvana i iznutra. FF Press, Zagreb (2002)
17. Langacker, R.W.: Cognitive Grammar: A Basic Introduction. Oxford University Press, Oxford (2008)
18. Langacker, R.W.: Subjectification and grammaticization. In: Langacker, R.W. (ed.) Grammar and Conceptualization, pp. 297–315. Mouton de Gruyter, Berlin/New York (2000)
19. Langacker, R.W.: Subjectification, grammaticization, and conceptual archetypes. In: Athanasiadou, A., Canakis, C., Cornillie, B. (eds.) Subjectification: Various Paths to Subjectivity, pp. 17–40. Mouton de Gruyter, Berlin/New York (2006)
20. Ljubešić, N., Klubička, F.: {bs,hr,sr}WaC – Web corpora of Bosnian, Croatian and Serbian. In: Bildhauer, F., Schäfer, R. (eds.) Proceedings of the 9th Web as Corpus Workshop (WaC-9), pp. 29–35. Association for Computational Linguistics, Stroudsburg (2014)
21. Rychlý, P.: A lexicographer-friendly association score. In: Sojka, P., Horák, A. (eds.) Proceedings of Recent Advances in Slavonic Natural Language Processing, pp. 6–9. Masaryk University, Brno (2008)
22. Evert, S.: The Statistics of Word Cooccurrences: Word Pairs and Collocations. Ph.D. dissertation, University of Stuttgart (2005)

23. Lebedeva, L.A.: Ustojchivye sravnenija russkogo yazyka: Kratkij tematicheskij slovar' [Russian fixed similes: A short thematic dictionary]. Flinta, Moscow (2011)
24. Parizoska, J., Novoselec, Z.: Idiom variation and grammaticalization: a case study. In: Peti-Stantić, A., Stanojević, M.-M. (eds.) Language as Information, pp. 179–192. Peter Lang, Frankfurt am Main (2014)

Cognitive Processing of Multiword Expressions in Native and Non-native Speakers of English: Evidence from Gaze Data

Victoria Yaneva(✉), Shiva Taslimipoor, Omid Rohanian, and Le An Ha

Research Institute in Information and Language Processing, University of Wolverhampton, Wolverhampton, UK
{v.yaneva,shiva.taslimi,omid.rohanian,ha.l.a}@wlv.ac.uk

Abstract. Gaze data has been used to investigate the cognitive processing of certain types of formulaic language such as idioms and binominal phrases, however, very little is known about the online cognitive processing of multiword expressions. In this paper we use gaze features to compare the processing of verb - particle and verb - noun multiword expressions to control phrases of the same part-of-speech pattern. We also compare the gaze data for certain components of these expressions and the control phrases in order to find out whether these components are processed differently from the whole units. We provide results for both native and non-native speakers of English and we analyse the importance of the various gaze features for the purpose of this study. We discuss our findings in light of the E-Z model of reading.

1 Introduction

A large body of research supports the idea that words which often occur together (e.g. "fast food", "distance learning", "break the ice") are stored in the mental lexicon as whole units as opposed to single words [2,3,16,20]. It has been suggested that the long term memory stores these frequently occurring "formulaic" units in order to alleviate the burden that language comprehension poses on the short-term memory, a resource with a comparatively smaller span [3]. Such an approach to facilitating language processing could provide an explanation of the fact that a large proportion of the spoken and written language is formulaic: some corpus studies claim that between 52% and 58% of the language in the analysed corpora follows a formulaic pattern [7], and other studies claim that this figure is around 32% [9]. Furthermore, several eye tracking studies, as discussed in Sect. 2, provide evidence of processing advantage for idioms over non-idiomatic phrases, where the faster processing of the phrases is used as a proxy to measuring faster lexical access.

While research studies using different approaches support the idea that formulaic language is a specific form of a "shortcut" to language processing, many questions about the stages of processing of such phrases remain unanswered. For example, it is still uncertain whether non-native speakers with a high degree of

R. Mitkov (Ed.): Europhras 2017, LNAI 10596, pp. 363–379, 2017.
https://doi.org/10.1007/978-3-319-69805-2_26

proficiency store formulaic sequences as units in their mental lexicon or not. A study by [20] reported no difference in the duration of gaze fixations between idiomatic and control phrases read by non-native speakers. In another study by [16] non-native speakers produced fewer fixations while reading idioms compared to control phrases, but there was no difference in the duration of these fixations. Another gap in the current research is that the few existing eye-tracking studies for formulaic language focused specifically on idioms and very little is known about the processing of other types of phraseological units. The selection of appropriate phrases as experimental stimuli is yet another under researched area. Some of the early eye tracking studies investigating formulaic units (e.g. [20]) did not control for the syntactic structure of the phrases used as stimuli, which may have biased some of their results. Last but not least, all eye-tracking studies investigating formulaic language, that we are aware of, used stimuli that were crafted for the purpose of the research as opposed to naturally occurring examples from corpora.

In this study, we use gaze data from native and non-native speakers of English to investigate whether multi-word expressions (MWEs) have a processing advantage over control phrases. As opposed to designing the target phrases ourselves, we extract these from the GECO corpus[1] [4], a large eye-tracking corpus containing gaze data from native and proficient non-native readers. The use of this data allows the comparison of naturally occurring phrases, as well as the use of more gaze features compared to previous research. We control for the syntactic structure of the investigated phrases by focusing on MWEs and control phrases following a verb and noun (V + N) and verb and particle (V + P) part-of-speech pattern, which do not contain other words in between.

While very informative, the use of eye tracking as an approach for investigating formulaic language is not straightforward. One of the reasons for this is that the very nature of formulaic units challenges the use of the word as a traditional unit of analysis in eye-tracking research [2]. For example, idioms have been described as "superlemmas", entries that represent the phrase as a whole but are linked to each component word [18]. One way to overcome this problem is the so called *hybrid* approach where both the behaviour of the whole phrase and the behaviour of its component parts are analysed [2]. To account for this, as suggested by the existing literature discussed in Sect. 2, we compare both the whole units (MWEs versus control phrases), as well as the last word of the units (either noun versus noun or particle versus particle) in order to identify whether the native and non-native readers differ in the stage at which they recognise the unit (the so called "completion of familiarity check"). We discuss this process in light of the E-Z model of reading [13].

The annotation of the MWEs used in this study is available at: https://github.com/shivaat/mwe-geco.

The rest of this paper is organised as follows. Section 2 presents the E-Z model of reading and related work on using gaze data for the investigation of

[1] The GECO corpus can be downloaded freely at: http://expsy.ugent.be/downloads/geco.

formulaic language. Section 3 presents the data used in this study, while Sect. 4 presents the gaze features. The experiments are described in Sect. 6 and the main results are discussed in Sect. 7. Finally, Sect. 8 summarises the main findings of this study and introduces potential directions for future work.

2 Processing of Formulaic Language and the E-Z Model of Reading

Eye tracking is a process where an eye-tracking device measures the point of gaze of an eye (gaze fixation) or the motion of an eye (saccade) relative to the head and a computer screen [6]. Fixations are eye movements which stabilise the retina over a stationary object of interest, which, in the case of reading research, is the written text and its units (letters, words, phrases, etc.). Gaze fixations and revisits (go-back fixations to a previously fixated object) have been widely used as measures of cognitive effort by taking into account their durations and the places in text where longer fixations occur [6].

The most prominent model of reading to date is arguably the E-Z Reader [12–14]. The model has several versions, which has introduced some changes in the use of terminology (e.g. earlier versions of the model use terms such as "familiarity check" and later versions of the model (e.g. E-Z Reader 7) refer to the same phenomenon as "first stage of lexical access" or "L1"). We have done our best to explain such variability in the use of the terminology.

The central assumptions of the model are that: (1) the signal to move the eyes to the right is given at the stage of word identification; and (2) attention is allocated from one word to the next in a strictly serial fashion [14]. The model thus has five stages: familiarity check, lexical access, early saccadic programming, late saccadic programming and saccadic movement. In later versions of the model the first two stages are referred to as "early visual processing" and "word identification", which is divided into stages of early and late lexical access. In our review we focus on these two stages as they are most relevant to our research.

During early visual processing, visual features from the printed page are projected from the retina to the visual cortex so that the objects on the page (i.e., the individual words) can be identified [14]. Early visual processing is most rapid if the word is fixated near its center and thus the time needed to encode a word increases with word length. At this stage word-boundary information is obtained, which is needed for the programming of saccades to upcoming words.

The word identification process starts with the focus of attention to that word and is completed in two stages, reflecting early and late stages of lexical processing. The first stage, also referred to as "familiarity check", corresponds to identifying the orthographic form of the word, where the phonological and semantic forms are not yet fully activated. This activation occurs during the second stage of lexical processing and thus corresponds to what is typically known as "lexical access". The time required to complete the familiarity check is a linear function of the natural logarithm of the word's frequency and its predictability within a given sentence or phrase context. As most of the orthographic recognition has been completed during the first stage, the time required to complete the second stage of lexical processing is more influenced by a word's predictability [14]. Unlike with the first stage of lexical processing, word's predictability fully affects the second stage: "Words that can be predicted with complete certainty within a given sentence context will require no time in this second stage (i.e., if predictability = 1, then t(L2) = 0 ms)" [14].

This is particularly relevant to the investigation of the cognitive processing of MWEs and has been discussed in several studies focusing on idioms: "It is proposed that when a MWE (e.g. *the black sheep of the family*) is read, the constituent words become more predictable as they progress through the phrase, and the final word of the string (Word n) is almost redundant" [15].

In another study on idiom processing ([20]) the findings are also discussed in light of the E-Z Reader. The reported results showed processing advantage for idioms for native speakers (e.g. "*honesty is the best policy*") compared to novel phrases (e.g. "*it seems that his policy of...*"). For non-native speakers this held true only for number of fixations but not for fixation durations (these two were the only gaze features used in the study). The authors argue that the processing advantage was observed because the familiarity check was completed earlier in the idiom condition due to the high predictability of the terminal word. However, there was no explicit comparison of the terminal words in the two conditions. This study was a seminal one for the field but has been criticised for a number of shortcomings such as using only one measure of processing time (fixation duration), embedding the target words into phrases with varying syntactic structure and varying length and not controlling whether the idioms used in the study were actually known to the non-native readers, with a post-test that strongly suggested half of them were not [15].

Another study by [16], also focusing on idioms, investigated their processing by native and non-native speakers in a biasing story context. The stimuli were three types of phrases, which were either idioms ("*at the end of the day*" - eventually), literal expressions ("*at the end of the day*" - in the evening) or matched novel phrases ("*at the end of the war*"). The authors investigated whether there was processing advantage for the entire unit, as well as its components before and after the recognition point (the point at which the expression becomes uniquely recognisable as idiomatic) [16]. This was done in order to test the *configuration hypothesis* [19], according to which individual words and their meanings are activated until the recognition point has been reached. Once it has been reached, the figurative meaning is accessed and the literal one is no longer viable. The findings of [16] supported the processing advantage of idioms for native speakers, which was found only in the late processing features (total reading time and fixation count). In contrast, the non-native speakers did not read the idioms faster than the novel phrases and required more time to retrieve figurative senses than literal ones, especially in words that were before the recognition point.

To the best of our knowledge, the only eye tracking study on formulaic language different from idioms is a study on binominal expressions (e.g. "*bride and groom*") [17], which aimed to find out whether readers were sensitive to the frequency with which phrases occur in language. The results indicated that first pass reading time, total reading time and fixation count were all affected by phrase length, proficiency, phrase type and phrasal frequency in both native and non-native readers.

The three eye tracking studies presented in this section give an important insight into the processing of formulaic language, however, they predominantly focused on idiomatic expressions with varying length (up to eight words) and used a very limited number of gaze features. Furthermore, the control phrases were designed in a way to be as similar as possible to the idiomatic ones but to have literal meaning, which resulted in having control phrases with lower frequency than the idiomatic ones [15]. In an attempt to overcome these shortcomings and to go beyond the state-of-the-art, we present an experiment where: (i) we compare MWEs and control phrases extracted from a corpus as opposed to target phrases designed specifically for this study, (ii) we control for their length and syntactic structure by focusing on two-word MWEs that are either verb - noun or verb - particle combinations, (iii) investigate a larger number of gaze features.

The next sections present the data, gaze features and experimental analysis of our study.

3 Data

This section describes the corpus used in this study, as well as the procedure followed for the annotation of the MWEs.

The GECO corpus. The GECO corpus [4] used in this study is, to the best of our knowledge, the most recent eye tracking corpus for English, which: (i) contains gaze data from a natural reading task (as opposed to e.g. single sentences), (ii) is long enough to contain a sufficient number of MWEs, and (iii) contains paired gaze data from native and non-native readers.

The text of the corpus is a novel by Agatha Christie entitled "The Mysterious Affair at Styles", the English version of which contains 54,364 tokens and 5,012 unique types. The novel was selected based on the fact that its word frequency distribution was the most similar to the one in natural language use, as observed in the Subtlex database [4]. The novel was read by 14 English monolingual undergraduates from the University of Southampton and 19 Dutch (L1) - English (L2) bilingual students at Ghent University (intermediate and advanced). The two groups were matched on age and education level. The monolingual participants read only the English version of the novel, which amounted to a total of 5,031 sentences. The bilingual participants read Chaps. 1–7 in one language and 8–13 in the other in a counterbalanced order, thus reading 2,754 Dutch sentences and 2,449 English sentences. The eight bilingual participants who read the first part of the novel in English read 2,852 English sentences. Eye tracking data was collected for both the English version of the novel and its translation in

Dutch; however, in this study we only focus on the data about English. All participants completed a battery of language proficiency tests, as a result of which two bilinguals were classified as lower intermediate, ten were classified as upper intermediate and seven were scored as advanced L2 language users according to the LexTALE norms [11]. Full details about the method and procedure used for the development of the corpus could be found in [4].

Annotation of the MWEs and Control Phrases. MWEs have been investigated based on their many different characteristics such as fixedness [8], non compositionality [1], and semi-productivity [21]. We have used these properties as the main guidelines for annotating MWEs, specifically following the guidelines provided by the PARSEME project on identifying verbal MWEs.[2] In those guidelines, MWEs are defined as semantically non-compositional sequences of words with the following compulsory properties: (i) their component words include a head word and at least one other syntactically related word; (ii) they show some degree of orthographic, morphological, syntactic or semantic idiosyncrasy with respect to what is considered general grammar rules of a language (collocations are excluded); (iii) at least two components of such a word sequence have to be lexicalised.

Two annotators with linguistic background labelled the GECO corpus for Verb + Noun and Verb + Particle constructions following the guidelines. We have considered cases where the components of an MWE can occur with at most three words in between. The kappa inter-annotator agreement is $k = 0.7864$. We have resolved the annotation differences by employing a third annotator to decide in cases of disagreement.

We extracted from the corpus all patterns of Verb + Noun and Verb + Prepositions (and Verb + a list of other particles such as *up, down, over, etc.*) with no other words between the components. For the V + P pattern this resulted in a total of 1,220 Control phrases and 168 MWEs. Examples of V + P MWEs include "turned out" and "went on", while "stayed at" and "went in" are examples of control phrases. For the V + N pattern there were 524 Control phrases and 36 MWEs, where "catching sight" and "brought home" are examples of MWEs and "heard footsteps" and "achieved triumphs" are examples of control phrases.

The annotated MWEs and Control phrases are available at: https://github.com/shivaat/mwe-geco.

4 Gaze Features

The GECO corpus contains a number of early and late gaze features, out of which we selected six that have been widely used in general reading research. For comparison, previous studies investigating formulaic language through gaze data have used smaller number of features: two features (*fixation duration* and *fixation count*) in the case of [20] and three features (*first pass reading time,*

[2] https://typo.uni-konstanz.de/PARSEME/images/shared-task/guidelines/PARSEME-ST-annotation-guidelines-v6.pdf.

total reading time and *fixation count*) in the case of [16]. All gaze features were averaged over 14 readers for the monolingual data and 19 readers for the bilingual data and are reported in milliseconds or in counts. The features used in this study are as follows.

Word First Fixation Duration is the duration of the first fixation that was on the current word. It is an early measure of word processing and is informative of lexical access and early syntactic processing, as well as oculomotor processes and visual properties of the region [5]. *Word Fixation Count* is the total number of fixations falling on the current word. *First Run Fixation Count* is the number of all fixations in a trial falling in the first run of the word. *Word Go Past Time* is the summation of all fixation durations from when the current word is first fixated until the eyes enter a word with a higher word identification number. *Word Total Reading Time* is the summation of all fixation durations on the current word, including refixations of the region after it was left. *Word Skipping Probability* is the probability that a word may be skipped, i.e. not fixated. A word is considered skipped if no fixation occurred in first-pass reading.

Late measures such as *Word Total Reading Time* or *Word Fixation Count* account for late syntactic processing, textual integration processes, lexical and syntactic/semantic processing and disambiguation in general [5].

The distribution of each gaze feature for the V + N and V + P MWEs and Control phrases for both native (L1) and non-native (L2) speakers are presented in Appendix A.

5 Experimental Design

In the experiments presented below we set out to find out whether there is a processing advantage for MWEs compared to control phrases (Experiment 1) and whether the completion of the familiarity check happens earlier for MWEs than for control phrases (Experiment 2). We also discuss the differences between early and late gaze features for the two groups of phrases in order to draw conclusions about the early and late stages of processing of the phrases.

In Experiment 1 we test whether: (i) *native* speakers process whole MWEs differently from whole control phrases and whether ii) *non-native* speakers process whole MWEs differently from whole control phrases. In order to account for the processing of the entire unit we add the values of the gaze features of its component parts together (either V + P or V + N, respectively) for each participant group. We do this separately for each gaze feature. For example, if in the phrase "shook hands" the verb "shook" has a *First Fixation Duration* of 149 msec and the noun "hands" has a *First Fixation Duration* of 189 msec, then the entire phrase has a *First Fixation Duration* of 338 msec. We compare the whole units within groups in order to find out whether there is processing advantage for MWEs over control phrases, as suggested by the related work.

In Experiment 2 we focus only on the last part of the MWEs and the Control phrases, namely the nouns and particles. We compare their processing within groups based on the six gaze features in order to find out whether nouns and particles which belong to MWEs are processed faster and skipped more often compared to nouns and particles from the control phrases. As suggested by the literature discussed in previous sections and the E-Z model in particular, such faster processing of the last word of the MWE would be an indication of an earlier completion of the familiarity check stage of the phrase processing.

The results of our experiments are presented in the next section.

6 Results

This section presents the statistical analysis results for entire MWEs versus Control phrases, as well as those for the last words of the MWEs and the last words of the Control phrases.

6.1 Experiment 1: MWEs Versus Control Phrases

This section presents a comparison between a number of gaze features for V + N and V + P MWEs and Control phrases. The gaze feature values for the whole phrases are computed by adding the values of each individual word in the phrase. The Control phrases also follow the V + N and V + P patterns, but were not classified by the annotators as MWEs based on the annotation guidelines.

Monolingual Data. A Shapiro-Wilk test revealed that the data for the majority of the gaze features for V + N and V + P phrases was non-normally distributed; hence, we used a Wilcoxon Signed Rank test in order to compare the two types of phrases (MWEs versus Control phrases).

For V + N combinations, the analysis revealed that there were statistically significant differences for all gaze metrics except for First Fixation Duration ($Z = -1.854$, $p = 0.064$) and Skipping Probability ($Z = -1.738$, $p = 0.082$). The results for the rest of the features were as follows (two-tailed): Fixation Count ($Z = -3.166$, $p = 0.002$); First Run Fixation Count ($Z = -2.499$, $p = 0.012$); Go Past Time ($Z = -3.441$, $p = 0.001$), and Total Reading Time ($Z = -2.906$, $p = 0.004$). Table 1 shows the Median values of each gaze feature for both types of phrases.

These results indicate that the processing of V + N MWEs indeed takes less time and less fixations compared to the processing of control V + N phrases.

The case was similar for V + P combinations, where the Wilcoxon Signed Rank test revealed statistically significant differences for all features (two-tailed), except Skipping Probability ($Z = -0.587$, $p = 0.557$). The results for the rest of the features were as follows (two-tailed): Fixation Count ($Z = -3.646$, $p = 0.000$); First Run Fixation Count ($Z = -2.934$, $p = 0.003$); First Fixation Duration ($Z = -2.871$, $p = 0.004$); Go Past Time ($Z = -2.640$, $p = 0.008$), and Total Reading Time ($Z = -3.996$, $p = 0.000$). The Median values are presented in Table 1. Interestingly, the median value for First Fixation Duration is higher for the V + P MWEs (259.89) than the V + P control phrases (258.32), which is the only feature indicating that the MWEs are more challenging to process than the control phrases.

Table 1. Median values for MWEs and Control phrases for **monolingual** participants (added feature values for both words in a phrase) note that Skipping Probability > 1 because it represents the added skipping probability for each word in the phrase.

	V + N MWEs	V + N Control	V + P MWEs	V + P Control
Fixation Count	1.67	1.93	1.43	1.5
First Run Fixation Count	1.48	1.62	1.29	1.3
First Fixation Duration	296.54	310.57	259.89	258.32
Go Past Time	377.18	482.82	354.03	367.34
Total Reading Time	345.86	402.2	299.39	323.86
Skipping Probability	1	0.79	1.07	1.07

Bilingual Data. A Shapiro-Wilk test signified a non-normal distribution of the data so, similar to the case with the monolingual participants, a Wilcoxon Signed Rank test was used to compare the V + P and V + N MWEs and control phrases for bilingual participants.

For V + N combinations the test revealed similar results to those with the monolingual participants: MWEs are processed more efficiently than control phrases. The only exceptions were again First Fixation Duration, which did not yield a significant result ($Z = -0.707$, $p = 0.48$) and Skipping Probability ($Z = -0.188$, $p = 0.851$). The results for the rest of the features were as follows (two-tailed): Fixation Count ($Z = -2.821$, $p = 0.005$); First Run Fixation Count ($Z = -2.636$, $p = 0.008$); Go Past Time ($Z = -3.158$, $p = 0.002$), and Total Reading Time ($Z = -4.509$, $p = 0.000$). The Median values are presented in Table 2.

For V + P combinations there was no difference on the First Fixation Duration measure ($Z = -1.414$, $p = 0.158$) and Skipping Probability ($Z = -0.023$, $p = 0.981$). It was interesting to note that the Go Past Time measure was significantly lower for the Control phrases ($Z = -2.645$, $p = 0.008$). The rest of the features differed significantly between MWEs and Control phrases in favour of MWEs being easier to process: Fixation Count ($Z = -3.314$, $p = 0.001$); First Run Fixation Count ($Z = -2.881$, $p = 0.004$); Total Reading Time ($Z = -3.381$, $p = 0.001$). The Median values are presented in Table 2.

Conclusions for MWEs Versus Control Phrases. The comparison between V + N and V + P MWEs and control phrases using both monolingual and bilingual gaze data reveals that, much in line with previous research on other formulaic sequences (e.g. idioms), the MWEs are generally processed with lower numbers of fixations and lower reading times. Another finding, which relates to previous research is that early gaze measures and First Fixation Duration in particular, were not discriminative between formulaic and non-formulaic phrases. While Skipping Probability is not a discriminative feature, V + P combinations are skipped a lot more often than V + N combinations and the value of the Median for Skipping Probability is higher in cases where the phrase is a MWE. In terms of differences between monolingual and bilingual participants, we notice

Table 2. Median values for MWEs and Control phrases for **bilingual** participants (added feature values for both words in a phrase) Note that Skipping Probability > 1 because it represents the added skipping probability for each word in the phrase.

	V + N MWEs	V + N Control	V + P MWEs	V + P Control
Fixation Count	2.28	2.33	1.8	1.89
First Run Fixation Count	1.74	1.89	1.56	1.56
First Fixation Duration	349.67	358.7	309.56	303.11
Go Past Time	497.56	595.47	468.07	451.61
Total Reading Time	484.11	248.28	400.6	404.1
Skipping Probability	0.67	0.67	1	0.9

that while bilingual participants also process MWEs more efficiently, they have Go Past measures lower for control phrases for the V + P pattern, meaning that they spent longer integrating the meaning of the MWEs with information previously read.

6.2 Experiment 2: Last Word of the MWEs Versus Last Word of the Control Phrases

In this section we present a comparison between the last words of each unit (nouns from MWEs versus nouns from control phrases and particles from MWEs versus particles from Control phrases). This comparison is motivated by findings from previous research, which state that due to predictability effects, the last words in formulaic sequences are processed through fewer and shorter fixations and are skipped more often than those in non-formulaic ones.

Monolingual Data. A Wilcoxon Signed Rank test was used to first compare the nouns (N) which were part of MWEs and those which were part of Control phrases, where a processing advantage was revealed for the former.

Again, there were statistically significant results for all features except First Fixation Duration ($Z = -1.147$, $p = 0.251$). Interestingly, in this case Skipping Probability was a discriminative feature, showing that nouns in MWEs were skipped significantly more often than those in Control phrases ($Z = -2.187$, $p = 0.029$). The results for the rest of the features were as follows (two-tailed): Fixation Count ($Z = -2.950$, $p = 0.003$); First Run Fixation Count ($Z = -2.123$, $p = 0.034$); Go Past Time ($Z = -3.441$, $p = 0.001$), and Total Reading Time ($Z = -2.388$, $p = 0.017$). The Median values are presented in Table 3.

Interestingly, for particles (P), the results show that none of the features are discriminative enough between particles which are part of MWEs and those from the Control phrases. A possible explanation for this is that both are skipped often and processed using very few and very short fixations. The results are Fixation Count ($Z = -1.343$, $p = 0.179$); First Run Fixation Count ($Z = -1.255$,

Table 3. Median values for Ns and Ps for **monolingual** participants

	N MWEs	N Control	P MWEs	P Control
Fixation Count	0.86	0.93	0.57	0.5
First Run Fixation Count	0.78	0.85	0.5	0.46
First Fixation Duration	164.35	161.14	100.61	91
Go Past Time	197.64	246.6	129.17	123.89
Total Reading Time	179.82	198.92	110.36	100.84
Skipping Probability	0.43	0.36	0.64	0.69

$p = 0.209$); First Fixation Duration ($Z = -1.132$, $p = 0.257$); Go Past Time ($Z = -0.120$, $p = 0.904$), and Total Reading Time ($Z = -1.105$, $p = 0.269$); and Skipping Probability ($Z = -0.231$, $p = 0.818$). The Median values are presented in Table 3.

Bilingual Data. The comparison between the last words of the MWEs and the Control phrases was repeated using gaze data from bilingual readers in order to identify potential differences in their processing.

Contrary to what we found for monolingual participants, the bilingual ones read the nouns in MWEs and Control phrases with a similar number of fixations and fixation durations. This reveals that the predictability effect was significantly lower for readers to whom English was not a first language. The only statistically different comparison was found for Go Past Time ($Z = -2.781, p = 0.005$). The results for the rest of the features were: Fixation Count ($Z = -1.248$, $p = 0.212$); First Run Fixation Count ($Z = -0.314$, $p = 0.754$); First Fixation Duration ($Z = -0.063$, $p = 0.95$); Total Reading Time ($Z = -1.618$, $p = 0.106$); and Skipping Probability ($Z = -0.492$, $p = 0.623$). The Median values are presented in Table 4.

Table 4. Median values for Ns and Ps for **bilingual** participants

	N MWEs	N Control	P MWEs	P Control
Fixation Count	1.3	1.11	0.7	0.67
First Run Fixation Count	0.9	0.9	0.6	0.56
First Fixation Duration	179.73	179.58	122.56	112.11
Go Past Time	246.33	287.44	167.56	157
Total Reading Time	257.67	248.26	146.95	135.6
Skipping Probability	0.3	0.3	0.6	0.6

For Particles the results were similar to those for the monolingual data and to the results for Nouns for the bilingual participants: there were no significant differences found. This suggests that particles which were parts of MWEs were processed similarly to particles which were from control phrases: Fixation Count ($Z = -1.474$, $p = 0.14$); First Run Fixation Count ($Z = -0.661$, $p = 0.509$); First Fixation Duration ($Z = -0.628$, $p = 0.53$); Go Past Time ($Z = -1.666$, $p = 0.096$); Total Reading Time ($Z = -1.231$, $p = 0.218$); and Skipping Probability ($Z = -1.088$, $p = 0.277$). The Median values are presented in Table 4.

Conclusions for Last Word of the MWEs Versus Last Word of the Control Phrases. The results from the statistical analysis indicated that native speakers show a processing advantage for nouns which are a part of MWEs compared to nouns in Control phrases. This was not the case, however, with non-native speakers, who did not find these nouns more predictable than the nouns in the Control phrases. With regards to particles, both monolingual and bilingual gaze data revealed that these are often skipped and processed equally efficiently when they are a part of MWEs and when they are not.

7 Discussion

The analysis of the data presented in the previous section revealed important findings about the processing of MWEs by native and non-native speakers. We discuss these findings in the context of previous eye-tracking research for idioms and in light of the E-Z model of reading presented in Sect. 2.

Processing Advantage for MWEs. In line with previous research on idioms (e.g. [15,16]), MWEs were processed with fewer fixations and shorter fixations compared to Control phrases for native readers. In contrast with idiom research though, where non-native readers did not read idioms more efficiently compared to novel phrases, our findings suggest that in the case of V + N and V + P MWEs such processing advantage exists for non-native readers, too. The effect was significant for both V + N and V + P phrases. The majority of the features (except First Fixation Duration) showed that there was a clear processing advantage for the formulaic phrases as whole units for both groups of readers. As shown by the median values, MWEs of the type V + P had a higher skipping probability than those of the V + N type, especially when they were part of a MWEs. The latter was not unexpected given the effect of word length on parafoveal word recognition (particles are usually shorter than nouns) and the overall processing advantage for MWEs.

Completion of the Familiarity Check. An interesting finding emerged when analysing the last word of the MWEs of the V + N type. As expected, native speakers showed a processing advantage for nouns which were a part of MWEs compared to nouns in Control phrases and skipped them more often, but this was not the case with non-native readers. One possible explanation for this difference is that since native speakers have a higher exposure to the English language, they used the first word of the MWE as a disambiguating region and were better able to predict the second part of the MWEs due to familiarity with the phrases.

The E-Z model of reading explains this as a completion of the familiarity check earlier in the case of MWEs compared to Control phrases. While the non-native readers did show a processing advantage for MWEs over Control phrases, the first word of the MWE did not act as a disambiguating region for them and thus the familiarity check was not completed earlier than with the Control phrases. It is then possible that the processing advantage for MWEs for non-native readers occurred due to higher familiarity with the overall phrase in a way that allows both words to be processed using fewer and shorter fixations. Since no disambiguation and facilitated semantic access occurred after reading the first word, it could be suggested that the MWEs were not yet entrenched as whole units in the mental lexicon of the non-native participants. Further analysis is thus necessary in order to explain the source of the processing advantage for the whole N + P phrases over Control phrases for non-native readers and to further investigate at what stage these phrases begin being stored as "wholes".

Unsurprisingly, the processing of the last word in the V + P combinations was no different for MWEs and Control phrases for both native and non-native speakers. The most likely explanation for this is that particles are processed parafoveally in both types of phrases and are thus skipped at a very high rate, as shown by the median values in Tables 3 and 4.

Stages of Processing. The discriminative power of the different gaze features used in this study is informative of the stages of processing where the differences between MWEs and Control phrases occur. Early gaze features such as First Fixation Duration were not discriminative between the two types of phrases, which means that the two types of phrases (MWEs and Control) evoked similar orthographic recognition mechanisms. Thus, the differences in the processing of the MWEs occurred at the later stages of lexical and syntactic processing, as evidenced by late features such as Fixation Count, First Run Fixation Count, Go Past Time and Total Reading Time (if the familiarity check was completed earlier and the last word was skipped more often, then the differences in the late gaze features are expected). Even though previous research on formulaic language using gaze data did not utilise as many gaze features and focused on longer phrases, similar findings have been reported with regards to early features: "It was concluded that early eye-tracking measures might not be suitable for the investigation of longer multi-word sequences (some idioms used in the study were up to eight words in length), a that a combination of late measures should be used instead" [15]. The present study shows that this is also the case for shorter MWEs consisting of two words.

Finally, analysis of the skipping probability revealed that even though this feature was not discriminative for the whole phrases, the Median values show that V + P combinations are skipped more often than V + N combinations and this is especially the case when the phrase is a MWE. Again, this can be explained with the parafoveal processing of the particles.

Limitations. The main limitation of this study is related to the small number of participants whose gaze data was analysed. We argue that this is a characteristic of most eye-tracking studies and especially the ones which use eye-tracking corpora. By comparison, the Dundee corpus [10], which is the only other eye-tracking corpus for English of a similar size that we are aware of, contains gaze data from only 10 people. Due to the small number of participants, we were not able to conduct between-group comparisons as individual differences in such small samples could not have been properly accounted for. One possible way to solve this in our future work would be to build individual models for each participant.

Another limitation is the fact that the length in characters of the compared examples was not controlled for, however, this was not feasible given that the aim of this study was to compare data from naturally occurring examples from corpora as opposed to carefully designed laboratory stimuli. The division of the examples into V + N and V + P partially accounts for this as we compare phrases with the same part-of-speech patterns.

8 Conclusions and Future Work

We presented an initial study towards investigating the processing of MWEs versus control phrases in native and non-native speakers of English using gaze data from a large corpus. We focused on MWEs following verb + noun and verb + particle part-of-speech patterns and discussed our findings in the context of previous research on idioms and the E-Z model of reading. Our results indicate that both native and non-native speakers show a statistically significant processing advantage for MWEs compared to Control phrases as measured by a number of gaze features. However, the analysis of the last word from each phrase showed that while native readers complete the familiarity check of the phrase after reading the first word, non-native readers do not exhibit a similar pattern and more research is needed in order to investigate the source of the processing advantage for MWEs in non-native readers. Feature analysis revealed that the differences in the processing of the MWEs and the Control phrases occur at the later stages of syntactic, semantic and lexical processing, as opposed to the stages of early lexical processing.

Future work includes analysis of the relationships between the gaze data and several factors which may interact with it such as frequency, length, familiarity, predictability, etc. A suitable approach to investigating this would be mixed-effects modelling. Other avenues for future research include the investigation of other types of MWEs including ones which contain other words in between, as examples of these were fairly frequent within the GECO corpus.

A Appendix: Distribution of Gaze Features

Tables 5, 6, 7 and 8 present the distribution of each gaze feature for the V + N and V + P MWEs and Control phrases for both native (L1) and non-native (L2) speakers.

Table 5. Eye-tracking data statistics for V + N MWE

Gaze features	Mean		SD		Variance	
	L1	L2	L1	L2	L1	L2
First Run Fixation Count	1.49	1.77	0.26	0.30	0.07	0.091
Word First Fixation Duration	299.8	351.1	58.14	69.2	3380	4784
Word Go Past Time	433.5	543.4	137.6	206.7	18942	42733
Skipping Probability	0.9	0.67	0.22	0.27	0.05	0.07
Word Fixation Count	1.73	2.3	0.41	0.6	0.17	0.37
Total Reading Time	365.16	501.54	96.81	155.4	9372	24137

Table 6. Eye-tracking data statistics for V + P MWE

Gaze features	Mean		SD		Variance	
	L1	L2	L1	L2	L1	L2
First Run Fixation Count	1.33	1.57	0.32	0.38	0.1	0.15
Word first Fixation Duration	262.9	314.9	64.3	76.5	4140	5851
Word Go Past Time	393.7	507.9	159.6	228.1	25468	52053
Skipping Probability	1.04	0.92	0.23	0.3	0.05	0.08
Word Fixation Count	1.55	1.93	0.5	0.6	0.22	0.41
Total Reading Time	325.28	426.15	110.9	143.53	12296	20600

Table 7. Eye-tracking data statistics for V + N Control Phrases

Gaze features	Mean		SD		Variance	
	L1	L2	L1	L2	L1	L2
First Run Fixation Count	1.67	1.94	0.43	0.5	0.18	0.26
Word first Fixation Duration	314.9	358.1	71.81	81.8	5157	6691
Word Go Past Time	520.4	657.6	221.5	328.4	49085	107875
Skipping Probability	0.81	0.67	0.31	0.33	0.09	0.11
Word Fixation Count	2.03	2.45	0.69	0.83	0.47	0.69
Total Reading Time	429.17	259.88	159.73	126	25513	15877

Table 8. Eye-tracking data statistics for V + P Control Phrases

Gaze features	Mean		SD		Variance	
	L1	L2	L1	L2	L1	L2
First Run Fixation Count	1.33	1.57	0.33	0.39	0.11	0.16
Word first Fixation Duration	258.5	305.8	63.7	77.2	4052	5967
Word Go Past Time	389.3	491	156.9	213.9	24631	45773
Skipping Probability	1.06	0.92	0.26	0.29	0.07	0.09
Word Fixation Count	1.57	1.93	0.48	0.63	0.22	0.4
Total Reading Time	329.88	425.26	107.88	152.77	11637	23338

References

1. Baldwin, T., Kim, S.N.: Multiword expressions. In: Indurkhya, N., Damerau, F.J. (eds.) Handbook of Natural Language Processing, 2nd edn, pp. 267–292. CRC Press, Boca Raton (2010)
2. Carrol, G., Conklin, K.: Eye-tracking multi-word units: some methodological questions. J. Eye Mov. Res. **7**(5), 1–11 (2015)
3. Conklin, K., Schmitt, N.: The processing of formulaic language. Annu. Rev. Appl. Linguist. **32**, 45–61 (2012)
4. Cop, U., Dirix, N., Drieghe, D., Duyck, W.: Presenting GECO: an eyetracking corpus of monolingual and bilingual sentence reading. Behav. Res. Methods **49**(2), 602–615 (2017). http://dx.doi.org/10.3758/s13428-016-0734-0
5. Demberg, V., Keller, F.: Data from eye-tracking corpora as evidence for theories of syntactic processing complexity. Cognition **109**(2), 193–210 (2008)
6. Duchowski, A.: Eye Tracking Methodology: Theory and Practice, 2nd edn. Springer, London (2007). doi:10.1007/978-1-84628-609-4
7. Erman, B., Warren, B.: The idiom principle and the open choice principle. Text-Interdiscip. J. Study Discourse **20**(1), 29–62 (2000)
8. Fazly, A., Stevenson, S.: A distributional account of the semantics of multiword expressions. Ital. J. Linguist. **1**(20), 157–179 (2008)
9. Foster, P.: Rules and routines: a consideration of their role in the task-based language production of native and non-native speakers. In: Researching Pedagogic Tasks: Second Language Learning, Teaching, and Testing, pp. 75–93 (2001)
10. Kennedy, A., Pynte, J., Murray, W.S., Paul, S.A.: Frequency and predictability effects in the dundee corpus: an eye movement analysis. Quart. J. Exp. Psychol. **66**(3), 601–618 (2013)
11. Lemhöfer, K., Broersma, M.: Introducing LexTALE: a quick and valid lexical test for advanced learners of English. Behav. Res. Methods **44**(2), 325–343 (2012)
12. Rayner, K., Duffy, S.A.: Lexical complexity and fixation times in reading: effects of word frequency, verb complexity, and lexical ambiguity. Mem. Cognit. **14**(3), 191–201 (1986)
13. Rayner, K., Pollatsek, A., Ashby, J., Clifton Jr., C.: Psychology of Reading. Psychology Press, San Diego (2012)
14. Reichle, E.D., Rayner, K., Pollatsek, A.: The E-Z reader model of eye-movement control in reading: comparisons to other models. Behav. Brain Sci. **26**(4), 445–476 (2003)

15. Siyanova-Chanturia, A.: Eye-tracking and ERPs in multi-word expression research: a state-of-the-art review of the method and findings. Ment. Lex. **8**(2), 245–268 (2013)
16. Siyanova-Chanturia, A., Conklin, K., Schmitt, N.: Adding more fuel to the fire: an eye-tracking study of idiom processing by native and non-native speakers. Second Lang. Res. **27**(2), 251–272 (2011)
17. Siyanova-Chanturia, A., Conklin, K., Van Heuven, W.J.: Seeing a phrase "time and again" matters: the role of phrasal frequency in the processing of multiword sequences. J. Exp. Psychol. Learn. Mem. Cogn. **37**(3), 776 (2011)
18. Sprenger, S.A., Levelt, W.J., Kempen, G.: Lexical access during the production of idiomatic phrases. J. Mem. Lang. **54**(2), 161–184 (2006)
19. Tabossi, P., Zardon, F.: The activation of idiomatic meaning in spoken language comprehension. In: Idioms: Processing, Structure, and Interpretation, pp. 145–162 (1993)
20. Underwood, G., Schmitt, N., Galpin, A.: The eyes have it. Formul. Seq. Acquis. Process. Use **9**, 153 (2004)
21. Villavicencio, A.: Verb-particle constructions and lexical resources. In: Proceedings of the ACL 2003 Workshop on Multiword Expressions: Analysis, Acquisition and Treatment - Volume 18, MWE 2003, pp. 57–64. Association for Computational Linguistics, Stroudsburg, PA, USA (2003)

Theoretical and descriptive approaches to phraseology

Verb-Object Compounds and Idioms in Chinese

Adams Bodomo[1], So-sum Yu[2], and Dewei Che[1(✉)]

[1] University of Vienna, 1090 Vienna, Austria
dewei.che@univie.ac.at
[2] Hong Kong, China

Abstract. This paper addresses central issues about the nature of a construction in the Chinese language that is referred to as Verb-Object Compounds (VOCs). It has long been noted that the relationship between the two or more morphemes of VOCs is partly morphological and partly syntactic in the sense that, on the one hand, they do combine to form a 'word-like unit', but on the other hand, some degree of separation is possible between the two parts [4, 8, 9, 10, 12, 16, 17, 22, among others]. The VOC has triggered intense interest and rigorous research on the issue of wordhood in Chinese due to its disharmonious behaviour shown in the two separate modules of syntax and morphology. However, these previous discussions mainly focus on the criteria that can identify a word in Chinese. This paper, rather than belabouring the issue of refining these criteria or proposing new ones, centres on the fact that this type of compound exhibits properties in syntax, as well as lexical features in morphology and semantics. The description and analysis of the syntactic and morphological characteristics of VOCs then provide a foundation for a generalized account of the representation of VOCs and Verb-Object (VO) idioms within the grammatical framework of Lexical-Functional Grammar (LFG).

Keywords: VOCs · Lexis · Constituency · Semantics · Correspondence · LFG

1 Introduction

Bloomfield [2] subdivides compounds into syntactic and asyntactic varieties. According to this treatment, a construction such as *runaway* is syntactic, because it parallels a pattern of English syntax, that of [verb + preposition]. The pattern [preposition + verb], however, is not found in the grammar, so *outsell* is an asyntactic compound. Chinese VOCs display exactly the syntacticity described above, reflected in Li and Thompson [17]'s statement that '[t]he verb-object compound, as its name indicates, is composed of two constituents having the syntactic relation of a verb and its direct object'. The syntacticity they demonstrate means that they are not always easy to distinguish from VPs, as they often seem to fill in the same syntactic slot in the

S. Yu—Independent Scholar.

R. Mitkov (Ed.): Europhras 2017, LNAI 10596, pp. 383–396, 2017.
https://doi.org/10.1007/978-3-319-69805-2_27

sentence. This is partly because Chinese is an SVO language: the compounds reflect the SVO sentential pattern in their internal structure.

The source of dispute among linguists in past studies is the lexical (vs. phrasal) status of the Chinese VOC. For instance, one may consider *xi-zao* {wash-bath}[1] 'to bathe' as a lexical word. However, it can appear as a syntactic phrase as in (1)[2].

(1) *ta* *xi-le* *lang-ci* *zao.* [Mandarin]
3.SG wash-PERF two-CL bath
'He has bathed twice.'

An example of a construction of the same type in Cantonese can be seen in (2), in which the VOC, *jau-seoi* {swim-water} 'to swim', is separated by an aspectual marker and a duration phrase.

(2) *ngo* *jau-zo* *jat-go* *zungtau* *seoi* [Cantonese]
1.SG swim-PERF one-CL hour water
'I've swum for an hour'.

The VOC is peculiar in status in the sense that it is often treated as a word since the two constituting elements always go together as a composite form, yet it also allows some other elements to be inserted in the middle, making it appear to be a phrase.

The main objective of this paper is to show that although, syntactically, certain Mandarin and Cantonese VOCs can be interrupted in some contexts in which the verbal constituent acts as a predicate and the nominal constituent becomes a syntactic object, semantically, and in some morphological aspects, these VOCs are still like single lexical items with unitary lexical semantics. In accordance with this observation, formal representation of VOCs within the syntactic framework of Lexical-Functional Grammar (LFG) will be presented. We will first propose syntactic diagnostics for the object status of O in Sect. 2. We then propose formal morphological tests in Sect. 3 and suggest further semantic properties in Sect. 4 for the word status of VO. Section 5 will propose the representation of VOCs through the mechanism of LFG. Section 6 concludes the paper with a summary of our proposed analyses.

---

[1] Curly brackets are used in the text to enclose the morpheme-for-morpheme translation of verb-object phrasal structures or that of Verb-Object Compounds. Although sometimes the constituents of a VOC themselves do not carry unequivocal meanings as they might be bound morphemes, glosses most appropriate to the context are given for illustrative purposes.

[2] Symbols and abbreviations used in this paper: * = Ungrammatical; 1 = First Person; 2 = Second Person; 3 = Third Person; A = adjective; ADJ = adjunct; ADV = adverb; ADVP = adverbial phrase; Ag = Agent; AP = adjectival phrase; ASP = aspect; CL = classifier; D = determiner; DE = genitive marker in Mandarin; DP = determiner phrase; EXP = experiential verbal particle; Exp = experiencer; GE = genitive marker in Cantonese; N = noun; NEG = negative marker; NP = noun phrase; NUM = number; OBJ = object; PERF = perfective verbal particle; PERS = person; PL = plural; PRED = predicate; PRO = pronoun; S = sentence; SG = singular; SUBJ = subject; V = verb; VP = verb phrase.

2 Syntactic Diagnostics

The term Verb-Object Compound suggests that a compound is derived from a syntactic verb-object construction – which is an implication for which no evidence has been offered. In order to say that the nominal is a syntactic object, we have to first examine what an object is like in Chinese. In this section we will discuss, specifically from the syntactic point of view, what an object is in Mandarin and Cantonese. In illustrating the syntactic features of objects, the syntactic behaviors that a VOC can engage in will also be shown.

2.1 Topicalization

Objects in Mandarin and Cantonese, usually realized by nominal elements, occur after the verb in simple declarative sentences, as is the case in (3).

(3) a. *ta bu hui xi yifu*. [Mandarin]
3.SG NEG know wash clothes
'He doesn't know how to wash the clothes.'
b. ***yifu** ta bu hui xi.*

The object *yifu* 'clothes' follows the verb *xi* 'to wash'. However, when there is emphasis, the object can be preposed by topicalization, which has the effect of putting the NP in focus [21], as in (3b).

This kind of topicalization case is also exhibited by VOCs, as shown in (4).

(4) *loeng nei zung m cung* [Cantonese]
shower 2.SG still NEG wash away
'Why have you still not taken a bath?'

The nominal *loeng* 'shower' is displaced from the position after the verbal *cung* 'to wash away' and is topicalized like a normal object.

2.2 Modification

Between a verb and a grammatical object, we can insert certain modifiers (neutral between adverbials and adjectives), as in (5).

(5) *wo he-guo yi-ci jiu.* [Mandarin]
1.SG drink-EXP one-CL wine
'I drank wine once.'

A frequency phrase *yi-ci* {one-time} 'once' is put between the verb *he* 'to drink' and the object *jiu* 'wine', giving information about the frequency of the action of drinking wine. The same phenomena are also observed in VOCs, as can be seen in (6).

(6) *tamen meitian ban liang-ci zui.* [Mandarin]
3.PL every-day mix two-CL mouth
'They quarrel twice a day.'

Besides adverbials and adjectives, a possessive phrase may also occupy that position, as in the case of (7), where *tau-cin* {steal-money} 'to steal money' is the VO phrase.

(7) *keoi tau ngo ge cin.* [Cantonese]
3.SG steal 1.SG GE money
'S/he steals my money.'

This type of projection of referentiality can also be found in VOCs, like the one in (8).

(8) *ta sheng wo de qi.* [Mandarin]
3.SG produce 1.SG DE air
'He is angry with me.'

The possessive pronoun, *wo de* 'my', comes between the two elements of the VOC *sheng-qi* {produce-air} 'to get angry'. It is syntactically the possessor of the nominal *qi* 'air', but semantically it is the same entity towards which the emotion or action expressed by the VOC is directed.

The description provided in this section has shown that the nominal element of a VOC exhibits the syntactic properties of a normal object. Hence, it is reasonable to treat the nominals of VOCs as syntactic objects for the various patterns attested.

3 Morphological Tests

In this section, we will investigate the morphological properties of VOCs with respect to the manifestation of one well-formedness condition for morphological structures – the Coordination Test.

Many studies have used coordination as a test for unithood [3, 7, 18]. It is generally assumed that coordination is a syntactic construction: two (or more) phrase structure nodes are immediately dominated by a phrase structure node of the same category as its daughters [19].

This means that only X^0 (words) and their projections can be conjuncts in a coordinate structure. Consequently, while syntactic categories can be conjoined by syntactic conjunctions, stems and affixes normally cannot [20]:

(9) (a) Mary outran and outswam Bill.
(b) *Mary outran and -swam Bill.

(10) (a) John's joyfulness and cheeriness kept us going.
(b) *John's joyful- and cheeriness kept us going.

The simplest explanation for this constraint is that morphological constituents, being formed in the lexical component, must have intrinsic lexical content. Conjunctions, being syncategorematic categories [7], which necessarily occur only in conjunction with certain other words, lack such content and thus are not available in word formation.

Before illustrating how coordination can serve to show the morphological nature of VOCs, let us dispel some apparent counterexamples to the generalization that only syntactic constituents can be coordinated. Certain prefixes in English can be coordinated, as shown in (11).

(11) (a) *pre* and *post* World War II
(b) *pro* and *anti* abortion
(c) *super* and *supra* national

These prefixes (in italics) have 'the phonological status of independent words: they bear stress, they have either schwa or long vowels in final position, etc.' [1: 221]. Simpson [20] and Alsina [1] suggest that the phonological salience of these English prefixes explains their appearance in conjunctions. They may be ambiguously analyzable as prefixes or independent words, as proposed by Di Sciullo and Williams [11].

It is usually said that coordination involves parallel constructions sharing an identical grammatical function, but as Her [14] has pointed out, coordination does require more than parallel grammatical functions.

(12) *I admire Mary and honesty. [14: 184]

Sentence (12) is ill-formed because 'Mary' and 'honesty' are not semantically compatible as conjoined elements. Therefore, besides the 'parallel grammatical functions' requirement, semantic compatibility may also be a constraint conditioning the well-formedness of coordinate structures.

The unitary nature of the two constituting elements of a VOC is apparent in the phenomenon of conjoining. To conjoin sentences in Cantonese, the word *tung* 'and' (*he* for Mandarin) can be used. Firstly, let us take two verb phrases in (13) as an example:

(13) *paa saan* / *paa sek*
climb mountain / climb rock
'to climb mountains' 'to climb rocks'

We can join the two verb phrases by deleting the head verb *paa* 'to climb' of the second verb phrase and using the conjunction *tung* 'and' to link them up as in (14):

(14) *paa saan tung sek*
climb mountain and rock
'to climb mountains and rocks.'

The two verb phrases here can be conjoined like the above because the nominals, *saan* 'mountain' and *sek* 'rock' in these two phrases, are subcategorized for by the common matrix verb *paa* 'to climb'.

However, it is impossible for us to conjoin the verb phrase *paa saan* {climb mountain} 'to climb mountains' and the VOC *paa-tau* {climb-head} 'to overtake' shown here:

(15) (a) *paa saan paa-tau*
climb mountain climb-head
'to climb mountains' 'to overtake'
(b) **paa saan tung tau*

The ungrammaticality indicated results from the deletion of the lexical head of the VOC *paa* 'to climb' and hence the destruction of the lexical content/meaning of the VOC *paa-tau* {climb-head} 'to overtake'. The expression in (b) illustrates that when the VOC *paa-tau* {climb-head} 'to overtake', takes a conjoined NP, the only possible reading is the literal, i.e. 'to climb somebody's head', which does not make sense.

4 Semantic Features

Coordination tests have hinted at the morphological nature of VOCs. We will now go on to cite further a feature of modification to support the view that the verbal and the nominal constituents of a VOC form a single coherent semantic unit.

The noun in a verb phrase can be preceded and modified by a nominal classifier (indicating quantity) or a verbal classifier (indicating frequency) since it is a genuine object of the phrase which is syntactically and semantically modifiable. For instance, the verb phrase *tiao shui* {carry water} 'to carry water' can be modified by nominal classifiers like *yi-tong* {one-bucket}, as in (16).

(16) *ta tiao-guo yi-tong shui.* [Mandarin]
3.SG carry-EXP one-CL water
'S/he has carried a bucket of water'

However, the VOC *suo-shui* {shrink-water} 'to shrink through getting wet' cannot be modified by the same classifier, as shown by the unacceptability of (17).

(17) **zhe chenshan suo-guo yi-tong shui.*
This shirt shrink-EXP one-bucket water

Since the nominal *shui* 'water' is part of the VOC (morphological construct) *suo-shui* {shrink-water} 'to shrink through getting wet', this explains why it cannot be quantified by a nominal classifier, as a noun normally can. Given that neither the verbal nor the nominal alone can convey the non-compositional meaning of VOCs, both constituents are indispensable in completing the unithood of a VOC.

Previous analyses of Chinese VOCs have been suggested by various scholars including Huang [15] and Her [14]. In the interest of space we cannot present them here, though they are treated in our previous works (e.g. [4, 9, 22]).

5 An Analysis of VOCs

This VOC analysis is based on Bresnan's [5] work on idioms within the LFG framework. Again, we have an extensive discussion of this in our previous works. Given the fact that the surface syntactic structure offers no adequate solution to the ambiguity of VO idioms and since the nature of VOCs is in many ways similar to that of idioms, the natural place to explore next within the LFG framework is the argument-structure (a-structure).

Representation of VOCs and VO idioms in a-, c-, f-Structures[3]. We now move on to a concise representation of a VOC and a VO idiom in a-, c-, f-structures and the establishment of the mappings between these three parallel and inter-connected planes. To concretize the analysis, we will take the Cantonese sentence in (18) and the Mandarin sentence in (19) for illustration. Sentence (18) contains the separated VOC *jau-seoi* {swim-water} 'to swim' and (19) is made up of the VO idiom *chi-cu* {eat-vinegar} 'to be jealous'.

(18) *ngo jau-zo zan seoi.* [Cantonese]
1.SG swim-PERF for-a-while water
'I have swum for a while.'

(19) *ta changchang chi gan cu.* [Mandarin]
3.SG always eat dry vinegar
'He always gets jealous for no reason.'

Two points to note on the idiomatic VO utterance in (19) are, first, the adjective *gan* 'dry' is in fact not to be taken to modify the nominal *cu* 'vinegar', but the entire construction; second, the adjective is invariable, since it cannot be substituted for by the opposite, *shi* 'wet', or other adjectives. The adjective *gan* 'dry', here actually has scope over the entire construction, so the sentence in (19) would mean 'He is jealous for no reason' but not something literal like 'He eats dry vinegar', which is even a hardly interpretable expression. It acts like an adverbial meaning 'unreasonably' rather than an adjective merely meaning 'dry'. The impossibility of modification by a 'true' nominal modifier and the fact that whatever comes between the head verb and the nominal would be interpreted as applying to the whole idiomatic VO construction preserves the unitary nature of the idiom *chi-cu* {eat-vinegar} 'to be jealous'.

C-structure. A c-structure is a constituent phrase-structure tree expressing categories, surface precedence and immediate dominance relations. The first step in constructing a

[3] These structures are levels of representation in LFG. Readers unfamiliar with LFG are invited to consult introductory references such as Bresnan 2001 and Falk 2001.

c-structure for the example sentences is to provide annotated phrase structure rules (PSRs) as inputs. These rules consist of context-free skeletons annotated with schemata of functional equations which specify grammatical functions and direct the application of unification. The annotated PSRs necessary for (18) and (19) are stated in (20) and (21) respectively[4]:

(20) (a) S → DP VP
(↑ SUBJ) = ↓ ↑ = ↓
(b) DP → D
↑ = ↓
(c) VP → V ADVP NP
↑ = ↓ (↑ADJ) = ↓ (↑OBJ) = ↓
(d) ADVP → ADV
↑ = ↓
(e) NP → N
↑ = ↓

(21) (a) S → DP VP
(↑ SUBJ) = ↓ ↑ = ↓
(b) DP → D
↑ = ↓
(c) VP → ADVP V'
(↑ ADJ) = ↓ ↑ = ↓
(d) ADVP → ADV
↑ = ↓
(e) V' → V NP
↑ = ↓ (↑OBJ) = ↓
(f) NP → AP N'
(↑ ADJ) = ↓ ↑ = ↓
(g) AP → A
↑ = ↓
(h) N' → N
↑ = ↓

Lexical entries. In addition to information about syntactic functions, the grammatical representations of the example sentences also include information about such grammatical features as tense, aspect and number. This kind of information comes from the schemata in the lexicon. The lexical entries for the Cantonese example sentence are postulated in (22) and those for the Mandarin sentence are in (23).

[4] Space has limited the explanation of the functional annotations in each PSR. Please refer to Bresnan 2001:44–86 and Falk 2001:68–76 for an introduction to functional annotations in LFG.

(22)	(a) *jau-zo*	V	(↑ ASP) = PERF
			(↑ PRED)= 'SWIM<(↑ SUBJ)>(↑ OBJ)'
			(↑OBJ FORM) =*c*SEOI
	(b) *seoi*	N	(↑ FORM) = SEOI
	(c) *ngo*	D	(↑ NUM) = SG
			(↑ PERS) = 1
			(↑ PRED) = 'PRO'
	(d) *zan*	ADV	(↑ PRED) = 'zan'
(23)	(a) *chi*	V	(↑ PRED) = 'BE-JEALOUS<(↑ SUBJ)>(↑ OBJ)'
			(↑ OBJ FORM) =*c*CU
	(b) *cu*	N	(↑ FORM) = CU
	(c) *ta*	D	(↑ NUM) = SG
			(↑ PERS) = 3
			(↑ PRED) = 'PRO'
	(d) *gan*	A	(↑ PRED) = 'gan'
	(e) *changchang*	ADV	(↑ PRED) = 'changchang'

Note in particular the first two entries (22a, b & 23a, b). The crucial characteristic of VOCs is their single lexical semantics despite the noncontiguous positions of the verbal and the nominal. This property would have to be captured by lexical entries. For our Cantonese example sentence in (18), it is only the co-occurrence of the V and the N that yields the meaning of 'SWIM' for the VOC *jau-seoi* {swim-water}.

Similarly, for our example Mandarin expression in (19), the meaning 'BE-JEALOUS' for the VO idiom *chi-cu* {eat vinegar} can be obtained only with the co-occurrence of the V and the N. As shown in (22a, b), the binding force between the verbal *jau* and the nominal *seoi* comes from the constraining equation (↑ OBJ FORM) = *c*SEOI. A constraining equation, marked by subscripting the italic letter c to the equal sign, i.e. "=*c*", does not create a new attribute-value pair but constrains information coming from somewhere else. The attribute specified on the left-hand side of the equation is required to have the exact value specified on the right-hand side of the equation. Otherwise, the f-structure would be rendered ungrammatical. In other words, the constraining equation would invoke checking on that attribute at the final f-structure. So, the constraining equation (↑ OBJ FORM) = *c*SEOI requires that the FORM attribute of the OBJ function be present with the value 'SEOI', the FORM value uniquely stipulated on the nominal *seoi*. This ensures that the reading of 'SWIM' is only available with the co-occurrence of the lexical head, *jau*, and this designated nominal *seoi*. The constraining equation and hence the f-structure would be violated if either the value is not specified at all, or it is specified differently from what the constraining equation requires. The two pieces of lexically encoded grammatical information coming from the constraining equation and the functional equation (↑ FORM) = SEOI under the lexical entry of *seoi* represent the fact that the full meaning of the VOC in the example sentence (18) depends on the unification of information carried by the two components. The same approach is adopted for the Mandarin sentence in (19). The constraining equation (↑ OBJ FORM) = *c*CU in the lexical entry of the lexical head in (23a) simply requires that the value of the FORM attribute of its OBJ function must be 'CU' for the VO idiom to mean 'BE-JEALOUS'.

Note also that in the entries of (22a) and (23a), the OBJ function placed outside the angled brackets is the athematic syntactic argument subcategorized for by the lexical head *jau* 'to swim' and *chi* 'to eat'.

Annotated C-structure. With annotated rules in (20) and (21), and lexical entries in (22) and (23), annotated c-structure representations for sentences (18) and (19) can be drawn up in Figs. 1 and 2 respectively.

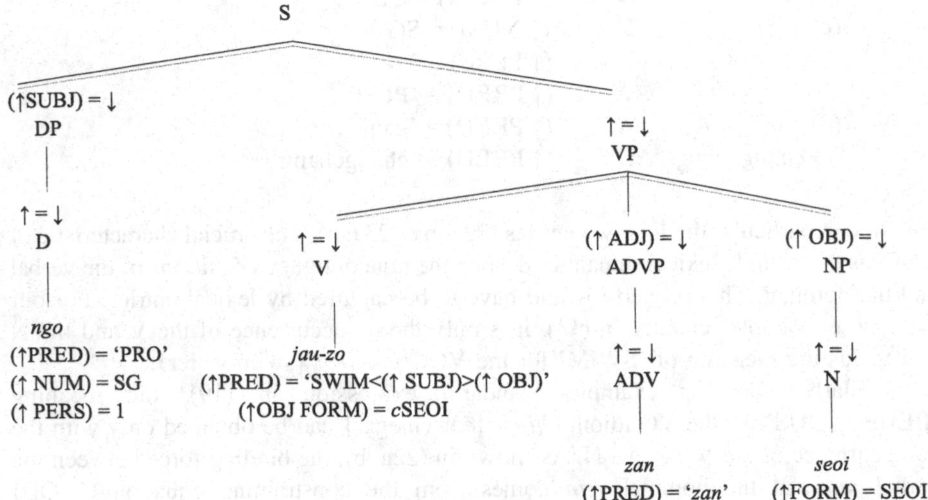

Fig. 1. C-structure

F-structure. The f-structure is also basic in the three-level representations in LFG. The c-structures in Figs. 1 and 2 are now represented as f-structures as follows in Figs. 3 and 4 respectively.

The f-structures in Figs. 3 and 4 specify that the predicate-argument structures of the sentences contain one thematic argument, the SUBJ function, and one athematic argument, the OBJ function. The contents of these arguments are also specified in the outermost f-structures by the inner f-structures assigned as the values to the attributes SUBJ and OBJ. The ADJ function, carrying the semantic content of '*zan* (for a while)' in Fig. 3 and '*changchang* (always)' in Fig. 4, is specified as an adjunct of the sentence, adding further information about the frequency or duration of the action to the entire VOC *jau-seoi* {swim-water} 'to swim' and the VO idiom *chi-cu* {eat-vinegar} 'be jealous of'. Whereas there is also an ADJ (whose PRED is '*gan*' (dry)) in the f-structure of the OBJ function in Fig. 4, unlike the former ADJ, this one is viewed as a syntactic adjunctive element to the OBJ only, since it is a nominal modifier even though its semantics of 'doing something for no reason' applies to the entire idiomatic VO compound. According to Bresnan [5: 50],

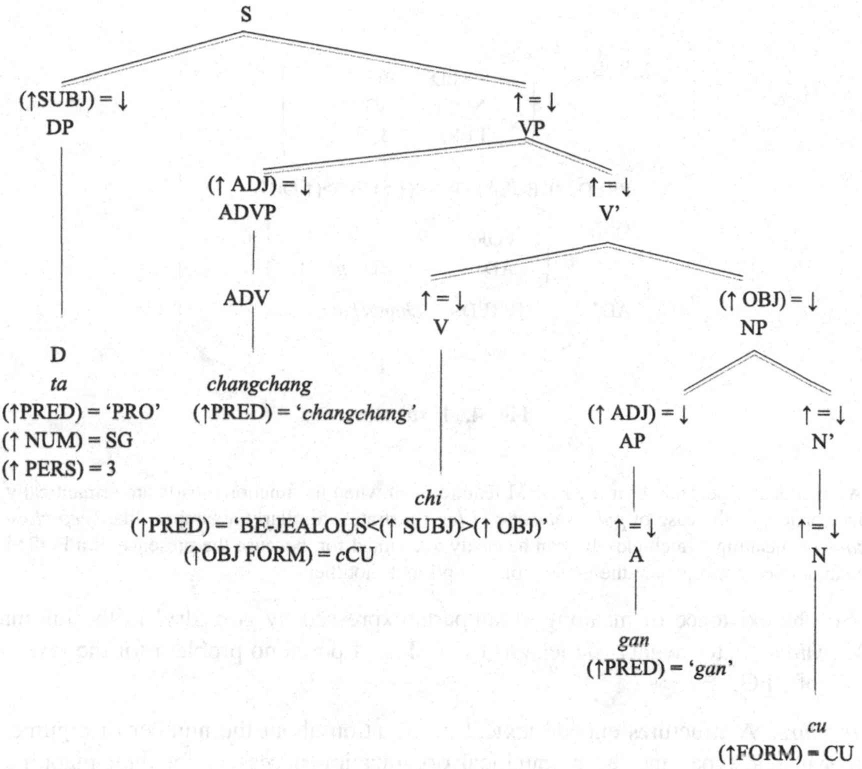

S

(↑SUBJ) = ↓
DP

↑ = ↓
VP

(↑ ADJ) = ↓
ADVP

↑ = ↓
V'

ADV

↑ = ↓
V

(↑ OBJ) = ↓
NP

D
ta
(↑PRED) = 'PRO'
(↑ NUM) = SG
(↑ PERS) = 3

changchang
(↑PRED) = '*changchang*'

(↑ ADJ) = ↓
AP

↑ = ↓
N'

chi
(↑PRED) = 'BE-JEALOUS<(↑ SUBJ)>(↑ OBJ)'
(↑OBJ FORM) = *c*CU

↑ = ↓
A

↑ = ↓
N

gan
(↑PRED) = '*gan*'

cu
(↑FORM) = CU

Fig. 2. C-structure

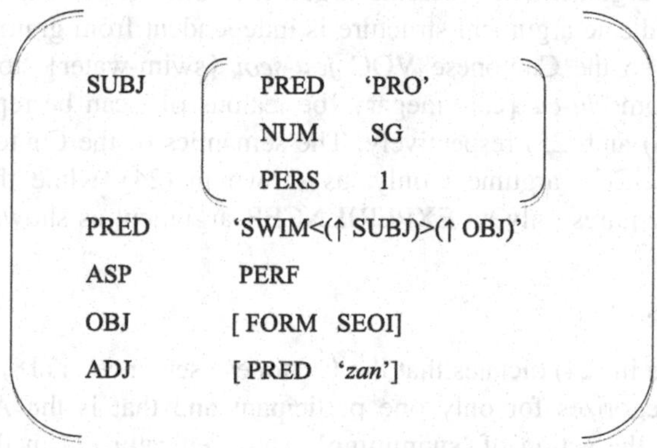

Fig. 3. F-structure

SUBJ [PRED 'PRO'
NUM SG
PERS 3]

PRED 'BE-JEALOUS<(↑ SUBJ)>(↑ OBJ)'

OBJ [FORM CU
ADJ [PRED '*gan*']]

ADJ [PRED '*changchang*']

Fig. 4. F-structure

A functional object can bear the FORM feature even when its functional parts are semantically interpreted, as the case of *pull [someone's] leg* illustrates. Similarly, examples like *keep close tabs on* meaning 'watch closely' can be easily accounted for, because the presence of a FORM feature does not preclude the generation of optional modifiers.

So, the existence of meaningful subparts expressed by *gan* 'dry' in the idiomatic VOC *chi-cu* {eat-vinegar} 'be jealous of' in Fig. 4 poses no problem for the lexicalist theory of LFG.

A-structure. A-structures encode lexical information about the number of arguments, their syntactic type, and the hierarchical organization necessary for their mapping to syntactic structure[5]. The nominals of the VOC and the VO idiom here, *seoi* 'water' and *cu* 'vinegar', are syntactic (grammatical) objects but not 'logical objects': they do not correspond to an argument in predicate argument structure. In the lexicalist theory assumed here, predicate argument structure is independent from grammatical function assignments, and so the Cantonese VOC *jau-seoi* {swim-water} 'to swim' and the Mandarin VO idiom *chi-cu* {eat-vinegar} 'be jealous of', can be represented by the a-structures in (24) and (25) respectively. The semantics of the Cantonese VOC verb necessitates an AGENT argument only, as shown in (24), while that of the Mandarin VO idiom requires only an EXPERIENCER argument as shown in (25).

(24) *jau* < Ag >
(25) *chi* < Exp >

The a-structure in (24) dictates that the Cantonese sentence in (18) has a predicator *jau* which subcategorizes for only one participant and that is the AGENT *ngo* 'I', which carried out the action of 'swimming'. The predicator *chi* in the a-structure in (25) for the Mandarin utterance in (19) also requires only one participant which is the EXPERIENCER *ta* 'he', that undergoes the psychological state of 'being jealous'.

[5] The Universal Hierarchy identifies the most prominent argument which can be selected as the logical subject, and is: agent > beneficiary > experiencer/goal > instrument > patient/theme > locative.

6 Conclusion

Through the use of formal syntactic and morphological diagnostics in addition to the demonstration of several semantic features, it has been shown that VOCs exhibit both syntactic and morphological properties. In this respect, they share some properties with VO idioms. In view of problems found in previous studies that attempted to accommodate VO idioms within the theoretical construct of LFG, we have presented a proposal of viewing the nominal element of a VOC as an athematic argument in the a-structure in LFG. It has been shown here that through the lexical specifications in LFG, specifically the constraining equation on the lexical head, we are in a position to plausibly represent the syntactic and semantic features of the VOCs.

Acknowledgements. The authors thank Prof. John Rennison for native-English speaking proof-editing of our paper in accordance with the requirements of the editors of this volume in which our paper appears. Research, writing, and conference presentation of the paper are funded by the University of Vienna, GADS Research Platform.

References

1. Alsina, A.: Causatives in Bantu and Romance. In: Alsina, A., Bresnan, J., Sells, P. (eds.) Complex Predicates, pp. 203–246. CSLI Publications, Stanford (1997)
2. Bloomfield, L.: Language. Allen and Unwin, London (1935)
3. Bodomo, A.: Serial verbs as complex predicates, in Dagaare and Akan. In: Maddieson, I., Hinnebusch, T.J. (eds.) Language History and Linguistics Description in Africa: Trends in African Linguistics, vol. 2, pp. 195–204. Africa World Press, Trenton (1998)
4. Bodomo, A.: The syntax of nominalized complex verbal predicates in Dagaare. Studia Linguistica **58**(1), 1–22 (2004)
5. Bresnan, J.: The passive in lexical theory. In: Bresnan, J. (ed.) Mental Representation of Grammatical Relations, pp. 3–86. MIT Press, Cambridge (1982)
6. Bresnan, J.: Lexical-Functional Syntax. Blackwell Publishers Inc., Massachusetts (2001)
7. Bresnan, J., Mchombo, S.A.: The lexical integrity principle: evidence from Bantu. Nat. Lang. Linguist. Theory **13**, 181–254 (1995)
8. Chao, Y.R.: A grammar of spoken Chinese. University of California Press, California (1968)
9. Che, D.W.: The syntax of particles in Mandarin Chinese. Ph.D. dissertation, The University of Hong Kong (2014)
10. Chi, T.R.: A Lexical Analysis of Verb-Noun Compounds in Mandarin Chinese. The Crane Publishing Co. Ltd., Taipei (1985)
11. Di Sciullo, A., Williams, E.: On the Definition of Word. MIT Press, Cambridge (1987)
12. Elenbaas, M.: The synchronic and diachronic syntax of the English verb-particle combination. Ph.D. dissertation, Radboud Universiteit, Nijmegen (2007)
13. Falk, Y.N.: Lexical-Functional Grammar: An Introduction to Parallel Constraint-Based Syntax. CSLI Publications, Stanford (2001)
14. Her, O.S.: Interaction and Variation in the Chinese VO Construction. The Crane Publishing Co. Ltd., Taipei (1997)
15. Huang, C.R.: A unification-based analysis of lexical discontinuity. Linguistics **28**, 263–307 (1990)

16. Huang, C.T.J.: Phrase structure, lexical ambiguity, and Chinese compounds. J. Chin. Lang. Teach. Assoc. **19**(2), 53–78 (1984)
17. Li, C.N., Thompson, S.A.: Mandarin Chinese: A Functional Reference Grammar. University of California Press, Berkeley (1981)
18. Mohanan, T.: Multidimensionality of representation: NV complex predicates in Hindi. In: Alsina, A., Bresnan, J., Sells, P. (eds.) Complex Predicates, pp. 431–472. CSLI Publications, Stanford (1997)
19. Sag, I.A., Gazdar, G., Wasow, T., Weisler, S.: Coordination and how to distinguish categories. Nat. Lang. Linguist. Theory **3**, 117–171 (1985)
20. Simpson, J.: Warlpiri Morpho-Syntax: A Lexicalist Approach. Kluwer Academic, Dordrecht (1991)
21. Tang, T.C.: Bingyu de jufa yu yuyi gongneng [The syntactic and semantic functions of object]. In: Tang, T.C. (ed.) Guoyu yufa yanjiu lunji [Studies on Mandarin Syntax], pp. 81–98. Student Book Co. Ltd., Taipei (1979)
22. Yu, S.S.: Discontinuous verb-object compounds in Cantonese and Mandarin. (Thesis). University of Hong Kong, Pokfulam, Hong Kong SAR (2003). http://dx.doi.org/10.5353/th_b2922486

Korean Morphological Collocations: Theoretical and Descriptive Implications

Mi Hyun Kim and Alain Polguère(✉)

ATILF, CNRS, Université de Lorraine, Nancy, France
mihyun.kimb@gmail.com, alain.polguere@univ-lorraine.fr

Abstract. Phrasemes are often characterized as constrained multiword expressions, like *spill the beans* (idiom) or *black coffee* (collocation), and the very term *phraseology* seems to imply that this phenomenon is restricted to phrases only. Consequently, morphological compounds, like *highbrow* or *bookstore*, are usually excluded from the scope of phraseological studies. Phrasemes, however, are not necessarily phrases (syntactically connected wordforms). In Korean, in particular, many compounds have to be analyzed and modeled as phrasemes. Like their phrasal counterparts, Korean compound phrasemes can be either semantically compositional or non-compositional. This paper deals with the first class of such compounds, which we term *morphological collocations*. It begins with a presentation of basic phraseological notions (Sect. 1). Then, Korean morphological collocations are introduced (Sect. 2), followed by descriptive repercussions exemplified with the lexicographic modeling of the phraseology of Korean nouns denoting body elements (Sect. 3). The conclusion summarizes theoretical and practical implications of this study (Sect. 4).

Keywords: Functional *vs.* morphological collocation · Korean · Body element

1 Background Notions

Before we start, we need to clarify important notions on which this paper is based, focusing on the notion of functional collocation (Sect. 1.1). Considerations on language discrepancies in regards to collocational phenomena will follow (Sect. 1.2).[1]

1.1 Functional Collocations

It is a well-known fact that the literature on phraseology features two distinct, though related notions of collocations, that can be termed:

- *frequency-based collocations* [1,2];
- *functional collocations* [3,4].

[1] We are deeply grateful to EUROPHRAS 2017 anonymous reviewers for their comments on an earlier version of the present paper.

R. Mitkov (Ed.): Europhras 2017, LNAI 10596, pp. 397–411, 2017.
https://doi.org/10.1007/978-3-319-69805-2_28

While frequency-based collocations can loosely be characterized as word combinations that are recurrent in texts, the notion of functional collocations is better understood in reference to how they are typically produced by the Speaker.[2] As our study is based on functional collocations, it is important that we propose a definition of this latter notion.

> A *collocation* – in the functional sense – is a linguistic expression AB (or BA) that the Speaker assembles by freely selecting A to express its meaning 'A', while B is selected in order to express a particular meaning 'm' according to combinatorial constraints imposed by A.
>
> A collocation is thus a semi-phraseological expression. A is called the *base* of the collocation and B the *collocate* of the base A.

For instance, *puppy love* 'intense and often short-lasting love of a very young person' is a collocation whose base is the noun *love* and collocate *puppy*. Clearly, *puppy* is here functionally dependent on *love*: it is a combinatorial property of the lexeme LOVE_N to select *puppy* as syntactic modifier as a means of expressing the specific meaning '[love] that is intense and often short-lasting, as experienced by a very young person'.[3]

The above definition of the notion of functional collocation shows that collocations are semantically compositional (though phraseological) expressions: they are assembled by the Speaker. In this respect, they are distinct from idioms, such as *blow the whistle*, *can of worms*, *on the spot*, etc. Idioms are not Speaker's constructs: they are full-fledged lexical units, that happen to be formally expressed by phrases instead of wordforms.[4]

Though extremely varied in terms of formal structure and semantic content, many collocations are based on universal **collocational patterns** known as *standard syntagmatic lexical functions* [5–7]. The system is too rich to be introduced here; suffice it to indicate that standard syntagmatic lexical functions are used to encode collocations controlled by the keywords of lexicographic articles [4].

Let us examine two well-known collocational patterns and their encoding by means of lexical functions, illustrating each case with collocations whose base is SIGH_N – i.e. collocations that are encoded in the lexicographic article for SIGH_N in order to account for its combinatorial properties.[5]

- Syntactic modifiers expressing intensification of the keyword's meaning are encoded by the lexical function Magn; in the article for SIGH_N, this gives:

  Magn: *audible*; *deep*, *profound*

---

[2] The term *Speaker*, written with an initial capital, refers to the producer of a given utterance, in contrast with *speaker of a language*.

[3] The lexicographic name of a lexical unit – i.e. its basic form as headword of a lexicographic article – is written here in small capitals. The part of speech (N[oun], V[erb], etc.) is specified in subscript when necessary: LOVE_V *vs.* LOVE_N.

[4] See Sect. 2.1 below for a definition of the notion of wordform.

[5] Collocations encoded below were extracted from the article for SIGH_N in the *The BBI Combinatory Dictionary of English* [8].

- Support verbs[6] that take the keyword as first complement and the keyword's first actant as subject are encoded by the lexical function Oper_1; in the article for SIGH$_N$, this gives:

  Oper_1: *to give, to let out* [*a* ~]; *to breathe, to heave* [*a* ~] | for ~ of relief

Lexical functions have been extensively used to formally encode collocations in lexical models such as: (i) *Explanatory Combinatorial Dictionaries* [9] and (ii) *Lexical Systems*, i.e. lexical networks structured by the system of Meaning-Text lexical functions [10].

1.2 Language-Dependent Properties of Collocational Patterns

An interesting and challenging aspect of collocational patterns is that – though universal in principle – they are influenced by the grammatical characteristics of each individual language. For instance, while Magn collocates (intensifiers) of nouns are prototypical syntactic modifiers, they are often not presented as such in Korean dictionaries when the collocate is an adjectival predicate. In Korean, the default syntactic position of an adjectival predicate is that of syntactic governor of the sentence, with the first semantic actant of the adjective expressed as grammatical subject. Consequently, (1a) below is a much more natural way of presenting a collocation in a Korean collocation dictionary than (1b):

(1) a. *Gaseumi pungmanhada*
bosom+SUB be.ample+PRES+DECL
'Somebody has a large bosom'
b. *pungmanhan gaseum*
be.ample+MOD bosom
'large bosom'

To some extent, the notion of Magn has to be somehow tailored for Korean, by considering that a prototypical Magn is either a syntactic modifier of the keyword or, in the case of predicative adjectives, a syntactic governor of the keyword, that functions as its grammatical subject.

The present paper is dealing with another, far more striking, specificity of collocational phenomena in Korean: the omnipresence of *morphological collocations.* The existence of morphological collocations has strong implications on the structuring of the Korean lexis, that ought to be taken into consideration both for lexicographic modeling and for the processing of Korean phraseology.

Phraseological discrepancies between natural languages are the first target of comparative approaches to the study of collocations. This paper is based on the outcome of research focusing on the comparison between Korean and French collocations [11].[7] We believe that the specific problems posed by morphological

---

[6] Support (or light) verbs are collocates that act as syntactic governors of the keyword without adding any significant meaning to it in the context of the collocation.

[7] On collocations for this language pair, see for instance [12].

collocations in Korean, as well as the notion of morphological collocation, have been overlooked in the past and we hope our work will partly remedy this situation.

2 Morphological Collocations in Korean

2.1 Phraseologization in Wordforms

We have introduced collocations in Sect. 1 as a special type of compositional phrasemes. The notion and the classification of phrasemes, including collocations, was explained at the level of phrases. Multilexicality, the first necessary condition for phrasemes, is generally applied in the context of phrase. In this section, we show that phraseologization in Korean is also possible at the level of *wordforms* and that Korean compound lexemes can be analyzed as phrasemes. Note that, in our terminology, a wordform is not just a *word form* (a linguistic signifier). It is a full-fledged linguistic sign: i.e. a triplet constituted of a given signified, a given signifier and a given combinatorics.[8] Wordforms can thus be conceived of as "desambiguated word forms."

To illustrate phraseologization in Korean wordforms, we start with collocations controlled by the lexeme BI 'rain' (i.e. collocations whose base is BI). In particular, we are focusing on collocations expressing the de-intensification of the meaning of this lexeme, such as in (2) below.

(2) *biga* *buseulgeorinda*
rain+SUB produce.lightly+PRES+DECL
'The rain is light'

In (2), the verb BUSEULGEORIDA[9] is selected restrictedly – according to BI's combinatorial properties – to express simultaneously 'takes place', i.e. to function as syntactic governor of the sentence, and to de-intensify the meaning of BI. In terms of Meaning-Text lexical functions, it corresponds to the configuration of standard lexical functions $\mathsf{AntiMagn}+\mathsf{Func}_0$.

De-intensification of the noun BI can also be expressed as a single AntiMagn, using the verb BUSEULGEORIDA as collocative modifier:

(3) *buseulgeorineun* *bi*
produce.lightly+MOD rain
'light rain'

As shown by the literal translation of (3), this is not unlike English, and it corresponds to prototypical expressions of (de-)intensifier collocates (Magn and

[8] "A wordform is a segmental sign that is more or less autonomous in [a given natural language] L and not representable in terms of other (previously established) wordforms" [13, p. 30].

[9] *Buseulgeor**ida*** is the infinitive of the verb – and its lexicographic name (BUSEULGEORIDA) –, while *buseulgeor**inda*** in (2) is a tensed form (present).

AntiMagn). Now, there exists in Korean a third option for expressing the de-intensification of BI – and of many other lexical units –, that is not available as such in English: a morphological, rather than syntactic structure.

The verb BUSEULGEORIDA is morphologically derived from the so-called *ideophonic* (reduplicated) adverb BUSEULBUSEUL – by means of the derivational suffix -GEORI (-DA being the inflectional suffix for the infinitive).[10] It is possible in Korean to produce a collocation synonymous to (3) by **compounding** the adverbial root BUSEUL- to the noun BI, as morphological modifier, as shown below.

(4) *buseulbi*
thinly+rain
'light rain'

This type of morphological construct is called *asyntactic compound* in publications on Korean grammar [16–18] because its compounding pattern, $\texttt{Adv}_{\texttt{root}}$+N, does not have a syntactic counterpart: adverbs cannot be nouns modifiers in a phrase. It is important to stress the fact that the root of reduplicated adverbs participate somewhat productively in compounding [14, p. 218].

Let us examine now two morphological compounding patterns that are even more productive than $\texttt{Adv}_{\texttt{root}}$+N in Korean.

A. Compound adjectival modifier of a noun: Adj+MOD+N

(5) a. *keunbi*
be.big+MOD+rain
'heavy rain'

b. *danbi*
be.sweet+MOD+rain
'timely rain'

B. Compound nominal modifier of a noun: N+N

(6) a. *jangdaebi*
stick+rain
'torrential rain'

b. *iseulbi*
dew+rain
'fine rain'

These two types of compounds are customarily called *syntactic compounds* as their morphological structures mirror corresponding syntactic structures: both adjectives and nouns can be noun modifiers in phrases.

Notice that asyntactic compounding patterns such as $\texttt{Adv}_{\texttt{root}}$+N – see (4) above – may have syntactic phrasal counterparts provided a verb is derived from the adverb by means of the -GEORI suffix, this derived verb being the phrasal modifier of the noun, as in example (3) above. To better contrast these two alternative realizations, one can compare the wordform in (7) and its phrasal counterpart in (8):

[10] Adverbs with inherent reduplication – such as BUSEULBUSEUL – lose their reduplication when combined with the derivational suffix -GEORI [17, p. 206]. For more on the loss of the reduplication in adverbs, see [15, p. 529].

(7) ***sandeul****baram* [Asyntactic morphological collocation $\texttt{Adv}_{\texttt{root}}$+N]
softly+wind
'light wind'

(8) ***sandeulgeorineun*** *baram* [Phrasal collocation $\texttt{V} \xleftarrow{\texttt{mod.}} \texttt{N}$]
produce.softly+MOD wind
'light wind'

As illustrated with the above examples, both asyntactic and syntactic compounding in Korean can give rise to semi-phraseological units, i.e. collocations whose base is their morphological head: *buseul**bi***, *keun**bi***, *dan**bi***, *jangdae**bi***, *iseul**bi***, etc. These semantically compositional phrasemes are by no means lexicalized entities (=lexical units). In other words, it would be very counterintuitive to consider a proliferation of quasi-synonyms of BI: *BUSEULBI, *KEUNBI, *DANBI, *JANGDAEBI, *ISEULBI, etc. One should rather envisage a single lexical unit BI, that controls (i.e. is the base of) multiple collocations that are constructed either syntagmatically (9) or morphologically (10):

(9) *buseulgeorineun bi*
produce.lightly+MOD rain
'light rain'

(10) *buseulbi*
lightly+rain
'light rain'

We shall call constructs such as (9) *phrasal collocations* and constructs such as (10) *morphological collocations*

Morphological collocations are multilexical, semantically compositional and non-free (more precisely, semi-fixed) expressions, same as phrasal collocations. Discrepancy in the level of phraseologization makes it necessary to distinguish between morphological collocations and two types of formally comparable compounds: free compounds (Sect. 2.2 below) and lexicalized compounds (Sect. 2.3).

2.2 Free Compounds

The term *morphological collocation* is strictly restricted to compounds that are indeed semantically compositional **and semi-phraseological** (semi-fixed). Morphological collocations have to be distinguished from *free compounds* [19, p. 274]. The latter are compounds freely assembled by the Speaker, based on morphological rules of the grammar, the choice of each element of the compounds to lexicalize the corresponding meaning being performed independently. (There is no base-collocate functional organization in free compounds.)

Wordforms (11a) below are free compounds whose morphological head is *bi* 'rain'; conversely, (11b) shows free compounds with *yeoreum* 'summer' as morphological modifier:

(11) a. *sigol**bi***; *saebyeok**bi***; *bam**bi***
countryside+rain; dawn+rain; night+rain
'countryside/dawn/night rain'

b. ***yeoreum**naj*; ***yeoreum**bam*; ***yeoreum**eumsik*
summer+day; summer+night; summer+food
'summer day/food/night/food'

As stated earlier, these compounds are made up of two nouns that are chosen unrestrictedly by the Speaker. The two nominal components are freely selected and combined according to Korean grammatical rules that build `N+N` wordforms.

2.3 Lexicalized Compounds

In contrast with free compounds, *lexicalized compounds* – e.g. the Korean compounds listed in (12a–c) below – are not assembled by the Speaker. They are diachronically lexicalized and belong to the lexicon prior to their use.

(12) a. *jakeunabeoji*
be.small+MOD+father
'uncle younger than one's father'
b. *keunabeoji*
be.big+MOD+father
'uncle older than one's father'
c. *heulkbi*
soil+rain
'dust storm'

Languages differ considerably as regards to compounding. While Korean – like Chinese [20], German, etc. – manifests both free and lexicalized compounding, other languages, such as French, possess only the latter type of compounding – see the French lexicalized compounds in (13a–b).[11]

(13) a. *tire-bouchon*
[it] pulls+cork
'corkscrew'
b. *grand-père*
big+father
'grandfather'

The idiomaticity of lexicalized compounds has been extensively studied by Korean linguists at the expense of free compounds. This may explain why Korean morphological collocations – on which we focus here – are also barely studied and are modeled in an erratic way (Sect. 3.2): morphological collocations can be viewed as phraseology that "takes advantage" of the presence of free compounding in the grammar of the language.

This concludes our presentation of the notion of morphological collocation in Korean and its comparison with related phrasal and morphological constructs; see Annex at the end of the paper for a synthetic recapitulation of important

[11] Of course, it is possible to generate new compounds in French, that will be considered neologistic until they eventually become lexicalized.

notions that have just been introduced.[12] We can now proceed with the topic of the modeling of Korean collocations.

3 Descriptive Implications: Korean Body Element Nouns

3.1 Lexicon of Body Element Nouns in Korean

To show phraseologization in wordforms as well as in phrases in Korean, we choose the lexicon of *body element nouns.*[13] The scope of this study is restrited to human external body element nouns, that are neutrally used: IP 'mouth' (not its familiar counterpart JUDUNGI), BAE 'belly' (not WI 'stomach', that denotes an internal body element), etc. We extracted about 200 entries that designate human external body elements from the entries of *Pyojun Gukeo Daesajeon*, hereafter PGD[14] – see Table 1.

Table 1. Localization of external body elements denoted by entries in PGD

Head	Limbs	Trunk	Whole body
103 entries	44 entries	30 entries	18 entries

Body element nouns draw our attention not only by their lexical abundance but also by the abundance of phraseology they display. First of all, they control a lot of collocations that describe quantification, position, appearance, function, structure, mobility, etc. of body elements:[15]

(14) a. *soni* *gopda*
hands+SUB be.comely+INF
'hands to be beautiful'

---

[12] For lack of space, we leave aside the interaction of the above classification of compounds with interesting descriptive notions that have been put forward in the study of semantic classes of compounds. Such is the case of the distinction between *endocentric compounds* – compounds whose semantic head is lexicalized in the compound structure (e.g. *draw**bridge***, for '**bridge** that ...') – and *exocentric compounds* – compounds that do not display such lexicalization of their semantic head (e.g. *pickpocket*, for '**thief** that ...'). On the distinction between these two semantic classes of compounds, see [21–23].

[13] We deliberately use the term *body element* rather than *body part*, as the former is a more general term than the latter. For instance, a leg is a body part, but not a tooth or an eye. By contrast, legs, teeth, eyes, etc. are all body elements.

[14] *Pyojun Gukeo Daesajeon* 'Standard dictionary of Korean language', National Institute of Korean Language, http://stdweb2.korean.go.kr/main.jsp.

[15] For a semantic classification of the collocations controlled by Korean body element nouns, see [11], where a list of 725 phrasal collocations controlled by body element nouns is presented.

b. *soneul* *naemilda*
hands+ACC hold.out+INF
'to hold out hands [to shake hands]'
c. *soneul* *naejeosda*
hands+ACC wave+INF
'to wave hands in order to deny'
d. *soneul* *heundeulda*
hands+ACC wave+INF
'to wave hands in order to greet'

A considerable number of Korean **idioms** also include body element nouns:[16]

(15) a. *soni* *keuda*
hands+SUB be.big+INF
'to be generous'
b. *soni* *jakda*
hands+SUB be.small+INF
'to be stingy'
c. *soni* *maepda*
hands+SUB be.spicy+INF
'hit done with the hands to be painful'
d. *soneul* *nohda*
hands+ACC put+INF
'to stop the work'
e. *soneul* *ssisda*
hands+ACC wash+INF
'to cut off negative relations'

Expressions such as (15a, b, d, e) above are in fact structurally (and semantically) ambiguous: *soni keuda*, for instance, can be analyzed either as a collocation that describes the dimension of hands or, as glossed in (15a), as an idiom.[17]

This study focuses on the description of morphological collocations controlled by Korean body element nouns, i.e. semi-phraseological compounds whose semantic pivot is a body element noun (Sect. 2 above).

3.2 Inconsistencies in Dictionaries and Lexical Resources

In a lexicographic project, identifying which lexical items should appear as dictionary entries is more perplexing when one treats compounds or derivatives in languages where compounding and derivation are highly productive. As we have seen in Sect. 2, there are three main types of compounds in Korean. These compounds need to receive lexicographic description that reflect their respective status, which is far from being the case is standard dictionaries. For example, we

[16] H.-S. Kim constructed a list of 2,585 Korean idioms, of which 798 idioms include body elements nouns [24].
[17] Only *soni maepda* (15c) does not display such ambiguity.

can find as **entries** in PGD the following lexical items that designate the nose and nose elements:[18]

Table 2. Entries for nouns denoting nose and nose elements in PGD

ko 'nose'
koan (nose+inside) 'inside of the nose'
koeonjeori (nose+surround) 'side of the nose'
koheori (nose+middle part) 'middle part of the nose'
kokkeut (nose+tip) 'tip of the nose'
kosbangul (nose+bell) 'rounded sides of the nose'
kosdae (nose+stem) 'nasal bridge'
kosdeung (nose+upper part) 'nasal bridge'
kosgumeoong (nose+hole) 'nostril as opening'
kosmaru (nose+ridge) 'ridge of the nose'
kosnal (nose+blade) 'nasal bridge'
kossok (nose+inside) 'inside of the nose'
koteol (nose+hair) 'nose hair'

Even though PGD treats all these compounds as entries, their lexical status are not same. Some compounds, like *koan* 'inside of the nose' and *koeonjeori* 'side of the nose', can be analyzed as free compounds. Speakers can assemble them freely: *ipeonjeori* (mouth+side), *ipan* (mouth+inside), etc. Other compounds, like *kosbangul* 'rounded sides of the nose' and *kosnal* 'nasal bridge', are better analyzed as lexicalized compounds.

In addition to compounds such as those presented in Table 2 above, one can find in PGD compounds that describe shapes of the nose and that are of two different structural types.

Firstly, there are compounds that consist of adjectival or adverbial root and *ko* 'nose' – i.e. based on the $\texttt{Adj/Adv}_{root}\texttt{+N}$ compounding pattern:

(16) a. *oddukko*
highly+nose
'high-bridged nose'
b. *napjakko*
flat+nose
'flat nose'
c. *ppyojokko*
pointedly+nose
'pointed nose'

These compounds are semi-phraseological units, i.e. morphological collocations. Take *napjakko*, for example. The standard way to describe its lexicalization

[18] Entries are listed in alphabetical order of transliterations.

is to consider that the Speaker chooses the base of the collocation – in our case, *ko* 'nose' – and then the collocate *napjak* is selected according to this base in order to express the meaning 'that is flat' next to the base. Such compounds should be modeled as being "assembled" by the Speaker, due to their compositional (though semi-phraseological) nature; they should not possess their own lexicographic entry and should rather be accounted for as combinatorial properties of their base.

Secondly, there are compounds that consist of a noun and *ko* – i.e. based on the N+N compounding pattern:

(17) a. *maeburiko*
hawk.beak+nose
'aquiline nose'
b. *jumeokko*
fist+nose
'bulbous nose'
c. *deulchangko*
pushed.up.window+nose
'upturned nose'

In Korean compounds of the N+N form, the second noun is always a *semantic pivot* and the first noun is a modifier [25]. In (17a–c), the second noun (*ko*) is freely chosen by Speaker and the first noun (*maeburi*, *jumeok*, *deulchang*) is selected in a restricted way of express a specific type of nose shape. Such compounds should clearly be analyzed and modeled as morphological collocations.

In contrast, there exist some clearly lexicalized compounds that are not to be treated as compositional constructs, such as:

(18) *ddalgiko*
strawberry+nose
'rosacea (= chronic inflammatory condition of the nose)'

The semantic pivot of this compound is not the meaning expressed by *ko*, but the semanteme 'disease'. Lexicalized compounds like (18) are genuine lexical units in Korean, that have to possess their own entry in Korean dictionaries and other lexicographic models.

3.3 Proposal for Lexicographic Modeling of Korean Compounding

Even though all compounds mentioned in Sect. 3.2 possess their own entry in a Korean dictionary such as PGD, we have seen that they correspond to three distinct types of complex wordforms: free compounds like *koan* 'inside of the nose', morphological collocation like *maeburiko* 'aquiline nose' and lexicalized compound like *ddalgiko* 'rosacea'. This section examines how to model these different compounds in a coherent and systematic way.

First of all, it should be stressed that free compounds should not be registered as dictionary entries. Speakers can freely produce countless compounds of that type according to general grammar rules of the language. For the sake of economy (and theoretical relevance), one should exclude from lexical models' wordlist free compounds, such as *koan*, *koeonjeori*, *kokkeut* and *kossok* listed in Table 2 above.

Morphological collocations, as well, do not possess a status of a full-fledged lexical unit. They are assembled by the Speaker according to combinatorial properties of their base. We therefore propose to describe not only phrasal collocations, but also morphological collocations in the entry for the base, as shown in Table 3.

Table 3. Phrasal and morphological collocations to appear in the entry for KO 'nose'

KO 'nose'
~*ga oddukhada* 'nose to be high-bridged'
~*ga napjakhada* 'nose to be flat'
~*ga mungtukhada* 'nose to be blunt'
~*leul golda* 'to snore'
~*leul japda* 'to hold one's nose [for protection against a bad smell]'
(...)
oddok~ 'flat nose'
napjak~ 'high-bridged nose'
ppyojok~ 'pointed nose'
jumeok~ 'bulbous nose'
maeburi~ 'aquiline nose'

Lexicalized compounds, finally, are non-compositional prefabricated morphological phrasemes[19], and they have to possess their individual entry in lexical models.

To sum up, a proper diagnosis of the linguistic nature of compounds has strong incidence on the structure and content of dictionaries and lexical databases. Let us look back at the statistics presented in Table 1 (Sect. 3.1). According to our classification of compounds, we can exclude about 20 lexicographic entries from the 103 entries in PGD that denote elements of the head: free compounds like *ipsok* 'inside of the mouth' and morphological collocations like *wisni* 'upper teeth' – the latter being accounted for in the entry for their base.

4 Conclusions

The aim of the present study was to examine Korean compounds from a phraseological point of view. This study has shown that phraseologization is possible in compound wordforms as well as in phrases.

[19] Morphological phrasemes are called *morphophrasemes* by D. Beck and I. Mel'čuk [26].

The principal theoretical implication of this study is the distinction of Korean compounds according to the same criteria of phraseologization, i.e. restrictedness and compositionality. Korean has not only free compounds (*koan* 'inside of the nose') and lexicalized compounds (*ddalgiko* 'rosacea'), but also semi-restricted and compositional compounds (*napjakko* 'flat nose'), that we term *morphological collocations*.

This research has several practical applications. Firstly, it helps to understand how to describe different types of compounds according to their lexical status in a systematic and exhaustive way in dictionaries, or any lexical resources. Secondly, it contributes to an efficient teaching and learning method of morphological collocations: teaching or learning morphological collocations along with phrasal collocations under the base will be more efficient than teaching or learning these compounds separately.

Annex: Korean Constructs Introduced in Sect. 2

Constructs	Examples
Phrasal collocation	비가 부슬거리다 *biga* *buseulgeorida* rain+SUB produce.lightly+INF 'The rain is light' 부슬거리는 비 *buseulgeorineun* *bi* be.thin+MOD rain 'light rain'
Morphological collocation	부슬비 *buseulbi* thinly+rain 'light rain' 큰비 *keunbi* be.big+MOD+rain 'heavy rain' 장대비 *jangdaebi* stick+rain 'torrential rain'
Free compound	밤비 *bambi* night+rain 'night rain'
Lexicalized coumpound	흙비 *heulkbi* soil+rain 'dust storm'

References

1. Sinclair, J.: Beginning the study of lexis. In: Bazell, C.E., Catford, J.C., Halliday, M.A.K., Robins, R. (eds.) In Memory of J.R. Firth, pp. 410–430. Longman, London (1966)
2. Sinclair, J.: Corpus, Concordance, Collocation. Oxford University Press, Oxford (1991)
3. Hausmann, F.J.: Le dictionaire de collocations. In: Hausmann, F.J., Reichmann, O., Wiegand, H.E., Zgusta, L. (eds.) Wörterbücher: ein internationales Hanbuch zur Lexicographie/Dictionaries: An International Encyclopaedia of Lexicography/Dictionnaires: Encyclopédie internationale de lexicographie. Handücker zur Sprach- und Kommunikationswissenschaft, Band 5.1, pp. 1010–1019. Walter de Gruyter, Berlin, New York (1989)
4. Mel'čuk, I.: Collocations and lexical functions. In: Cowie, A.P. (ed.) Phraseology. Theory, Analysis, and Applications, pp. 23–53, Oxford University Press, Oxford (1998)
5. Mel'čuk, I.: Lexical functions: a tool for the description of lexical relations in the lexicon. In: Wanner, L. (ed.) Lexical Functions in Lexicography and Natural Language Processing. Language Companion Series 31, pp. 37–102. John Benjamins, Amsterdam, Philadelphia (1996)
6. Mel'čuk, I.: Lexical functions. In: Burger, H., Dobrovol′skij, D., Kuhn, P., Norrick, N. (eds.) Phraseologie/Phraseology: Ein Internationales Handbuch Zeitgenössischer Forschung/an International Handbook of Contemporary Research, pp. 119–131. Walter de Gruyter, Berlin, New York (2007)
7. Polguère, A.: Lexical function standardness. In: Wanner, L. (ed.) Selected Lexical and Grammatical Issues in the Meaning-Text Theory. In Honour of Igor Mel'čuk. Language Companion Series 84, pp. 43–95. John Benjamins, Amsterdam, Philadelphia (2007)
8. Benson, M., Benson, E., Ilson, R.F.: The BBI Combinatory Dictionary of English. John Benjamins, Amsterdam, Philadelphia (2010). Third edition expanded and revised
9. Mel'čuk, I.: Explanatory combinatorial dictionary. In: Sica, G. (ed.) Open Problems in Linguistics and Lexicography, pp. 225–355. Polimetrica, Monza (2006)
10. Polguère, A.: From writing dictionaries to weaving lexical networks. Int. J. Lexicography **27**(4), 396–418 (2014)
11. Kim M.-H.: Étude contrastive de la phraséologie des noms d'éléments du corps en coréen et en français. Ph.D. dissertation, Université de Lorraine, Nancy (2017)
12. Lee, S.-H., Im, H.-B., Hong, C.-S.: Dagukeo yeoneo daejo yeonguleul wihan DB guchukgwa uimiburyuui hwalyong – hanbul daejoleul jungsimeuro. 'Construction of DB and application of semantic class for the contrastive study of multilingual collocations – focus on the contrast between Korean and French'. Peurangseueomungyoyuk **31**, 197–220 (2009)
13. Mel'čuk, I.: Semantics from Meaning to Text. Studies in Language Companion Series 129, vol. 1. John Benjamins, Amsterdam, Philadelphia (2012)
14. Kim, I.-B.: Gukeo Hapseongeo Yeongu. 'Study of Korean Compounds'. Yeokrak, Seoul (2000)
15. Kim, C.-S.: Hangukeo Hyeongtaeron Yeongu. 'Study of Korean Morphology'. Taehaksa, Seoul (2008)
16. Ko, Y.-K., Koo, B.-G.: Urimal Munbeopron. 'Grammar of Our Language', 2nd edn. Jipmundang, Seoul (2009)

17. Nam, K.-S., Ko, Y.-K.: Pyojungugeomunbeobron. 'Standard Korean Grammar', 3rd edn. Tapchulpansa, Seoul (2011)
18. Ko, Y.-K.: Gukeohyeongtaeronyeongu. 'Study of Korean Morphology'. Seoul National University Press, Seoul (1999)
19. Mel'čuk, I.: Semantics: From Meaning to Text. Studies in Language Companion Series 135, vol. 2. John Benjamins, Amsterdam, Philadelphia (2013)
20. Nguyen, É.V.T.: Unité lexicale et morphologie en chinois mandarin. Vers l'élaboration d'un Dictionnaire Explicatif et Combinatoire du chinois. Ph.D. dissertation, Université de Montréal, Montreal (2006)
21. Gross, G.: Les expressions figées en français: noms composés et autres locutions. Ophrys, Paris (1996)
22. Bauer, L.: Typology of compounds. In: Lieber, R., Štekauer, P. (eds.) The Oxford Handbook of Compounding, pp. 343–356. Oxford University Press, Oxford (2009)
23. Haspelmath, M., Sims, A.D.: Understanding Morphology, 2nd edn. Routledge, London, New York (2010)
24. Kim, H.-S.: Hangukeo Sukeo Yeongu. Study of Korean Idioms. Hangukmunhwasa, Seoul (2011)
25. Kim, G.-H.: Gwanhyeong guseongui tongeo hyunsanggwa euimi gwangye. 'Syntax and semantic relation of modifier construction'. Hangeul **209**, 59–97 (1990)
26. Beck, D., Mel'čuk, I.: Morphological phrasemes and Totonacan verbal morphology. Linguistics **49**(1), 175–228 (2011)

Computational approaches to phraseology

Towards Comprehensive Computational Representations of Arabic Multiword Expressions

Ayman Alghamdi[1(✉)] and Eric Atwell[2]

[1] Umm Al-Qura University, Mecca, Kingdom of Saudi Arabia
scaaa@leeds.ac.uk
[2] University of Leeds, Leeds, UK
e.s.atwell@leeds.ac.uk

Abstract. A successful computational treatment of multiword expressions (MWEs) in natural languages leads to a robust NLP system which considers the long-standing problem of language ambiguity caused primarily by this complex linguistic phenomenon. The first step in addressing this challenge is building an extensive reliable MWEs language resource LR with comprehensive computational representations across all linguistic levels. This forms the cornerstone in understanding the heterogeneous linguistic behaviour of MWEs in their various manifestations. This paper presents a detailed framework for computational representations of Arabic MWEs (ArMWEs) across all linguistic levels based on the state-of-the-art lexical mark-up framework (LMF) with the necessary modifications to suit the distinctive properties of Modern Standard Arabic (MSA). This work forms part of a larger project that aims to develop a comprehensive computational lexicon of ArMWEs for NLP and language pedagogy LP (JOMAL project).

Keywords: Multi-Word Expressions · Language resource · Computational representations · Annotation

1 Introduction

Multi-Word Expressions MWEs are a heterogeneous phenomenon in human languages which pose different types of serious challenges particularly in the fields of Natural Language Processing NLP and in language pedagogy LP. This is because MWEs are considered as one of the key factors that contribute to the long-standing language ambiguity problems which is one of the most crucial setbacks that most NLP tasks face. Sag et al. [1] emphasise that 'like the issue of disambiguation, MWEs constitute a key problem that must be resolved in order for linguistically precise NLP to succeed'. However, in recent years much research has been conducted in this area which aims to scientifically study this phenomenon to discover new methods and approaches that aim to determine the best computational practice in MWEs processing based on state-of-the-art techniques and tools developed in NLP, machine learning and artificial intelligence research. These efforts cover a wide range of topics related to MWEs which includes but is not limited to extraction models, computational representations,

R. Mitkov (Ed.): Europhras 2017, LNAI 10596, pp. 415–431, 2017.
https://doi.org/10.1007/978-3-319-69805-2_29

linguistic analysis and classifications. The first step and the foundation stone of these studies is the availability of reliable representative open source MWE LRs which pave the way for interested researchers to experiment and analyse various types of these lexical units in order to find out the best computational treatment and ultimately improve various NLP applications output.

Moreover, these LRs can be embedded in the implementations of various NLP and ML tools that take MWEs knowledge into account and which assist considerably in the task of tackling language ambiguity related problems. However, while many well developed MWEs lexicons are freely available for English and other modern European languages, Arabic is still suffering from lack of computational comprehensive MWE LRs. Most of the existing Arabic MWEs lexicons are either very limited in terms of their scale or annotations features or they are not freely available as an open source project which makes it difficult for most researchers to benefit from them. This project aims to remedy this deficiency by constructing a large scale Arabic MWEs lexicon with detailed computational representations at different linguistic levels based on state-of-the-art extraction methods and international standards for MWE computational representations. The current paper reports part of this project which focuses on describing a framework for computational representations and annotations across various linguistic levels.

2 Related Work

Several projects have attempted to create an electronic database for different types of MWEs developed for various purposes; for instance, the SIGLEX-MWE website lists more than 22 MWE LRs in different languages which are open source projects that are available for free download[1]. In their on-going project -which is led by a multidisciplinary scientific network devoted to European MWEs- Savary et al. [2] provide a summary about their latest research results and activities related to the computational treatments of MWEs. However, as part of their project, Losnegaard et al. [3] and Rosén et al. [4] conducted an intensive survey of all the available MWEs LRs based on the use of an online questionnaire which was designed to obtain detailed information about all the existing electronic MWEs resources. The preliminary results of the survey are publicly accessible as an online updated spreadsheet[2]. Based on the main classifications of the study questionnaire[3] with minor modifications, the MWEs lexicons were grouped into five categories as can be seen in Table 1.

These MWEs lexicons represent a variety of LRs types in relation to their domain, phrase length, linguistic annotation, size and degree of accessibility; however the result related to Arabic MWEs lexicons shows only four MWE LRs developed by [5, 6, 7]. Unfortunately, they are not publicly accessible through the web which make it difficult

[1] http://multiword.sourceforge.net/PHITE.php?sitesig=FILES&page=FILES_20_Data_Sets.

[2] https://sites.google.com/site/mwesurveytest/home.

[3] The survey online form. https://goo.gl/eYz8qL.

Table 1. The main categories of MWE LRs

MWEs lexicon	LRs Nu	Percentage
Treebank with MWE annotations	12	11
MWE lexicons	48	45
Monolingual list of MWEs	13	12
Multilingual resources	15	14
Others (for all the LRs out of the previous categories)	19	18

for us to find out more details about their scale or what type of linguistic annotation is associated with them.

Another Arabic MWEs list was developed by Attia [8] in the process of creating an Arabic version of the Xerox Linguistic platform which was initially developed by Butt [9] and Dipper [10] for writing languages grammar rules and performing various linguistic analyses based on the Lexical Functional Grammar theory [11]. In the process of building the MWE Transducer, Attia managed to extract a list of 2826 Arabic MWEs items which were then classified into four main categories based on the classifications of MWEs presented by Sag et al. [1], as can be seen in Table 2 along with examples:

Table 2. Arabic MWEs classifications with examples.

Classifications	ArMWEs	Translation
Compositional expressions	*ġalāf alkatāb*[a], غلاف الكتاب	Book cover
Non-compositional expressions	*raj' bakfī ḥanīn*,رجع بخفي حنين	Kick the bucket
Fixed Expressions	*'išāra almarūr*, إشارة المرور	Traffic light/lights
Semi-fixed Expressions	*ṣabāḥ alḳayr*, صباح الخير/الخيرات	Good morning
Flexible Expressions	*takfīḍ sar'a almarkba*, تخفيض سرعة المركبة	Slow the car down

[a] The German standard DIN 31636 is used for rendering Romanized Arabic

In this project, several types of MWEs are excluded from the extracted list including compound nouns, verbal and prepositional phrases. In addition, there was no intention to create lexical representations for MWEs listed because the sole aim was to improve the linguistic analyser system by accommodating several types of MWEs. It is worth mentioning here that the experiment's findings in this research emphasise the major positive role of accommodating MWEs LR in the final system output which was less ambiguous with a higher degree of precision which again highlights the importance of creating a large scale Arabic MWE LR which will help in the improvement of many Arabic NLP tasks.

Bounhas and Slimani [12], implemented another hybrid model for extracting compound nouns and also proposed new algorithms to reduce morphological and syntactic ambiguities during the MWE extraction process. Their model was constituted

Table 3. Arabic compound nouns classifications with examples

Compound noun classifications	Examples	Examples
Annexation compound noun	سيارة رجل غني	The car of a rich man
Adjective compound noun	بيت كبير	Big house
Substitution compound noun	هذه السيارة	This car
Prepositional compound noun	نوع من الحلوى	A kind of sweet
Conjunctive compound noun	القط والفأر	The cat and the mouse
Compound nouns linked by composite relations	الاستمرار لحوالي سنة	To persist for about one year

of three phases starting from the morphological analysis, followed by the sequence identifier and syntactic parser. The final result was filtered based on statistical information. The extracted items were classified into six categories according to different types of Arabic compound nouns as shown in Table 3.

To evaluate their model, the final list of MWEs was compared to a previously well-developed MWEs list and the result shows an improvement in the extracting accuracy in comparison with previous experiments applied on Arabic MWEs extractors in the same domain.

A more recent study carried out by Hawwari et al. [13] aimed to build a list of MWEs collected manually from existing written Arabic MWEs dictionaries to automatically annotate an Arabic corpus using a pattern-matching algorithm to help in the automatic statistical identification of MWEs in running text. Their final list was categorised into five groups based on syntactic constructions as can be seen in Fig. 1.

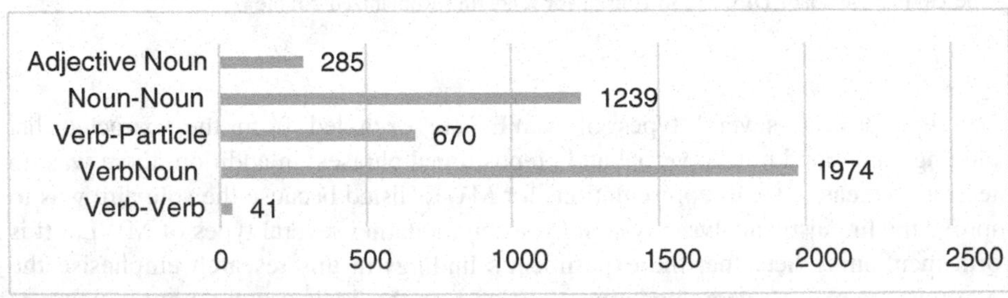

Fig. 1. Syntactic constructions of Arabic MWES in [13].

In their following study Hawwari et al. [14] presented a framework for the classification and annotation of Egyptian Arabic MWEs. Their focus was on representing different types of MWEs in the Egyptian dialect. It is worth considering here that several of the annotation features suggested in this study are applicable with several modifications to MWEs in MSA which are this study's main concern. The classifications and annotation cover different linguistic levels such as morphological, syntactic, semantic and pragmatic features of MWEs. The developed framework builds on previous research applied to other languages e.g. [15, 16]. Another study by Al-Sabbagh et al. [6] aims to build Arabic modal multiword expressions to accelerate the automatic extraction process and represents variation patterns of modal MWEs in Arabic. Based on Palmer et al. [17] cross-lingual taxonomy of modality senses, they classify the extracted MWEs items into 7 categories as follows: (un)certainty, evidentiality, obligation, permission, commitment, ability and volition. Table 4 shows examples of MWEs classifications. Although, the author stated that the final LR is available for free download, we could not find a copy or working link for this MWE lexicon.

Table 4. Examples of AM-MWEs from Al-Sabbagh et al. [6]

AM-MWEs	English translations
نويت	I intend
يمكنني	I can
أعتقد	I think
هناك احتمال بأن	It is possible

Bar et al. [18] developed a relatively small manually annotated list of MWEs as a gold standard list in the process of tackling the problem of automatic extraction and classifications of MWEs. They implemented deterministic pattern-matching algorithms in the detection process of various types of continuous and non-continuous MWEs; they found that the use of only shallow annotated data results in major improvements in the automatic boundary detection on the token level of MWEs.

Overall, in the developments of the current lexicon we build on all the previous attempts in the extractions and the lexical representations of ArMWEs, aiming to reach an innovative large scale Arabic MWE lexicon with comprehensive computational representations at various linguistics levels.

3 Properties of MWE Computational Representations

Based on the main project objectives, the annotation scheme had to be easy to integrate in different types of NLP systems, following the state-of-the-art standards in lexical mark-up research. In addition, the adopted scheme is not restricted to any particular grammatical framework because of the reusability purposes as Odijk [19] emphasised:

> *'Lexical representations of MWEs that are highly specific to particular grammatical frameworks or concrete implementations are undesirable, since it requires effort in making such representations for each new NLP system again and again and the degree of reusability is low' (p. 189).*

Another essential property of the current representations is the flexibility which cuts across all types of ArMWEs and also covers discontinuous as well as contiguous phrases; it is also targeted to be human readable and equally adopted for NLP systems to accommodate different end users' needs. However, most of the previous studies on ArMWEs annotation schemes have prioritised certain types of expressions or language genres to the exclusion of others, so they are not appropriate for representing multiple kinds of ArMWEs in our lexicon, which should allow for permutations across various linguistic levels. The computational ArMWEs representations are encoded in Extensible Mark-up Language XML because it is the most flexible and also the most used method in the representations of computational LR. The final version will be converted into HTML pages for the purpose of publishing its content on the Internet.

In our project we also benefit from the international standard lexical mark-up framework LMF which was the result of 60 experts' contributions who worked for more than five years to develop lexical representations and standards for different types of computational LRs [20, 21]. The LMF describes the basic hierarchy of information of a lexical entry and also has specific provisions for MWEs, specifically a normative NLP MWE patterns extension, illustrated with examples in the form of a UML class diagram and XML hierarchy model [22]. It is important to note that adopting standardisation when building computational LR can be very beneficial specially in NLP oriented applications as Francopoulo [20] showed:

> *'The significance of standardization was thus recognized, in that it would open up the application field, allow an expansion of activities, sharing of expensive resources, reuse of components and rapid construction of integrated, robust, multilingual language processing environments for end-user' (p. 3).*

Furthermore, the developed representations system gives special attention to enriching the lexical entries with extensive linguistic information to allow for various types of end users and to prepare the LR for any potential use. Atwell [23] states that 'For developers of general-purpose corpus resources, the aim may be to enrich the text with linguistic analyses to maximize the potential for corpus reuse in a wide range of applications' (p. 4). In the following, a brief description of the type of users targeted in the JOMAL project is presented. This is followed by a detailed illustration of the adopted ArMWEs classifications and representations across different linguistic levels.

4 JOMAL Computational Representations

As mentioned previously, in the design of our lexicon annotation and classifications, this project takes into account the LMF core package and MWE patterns extension with the necessary deviations to facilitate the JOMAL reusability and connectivity to other LRs and various NLP systems and applications. This section describes the computational representations and the labels adopted for each MWEs class and propriety property with examples from Arabic corpora.

Throughout, we have made as much use of automated procedures as possible to reduce the time and effort of the annotation process. All the representations in the current version of this annotation scheme are classified into four main categories as follows: basic lexicon information, linguistic properties, pedagogical, and any other related information, which involves all the representations that do not belong to any of the previous three annotation groups.

4.1 Basic Lexicon Information

This class is mainly adopted from the MWE extension in LMF framework, and it expresses the main information about the JOMAL which can be useful for the LR end users. The attributes in the Global information class illustrate a brief abstract about the project which includes: label author, language coding and script coding. Main Lexical Entry is the core class for each lexical entry which involves written form, related form and lexicographic type. Other classes aim to represent the details of MWE components in their various linguistic manifestations.

Table 5. Basic lexicon information representations in JOMAL.

Class name	Subclasses and attributes
Lexical resource	
Global information	Label Comment Author Language coding Script coding

As can be seen in Table 5, the ID attribute which can be seen in most annotation classes was created to facilitate the linkage between shared annotation classes; thus they can be targeted by cross-reference links. The comments attribute is specified to provide any necessary information which might explain the annotation class. This information is encoded in XML; Fig. 2 shows an example of the XML fragment of the Global Information class:

```
<GlobalInformation>
   <feat att="label" val="Arabic Formulaic Sequences Lexicon"/>
   <feat att="comment" val="مدخل تفصيلي لخصائص التركيب في أمس الحاجة "/>
   <feat att="author" val="AymanAlghmdi"/>
   <feat att="languageCoding" val="ISO 639-3"/>
   <feat att="scriptCoding" val="ISO 15924"/>
</GlobalInformation>
```

Fig. 2. An example of lexicon information annotated in XML.

4.2 Linguistic Representations

The linguistic annotation classes are the core package of the JOMAL model which aims to provide a detailed linguistic description of each ArMWE in our lexicon. The annotations are classified into six main layers, each one is dedicated for linguistic levels starting from the shallow orthographic form of the lexical entry to the deep semantic and pragmatics features of MWE. The following subsections present a brief explanation of these linguistic annotations.

Basic Linguistic Description

The first five classes provide the basic linguistic description of MWEs which was adopted from the MWE pattern extension model in LMF standards [20], as shown in Table 6.

Table 6. Basic linguistic representations of MWE

Class name	Subclasses and attributes
Main lexical entry	Id Comment Written form Related form Lexicographic type
List of components	Component Related component
MWE pattern	Id Written template Comment
MWE node	Syntactic constituent Pattern type
MWE lex	Structure head Rank Lexical flexibility Graphical separator

The Main Lexical Entry class is the core class of each lexical entry and it is associated with all the annotation features. It also has several attributes related to written and related forms of MWE. For instance, the lexicographic types of the expressions represented by several labels as can be seen in Table 7 with examples from the lexicon.

Table 7. Examples of lexicographic types labels in JOMAL

Lexical Types labels	Examples	Translation
Compound noun	عيادة الطبيب	*Medical Practice*
Support verb	طفح الكيل	*Fed up*
Quotation	ضرب صفحاً	*Ignore*
Idiom	مقطوع من شجرة	*Cut from a tree*
Proverb	اضرب الحديد وهو حامي	*Hit the iron while it's hot*

The MWEs pattern instance is a shared resource which provides information about different lexical combination phenomena. This class is associated and explained by the list of components instance that contain all the expression constituent words. The node classes' aim is to represent the structure properties of the given phrase by providing information on syntactic constituent and pattern type. The first feature illustrates the written template form of the structure, for instance the syntactic constituents of the English phrase to take off is Verb_ Preposition or VP; an Arabic equivalent example can be seen in the phrase, أخذ عن which is also classified as VP structure. In Table 8, examples of syntactic constituents found in JOMAL are listed.

Table 8. Examples of syntactic constituents' classifications in JOMLA

Label	Example
Noun_Noun	تكميم الأفواه, *takmīm al'afwāh*
Verb_Noun_Preposition_Noun	تجمد الدم في عروقه, *tajmd addam fī 'arūqh*
Noun_Adjective	اليد المغلولة, *alyad almaǧlūla*
Noun_Adverb	الأيام بيننا, *al'ayām baynnā*
Noun_Preposition	التغطية على, *attaǧtya 'alā*
Preposition_Noun_Preposition	من أجل أن, *man 'ajl 'an*
Noun_Preposition_Noun	النوم في العسل, *annawm fī al'asl*

The pattern type represents the degree of phrase morphological, lexical and grammatical flexibility by using a scale of three levels as illustrated in Table 9.

Table 9. Pattern types classifications with Arabic examples

Flexibility degree	Example
Fixed MWE	رجع بخفي حنين, *raj' bakfī ḥanīn*
Semi-fixed MWE	أثلج/أثلجت صدره/صدرها, *'aṯlj/a'ṯljt ṣadrh/ṣdrhā*
Flexible MWE	أثقلته/أثقله/أنهكته الأعباء/الحمل/المسؤوليات، *'aṯqlth/a'ṯqlh/a'nhkth al'a'bā'/alḥml/almsu'ūlyāt*

The MWE lex class used to provide a reference to each lexical component in the list of components instance. It also provides lexical classifications of each list of components based on the possibility of allowing some substitutions in the lexical items. Hence two values are specified for each component: one for MWEs that can be alternated with other lexical items and the second one for other MWEs that have to be used with the same lexical items or what we called fixed MWEs. The Structure Head represents the first POS tag for the phrases and the rank attribute shows the components order and also any possible alternative orders. This feature is important particularly for Arabic because it has a high degree of flexibility in the order of sentence words. For instance, the MWE أقبلت عليه الدنيا has six components order possibilities shown in Table 10.

Table 10. An example shows the components order flexibility in ArMWEs

A	**الدنيا**	**2**	**عليه**	**3**	**أقبلت**	**1**
B	عليه	3	الدنيا	2	أقبلت	1
C	أقبلت	1	الدنيا	2	عليه	3
D	الدنيا	2	أقبلت	1	عليه	3
E	أقبلت	1	عليه	3	الدنيا	2
F	عليه	3	أقبلت	1	الدنيا	2

Orthographic Representations

As described in Table 11, the orthographic annotation contains five attributes which in turn have several values. Three attributes express the orthographic variety of the expression, which can be very useful particularly for NLP oriented users, as they enable them to extract the LR in various formats according to the targeted NLP or ML tasks. An example of these types of representation can be seen in the phrase أعياه الأمر which can be represented in various forms based on its orthographic features, as in Table 12.

To see an example of the previous annotation in XML, Appendix 1 illustrates the XML fragment which represents the ArMWE في أمس الحاجة, *fī ʾams alḥāja, in urgent need.*

Phonological Representations

At the Phonological layer of annotation, we provide a complete diacritization of each phrase which is an essential feature in Arabic phonology to express the most common pronunciation form of ArMWEs in MSA. This representation is also particularly important because of the absence of short vowel symbols in Arabic script, which also play a prime role at the syntactic and semantic analysis levels of the lexical units. Other attributes are devoted to represent other phonological variants when available and also a representation of the expression in IPA phonetic script.

Morphosyntactic Representations

For the Morphosyntactic representations we use a modified version of LMF morphological patterns extension to provide detailed descriptions of the Morphosyntactic feature of the phrase. This level of annotation is essential particularly for Arabic which has powerful derivational morphological features which result in different variations for each word which we aim to represent in JOMAL lexicon. With regard to the POS feature, expressions components are classified into five categories according to their POS tag. Table 13 shows the adopted morphological tag set with MWE examples of the headword POS.

Table 11. The linguistic annotation layers of JOMAL

Class name	Subclasses and attributes
Orthographic features	Id Comment DIN31635RenderingInPlainEnglish Normalised form Different spelling form
Phonological features	Id Comment Diacritization Phonetic form Phonological variants
Morphosyntactic features	Id comment Word form Root Derivation form (Lemma) Stem Morphological scheme Part of speech Grammatical features syntactic function
Semantic features	Id Comment Sense Semantic fields Idiomaticity degree Semantic relations
Pragmatics features	Id Comment Usage type User type

Table 12. An example of orthographic features of MWE أعياه الأمر, exhaust

Orthographic Features	**Expression example**
DIN31635RenderingInPlainEnglish	*'a'yāh al'amr*
Normalised Form	اعياه الامر
Different Spelling Form	أعياه الأمر

Table 13. Examples of the POS tags used in the morphosyntactic representations

POS tag	Example
Noun	البرج العاجي *albarj al'ājī*
Verb	التزم الصمت *attazm aṣṣamt*
Adjective	جنون العظمة *janūn al'aḏma*
Adverb	بين الحياة والموت *bayn alḥayā walmawt*
Preposition	على قدم المساواة *'alā qadm almasāwā*
Interjection	يا غالب يا مغلوب *yā ġālb yā maġlūb*

Table 14. Examples of morphological patterns and meanings of the word سمع

Morphological patterns	Meaning
سمع	Listen(Past tense verb)
يسمع	Listening (Present tense verb)
اسمع	Listen (Imperative tense verb)
مسموع	Heard
سماعة	Speaker
سامع	Listener (Singular)
سامعون	Listeners (Plural for male)
سامعات	Listeners (Plural for female)

The morphological features for each component are represented in a specific element. However, the morphological properties are essential and useful information to include in the MWEs representations because of the derivational and inflectional nature of Arabic morphology which means that words in Arabic are derived from specific roots, and usually the inflected words that share the same root belong to a common semantic field. Thus this feature helps to easily classify all the words that belong to the same root into semantically similar groups based on the common morphological root. Table 14 shows an example of an Arabic root with its morphological patterns and inflection forms.

The grammatical features class is targeted to represent four main properties, including number, gender, tense for verbs and person. Consequently, all these features involve several values which are represented in detail in the grammatical properties of each MWE component. Table 15 provides examples of these linguistic features in Arabic.

Table 15. Examples of Grammatical features annotation

Grammatical features	Values
Number	Signal, plural
Gender	Male, female, things
Tense	Past, present, imperative
Person	Third person

Semantic Representations

This level of annotation constitutes four main classes created for representing the sematic information of MWEs. The 'Sense Set' class represents the meaning variants of MWEs in different contexts associated with a corpus example that reflects the real use of the phrase. The 'Semantic Fields' class aims to group the phrases into several categories based on the main semantic fields. The idiomaticity degree feature is targeted to classify the MWEs into three categories based on the ambiguity levels of the phrase as follows: full opaque, semi opaque and compositional MWEs. Full opaque MWEs involve expressions that have no semantic relation between the general meaning of the phrase as a whole and its component parts, such as, على كف عفريت، على قدم وساق، طالت أظافره، *'alā kaf 'afrīt, 'alā qadm wasāq, ṭālt 'aḏāfrh.* Semantic Relations is a class representing the oriented relationship between Synset instances, where three types of relations are included: synonymy, antonymy, and polysemy.

Pragmatics Representations

The pragmatic annotation of MWE adds usage labels to MWEs that demonstrate the type of potential users or the possible situations in which this phrase can be used, such as academic, formal and informal uses of the MWE. These features help in the deep understanding of a MWEs' pragmatic behaviour.

4.3 Pedagogical Representations and Other Features

The aim of these representations is to make the most of JOMAL in any language pedagogy related applications. Thus this class provides valuable information in this regard which includes frequency attributes which show the popularity degree of the phrase. In addition, the source label presents information about the LRs where phrases were extracted from. The date label indicates the date of compiling the source corpus while the style label refers to the type of language genre such as standard, classical or other Arabic dialects. The type element represents whether the MWE was from written or speech corpus. As listed in Table 16 the last class of our representations model was created to include all the information that are beneficial for the LR end-users and cannot belong to any of the previous described annotation classes; for instance, the status of annotation compilation for each lexical entry and also the MWE Equivalent in Arabic dialects or the translation of MWE in other languages.

Table 16. Pedagogical representations and other features of MWEs

Pedagogical features	Id Comment Learnability levels Frequency Language type Voiced example Language source name Language source link
Other features	Id Comment Translation equivalent Dialectic equivalent Entry status levels

5 Conclusion and Future Work

In this paper, we present a detailed description of the lexical representations model that we applied in the development of a comprehensive ArMWEs lexicon for NLP and LP. In our model, we build on previous attempts and standards in the computational lexical representations of MWEs; moreover, we add several innovative annotation features that enhance the usefulness and the usability of JOMAL in various practical applications in NLP and LP. This work is a crucial and essential step towards more advanced and comprehensive research in the computational treatment of ArMWEs. This paper extends our earlier work on ArMWEs reported in [24, 25]. Future work will focus on building various tools and applications based on the developed lexicon to make the most out of it.

Appendix

XML fragment for the MWE, *fī ʾams alḥāja*, **في أمس الحاجة**

```xml
<LexicalEntry mwePattern="PreAdvNo">
        <feat att="partOfSpeech" val="preposition"/>
        <Lemma>
          <feat att="writtenForm" val=" في أمس الحاجة"/>
                      </Lemma>
        <ListOfComponents>
          <Component entry="A1"/>
          <Component entry="A2"/>
          <Component entry="A3"/>
        </ListOfComponents>
    </LexicalEntry>
    <LexicalEntry id="A1" morphologicalPatterns="AsTable">
        <feat att="partOfSpeech" val="prepostion"/>
        <Lemma>
          <feat att="writtenForm" val="في"/>
        </Lemma>
    </LexicalEntry>
    <LexicalEntry id="A2" morphologicalPatterns="AsTable">
        <feat att="partOfSpeech" val="verb"/>
        <Lemma>
          <feat att="writtenForm" val="آمس"/>
        </Lemma>
    </LexicalEntry>
    <LexicalEntry id="A3" morphologicalPatterns="AsTable">
         <feat att="partOfSpeech" val="noun"/>
        <Lemma>
          <feat att="writtenForm" val="الحاجة"/>
        </Lemma>
    </LexicalEntry>
<MWEPattern id="NdeFixedN">
      <MWENode>
        <feat att="syntacticConstituent" val="NP"/>
        <MWELex>
          <feat att="rank" val="1"/>
          <feat att="graphicalSeparator" val="space"/>
          <feat att="structureHead" val="yes"/>
        </MWELex>
        <MWELex>
          <feat att="rank" val="2"/>
          <feat att="graphicalSeparator" val="space"/>
        </MWELex>
        <MWELex>
          <feat att="rank" val="3"/>
          <feat att="graphicalSeparator" val="space"/>
          <feat att="grammaticalNumber" val="singular"/>
        </MWELex>
      </MWENode>
    </MWEPattern>
    <LinguisticFeatures>
      <OrthographicFeatures>
        <feat att="Id" val="mwe1"/>
        <feat att="Comment" val=" "/>
        <feat att="DIN31635InPlainEnglish" val="fī 'ams alḥāja "/>
        <feat att="Normalised Form" val="فى امس الحاجة"/>
        <feat att="Different Spelling Form" val=" "/>
      </OrthographicFeatures>
```

References

1. Sag, I.A., Baldwin, T., Bond, F., Copestake, A., Flickinger, D.: Multiword expressions: a pain in the neck for NLP. In: Gelbukh, A. (ed.) CICLing 2002. LNCS, vol. 2276, pp. 1–15. Springer, Heidelberg (2002). doi:10.1007/3-540-45715-1_1
2. Savary, A., Sailer, M., Parmentier, Y., Rosner, M., Rosén, V., Przepiórkowski, A., Krstev, C., Vincze, V., Wójtowicz, B., Losnegaard, G.S.: PARSEME–PARSing and multiword expressions within a European multilingual network. In: 7th Language and Technology Conference: Human Language Technologies as a Challenge for Computer Science and Linguistics LTC (2015)

3. Losnegaard, G.S., Sangati, F., Escartín, C.P., Savary, A., Bargmann, S., Monti, J.: PARSEME survey on MWE resources. In: Proceedings of the Tenth International Conference on Language Resources and Evaluation LREC, Portorož (2016)
4. Rosén, V., De Smedt, K., Losnegaard, G.S., Bejček, E., Savary, A., Osenova, P.: MWEs in Treebanks: from survey to guidelines. In: Proceedings of the Tenth International Conference on Language Resources and Evaluation LREC, Portorož (2016)
5. Cardey, S., Chan, R., Greenfield, P.: The development of a multilingual collocation dictionary. In: Proceedings of the Workshop on Multilingual Language Resources and Interoperability, pp. 32–39. Association for Computational Linguistics (2006)
6. Al-Sabbagh, R., Girju, R., Diesner, J.: Unsupervised construction of a lexicon and a repository of variation patterns for Arabic modal multiword expressions. In: EACL (2014)
7. Arts, T.: Oxford Arabic Dictionary: Arabic-English, English-Arabic. Oxford University Press, Oxford (2014)
8. Attia, M.A.: Accommodating multiword expressions in an Arabic LFG grammar. In: Salakoski, T., Ginter, F., Pyysalo, S., Pahikkala, T. (eds.) FinTAL 2006. LNCS, vol. 4139, pp. 87–98. Springer, Heidelberg (2006). doi:10.1007/11816508_11
9. Butt, M.: A Grammar Writer's Cookbook. CSLI, Vancouver (1999)
10. Dipper, S.: Implementing and Documenting Large-scale Grammars-German LFG. Inst. für Maschinelle Sprachverarbeitung, Univ. (2003)
11. Wanner, L.: Lexical Functions in Lexicography and Natural Language Processing. John Benjamins Publishing, Amsterdam (1996)
12. Bounhas, I., Slimani, Y.: A hybrid approach for Arabic multi-word term extraction. In: A Hybrid Approach for Arabic Multi-word Term Extraction, pp. 1–8. IEEE Press (2009)
13. Hawwari, A., Bar, K., Diab, M.: Building an Arabic multiword expressions repository. In: Proceedings of the 50th ACL, pp. 24–29. Citeseer (2012)
14. Hawwari, A., Attia, M., Diab, M.: A framework for the classification and annotation of multiword expressions in dialectal Arabic. In: Proceedings of the ANLP (2014)
15. Calzolari, N., Fillmore, C.J., Grishman, R., Ide, N., Lenci, A., MacLeod, C., Zampolli, A.: Towards best practice for multiword expressions in computational lexicons. In: Proceedings of the LREC (2002)
16. Tanabe, T., Takahashi, M., Shudo, K.: A lexicon of multiword expressions for linguistically precise, wide-coverage natural language processing. Comput. Speech Lang. **28**(6), 1317–1339 (2014)
17. Palmer, M., Gildea, D., Kingsbury, P.: The proposition bank: an annotated corpus of semantic roles. Comput. Linguist. **31**(1), 71–106 (2005)
18. Bar, K., Diab, M., Hawwari, A.: Arabic multiword expressions. In: Dershowitz, N., Nissan, E. (eds.) Language, Culture, Computation. Computational Linguistics and Linguistics. LNCS, vol. 8003, pp. 64–81. Springer, Heidelberg (2014). doi:10.1007/978-3-642-45327-4_5
19. Odijk, J.: Identification and lexical representation of multiword expressions. In: Spyns, P., Odijk, J. (eds.) Essential Speech and Language Technology for Dutch. Theory and Applications of Natural Language Processing, pp. 201–217. Springer, Heidelberg (2013)
20. Francopoulo, G.: LMF Lexical Markup Framework. ISTE Ltd., London (2013)
21. Francopoulo, G., Huang, C.-R.: Lexical markup framework: an ISO standard for electronic lexicons and its implications for Asian languages. Lexicography **1**(1), 37–51 (2014)
22. Francopoulo, G., George, M.: Language resource management-Lexical markup framework (LMF), ISO/TC (2008)
23. Atwell, E.: Development of tag sets for part-of-speech tagging. In: Ludeling, A., Kyto, M. (eds.) Corpus Linguistics: An International Handbook, pp. 501–526. Walter de Gruyter (2008)

24. Alghamdi, A., Atwell, E.: Constructing a corpus-informed listing of Arabic formulaic sequences ArFSs for language pedagogy and technology, Under review paper submitted to International Journal of Corpus Linguistics (2017)
25. Alghamdi, A., Atwell, E.: An empirical study of Arabic formulaic sequence extraction methods. In: Proceedings of the Tenth International Conference on Language Resources and Evaluation LREC, Portorož, pp. 502–506 (2016)

Frequency Consolidation Among Word N-Grams

A Practical Procedure

Andreas Buerki(✉)

Centre for Language and Communication Research,
Cardiff University, Cardiff, Wales, UK
buerkiA@cardiff.ac.uk

Abstract. This paper considers the issue of frequency consolidation in lists of different length word n-grams (i.e. recurrent word sequences) extracted from the same underlying corpus. A simple algorithm – enhanced by a preparatory stage – is proposed which allows the consolidation of frequencies among lists of different length n-grams, from 2-grams to 6-grams and beyond. The consolidation adjusts the frequency count of each n-gram to the number of its occurrences minus its occurrences as part of longer n-grams. Among other uses, such a procedure aids linguistic analysis and allows the non-inflationary counting of word tokens that are part of frequent n-grams of various lengths, which in turn allows an assessment of the proportion of running text made up of recurring chunks. The proposed procedure delivers frequency consolidation and substring reduction among word n-grams and is independent of any particular method of n-gram extraction and filtering, making it applicable also in situations where full access to underlying corpora is unavailable.

Keywords: Multiword expressions · Word n-grams · Corpus linguistics

1 Introduction

The present paper presents a procedure for frequency consolidation among lists of recurrent word sequences (i.e. word n-grams) of various lengths, as implemented in the software programme SubString [1]. Word sequences that occur again and again in largely the same form are often referred to as multi-word expressions (MWEs) and have been of considerable interest to corpus linguistics as well as natural language processing (NLP). In corpus linguistics, the availability of large language corpora and their machine-assisted processing led to the realisation that recurrent sequences are far more widespread than would be predicted on the basis of a model of linguistic knowledge that consists of a store of atomic items (words in the lexicon) and combinatory rules (the grammar). This in turn led to alternative models of linguistic knowledge and processing being proposed such as Sinclair's Idiom Principle [2], Pattern Grammar [3] or Lexical Priming [4]. The existence of large quantities of MWEs in language also influences and supports

R. Mitkov (Ed.): Europhras 2017, LNAI 10596, pp. 432–446, 2017.
https://doi.org/10.1007/978-3-319-69805-2_30

constructionist approaches to grammar (e.g. [5–7], and research in the field of formulaic language, which has attracted a great deal of recent research effort (for a recent overview see [8]). In NLP, MWEs are key to the success of many tasks including machine translation, speech synthesis or term extraction (e.g. [9–11]).

Methods of MWE extraction out of corpus material have therefore been an area of very significant research activity (cf. overviews in [12–14]). The present paper concerns a different but related task that has, by comparison, received scant attention to date. It is a specialized task but one that is key to challenges encountered in a number of situations as discussed below.

Frequency consolidation is applied where there are n-grams that are substrings of other n-grams: the frequency of occurrence of a shorter string is then reduced by the frequency of its longer superstring(s). Frequency consolidation thus works on the basis of extracted and filtered lists of MWEs and provides insight into the frequency structure of those MWEs. A simple case is illustrated in Fig. 1, where the two 3-grams *a nice day* and *have a nice* have their frequencies (in square brackets) consolidated with the 4-gram *have a nice day*. This results in the substrings *have a nice* and *a nice day* appearing with consolidated frequencies of 4 and 1 respectively since the six occurrences as part of the superstring *have a nice day* are removed. Substring reduction additionally occurs if a string receives a consolidated frequency count of zero (or below a certain cut-off frequency), resulting in its deletion and consequently a reduction in the number of substring types occurs.

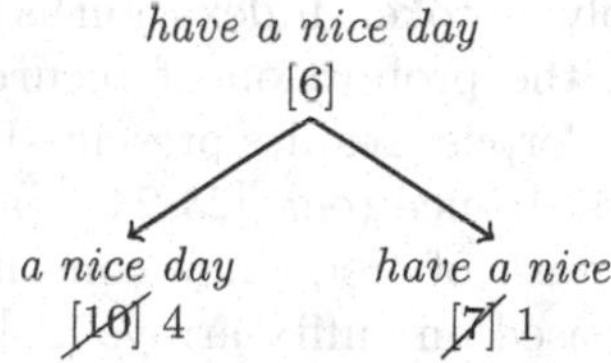

Fig. 1. A simple case of a frequency consolidation between word n-grams

An accurate frequency consolidation and substring reduction procedure is a prerequisite for an empirical assessment of the degree to which running text consists of MWEs; unless frequencies of different length MWEs are consolidated, no accurate figures of the proportion of running words that form part of MWEs can be derived. Although, as indicated above, this is a point of significant theoretical weight and is furthermore thought to vary notably between text types [2, p. 114], [15, p. 29-17], assessments of MWE-density (save for [18], see discussion below) have either relied on estimates based on a single length of n-grams (e.g. [16, pp. 993–997], [19, p. 67ff]), or have had to limit the amount of source material considered to manually countable amounts of text [17,20,21], thus severely limiting the empirical base on which conclusions are drawn. Clearly, neither of these options is satisfactory. An automatic frequency consolidation addresses this problem by making it easy to determine (and contrast) MWE-density across large amounts of language data. Further, in linguistic analyses of MWEs of various lengths it is often useful to have access to consolidated frequencies of a cluster of MWEs under investigation as this facilitates meaningful comparisons between MWEs of different lengths – an automatic consolidation procedure delivers such results quickly and accurately and in so doing simplifies and speeds up the task of linguistic analysis. Beside these two principal uses, frequency consolidation also reduces the number of n-grams that need to be managed or investigated in a study by eliminating redundant substrings. A word n-gram frequency consolidation procedure is therefore a useful tool when dealing with MWEs and their analysis for linguistic purposes.

The remainder of this paper is structured as follows: in Sect. 2, we take a look at earlier approaches to similar tasks. Then, in Sect. 3, a procedure to deal with frequency consolidation is proposed and documented in detail. In Sect. 4, the proposed procedure is evaluated using corpus data. Conclusions are presented in a final section. Since the procedure is in principle applicable to any type of word sequence (or indeed sequences of other elements) rather than specifically to MWEs, which are more narrowly defined, the general term word n-gram will be used to refer to sequences of words that make up the input to the procedure.

2 Related Work

In a pioneering early study, Altenberg and Eeg-Olofsson [22] used a frequency consolidation procedure involving token-indexation as part of their MWE extraction procedure to ascertain the proportion of recurrent word n-grams in the 500,000 word London-Lund Corpus (results presented in [18]). Procedures using indexation have been discussed since (e.g. [23,24, pp. 147–149]) and remain an important approach to the task of frequency consolidation. A special case of indexation are approaches based on suffix arrays [25] where n-gram extraction and the picking out of interesting n-grams (and possibly the discarding of others) are in effect queries to a corpus, converted to an indexed data structure. As far as could be ascertained, no frequency consolidation procedure of the sort outlined has been suggested for data stored in suffix arrays, although this would certainly be a possibility. Further, a Serial Cascading Algorithm was proposed by Smith (reported in [24, pp. 149–153]). It takes two passes over a corpus to extract, filter and then consolidate n-grams of various lengths. This approach, and indexation-based ones, are integral parts of MWE extraction procedures, that is, they necessarily take as input a corpus of texts, rather than a list of extracted n-grams and their frequencies. This has the advantage of producing results that are maximally faithful to the original context in which n-grams occur, resulting in high accuracy. The disadvantage is a loss of flexibility as these procedures cannot be applied in situations where full access to the underlying corpus material is unavailable, as is frequently the case, for example with the vast Google n-grams corpora [26], n-gram lists made available at the COCA website [27], or with corpora accessible only through corpus portals like the

Sketch Engine [28] or Wmatrix [29] which allow the creation of n-gram lists but not a full frequency consolidation (cf. discussion below).

Among approaches that are independent of a particular extraction procedure and can work with n-gram lists as input, Lü et al. [30] proposed a statistical substring reduction algorithm for fast and accurate 'removal of equal frequency n-gram substrings from an n-gram set' [30, p. 1]. Wible and Tsao [31, p. 29] proposed a similar procedure (referred to as horizontal pruning), where, in addition to the deletion of substrings that match the frequencies of their superstrings, substrings are also deleted if their frequencies are higher than those of the superstring(s), up to a certain maximum 'threshold proportion' [31, p. 29]; this results in a higher number of eliminated substrings. However, both approaches leave unconsolidated the frequencies of substrings that are not eliminated. Consequently, these procedures are suitable only for reducing the number of redundant material in data.

Example 1. (rendering of substrings in Sketch Engine)

settlements in the West Bank 5
... settlements in the West 5
... ... in the West 21
... ... in the 6,348
... ... the West 70
... ... settlements in the 7
... ... in the 6,348
... ... settlements in 9

The n-gram extraction function of the Sketch Engine [28] offers the option to 'hide/nest sub n-grams' [32]. As illustrated using the output shown in Example 1 below, this option groups any sub- (and sub-sub, etc.) strings under the longest extracted n-grams. Crucially, however, no adjustments to frequencies of substrings are made, so even though in Example 1, the substring *settlements in the West* does not occur outside of *settlements in the West Bank*, the substring is still listed with a frequency of 5. When hidden, all substrings (preceded by dots) are removed from lists, even when substrings are much more frequent than the top-level superstring, as illustrated by the string *the West.* Although this aids comparisons of MWEs of different lengths to some degree, the hiding of all substrings, even if more frequent than longer superstrings, and the lack of a consolidation of frequencies limits the usefulness of this approach – its strength lies mainly in providing analysts with a usefully re-arranged view of n-gram lists. The same appears to be case for the option to produce 'collapsed grams' within Wmatrix [29]: although currently this functionality is switched off, it is described as producing 'a tree structure with the longest n-grams on the left and shortest n-grams on the right'.

Other procedures approach the task of handling substrings from the point of view of finding the ideal length of an MWE in a cluster of word sequences that share a common core. Kita et al. [33] documented a procedure which assigns a cost measure to different length word n-grams (cf. also [34,35]). This results in the ideal (according to the measure) extent of an MWE receiving the highest score while leaving shorter or longer forms with lower scores. Sequences with lower scores are potentially eliminated depending on the threshold value set. A more recent proposal in this paradigm is put forward by Gries [36] and Gries and Mukherjee [37]: first, collocation strength for n-grams of different lengths is measured using Daudaravicius and Marcinkeviciene's gravity measure G [38]. Subsequently, the G-value of each extracted n-gram, starting with 2-grams, is compared to that of its immediate superstring(s) (i.e. n-grams that are one word longer). If the G-values of the superstrings are higher than that of the substring, the substring is removed, otherwise it is retained as a legitimate n-gram despite the existence of larger superstrings. Gries and Wahl propose a procedure involving 'the successive merging of bigrams to form word sequences of various lengths' [39]; while results depend on the setting of a sensible threshold number of successive merges (and this is likely difficult to get right), Gries and Wahl demonstrate using human ratings that MWEs resulting from early merges (vs. late merges) are more often rated as good MWEs. Wible and Tsao [31] documented a similar procedure making use of a normalized MI score. Approaches of this type are useful for allowing 'the length of each n-gram to emerge, as it were, from the data' [37, p. 522]. However, the output, while providing a filtered set of n-grams, does not provide consolidated frequencies for remaining n-grams and is therefore a slightly different task to the one discussed in this paper. Naturally, full access to the underlying corpus data are also required.

In summary, previous research has identified ways of dealing with aspects of substring reduction and frequency consolidation among word n-grams that lead to reductions in redundant substrings and the identification of the ideal length of an n-gram in a cluster as well as full frequency consolidations for cases where full access to the input text corpora is available. However, as far as could be ascertained, no procedure has been suggested to date that covers the uses outlined at the beginning and is sufficiently flexible to cope with situations where only n-gram lists are available as input. Such a procedure will be outlined in the next section.

3 The Procedure

To illustrate how the proposed procedure handles frequency consolidation among different length word n-grams, let us assume we have as input the n-grams given in Example 2 below. These will have been extracted from a corpus and their frequencies of occurrence in the corpus are indicated by the number following each n-gram.

Example 2. (example input to a frequency consolidation):

have a lovely time	15
have a lovely	58
a lovely time	44
have a	37,491
a lovely	101
lovely time	44

Example 3. (consolidated output):

have a lovely time	15
have a lovely	43
a lovely time	29
have a	37,433
a lovely	14

The 4-gram *have a lovely time* occurs with a frequency of 15. The 3-grams *have a lovely* and *a lovely time* occur 58 and 44 times respectively. 15 of those occurrences are, however, occurrences as part of the superstring *have a lovely time.* To get the consolidated frequency of occurrence for *have a lovely* and *a lovely time* (i.e. the occurrences of these 3-grams on their own, not counting when they occur in the longer string), we therefore deduct the frequency of their superstring (15) from their own frequency as shown as in Fig. 2, step 1. This results in a consolidated frequency of 43 for *have a lovely* (i.e. 58 – 15) and 29 for *a lovely time* (i.e. 44 – 15). The 2-grams *have a, a lovely* and *lovely time* are also substrings of *have a lovely time* and therefore also need to have their frequency reduced by 15, resulting in a frequency of 37,476 for *have a*, 86 for *a lovely* and 29 for *lovely time* (Fig. 2, step 2). In addition, *have a* and *a lovely* are substrings of *have a lovely* and therefore the frequency of *have a lovely*, which is now 43, needs to be deducted from their frequencies (Fig. 2, step 3). This results in a new frequency of 37,433 for *have a* $(37,476 - 43)$ and 43 for *a lovely* $(86 - 43)$. *a lovely* and *lovely time* are furthermore substrings of *a lovely time* and consequently need to have their frequencies reduced by that of *a lovely time* (i.e. by 29): the consolidated frequency of *a lovely* is now 14 (i.e. 43 – 29), that of *lovely time* is now zero. The final output of the frequency consolidation is given in Example 3. We note that *lovely time* is completely eliminated and does not appear in Example 3 since it has a consolidated frequency of zero. This type of substring reduction is an automatic consequence of the frequency consolidation. The example of the 'lovely time'-cluster also shows that the type of data provided in Example 3 can usefully complement the bare frequencies in Example 2 for purposes of a linguistic analysis. Although in this example the consolidated frequencies could easily be worked out at the time of analysis, in reality a cluster is not artificially isolated as in this example and the large net of sub- and superstrings that need to be considered makes a consolidation extremely laborious to work out manually.

The procedure as narrated above is expressed in pseudo code in Fig. 3. Iterative loops enable the processing of any (reasonable) number of different n-gram lengths, far beyond the three lengths of Fig. 2.

Assuming for a moment that Example 2 (above) represents the entire set of n-grams extractable from the underlying source text, the accuracy of results in Example 3 could be assessed by comparing the word count of the source text with the number of words bound up in Example 3, that is, the length in words of each n-gram, multiplied by its frequency and summed: $\sum(|n|^{1..n} \cdot f^{1..n})$. For Example 3, the numbers would match and confirm the accuracy of the

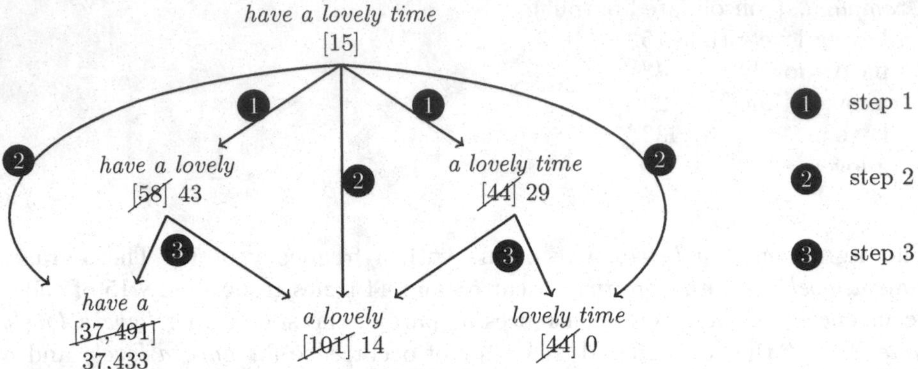

Fig. 2. Consolidation of n-grams in Example 2. Arrows indicate frequency subtractions: the frequencies at their starting points are deducted from the frequencies at their end points.

```
FUNCTION CONSOLIDATE(firstList, secondList)
   accept 2 arguments: firstList, secondList
   FOR each line IN firstList
      cut off frequency at the end of the line
      store frequency in Freq1
      store the rest in SearchLine
      search secondList for lines containing SearchLine
      IF matching lines are found THEN
         sum the n-gram frequencies of each matching line
         store the result in Freq2
         subtract Freq2 from Freq1 and store result in newFreq
         IF newFreq > 0 THEN
            replace frequency information in original line in
            firstList with newFreq
         ELSE
            delete original line from firstList
         END IF
      END IF
   END FOR
END FUNCTION

# the function is now applied to input lists
SET LongListIndex to the total number of input lists present
SET LongListMinusIndex to [LongListIndex - 1]
REPEAT
   CONSOLIDATE(List[LongListMinusIndex], List[LongListIndex])
   SET LongListIndex2 to [LongListIndex - 1]
   REPEAT
      CONSOLIDATE(List[LongListMinusIndex], List[LongListIndex2])
      SUBSTRACT 1 from LongListIndex2
   UNTIL LongListMinusIndex = LongListIndex2
   SUBTRACT 1 from LongListMinusIndex
UNTIL 1 > LongListMinusIndex
```

Fig. 3. Frequency consolidation algorithm in pseudo code. Input consists of lists of n-grams named List^1, List^2, $\ldots \text{List}^n$, where List^1 contains the shortest and List^n the longest n-grams. Lists consist of n-grams of one length, one n-gram (followed by its frequency) per line.

consolidation. Summing the word tokens bound up in Example 2, on the other hand, would result in the token inflation typical of unconsolidated n-gram lists. This simple assessment only works if the frequency consolidation procedure is applied to n-gram lists containing the complete set of extractable continuous n-grams in the source text, barring n-grams across sentence boundaries, and n-grams are extracted up to an n-gram length ($|n|$) where $|n|$ equals the number of words in the longest sentence. In applying the proposed procedure to real-life uses, where these conditions do not hold, we are faced with three challenges: (i) a reasonable maximum n-gram length must be set at which the procedure is nevertheless able to resolve overlapping n-grams; (ii) the correct functioning of the procedure must be maintained even if input n-gram lists were filtered before the application of frequency consolidation (for example by the application of frequency cut-offs, cut-offs based on statistical measures of association, or other filters designed to remove uninteresting n-grams); (iii) the question of how results can be verified when the source corpus word count can no longer be used as a target word count. The exclusion of n-grams across sentence boundaries, on the other hand, can be meaningful in many real-life contexts and is therefore retained as a precondition for the application of the procedure. The possible application of the proposed procedure to non-continuous n-grams is discussed in Sect. 4.

In dealing with the three challenges identified, we consider two more examples. Figure 4 presents the same n-gram cluster as Fig. 2 except that the 4-gram *have a lovely time* is absent. The absence of such resolving superstrings can be due to a previous application of a filter or a maximum n-gram extraction length of $|n| = 3$ (the resolving superstring in this case being of length $|n| = 4$). Considering the situation in Fig. 4, we observe that without the resolving superstring *have a lovely time* (greyed out), the consolidation fails to yield accurate results, producing a negative frequency for *a lovely*. The cause of this inaccuracy lies in the inflation of n-gram frequencies created by the unresolved overlap of *have a lovely* and *a lovely time*: there are fifteen extra, unwarranted, n-gram tokens in the system which push *a lovely* into negative frequency.

However, as shown in Fig. 5, unresolved overlaps do not necessarily cause negative frequencies. The consolidation here does not take the overlap resolving superstring *not at all certain* (in grey) into account. While the incorporation of the string in grey would lead to a somewhat different result (a result that is more faithful to the conditions pertaining in the source text), the consolidated frequencies in Fig. 5 nevertheless avoid n-gram frequency inflation (and consequently negative frequencies) and are therefore considered accurate here.

Concerning the three challenges of maximum n-gram length, filtered source lists and verification, we consequently note that, firstly, inaccuracies in consolidation manifest themselves as negative frequencies and hence the accuracy of the procedure can be assessed via instances of negative frequencies. Secondly, both filtering and maximum n-gram length determine the presence or absence of overlap-resolving superstrings and thus influence the accuracy of any particular frequency consolidation process. It is therefore important to retain the highest

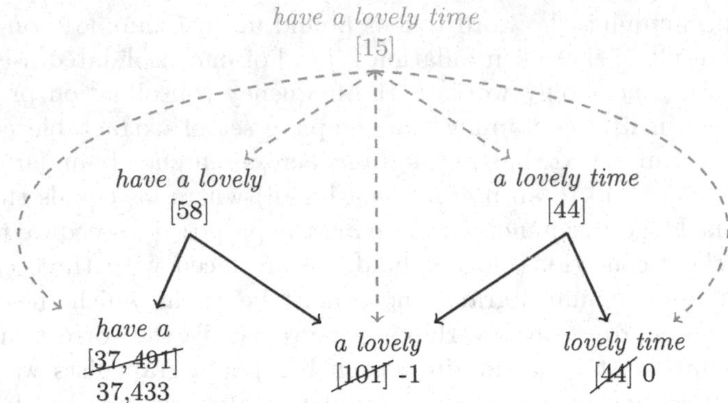

Fig. 4. Consolidation of a group of n-grams with missing resolving superstring (in grey)

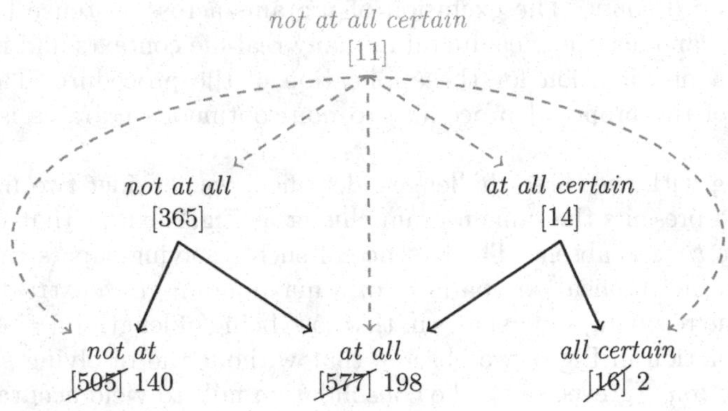

Fig. 5. Overlap without negative frequency. The overlap resolving superstring (in grey) is not considered in the consolidation shown.

number of overlap-resolving superstrings which would, if absent, cause negative frequencies. Such superstrings are hereafter referred to as *necessary superstrings.*

To safeguard the extraction of such necessary superstrings, n-grams should minimally be extracted up to length $|n| = 6$. In our test data set A (cf. Table 1 below), no missing superstrings longer than 6-grams were found to be the cause of negative frequencies. Given the extreme rarity of frequent, long n-grams, however, employing a maximum n-gram length below this length is unlikely to have a serious negative impact.

Further, the retention of necessary superstrings can be optimized by (temporarily) re-importing necessary superstrings that were eliminated by filters prior to frequency consolidation. This can be accomplished using an optional preparatory stage to the core algorithm. The preparatory stage scans filtered n-gram lists and constructs projected necessary superstrings. If these are not found among the n-grams of the filtered lists, it searches for them in the unfiltered state of the lists (which need to be supplied) and, if found, imports them back into the filtered lists. After the frequency consolidation and substring reduction process has concluded, the imported n-grams are easily eliminated by the re-application of the relevant filter(s), if desired. To avoid a situation where the imported n-grams themselves create a need for yet more necessary superstrings, only n-grams of length $|n| > 4$ (i.e. 5-grams and longer) are made available for re-import and since extensive testing showed that no necessary superstrings had frequencies of <1 per million tokens, no superstrings below that frequency are made available for re-import as part of the procedure.

4 Evaluation and Limitations

The application of the procedure to test data using parameters shown in Table 1 produced the figures in Table 2. For comparison, figures resulting from the application of Lü et al.'s SSR-algorithm [30] as implemented in Zhang's NGramTool [40] are also included. Looking at rows one and two of Table 2, the greater number of deleted substring types and tokens in row one compared to row two is made possible by the consolidation of frequencies even if frequencies of substring and superstring are not identical. This resulted in the deletion of additional substrings that featured consolidated frequencies greater than zero but below the minimum frequency (extraction parameters as per Table 1). The procedure is therefore effective in reducing the number of redundant substrings among extracted n-grams of various lengths as well as producing consolidated frequency values for all n-grams. This in turn facilitates and assessment of MWE-density: the number of word tokens that are part of the extracted word n-grams can be calculated by multiplying frequency with length for each word n-gram and summing the resulting figures. In case of the procedure in row one, this comes to 1,748,239. Given a corpus size of four million word tokens, this is a proportion of 43.7% of running words.

The number of inaccuracies in row one as measured by the number of n-grams with negative frequencies is modest compared to the overall number of types. This number is further reduced by the application of the preparatory

Table 1. Extraction parameters for test data

	Data set A	Data set B
Size	4 million tokens	29 million tokens
Language	German	English
Source	Swiss Text Corpus [41]	Wikipedia
Extraction	2-grams to 7-grams	2-grams to 9-grams
Filters	Additive stop list of the 200 most frequent word forms of German; min. freq. 4 per million words (16)	Additive stop list of the 200 most frequent word forms of English; min. freq. 2 per million words (58)

Table 2. Figures resulting from various procedure variants

Data	Proc	Types			Tokens		
		Before	After	neg-freq	Before	After	neg-freq
A	1	21,953	19,696	84	1,085,102	788,839	−962
A	2	21,953	21,535	-	1,085,102	1,072,077	-
A	3	21,953	19,627	52	1,085,102	787,204	−644
A	4	44,297	39,607	708	2,220,699	1,455,015	−36,639
A	5	22,116	19,961	106	1,569,771	1,163,707	−6,228
B	2	63,680	60,958	-	12,702,769	12,277,406	-
B	3	63,680	45,297	4,893	12,702,769	6,663,964	−956,542

Note. Procedure (Proc): 1 = without preparatory stage; 2 = SSR according to [30]; 3 = with preparatory stage; 4 = window of size n+1; 5 = window of size n + 1, filtered to remove n-grams that do not occur at all in continuous form. Numbers featuring negative frequencies are not included in numbers after procedure.

stage which yielded the figures in row three of Table 2. Here, a total of 261 previously filtered-out n-gram types were re-imported. The frequency filter was re-applied at the end of the process.

If we consider results from data set B (last two rows of Table 2), a similar pattern to procedures 2 and 3 applied to data set A emerges. It is worth noting, however, that n-grams with negative frequencies are proportionally higher in data set B (procedure 3); roughly 7.5% of unconsolidated types and tokens are given negative frequencies. This shows that, without recourse to the underlying corpus, consolidation can only approximate the a consolidation that takes into account the full context of n-grams within the source corpus and the accuracy of the procedure varies depending on the data set. An analysis of types with negative frequencies in set A furthermore showed that these were, with very few exceptions, 2-grams and the negative frequency was caused by the absence of resolving superstrings of length $|n| = 4$, which were not made available for re-import by the preparatory stage. If n-grams of length $|n| = 4$ had been admitted for re-import, the result would have been a higher number of types with negative frequencies, since the larger number of re-imported n-grams would in turn have created a need for yet more resolving superstrings.

To capture patterns with variable slots such as those shown in Examples 4 to 6, n-grams are often extracted within a window such that for n-gram length $|n|$, the window size is $n + 1$, $n + 2$, $\ldots n + n$, allowing intervening words to be skipped. To test how the proposed frequency consolidation procedure fares with discontinuous n-grams, lists with a window size of $n + 1$ (remaining parameters as per Table 1) were also extracted and frequency-consolidated using both the preparatory stage and the core algorithm. The result, shown in row four of Table 2, indicates a much lower accuracy of the procedure compared to continuous n-grams. However, applying a filter which only admits discontinuous n-gram types that are also attested in continuous form (such as those in Examples 4 to 6 where the variable slot is optional) yielded the figures in row five of Table 2 and performed acceptably on our accuracy measure. The proposed procedure therefore cannot be recommended for a frequency consolidation among discontinuous n-grams, although the inclusion of discontinuous n-grams that also appear in continuous form does not pose difficulties for the procedure.

Example 4. With the [occasional / sole / possible / notable] exception of

Example 5. the [provisional] IRA

Example 6. on [false / supposed / fabricated / 11 / two / fresh] charges of

Finally, it was mentioned above that all negative frequencies indicate inaccuracies in the substring reduction process. Normally, the converse also applies (i.e. all inaccuracies are indicated by negative frequencies), but there is one caveat: where a string that would have received negative frequency (such as *a lovely* in Fig. 4) is filtered out prior to the frequency consolidation process, the inaccuracy, though present, is not flagged up. To assess the extent of this under-reporting, test data set A was run through procedure 3 with one alteration: the 2-gram list, from which the vast majority of negative-frequency types stem, had no stop list applied and all n-grams with a minimum frequency of 2 were admitted. This resulted in a 2-gram list of 244,611 types compared to 16,764 types in the procedure that produced the figures of row three. The substring reduction process produced 53 types with negative frequencies, only one type more than the 52 types previously obtained in Table 2, row three. A further test applied a more severe 2-gram stop list that produced a 2-gram list of merely 9,554 types. The number of types with negative frequencies was only moderately affected, showing a count of 33. We can conclude that all negative frequencies indicate inaccuracies and that, while all inaccuracies are not necessarily indicated by negative frequencies, the figure is very close. The number of types with negative frequencies therefore remains an excellent indicator of the accuracy of a particular substring reduction process.

5 Conclusions

A frequency consolidation procedure was presented which is able to fully consolidate frequencies of word n-grams of various lengths to a high degree of accuracy. The output of the procedure can be used to gain fast and easy access to consolidated frequencies for linguistic analysis, to calculate the proportion of text that is part of recurring word n-grams and to reduce the number of redundant substrings in a data set (substring reduction). A means of assessing the accuracy of a particular substring-reduction process was also suggested. Preconditions for the application of the suggested procedure are the non-extraction of n-grams across sentence boundaries and the extraction of n-grams up to a reasonable length (a length of 6 is minimally suggested). It was also found that the procedure works best with continuous n-grams but can be used to consolidate n-grams with optional slots. The suggested procedure has several advantages over other existing attempts at frequency consolidation which are either inextricably linked to particular n-gram extraction procedures and therefore cannot be used where full access to source texts is unavailable or only deal with substring reduction or with the identification of an ideal n-gram length among a cluster of n-grams. The proposed procedure therefore facilitates the addressing important theoretical questions and practical challenges in the area of corpus-based MWE research, even in situations where existing other procedures are inapplicable. The procedure is implemented and available for use as part of the open source software programme SubString [1].

References

1. Buerki A.: SubString 0.9.9 (Computer Software) (2016). http://buerki.github.io/SubString/
2. Sinclair, J.: Corpus, Concordance, Collocation. Oxford University Press, Oxford (1991)
3. Hunston, S., Francis, G.: PatternGrammar: A Corpus-driven Approach to the Lexical Grammar of English. John Benjamins, Amsterdam (2000)
4. Hoey, M.: Lexical Priming: A New Theory of Words and Language. Routledge, London (2005)
5. Fillmore, C.J., Kay, P., O'Connor, M.C.: Regularity and idiomaticity in grammatical constructions: the case of let alone. Language **64**(3), 501–538 (1988)
6. Goldberg, A.E.: Constructions: A Construction Grammar Approach to Argument Structure. The University of Chicago Press, Chicago (1995)
7. Hilpert, M.: Construction Grammar and its Application to English. Edinburgh University Press, Edinburgh (2014)
8. Wray, A.: What do we (think we) know about formulaic language? An evaluation of the current state of play. Ann. Rev. Appl. Linguist. **32**, 231–254 (2012)
9. Villavicencio, A., Bond, F., Korhonen, A., McCarthy, D.: Editorial: introduction to the special issue on multiword expressions: having a crack at a hard nut. Comput. Speech Lang. **19**(4), 365–377 (2005)
10. Bouamor, D., Semmar, N., Zweigenbaum, P.: Improved statistical machine translation using multiword expressions. In: LIHMT 2011, pp. 15–20 (2011)
11. Ren, Z., Lü, Y., Cao, J., Liu, Q., Huang, Y.: Improving statistical machine translation using domain bilingual multiword expressions. In: Proceedings of the Workshop on Multiword Expressions: Identification, Interpretation, Disambiguation and Applications, pp. 47–54 (2009)
12. Rayson, P., Piao, S., Sharoff, S., Evert, S., Moirón, B.V.: Multiword expressions: hard going or plain sailing? Lang. Resour. Eval. **44**(1), 1–5 (2010)
13. Seretan, V.: Syntax-Based Collocation Extraction. Springer, Dordrecht (2011). doi:10.1007/978-94-007-0134-2
14. Pearce, D.: A comparative evaluation of collocation extraction techniques. In: Proceedings of the 3rd International Conference on Language Resources and Evaluation (LREC 2002), pp. 1530–1536 (2002)
15. Sinclair, J.: Trust the Text. Routledge, London (2004)
16. Biber, D., Johansson, S., Leech, G., Conrad, S., Finegan, E.: Longman Grammar of Spoken and Written English. Pearson Education, Harlow (1999)
17. Erman, B., Warren, B.: The idiom principle and the open choice principle. Text **20**(1), 29–62 (2000)

18. Altenberg, B.: On the phraseology of spoken English: the evidence of recurrentword-combinations. In: Cowie, A.P. (ed.) Phraseology: Theory, Analysis and Applications, pp. 101–122. Clarendon Press, Oxford (1998)
19. Mittmann, B.: Mehrwort-Cluster in der englischen Alltagskonversation: Unterschiede zwischen britischem und amerikanischem gesprochenen Englisch als Indikatoren für den präfabrizierten Charakter der Sprache, G. Narr, Tübingen (2004)
20. Sorhus, H.B.: To hear ourselves - implications for teaching English as a second language. Engl. Lang. Teach. J. **31**(3), 211–221 (1977)
21. Van Lancker, S.D.: When novel sentences spoken or heard for the first time in the history of the universe are not enough: toward a dual-process model of language. Int. J. Lang. Commun. Disord. **39**(1), 1–44 (2004)
22. Altenberg, B., Eeg-Olofsson, M.: Presentation of a project. In: Aarts, J., Meijs, W. (eds.) Theory and Practice in Corpus Linguistics, pp. 1–26. Rodopi, Amsterdam (1990)
23. Smadja, F.Z.: Retrieving collocations from text: Xtract. Comput. Linguist. **19**(1), 143–177 (1994)
24. O'Donnell, M.B.: The adjusted frequency list: a method to produce cluster-sensitive frequency lists. ICAME J. **35**, 135–169 (2011)
25. Church, K., Yamamoto, M.: Using suffix arrays to compute term frequency and document frequency for all substrings in a corpus. Comput. Linguist. **27**, 1–30 (2001)
26. Michel, J.B., Shen, Y.K., Aiden, A.P., Veres, A., Gray, M.K., Pickett, J.P., Hoiberg, D., Clancy, D., Norvig, P., Orwant, J.: Quantitative analysis of culture using millions of digitized books. Science **331**(6014), 176–182 (2011)
27. Davies, M.: N-grams data Corpus of Contemporary American English. http://www.ngrams.info. Accessed 12 June 2017
28. Kilgarriff, A., Baisa, V., Bušta, J., Jakubíček, M., Kovář, V., Michelfeit, J., Rychlý, P., Suchomel, V.: The sketch engine: ten years on. Lexicography **1**(1), 7–36 (2014)
29. Rayson, P.: A web-based corpus processing environment. http://ucrel.lancs.ac.uk/wmatrix/
30. Lü, X., Zhang, L., Hu, J.: Statistical substring reduction in linear time. In: Su, K.-Y., Tsujii, J., Lee, J.-H., Kwong, O.Y. (eds.) IJCNLP 2004. LNCS (LNAI), vol. 3248, pp. 320–327. Springer, Heidelberg (2005). doi:10.1007/978-3-540-30211-7_34
31. Wible, D., Tsao, N.L.: StringNet as a computational resource for discovering and investigating linguistic constructions. In: Proceedings of the NAACL HLT Workshop on Extracting and Using Constructions in Computational Linguistics, pp. 25–31 (2010)
32. Sketch Engine User Guide. https://www.sketchengine.co.uk/user-guide/user-manual/n-grams/. Accessed 10 June 2017
33. Kita, K., Kato, Y., Omoto, T., Yano, Y.: Mutual information vs. cost criteria. J. Nat. Lang. Proc. **1**(1), 21–33 (1994)
34. Frantzi, K., Ananiadou, S., Mima, H.: Automatic recognition of multi-word terms: the C-value/NC-value method. Int. J. Digit. Libr. **3**(2), 115–130 (2000)
35. Frantzi, K.T., Ananiadou, S.: Extracting nested collocations. In: Proceedings of the 16th conference on Computational linguistics, vol. 1, pp. 41–46 (1996)
36. Gries, S.T.: A bigram gravity approach to the homogeneity of corpora. In: Proceedings of Corpus Linguistics (2009)
37. Gries, S.T., Mukherjee, J.: Lexical gravity across varieties of English: an ICE-based study of n-grams in Asian Englishes. Int. J. Corpus Linguist. **15**(4), 520–548 (2010)
38. Daudaravicius, V., Marcinkeviciene, R.: Gravity counts for the boundaries of collocations. Int. J. Corpus Linguist. **9**(2), 321–348 (2004)

39. Gries, S., Wahl, A.: A new recursive approach towards multiword expression extraction and four small validation case studies. Paper Presented at Corpus Linguistics 2017, University of Birmingham, 25 July 2017
40. Zhang, L.: NGramTool (Computer Software) (2004). http://homepages.inf.ed.ac.uk/lzhang10/ngram.html
41. Bickel, H., Gasser, M., Häcki Buhofer, A., Hofer, L., Schön, C.H.: Schweizer Text Korpus - Theoretische Grundlagen, Korpusdesign und Abfragemöglichkeiten. Linguistik Online **39**(3), 5–31 (2009)

Combining Dependency Parsing and a Lexical Network Based on Lexical Functions for the Identification of Collocations

Alexandro Fonseca[1(✉)], Fatiha Sadat[1], and François Lareau[2]

[1] Computer Science Department, University of Quebec in Montreal, 201, President Kennedy Avenue, Montreal, QC H2X 3Y7, Canada
fernandes_da_fonseca.alexsandro@courrier.uqam.ca, sadat.fatiha@uqam.ca

[2] Linguistic and Translation Department, University of Montreal, C.P. 6128, succ. Centre-Ville, Montreal, QC H3C 3J7, Canada
francois.lareau@umontreal.ca

Abstract. A collocation is a type of multiword expression formed by two parts: a base and a collocate. Usually, in a collocation, the base has a denotative or literal meaning, while the collocate has a connotative meaning. Examples of collocations: *pay attention*, *easy as pie*, *strongly condemn*, *lend support*, etc. The Meaning-Text Theory created the lexical functions to, among other objectives, represent the meaning existing between the base and the collocate or to represent the relation between the base and a support verb. For example, the lexical function *Magn* represents the meaning *intensification*, while the lexical function *Caus*, applied to a base, returns the support verb that represents the causality of the action expressed in the collocation. In a dependency parsing, each word (dependent) is directly associated with its governor in a phrase. In this paper, we show how we combine dependency parsing to extract collocation candidates and a lexical network based on lexical functions to identify the true collocations from the candidates. The candidates are extracted from a French corpus according to 14 dependency relations. The collocations identified are classified according to the semantic group of the lexical functions modeling them. We obtained a general precision (for all dependency types) of 76.3%, with a precision higher than 95% for collocations having certain dependency relations. We also found that about 86% of collocations identified belong to only four semantic categories: *qualification*, *support verb*, *location* and *action/event*.

Keywords: Meaning-Text Theory · Lexical function · Collocation identification · Dependency parsing · Lexical network

1 Introduction

A collocation is a type of multiword expression (MWE) in which one of the constituents, the *base*, is chosen freely. The other component, the *collocate*, is chosen by a speaker contingent to the base to express a specific thought. Given

R. Mitkov (Ed.): Europhras 2017, LNAI 10596, pp. 447–461, 2017.
https://doi.org/10.1007/978-3-319-69805-2_31

the base, there are few possible words for the collocate (usually there is only one) that express the meaning intended by the speaker [1].

For example, in the collocation *strongly condemn*, the base is *condemn*. The collocate *strongly* adds the sense of *intensification* to the base's meaning. The meaning between the base and the collocate can be seen as a *predicate* applied to a *subject* that returns an *object* or *set of objects*. For example: *intensification(condemn)* = {*strongly*}.

Beyond the fact that the identification of collocations by a machine is a hard problem, what is the case for any other type of MWE, collocations add the difficulty of having a collocate whose meaning is usually idiomatic or connotative. For example, in the collocation *pay attention*, the collocate *pay* does not have the literal meaning of "*exchanging money for a good or service*".

However, in comparison to other types of MWEs, such as idioms, the different types of predicative meaning between the base and the collocate in a collocation can be categorized. The Meaning-Text Theory's (MTT) lexical functions (LF) [1,2] were created, among other things, to represent each of those meanings. For example, the LF *Magn* represents the meaning *intensification*, which is present in the following collocations: *strongly condemn*, *close shave*, *easy as pie*, *stark naked*, *skinny as a rake*, *rely heavily*, *thunderous applause*, etc. A LF has the form: LF(*base*) = {*collocate*}. For example: Magn (*applause*) = {*thunderous*}.

In some LFs, like Oper_1, subscripts are used to represent the semantic actant of the collocation's base [3]. The subscript used in the LF connecting a base and a collocate identifies if the subject of the verb is the one who is performing the action (subscript = 1), receiving the action (subscript = 2), etc.

Finally, simple LFs, like *Magn*, can be combined to other simple LFs to form complex LFs. Example: AntiMagn (*applause*) = {*scattered*}.

Some methods have been proposed for the identification of collocations. In general, they rely on two main approaches to extract collocation candidates: *n-grams* and *syntactic parsing*. In n-grams based methods, a window containing w words is extracted and all combinations of bigrams or trigrams inside this window are generated. Association measures (e.g. *log-likelihood*) are used to rank those n-grams to create a list of the most probable candidates, as in [4].

In methods based on syntactic parsing, word pairs having some specific syntactic relations are extracted. Usually, those methods rely on three types of word combinations: *verb-noun*, *adjective-noun*, and *noun-noun*. Association measures are used for ranking the best candidates.

In this paper, we propose a method for identifying collocations based on dependency syntactic parsing and we extract candidates belonging to 14 different dependencies (e.g. *subject-verb*, *adjectival modifiers*, *verb-object*, etc.), for French. For filtering the candidates we use a lexical network where words forming collocations are connected by LFs. Finally, we classify the identified collocations according to a semantic perspective for the LFs modeling them.

Our main objective is to precisely identify collocations, instead of having a ranking of probable collocations, as it is the case in methods based on association measures. Moreover, we intend to identify the main semantic groups to which the collocations belong. Finally, we believe that it is important to identify the syntactic dependencies that are more probable to be part in a collocation relation, since the MTT and the LFs are based on dependency syntax.

Another important point is the fact that most work related to distributional semantics deals with paradigmatic relations, such as synonymy and hyperonymy. Syntagmatic relations are mostly ignored [5]. Therefore, we believe that a study showing the semantic distribution of syntagmatic relations, encoded into collocations and LFs, may improve the studies related to distributional semantics.

2 Related Work

In general, works on collocation identification are based on a combination of parsing and statistical methods. The majority of those works are based on the ideas proposed by the following precursor works:

- [6] proposed a method for collocation extraction based on the frequency of n-grams (sequence of n words, where $n > 1$);
- [7] tested the use of more sophisticated association measures, based on the theory of mutual information;
- [8] proposed collocation extraction using an annotated corpus with parts of speech (POS) and statistical information, such as the standard deviation and the mean of the distance between words in a sentence.

In the next section, we present some work treating the identification of collocations based on LFs. In Sect. 2.2, we present a semantic classification for LFs, which we use in the classification of the identified collocations. In Sect. 2.3, we present the French Lexical Network, which is based on LFs. In Sect. 2.4, we present the ontology we developed for the representation of LFs and for encoding the French Lexical Network.

2.1 Extraction of Collocations Based on Lexical Functions

[9] uses parallel corpora in three languages, English, Spanish and Portuguese, in order to extract collocation candidates. After a preprocessing, a parsing based on Universal Dependencies [10][1] is applied to the corpora, producing files in the CONLL-X [11] format. From those files, candidates pairs having three types of dependency are extracted: *adjective modification* (*amod*) (*adjective-noun*), *nominal modification* (*nmod*) (*noun-noun*) and *verbal object* (*vobj*) (*verb-noun*).

A *t-score* association measure is applied in order to rank the candidates. Only the candidates having a t-score greater than 1 and a frequency higher than 10 are kept. Then, three models are created for each pair of languages (en-es, en-pt and es-pt) using *MultiVec* [12], an implementation of *word2vec* [13] for MWEs, and *BiSkip* [14], a word embeddings model which learns bilingual representations using aligned corpora. Those models are applied in the identification of equivalent collocations between a source and a target language.

[1] http://universaldependencies.org/introduction.html.

In [15], Kolesnikova evaluates 68 supervised classification algorithms (e.g. *Bayes Net*, *Bagging*, *AdaBoostM1*, etc.), for the classification, into different lexical functions, of several Spanish collocations having the pattern *verb-noun*.

For the construction of the training sets, *verb-noun* pairs are extracted automatically from a corpus. The most frequent pairs are selected and those representing collocations are manually annotated with their respective LFs. The pairs that are not collocations are annotated as FWC - (Free word combination).

For each pair *verb-noun*, hyperonyms are extracted from the Spanish WordNet. If no hyperonym is found for a verb or for a noun in a pair, it is excluded from the list. A training set is created for each LF. As a result, for example, the *Bayesian Logistic Regression* algorithm is the most efficient in the identification of collocations modeled by the FL $Oper_1$.

[16] uses *FrameNet* [17] to extract collocations having a support verb. Each frame is associated with lexical units that evoke it. For example, the *Judgment* frame is evoked by lexical units (LU) such as *accusation*, *critique*, etc. A LU that evokes a frame is a *target*. Text corpora associated with FrameNet are annotated with frame element and target names, such as *support verb*, *controller*, etc.

The method of [16] consists in automatically browsing an annotated corpus with frames and target words to locate the annotated verbs such as *Supp* (support verbs) and the target words associated with those support verbs. Each pair (*Supp*, *target*) is a collocation having a support verb and is associated with the LF *Oper*. A heuristic is employed in order to determine the *Oper* function's index: for example, if the subject of the support verb is an agent, a person, etc., the index of *Oper* is *1*, so the function is $Oper_1$.

[18] presents a method where classification algorithms are used to assign collocations to the LF that model them. Their method is based on the *K-nearest neighbor algorithm*, which can be used when prototypical collocations are defined for the LF that model them.

From the collocations given as examples, the algorithm can automatically classify other collocations. [18] present two other classification methods, based on *naive Bayes networks* to automatically assign LFs to collocations.

[4] presents *Colex*, a tool based on LFs that combines symbolic and statistical approaches for extracting terminological collocations for English. As in [15], the extracted collocations follow the pattern *verb-noun* and three types of grammatical relations: subj. + verb (*The program executes*), verb + direct object: (*[to] close a file*) and verb + indirect object (*[to] load into memory*).

The method for the extraction of candidates is the matching between rules that follow these relation types and the syntactic tree obtained for a parser applied to the sentences of an English corpus. Two association measures, *mutual information* and *log-likelihood* are employed in order to increase the precision.

2.2 Semantic Perspective for Lexical Functions

In [19], different classification of lexical functions are presented, which are called "perspectives". In the semantic perspective (SP), LFs are classified into ten main classes. We added two more in our ontology, *supportVerb* and *semanticallyEmptyVerb*. These two added classes are not semantic in a strict sense because they represent "semantically empty verbs". However, since a great number of collocations are formed by these types of verbs, we decided to add these two classes.

The 12 main classes are presented in Table 1.

Table 1. Semantic perspective classes for lexical functions

actionEvent	causativity	elementSet	equivalence
location	opposition	participants	phaseAspect
qualification	semanticallyEmptyVerb	supportVerb	utilizationForm

Some of the SPs are subdivided into subclasses. For example, phase/aspect is divided in *preparation*, *start*, *continuation*, *duration*, *reiteration*, etc. Examples of collocations and their respective LFs classified as phase/aspect:

- *déployer ses ailes* (*stretch the wings*): $\text{PreparReal}_1(\textit{ailes}) = \{\textit{déployer}\}$ - (*phase/preparation*);
- *adopter une attitude* (*adopt an attitude*): $\text{IncepOper}_1(\textit{attitude}) = \{\textit{adopter}\}$ - (*phase/start*);

Examples of LFs and collocations for the other SPs:

- action/event - *jouer du piano* (*play the piano*): $\text{Real}_1(\textit{piano}) = \{\textit{jouer}\}$;
- causativity - *par politesse* (*out of politeness*): Propt(*politesse*) = {*par*};
- location - *sur le lit* (*on the bed*): $\text{Loc}_{in}(\textit{lit}) = \{\textit{sur}\}$;
- opposition - *bref délai* (*short delay*): AntiMagn(*délai*) = {*bref*}. In this example, the opposition is not between the base (*délai*) and the value (*bref*). Instead, it is an opposition of the intensification relation: Magn(*délai*) = {*long*} $\rightarrow$ AntiMagn(*délai*) = {*bref*};
- participants - *siège vacant* (*vacant seat*): $\text{A}_2\text{NonReal}_1(\textit{siège}) = \{\textit{vacant}\}$;
- qualification - *politique efficace* (*effective policy*): Ver(*politique*) = {*efficace*};
- semant. empty verb - *être victime* (*to be a victim*): Pred(*victime*) = {*être*};
- support verb - *courir le risque* (*take the risk*): $\text{Oper}_1(\textit{risque}) = \{\textit{courir}\}$;
- utilization/form - *par avion* (*by plane*): Instr(*avion*) = {*par*}.

The SPs *element/set* and *equivalence* represent paradigmatic relations. Therefore, there are no collocations classified in those classes. Examples of LFs and paradigmatic relations for those classes:

- element/set (hyperonymy, meronymy, etc.) - *chat/félin* (*cat/feline*): Hyper(*chat*) = {*félin*};
- equivalence (syntactic conversion) - *acclamation/acclamer* (*acclamation/to acclaim*): $\text{V}_0(\textit{acclamation}) = \{\textit{acclamer}\}$;

2.3 The French Lexical Network

The French Lexical Network (FLN) [20] is, to our knowledge, the only lexical network based on LFs. It has been built manually by a lexicographic team of around 15 people, as part of the project *RELIEF*[2]. Lexicographic strategies used to extract linguistic information from corpora and build the network are based on the Explanatory Combinatorial Lexicology [21]. It makes extensive use of the *Digital Thesaurus of the French Language*[3] (in French, *Trésor de la Langue Française informatisé*) [22] as a lexical database for lexicographic information.

In the FLN, each word is represented together with its possible meanings, each meaning being a lexeme of a word. Each lexeme is represented by the word form and a combination of Romans and Arabic numbers. For example, the word "*vêtement*" (*clothing*) has five meanings inside the FLN: $vêtement_{I.1}$, $vêtement_{I.2}$, $vêtement_{II}$, $vêtement_{III.1}$ and $vêtement_{III.2}$

In the FLN, the paradigmatic and syntagmatic relations between lexemes are represented by LFs. For example, between "*petit*" (*small*) and "*grand*" (*big*) there is the LF *Anti* (antonymy) connecting them. Or between "*très*" (*very*) and "*grave*" (*serious*) there is the LF *Magn* connecting them.

2.4 The FLN in an Ontology Format

We have developed a lexical ontology, called *lexical function ontology model* (*lexfom*) [23] to represent LFs and lexical relations based on LFs and we have applied this ontology in the transformation of the FLN to an ontology format.

Having the FLN in an ontology format facilitates the access of its content, allow its combination with other lexical resources on the semantic web and sets a standard that can be followed by other lexical networks based on LF for other languages. Lexfom has four modules:

- *Lexical functions representation* (*lfrep*): represents the individual properties of a LF, such as syntactic actants, if it is a simple or complex LF, etc.;
- *Lexical functions relation* (*lfrel*): represents a syntagmatic or paradigmatic relation, indicating the base and the value of the relation;
- *Lexical functions family* (*lffam*): represents a syntactic classification of LFs;
- *Lexical functions semantic perspective* (*lfsem*): represents the semantic perspectives for LFs, presented in the Sect. 2.2.

The FLN in ontology format contains about 8,000 different syntagmatic and about 46,000 different paradigmatic relations between lexemes. Moreover, our ontology represents about 600 different LFs, where 500 are complex LFs and 100 are simple LFs. In this ontology, LFs like, for example, $Oper_1$, $Oper_2$ and $Oper_3$ are considered as different LFs.

He have then created a Java API to access the FLN in an ontology format. For the present paper, the relevant API's functions are:

[2] http://www.atilf.fr/spip.php?article908.

[3] http://www.atilf.fr/spip.php?rubrique77.

- searchSyntagRelation(gov, dep) → LF(*base*, *collocate*): the pair (*governor*, *dependent*) (or any pair of words) are searched in the part of the ontology representing the syntagmatic relations (SR). If there is at least one SR between them, the result of the query returns the LF connecting them and which one is the base and the collocate in this relation.
  Example: searchSyntagRelation(*pose*, *questions*) → Oper_1(*questions*, *pose*);
- searchSemPerspective (LF) → semanticPerspective: returns the semantic perspective of a LF. Example: searchSemPerspective(Oper_1) → *supportVerb.*

3 Methodology

We present our method for extracting collocation candidates from a corpus and identifying them as true collocations. Figure 1 presents our methodology. The sequence of steps is as follows:

- Pre-processing of the corpus: tokenization, POS-tagging and lemmatization;
- A dependency parsing is applied and a file in the CONLL-X [11] format is generated (next two steps);
- The pairs (*gov*, *dep*) are extracted from the CONLL-X file according to some specific dependency types;
- The pairs extracted are matched against our ontology representing the FLN and a list of collocation candidates is generated;
- All the candidates are manually analyzed and a collocations list is generated;
- The collocations are classified accordingly to the SP of their LFs.

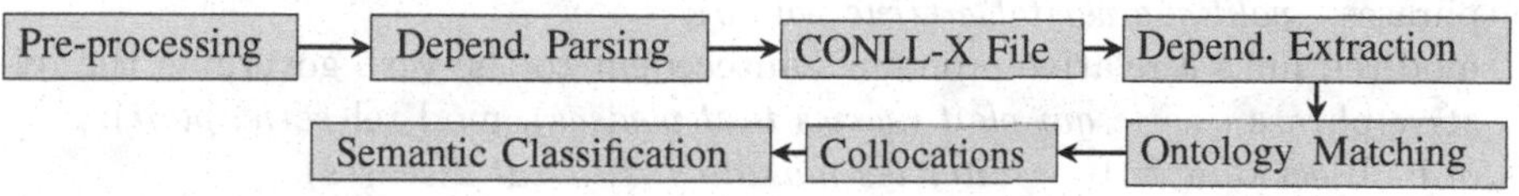

Fig. 1. The Pipeline for the extraction of candidates and the identification and classification of collocations.

In Sect. 3.1, we present the steps from the dependency parsing to the CONLL-X file generation. In Sect. 3.2, we show how the ontology matching is used to generate a list of collocations. In Sect. 3.3, we show how the identified collocations are semantically classified.

3.1 Use of Dependency Syntax to Extract Candidates

After the preprocessing, a dependency parser (MaltParser[4]) is applied. According to [24], the MaltParser's accuracy for French is around 89%. They showed

[4] http://www.maltparser.org/.

that MaltParser is about 1 to 2 p.p. less precise than Berkeley Parser[5] and MSTParser[6], but it is about 12 to 14 times faster. The parsing generates a file in the CONLL-X format, where each token in a phrase is represented by a row containing 10 columns. The most important for this work are:

- an ID (position) of the token in the phrase;
- surface form; – lemma; – POS; – dependency type;
- dependency head ID in the phrase (zero if the token is the root in the phrase).

We extract the collocation candidates from the CONLL-X file. We extract only word pairs having between them the following dependency relations [25]:

- a_obj: argument introduced by "à" - *à fond* (*thoroughly*);
- arg: argument (expressions connected by a preposition) - *comme tout* (*like any other*);
- ats: predicative adjective or nominal over the subject (*attribut du sujet*) - *être victime* (*to be a victim*);
- aux_caus: causative auxiliary verb - *faire dégager* (*to make clear*);
- aux_tps: tense auxiliary verb (*auxiliare de temps*) - *avoir vu* (*have seen*);
- coord: links a coordinator to the immediately preceding conjunct - in the phrase "*le garçon et la fille*" (*the boy and the girl*), there is a *coord* relation between the coordinator *et* and the preceding conjunct *garçon*;
- de_obj: argument introduced by "de" - *souvient de* (*remembers*);
- dep: unspecified dependency - *très grave* (*very serious*);
- dep_coord: links a conjunct to the previous coordinator - in the phrase above, given as example for the dependency *coord*, there is a *dep_coord* relation between the conjunct *fille* and the previous coordinator *et*;
- mod: modifiers (adjectival, nominal and adverbial) other than relative phrases - *politique véritable* (*true policy*);
- mod_rel: links a relative pronoun's antecedent to the verb governing the relative phrase - *série qui plaît* (*series that pleases*), mod_rel(*série*, *plaît*);
- obj: object of a verb - *traiter les maladies* (*to treat diseases*);
- p_obj: arg. introduced by another preposition - *sur la table* (*on the table*);
- suj: subject of a verb - *le bateau naviguait* (*the boat was sailing*).

Most of the recent work based on parsing use the tag sets provided by the Universal Dependency (UD) project [10]. The aim of this project is to have a tag set of dependencies that are the same for all languages and facilitate the sharing and comparison of information.

The dependencies used in this paper are not the same as the dependencies used in UD. Our method is based on a lexical network based on LFs, which, for the moment, only exists for the French language. For MaltParser, the only French language model available[7] was developed before the UD creation.

---

[5] http://www.eecs.berkeley.edu/~petrov/berkeleyParser.

[6] http://mstparser.sourceforge.net.

[7] http://maltparser.org/mco/french_parser/fremalt.html.

The use of a dependency parser can improve precision in the identification of collocations for two reasons. The first one, the relation between a base and a collocate in a collocation is a dependency relation. The second one, a parser can identify with good accuracy dependency relations between words that are some words apart, what a method based on a window of n words may fail to identify.

3.2 Use of the FLN to Filter Candidates

From the CONLL-X files, each pair (*gov*, *dep*) having one of the 14 dependencies types where matched against our ontology representing the syntagmatic relations extracted from the FLN. We used the lemmas of each *gov* and *dep* in the search.

A match means that the pair having a dependency relation in a phrase also has a syntagmatic relation in the French language and is possibly a collocation. Our search in the ontology returns also the LF connecting the pair. This allows us not only to identify collocations but also identify the LF modeling the relation.

For the positive matches against our ontology, we keep the following information: the surface forms of the *gov* and *dep* words, their lemmas, the LF connecting them in the ontology, the information about which word is the base and which one is the collocate and the syntactic dependency between them in the text.

Due to the lack of resources, we could not make the analysis on the negative matches, that is, the true collocations in the corpus that are not present in the FLN. For this type of analysis, we would need a French corpus annotated with collocations and LFs, what is not yet available. For the same reason we measure our results by precision only, without calculating the recall.

For some pairs, we can have more than one LF connecting them. As an example, the pair (*adopter*, *politique*):

- IncepOper_1 (*politique*) = {*adopter*};
- Real_{1-I} (*politique*) = {*adopter*};

3.3 Semantic Classification of Collocations

For each match, we search for the SP of each LF modeling the collocation. Since LFs can be complex, i.e., formed by the combination of two or more simple LFs, a LF can have more than one SP and as a consequence, the collocation modeled by this LF will be classified in more than one semantic group.

For example, the complex LF $FinReal_1$ is composed by the LF *Fin*, whose SP is "*actionEvent*", subclass "*disparation/existencial cease*", and by the LF $Real_1$, whose SP is "*actionEvent*", subclass "*utilization/typical operation*". Therefore, the French collocation "*abandoner la politique*" (*to quit politics*), which is modeled by the LF $FinReal_1$ ($FinReal_1$ (*politique*) = {*abandoner*}), will be classified in two semantic subclasses of *actionEvent*. This feature can be useful, for example, in a multi-labeling classification system that uses collocations to identify multi-classes of a phrase or document.

In the case of pairs having more than one LF, we choose to classify them according to the first LF returned.

4 Experiments and Analysis of Results

We use and exploit the EuroSense corpus [26] in our experiments. EuroSense is a multilingual parallel corpus, containing sentences in 21 languages. We extract all French phrases (about 1.8 million) contained in EuroSense.

The next step is the preprocessing: all phrases are segmented and POS tagged using the Apache OpenNLP[8] (OpenNLPSegmenter and OpenNlpPosTagger). Then the lemmatization is performed with DKPRO LanguageToolLemmatizer[9]. MaltParser[10] is used as a dependency parser. Finally, we use DKPRO to generate a file containing all phrases in the CONLL-X format.

We perform two types of analysis. In the first one, we measure the collocation identification precision by dependency type. The objective is to evaluate for which dependencies we can obtain more collocations with higher precision. In the second one, we count how many collocations are identified by SP. The objective is to evaluate the most common semantic relations in French collocations.

We could not calculate the recall since this is a first study of this type for French and there is no corpus annotated with French collocations and LFs.

4.1 Collocations Classified by Syntactic Dependencies

Table 2 shows the candidates extracted and collocations correctly identified by syntactic dependency. For each type of dependency, we have the total number of candidates extracted, the total number of true collocations and the precision (number of true collocations/number of candidates). We extracted 43, 629 collocation candidates and 33, 273 were identified as true collocations.

Since there are no available corpora annotated with collocations and LFs for the French, we calculated the precision manually, over all the collocation candidates extracted: each pair is observed and a human annotator decides if a pair is or not a collocation. Although we have many candidates, the number of different individual collocations is low since many are repeated many times, what facilitates the manual annotation.

Except for the *arg* dependency, that produced only seven collocations, we had the highest precision with the pairs having the *obj* (96.9%), *a_obj* (98.3%) and *p_obj* (95.6%) dependencies. In other words, the relations where the *dependent* is a *governor*'s object had the best precision overall.

The most similar work is the one from [9], presented in Sect. 2.1. Besides the fact that they deal with the extraction of bilingual collocations, what is a harder task, the difference is that they only use three dependencies: *amod*, *nmod* and *vobj*, which are less likely to produce errors because the governor and the dependent are adjacent to each other. Their average precision (for the three language pairs) are: 91.8% for *amod*, 90.6% for *nmod* and 86.2% for *vobj*.

To our knowledge, there is no other work, besides ours, on the extraction of French collocations using syntactic dependency or the FLN.

[8] https://opennlp.apache.org/.
[9] https://dkpro.github.io/.
[10] http://www.maltparser.org/.

Table 2. Precision for the extraction of collocations by syntactic dependency.

Dependency	nr. candidates	nr. true coll.	Precision
mod	20625	14240	0.690
dep	14015	11532	0.823
obj	4869	4720	0.969
suj	1249	688	0.551
mod_rel	1179	888	0.753
coord	605	442	0.731
ats	400	346	0.865
a_obj	300	295	0.983
dep_coord	246	13	0.053
p_obj	90	86	0.956
aux_tps	37	15	0.405
arg	7	7	1.000
aux_caus	7	1	0.143
de_obj	0	0	0
Total	**43629**	**33273**	**0.763**

In general, we expected to have a good precision for all types of dependencies since each candidate is matched against the collocations represented in the ontology and the ontology is based on the FLN, which is manually constructed. However, we had false positives due to parsing errors. The most common:

- errors connected to the verb "*être*" (*to be*). For example, in the phrase "*on est pêcheur de père en fils*" (lit. *we are fishermen from father to son*) the verb "*est*" is not syntactically dependent on "*père*". However, the parser found a dependency between them. And since "*être père*" (lit. *to be a father*) is a collocation in French ($Oper_{12}$ (*père*) = {*être*}), we had a false positive;
- errors connected to the verb "*avoir*" (*to have*). For example, in the sentence "*...transport des animaux vivants ait été décidée, même si nous aurions préféré...*" (lit. *transport of live animals has been decided, even if we would have preferred...*), the parser found a dependency (*mod*) between "animaux" and "aurions", what is false. It was considered a collocation since, in the FLN, there is the following relation: $Real_1$ ($animal_{I.2}$) = {$avoir_{I.1}$};
- errors with the verb "*pouvoir*" (*to be able to*). In many phrases, this verb was considered a noun and we had some false positives because, for example, "*tenir le pouvoir*" (*to keep the power*) is a collocation;
- the word "*car*" (*because*), which is also a colloquial word for "*autocar*" (*coach* or *bus*), was often tagged as a noun, appearing incorrectly as a collocation in expressions like "*dans le car*" (*inside the car*). For the pairs having the dependency *dep_coord*, "*dans le car*" was the most common candidate and this explains why candidates in this group had a low precision.

The first three types of errors respond for 95.7% of the errors, in the following proportion: "*pouvoir*" errors = 35.1%; "*avoir*" errors = 31.1%; "*être*" errors = 29.5%. The "*car*" errors correspond to 3.9% of the errors, while only 0.4% (43/10, 356) are due to other types of errors.

This error distribution means that it would be easy to decrease the error rate by concentrating an extra effort in dealing with dependencies having few types of words or having a more detailed analysis on the RLF's syntagmatic relations where those specific words appear.

4.2 Collocations Classified by Semantic Perspectives

The 33, 273 identified collocations were classified by the semantic perspective of their lexical functions. Since some collocations are modeled by complex LFs, they can be classified into more than one SP, which gives 35, 243 different instances of SP classifications. Table 3 shows the number of collocations identified, classified by each SP. For the SPs *actionEvent*, *phaseAspect*, *qualification* and *equivalence* we have also identified collocations for their subclasses.

Table 3. Number of collocations identified by semantic perspective.

semantic perspective	n. coll.	example	lexical function
qualification	11983		
intensity	5988	*très grave*	Magn(*grave*) = {*très*}
judgment	5940	*aller bien*	Bon(*aller*) = {*bien*}
inten+judg	55	*trop rapide*	AntiBon+Magn(*rapide*) = {*trop*}
supportVerb	8620	*donner un coup*	Oper_1(*coup*) = {*donner*}
location	6332	*dans le pays*	Loc_{in}(*pays*) = {*dans*}
actionEvent	3428		
utilizationTypOper	2846	*mettre l'accent*	Real_1(*mettre*) = {*accent*}
creation	580	*faire voler*	Caus(*voler*) = {*faire*}
disparExistCease	121	*l'avion atterrit*	FinFact_0(*avion*) = {*atterrir*}
imminence	5	*la tempête vient*	ProxFunc_0(*tempête*) = {*venir*}
semanticallyEmptyVerb	1693	*être similaire*	Pred(*similaire*) = {*être*}
utilizationForm	1410	*à vélo*	Instr(*vélo*) = {*à*}
phaseAspect	729		
start	632	*devenir mère*	IncepPred(*mère*) = {*devenir*}
continuation	77	*rester debout*	ContPred(*debout*) = {*rester*}
preparation	20	*déployer les ailes*	PreparReal_1(*ailes*) = {*déployer*}
semanticOpposite	647	*mauvais sens*	AntiBon(*sens*) = {*mauvais*}
causativity	362	*par politesse*	Propt(*politesse*) = {*par*}
participants (actants)	39	*cigarette allumé*	A_1Fact_0(*cigarette*) = {*allumer*}
Total	35243		

The most common SP for collocations were *qualification* (33.9%), *supportVerb* (24.4%), *location* (17.9%) and *actionEvent* (9.7%). These four SPs represent about 86% of all collocations identified.

The collocations classified into the group *qualification* were divided almost equally between the sub-groups *intensity* and *judgment*. As examples of collocations belonging to this group we have:

- "*crime odieux*" (*heinous crime*): Magn(*crime*) = {*odieux*} - (intensity)
- "*chiffre exact*" (*exact number*): Ver(*chiffre*) = {*exact*} - (judgment)

Among the collocations classified as *supportVerb*, the most common are the ones having LFs belonging to the $Oper_1$ "family". For example:

- "*poser une question*" (*to ask a question*): Oper_1(*question*) = {*poser*}

Almost all the collocations classified into the group *location* are modeled by the LF Loc_{in}. Examples of collocations belonging to this group:

- "*dans le pays*" (*in the country*): Loc_{in} (*pays*) = {*dans*}
- "*en semaine*" (*during the week*): ${Loc_{in}}^{time}$ (*semaine*) = {*en*}

For the collocations classified as *actionEvent*, the most common sub-groups were *utilizationTypicalOperation* (u/t.o) and *creation*. For example:

- "*donner la forme*" (*give shape*): CausFunc_1 (*forme*) = {*donner*} - (creation)
- "*mettre l'accent*" (*to accentuate*): Real_1 (*accent*) = {*mettre*} - (u/t.o)

This type of analysis and classification by semantic group could be useful in, for example, those applications related to distributional semantics:

- sentiment analyses: the identification of collocations in the semantic group *qualification* in a phrase may be useful in the identification of the sentiment expressed. Either positive, if the collocation is modeled by the LFs *Bon* or *Ver*, or negative, if modeled by the LFs *AntiBon* or *AntiVer*;
- text classification: the presence of a specific collocation in a specific semantic group may help in the identification of the topic of a sentence.

5 Conclusion and Future Work

In this paper, we presented a method for identifying collocations from a corpus. To decide which candidate is a true collocation, we performed a search in a lexical network based on lexical functions, the French Lexical Network (FLN), using a lexical ontology that we developed to access the information in the FLN.

More than searching for collocations, we also obtained the lexical functions connecting the base and the collocate and each lexical function's semantic(s) perspective(s). We calculated the precision of the identified collocations for each type of dependency and we compared the total number of collocations by semantic perspective. For some dependency relations, we had a precision higher than 95%. And we analyzed that, if we deal properly with punctual issues, like some parsing errors, we can achieve a precision close to 100%.

As future work, we intend to combine our method with machine learning algorithms based on word embeddings. Machine learning works well for collocations having a frequency higher than a certain threshold. We believe that the use of a lexical network where the relations of collocations (syntagmatic relations) were manually annotated by lexicographers will help in the identification of less frequent collocations, improving the performance.

Also, we expect to extend this method to a lexical network based on lexical functions for English (under construction), and apply it to the translation of collocations for the pair English-French. Finally, we intend to create a French corpus annotated with collocations and lexical functions, to allow future automatic evaluation of precision and recall in the identification of collocations.

References

1. Mel'čuk, I.: Collocations and Lexical Functions. Phraseology. Theory, Analysis and Applications, pp. 23–53 (1998)
2. Mel'čuk, I.: Vers une linguistique sens-texte. Leçon Inaugurale. Collège de France, Paris (1997)
3. Mel'čuk, I.: Actants in Semantics and Syntax II: Actants in Syntax, vol. 42, pp. 247–291. de Gruyter, Berlin
4. Orliac, B.: Colex: Un outil d'extraction de collocations spécialisées basé sur les fonctions lexicales. Terminology **12**, 261–280 (2006)
5. Sahlgren, M.: The Word-Space Model: Using Distributional Analysis to Represent Syntagmatic and Paradigmatic Relations Between Words in High-dimensional Vector Spaces. SICS Dissertation Series. Department of Linguistics, Stockholm University (2006)
6. Choueka, Y.: Looking for needles in a haystack or locating interesting collocational expressions in large textual databases. In: Fluhr, C., Walker, D.E. (eds.) RIAO, pp. 609–624. CID (1988)
7. Church, K.W., Hanks, P.: Word association norms, mutual information, and lexicography. Comput. Linguist. **16**(1), 22–29 (1990)
8. Smadja, F., McKeown, K.R., Hatzivassiloglou, V.: Translating collocations for bilingual lexicons: a statistical approach. Comput. Linguist. **22**(1), 1–38 (1996)
9. Garcia, M., García-Salido, M., Alonso-Ramos, M.: Using bilingual word-embeddings for multilingual collocation extraction. In: Proceedings of the 13th Workshop on Multiword Expressions (MWE 2017), pp. 21–30. Association for Computational Linguistics, Valencia, April 2017
10. McDonald, R.T., Nivre, J., Quirmbach-Brundage, Y., Goldberg, Y., Das, D., Ganchev, K., Hall, K.B., Petrov, S., Zhang, H., Täckström, O., Bedini, C., Castelló, N.B., Lee., J.: Universal dependency annotation for multilingual parsing. In: ACL (2), pp. 92–97. The Association for Computer Linguistics (2013)
11. Buchholz, S., Marsi, E.: CoNLL-X shared task on multilingual dependency parsing. In: Proceedings of the Tenth Conference on Computational Natural Language Learning, CoNLL-X 2006, pp. 149–164. Association for Computational Linguistics, Stroudsburg (2006)

12. Berard, A., Servan, C., Pietquin, O., Besacier, L.: Multivec: a multilingual and multilevel representation learning toolkit for NLP. In: Calzolari, N., Choukri, K., Declerck, T., Goggi, S., Grobelnik, M., Maegaard, B., Mariani, J., Mazo, H., Moreno, A., Odijk, J., Piperidis, S. (eds.) Proceedings of the Tenth International Conference on Language Resources and Evaluation (LREC 2016). European Language Resources Association (ELRA), Paris, May 2016
13. Mikolov, T., Chen, K., Corrado, G., Dean, J.: Efficient Estimation of Word Representations in Vector Space. CoRR, abs/1301.3781 (2013)
14. Luong, T., Pham, H., Manning, C.D.: Bilingual word representations with monolingual quality in mind. In: Proceedings of the 1st Workshop on Vector Space Modeling for Natural Language Processing, pp. 151–159 (2015)
15. Kolesnikova, O.: Automatic Extraction of Lexical Functions. Ph.D. thesis directed by Alexander Gelbukh, Instituto Politecnico Nacional - Centro de Investigacion en Computacion, Mexico, DF (2011)
16. Ramos, M.A., Rambow, O., Wanner, L.: Using semantically annotated corpora to build collocation resources. In: Proceedings of LREC, pp. 1154–1158 (2008)
17. Fillmore, C.J.: Scenes-and-Frames Semantics. Fundamental Studies in Computer Science, vol. 59. North Holland Publishing, Dordrecht (1977)
18. Wanner, L., Bohnet, B., Giereth, M.: What is beyond collocations? Insights from machine learning experiments. In: Corino, C.O.E., Marello, C. (eds.) Proceedings of the 12th EURALEX International Congress, pp. 1071–1087. Edizioni dell'Orso, Torino, September 2006
19. Jousse, A.-L.: Modèle de structuration des relations lexicales fondé sur le formalisme des fonctions lexicales. Ph.D. thesis. Directed by Sylvain Kahane et Alain Polguere, Université de Montréal et Université Paris Diderot (Paris 7) (2010)
20. Lux Pogodalla, V., Polguère, A.. Construction of a french lexical network: methodological issues. In: First InternationalWorkshop on Lexical Resources, WoLeR 2011, Ljubljana, Slovenia, pp. 54–61, August 2011
21. Mel'čuk, I., Clas, A., Polguère, A.: Introduction à la lexicologie explicative et combinatoire. Duculot, Louvain-la-Neuve (1995)
22. Dendien, J., Pierrel, J.-M.: Le trésor de la langue française informatisé: un exemple d'informatisation d'un dictionnaire de langue de référence. Traitement Autom. Lang. (TAL) **44**, 11–37 (2003)
23. Fonseca, A., Sadat, F., Lareau, F.: Lexfom: a lexical functions ontology model. In: Proceedings of the Fifth Workshop on Cognitive Aspects of the Lexicon (CogALex), COLING, Osaka, pp. 145–155 (2016)
24. Candito, M., Nivre, J., Denis, P., Anguiano, E.H.: Benchmarking of statistical dependency parsers for french. In: Proceedings of the 23rd International Conference on Computational Linguistics: Posters, COLING 2010, pp. 108–116. ACL, Stroudsburg (2010)
25. Candito, M., Anguiano, E.H., Seddah, D.: A word clustering approach to domain adaptation: effective parsing of biomedical texts. In: Proceedings of the 12th International Conference on Parsing Technologies, Vancouver, Canada, pp. 37–42 (2011)
26. Raganato, A., Bovi, C.D., Collados, J.C., Navigli, R.: Eurosense: automatic harvesting of multilingual sense annotations from parallel text. In: Proceedings of 55th annual meeting of the Association for Computational Linguistics (ACL 2017), Vancouver, Canada (2017)

12. [illegible] a multilingual and [illegible] toolkit [illegible]. In: [illegible] Proceedings of the [illegible] International Conference on Language Resources and Evaluation (LREC 2016). European Language Resources Association (ELRA) [illegible] 2016
13. [illegible] of Word [illegible] (2013)
14. [illegible] Workshop on Vector Space [illegible] (2013)
15. [illegible] Computational [illegible] (2011)
16. [illegible] (1997)
17. [illegible] (2010)
18. [illegible] beyond conventional [illegible] In: Cortina, [illegible] Edizioni dell'Orso [illegible]
19. [illegible]
20. [illegible]
21. [illegible]
22. [illegible] (2003)
23. [illegible] In: Proceedings of the [illegible] Workshop on [illegible]
24. [illegible] In: Proceedings of the 22nd International Conference on Computational Linguistics [illegible] (2008)
25. [illegible] In: Proceedings of the 12th [illegible]

Author Index

Printed in the United States
By Bookmasters